HIDDEN®
Carolinas

"Provides a thoughtful look at the region's culture and quirks. . . .Ritz picks out charming hotels, eating spots that locals like, and sights a visitor might overlook."
—*Raleigh News & Observer*

"A well-written and thorough guide for those who want to get deeper into the Carolinas than they can with the broader-brush competition."
—*Atlanta Journal and Constitution*

"Charts a course of discovery through many of the South's best-loved destinations."
—*Knoxville News-Sentinel*

"The definitive guide to North and South Carolina, featuring both well-known places and little-known finds."
—*Allentown Morning Call*

HIDDEN®

Carolinas

Stacy Ritz

SECOND EDITION

Ulysses Press®
BERKELEY, CALIFORNIA

Published by:
ULYSSES PRESS
P.O. Box 3440
Berkeley, CA 94703-3440

Library of Congress Catalog Card Number 97-60063

ISBN 1-56975-104-8

Printed in Canada by Best Book Manufacturers

10 9 8 7 6 5 4 3 2

EDITORIAL DIRECTOR: Leslie Henriques
MANAGING EDITOR: Claire Chun
PROJECT DIRECTOR: Lily Chou
COPY EDITOR: David Sweet
EDITORIAL ASSOCIATES: Natasha Lay, Phoebe McClure
    Aaron Newey, Nicole O'Hay
TYPESETTER: Kenya Ratcliff
CARTOGRAPHER: Stellar Cartography, Lawrence, Kansas
COVER DESIGN: Sarah Levin and Sara Glaser
INDEXER: Sayre Van Young
COVER PHOTOGRAPHY: Front: B. Beerman/SuperStock
    Circle and back: Mark Gibson
ILLUSTRATOR: Hanako Wakiyama
CONTRIBUTORS: Lee Micheaux, David Hume,
    Sharlene Zwing

Distributed in the United States by Publishers
Group West, in Canada by Raincoast Books,
and in Great Britain and Europe by World
Leisure Marketing

For Sharlene Zwing,

and for Joanna Pearlman,
always a positive force

Acknowledgments

As this book enters its second edition, I am indebted to a growing family of researchers, sources and friends whose perseverance and enthusiasm made publication possible. My deepest thanks goes to native Carolinian Lee Micheaux, who devoted many nights and weekends to the North Carolina part of this project, and to David Hume for his exhaustive work on the South Carolina portion.

Sincerest thanks to everyone at Ulysses Press. First, to managing editor Claire Chun, whose dedication and perseverance are nothing short of extraordinary. Then to editorial director Leslie Henriques, for her compassion and encouragement, and to publisher Ray Riegert, who first proposed the idea for this book. Project director Lily Chou and copy editor David Sweet kept things on an early timeline, as did editorial associates Natasha Lay, Aaron Newey and Nicole O'Hay. Thanks also to Sarah Levin and Sara Glaser for their cover design, and to Hanako Wakiyama for her illustrations.

Across the Carolinas, I owe thanks to Susan George for a great night out in Chapel Hill, to Cathy Butler for a great day in Chatham County, and to Howard and Linda Sherman for showing me their native Charleston by water. Amy Blyth also lent assistance in Charleston, Cherie Had helped out in Columbia, and Bob Miller was a superb source in the Smokies.

Close to home, I owe sincerest thanks to Vicki Goldstein for her enduring friendship, faith and inspiration; and to my soul mate and husband, David, who went on (nearly) every trip, endured snowstorms and drove me thousands of miles around the Carolinas.

What's Hidden?

At different points throughout this book, you'll find special listings marked with a hidden symbol:

◀ HIDDEN

This means that you have come upon a place off the beaten tourist track, a spot that will carry you a step closer to the local people and natural environment of the Carolinas.

The goal of this guide is to lead you beyond the realm of everyday tourist facilities. While we include traditional sightseeing listings and popular attractions, we also offer alternative sights and adventure activities. Instead of filling this guide with reviews of standard hotels and chain restaurants, we concentrate on one-of-a-kind places and locally owned establishments.

Our authors seek out locales that are popular with residents but usually overlooked by visitors. Some are more hidden than others (and are marked accordingly), but all the listings in this book are intended to help you discover the true nature of the Carolinas and put you on the path of adventure.

Write to us!

If in your travels you discover a spot that captures the spirit of the Carolinas, or if you live in the region and have a favorite place to share, or if you just feel like expressing your views, write to us and we'll pass your note along to the author.

We can't guarantee that the author will add your personal find to the next edition, but if the writer does use the suggestion, we'll acknowledge you in the credits and send you a free autographed copy of the new edition.

ULYSSES PRESS
3286 Adeline Street, Suite 1
Berkeley, CA 94703
E-mail: ulypress@aol.com

Contents

Maps

Special Features

OUTDOOR ADVENTURE SYMBOLS

The following symbols accompany national, state and regional park listings, as well as beach descriptions throughout the text.

▲	Camping		Waterskiing
	Hiking		Windsurfing
	Biking		Canoeing or Kayaking
	Horseback Riding		Boating
	Swimming		Boat Ramps
	Snorkeling or Scuba Diving		Fishing
	Surfing		

ONE

Carolinas Wandering

On one end of the Carolinas there is the ocean, a great vault of fabulous blue heaving against wispy islands and shores of monstrous dunes. On the other end are mountains, broad and green and towering, acutely silent, eternally cool, wrapped in mist and a halo of clouds.

In between the water and peaks are foothills and farmlands, corn and tobacco fields running into crisp sky, sprinklings of white-washed clapboard, no-name roads rouged with clay, and far-reaching forests of palmetto and slash pine where white-tailed deer and bald eagles reside.

The land is not only eclectic but vast. Together, North and South Carolina cover some 82,811 square miles—considerably more than all the New England states combined. To cross the Carolinas by car is to pass through many dimensions, to enter many eras and to observe many ways. The scenery is forever changing, from wild and watery swamps to subtle, sunlit plantations, from cultured cosmopolitan cities to wooded mountain hollows where folks carve their own dulcimers. Not far from bustling Charlotte, North Carolina, there's a quiet western town where no cars—only horses—are allowed on Main Street. The surf-and-beer scene of North Carolina's Outer Banks is but a few country miles from the cotton towns where Tammy Wynette rules the radio and Baptist preachers reign on Sunday mornings.

New South ideas prevail in larger cities, but elsewhere the Old South thrives. Sweet tea is sipped on front porches. Blue crabs are caught in the tidal marshes. Cotton and apples are picked in the fall. Pecan trees make music during afternoon storms, their nuts clacking in the wind. White magnolia blossoms perfume the roadsides and gardens. And in true Southern fashion, everyone asks how you're doing.

There is much history in the Carolinas. Wilbur and Orville Wright took their first flight from a hellish sand dune on the Outer Banks. The country's first English child was born a few miles away. The first hunk of North American gold was found in a North Carolina creek, though the finder chose to use it as a doorstop.

Beautiful Charleston, South Carolina, is one of the United States' oldest cities, founded in 1670 and saturated with early Americana; some 4000 historic buildings fill its downtown, many dating to the 1700s. Horse-drawn carriages convey visitors along ancient cobbled streets, and Gullah women, African-American descendants

1

of plantation slaves, weave sweetgrass baskets on the sidewalks. Lofty antebellum plantations, with their lavish gardens, dot the coastal plain of South Carolina.

It is for these reasons—compelling history, scenery and the Southern state of mind—that so many travelers keep finding the Carolinas. Every year, more than nine million visitors find Great Smoky Mountains National Park in North Carolina—twice as many as those who go to the Grand Canyon, making it the nation's most-visited national park. About 12 million visitors make an annual trip to Myrtle Beach to soak up sun and swim in the sea. Some 20 million travelers take North Carolina's Blue Ridge Parkway, and why not? The road is a glorious ride amid bluish mountain peaks, with not a single stop sign or traffic light along the way.

Hidden Carolinas is designed to help you explore these two great states. It will lead you to countless popular spots, offering advice on how best to enjoy them, then take you to off-the-beaten-path locales, places usually known only to locals. The book will tell the story of the region's history, its flora and fauna. Each chapter will suggest places to stay and eat, to sightsee and shop, and to enjoy the outdoors and the nightlife, covering a range of tastes and budgets.

The book sets out in Asheville, North Carolina, taking visitors in Chapter Two through this lovely Blue Ridge city and gateway to North Carolina's mountains. Chapter Three wanders along the state's Southern Mountains sprinkled with small towns and filled with waterfalls. From there, Chapter Four picks up the Great Smoky Mountains of North Carolina, including the tourist towns of Maggie Valley and Cherokee, and the Cherokee reservation. Chapter Five presents a driving tour along the North Carolina portion of the Blue Ridge Parkway, one of the nation's most appealing roads.

Chapter Six heads up into the High Country, the mountainous northwestern corner of North Carolina with both popular resort areas and far-flung hamlets. Chapter Seven wanders east through North Carolina's Piedmont, home to several big cities and nearly six million people. Chapter Eight runs down the North Carolina coast, with its rich maritime mood and dramatic barrier isles known as the Outer Banks. Chapter Nine moves southward along South Carolina's coast, through the sands and golf courses of Myrtle Beach to old-world Charleston and the megaresort called Hilton Head. Finally, Chapter Ten wanders across inland South Carolina, with its fields of cotton and deep pine woods, and foothills culminating in westerly mountains and lakes.

What you choose to see and do is up to you. Whether you prefer to park your towel in the sand or picnic on a plantation, wander through stately sculpture gardens or stroll glittering city streets, swing a golf club or wade in a mountain creek, you will find your place in the Carolinas.

▼▼▼▼▼▼▼▼▼▼▼▼▼▼

The Carolinas Story

GEOLOGY

The Southern Appalachians are old mountains, much older than the Himalayas or even the Swiss Alps. They were created half a billion years ago, during the Paleozoic period, when two enormous land masses collided to form the supercontinent of Pangea. Where they crashed, the land exploded in a torrent of high, ragged mountains that resembled today's Himalayas. When Pangea later broke apart, the mountains formed a dramatic, easterly wrinkle down the side of a

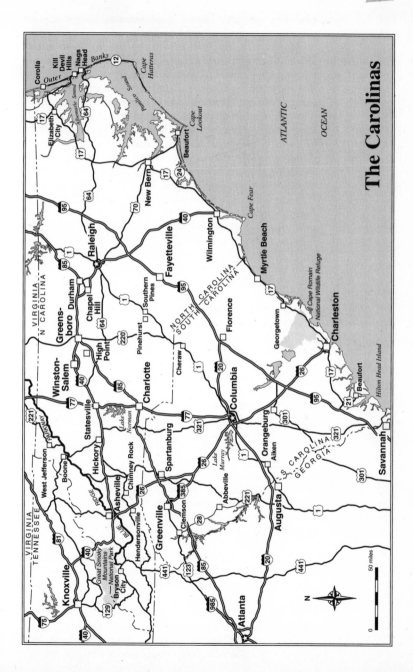

The Carolinas

mountains formed a dramatic, easterly wrinkle down the side of a land mass—the future North America.

Over the eons, erosion wore away and rounded the mountains' sharp peaks, and a luxuriant blanket of vegetation spread across their shoulders and valleys. Today's Southern Appalachians are foremost green and flourishing, with double and triple canopies of forest carpeted with ferns and pillow-soft layers of leaves and filled with flowers nearly all year. In winter, though, the mountains become rocky skeletons, revealing their ancient beginnings of granite, gneiss and schist. Wandering through these mountains, which run along the western sides of North and South Carolina, it is easy to believe their age, for the rocky outcroppings and gorges look primeval and the summits honed by interminable time.

What were originally pools of water between the Appalachian ridges have now become wind gaps, and there is many a summit where you can sit high above the world and hear the winds sing. Wind and water constantly shape and reshape the mountains, sometimes carving bizarre and haunting profiles. Chimney Rock in North Carolina is a great pedestal of granite, 225 feet high and poking into blue sky, its summit offering views of wind-etched ravines all around. North Carolina's Grandfather Mountain, another freak of wind and erosion, most resembles a patriarch lying on his back, bushy brows and goatee aimed toward heaven.

The crystalline nature of Appalachian rocks has made many a Carolinian rich. In the late 1800s, rubies were discovered in the mountains of North Carolina, including pigeon-blood rubies, the rarest rubies in the world. Commercial mines thrived for a while and then closed. Today's visitors, however, can still pan for rubies and sapphires, garnets, kyanite, moonstone and other stones and minerals, though few strike it big. Half the country's supply of feldspar, a chalky rock used in everything from dinner plates to house paint, comes from the small Appalachian town of Spruce Pine, North Carolina.

Go to the Outer Banks, and you can hang-glide off a giant pillar of sand 15,000 years old.

East of Appalachia lies an immense expanse of foothills known as the Piedmont. In geologic terms it is called the Fall Line, named for the line of waterfalls, rapids and rivers that course through on their way from mountains to sea. Carolinas' towns grew around these agitated waters, harnessing their energy for the water wheels of industry. The Piedmont is even older than the Appalachians, having existed before the collision of continents into Pangea.

The Coastal Plain, which lies east of the Appalachians along the Carolinas' seaboard, was once covered by the Atlantic Ocean, and today the earth bears traces of sea sediment. Not until about 15,000 years ago did the coast and its barrier islands begin to take their current shape. Near the end of the Ice Age when the sea level subsided, wicked ocean winds drove sandbars up into lofty dunes. When the sea rose at the end of the Wisconsin Advance, the waves pushed the dunes close to shore.

There they remain today, a strand of barrier islands running the length of the Carolinas, forever windwhipped and at the mercy of currents and tides. The wildest isles are the Outer Banks of North Carolina, where dunes reach 150 feet high and look like something from the Mojave Desert, and where Mother Nature is constantly moving islands around, without the slightest concern for human development.

Nowhere is Carolinas' flora more abundant than in the mountains. Across the Blue Ridge and Great Smoky Mountains of North Carolina are fantastic forests of maples, hickories, sourwoods, poplar and elms, sycamores, sweet gums and Carolina silverbells. Caverns of hemlock conceal creeks and streams and run for thousands of feet down mountains. Pines and oaks protrude from windier slopes and outcroppings. Fraser fir and red spruce, rarely found south of Maine, grow on the highest points. There is so much green, and so little development, that the very air takes on a moist, Edenic tint.

FLORA

Flowers fill the mountain scenery with flamboyant color, starting on the lowest slopes in March and ending on the loftiest peaks with a September finale. Take a spring ride along North Carolina's Blue Ridge Parkway and you will witness trilliums, lady's slippers, jack-in-the-pulpits and showy orchids. Millions of mountain laurel shrubs release their pinkish blossoms, fountains of flowers gushing from cliffsides. Dogwood trees, which are native to the forests and also planted profusely around Carolinas' gardens, put out their pearlwhite blossoms in spring.

Solomon's seal comes along in May, though nothing is so splendid as the opening of the Catawba rhododendrons around mid-June. The mountain shrubs with their purple-pink blooms grow so thick they look like shimmering rose-hued seas. Mountain laurel and flame azaleas, their blooms a blazing orange, crowd in with the rhododendron for extra extravagance.

The lower forests of South Carolina's Upcountry, where elevations average about 2000 feet, are dominated by poplar, oak and pine trees, and there are sprinklings of fraser magnolias, also called umbrella trees for their thickleaf canopies that protect from rain. Their supple white blossoms emerge in April and May, and breathe sweetness into the forest air. Here also are rare Oconee bells, found only around the Carolinas and Georgia, each with five white petals inset with yellow and shaped like bells.

Scruffy forests of pine and oak and sandhills run across the Carolinas' Piedmont and coastal plain. The longleaf pine is North

Carolina's state tree, though its name is too enchanting for its look: tall, skinny and ruddy-colored, with bristly limbs and shingly bark, and sprays of dark green needles. South Carolina's state tree, the palmetto, is no more beautiful, being similarly dull in color and design.

All across the Carolinas, kudzu overtakes whole trees and cars and hills. Kudzu is pretty but treacherous: the vine and its heart-shaped leaves grow rapidly, as much as a foot a day, swallowing everything in its path, including native foliage that animals need to survive. Kudzu came from Asia to the South in the 1870s, when farmers planted it to enrich their soil and the federal government used it to control riverbank erosion. By the time everyone learned of its destructive nature, it was too late. Now kudzu is called "The Scourge of the South."

Walk among Charleston's gardens and you will breathe the sweet scent of the Carolinas.

Only the hardiest flora survive along the shifting, sun-beaten dunes of North Carolina's Outer Banks. Arrowleaf morning glory, with its leathery leaves and funnel-shaped flowers, is a vine that climbs the dunes. Virginia creeper will grow almost anywhere but has a dull green flower—not exciting. Sea purslane and blanket-flowers also survive along the salt-washed beaches.

North Carolina's coastal plain is completely different. Lonesome pine woods stretch for miles, and there are vast wetlands whose rich, mucky soils harbor dazzling wildflowers, seas of saw grass, woods of pine and oak, and rare carnivorous plants. There is a chunk of woods, Croatan National Forest, that boasts five insect-eating plants, including the Venus flytrap, the pitcher plant, and the butterwort, which washes its victims in anesthesia.

The myrtle trees of Myrtle Beach, South Carolina, are wax myrtles. The area's first settlers found the shrubby, wind-tolerant plants growing along the shores. Today, there are also many crepe myrtles, much prettier than wax myrtles, with buttery-smooth, chalk-white trunks and spidery limbs tasseled with white and lavender blossoms in summer. Fat, fluffy hydrangeas, whose pink and blue blooms look like powder puffs, decorate local gardens, as do velvety white gardenias.

South of Myrtle Beach across the watery Lowcountry, bald cypress trees cling to the sides of swamps and black rivers, and reedy tidal grass spills across horizons. The limbs of the live oak, so magisterial and primal, draped in ethereal moss, stretch across the Lowcountry sky. They cover roadways, sometimes for miles, a cool, dark tunnel of filigreed greenery. Within Lowcountry gardens and plantations, particularly around Charleston, grow vigorous plantings of jasmine and honeysuckle, Carolina jessamine and tea olive, daphne and sweet bay. There are walls of wisteria and pittosporum, gardens of roses and stands of magnolias.

Once there were bison, cougars and elk in the Carolinas mountains, but white settlers hunted them to extinction. There are still black bears, wild turkeys, foxes, bobcats, mink and white-tailed deer in the mountains, particularly in North Carolina's Great Smoky and Blue Ridge mountains.

The bears are big, up to 300 pounds, and there are about 400 who live in Great Smoky Mountains National Park. During the winter, they snooze in their dens. When they awake in spring, they are naturally quite ravenous and go foraging for nuts, berries, insects and small animals. Unfortunately, despite warnings to the contrary, park visitors sometimes feed the bears, which causes the burly creatures to become aggressive. A pushy, hungry bear is not something you want to encounter on a hiking trail.

Even worse, the bears become easier prey for poachers—increasingly a problem, as bear body parts, from the paws to the teeth, bring big bucks on the black market. In Asian markets, the gallbladder of a black bear is worth up to US$2000, and rangers in Great Smoky Mountains National Park have found massive bear carcasses, intact except for the tiny gallbladder.

The Smokies are also plagued by non-native, exotic wild hogs whose ancestors escaped from a nearby hunting preserve in 1912 and invaded the mountain forests. They compete with bears and other animals for food, breed huge litters and have virtually no enemies. About 2000 hogs live in the Smokies, though you will rarely see them, since they are nocturnal.

You probably will see a woodchuck, possibly two, as the furry groundhogs love to burrow in the mown green roadsides of the Great Smoky Mountains National Park. Ruffed grouse, brownish birds about the size of chickens, are also common in the park. Beavers, once gone from the Smokies, have reappeared but are still scarce.

Even if you don't make it to the mountains, you may see a white-tailed deer, wild turkey or a fox, especially a red fox, which all thrive in forests across the Piedmont and coastal plains.

Trout, particularly rainbow and brown trout, fill the rivers, creeks and streams that flow seaward across the Carolinas. In the lakes you will find bass, catfish, sunfish, croaker and bream. And the sea holds such good-to-eat fish as flounder, whiting, Spanish mackerel, gray sea trout, small bluefish, sheepshead and cobia.

Tundra swans winter in the lakes along the Carolina coast; some 45,000 gather at North Carolina's Lake Mattamuskeet National Wildlife Refuge. Otters live in the rivers. Muskrat and bobcat roam coastal forests. Alligators prowl the lakes, marshes and streams.

There are thousands of shorebirds, snow geese and hooded mergansers, wood ducks, sandpipers and herons, common brown pelicans and egrets. There are raptors, too, such as bald eagles and osprey, also called fish hawks, who pluck fish from the water. There is nothing quite like watching an osprey glide by with a plump, silvery fish fluttering in its razor-sharp talons.

HISTORY   **NATIVE PEOPLE** Most Carolina histories recount only the last 400 years, when white men conquered these coasts and mountains. Far more fascinating are the 10,000 years before, when the first Carolinians arrived. Near the end of the Ice Age, they made their way from Asia across a ribbon of land today covered by the Bering Strait. They arrived in what is now North America and spread across the continent in a sea of humanity.

Some walked thousands of miles over several years, following the wild game animals and the warmth that beckoned from the south. They were of many tribes and languages, dress, religion and government. In the Carolinas, the Hatteras and Yammassee tribes settled along the coast; the Catawba, Chowanoc, Waxhaw and Tuscarora found homes in the Piedmont sandhills and forest; and the Cherokee took to the mountains.

The Cherokee became the mightiest and most populous tribe. They were taller, more rugged than the people of other tribes, and they were brilliant hunters and marksmen. The women gathered nuts, berries and vegetables—potatoes and mushrooms, chestnuts and hickory nuts, huckleberries and mulberries—using them for food and medicine. At least 2000 years ago, the Cherokees were growing gardens of corn, beans, pumpkins and squash.

Most native tribes were not nomadic, but lived in permanent homes of log, split canes and twigs that were covered with grass and clay (despite the pervasive tepees advertised around the Carolinas today). Every family had a hothouse where they holed up on the coldest winter days; partly underground and encased in thick earthworks, it had a fire inside that burned all the time. Their villages were clustered alongside streams and at the mouths of rivers rich with trout, redhorse and catfish. The men hunted deer, bear, wild turkey and bison.

There were wars between tribes, but for the most part the earliest Carolinians lived a peaceful existence. The Cherokee had a national government with a board of nine men, as well as seven women, whose specific duties included deciding the fate of war prisoners. There were seven clans with names such as Wild Potato, Bird and Long Hair. Women could fight and vote.

Despite all this, the Europeans considered them savage. When the first white men and women arrived in the mid-1500s, there were about 35,000 native people living in the Carolinas. Three hundred years later, there were fewer than 2000.

EUROPEAN SETTLEMENT   The Spanish first found the Carolinas in Francisco Cordillo's 1521 expedition along the coast. Five years later, a Spanish judge named Vasquez de Ayllón brought 500 men, women and children from Santo Domingo Island to what is now Georgetown, South Carolina, and tried to establish a colony. The judge died, disease and starvation set in and the weather was unusually nasty; 150 survivors fled back to Santo Domingo.

Not until 1584 was there another Carolina colony, when Sir Walter Raleigh dispatched two English ships carrying 107 men to the shores of North Carolina. Upon arriving on today's Outer Banks, Captain Arthur Barlowe wrote of a land overflowing with grapes and with the "beating and surge of the sea," and "woods full of deer, conies, hares and fowl . . . in incredible abundance." He also wrote of a native man, perhaps of the Hatteras or Yamasee tribe, who came aboard a ship, was given clothing and food, then returned with a bounty of fish for the colonists.

It was the European hunting methods that brought the local bison population to extinction.

But winter soon set in and the men ran low on food and supplies. Before a year was over, they returned to England. A second colony came in 1587, this time with women, and within a few months the first English child was born in North America. Her name was Virginia Dare, and though it is a common name today, appearing on everything from roads to inns, no one knows the fate of the girl. This second colony also ran low on food and supplies and dispatched a ship to England, but the ship got caught up in the war with Spain and could not return for three years. By then, the settlers were gone. They became known as the lost colony.

The white settlers who first made permanent homes in the Carolinas came down from Virginia in the 1650s. Most were planters with hopes of owning huge hunks of land, which they found and secured along North Carolina's fertile coastal plain. Crude farming and fishing outposts sprang up alongside rivers and sounds.

South Carolina's first lasting colony came in 1670, when the English built a coastal settlement and called it Albemarle Point. Ten years later they moved to a nearby peninsula and named it Charles Town, today's Charleston. French, English and Irish immigrants came to town and got rich trading deerskins, sugar and rum, and the trading port quickly became the center of the Carolina Colonial universe—a cultural, artistic, affluent mecca with grand homes and formal gardens.

As European settlers spread out, they pushed aside the native Carolinians. Entire tribes were eliminated by disease, while others were driven westward to the rugged Carolina mountains. Still others, such as the Yamasee, fought bloodily but unsuccessfully for their land, eventually fleeing to Florida in 1718, where they were later obliterated.

Pirates also waged war with colonists, terrorizing the coastal cities in the early eighteenth century. Blackbeard, Stede Bonnet and many other buccaneers, including several women, found the hidden coves and blackwater swamps of the Carolinas perfect lairs. Blackbeard was killed in 1718 at Cape Fear, North Carolina, by a British Navy lieutenant; Bonnet was captured at the same time, shipped to Charleston, and hung.

The early 1700s also brought the beginning of Southern plantation life. South Carolina's fertile, watery fringe made it perfect for rice growing, and by the mid-1700s, plantations covered much of the coast. Most planters grew indigo and cotton, as well, though all these crops were labor-intensive.

And so some of history's bleaker moments were played out in the Carolinas as thousands of Africans were shipped here and enslaved on plantations. Charleston boasted the busiest slave markets around, and South Carolina's economy was built on rice and slavery. By 1775, black slaves outnumbered white South Carolinians by 30,000, though they were unable to overthrow their oppressors. Reminders of those times are evident today in the grim former slave quarters and the nameless tombstones of slave cemeteries.

There are many reminders, too, of the Revolutionary War, particularly in South Carolina, where several battles and skirmishes were fought. British troops failed to capture Charleston in 1776, but succeeded in 1780. Shortly thereafter, the British were defeated by Continental forces at Kings Mountain and then at Cowpens, both in northwestern South Carolina.

CIVIL WAR AND RECONSTRUCTION   No event so shaped the Carolinas as did the Civil War, simply called "The War" around both states today. The shooting started in Charleston on April 12, 1861, a most appropriate place for the war's beginning, as the city coquettishly called itself the "Cradle of Secession." Union General

TAR HEELS

It was around the time of the Revolutionary War that North Carolinians were named Tar Heels. One story says that a British general remarked after intense fighting that "those Carolina boys stick in there like they've got tar on their heels." Another version is that General Cornwallis' troops crossed the Tar River (where turpentine mills dumped their waste) and emerged with the black stuff on their feet. Cornwallis is said to have observed that "anyone who wades in a Carolina stream would get tar heels."

William Tecumseh Sherman called South Carolina the "hellhole of Secession" and vowed to crush the state, the first to secede the Union and the premier champion of slavery.

North Carolina was the last state to secede, having opposed secession until May 1861, when it was asked to send troops to the Union Army. Instead, North Carolina sent 125,000 men to fight with the Confederacy—about a quarter of the entire Confederate Army—and lost more soldiers by war's end than any other Southern state.

Sherman kept his promise about South Carolina. In 1865, during the war's final months, he and 61,000 troops swept across the state, demolishing railroad lines, burning fields and plantations, blackening the sky with columns of smoke. Sherman set fire to Columbia, the state capital, and wiped out 84 city blocks. His troops then spent three days getting drunk, plundering and raping.

The troops never reached Charleston, having been held back by the Lowcountry's mucky labyrinth of swamp, creeks and rivers, but the city fell anyway. A Union siege begun in 1863 left the city in shambles by February 1865, when the Confederate flag was permanently lowered over Charleston.

Post-war, the Carolinas were mostly a wasteland. Plantations, abandoned or reduced to cinders, covered the Piedmont and coastal plain. Cities lay in ruins. Slaves were technically free but enjoyed few economic or social rights. The Ku Klux Klan reared up, horribly, from the Civil War wreckage to begin its secretive tyranny. Federal law guaranteed African-Americans the right to vote, go to school and own land, but the Klan believed otherwise. Many Carolinian blacks died at the bad end of a hanging rope, in the sweaty darkness of a Southern night.

North Carolina planters divvied up their land and rented portions to sharecroppers, many of whom were former slaves. Three decades after the war, cotton and tobacco dominated the land, and mills populated the towns and cities. Forests were logged and the wood turned into tables, chairs and desks, and soon North Carolina became a hub of furniture making. Textile mills spilled over into South Carolina, where hydroelectricity was the new source of energy and where destitute farmers were desperate for work. By 1900, thousands had left the fields for the mills.

MODERN TIMES   Twentieth-century North Carolina is still dominated by furniture and tobacco manufacturing, though the latter—a perilous, controversial business—continues to trouble the state. In the 1950s, North Carolina focused on technology and engineering, opening the Research Triangle Park between Raleigh and Durham to attract industry. Today, the 6800-acre park is a high-tech haven whose tenants include IBM, Burroughs-Wellcome and Northern Telecom. The drug AZT was created here, and several researchers have received the Nobel Prize for their findings.

Greensboro, North Carolina, was the seat of social reform in 1960, when four black students staged a sit-in at an F. W. Woolworth lunch counter. It sparked lunch-counter sit-inns across the nation, and helped bring about the Civil Rights Act of 1964.

The Carolinas' most progressive city, Charlotte, North Carolina, is today a sparkling New South hub with a burgeoning banking and insurance industry and a sleek downtown. It is often compared to Atlanta—and unfairly, since Charlotte lacks the crime, congestion and urban chaos of the big Georgia city to the south.

South Carolina's hub of business and technology can be found at Greenville and Spartanburg, in the state's hilly Upcountry. In 1994, nearby Greer was chosen over dozens of other cities worldwide as the site of BMW's newest auto manufacturing plant.

As for Charleston, that grand antebellum dame by the sea has emerged as one of the top tourist cities in the nation, its downtown saturated with marvelous Old South architecture and New South cafes and boutiques. National magazines have recently named Charleston among the top ten destinations in the United States, and its historic inns among the country's most desirable.

Indeed, since the turn of the century, tourism has defined the Carolinas. Mountain resort towns have long drawn thousands of summer visitors to their fabulously forested, cool environs, and today they draw millions. Beaches attract sun-and-sand seekers and, lately, anyone who wants to swing a golf club. More than 100 golf courses are along the South Carolina coast, with Myrtle Beach leading the pack with more than 80 golf courses. Winter retreats such as Aiken, South Carolina, attracted Northerners after the Civil War—"Yankee" aristocrats built grand mansions and called them cottages, and called themselves "The Winter Colony."

Perhaps the greatest statement about modern Carolinas tourism is that Carolinians themselves do much of the wandering, preferring the beauty and familiarity of their own states to any others.City people head for the mountains in summer; mountain folk drive over to the beaches, seeking out the secluded isles and hidden coves of the Lowcountry in South Carolina and the Outer Banks in North Carolina. Just about everyone makes a pilgrimage to Charleston, usually in spring or fall, to walk among the ancient cobbled streets and redolent gardens.

▼▼▼▼▼▼▼▼▼
Where to Go

Choosing the Carolinas as a vacation destination is easy; deciding where to go is another matter. The two states are so vast and varied that it would take many visits to experience all they have to offer. To help you decide, here are brief descriptions of the regions presented in this book, but they are only teasers. To get the big picture, read the more detailed introductions to each chapter, then delve into the material on the particular regions that appeal to you most.

Asheville, North Carolina, is ringed with Blue Ridge mountains and filled with beautiful old architecture, moneyed neighborhoods and a young, hip population. Only 65,000 people live in this city where, in the 1880s, George Vanderbilt built his exquisite Biltmore Estate, today the country's largest private home and a major Carolinas attraction. Asheville is the gateway to North Carolina's mountains; the Blue Ridge Parkway runs alongside the city, and the Great Smoky Mountains are barely 30 miles to the west.

North Carolina's **Southern Mountains** start just south of Asheville and run west more than a hundred miles. Two-lane Route 64 is the main thread through this deeply wooded region where heights average 2000 to 3000 feet. Waterfalls, apple orchards and national forests fill the scenery, and there are a few small resort towns, some with chichi shops and golf courses, others with downhome appeal.

The western edge of North Carolina explodes with the lush, green, misty peaks of the **Great Smoky Mountains**. Most lie within Great Smoky Mountains National Park. Split between North Carolina and Tennessee, it's the country's most popular national park, with more than nine million annual visitors. Old homesteads and grist mills and farms, extraordinary vistas of valleys and mountain ranges, and rich, dazzling plant and animal life await in this cool and luxuriant place. Old-time resort towns just outside the park offer venerable lodging and dining, plenty of outdoor pursuits and Southern hospitality.

A scenic road across mountain peaks, the **Blue Ridge Parkway** runs from the Smokies northeast all the way into Virginia. There are 252 miles of this national parkway in North Carolina, all offering postcard views, whether they be of a century-old log cabin framed in split-rail fence, a mountain lake enveloped in evergreens, cold-running streams filled with trout, or apple orchards cascading into valleys. No stop signs, no traffic lights and barely any development—just dozens of historic and scenic stops.

You can exit the parkway right into the resort towns of the **High Country**. North Carolina's highest mountains are here, with 6684-foot Mount Mitchell, tallest mountain east of the Mississippi, ruling the scenery. Little Switzerland, Linville and Blowing Rock are some of the scenic, elite hamlets sprinkled across the High Country, and there is the slightly larger city of Boone, named for the frontiersman who once blazed the buffalo trails through these parts. The High Country is North Carolina's hub of snow skiing, and summer headquarters for golf and tennis, hiking and fishing, fine dining and just plain living well.

The Piedmont makes up that great swath of central North Carolina, painted with clay, covered with foothills and tobacco fields, and studded with the Carolinas' major population centers. Nearly six million people call the Piedmont home, most living in

Winston-Salem, Charlotte, Raleigh, Durham or Chapel Hill. Picturesque college campuses, burgeoning banking, insurance and high-tech industries, furniture and tobacco factories, and lovely old Southern homes dominate the region, though rambling countryside and Old South ways are easy to find.

Stretching nearly 300 miles between Virginia and South Carolina, the **North Carolina Coast** is a wonderful tapestry of rivers and sounds and scrub pine forest, pretty old fishing villages and a necklace of barrier isles called the Outer Banks. The Banks boast long, lonesome beaches and popular ones, too, and constant winds that whip the sand into the East Coast's highest dunes. Ferry boats deliver visitors and their cars to various islands.

The **South Carolina Coast** encompasses 200 miles of rivers and swamps, silver sand beaches and long-lasting forests, towns dating to the 1600s and Civil War plantations. Myrtle Beach, on the north end, has the prettiest beaches, the kitschiest ambiance and more than 80 golf courses. South of here is the Lowcountry, a watery world of tidal creeks and savannahs where rice and indigo plantations once thrived, and where today shrimp and crab are abundant. Charleston—old, elegant and supremely Southern—is the heart of the Lowcountry, and then there is the pretty town of Beaufort and the exclusive resort island of Hilton Head, where golfing reigns supreme.

Inland South Carolina starts with the appealing capital, Columbia, then spreads out to handsome, moneyed Aiken and its thoroughbred horse culture. It also takes in the northwestern corner of the state, called the Upcountry, with low, green mountains, lakes cupped in evergreen spires, and dozens of hidden places to discover.

When to Go

▼▼▼▼▼▼▼▼▼

The Carolinas rarely get extremely cold or hot, but stay comfortable most of the time—in the 80s during summer and 60s during spring and fall. In winter, the mercury drops down in

SEASONS

the 30s and 40s, lower in the mountains and higher on the coast, and rain is frequent.

Spring and fall bring some of the most pleasant days and nights in all but the highest regions of the Carolinas. The weather is typically dry and sunny, the flowers blooming in spring and leaves blazing orange, purple and red in fall, creating a crisp, colorful experience. This is high season for the mountains, when the most visitors take to the winding roads. It's also peak time in certain coastal cities, such as New Bern, North Carolina, and Charleston, South Carolina, when the gardens put on a spectacular show.

The mountains are glorious in summer, with their light-sweater nights, T-shirt days and endless shades of green. Summer rain comes suddenly and frequently in the mountains, particularly the

Great Smoky Mountains, but it rarely lasts long—usually just minutes—and the sun is back in all its warmth and glory.

People in the Piedmont region of North Carolina and across inland South Carolina head for the mountains on summer weekends to escape the still, humid heat of the cities, where temperatures can creep up into the 90s. On winter weekends, the same folks go to the mountains to ski. The downhill and cross-country action typically starts in December and runs until mid- or late March, with December and March bringing the warmest ski weather.

> When visiting the East's highest peak, Mount Mitchell, North Carolina, dress warmly. This wind-lashed summit has seen snow year-round. Temperatures can drop 10° in an hour, 20° in three hours.

Beaches along the Carolinas' coast are generally packed from Memorial Day to Labor Day, when temperatures average in the mid- to high 80s but the beaches are cooled by constant wind. On North Carolina's Outer Banks, the breeze is so dependable that many beachfront cottages don't bother with air conditioning. Water temperatures are another story—usually reaching the mid- to upper 70s, but rarely 80°.

Hurricanes, though they can be devastating, need not keep one away from the coast. Usually developing in September, hurricanes have also been known to occur earlier or much later. Unlike many other weather phenomena, they come with plenty of warning, allowing visitors to either batten down or depart for inland locations and higher ground. Besides, September can be a wonderful time on a Carolinas' beach. The kids are back in school, the rates have dropped considerably but the temperature only a little, and the sands are much more secluded.

CALENDAR OF EVENTS

Ever been to a grits festival, an opossum creep, a parade of pigs, or a mountain sweet talk play? Now's your chance. Annual events in the Carolinas are folksy, friendly fests where you'll get to know the local people and instantly feel at home.

Check with local chambers of commerce (listed in regional chapters of this book) to see what will be going on when you are in the area. Below is a sampling of some of the bigger events, and some home-style ones, too.

High Country Christmas at the Homestead, is a traditional eighteenth-century holiday celebration, and re-enacted in Boone, North Carolina.

JANUARY

Piedmont In Greensboro, North Carolina, you can peruse custom cars at the **World of Wheels** expo. Hickory, North Carolina, celebrates **Art in the Mart** with exhibits of painting, sculpture and other artwork at the Hickory Furniture Mart. Pinehurst, North

Carolina's **Jazz Fest in January** is a three-day musical gala at the grand old Pinehurst Resort.

South Carolina Coast   Get your steamed oysters by the bucket at Charleston's **Lowcountry Oyster Festival**, held on the lawns of Boone Hall Plantation.

FEBRUARY   **Piedmont**   Antique hounds won't want to miss Waxhaw's **Antique & Collectible Show**, featuring local and regional dealers.

North Carolina Coast   A Revolutionary War skirmish is replayed at the anniversary **Celebration of the Battle of Moores Creek Bridge,** located northwest of Wilmington.

Inland South Carolina   **Africa Alive** uses art, drama and dance to tell the story of early African culture. The event is held at the Museum of York County in Rock Hill.

MARCH   **North Carolina Coast**   Wilmington hosts a month-long **Southern Lights Festival** with music, performing arts, golf tournaments and other events.

South Carolina Coast   One of Charleston's biggest events, the **Festival of Houses and Gardens,** includes tours of more than 100 historic private homes and their gardens, as well as churches. Afternoon teas, oyster roasts, garden galas and walking tours are among the many events, which last from mid-March to mid-April. Around the same time, Charleston's **Courtyard Tearoom** offers tastings of Lowcountry cuisine, such as she-crab soup, okra soup and shrimp paste sandwiches, in a Confederate home. On Hilton Head Island, the world's top women tennis players compete in the **Family Circle Magazine Cup,** which usually runs from late March through early April.

Inland South Carolina   One of South Carolina's biggest events, the **Aiken Triple Crown,** takes place on three consecutive March weekends. The venue is Aiken, the heart of thoroughbred racing country. Over in Barnwell, visit the **Opossum Creep Festival** and have a taste of opossum and coon (that's raccoon to you), ride carnival rides, see a horse show, and shop for arts and crafts.

APRIL   **Asheville**   The Biltmore Estate's **Festival of Flowers** is a dazzling, colorful affair, with spring blooms filling the formal gardens and interior of Asheville's famed chateau.

Southern Mountains   What more compelling place than Chimney Rock Park to celebrate Easter? The **Chimney Rock Park Easter Sunrise Service,** held at the spine-tingling top of the rock, is nondenominational.

Piedmont   Civil War times are relived at Durham, North Carolina's **Bennett Place Surrender Reenactment Program.** In Southern Pines, North Carolina, the **Springfest/Tour De Moore**

features 30- and 100-mile bike races, crafts, food and entertainment. Dozens of "turners and burners" gather for the annual **North Carolina Pottery Conference** in Seagrove, North Carolina.

North Carolina Coast   Wilmington goes all out for azaleas, with a parade, home and garden tours, and live entertainment during the **North Carolina Azalea Festival**.

Inland South Carolina   Lovely Edisto Memorial Gardens in Orangeburg explodes with roses in spring, offering festivities such as canoe racing, an arts-and-crafts fair and food during its three-day **South Carolina Festival of Roses**. The **World Grits Festival** in St. George has lots of gritty trappings, including grits grinding, a grits-eating contest and corn-shelling contest. In Springfield, frogs are hopping and eggs are cracking at the **Governor's Frog Jump & Egg Striking Contest** on Easter weekend. (The egg strike is a long-time local tradition wherein each contestant holds a hard-boiled egg on end and taps—or strikes—the egg against another contestant's. The person holding the last unbroken egg wins.) Pickens celebrates the blooming of the azaleas with its **Azalea Festival**, featuring a classic car show, food booths, arts and crafts, and entertainment.

MAY

Asheville   Northeast of Asheville, the **Black Mountain Folk Festival** centers around crafts, dance and food.

Piedmont   Tanglewood Park, located south of Winston-Salem in Clemmons, North Carolina, hosts its ever-popular **Steeplechase at Tanglewood**. Over at the Charlotte Motor Speedway in Concord, North Carolina, there's big excitement generated during the **Coca-Cola 600** race.

North Carolina Coast   All the action's up high at the **Hang Gliding Spectacular** competitions and show in Nags Head.

South Carolina Coast   The **Myrtle Gras of Myrtle Beach** is a jazzy fest by the sea with Nawlins'-style music, food and a parade. Little River has its **Blue Crab Festival**, one of the coast's biggest events, with more than 150 booths and exhibits and plenty of fresh, flaky blue crab. Charleston's most acclaimed annual gala, **Spoleto Festival**, is a three-week musical extravaganza focusing on opera but also featuring jazz, ballet, chamber music, theater, late-night cabaret—and lots and lots of parties. The Lowcountry's rich Gullah heritage is celebrated during the three-day-long **Gullah Festival** in Beaufort. Storytelling, basketmaking, fine art, dance and music are just some of the activities.

Inland South Carolina   Ever heard of a custom-built lobster race-track? You have now. The one in the town of Aiken is the site of the **Lobster Race and Oyster Fest**, where you can watch the crustaceans crawl down a track, listen to big band music, peruse arts and crafts, and savor fresh-cooked seafood (read lobster).

JUNE

Great Smoky Mountains Pretty downtown Dillsboro, North Carolina, is lined with art, craft and food vendors as well as side-walk entertainers during the **Dillsboro Heritage Festival**.

High Country When the world's largest wild rhododendron gardens bloom on Roan Mountain, Bakersville folks hold the **North Carolina Rhododendron Festival**, with a 10K race, golf tournament and carnival rides. Nature lovers and photographers won't want to miss the **Grandfather Mountain Nature Photography Weekend**, with lectures and contests on the mountain in Linville, North Carolina. Arts and crafts are the highlight of **Art in the Park** at Blowing Rock, North Carolina.

North Carolina Coast Nags Head celebrates June with the **Rogallo Kite Festival**, featuring kite-flying workshops and competitions. Beaufort's **Annual Old Home Tours** are a wonderful way to see inside some of North Carolina's most beautiful historic houses.

South Carolina Coast Myrtle Beach's **Sun Fun Festival** is a week-long parade of events: sporting contests, beauty pageants, sand-castle-building contests, outdoor concerts and fireworks. **Harborwalk** at Georgetown is a riverside party with live music, artwork and Lowcountry fare.

JULY

Many communities celebrate the **Fourth of July** with parades, fireworks and other festivities.

Great Smoky Mountains Waynesville, North Carolina, hosts its popular **Folkmoot, U.S.A.**, highlighted by international music and dance. The town also has a July **Street Dance** accompanied by mountain and bluegrass music and Southern cooking.

High Country Grandfather Mountain's famous **Highland Games & Gathering of Scottish Clans** draws thousands of people to the scenic mountainside in Linville, North Carolina. Highland dancing, athletic competitions, Scottish fiddling and harps, piping and drumming, Celtic jam, and Scottish folk music fill four days of celebration.

Piedmont In Durham, North Carolina, the **Duke Homestead Curing Barn Party** relives tobacco's earliest days. Live entertainment and food come with the party.

North Carolina Coast The **Wright Kite Festival** in Kill Devil Hills is held on the spot where Wilbur and Orville Wright took their first flight. The Outer Banks beaches of Ocracoke Island are the site of the **Ocracoke Sand Sculpture Contest**. Gospel singing and croakers team up at the **Pamlico County Croaker Festival** in tiny seaside Oriental. Arts and crafts and a parade are also on the agenda. (A croaker is a small, white-fleshed fish that, well, *croaks* when you catch him.) On Wrightsville Beach, there are volleyball tournaments, sand-sculpting contests, boogie-board contests and wind-surfing at the **Surf, Sun & Sand Celebration**.

Inland South Carolina   Get out your clogging shoes and head to
Hillbilly Day in Mountain Rest, where the countrified fun includes
square dancing, clogging, live country music and Southern crafts.
Gaffney pays homage to the peach during the ten-day **South Carolina Peach Festival**, with concerts by nationally known musicians,
truck and tractor pulls, and lots of peachy eats. Watermelons more
your style? Pageland hosts the **Watermelon Festival**, where events
range from melon-eating and seed-spitting contests to rodeos.

Great Smoky Mountains   Autoharps, fiddles, dulcimers and
banjos make sweet music during the **Smoky Mountain Folk Festival** on Lake Junaluska, located near Waynesville, North Carolina.
Blue Ridge Parkway   The **World Gee Haw Whimmy Diddle
Contest** at the Folk Art Center in Oteen is all about whimmy
diddles, an Appalachian folk toy that's a stick with notches along
one side and a propeller on the end. Take another stick, rub it along
the notches, and the propeller turns, making a "gee haw" sound.
Besides the contest—who can make the most gees and haws in
twelve seconds—there are crafts, food and music.
North Carolina Coast   Fresh, summery seafare will water your
mouth at the **Corolla Seafood Festival** on the northern Outer
Banks. Down on the Cape Fear Coast, Snead's Ferry dishes up
pearly pink shellfish at the **Annual Shrimp Festival**, which includes
a parade, arts and crafts booths and entertainment.

AUGUST

Asheville   The life and works of novelist Thomas Wolfe, the late
Asheville native, take center stage during the **Thomas Wolfe Festival** from late September through early October.
Southern Mountains   Hendersonville's **North Carolina Apple Festival** features four days of celebrating over the Labor Day weekend. There's a jazz concert, a gem and mineral show, food and art
booths, and a King Apple Parade.
Great Smoky Mountains   The **Mountain Life Festival**, held in
Great Smoky Mountains National Park features demonstrations of
weaving, spinning, quilting, open-hearth cooking and the making
of apple butter and hominy.
Piedmont   Kernersville, North Carolina, holds the **Honeybee Festival**, with art, food and music honoring the state insect. **Mayberry
Days** in Mount Airy, North Carolina—the setting fictionalized in
The Andy Griffith Show—offers down-home fun: pie-eating con-
tests, pig-pickin' cookouts and Opie's Backyard playground where
kids can go worm-digging and play hopscotch. Durham, North
Carolina, home of Carolina blues, hosts the **Bull Durham Blues
Festival** with two days of bluesy music and plenty to eat.
South Carolina Coast   Charleston hosts the **Scottish Games and
Highland Gathering**, complete with medieval competitions, bag-
pipe playing and Scottish dancing.

SEPTEMBER

Inland South Carolina   One of the state's biggest mountain parties, the **Cherokee Foothills Festival** in Fair Play has a juried arts-and-crafts show, live music and plenty of homegrown food.

OCTOBER   Octoberfests are in full gear around the Carolinas, with most offering German food and beer and oompah-pah music.

High Country   Banner Elk, North Carolina, holds the **Wooly Worm Festival**, where locals turn out to race caterpillars on strings, after which there is plenty of food and drink and music.

Piedmont   The biggest barbecue bash around is Lexington, North Carolina's **Barbecue Festival**, where dozens of Carolina cooks take to the streets with their pigs and smokers. There's a barbecue cook-off, arts and crafts, and a parade of pigs.

North Carolina Coast   Thousands of mum lovers stream to the town of Wilmington for the **Chrysanthemum Festival** at Tryon Palace. Down in tiny Shallotte, on the Southern part of the Cape Fear coast, there's the **North Carolina Oyster Festival**.

South Carolina Coast   Owners of beautiful old Beaufort homes open their doors to visitors for the **Fall Tour of Historic Homes**. You can continue your tour down on Edisto Island during **Edisto's Golden Age**, which offers visits to churches and plantations dating to the early 1700s.

Inland South Carolina   If you're into okra, go to the **Okra Strut** in Irmo and enter the okra-eating contest. Prefer collard greens? Then check out the **Collard Festival** in Gaston, which has a granny pageant, carnival and crafts. Fountain Inn, in South Carolina's Upcountry, sponsors the **Aunt Het Festival**, where nineteenth century–style fun includes weaving and pottery demonstrations and an antique auto show.

NOVEMBER   **Asheville**   The much-celebrated **Candlelight Christmas at Biltmore Estate**, where the beautiful Asheville chateau is elaborately decorated in Victorian holiday style, begins in the middle of November and runs through early January.

Piedmont   Seagrove, North Carolina, holds its **North Carolina Traditional Pottery Festival**, where artistically inclined browsers can choose from dozens of styles and artists.

South Carolina Coast   Sea island history is remembered during the **Heritage Celebration** on St. Helena Island, with activities such as a fish fry, oyster roast and "traditional spirituals."

DECEMBER   Candlelight and historic home tours, parades and Santa festivals prevail across North and South Carolina communities throughout December, culminating in New Year's Eve galas.

Asheville   **New Year's Eve Celebration** at the Grove Park Inn starts on December 30 and continues for three days, with highlights including a mountain theme party and nonstop dining and entertainment.

Piedmont   Centuries-old Moravian customs are featured in Winston-Salem during **Old Salem Christmas**, where visitors can observe Christmas candles being made and attend "lovefeasts," which (before you get too excited) are meals of sweetened buns and coffee.

North Carolina Coast   The **First Flight Anniversary Celebration** in Kill Devil Hills commemorates Wilbur and Orville Wright's history-making flight. Wilmington's Tryon Palace is lavished with Colonial holiday decor most of the month for the **Tryon Palace Christmas Celebration**, featuring home and garden tours and a wassail bowl.

Inland South Carolina   The cities of Columbia and Greenville bring in the New Year in a big way. **First Night Columbia** and **First Night Greenville** feature a lineup of musical and performing-arts events, downtown art fests and a finale of fireworks in an alcohol free environment.

For information on North Carolina, contact the **North Carolina Division of Travel & Tourism**. ~ 430 North Salisbury Street, Raleigh, NC 27611; 919-733-4171, 800-847-4862. For a free copy of the *North Carolina Scenic Byways* booklet, which describes hidden roads and off-the-beaten-path trails all around the state, contact the **North Carolina Department of Transportation**. ~ P.O. Box 25201, Raleigh, NC 27611; 919-733-2920.

▼▼▼▼▼▼▼▼▼▼
Before You Go

VISITORS CENTERS

In South Carolina, the **South Carolina Division of Parks, Recreation & Tourism** is the place for general information. ~ 1205 Pendleton Street, Columbia, SC 29201; 803-734-0122, 800-868-2492, fax 803-734-0133. Most Carolinas cities and small towns have visitor information centers or chambers of commerce; many of them are listed in *Hidden Carolinas* under the appropriate regions.

Packing for the Carolinas depends a lot on when and where you visit. In summer, you can get by in most areas with light, casual clothing, some shorts and cool slacks, T-shirts and cotton blouses, a bathing suit (two, if you're beach bound), sandals and sturdy, comfortable walking shoes, and something a little dressy for night. If you're headed for the mountains, definitely pack a sweater or lightweight jacket for those cool summer nights.

PACKING

For big-city forays, you can take along fancier clothes for ultra-deluxe dining, but very few places require coat and tie. Dress is more conservative in small towns, particularly those with laws prohibiting the sale of alcohol and where Sunday churchgoing is de rigueur. Short-shorts and micro-skirts are not.

Spring and fall call for more substantial wear: jeans and a sweatshirt, sweatpants and a warm jacket. Bring your warmest clothes in winter: thick sweaters and socks, hats and gloves, down jackets and ski clothes, especially if you're headed for the mountain slopes. Heavy-soled hiking boots come in handy even in the cities, where winter rains are dependable. Take along an umbrella and raincoat, any time or place you visit.

Though the Carolinas are not the Caribbean, you can get just as impressive a sunburn here. Bring a good sunscreen, especially to the beach, where sand and water reflect the sun's rays more intensely. If you'll be on the Outer Banks, pack protective sunglasses to shield your eyes from constant winds and occasional airborne sand. Polarized glasses, which help you see beneath the water's surface, are extra helpful if you're going fishing.

Mosquito repellent is essential in summer, particularly in the coastal forests and swamps. If you plan to do any hiking in the wetlands or crabbing in the tidal marshes, wear canvas shoes that you don't mind wading in.

Bring along a camera; mountain sunsets and seaside sunrises are sensational. Binoculars enhance both birdwatching and beachwatching. Good street and road maps are a must. Many roads in the Carolinas are winding and poorly marked (or unmarked), but these offer some of the most scenic, worthwhile wandering. Anyway, if you get lost, Carolinians will gladly point you in the right direction.

LODGING   Lodging in the Carolinas ranges from log cabins hidden in the woods to grand old mountainside inns, from funky seaside cottages to lavish beachfront hotels with fantasy gardens and swimming pools. Charleston, South Carolina, is a haven of exquisite lodges and inns, many more than 100 years old, including the John Rutledge House, which Rutledge built in 1763 for his bride.

Bed and breakfasts abound throughout both states. Some are in historic farmhouses or port town mansions with rambling quarters and plenty of space and privacy for guests. Other places are small homes with a spare room or two, with plenty of space for the host family but little seclusion or privacy for guests. Be sure to ask whether a bed and breakfast is a real inn or not. All of the bed and breakfasts listed in this book offer generous, private quarters for guests.

Chain motels line most main thoroughfares and mom-and-pop enterprises still successfully vie for lodgers in every region. Large hotels with names you'd know anywhere appear in most cities of any size. All along the Carolinas' coast, you'll find old-fashioned beach houses, many on stilts, where the salt-laden wind blows in off the water and the seagulls screech along the surf. Many are available by the week-only in summer but offer rates in the budget to moderate range.

State park cabins and villas, usually in the woods or along the shore, offer some of the least expensive lodging in the Carolinas. Naturally, it is some of the hardest to procure. You may have to book a year in advance—and then settle for your second or third choice of dates. Weekly stays are usually required in high season.

Whatever your preference and budget, you can probably find something to suit your taste with the help of the regional chapters in this book. Remember, rooms are often scarce and rates steepest in the high season—spring through fall in the mountains and on the beaches, spring and fall (but not summer) in Charleston. Ski season is also peak time in North Carolina's High Country. Across the North Carolina Piedmont and inland South Carolina, most cities offer constant year-round rates.

Off-season rates are often drastically reduced in many places (ultra-deluxe summer rooms on Myrtle Beach, for instance, are budget-priced in winter), allowing for a week's, or even a month's, stay to be a real bargain. Then, of course, there may be nasty weather. Whatever you do, plan ahead and make reservations, especially in the prime tourist seasons.

Accommodations in this book are organized by region and classified according to price range. Rates referred to are high-season rates, so if you are looking for low-season bargains, it's good to inquire. *Budget* lodgings generally are less than $60 per night for two people and are satisfactory—clean but modest. *Moderate*-priced lodgings run from $60 to $100; what they have to offer in the way of luxury will depend on where they are located, but they tend to offer larger rooms and more attractive surroundings. For a *deluxe* accommodation, you can expect to spend between $100 and $130 for a double; you'll generally find spacious rooms, a fashionable lobby, a restaurant or two, and perhaps some boutiques. *Ultra-deluxe* facilities, priced above $130, are a region's finest, offering all the amenities of a deluxe hotel plus plenty of resort extras such as a health club and spa, 24-hour room service and gourmet dining.

If you crave a room facing the mountainside or the sea, be sure to ask specifically. Be warned that "waterfront" can mean sound or inlet or even a creek in some cases. If you are trying to save money, lodgings a block or so from the beach, or in town instead of on the mountain, usually offer lower rates. The savings are often worth the short stroll to the beach or scenic ride up the mountain.

DINING

Southern fare, from New South nouveau and Old South country cooking to Lowcountry cuisine, stars at Carolinas restaurants everywhere. In big cities and college towns, you won't have trouble finding just about any kind of eatery, from ethnic to European to vegetarian. (For more on local fare, see the section titled "Carolinas Cooking" in this chapter.)

Within a particular chapter of *Hidden Carolinas*, restaurants are categorized geographically, with each entry describing the establishment according to price. Dinner entrées at *budget* restaurants usually cost $9 or less per person. The ambiance is less formal, service usually speedy and the crowd is often a local one. *Moderate*-priced restaurants range between $9 and $16 at dinner; surroundings are casual but pleasant, the menu offers more variety and the pace is usually slower than at budget eateries. *Deluxe* establishments tab their entrées from $16 to $24; cuisines may be simple or sophisticated, depending on the location, but the decor is plusher and the service more personalized. *Ultra-deluxe* dining rooms, where entrées begin at $24, are often the gourmet places; here cooking has become a fine art and the service should be impeccable.

> In most major urban areas of the Carolinas, you can order alcohol by the glass any day of the week—though you must order it after 1 p.m. on Sunday.

Some restaurants change hands often and are occasionally closed in low season. Efforts have been made in this book to include places with established reputations for good eating. When possible, restaurants with seasonal schedules have been noted. Breakfast and lunch menus vary less in price from restaurant to restaurant than evening dinners.

LIQUOR

Now, about alcohol: Carolinas' laws on liquor consumption vary from town to town and county to county. Particularly in "dry" rural areas along the Bible Belt, alcohol sales are limited in some form or even altogether. Some places permit wine and beer sales but no hard liquor; others limit all liquor sales to package stores but no restaurants—and forget nightclubs. Sunday liquor sales are banned in many rural areas. Often, restaurants will permit you to bring your own alcohol, though sometimes only wine and beer. If a drink with dinner is important to you, call before dining out.

TRAVELING WITH CHILDREN

The Carolinas are a wonderful place to bring children. The prevailing Southern culture focuses not just on hospitality but on the family, and the most activities, lodging and restaurants accommodate children. Two major North Carolina ski resorts are geared toward families, and what child wouldn't love a city (Myrtle Beach) with 26 mini golf courses? Then there are miles of beaches, dozens of lakes and hundreds of parks perfect for family travelers.

Some Carolinas' inns, guesthouses and bed and breakfasts don't accept children, so be sure of the policy when you make reservations. If you need a crib or cot, arrange for it with your hotel ahead of time.

If you are traveling by air, try to reserve bulkhead seats where there is plenty of room. Take along extras you may need, such as diapers, changes of clothing, snacks and toys, or small games. When traveling by car, be sure to take along the extras, too. Make sure you have plenty of water and juices to drink; dehydration can be a subtle problem.

A first-aid kit is a must for any trip. Along with adhesive bandages, antiseptic cream and something to stop itching, include any medicines your child's pediatrician might recommend to treat allergies (particularly if you visit in spring), colds, diarrhea or any chronic problems your child may have.

At the beach, take extra care with children's skin the first few days. Tender young skin can suffer severe sunburn before you know it. Hats for the kids are a good idea, along with liberal applications of a good sunscreen. Never take your eyes off children at the shore.

All-night stores are scarce in rural areas, and stores in small towns often close early. You may go a long distance between stores that can supply you with essentials, so be sure to be well-stocked with diapers, baby food and other necessities when on the go.

Many towns, parks and attractions offer special activities designed just for children. Consult local newspapers and/or call the numbers in this book to see what's happening where you're going.

GAY & LESBIAN TRAVELERS

The Carolinas are not known for their broadmindedness (this *is* the South) and there are, undoubtedly, deeply rural places where gay and lesbian travelers will not feel comfortable. However, in many areas they will not only feel comfortable but especially welcome. And several regions are fast emerging as gay and lesbian hot spots.

It is within these regions that *Hidden Carolinas* will steer you to gay-friendly and gay-specific lodging, dining, shopping and nightlife. In Chapter Two, you'll find gay-friendly lodging, bookstores and night spots in the dynamic city of Asheville. The big cities of Piedmont, covered in Chapter Seven, offer lots of danceclubs and other popular night spots for gay and lesbian travelers.

Gay headquarters on North Carolina's coast is Wilmington; check Chapter Eight for gay-friendly lodging, nightlife and beaches in this progressive coastal town. Across the line in South Carolina, Charleston has a thriving community of gay artists, writers and affluent nine-to-fivers. Their favorite lodges, night spots and beaches are outlined in Chapter Nine.

For gay and lesbian happenings around the Carolinas, pick up a copy of the *Front Page*, a free bi-weekly available in bookstores, cafes and gay nightclubs. ~ 919-829-0181.

SENIOR TRAVELERS

The Carolinas are an ideal place for older vacationers; countless museums, historic sights and even restaurants and lodges offer senior discounts that cut a substantial chunk off vacation costs.

Text continued on page 28.

Carolinas Cooking

Eating is a serious pastime in the Carolinas. Carolinians grow their crops in big fields, buy food by the bushel, make sweet tea by the gallon and carry pies and tomatoes to the neighbors. They spend weeks canning, curing and freezing, and, if war were to strike, they could no doubt survive for years on their pantries.

Mountain fare is typically meaty and vigorously prepared. Finer restaurants offer spicy duck sausage, pan-seared venison, hickory-smoked pork tenderloin, perhaps elk and antelope. Country kitchens serve pot roast, juicy and falling apart, peppery fried chicken, creamed corn and chicken and dumplings, and mashed potatoes piled with butter and cream and whipped into waves.

Trout are caught in the icy mountain streams and prepared every way, from the whole fish seasoned and baked with lemons to a filet that's pan-fried, topped with shrimp or crab. Alas, the fish is so small and delicate that you may often find yourself picking through pin-size bones, and wondering if it might have been wiser to order the country ham, salt-cured and smoked with oak, hickory and apple wood, and served in sweet pink loaves.

Old-time coffee shops start the day with steak and eggs, fat buttermilk pancakes framed in skinny sausage links, and mountain-ground grits dripping with butter. New Age coffeehouses have flaky croissants, muffins studded with Carolina apples, and little cups of energizing espresso.

Vegetarian and nouveau eateries and microbreweries are best found in big cities and college towns across the central Carolinas. Here, also, are fine French restaurants and exuberant ethnic eats—fiery Caribbean and Latin salsas, saffron-suffused Spanish and vinegary, robust German. There is also great soul food, African-American stews and meats and pies that really do comfort the soul.

Barbecue is cult food in the Carolinas, with Civil War–style debates waged over which is best. Depending on who you talk to, the pork should be finely chopped, sliced paper thin or served in big chunks. The sauce should be thin and vinegar-based, or thick and tomatoey. And coleslaw never—or always—goes on the sandwich, simply called a "barbecue."

No cuisine is so singular as that of the Lowcountry, on South Carolina's coast. Lowcountry cooking draws strongly from the sea, and from the tidal marsh and flats that feed the land. Oysters plucked from the mudflats are cooked in a thin, hot, milky bath called oyster stew. The pearly morsels of the blue crab are turned into she-crab soup, thick as pudding and white as a magnolia blossom. Sweet shrimp are sauced and barbecued, ladled over creamy grits and crowned with melted cheddar cheese.

In the town of St. Helena Island, formerly Frogmore, locals brew big cauldrons of shrimp, blue crabs, spicy sausage, corn on the cob, potatoes and onions, and invite all the neighbors over. Few restaurants serve Frogmore Stew, also called Lowcountry Boil, so unless you're lucky enough to be invited to a Lowcountry home, you'll probably never experience this zesty taste of the sea.

Charleston, where food is crucial to the culture, is the capital of Lowcountry cuisine. "Cooking was always a fine art in Charleston, and a lady was expected to keep her own recipe books, know how to supervise servants, and entertain lavishly," notes Robert Rosen in his book, *A Short History of Charleston*. And today, "Charlestonians still prefer a party to any other activity."

Many Charleston cookbooks have recorded centuries of local recipes, though none is so well regarded as *Charleston Receipts* ("receipt" is a take on the word "recipe"), published in 1950 by the Junior League of Charleston. The league's most recent endeavor, *Party Receipts*, gives the recipe for Jeannie Nissen King's wonderful cheese spread using Clemson blue cheese, made on the campus of Clemson University in South Carolina's Upcountry. You can also use regular blue cheese or, even better, Gorgonzola.

CLEMSON BLUE CHEESE AND OLIVE PASTE

8 ounces black olives, pitted
4 cloves garlic, mashed
¼ cup chopped pecans or walnuts
6 tablespoons olive oil or more, as needed
¾ pound Clemson blue cheese or Roquefort or Gorgonzola
French bread or assorted crackers

Place the olives, garlic, nuts and olive oil in the bowl of a food processor and process with on/off pulses until the mixture is finely chopped and blended. Add the blue cheese and pulse until blended to a smooth consistency. The paste should be some-what moist from the oil. Add more olive oil by the tea-spoon, if necessary. Refrigerate until 15 minutes before serving (the paste will keep for up to a week in the refrigerator, and several months in the freezer). To serve, spread on slices of French bread or on crackers.

Makes 10 to 12 servings.

And many older travelers from hotter climes flock to the Carolina mountains for its cool summers.

The **American Association of Retired Persons** (AARP) offers membership to anyone 50 or over. Benefits of AARP membership include travel discounts with a number of firms. ~ 3200 East Carson Street, Lakewood, CA 90712; 310-496-2277.

Elderhostel offers reasonably priced, all-inclusive educational programs at a variety of Carolinas' locations throughout the year. ~ 75 Federal Street, Boston, MA 02110; 617-426-8056.

Be extra careful about health matters. In addition to the medications you ordinarily use, it's a good idea to bring along the prescriptions for obtaining more. Consider carrying a copy of your medical record with you—including your medical history and current medical status as well as your doctor's name, telephone number and address. Make sure that your insurance covers you while you're away from home.

DISABLED TRAVELERS

Many travel destinations throughout the Carolinas are fully accessible to travelers with disabilities. Every state park campground in South Carolina has two wheelchair-accessible sites that can be reserved in advance. The city of Myrtle Beach provides beachgoing wheelchairs. Many museums, botanical gardens and even mountain parks are designed with wheelchair visitors in mind. Plenty of wheelchair visitors have ridden the half-mile concrete ramp up to the top of Clingman's Dome, which is the highest spot in Great Smoky Mountains National Park.

Access North Carolina, a travel booklet with detailed wheelchair-access information on state attractions, is available free from **Independent Living**. ~ P.O. Box 26053, Raleigh, NC 27611; 919-733-5407.

Helpful information on traveling with disabilities is available from several national groups, including the **Society for the Advancement of Travel for the Handicapped**. ~ 347 5th Avenue, Suite 610, New York, NY 10016; 212-447-7284. Also try **Travel Information Service of Moss Rehab Hospital**. ~ 1200 West Tabor Road, Philadelphia, PA 19141; 215-329-5715. Information is also available at **Mobility International USA**. ~ P.O. Box 10767, Eugene, OR 97440; 503-343-1284. Or contact **Flying Wheels Travel**. ~ P.O. Box 382, Owatonna, MN 55060; 800-535-6790.

Travelin' Talk, a network of people and organizations, will provide information for travelers with disabilities. ~ P.O. Box 3534, Clarksville, TN 37043; 615-552-6670.

The travel guide *Traveling Like Everybody Else: A Practical Guide for Disabled Travelers*, by Jacqueline Freedman and Susan Gersten, lists tour operators and provides information on many other resources.

Passports and Visas   Most foreign visitors need a passport and tourist visa to enter the United States. Contact your nearest U.S. Embassy or Consulate well in advance to obtain a visa and to check on any other entry requirements.

Customs Requirements   Foreign travelers are allowed to carry in the following: 200 cigarettes (1 carton), 50 cigars or 2 kilograms (4.4 pounds) of smoking tobacco; one liter of alcohol for personal use only (you must be 21 years of age to bring in alcohol); and US$100 worth of duty-free gifts that may include an additional 100 cigars. You may bring in any amount of currency, but must fill out a form if you bring in over US$10,000. Carry any prescription drugs in clearly marked containers. (You may have to produce a written prescription or doctor's statement for the customs officers.) Meat or meat products, seeds, plants, fruits, and narcotics may not be brought into the United States. Contact the **United States Customs Service** for further information. ~ 1301 Constitution Avenue NW, Washington, DC 20229; 202-927-6724.

Driving   If you're visiting from another country and plan to rent a car, an international driver's license should be obtained before arriving in the United States. Some car rental agencies require both a foreign license and an international driver's license. Many also require a lessee to be at least 25 years of age; all require a major credit card.

Currency   United States money is based on the dollar. Bills come in denominations of $1, $5, $10, $20, $50 and $100. Every dollar is divided into 100 cents. Coins are the penny (1 cent), nickel (5 cents), dime (10 cents) and quarter (25 cents). Half-dollar and dollar coins are rarely used. You may not use foreign currency to purchase goods and services in the United States. Consider buying traveler's checks in dollar amounts. You may also use credit cards affiliated with an American company such as Interbank, Barclay Card and American Express.

Electricity and Electronics   Electric outlets use currents of 110 volts, 60 cycles. For appliances made for other electrical systems, you need a transformer or other adapter. Travelers who use laptop computers for telecommunication should be aware that modem configurations for U.S. telephone systems may be different from their European counterparts. Similarly, the U.S. format for videotapes is different from that in Europe; U.S. Park Service visitors centers and other stores that sell souvenir videos often have them available in European format.

Weights and Measures   The United States uses the English system of weights and measures. American units and their metric equivalents are: 1 inch = 2.5 centimeters; 1 foot (12 inches) = 0.3 meter; 1 yard (3 feet) = 0.9 meter; 1 mile (5280 feet) = 1.6 kilometers; 1 ounce = 28 grams; 1 pound (16 ounces) = 0.45 kilograms; 1 quart (liquid) = 0.9 liter.

▼▼▼▼▼▼▼▼▼▼▼▼▼▼
Outdoor Adventures

CAMPING

The Carolinas offer a wide variety of camping opportunities, from primitive camping in wilderness areas to recreational vehicle parks that resemble fashionable resorts. For a listing of North Carolina state parks and recreations areas, contact **North Carolina State Parks and Recreation Division**. ~ 512 North Salisbury Street, Raleigh, NC 27611; 919-733-4181. In South Carolina, write or call the **South Carolina State Parks**. ~ 1205 Pendleton Street, Columbia, SC 29201; 803-734-0122.

Information on camping in national forests in North Carolina is available from the **U.S. Forest Service**. ~ P.O. Box 2750, Asheville, NC 28802; 704-257-4200. If you're visiting the Smokies, contact the **Great Smoky Mountains National Park**. ~ Gatlinberg, TN 37738; 423-436-1226. For South Carolina national forests, contact the **U.S. Forest Service**. ~ 4931 Broad River Road, Columbia, SC 29210-4021; 803-561-4000.

An accommodations directory published by the **North Carolina Division of Travel & Tourism** lists public campgrounds and cabins across the state. ~ 430 Salisbury Street, Raleigh, NC 27611; 919-733-4171, 800-847-4862. The **North Carolina Campground Owners Association** publishes a guide to numerous privately owned campgrounds. ~ 1418 Aversboro Road, Garner, NC 27529; 919-779-5709.

The **South Carolina Campground Owners Association** puts out an annual *South Carolina Camping Guide* that lists more than two dozen private campsites across the state. Also, see the "Beaches & Parks" section in each chapter of this book to discover where camping is available in various areas of the Carolinas. ~ Associated Services, P.O. Box 1184, Irmo, SC 29063; 803-238-5636.

PERMITS Primitive campsites are provided in certain state parks and recreation areas. You need a permit for wilderness camping away from designated sites in national forests and in certain wilderness areas of state parks and seashores. To obtain permits and

◆◆

SNOW HEELS

As winter blankets the mountains of North Carolina, ski season heats up. Ski enthusiasts head for the High Country, where Sugar Mountain, Beech Mountain, Hawksnest and Appalachian Mountain offer the best downhill action. Much of the snow is machine-made and can sometimes get icy, though daily grooming helps keep the runs smooth and navigable. Specifics on individual resorts are listed in Chapter Six. For additional ski information, contact High Country Host. ~ 1700 Blowing Rock Road, Boone, NC 28607; 704-264-1299, 800-438-7500.

information, contact individual sites, as found in the "Beaches & Parks" sections of the regional chapters of this book.

Boating is one of the more popular activities in the Carolinas. You can bring your own boat and travel the Intracoastal Waterway or laze away the day on a quiet lake with a fishing pole. And if you have no boat, you can rent or charter a craft of just about any size or speed. Various chapters in this book offers suggestions on how to go about finding the vessel of your choice. Most marinas and other rental agencies will arm you with maps in advance. **BOATING**

A *Coastal Boating Guide* to North Carolina is available from the **North Carolina Department of Transportation Map Section**. ~ P.O. Box 25201, Raleigh, NC 27611; 919-733-7600. For information on boating regulations in South Carolina, contact the **Boating and Titling Division of the South Carolina Department of Natural Resources**. ~ P.O. Box 167, Columbia, SC 29202; 803-734-3888.

Or, if you're planning a trip along the Intracoastal Waterway, consider buying the *Mid-Atlantic Waterway Guide* (Communication Channels, Inc.), which details sounds, bridges, bays and connecting rivers through Virginia, North and South Carolina, and Georgia. Other charts are available through **Land Resources**. ~ 2221 Divine Street, Columbia, SC 29205; 803-734-9100.

Even in winter, you'll find diehard surfers and windsurfers riding the waves in their wetsuits. Swimming, waterskiing, jetboating and floating on inflatable rafts are popular activities in the summer. **WATER SAFETY**

People have drowned in Carolinas waters, but drownings are easily avoided when you respect the power of the water, heed appropriate warnings and use good sense.

Wherever you swim, never do it alone. Always swim in designated areas, preferably where there are lifeguards. On the ocean, always face the incoming waves. They can bring unpleasant surprises even to the initiated. If you go surfing, learn the proper techniques and how to spot dangers from an expert before you start out. Respect signs warning of dangerous currents and undertows. North Carolina's Outer Banks are particularly prone to rough seas and strong currents, so be aware when swimming there. If you get caught in a rip current or any tow that makes you feel out of control, don't try to swim against it. Head across it, paralleling the shore. Exercise caution in the use of floats, inner tubes or rafts; unexpected currents can quickly carry you out to sea.

There are some jellyfish that inflict a mild sting, but that is easily treated with an over-the-counter antiseptic. If you go oystering or crabbing, swim in or wade in murky waters where shellfish dwell, wear canvas or rubber boots to protect your feet.

If you're going canoeing or whitewater rafting, always scout the river from land before the first trip, and check available literature. Rivers may have danger areas such as falls, boulders, rapids and dams.

FISHING & CRABBING

Sitting near dead center on the Atlantic coast and sharing two big migratory basins—the Mid-Atlantic Bight and the South Atlantic Bight—the Carolinas offer some of the East Coast's best fishing. As well, the network of sounds, basins and estuaries provide breeding and feeding grounds for dozens of fish and shellfish.

Unfortunately, like most areas along the Atlantic, commercial overfishing and rising consumer demand has in recent years taken its toll, reducing the populations of several types of fish. Gray trout, red drum, black sea bass and summer flounder are being caught faster than they can replace themselves. Grouper, snapper, spot, bluefish and striped bass are among those species classified as "stressed." Recent regulations banning certain commercial fishing (but not recreational sportfishing) are intended to replenish the waters.

Still, nearly 1.7 million sport anglers take to the Carolinas' coastal waters every year, and with considerable success, catching more than 26 million fish. King mackerel, Southern flounder, Spanish mackerel and croakers are still abundant, as are blue crabs.

Crabbing is a major pastime, particularly in South Carolina's Lowcountry. It's an easy and inexpensive endeavor, requiring some string, a weight, some chicken parts and a dip net. Tie the weight and chicken onto the string, throw it out in the creek or tidal flats, wait for a blue crab to mosey along, and scoop him out with the net.

Inland, lakes and streams offer excellent angling. You can flyfish for trout, or use a rod 'n' reel baited with anything from corn kernels and crickets to nightcrawlers. You can also try for catfish, bream, bass and sunfish—all part of many Carolinians' diet.

If you'd like to try a kind of fishing that's new to you, you will find guided services available just about everywhere boats are rented and bait sold. Charter fishing is the costliest way to go out to sea; party boats (also called head boats) take a crowd but are less expensive and usually great fun. On rivers, lakes and tiny hidden streams, guides can show you the best place to throw a hook or skim a fly.

In North Carolina, you don't need a license to fish in saltwater (though state officials have long proposed the idea), but you do need one for freshwater fishing. Occasionally, special stamps, such as trout stamps, are required as well. Fishing licenses and stamps are available from local bait-and-tackle stores and from the Licensing Section of the **North Carolina Wildlife Resources Commission**. ~ 322 Chapanoke Road, Raleigh, NC 27603; 919-662-4370.

No matter where you fish in South Carolina—saltwater or freshwater—you'll need a license, available from many bait-and-tackle shops and marinas. Or, contact the **Licensing Division of the South Carolina Department of Natural Resources.** ~ P.O. Box 11710, Columbia, SC 29211; 803-734-3838.

TWO

Asheville

George Vanderbilt called Asheville "the most beautiful land in the world." The year was 1888, and it was no shallow praise from a savvy tycoon who had traveled to Europe more than a dozen times. But then, Vanderbilt was certainly not the first to be charmed by this North Carolina place, set in a bowl of Blue Ridge Mountains, painted with persistent clear skies, emblazoned in summer with lavender bursts of rhododendron and in autumn with the fire-red of maples.

"Eden Land" is what the area's first permanent settlers called Asheville. Arriving in 1785 from northern Ireland, they were mainly Scottish-Irish immigrants who couldn't make a living after the British slapped steep tariffs on wool. No longer in the sheep business, they turned hardy mountaineers who built crude wood shacks, hunted the depths of surrounding forests and farmed small garden patches. One local frontierswoman, Elizabeth Patton, caught the eye of an itinerant frontiersman named Davy Crockett. The couple was wed in the town of Asheville, incorporated in 1797 and named after North Carolina Governor Samuel Ashe.

Asheville's fate as a thriving crossroads and summer escape was set in the 1820s when pioneers carved the Buncombe Turnpike toll trail from the Eastern Seaboard to western South Carolina. It ran right through the middle of town and brought hundreds of wagons and stagecoaches, and drovers herding cattle and flocks of turkeys headed for southern markets. The passers-through left, telling of a "Land of Sky," where mountains lapped at the clouds and the air was cooler and kinder than most.

The Civil War plunged Asheville into decline, putting its resort destiny on brief hold, but by the 1880s the town was turning into a summer social mecca. In 1883 the local newspaper pronounced Asheville the "Paris of the South," raving about its art studios and extravagant parties, 1000-volume library above the drugstore, hunting forays and railroad excursions.

A train brought George Vanderbilt from New York to Asheville in the late 1880s, and with Vanderbilt money he bought several mountains and began building what would come to be recognized as one of the world's most beautiful estates. Designed after the grand French chateaux he had come to love during his travels, today Vanderbilt's fabulous Biltmore Estate is one of the Carolinas' most-visited attractions. Vanderbilt eventually bought 125,000 acres and founded the country's first forestry school; much of the land is now Pisgah National Forest, a vast tract of woods running west of Asheville.

Like Vanderbilt, Edwin Wiley Grove was so smitten with Asheville that he put his fortune there. The St. Louis inventor of Grove's Tasteless Chill Tonic created the Grove Park Inn as a monument to himself, opening the great granite resort in 1913 before a throng of dignitaries. It was—and still is—an extraordinary place, earthy and elegant, roosting atop Sunset Mountain, its rock-studded facade glinting mightily in the mountain sun.

Many of the architects, masons and other minds behind the Grove Park Inn and Biltmore Estate also turned their talents on downtown Asheville. The result is obvious today: a tremendous blend of styles, from Byzantine and Florentine to Romanesque and Art Deco. Though many buildings fell into near-ruin after the Depression, they have been (and are still being) vigorously revived, so that downtown Asheville today has a fresh-scrubbed, vibrant look.

And while the extravagant bluebloods of the 1890s polished Asheville with money and affluence, the New Age and espresso crowds of the 1990s have bestowed a distinctly bohemian edge. Pretty and gritty coffeehouses, trendy bistros, "smokefree" nightclubs and retro boutiques crowd this ever-growing stronghold of American counterculture. Dozens of galleries showcase Appalachian art and music, from mountain pottery to hand-carved dulcimers. Everything in Asheville is on a small scale—the population is only 65,000—and rarely crowded. A number of national magazines have lately listed Asheville as one of the top ten U.S. cities to live in. Some have suggested that a large measure of Asheville's appeal is derived from what the city *doesn't* have. Exulted one transplanted Atlanta artist: "I like Asheville because there's no traffic, pollution, serious crime. For the first time in my life, I don't lock my doors at night."

Asheville is also a perfect place to start the Carolinas' experience, not only because it's good-looking and hip, but because it's the gateway to the mountains. North Carolina's southern mountains and South Carolina's Upcountry spread out beneath the city like a rippled apron. The Blue Ridge Parkway, that slow, wonderful glide past hundreds of awe-inspiring peaks, cuts along the eastern side of Asheville and squiggles its way west to Great Smoky Mountains National Park. Mt. Mitchell, eastern America's highest peak at 6684 feet, is only 30 miles from Asheville, right off the parkway.

Many people bent on seeing those mountains, however, inevitably get sidetracked in Asheville, spending days instead of hours, finding there's more to do than they had imagined. At day's end, they will hopefully find themselves on the terrace of the Grove Park Inn, where they can watch the sun put down behind the soft peaks of the Blue Ridge, leaving a purple afterglow across this most beautiful land.

▼▼▼▼▼▼▼▼▼▼▼▼▼▼
Downtown Asheville

From Route 240, the main approach to downtown Asheville, visitors are delivered to a place of neatly tended blocks with broad, tidy streets, the most stylish of buildings, and a palpable air of business. Great church domes glimmer beneath the glass silhouettes of slender midrises, and sensuous Art Deco facades ramble beneath oaks and dogwoods. Entire blocks look like 1990s beat scenes, with youths garbed in tie-dye and army-issue boots, their hands warming little cups of double espresso. Gallery windows tempt with clever artwork, and bakeries and coffeehouses send good smells into the street.

SIGHTS

Downtown Asheville is entirely enjoyable, easy to walk and offers plenty for the eye, palate and shopping list. You won't even have trouble finding a parking space—without a meter, if you're lucky. Park near **Pack Square**, known simply as "The Square" in the 1820s when the Buncombe Turnpike (a loose term for a wagon trail) ran through town and brought in all sorts of business. Back then The Square was often filled with livestock on its way to the market; today it is a public park punctuated by a granite obelisk monument to Zebulon Baird Vance, whose law practice once stood on the spot. ~ Corner of Patton Avenue and Broadway.

The park came to the city compliments of George Willis Pack, a Cleveland lumberman who brought his sick wife to Asheville in 1883, hoping the cool, dry air would make her feel better. He took a liking to the town, buying up land and erecting buildings he would later donate to the people. One of these was the 1926 library, now **Pack Place**, Asheville's showpiece center for art, science and culture. There are two performing arts spaces, as well as four museums easily seen in a day. Buy a ticket for just one museum, or save money with a combination ticket. All museums are closed Sunday and Monday. Admission. ~ 2 Pack Square; 704-257-4500.

Least impressive of the museums, the **Asheville Art Museum** has several small galleries that are home to a small permanent collection, mostly twentieth-century pieces, including bronze sculpture, serigraphs, lithographs and screen-printing. Next door, The Health Adventure is great for kids. In "Cartilage Hall" they can put together the model of a man—bones, organs and all. In the "Creative Playspace" they can climb through tunnels and captain a tugboat.

Adults will be more taken with the **Colburn Gem & Mineral Museum,** where walls glitter with exhibits of thousands of precious stones and manuscripts tell of the state's stone age. In case you did not know, North Carolina was the country's top producer of gold until California's rush in 1849. In the 1800s, more than 100 mines were open in the Piedmont area; today, the world's largest granite quarry—a mile long and 1800 feet wide—is still in operation near Mt. Airy, in the northern Piedmont. The museum is named for Burnham Standish Colburn, the local man who had the world's largest collection of hiddenite.

Stop by the **Asheville Gifts and Welcome Center** for walking-tour maps of the city. ~ 14 Battery Park. For more detailed information on Asheville, visit the **Asheville Convention and Visitors Bureau**. ~ 151 Haywood Street; 704-258-6111, 800-257-1300.

Not in the same building but actually part of the Pack Place museum family, the YMI **Cultural Center** houses a small but accomplished exhibit of African-American art within its historic brick walls. The handsome Tudor building dates to 1892, when George Vanderbilt decided the "Negro" craftsmen who worked on his Biltmore Estate should have a community center. The craftsmen built this Young Men's Institute, then they bought it from Vanderbilt in 1905. Over the years it went from western North Carolina's hub

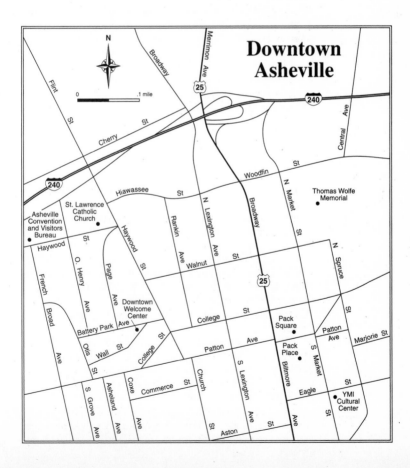

for black art and culture to abandonment back to flourishing cultural center. Today, the permanent artifacts include tribal masks and sculptures; traveling exhibits tend to be of stellar quality. Admission. ~ Market and Eagle streets; 704-252-4614.

In the early 1900s, Asheville's architectural aura was being helped along by places like the **First Baptist Church**. Its gigantic rust-colored dome lends a European air to the city skyline; its steps and portico of Italian pink marble excite up close. The church was designed after the great domed cathedrals of Florence, and its well-known architect, Douglas Ellington, clearly understood Florentine design. If you go inside you can see the stained glass all around the sanctuary, and the pipe organs and chandeliers that are overwhelming in size. ~ 5 Oak Street; 704-252-4781.

The city's other big and beautiful church is **The Basilica of St. Lawrence, D.M.**, built early this century in exotic Moorish style, with an incredible elliptical dome of tile and concrete. Rafael Gustavino, an Italian who was familiar in Moorish ways, worked on Biltmore House before designing the church. He died in 1908 and was buried in the church. ~ 97 Haywood Street; 704-252-6042.

A few blocks east, huddling in the shadows of Asheville's more statuesque buildings, the **Thomas Wolfe Memorial** is the dim and drafty boardinghouse that forged the life of author Thomas Wolfe. "In winter, the wind blew howling blasts under the skirts of (the house): its back end was built high off the ground on wet columns of rotting brick." So wrote Wolfe in *Look Homeward, Angel*, his first and most acclaimed autobiographical novel, in which he depicted a sad and strange childhood in the boardinghouse, watching the traveling salesmen pass through, enduring the social and racial turmoil of a city not fully recovered from the Civil War.

Wolfe's internal turmoil was fueled by his parents' endless bickering; his mother was a workaholic miser who ran the boarding-

UNIQUE ASHEVILLE EXPERIENCES

- Spend a day—or two—at **Biltmore Estate,** George Vanderbilt's lavish tribute to French chateaux. *page 44*
- Join generations of the rich and well known and check into the **Grove Park Inn**, with its fabulous stone and clay architecture set astride Sunset Mountain. *page 48*
- Enjoy sumptuous Carolina cuisine at **Gabrielle's,** an exquisite dining retreat hidden outside downtown Asheville. *page 50*
- Play the world's third-longest golf hole—the 17th hole at **Black Mountain Golf Club.** *page 52*

house, while his father was an alcoholic stonecutter who hated the house and its flow of transients. Wolfe's father lived across the street with seven of the children; only Tom lived with his mother in the boardinghouse, taking his meals alone in a cubbyhole to maximize space for boarders, sleeping in whatever bedroom was available at day's end.

The house, a State Historic Site, is nearly as it was when six-year-old Wolfe moved there in 1906. A guide will walk you through the 20-plus rooms with their stark white walls, including the "antiseptic cold and gloomy" parlor Wolfe wrote about. The furnishings and cookware, mainly original, include the medallion bed where Wolfe was born and his old Remington typewriter, retrieved by his siblings from his New York apartment. He did most of his writing after moving to New York, and he also died there at age 38 of a rare tuberculosis of the brain. Before his death he returned to Asheville and found good feelings, writing of "the cool sweet magic of starred mountain night, the huge attentiveness of dark, the slope, the trees, the living silence of the houses waiting. . . ." Closed Monday from November through March. ~ 52 Market Street; 704-253-8304.

Downtown's most chic lodging is at **Haywood Park Hotel**. Elegant in a minimalist way, its style is crisp and airy with lots of open space, from the soaring lobby with white pillars, brass rails and curved staircases to the 33 impeccable suites with deep closets and baths of Spanish marble. ~ Located at 1 Battery Park Avenue; 704-252-2522, 800-228-2522, fax 704-253-0481. DELUXE TO ULTRA-DELUXE.

LODGING

Next door to the Thomas Wolfe Memorial, the **Radisson Hotel Asheville** is tall, sleek and corporate-looking. A $3 million renovation in 1993 provided luxurious carpets and draperies and Queen Anne reproduction furnishings. Nearly all of the 281 rooms and seven suites have a sweeping view of the city with a backdrop of Blue Ridge Mountains. There's an outdoor pool for warm-weather swimming and several places for dining, including a penthouse restaurant and lounge—great spots for sunset watching. ~ 1 Thomas Wolfe Plaza; 704-252-8211, 800-333-3333. MODERATE TO DELUXE.

On the northern fringe of downtown and impossible to miss, **Beaufort House Bed and Breakfast** is daubed with deep salmon, white and burgundy, decorated with bay and arched windows and a big gazebo with wraparound porch. The Queen Anne confection, designed in 1894 by famed local architect A. L. Melton, is formal inside; its polished wood walls gleam and its luxuriant bedrooms are rich with antiques, lace and carved woods. Each is completely different, from the two-bedroom suite that takes up the top floor to the carriage house with loft bedroom and kitchen. ~ 61 North Liberty Street; 704-254-8334, 800-261-2221, fax 704-251-2082. DELUXE TO ULTRA-DELUXE.

◀ HIDDEN

DINING

Joining the bistro mania that's clutching the country, **Café on the Square** is a smart-looking spot done in black-and-white Art Deco, with a glass wall overlooking Pack Square. It's always thronged with locals who come to eat bistro bites like chipotle-rubbed pork tenderloin and pecan-crusted chicken. Start with butternut squash and brie soup crowned with puff pastry—it's wonderful. Closed Sunday. ~ 1 Biltmore Avenue; 704-251-5565. MODERATE TO DELUXE.

Across the way, **Beanstreets** coffeehouse is where the suit-and-tie crowd readies itself for the early morning shock of business. The espresso and cafe mochas do the trick, accompanied by a bowl of fruit, scone or French bread with brie. Even better are the simple, home-cooked lunches—chicken 'n' dumplings and other thick stews and soups, and sandwiches made with just-baked bagels, croissants and baguettes. The atmosphere is bright and gallerylike, with walls showcasing local art. ~ 3 Broadway; 704-255-8180. BUDGET.

Plush, cozy and candlelit, **23 Page** is a nouvelle niche where patrons can enjoy such dishes as vodka-soaked salmon with black poppyseed buerre blanc or cashew-crusted grouper with mango basil sauce. The soups and salads are unusual and unusually good, too; try the smoked duck breast on ramen slaw with fried wonton. Dinner only. ~ 1 Battery Park Avenue, in the Haywood Park Hotel; 704-252-3685. MODERATE TO DELUXE.

When you must have Northern Italian, you need look no further than **Vincenzo**. The veal chop Milanese, the salmon-and wild mushroom cannelloni, and the penne pasta with tasty charbroiled chicken, roasted peppers, spinach and pepperoni are all very good. The bright and bustling trattoria has a piano bar. ~ 10 North Market Street; 704-254-4698. MODERATE.

Locals love **Flying Frog Cafe**. The festive and eclectic restaurant, bathed in burgundy and black, serves a hot mix of Indian and French island cuisine from its open kitchen. The "Rasta Pasta" is spiked with jerk chicken or shrimp; the roasted duckling is served on a bed of bay leaves and onions; and the tandoori will, no doubt, start you salivating. Closed Tuesday. ~ 76 Haywood Street; 704-254-9411. MODERATE TO DELUXE.

Laughing Seed Café is a vegetarian haunt, ridiculously popular and overcrowded at lunch and sometimes dinner, so go early or late. The food, imaginative, colorful and super fresh, is worth any inconvenience. Try the Thai garlic soup, black-bean chili or Caribbean quesadillas with avocado and pineapple. Wash it down with a fruit smoothie or an organic beer or wine. ~ 40 Wall Street; 704-252-3445. MODERATE.

SHOPPING

Downtown has it all—antique stores by the dozen, vintage boutiques, great bookstores with basement coffeehouses, and myriads of galleries showcasing Appalachian art and crafts.

The Chocolate Fetish is known for its ragingly good truffles, though the indulgence also includes caramels and barks, and hand-dipped chocolate turtles. ~ 36 Haywood Street; 704-258-2353.

Wonderfully worn and inviting, **Malaprop's Bookstore and Cafe** is Asheville's counterculture central. Wood floors creak and shelves sag with the weight of books on everything from African dance to modern goddesses. A great source for gay and lesbian literature and regional travel maps, Malaprop's has a basement cafe where all the cool people go. ~ 61 Haywood Street; 704-254-6734.

For a rundown on clubs and bands, pick up a free copy of *Out 'n About* magazine from one of the local shops or restaurants.

If you're an antique hound, find the block of **Lexington Avenue** between Walnut and Woodfin streets. Within dozens of stores, relics run the gamut from Renaissance busts and miniatures and life-size carousels to American Indian baskets, bassinets and sleds. The quality ranges from heirloom to cast-off.

Mystic Eye advertises "non-ordinary clothing, sublime eccentric." Translation: gauzy, flowing dresses; patchwork jeans; wide belts; crystal jewelry, oils, candles and the like. ~ 30 North Lexington Avenue; 704-251-1773.

Downtown Books & News carries the kind of alternative publications you won't see in any of the chain stores. Underground magazines and newspapers, experimental sex books, pot-growing manuals and even free coffee while you browse. ~ 67 North Lexington Avenue; 704-253-8654.

The **Wall Street Shops** is a pedestrian mall that's trying to happen but hasn't yet. ~ Wall Street between Battery Park Avenue and Otis Street. There are a few finds here, namely **Folklore**, which has painted masks, flying wood dragons, flowing dresses and other stylish items from Africa, India and Asia. ~ 10 Wall Street; 704-252-4336.

There are big night moves in downtown Asheville, lots of live music, wildly varied, with young but sophisticated crowds.

NIGHTLIFE

Clean, classy and extremely cool, **Be Here Now** has hosted Leon Russell, Mike Cross and Michelle Shocked. The spacious, smoke-free "pub, dance and concert hall" showcases national and regional talent with a vast array of music, from spicy Cajun and unplugged concerts to Irish bagpipes and mandolins. Cover. ~ 5 Biltmore Avenue; 704-258-2071.

At **Beanstreets** coffeehouse, you can sink into a sofa and hear some poetry read, or listen to some rhythm-and-blues or acoustic. ~ 3 Broadway; 704-255-8180.

Hidden down a side alley, its entrance obscured by chatty, smoking youths in retro garb, is the extremely hip **Vincent's Ear.** Impromptu ensembles, acoustic or heavy metal music—virtually anything goes at this bizarre bi-level beer and coffeehouse. Rarely a

◄ HIDDEN

cover. Jazz is featured on weekends. In warm weather, most of the action's outside on the patio bar. ~ 68-B North Lexington Avenue; 704-259-9119.

Gatsby's is publike and classy, with smooth wood booths and floors, an exposed brick wall and velvet draperies providing a great backdrop for the bands, which play everything from rhythm-and-blues and classic rock-and-roll to swing and alternative. Cover. ~ 13 West Walnut Street; 704-254-4248.

HIDDEN ▶ If old-time bluegrass and country cloggin' strike your fancy, duck inside **Mountain Smokehouse**. Shows are held on Friday and Saturday night, and they come with or without dinner. Cover. ~ 20 South Spruce Street; 704-253-4871.

GAY SCENE **O'Henry's** is smack in downtown Asheville, though it feels more like a neighborhood bar, an afternoon and evening meetingspot for gay professionals. ~ At 59 Haywood Street; 704-254-1891.

Asheville's gay nightlife central is a trio of bars—**Hairspray Cafe**, **The Barber Shop** and **Club Metropolis**—sharing the same roof and sometimes the same clientele, though lesbians do indeed prefer the '50s-motif Hairspray while gay men head for the publike Barber Shop (sorry, no haircuts—just plenty of 'dos). Metropolis is a Thursday-through-Saturday disco and showbar with frequent drag shows. Straights are lately trickling in, says the clubs' owner, "a few really cool, hip, straight people." Cover only at Club Metropolis. ~ 38 North French Broad Avenue; 704-258-2027.

Scandals likewise draws young gay men and women to its trilevel disco and showbars, except on Thursday, when "Alternative Night" brings in a straight clientele. Cover. ~ 11 Grove Street; 704-252-2838.

▼▼▼▼▼▼▼▼▼▼
Asheville Area

Just outside downtown lie Asheville's better homes and gardens, gorgeous old inns and well-tended house museums, curling streets and their canopies of ancient oaks.

SIGHTS Start exploring on the northeast corner of downtown, taking Charlotte Street to Macon Avenue and working your way north through luxuriant wooded neighborhoods where, if you listen closely, you can hear the servants polishing the silver. Soon you will come upon the place where perhaps more silver has been polished over time than anywhere else, the **Grove Park Inn**, Asheville's legendary haunt of the wealthy and well-known.

Newspaper editor Fred Seely first had the idea for an earthy but luxurious inn crafted of natural material to match nature. In 1912 he took his idea for "organic architecture" to his father-in-law, E. W. Grove, who had made millions by inventing Grove's Tasteless Chill Tonic and Grove's Bromo-Quinine (potions whose benefits remain questionable today). Grove had as much ego as money, so he commissioned the inn as a monument to himself. Italian stonemasons and tons of Appalachian granite were brought in, and artists and craftspeople created natural-style furnishings. Within a year the 150-room resort opened to a slew of celebrities. Soon everyone who was anyone wanted to come to the Grove Park Inn

Today the inn is much bigger—510 rooms, thanks to the additions of two wings in the 1980s—although its "organic" character remains largely intact. Sitting astride Sunset Mountain, its rocky face looks to downtown Asheville and the Pisgah Mountains, its famous hood of red-clay roof drooping over the granite like folds of dough.

Even if you don't stay here (which you must), you should have a look around the place. If it's late in the day, find a chair on **Sunset Terrace**, order a cocktail and watch the sun vanish behind Mt. Pisgah. ~ 290 Macon Avenue; 704-252-2711.

The **Estes-Winn Automobile Museum** is in the unlikeliest of ◄ HIDDEN
places: at the dead end of a strip of historic shops next door to the

Asheville Area

Grove Park Inn. The antique cars are queued up and polished to a high sheen, and date back to the inn's opening in 1913. There's a horse-drawn carriage from 1890, and a 1927 La France fire engine that was used to put out Asheville fires. Closed Sunday in the winter. ~ At the Homespun Shops, 111 Grovewood Road; 704-253-7651.

The **Botanical Gardens at Asheville** are like a secret hideout, with dark caverns of forest, tiny footbridges arching beneath enormous trees, streams trickling through beds of soft leaves, and cool air given over to birdsong. Covering two square miles, it's a great introduction to Appalachian greenery: giant sycamores, rock cap ferns, paper birches, largeleaf magnolias and many other species are labeled within the area. A Garden for the Blind identifies plants in Braille. ~ 151 W. T. Weaver Boulevard; 704-252-5190.

HIDDEN ►   The **Smith-McDowell House-Museum** is said to be "Asheville's oldest brick home," built around 1840, though certainly not on a grand scale. It is, however, most definitely a warm and inviting home, with good-size rooms for entertaining and just sitting by the fire—indeed a place one would liked to have lived in back then. You'll learn how the home was restored by Asheville-Buncombe Technical College students, as you wander through rooms with rich period wallpapers and furnishings, and pretty vintage clothes draped here and there. Closed Sunday and Monday from April through December; closed Saturday through Monday from January through March. Admission. ~ At 283 Victoria Road, on the Asheville-Buncombe Technical College campus; 704-253-9231.

The **Biltmore Estate** is the reason tens of thousands of people come to Asheville every year. This theme park of historic homes—complete with winery, tremendous gardens, fine restaurants and shops, and history to match—is one of the most-visited attractions in the Carolinas. The Biltmore House itself, a sensational French-style chateau, is, of course, the point of it all. When first seen from the long, poplar-lined drive, its architecture is so exquisite it's hard to believe the place is real. Indeed, from the first encounter with the elaborate facade to the last hour spent in the rose garden where sweet buds tower above, the eye is enchanted time and time again. Which is precisely how George Vanderbilt planned it.

Vanderbilt was 26 when he commissioned the Biltmore Estate in 1888. Despite his youth, he had traveled the world many times over, enjoying the bounty of Vanderbilt money. In the French wine country he found the architecture he loved most—sixteenth-century chateaux—and he brought it to Asheville. He hired famed architect Richard Morris Hunt, educated at Paris' École des Beaux-Arts, to build his masterpiece. Then he hired one Frederick Law Olmsted, mastermind of landscape, to create the formal gardens.

It took six years to build the 255-room mansion, and, when it opened in 1895, it was the largest private home in all the United

States—a designation it still enjoys today. Vanderbilt filled his home with handsome furnishings and masterworks he had acquired during his travels, and made it comfortable for guests. Central heat, electric lights and indoor bathrooms—unheard of at the time—were installed, and so was an indoor swimming pool, bowling alley and gymnasium. From the marble terraces, misty mountain views went on forever.

Upon returning home from a visit to the house, author Paul Leicester Ford recalled that ". . . as I read the proofs of this book I have found more than once that the pages have faded out of sight and in their stead I have seen Mt. Pisgah and the French Broad River, or the ramp and the terrace of the Biltmore House. . . ."

The panoramas endure, as does the grandeur of the house. Yet despite the colossal magnitude and elaborate design, the chateau is neither cold nor aseptic but full of warmth and light and air. As you step through the great Entrance Hall and into the Winter Garden, sunshine streams through a glass-paned rotunda, and greenery spills from pots. In the stupendous Banquet Hall, the acoustics are so perfect that two people seated at opposite ends of the long table can speak normally and hear each other.

Every room has something of intrigue. Walls of Spanish leather in the Breakfast Room. Bizarre murals, painted by former guests, in the underground Halloween Room. The two-lane Bowling Alley of hard maple and pine, possibly the oldest lanes in the world. The bright red baroque decor of Vanderbilt's bedroom; the yellow and purple designs of his wife, Lila's, room.

The tour of the house is self-guided, though there are docents everywhere (only a few of the 450 full-time employees are running the place) hoping someone will ask them a question. For an additional fee, you can hear a narrated tour over headphones, or you can pay even more and take a guided behind-the-scenes tour. The latter is best done on a second visit to Biltmore Estate. There's just too much to see the first time.

After the house there are The Gardens, formal and Italian, marbled with pebbled paths, decorated with reed-filled ponds and statuary, and dotted with shaded benches for contemplating the surroundings. Then there's The Winery, an enjoyable five-mile drive from the house (it's three miles from the main gate to the house), where you'll get a tour of the fermenting, aging and bottling rooms, and taste some Biltmore Estate vintages. The Winery, opened in 1985, is a new endeavor.

Some general advice for visiting: Wear comfortable shoes, take frequent breaks (the courtyard at the Stable Cafe is a good place) and plan to spend most of the day. Most of the estate is wheelchair accessible, including The Gardens. Three on-site restaurants offer lunch: **The Stable Cafe** has good budget-priced sandwiches, salads

Text continued on page 48.

Oteen and Black Mountain

Due east of Asheville is the small town of Black Mountain and the even smaller Oteen. Oteen is known for the annual World Gee Haw Whimmy Diddle Contest. Black Mountain is known for folk art and antique shops and religious retreats.

You'll come to Oteen first, along Tunnel Road, right before the Blue Ridge Parkway. There's not much doing around Oteen, save for the third weekend of August when everyone brings out their whimmy diddles and starts geeing and hawing.

A whimmy diddle is an Appalachian folk toy that's basically a stick with notches cut along the top and a propeller on the end. Rub the notches up and down with another stick and the propeller turns. The gee and haw come in when you rub along the right or left of the notches (gee is right; haw is left), making sounds a lot like a donkey might make.

The contest, held on the parkway at the Folk Art Center, is to see who can make the most gees and haws in twelve seconds. For information on the next World Gee Haw Whimmy Diddle Contest, call 704-298-7928.

A few miles farther east, set deep in the greenery of the Swannanoa Valley, Black Mountain calls itself the "Front Porch of Western North Carolina." The pretty little place of red-brick buildings actually has a lot of front porches, set off the road and attended by folks in rockers whiling away the lazy Southern days.

You, too, can relax on a porch if you stay at the lovely **Red Rocker Inn**. The rooms are country cozy, and have names like "Aunt Madge's Bedroom" and "Grandpa's Bedroom." Innkeepers Pat and Fred Eshleman are famous for serving bountiful country dinners—roast pork with cornbread stuffing, mountain trout with almond butter, squash casserole, buttermilk biscuits. You can enjoy dinner even if you don't stay here, but you have to have a reservation. Pat does the serving; Fred says grace. After the main course, go for a piece of Black Mountain Mud Pie or X-rated Chocolate Cake. You won't regret it. Closed November through mid-April. ~ 136 North Dougherty Street; 704-669-5991, 888-669-5991. BUDGET TO DELUXE.

For an affordable lunch, there are more scrumptious eats at **Monte Vista Hotel**, where you can fill up on fried chicken and mashed potatoes, fresh vegetables and pecan pie. The dining room of the 1919 hotel is a simple Southern affair, and the lobby is decorated with antiques and Appalachian art. ~ 308 West State Street; 704-669-2119. BUDGET.

You can forage for your own antiques and mountain art right down from the Monte Vista. Historic State and Cherry streets and the blocks surrounding them offer plenty of shopping possibilities. **Vern & Idy's** is known for its functional stoneware pottery and one-of-a-kind dolls. ~ 414 West State Street; 704-669-2370. **Seven Sisters Gallery/Shop**, carries fine pottery, glass and fiber art, jewelry and wood crafts representing hundreds of regional and national artists. ~ 117 Cherry Street; 704-669-5107.

Song of the Wood is devoted to the music of the mountains. The collection of dulcimers here is excellent. ~ 203 West State Street; 704-669-7675. **Second Look Books** stocks those great old reads you had forgotten about, including many out-of-print books by Southern authors. ~ 103 Cherry Street; 704-669-8149.

Over on Broadway, **Treasures & Trivia** offers crystal and porcelain, lamps and furniture fashioned in Victorian, English and Early American styles. ~ 106 Broadway; 704-669-5190.

The **Black Mountain Antique Mall** is a treasure trove of pottery, furniture, glassware and collectibles. Best of all are the quilts, some dating to the 1700s, that start around $40 and go up to $50,000.

Besides being a hub of antiques, Black Mountain is also home to numerous **traditional and alternative religious camps**. It started back in the early 1900s, when Presbyterians settled into nearby Montreat. Seeing the far-flung mountains as a good place to renew one's spiritual sense, others soon followed: first the Baptists and then the YMCA, later the Disciples of Christ, the African Methodist Episcopalians, Freewill Baptists and lots of others. Thousands of people now come to Black Mountain every summer for retreats—there are now upwards of 15 of them, more than any other small town in America. ~ 100 Sutton Avenue; 704-669-6218.

and great Southern desserts; **Deerpark Restaurant**, open March through December, offers full-course fare at moderate to deluxe prices. **The Bistro** at the winery features gourmet pizzas, home-made pastas, breads and salads—all at a moderate price.

If at all possible, visit Monday through Thursday; Fridays, week-ends and holidays are more crowded. Most crowded is the whole month of December, when the house is elaborately decorated for the holidays, and the popular candlelight tours take place. Least congested is January through March, though The Gardens aren't much to look at then. Admission. ~ Route 25, off Route 40, south of downtown; 704-255-1700, 800-543-2961.

If you have a drop of stamina left, take a stroll around **Historic Biltmore Village**. The pretty cottages of red brick and stucco are the work of Vanderbilt, who bought the town of Best in 1889 and fashioned it as the attendant village of his Biltmore Estate. Many of his 80 employees lived here in the early 1900s; there was once a school, post office, church, train depot and even a hospital. The buildings have been given over to shops and restaurants, making it a prime place to visit. ~ Just west of Biltmore Estate and bounded roughly by Biltmore Avenue, Brook Street and All Souls Crescent.

LODGING   Mountainside elegance, perhaps the ultimate to be found in the Carolinas, is why people have been finding the **Grove Park Inn** for most of this century. Built of native granite and rich in local lore, it is high on amenities, low on snobbery. Things were not always this way at the Grove Park. When it opened in 1913, children were forbidden upstairs near the bedrooms and adults were forbidden to wear shoes after 10 p.m., for fear they would disturb a sleeping guest. Kids are not only welcome today, they have their own activities program (kids under 16 stay free). For adults, there's a championship golf course, tennis, racquetball and squash courts, indoor and outdoor pools, several excellent restaurants, nightclubs and lounges.

The rooms number 510, including 142 in the original inn, with decor ranging from simple, earthy and comfortable to quite lavish. Many have mountain views that are stunning. Some of the original hammered-copper light fixtures decorate the historic rooms. The Great Room lobby, furnished with some of the famous original Roycrofters pieces, has stone fireplaces so enormous you can fit a whole tree. The staff can't seem to do enough for you. It's all the things you expect from a luxurious inn, but don't always find. ~ 290 Macon Avenue; 704-252-2711, 800-438-5800, fax 704-252-6102. ULTRA-DELUXE.

In Asheville's lovely and historic Montford neighborhood, the **AppleWood Manor Inn** is set among two acres of rolling lawn and gardens. A favorite of straight and gay professional couples, the 1910 Colonial Revival home has four guest rooms furnished in

HIDDEN ►

tasteful, homestyle decor, plus a cottage with kitchen. Three of the bedrooms have balconies and wood-burning fireplaces. Innkeepers Johan and Coby Verhey go all-out for breakfast, serving delicious fare such as orange nutmeg French toast. ~ 62 Cumberland Circle; 704-254-2244; 800-442-2197, fax 704-254-0899. MODERATE TO DELUXE.

Richmond Hill Inn looks theatrical sitting high atop a hill, with dark silhouettes of mountains hovering behind and the lights of downtown Asheville glittering below. A beautiful, 12-room Queen Anne building presides over the grounds, complete with a rippling mountain brook, waterfalls and pretty parterre gardens. Fifteen rooms, opened in 1996, rest among the gardens, and nine cottages are uphill from the manse. Every room is desirable, offering plenty of space, plush furnishings and modern amenities such as cable TV and telephones. Dine at the inn's casual garden pavilion or the elegant, haute Gabrielle's. ~ 87 Richmond Hill Drive, off Route 251, 3 miles north of downtown Asheville; 704-252-7313, fax 704-252-8726. ULTRA-DELUXE.

> F. Scott Fitzgerald holed up in the Grove Park Inn in 1935 and 1936—he made the inn his Asheville home and wrote several short stories.

Less than a mile from the Biltmore Estate, the **Cedar Crest Inn** enjoys a splendid location on a hill amid four acres of gardens and forest. The interior of the 1891 Queen Anne home is a feast for the eyes, with gorgeous stained glass, polished antiques, rich rugs and elaborate woodworking, some of which was carved by Biltmore artisans. There are nine bedrooms and a 1915 bungalow—all are completely different but beautifully decorated, from the canopied ceilings to the deep clawfoot tubs. Silver breakfast service and afternoon tea and lemonade are included in the rates. ~ 674 Biltmore Avenue; 704-252-1389, 800-252-0310, fax 704-253-7667. DELUXE TO ULTRA-DELUXE.

For years, families have been finding **Pisgah View Ranch** a wonderful way to experience the mountains. It's way out in the woods, surrounded by 2000 acres of tall trees and wending creeks and stellar views of Mt. Pisgah. Accommodations are in rustic cabins; meals, famously large, are served family style. After supper there's square dancing, storytelling and bingo. During the day, kids can chase butterflies, swim in the pool, ride horses and go hiking. Rates include three daily meals and most activities. Closed November through April. ~ Off Route 151, Candler; 704-667-9100. ULTRA-DELUXE.

◄ HIDDEN

The **Sunset Terrace** of the Grove Park Inn is the place to be when the sun goes down. The breezy veranda opens to a view of the mountainous countryside and offers hearty cuisine to match. Prime rib, North Carolina rainbow trout and veal medallions "Appalachia" (with sage and apple cider) are among the fine choices. ~ 290 Macon Avenue; 704-252-2711. DELUXE. Similarly spectacular views,

DINING

except behind glass, can be had at the hotel's formal **Horizons**. The fare is chichi Continental; the dress is coat and tie. ~ 290 Macon Avenue; 704-252-2711. ULTRA-DELUXE.

Grovewood Cafe resides in a storybook cottage with vines creeping up its stucco walls and flower-lined paths decorating the lawn. Mozart streams through the tiny dining room with white tablecloths and black lacquer chairs, and fare that is predominantly Continental. Start with the prosciutto-wrapped sea scallops. Then indulge in the blackened mahimahi served with cucumber noodles and beurre blanc, or try the vegetarian pasta. All soups, bread and desserts are homemade. Closed Sunday. ~ 111 Grovewood Road, next to the Grove Park Inn; 704-258-8956. MODERATE TO DELUXE.

Hathaway's is where you should have lunch at Historic Biltmore Village. The whole cottage smells of chocolate and coffee, but leave those for last. Slow-cooked soups, stacked sandwiches, salads and quiche are the regular bill of fare, and a daily special might be Grand Marnier French toast. In the morning, have a hot sticky bun. ~ 3 Boston Way; 704-274-1298. BUDGET TO MODERATE.

HIDDEN ▶   Inside Richmond Hill Inn, the handsome, cherry-paneled **Gabrielle's** is perfect for such Southern culinary formalities as mountain apple and Vidalia onion soup; and grilled Black Angus fillet with barbecue sauce, Dixie potatoes and smoked corn fritters. Menus change seasonally and you can order à la carte or the six-course "Chef's Table." Highly recommended. ~ 87 Richmond Hill Drive, off Route 251, three miles north of downtown Asheville; 704-252-7313. ULTRA-DELUXE.

HIDDEN ▶   For less extravagant dining at the Richmond Hill Inn that's still on the Southern side, consider the inn's **Arbor Grille** overlooking parterre gardens. ~ 87 Richmond Hill Drive, off Route 251, three miles north of downtown Asheville; 704-252-7313. MODERATE.

SHOPPING   For a look at the kind of stellar art and crafts produced by Appalachian artists, go to **Grovewood Gallery**. Furniture, blown glass, pottery, woven rugs, and wood and ceramic sculpture reflect a myriad of styles and eras, with many prices in the moderate range. Step next door, and you'll see some of the artists at work. ~ 111 Grovewood Road, across from the Grove Park Inn; 704-253-7651.

HIDDEN ▶   Herb heads will love **Gourmet Gardens Herb Farm**, where the varieties, from licorice basil to chocolate mint, seem endless. There's other good stuff, too, like scented geraniums, rosemary topiaries and faerie rings of wild thyme, flowers and moss. ~ 14 Banks Town Road, Weaverville; 704-658-0766.

Lightweaver offers "alternatives for the coming age," including American Indian–made dream-catchers, earrings, crystals and a good selection of books on New Age thought. ~ 10 Weaver Road; Weaverville; 704-658-0123.

Located southwest of downtown, the $5 million **Western North Carolina Farmer's Market** is considered one of the best produce places in the Carolinas. Allow a few hours to check out the 125-plus stands heaped with the season's freshest, from sweet corn and sourwood honey to apples and butter beans. There are also local-made crafts, jams and jellies, and a good lunch spot called Moose's Cafe. ~ 570 Brevard Road; 704-253-1691.

Rarely do big attractions have such inviting shops as you'll find at the **Biltmore Estate**. A few to explore while you're here:

The **Bookbinders Shop** has big, glossy and expensive coffee-table books, as well as guides on Victorian etiquette and gold embossed bookmarks.

The **Confectionery** stocks gourmet chocolates and candies, herbal teas, and hard-to-find cooking items like petit-four cups.

Elaborate wreaths, miniature towns and cities, and ornaments galore—what else would you expect from a place called **A Christmas Past**?

The **Toymaker** is mainly for someone who collects frilly dolls, model trains, miniatures and other pricey specialty toys (in other words, keep the kids out unless you plan to detach yourself from a bit of cash).

Just east of Biltmore Estate (and outside the admission gate), **Historic Biltmore Village** (bounded by Biltmore Avenue, Brook Street and All Souls Crescent) is a neighborhood filled with shops. Among the terrific places to scour for art is **New Morning Gallery**, a spacious loft showcasing thousands of works by local as well as national artisans. Handblown glass, delicate pottery, jewelry, vases, tables and furniture are among the many offerings here. ~ 7 Boston Way; 704-274-2831.

A block away, it's tough to miss **Bellagio**, whose windows reveal the sassiest apparel and jewelry. Inside, take a look at the outrageous furniture. ~ 5 Biltmore Plaza; 704-277-8100.

The **Early Music Shop** showcases the instruments of Appalachia—hammered dulcimers, Celtic harps and wooden drums—and carries recordings ranging from mountain to New Age music. ~ 3 Biltmore Plaza; 704-274-2890.

Focusing on the out-of-doors, **The Compleat Naturalist** supplies stargazer books and guides on wildflowers, science kits for kids and the wildlife prints of artists such as Robert Batemen. ~ 2 Biltmore Plaza; 704-274-5430.

If you need a break from shopping, stop for tea at **Chelsea's Tea Room**, then peruse the fancy French and English gifts and the food hall filled with all things culinary. ~ 6 Boston Way; 704-274-4400.

Don't leave Asheville without visiting the **Folk Art Center**. It's the Carolinas' premier place for folk art, not the country kitsch too frequently encountered at roadside craft marts, but the earthy, ethereal works that reflect generations of working with natural elements. Save your money for this place; there seems no end to the terrific pottery, wood sculpture, quilts, baskets, jewelry and objets d'art. ~ Milepost 382, Blue Ridge Parkway; 704-298-7928.

NIGHTLIFE   The tri-level **Elaine's** is dark, carpeted and cozy. Live bands, playing country to classic rock, are featured on the weekend. ~ 290 Macon Avenue, at the Grove Park Inn; 704-252-2711.

BEACHES   Though no major parks exist within Asheville, great forests begin
& PARKS   just beyond its borders. Pisgah National Forest and the Blue Ridge Parkway afford many possibilities for picnicking, camping, hiking, fishing and superior exploring. For details, see Chapter Three and Chapter Five.

▼▼▼▼▼▼▼▼▼▼▼▼▼▼   Asheville's most picturesque course is the 18-hole
Outdoor Adventures   Donald Ross design at the **Grove Park Inn**. Try
to schedule a late afternoon game so you'll catch
GOLF   the mountain sunset. ~ 290 Macon Avenue; 704-252-2711, 800-438-5800. Try other area courses at the **Great Smokies Holiday Inn Sunspree Resort**. ~ 1 Holiday Inn Drive, off Route 240, Asheville; 704-254-3211. Also try the **Buncombe County Golf Course**. ~ River Road, Asheville; 704-298-1867. In Weaverville try **Reems Creek Golf Course**. ~ Pink Fox Road, Weaverville; 704-645-4393. If you play the 17th hole at the **Black Mountain Golf Club**, you'll have played the world's third-longest hole (distance: 747 yards; par: 6). ~ 106 Montreat Road, Black Mountain; 704-669-2710.

TENNIS   At the city-owned **Ashton Park Tennis Center**, you'll find 12 clay courts. ~ Hilliard Avenue between French Broad Avenue and Klingman Street, Asheville; 704-255-5193. The beautiful **Grove Park Inn** has six outdoor and three indoor courts. ~ 290 Macon Avenue; 704-252-2711.

BIKING   Mountain biking is most popular around Asheville, which means heading away from downtown. For excellent bike-trail maps, contact the North Carolina Department of Transportation's Bicycle Program. ~ P.O. Box 25201, Raleigh, NC 27611; 919-733-2804.

If you get on the **Blue Ridge Parkway** around Milepost 382 five miles east of Asheville, you can ride southwest through Pisgah National Forest toward Mt. Pisgah, 27 miles away. Or, you can head northeast to Mt. Mitchell, about 30 miles away. The parkway's gently sloping curves and mountain vistas are a bicyclist's dream, though you should avoid the peak spring and fall seasons, when the road is jammed with cars. Also, be sure to stay on the paved road; bicycles are prohibited from parkway trails.

Pisgah National Forest, which sprawls west of Asheville, also offers biking possibilities. For information on where to ride, contact the District Ranger. ~ 1001 Pisgah Highway, Pisgah Forest; 704-877-3265.

North of Asheville, Route 251 follows the French Broad River and affords wonderful cycling. From the town of Woodfin north to Marshall, it's about a 26-mile round-trip ride.

Bike Rentals You can rent mountain bikes from Hearns Cycling and Fitness. ~ 34 Broadway; 704-253-4800. Mountain bikes are also available from Pro-Bikes. ~ 793 Merrimon Avenue; 704-253-2800. Or you can try Liberty Bikes. ~ 1987 Hendersonville Highway, Asheville; 704-684-1085.

In Black Mountain, rentals are available at Black Mountain Bicycle. Are you up for trying their tandem mountain bike? ~ 108 Black Mountain Avenue; 704-669-5969.

All distances listed for hiking trails are one way unless otherwise noted.

HIKING

One of the most enjoyable trails in Asheville is the one at the Botanical Gardens of Asheville (.6 mile), an easy stroll along gravel trails and others strewn with pine needles.

Five miles east of Asheville at the Blue Ridge Parkway's Folk Art Center, you can get on the Mountains-to-Sea Trail (7.5 miles), following the parkway northeast for a moderately difficult trek. In spring, the views of wildflowers are spectacular.

Adventure sports are limited within Asheville proper, but they abound in the nearby mountains. For information on whitewater rafting, skiing, canoeing and fishing, see Chapters Three, Four, Five and Six.

▼▼▼▼▼▼▼▼▼▼
Transportation

Perched along the eastern rim of the Blue Ridge, Asheville is the gateway to North Carolina's mountains. It's at the junction of Route 26, which runs northwest from Columbia, South Carolina, and Route 40, which cuts west from Wilmington on the North Carolina seacoast, arching through Raleigh, Durham and Winston-Salem. Route 40 continues west and north from Asheville into Knoxville, Tennessee. The Route 240 connector loops through downtown Asheville.

CAR

The Blue Ridge Parkway skirts the eastern side of Asheville and heads south to Cherokee, situated at the entrance to the Great Smoky Mountains National Park.

Asheville Regional Airport, off Route 26 about 15 miles south of downtown Asheville, is served by Atlantic Southeast, ComAir, Delta Airlines, USAir and USAir Express. Clean and well run, the attractive little airport is flanked by thick forest.

AIR

Shuttle service from the airport to town is available from **Asheville Limousine Service.** ~ 704-667-0758. Also try **Roberts Cab & Transportation.** ~ 704-683-1051.

BUS

Greyhound Bus Lines offers bus service to Asheville from various points around the South. ~ Two Tunnel Road; 704-253-5353, 800-231-2222.

CAR RENTALS

Avis Rent A Car (800-331-1212), **Budget Rent A Car** (800-527-0700), **Enterprise Rent A Car** (800-325-8007) and **Hertz Rent A Car** (800-654-3131) have locations at Asheville Regional Airport.

PUBLIC TRANSIT

The **Asheville Transit Authority** provides bus service throughout the city. ~ 704-253-5691.

TAXIS

Asheville taxi companies include **Brewer Lake Cab Company** (704-252-1913), **J & H Cab Service** (704-686-5920), **Jolly Taxi Company** (704-253-1411), **New Blue Bird Taxi Company** (704-258-8331) and **Yellow Cab** (704-253-3311).

THREE

The Southern Mountains

Along the southern rim of the Blue Ridge, a thread of asphalt uninspiringly dubbed Route 64 meanders through mountains and forests of remarkable beauty and mood. Wind swishes through giant boughs of trees, waterfalls thunder from a far cliff, slick white granite plummets into deep gorges. The lush scenery is broken only by towns, some small and simple with their old-time soda fountains and folks on front porches, others large and showy with their posh shops, plush golf courses and scads of noveaux riches.

These are North Carolina's Southern Mountains, linked by Route 64 and stretching south of Asheville, from compelling Chimney Rock Park on the east to the unadorned gem-mining town of Franklin on the west. Angling off from Route 64 are numerous back roads with endless hidden possibilities, from the lonesome silhouette of a tobacco barn to the sawdust-floored country store where the proprietor gives you free apples. "Sweetest in the Appalachians," she says.

Long before the apples and country stores, the Southern Appalachians belonged to the Cherokees. Their homes of bark and twigs and clay mud were clustered at the mouths of mountain streams, where the American Indians fished for trout, catfish and redhorse. In the Edenic forest around them, they hunted deer, wild turkey, rabbit, groundhog and other game, and picked mushrooms, blackberries and chestnuts. Their tranquil existence was interrupted only occasionally by skirmishes with the Creeks and other tribes. Until the white man came.

Around 1540, Spanish explorer Hernando de Soto journeyed to the mountains looking for gold. He made his way along the Cullasaja River (bastardized from the Cherokee *Kulsetsiyi*, meaning "honey locust place"), stopping at what are now the towns of Highlands and Franklin. In Franklin he encountered the Cherokee village of Nikwasi but, finding no gold, he continued west to the Mississippi. Too bad de Soto wasn't looking for rubies or sapphires, since the rocky earth around Nikwasi was littered with them. More than 300 years later, state geologists did discover the gems and numerous others, and miners overran the area looking for their own motherlode. Today, there are few big gems left in Franklin but many mines where visitors can try their luck. As for Nikwasi, it is an abandoned hump of roadside ground, lost in the oblivion of town traffic.

In the centuries following de Soto, white settlers continued to trickle in to the Southern Mountains. In 1819, a treaty was forced on the Cherokees that pushed them west to the Nantahala Ridge, just outside the Southern Mountains. With American Indians out of the way, hardy farmers and other gutsy pioneers could settle in the rugged mountains. They cleared small valley patches and built log cabins with fieldstone chimneys. They planted corn and sorghum, raised hogs and chickens, and wove baskets.

Wealthy planters and businessmen arrived, too, many from Charleston and New Orleans, and established vast plantations and summer estates in Hendersonville and Flat Rock, just south of Asheville. One of the most famous estates is Connemara, built in 1838 by Charlestonian Christopher Memminger, who later became Treasury Secretary for the Confederacy. More than a hundred years later, Carl Sandburg bought the simple frame farmhouse in Flat Rock, surrounded by 240 acres of sloping lawns and mountain vistas. The author, poet, political activist and social reformist spent the last 22 years of his life there, inspired and captivated by the southern Blue Ridge. His dark, cramped writing room is part of the tour at his farm, now registered as a National Historic Site.

With the 1860s came the Civil War, but its effect on the Southern Mountains was more psychological than physical. Young soldiers left for distant battlefields and never returned. Union sympathies were strong, and families and communities fought bitter philosophical wars. News of the war's end in 1865 took awhile to reach remote mountain towns, and the final surrender of Confederate forces in North Carolina supposedly took place deep in the Southern Mountains, in Macon County.

Reconstruction brought prosperity and, more specifically, the railroad, which provided release from rural life. Hotels were built to accommodate new summer visitors arriving by train, while cabins were constructed for immigrants coming to work the ore and mineral mines. Loggers found the railroad easy transport for their wood and, by the early 1900s, the mountains had been transformed into one big lumber camp. The forests were stripped with abandon until 1916, when the federal government began buying chunks for national forests.

Today, there's little evidence of logging scars, though some lumber companies stayed in business until the 1950s. Indeed, the Southern Mountains are for the most part a place of nature, with dense, far-reaching forests and horizons dotted with green summits. The most fantastic summit, magnificent Chimney Rock, is the starting point for the Southern Mountains tour in the east. From the windy, moodheightening plateau of Chimney Rock you can look down upon beautiful Lake Lure framed in verdant forest.

Farther west, apple orchards decorate the valleys and hills of Henderson County, home to 70 percent of North Carolina's apple crop.

In the autumn months, pumpkins grow in vast patches between the orchards, and you can stop alongside the road and select your own big orange ball.

The county seat of Hendersonville has a commercial veneer but a historic downtown with rows of pretty old homes and antique shops and galleries. Next door, tiny, old-moneyed Flat Rock is immensely appealing with its antebellum manses tucked into forest clearings. Westward awaits one of the most scenic drives in the Carolinas: Route 64's slow, twisting glide through misty, sun-streaked woods loaded

Southern Mountains

15 miles

POINTS OF INTEREST

Ⓐ Bridal Veil Falls
Ⓑ Carl Sandburg Home
Ⓒ Chimney Rock Park
Ⓓ Cradle of Forestry in America
Ⓔ Dry Falls
Ⓕ Holmes State Educational Forest
Ⓖ Jackrabbit Mountain Recreation Area
Ⓗ Joyce Kilmer Memorial Forest
Ⓘ Looking Glass Falls
Ⓙ Pearson's Falls
Ⓚ Sliding Rock
Ⓛ Standing Indian Mountain Recreation Area
Ⓜ Whitewater Falls

with waterfalls and wildlife, much of it protected within the 500,000-acre Pisgah National Forest. There are only a few intermissions, like the busy little town of Brevard and the affluent nests of Cashiers and Highlands.

Brevard is tiny and unassuming, home to only 5300 people, but surrounded by forests filled with hundreds of waterfalls. "Land of Waterfalls" is how Brevardians advertise their town. Downtown, whitewashed clapboard and red-brick homes help create a soothing Southern scene.

Around Cashiers and Highlands are developments of recent invention, which seem overrun by Floridians determined to escape their sweltering summers, and which look suspiciously like Florida's own country club communities with their Disneyesque flower beds and faceless condominiums and townhouses. Fairways and greens are etched into the mountainsides, and tennis courts are parked in the valleys.

The "planned" look comes to an abrupt end a bit west in Franklin, a simple Southern town with dozens of stores selling gems and minerals. Just north of Franklin in the Cowee Valley, rock hounds can pan for gems in real and imitation mines.

In between the better-known Southern Mountain towns are quirky places with quirky names like Bat Cave, whose blackened hollows harbor more salamanders than bats, and Zirconia and Sapphire, hamlets that recall the days before only tourists panned for gems.

Whether you search for the offbeat or the ordinary, the gem mine or the hidden sightseeing gem, the challenge of a golf fairway or a steep mountain trail, you will likely find it in these Southern Mountains.

▼▼▼▼▼▼▼▼▼▼▼▼▼▼
Chimney Rock Area

"I could stay all day and look across here," exalted one visitor upon reaching the top of Chimney Rock. It is a common sentiment, given the scale of this great granite pedestal with a sea of forest at its feet. The view from the rock's wind-polished, 225-foot-high summit is of sculpted peaks in every direction—on clear days the vistas stretch more than 75 miles—and the deeply etched ravines of Hickory Nut Gap and glassy blues of Lake Lure.

SIGHTS

The top of Chimney Rock offers much more than a view. Indeed, the moment you step off the narrow catwalk (don't look down on the way up) and onto the rock's plateau, the feeling hits: a vertiginous, leg-weakening, wind-against-body feeling that you won't forget, at least not anytime soon.

This was how Lucius Morse felt when he first climbed the chimney-shaped rock in the early 1900s, so he bought it. The doctor from St. Louis bought some of Chimney Rock Mountain, a total of 64 acres, and set about turning it into a park. Today, **Chimney Rock Park** covers 1000 acres of spectacular scenery. Though the rock is its centerpiece, the park offers miles of trails to various vistas that become more amazing as you hike. Trails are usually iced over in winter, and the park's waterfalls are at least partly frozen into sheets of ice. Admission. ~ Route 64-74A, in the town of Chimney Rock; 704-625-9611, 800-277-9611.

The park entrance is in the little town of Chimney Rock; from the entrance, three miles of narrow pavement corkscrew up through forest so thick it's dark on the brightest of days. On the way is a small **nature center** with displays on park geology, flora and fauna, and several picnic areas and playgrounds.

At the top of the road you come to an elevator shaft and a sign explaining that it took eight tons of dynamite and 18 months to blast the 258-foot-high hoistway for the shaft, which tunnels right through the middle of a solid rock mountain. The elevator rockets up through 26 stories of rock in 30 seconds before depositing visitors in a gift shop, where they learn that scenes from the movie *The Last of the Mohicans*, starring Daniel Day-Lewis and Madeleine Stowe, were shot at Chimney Rock. You can buy a T-shirt, actual photos of the actual filming (imagine!) and even a colorful brochure describing where various scenes were filmed—all items attesting that you were where the movie was made.

Here also is a snack bar where a glass wall lined with barstools looks across mood-altering mountain scenery. Outside the eatery are trailheads to Chimney Rock and to the **Opera Box**, a granite overhang whose graffiti-covered railing is all that separates you from a big plunge into a rocky abyss. A few steps up, **Devil's Head** perch lets you gaze across to the brooding profile of what looks like a Buddha's head balanced on a cliff.

Wheelchair travelers can go as far as the observation deck just below Chimney Rock, but, unfortunately, cannot reach the top of the rock, nor explore any trails. The views from the deck, however, are worth the price of admission.

After exploring the park, drive back down the mountain for a walk around the town of **Chimney Rock**. It won't take long, considering that it's only a block long. Main Street attractions include Bubba's General Store and Ford's Ice Cream, the latter having worn-

---

✔ CHECK THESE OUT—UNIQUE SIGHTS

- Climb the great granite pedestal that gives **Chimney Rock Park** its name, then marvel at the magnificent views. *page 58*
- Don't expect bats at **Bat Cave Preserve**, but do expect to encounter rare salamanders, threatened warblers and strange spiders on this wonderful walk in the woods. *page 60*
- Wander the peaceful **Carl Sandburg Home and farm**, ringed with lake and Blue Ridge Mountain views, where the Pulitzer-winning author put ideas on paper. *page 65*
- Love lilies? Admire the Venezuela poppy, water lettuce, froebelise and other flamboyant flowers at **Perry's Water Gardens**. *page 86*

out benches lined with locals watching passersby. There's also the Riverrun, a shop that sells simple gifts and boiled peanuts and has a rock garden for sitting and watching the river. ~ Route 64-74A.

From here it's about five miles southeast on Route 64-74A to lovely **Lake Lure**, which, like Chimney Rock Park, exists because of Dr. Lucius Morse. In 1926, Morse built a dam across the Rocky Broad River, corralling its waters into 1500 acres beneath the brow of Rumbling Bald Mountain. The instant lake meant instant lake-front property, and the area developed into a resort community. Now, pretty summer cabins rest beneath spires of evergreens along more than 25 miles of shoreline, and there's the small but much-esteemed **Lodge on Lake Lure**. ~ Charlotte Drive, off Route 64-74A; 704-625-2789.

Near the lodge are the **Bottomless Pools**. The phenomenon is caused by fractures in the ancient granite gneiss, which trap water on its way down the mountain to Lake Lure. Drop a twig into one of the three pools and it will stay there a very long time, swirling round so fast you can barely see it. Since Dr. Morse opened the pools in 1916, and *Ripley's Believe It or Not!* reported on them in the 1930s, the oddities have been attracting curious tourists. After seeing the pools and their respective waterfalls, there's really little to do other than enjoy the wooded trails—but you can do that almost anywhere in the Southern Mountains. Closed December through mid-March. Admission. ~ On Route 64-74A, Lake Lure; 704-625-4275.

The Bottomless Pools look like liquid tornadoes captured inside deep craters.

Back northwest on Route 64-74A just past Chimney Rock, in a wooded hamlet along the Rocky Broad River, you may or may not see signs for the town of **Bat Cave**. That's because fans of the Caped Crusader have lately taken to pilfering the signs, perhaps carting them off to their own secret bat cave, never to be seen again. As quickly as the town can replace them, they disappear. Even worse, many visitors who do manage to find the town come to see bats in a cave, which is not possible. ~ Intersection of Route 64-74A and Route 9.

HIDDEN ►

There is, in fact, a real Bat Cave (which the town of 457 residents is named for) located on the north slope of Hickory Nut Gorge. The property is protected and partly owned by The North Carolina Nature Conservancy. The Conservancy offers field trips to the 93-acre **Bat Cave Preserve**, designated a National Natural Landmark, from June through September. However, these days visitors are only allowed as far as the mouth of the cave so they rarely see any bats. Years ago many bats inhabited the cave but now there are only a few, thanks to pesky human explorers. Bats disturbed during hibernation often die, since they store only a limited amount of food. The critically endangered Indiana myotis bat, once a resident here, did not survive the years of human visits.

HIDDEN ►

Don't let the absence of bats dissuade you from taking this field trip: The two-hour hike is a wonderful walk in the woods, with opportunities to see waist-high wildflowers and 60-foot canopies of gnarled oak; many species of birds, including threatened warblers; and strange spiders and salamanders. The rare, red-and-white crevice salamander loves the rocks around Bat Cave and is usually spotted on the tour. The cave itself, the guide will tell you, is actually part of an elaborate network of granite fissure caves whose passageways run for more than a mile—making it one of the world's longest caves of the type. During the summer, tours can be arranged by contacting Sarah Lawter, owner of the Bat Cave Apple House fruit stand. ~ Route 64-74A, Bat Cave; 704-625-4311. During the winter, you should contact The North Carolina Nature Conservancy. There is a fee for the tour. ~ 4011 University Drive, Suite 201, Durham, NC 27707; 919-403-8558.

From Bat Cave you can head north to Asheville (see Chapter Two) on Route 74, a pleasant country drive with views across ravines carpeted with ferns and whitewashed homes with clothes strung on backyard lines. Or, you can stay in the Southern Mountains and drive southwest on Route 64 through apple country. This is **Henderson County**, North Carolina's number-one apple producer, where orchards of Rome Beauties and Golden Delicious, Gingergolds and Jonagolds, and many other popular varieties and hybrids ripple across a horizon of hills. In the spring, apple blossoms sweeten the air; in the fall, scarlet globes decorate the trees like Christmas ornaments. This is when signs invite you to pick your own fruit; tote a basket home and your car will smell of apples for many days. In the pint-size community of **Apple Valley**, about four miles west of Bat Cave, you can also select a pumpkin from one of the roadside patches. ~ Route 64.

LODGING

Small and pleasant, **Evening Shade** consists of several clapboard buildings parked above the boulder-studded Broad River, with green lawn cascading down to the water's edge. Rooms have paneled walls, small TVs and air conditioning—all in all quite rustic, but impeccable—and there are balconies peeking down to the river. A few rooms have kitchenettes. Closed end of October until April 1st. ~ Route 64-74A, Chimney Rock; 704-625-4774. BUDGET.

When Colonel Tom Turner opened an inn in 1890, he named it after the book *Esmeralda* by Frances Hodgson Burnett. No doubt it sealed the fate of the **Esmeralda Inn** as a literary and film haunt. Lew Grant finished *Ben Hur* in room number nine. Numerous silent movies were made in the area and their stars—Mary Pickford, Gloria Swanson and Clark Gable—stayed at the Esmeralda. Though the original building burned in 1916, it was rebuilt a year later, and today the three-story house of rough-hewn wood is warm and unassuming. The lobby offers rustic ambiance with its big stone fireplace and balconies of yellow poplar logs, and the 13 bedrooms invite with simple furnishings, old-fashioned sinks and painted plank walls. Continental breakfasts are included in the rates. Closed mid-December through mid-March. ~ Route 64-74A, Chimney Rock; 704-625-9105. BUDGET TO MODERATE.

If a place with a lake *and* mountain view sounds appealing, check into **The Lodge on Lake Lure**. Secluded and entirely comfortable, the venerable lodge was built in the 1930s shortly after Dr. Lucius Morse put a dam across the Rocky Broad River and created 1500-acre Lake Lure. The 12 rooms are all attractively decorated, with private bath, and a glass atrium dining room has sweeping views of the lake—and those peaks. A complimentary breakfast is served here. A paddleboat and canoes are provided for guest use. ~ Charlotte Drive, off Route 64-74A, Lake Lure; 704-625-2789, 800-733-2785, fax 704-625-2421. MODERATE TO DELUXE.

HIDDEN ► Half a mile southwest of Bat Cave, a gravel trail angles off Route 64 and curls for a mile through deep forest to the top of Hickory Nut Gorge. Here a secret hideaway called **Hickory Nut Gap Inn** sits high on a mountain in a grassy clearing, with only peaks and valleys and woods filling the landscape. In the 1940s and 1950s, Trailways Bus Company founder Herman Hardison built a weekend retreat here on 5000 acres. Now there are 40 acres and a rambling ranch house with six attractive bedrooms done in different woods, from maple to black walnut to cherry. The living room has a huge vaulted ceiling, and the screened breakfast porch affords mountain views. But the clincher is the basement bowling alley (regulation size), where garage bands used to practice on weekends. Lynyrd Skynyrd was once among those tuning their guitars. Rates include a continental breakfast. ~ Off Route 64, Bat Cave; 704-625-9108. MODERATE TO DELUXE.

DINING Inside Chimney Rock Park is a **snack bar** with the best view of any restaurant around. Grab a tray and order from the menu of filling, HIDDEN ► tasty deli sandwiches, pasta salads, homemade chili and soups, hot chocolate and fruit spritzers. Then grab a stool at the bar—glass walls face into the rock-etched Blue Ridge Mountains and Hickory Nut Gorge below. If you're planning to hike in the park, the eatery will prepare a picnic. ~ Route 64-74A; 704-625-4764. BUDGET.

Occupying a tin-roofed, low-slung building between road and river, **Crabby Bill's Old Time Oyster Bar** is popular, crowded and cluttered. Locals come for the fresh, no-frills seafood, everything from steamed Maine lobster and pan-fried flounder to grilled trout and oysters several ways, as well as alligator tail and fried chicken. Order and pay at the battered bar, then roll up your sleeves and have a seat at one of the long wooden tables inside, or outside overlooking the forested Rocky Broad River. Closed Tuesday. ~ Route 64-74A, Chimney Rock; 704-625-1302. MODERATE.

The veranda at the historic **Esmeralda Inn** is a wonderful place for a meal. Cooled by slow swirling fans and big shade trees, it features local fare with flair: rainbow trout sautéed with almonds and a wine sauce, seared smoked filet of beef and quail baked in burgundy sauce with pecans. There are pasta and chicken dishes as well, and traditional French cuisine. For lunch, you can choose a fancy sandwich or salad. Closed mid-December through mid-March. ~ Route 64-74A, Chimney Rock; 704-625-9105. MODERATE.

About four miles west of Bat Cave on Route 64, a speck of a town called Apple Valley, not found on many maps, invites you to pick your own fruit.

You can have your fish and beef with a water view at **Jimmy's Original Seafood and Steaks**, a log cabin parked right on Lake Lure. Locals and tourists alike stream in for lunch and dinner, where everchanging offerings might include pecan-crusted trout, shrimp scampi, roasted prime rib or grilled ribeye. In the summer, sit out on the patio. Closed January. ~ Route 64-74A at Route 9, Lake Lure; 704-625-4075. MODERATE TO DELUXE.

Right in "downtown" Chimney Rock, **Bubba O'Leary's General Store** is a big and bright emporium flooded with bluegrass music and stocked with everything from weathervanes and kitchenware to Pointer Brand overalls. ~ Route 64-74A; 704-625-2479.

SHOPPING

A few steps down the street and up a flight of stairs, **Featherheads** carries works by numerous artists, most from North Carolina. Mandalas and medicine wheels, handmade kites and twig pens are among the unusual works. ~ Main Street, above Goodwin's store; 704-625-1175.

◄ HIDDEN

If your tastes lean toward country-style gifts, you literally could spend a day at **A Day in the Country**. Quilts and afghans, jams and jellies, Christmas decor, baskets, antiques, dolls, pottery and more crowd into this 10,000-square-foot mecca. ~ Sugar Loaf Road, south of Route 64, Bat Cave; 704-692-7914.

There's not any. The closest nightlife (and it's limited) is in Flat Rock and Hendersonville, about 20 minutes away. Another 20 minutes north in Asheville (see Chapter Two), you'll find plenty to satisfy night owls.

NIGHTLIFE

An enviable location in the Blue Ridge foothills, an elevation (2200 feet) that guarantees chamber-of-commerce weather year-round, valleys that explode with apple orchards—these are the reasons people have been coming to Hendersonville and Flat Rock for over 150 years. The wealthy in particular have always liked the area; their grandiose antebellum and modern homes grace the neighborhoods. There are eight golf courses and nearly a dozen performing-arts groups in a county of only 75,000 people. And there are plenty of

Hendersonville & Flat Rock Area

creative ways to spend your money, whether on fine dining or exclusive shopping.

SIGHTS   You can start your spree in **Hendersonville**. The city of 9400 actually has two very different sides: the chaotic sprawl of strip malls and fast-food chains that creeps ever closer to Asheville; and the tranquil, affluent-feeling downtown where brick streets are edged with a panorama of flowers, and antique shops and galleries are sequestered beneath pretty awnings. The latter can be found just south of Route 64 in the historic district near **Main Street**, where more than 40 shops and eateries line ten square blocks.

Presiding over the area is the historic **Henderson County Courthouse** with its massive Corinthian columns, striking gold dome and lawn edged with tulips. ~ Corner of Main Street and 1st Avenue. (The new working courthouse is at 200 North Grove Street.)

The most exciting time downtown is the four days around Labor Day weekend (Friday through Monday) when the streets are transformed into a sea of fragrant scarlet for the North Carolina Apple Festival. There's mountain folk dancing, apple art and apple cuisine, and the wild and wacky King Apple Parade.

Information on the festival and all area sightseeing is available on the south end of historic Main Street at the **Henderson County Visitors Information Center**. ~ 201 South Main Street, Hendersonville; 704-693-9708.

A few minutes south of Hendersonville on Route 25 is **Flat Rock**, a town lying within a huge granite outcropping—hence the name. Little of the rock is visible, having been blasted out by developers or covered with thick woods. In fact, the town feels like a neighborhood in a forest. Within its four square miles of dense greenery are gracious nineteenth-century English country and antebellum homes, their lawns lined with boxwood hedges, their winding stone driveways laid by slaves.

The luxurious summer homes began to take shape in the early 1800s when the first aristocrats arrived from Charleston. In 1825, Charlestonians Susan and Charles Baring bought several hundred acres, fashioned it as an English country estate, and called it "Mountain Lodge." The wealthy rice planters set aside some land for a deer hunting club and invited their friends to come for the summer. In 1833 they built a chapel and rectory, but attendance was by invitation only. Authors Kenneth and Blanche Marsh, in their book *Historic Flat Rock*, tell how Susan "would allow no one to enter the church before the Barings' bright yellow carriage arrived. . . . The carriage door was opened by a footman, and Susan descended on her husband's arm. She then was preceded into the church by her maid carrying Susan's prayer book and a large turkey fan on a velvet cushion. . . . As soon as the Barings were seated, the bell would ring and the service could begin."

The Barings are buried in a vault beneath the church, which is now the **Episcopal Church of St. John in the Wilderness**. Don't miss this exquisite old building, enveloped in tall trees that throw long shadows on its tawny tower and fluted eaves. According to the Barings' specifications, Charleston architect Edward Jones designed the church as an English rural chapel, with a tremendous ceiling of beamed pine arches and glittering windows of stained glass. On the pews, brass plates bear the names of many nineteenth-century parishioners.

From the church, terraces of hemlock run down to a **little cemetery** where monuments are etched with the names of Flat Rock's earliest rich and famous, including Christopher Gustavus Memminger, the first Treasury Secretary of the Confederacy. ~ Route 25, Flat Rock; 704-693-9783.

Less than a mile south of the church, Memminger built a summer house that was eventually purchased by Carl Sandburg. The **Carl Sandburg Home** is a big white farmhouse, simple and weathered, set on a hill above a lake, with forest and then Blue Ridge Mountains and puffs of clouds in the distance. I could not imagine a more perfect setting for putting ideas on paper. Which, of course, is what Sandburg did here the last 22 years of his life.

An eighth-grade graduate who traveled as a hobo, then fought in the Spanish-American War, Sandburg became a poet, novelist, social commentator and political activist, among other things, although perhaps his most famous works are his Pulitzer Prize–winning biographies of Abraham Lincoln. In 1945, Sandburg had already won the Pulitzer when he and his wife, Paula, bought the 240-acre farm for $40,000. With it came 30 structures, including several barns and a pair of mountains and lakes. They called it Connemara, after the Connemara Mountains of Ireland. Sandburg was actually Swedish; his high, chiseled cheekbones and folksy, blond countenance are found in photos throughout the house.

Connemara is now a National Historic Site, a very popular one in fact. Guided, 25-minute tours of the house are given at various

LOVER'S LEAP

From downtown Hendersonville, take Laurel Park Highway west, winding through manicured neighborhoods with grand homes, until you ascend Jump Off Mountain. At the top is a lookout point called **Jump Off Rock**, so named because a young Cherokee woman took the big leap after her lover, a Cherokee chieftain, was killed in tribal wars—or at least that's the story. Today, you'll want to stay firmly on the big flat rock and well behind the guardrail, and enjoy the bluish peaks that seem to race across the horizon.

times throughout the day, but they fill up fast. Call before you go, then show up early. Wheelchair travelers have access to most sights, though some of the wooded trails are too narrow and bumpy to be navigated.

Visitors are often surprised to find the house is not fancy, but plain, even austere. Unlike most other Flat Rock residents, the Sandburgs eschewed the perks of wealth and fame, preferring to live modestly. Most impressive in the house is the books, more than 10,000 volumes spanning floor to ceiling in various rooms, that the Sandburgs spent much time reading and discussing. During the late evening and early morning hours, however, Sandburg wrote in a dim, cluttered attic chamber. He penned his only novel, *Remembrance Rock*, here. His green visor, left over from his days as a writer for the *Chicago Daily News*, rests on his desk, as does one of his cigars.

The entire house is virtually unchanged since the Sandburg days. *Newsweek* and *National Geographic* magazines, dating to the 1940s, are stacked everywhere (Sandburg refused to discard any reading material). In the dining room is the old Zenith television that Sandburg called the "thief of time," and watched only for news.

Paula and the Sandburg's daughters, Helga, Margaret and Janet, spent long days at the barn raising champion goats. Paula's well-bred herd, which numbered up to 200 and included famous Chikaming goats, earned her a worldwide reputation among goat traders and earned the couple a good living. Despite her business success, however, Carl Sandburg still traveled the lecture circuit, earning thousands of dollars for his appearances. He hated traveling, and while on the road wrote yearningly to Paula, to "speak to me of the drag on your heart, the iron drag of the long days."

From the house it's a short stroll through towering mountain ash and pines to the tin-roofed **main goat barn**, where you'll find descendants of Paula's original herds. Surrounding yards are filled with more animal life: swallows swoop in and out, a lavender-eyed cat goes on the prowl, chickens scratch around the dirt. Children especially enjoy the barn area, where they can pet the plump, bleating goats and sometimes even watch them being milked. The goats' milk is used for cheese-making demonstrations. The cheese, marinated in herbs and olive oil and aged a month, is especially rich and musky. If you are a fan of goat cheese, you will love these wedges.

There is much more to see at the Sandburg property, including a greenhouse and a silo (which the Sandburgs never used), a gazebo and a barn garage. Take a look at the copper-colored 1962 Willy's Jeep in the garage; Sandburg received it as a gift from the makers of *The Greatest Story Ever Told* after he helped write the movie script. Here also is Paula's set of farm wheels: a 1951 Ford tractor.

Carl Sandburg died in his bedroom at Connemara of a stroke in 1967. He was 90. In 1969, Paula deeded the property to the federal government as a historic site. She died nine years later. Today, daughters Margaret and Janet live in nearby Asheville. Admission. ~ Little River Road, just off Route 25; 704-693-4178.

Route 176 south of Flat Rock offers a peaceful, bucolic side trip through mountains marbled in forest and streams. After 12 miles you unexpectedly come upon **Saluda**, a tiny, two-block town   ◄ *HIDDEN* of the quaintest order, sitting right against the railroad tracks. Its Main Street is decorated with a little general store, a bakery, antique stores, and a renovated train depot where local artists sell unusual and traditional works. A crossroads between South Carolina and Georgia, Saluda was known among railroaders as having the steepest standard gauge tracks in the country. The tracks climb 600 feet up Saluda Mountain in just three miles, a grade of 4.8. A **historical marker** right next to the tracks notes this trivia.

South of Saluda, Route 176 is a switchback trail that launches into a web of thick forest. Soon you'll see a sign announcing **Tryon**,   ◄ *HIDDEN* "The Friendliest Town in the South." Folks here do seem friendly, though one suspects they'd also be a little off kilter, considering the whole town is lopsided, its brick buildings actually tilting against a mountain.

Grab a paper, stroll down the steeply angled Main Street, browse the gift shops and have lunch at one of the eateries. If you explore much south of town, you'll run into South Carolina, only a half-mile from Tryon.

Continuing the westward tour of the South Mountains, head back north to Hendersonville and then west on Route 64 toward Brevard. Immediately west of town, the **Oakdale Cemetery** contains a piece of literary intrigue. The **marble angel** atop the grave   ◄ *HIDDEN* of Margaret Johnson, wife of a local preacher, closely resembles the one in Thomas Wolfe's book *Look Homeward, Angel*. Wolfe's fictional angel was carved by Gant, a character based on Wolfe's own father, who was a mason. The Asheville author chose the angel because his father, frustrated that he could not sculpt one, was forced to import European angel monuments for his clients. No one's sure exactly which angel inspired Wolfe, though Mrs. Johnson's compelling monument—her wings spread high and finger pointed toward heaven—is hauntingly similar to the one in the book. You can see the angel from Route 64; follow the cemetery roads back to where she stands, enclosed by a wrought-iron fence.

Charles Kuralt once stayed at **The Claddagh Inn** while researching   **LODGING** local Americana. It was perfect for such research, since the turn-of-the-century, sunshine-yellow house radiates solace and warmth. Old wooden rockers invite from a rambling porch shaded with trees. The 14 bedrooms, all with private baths, are decorated with fine antiques and soothing colors. And the breakfasts, included in the rates, are like those you'd have on a farm: eggs, bacon and sausage, apple cinnamon pancakes and almond French toast, muffins and peach crisp. ~ 755 North Main Street, Hendersonville; 704-697-7778, 800-225-4700, fax 704-697-8664. MODERATE.

Next door to the Claddagh and equally as inviting, **The Waverly Inn** has been hosting guests since the early 1900s. In the late 1800s, the three-story frame house was restored, and now the 13 guest rooms with private baths gleam with pretty four-poster canopy beds, clawfoot tubs and pedestal sinks. One room has a sun porch. Guests enjoy getting acquainted with one another during the early-evening social hour. All-you-can-eat breakfasts are cooked to order. ~ 783 North Main Street, Hendersonville; 704-693-9193, 800-537-8195, fax 704-692-1010; e-mail waverlyinn@ioa.com. MODERATE TO DELUXE.

HIDDEN ►   Outside of town, at the crest of a mountain surrounded by skyline views, **Echo Mountain Inn** offers an escape to the woods. There are four buildings, including a frame-and-stone main house built in 1896, with 34 rooms and suites, decorated in simple French-country style, with balloon valances. Many rooms have working fireplaces and wonderful mountain views, and most have air conditioners. There's a swimming pool, plenty of hiking trails and a restaurant with fine dining. ~ 2849 Laurel Park Highway, Hendersonville; 704-693-9626, 888-324-6466, fax 704-697-2047. MODERATE TO DELUXE.

Secluded, wooded and on a 30-acre lake, **Highland Lake Inn** is where burned-out professionals come to unwind. Families and couples also find these 180 acres relaxing. There are horses in the barn and plenty of trails for riding, canoes down by the lake, a swimming pool for cooling off in summer, and an organic garden of berries and herbs, most of which end up in the inspired dishes served by the inn's restaurant. Accommodations are in various

----

✔ CHECK THESE OUT—UNIQUE LODGING

- *Budget:* Relax riverside at **Evening Shade**, a sprinkling of simple clapboard buildings overlooking rock-studded Broad River. *page 61*
- *Moderate:* Indulge in downy quilts, perfumed bath potions and extravagant breakfasts at the beautifully decorated **Flat Rock Inn**. *page 69*
- *Deluxe to ultra-deluxe:* Retreat to the woods without roughing it at **Millstone Inn**, a stylish, elegant home set beside a mountain. *page 80*
- *Ultra-deluxe:* Unpack for a while at **High Hampton Inn and Country Club**, fashioned like a big mountain cabin, but with every imaginable amenity and outdoor pursuit. *page 80*

Budget: under $60 Moderate: $60–$100 Deluxe: $100–$130 Ultra-deluxe: over $130

simple, generous-size cabins and cottages amid the trees, plus a modern main lodge and inn. A nine-hole golf course is across the street. ~ Highland Lake Road, between Routes 25 and 176, Flat Rock; 704-693-6812, 800-762-1376. MODERATE TO DELUXE.

Occasionally there is a place so pleasing in mood and design you really hate to leave. **Flat Rock Inn** is that place, no doubt because owners Sandi and Dennis Page spent much of their lives staying in guesthouses and seeing things from a guest's point of view. Their three-story, 1888 house is beautifully decorated and inviting, with four large, lovely, high-ceiling bedrooms and big baths, and much attention to detail, from the perfumed potions set beside the clawfoot tubs to the downy quilts and linens that envelop you at night. Every room has either an air conditioner or a ceiling fan. Sandi's bountiful breakfasts, included in the rate, look like they might grace the cover of *Gourmet* magazine. Closed in January. ~ 2810 Greenville Highway, Flat Rock; 704-696-3273, 800-266-3996. MODERATE.

Built in the early 1900s by the Southern Railway as a summer retreat for its clerks' union, the **Orchard Inn** now hosts travelers in search of seclusion. Hidden atop a mountain, the pale yellow farmhouse presides over sweeping green lawns swirled with wildflowers, with the peaks of the Warrior Mountain Range unfolding in the distance. The twelve guest rooms are informal with their wood floors and throw rugs or carpeting, simple antiques, and works by local artisans. Three spacious cottages, with private decks and fireplaces, overlook the woods or the mountains. ~ Route 176, one mile east of Saluda; 704-749-5471, fax 704-749-9805, 800-581-3800. DELUXE TO ULTRA-DELUXE.

◄ HIDDEN

In the tiny, little-known town of Tryon, a half-mile north of the South Carolina line, **Pine Crest Inn** seems purposefully hidden from civilization. That's likely what drew guests F. Scott Fitzgerald and Ernest Hemingway to this classy former hunt club in the woods. Cottages of forest green crouch beneath spidery trees, and French doors open onto shaded verandas. A main lodge gleams with polished wood and stylish country motif, while a woodcutter cottage, swayback cabin and stone cottage offer unusual places to sleep. Most rooms have fireplaces; all have cable TV, telephones and private baths. ~ 200 Pine Crest Lane, Tryon; phone/fax 704-859-9135, 800-633-3001. DELUXE TO ULTRA-DELUXE.

◄ HIDDEN

If you want to enjoy an exceptional meal in Hendersonville, you will inevitably be introduced to the name Tom Young. The culinary instructor, chef and owner of **Expressions** is famed for his fine productions of seasonal specialties served in an elegant bistro in historic downtown Hendersonville. Offerings change nightly but might include appetizers such as duck liver pâte with *bruschetta* or

DINING

smoked trout with horseradish cream, and entrées like grilled swordfish with artichoke relish or roasted Manchester Farms quail with goat cheese, sun-dried tomatoes and hickory-smoked bacon. Lunch is served Tuesday through Saturday. Closed Sunday. ~ 114 North Main Street, Hendersonville; 704-693-8516. DELUXE.

For light eats and a choice of over 125 beers, duck into **Hannah Flanagan's Pub**. A classy place of brass and brick and well-polished wood floors, it serves good sandwiches, homemade soups and salads (try the 40 Shades of Green Salad) from late morning till late night. ~ 300 North Main Street, Hendersonville; 704-696-1665. BUDGET.

HIDDEN ▶   Built in 1881, **Poplar Lodge** is a popular place of immense proportions, with massive walls of poplar wood and soaring fieldstone fireplaces, and a dimly lit, hearthside atmosphere for dining. No longer a lodge, the restaurant offers big and tender pricey steaks, grilled chicken and tuna, pan-fried mountain trout, and a salad bar whose items extend well beyond lettuce and veggies (sardines, pepperoni, smoked oysters, fresh apples, artichoke hearts, to name a few). ~ 2360 Heron Road, Hendersonville; 704-692-9191. DELUXE.

HIDDEN ▶   In a pretty dining room and glass-walled porch in the woods, **Highland Lake Inn** serves breakfast, lunch and dinner—some of the freshest, most innovative cooking around. Chef Larc Lindsey need only look as far as the inn's organic farm for herbs, fruits and vegetables to grace his plates. The food is always different, depending on what's in season, but here's a sampling of dinner: okra over tomato creole; warm curried cucumber vermicelli; grouper stuffed with Maryland lump crab and served with tarragon cream; and apple-smoked turkey scaloppini stuffed with wild mushrooms and served with a cranberry port wine sauce. Don't miss it. ~ Highland Lake Road, between Routes 25 and 176, Flat Rock; 704-693-6812. DELUXE.

HIDDEN ▶   Sitting near the railroad tracks, **Sidestreet Pizza** emits enticing Italian food smells from the front door. The thick- and thin-crust pizzas and toasted subs do live up to their smells; the "white pizza" with olive oil, garlic and cheese is unusually tasty. You can order out or eat on a wooden table with views of a jukebox and mirrored beer plaques. Closed Tuesday and Wednesday. ~ 201 South Trade Street, Tryon; 704-859-5325. BUDGET.

A meal at the **Pine Crest Inn** is one befitting a former hunt club: robust and meaty, steeped in sauces and arranged imaginatively on the plate. There's filet mignon served with wild mushrooms and potato-and-parmesan custard; roast breast of duck stuffed with spinach and roasted garlic; salmon crusted in brioche with fava beans and a yellow tomato bouillon. The dining room, with its heavily beamed ceiling, big stone hearth and crystal-topped tables, feels transported from the English countryside. ~ 200 Pine Crest Lane, Tryon; 704-859-9135. ULTRA-DELUXE.

The best shopping is in downtown Hendersonville, home to more **SHOPPING** than three dozen shops and galleries. Concentrate first on Main Street.

If you're even slightly interested in cooking, check out the wonderful kitchenry, specialty foods, and underground wine cellar at **Purple Sage**. It's owned by Tom Young, chef and restaurateur of the highly regarded Expressions, just down the street. ~ 416 North Main Street, Hendersonville; 704-693-9555.

Treasures Retrieved is an emporium of eclectic, eccentric jewelry and clothes, as well as folk art and birdhouses. ~ 1291 North Ridge Road, Hendersonville; 704-685-7900.

> Tryon gets its news from *The Tryon Daily Bulletin*, whose masthead reads "The World's Smallest Daily Newspaper,"—it's been printed on 8½" by 11" paper since 1928. Circulation is 4700.

Much of Henderson County's apple crop is turned into jams, jellies, relishes and pies, which you can sample at the old-time **Curb Market**. Established in 1924 with only eight farmers selling from beneath umbrellas, the market today has 137 vendors offering all sorts of fruits, vegetables and home-style goods, from aprons and afghans to wreaths and walking sticks. Open Tuesday, Thursday and Saturday from June through November; open Tuesday and Saturday December through May. ~ 221 North Church Street, Hendersonville; 704-692-8012.

The local night scene is limited to a beer and light tunes or the per- **NIGHTLIFE** forming arts, the latter of which happen to be some of the best in the Carolinas. Actually, some say **Flat Rock Playhouse** is the best, certainly at least when it comes to summer stock theater. Opened in 1952 and made North Carolina's State Theater in 1961, it hosts the ever-popular Vagabond Players, who started in New York in 1937. Musicals, comedies and occasional drama from Broadway and London play here. The season runs from late May to mid-October. ~ Route 25, Flat Rock; 704-693-0731.

The **Hendersonville Symphony Orchestra** presents several concerts a year, often featuring local and national guest artists. Location varies, so call for information. ~ 704-697-5884.

One of the most popular nightspots in Hendersonville, **Hannah Flanagan's Pub,** occasionally hosts weekend acoustic bands. Naturally, you'll want to order a beer—there were over 125 brands at last count. ~ 300 North Main Street, Hendersonville; 704-696-1665.

The bar at **Poplar Lodge**, comfortably cluttered with everything ◄ *HIDDEN* from barber poles and bicycles to an overhead train, is a fun place for a drink. ~ 2350 Hebron Road, Hendersonville; 704-692-9191.

HOLMES EDUCATIONAL STATE FOREST A marvelous introduc- **BEACHES** tion to the Carolinas' mountain flora, the 235-acre forest has **& PARKS** "talking trees" that tell about their origins and uses, and how they interact with animals and other plants. Simply push the button on ◄ *HIDDEN* an oak, hickory, tulip poplar or other hardwood, and a recording will give you the lowdown on the tree. The "Talking Tree Trail" is an easy half-mile, and there's a longer, three-mile "Forest Management Demonstration Trail" (which should be called something less stiff, like "Getting to Know Your Forest") where you can see exactly how big an acre is and learn other woodsy details. The forest also has a Christmas tree plantation, a wetland and a pond. Closed Monday; closed late November through mid-March. Facilities include picnic tables and covered shelters, restrooms (only picnic areas, restrooms, and the half-mile Crab Creek Trail are wheelchair accessible) and two amphitheaters. The closest convenience store is three miles away and the nearest restaurants are about nine miles away in Hendersonville or Brevard. ~ From downtown Hendersonville, take Kanuga Road (which becomes Crab Creek Road) southwest for nine miles, a scenic drive through rolling hills and valleys; 704-692-0100.

▲ There are 15 semi-primitive tent sites, plus a group area, with cold-water showers; no fee. The campground is just a short stroll from the parking area.

▼▼▼▼▼▼▼▼▼▼
Brevard Area

As Route 64 west leaves the suburban sprawl of Hendersonville behind, there is a welcome coolness in the air—and then forest, moist, quiet and dappled with sun filtering through 40-foot canopies of red oak and yellow and white pine, and rhododendron and flame azaleas coloring the roadsides. You know you are out of the city and in the country when you see signs for "Hunters' Dog Boxes" (the kind that goes on the back of a pickup truck to hold the hunting dogs). You'll also know when you see the signs for Pisgah National Forest.

SIGHTS

Pisgah National Forest is protected today because of George Vanderbilt, who in the late 1800s purchased several forests, totaling 125,000 acres, extending west from his famous Biltmore House in Asheville. Vanderbilt hired a friend named Gifford Pinchot, who had studied forestry in France, to manage and protect the area—and thus laid the groundwork for the first national forest. Not long after Vanderbilt died in 1914, the federal government acquired most of the forest and turned it into a game preserve, eventually more than tripling its size.

Pinchot was succeeded by Dr. Carl Schenck, a German forestry pioneer who created the Biltmore Forestry School. From the turn-of-the-century until 1914, his students ran a trout hatchery, studied selective logging, and lived in rundown, deserted logging camps, giving them names such as Hell Hole and Rest for the Wicked.

Today, the school has been re-created as the **Cradle of Forestry in America**, a National Historic Site spanning 6500 acres of the Pisgah National Forest. Most areas here are wheelchair accessible, including the one-mile Biltmore Campus Trail and the remnants of

Hell Hole, plus woodcarvers, basketmakers, weavers, quilters and blacksmiths demonstrating their skills. There's also the Black Forest Lodge, one of several buildings designed by Schenck to resemble Germany's Black Forest cottages. Schenck's hired rangers lived in these cottages while fending off illegal loggers and trappers. Admission. ~ Route 276, north of Route 64; 704-877-3130.

You can learn all about Schenck, Pinchot and Vanderbilt and their progressive forestry ideas in a film shown in the 15,000-square-foot **Visitors Center**. Kids will love the hands-on and high-tech exhibits including touch-screen videos, puppets and puzzles relating to forests, and a helicopter with a "virtual reality" screen that allows them to put out a forest fire. Another outstanding exhibit teaches kids about trees as they explore the trunk, branches and root system in a life-size replica. Visit the historic site between mid-April and October, since it's closed the rest of the year.

Heading south back on Route 276, take the turnoff for **Pisgah Forest State Fish Hatchery**. This is a highly interesting and strange place, especially if you've never seen thousands of multi-size trout swimming furiously in tanks called "raceways." Kids love feeding the fish, which attack the food (a mixture of fish meal and vitamins), piranha-like. About 425,000 trout are raised at the hatchery every year and released into surrounding streams, which sounds like a lot, until you consider only 20 percent of North Carolina's streams are "non-native," meaning they're eligible for farm-raised fish. In other words, if you do catch a local trout, chances are it was born in a stream, not here in a tank. ~ Route 475; 704-877-3121.

Returning to Route 64, continue westward through Pisgah Forest to **Brevard**, which calls itself "Land of Waterfalls" and "Home of the White Squirrel," for the white squirrels, rare in this part of the world, that live in city parks. Brevard is also the seat of Transylvania County, a name supposedly unrelated to vampires or any place in Europe, but derived from "trans," meaning across, and "sylvania," meaning the woods. The *Transylvania Times* is the local newspaper.

Brevard used to hold a festival called "Transylvania Mania," complete with a Dracula look-alike contest. The event is now called "Halloweenfest."

There are no waterfalls in Brevard proper, but there is a busy little town center and a main street whose western end dramatically frames a mountain. As you come into town, take a look at the lovely **Brevard College**, where distinguished Federal-style buildings of red brick and white columns assemble on rambling green lawns planted with brilliant flowers. ~ On North Broad Street; 704-883-8292.

Home to 5800 people, the town gets its name from Ephraim Brevard, a surgeon and Revolutionary War colonel who died of battle wounds in 1781 at the age of 37. The colonel never actually set foot in Brevard, but he was well known here and throughout the South. It's not known whether he loved music, but one hopes he did, since his town is best known for the Brevard Music Festival, which for seven weeks every summer draws national and international performers and thousands of spectators from surrounding counties and states. It's held at the **Brevard Music Center**, which was founded in 1936 and moved to its present locale ten years later. ~ West Probart Street; 704-884-2019.

More local history, as well as suggestions on things to see and do, are available from the **Brevard Chamber of Commerce**. The person to see here is Esther Wesley, who's been answering questions for the chamber of commerce for over 20 years now. Closed Sunday. ~ 35 West Main Street; 704-883-3700, 800-648-4523.

LODGING

HIDDEN ▶

Key Falls Inn is a fine old Victorian farmhouse, built in 1860 and splendidly restored, with a stream and waterfall cascading through the property. Owners Janet Fogleman and her parents, Clark and Patricia Grosvenor, have put antiques nearly everywhere in the house, including in the four tastefully decorated bedrooms and one suite, all with private baths. There are porches for watching the mountains, and 35 acres of luxuriant grounds, including thick boxwood and azalea gardens and a tunnel of rhododendron leading to a bridge over the waterfall. The rates include full farm-style breakfasts and afternoon tea. ~ Everett Road, off Old Route 64; 704-884-7559. BUDGET TO MODERATE.

The **Inn at Brevard** stands out along Main Street, its crisp white exterior accented with intensely blue awnings. Inside the turn-of-the-century mansion is a slightly worn but cozy atmosphere, with creaking red carpeted and five entirely different bedrooms, including two with shared bath. One rather dim room has walls of knotty pine paneling and cinnamon-colored carpet; another is bright and airy with a window seat; a third is a spacious suite. Room rates include breakfast. An adjacent two-story motel has ten more rooms. Open Easter through Thanksgiving. ~ 410 East Main Street; 704-884-2105, fax 704-966-9210. MODERATE TO ULTRA-DELUXE.

DINING

The dining rooms at the **Inn at Brevard** are open for dinner on Friday and Saturday nights, and for brunch on Sunday. The menus include pan-fried trout, fried chicken, mashed potatoes, fresh stewed vegetables and other Southern-style possibilities, perfect for this elegant turn-of-the-century setting. ~ 410 East Main Street; 704-884-2105. MODERATE TO DELUXE.

In a sparkling old white antebellum home with polished wood floors, **Oh! Susanna's** is a deli by day and full restaurant by night. Sandwiches come in half or whole and are far from plain; there's the Camptown Grinder loaded with meats and oil and vinegar, and the Swanee Ribber with tuna, swiss cheese and cucumbers. For dinner, try the pan-fried or broiled trout or penne pasta with chicken and broccoli. Dine inside or out on the porch under the maple trees. Wine and beer are available. ~ 230 West Main Street; 704-883-3289. BUDGET TO MODERATE.

Browsers should concentrate on the area around Main Street in downtown Brevard, a district sprinkled with some fine antique shops, boutiques and craft stores.

SHOPPING

The **White Squirrel Shop** is a curio shop with unusual gifts and antiques. ~ 2 West Main Street; 704-877-3530. **The Carolina Connection** is country-themed, with primitive furniture, birdhouses and woven throws. ~ 5 West Main Street; 704-884-9786.

If you're looking to trade in that book you just finished, make a stop at **The Book Nook**. The store stocks new and used books as well as T-shirts and locally made arts and crafts. ~ 15/17 South Broad Street; 704-883-9745.

If you brought your disco duds, put them away. Bring out the blue jeans and cowboy boots (you *did* pack them, right?).

NIGHTLIFE

If it's Thursday night, go to **Silvermont** for a real mountain hoedown, with old-time bluegrass and sometimes, if the local ladies are in the mood, clogging. As one resident puts it, the long-time event is "a bunch of local musicians who get together and just noodle away." ~ East Main Street; 704-884-3166.

On weekends, there's live music at several Brevard restaurants, ranging from country to easy listening to folk. Check out the entertainment at **The Falls Landing**. ~ 23 East Main Street; 704-884-2835. **Oh! Susanna's** also offers live entertainment on the weekends. ~ 230 West Main Street; 704-883-3289.

PISGAH NATIONAL FOREST 🎿 🚣 A 504,180-acre forest that extends far north into North Carolina's High Country and Piedmont regions, Pisgah is a wilderness of waterfalls, rocky outcroppings, thick caverns of ferns and spiraling trees, and several mountain ranges, including the Black Mountains, with a ceiling reaching more than 6000 feet. There's a vast array of wildlife, from black bears, red squirrels, ravens and hawks to ruffed grouse, whitetailed deer and the rare and tiny saw-whet owl, which lives only in spruce and fir forests higher than 5000 feet.

BEACHES & PARKS

Within the national forest, which reaches down into the Southern Mountains to the South Carolina line, there are many places for sightseeing, innertubing, camping out, swimming, fishing, rock climbing, waterfall watching and sliding. To simply drive through endlessly beautiful forest, take the **Forest Heritage National Scenic Byway**, a 77-mile loop along Routes 276, 64, 215 and 475.

Facilities include picnic sites, and hot showers at various locations. Good swimming is available at Lake Powhatan. The Davidson

Text continued on page 78.

Wandering the Waterfall Highway

They range from curtains of quiet water to fast-flowing flumes to liquid thunder. You can drive under or behind them, slide down them, or lodge your body beneath them and have the best shower massage of your life.

Most people, however, are content to simply stare at waterfalls, those indescribable tricks of nature: water freefalling its way to some darkened gorge or bright stream, crashing and fizzing before continuing on its way. Only the icy breath of winter can stop a waterfall, and it often does, suspending it in midair in a frozen sheet of silver fringed with icicles.

There are hundreds, possibly thousands, of waterfalls in the Southern Mountains, their names—Umbrella Falls, Bridal Veil Falls, Sliding Rock, Slippery Witch—suggesting a distinct form, beauty or treachery. Some are located right alongside the road; others are a short and scenic hike from the pavement. But most all are reached from Route 64, also known as the Waterfall Highway.

Start wandering the highway on the east end of the Southern Mountains in Chimney Rock Park. The park's number-one attention-getter is a stupendous chimney-shaped rock; number two is **Hickory Nut Falls**, one of the highest falls in the eastern United States with a straight-down drop of 404 feet, twice as long as Niagara, though significantly narrower. The easiest way to the bottom of the falls is via the Forest Stroll, a moderate, one-hour round-trip walk from the area just below the top parking lot. The two-hour Skyline Trail, which starts near Chimney Rock and whose views and steep steps will leave you breathless, leads to the top of the falls. Centuries-old chestnut oaks and hemlocks preside over this summit. This is a great spot for a picnic, and the folks down at the park's snack shop are happy to pack one—so ask before you go. Admission. ~ Route 64-74A in the town of Chimney Rock; 704-625-9611.

Westward on Route 64, then south on Route 176, between the tiny towns of Saluda and Tryon, look for the small sign for **Pearson's Falls**. A quarter-mile trail wends through carpets of ferns and trees dripping with bromeliads and orchids, delivering you to the granite terraces of the falls, where water tumbles 90 feet from step to step to step. These falls are out of the way and not so well known, so you will likely have them all to yourself. Enjoy.

If a painter were to portray a perfect waterfall, it would be **Looking Glass Falls**. Abroad, curving mantle of pure unbroken water, framed in granite ledges and speckled leaves of forest, flows 60 feet into a clear pool. This is a popular waterfall, close to the road, so you will likely share the moment with people snapping photos. ~ Route 276 north of Route 64, in Pisgah National Forest.

A spot that's even more crowded, but absolutely worth experiencing, lies two miles farther north on Route 276. Like it sounds, **Sliding Rock** is where water slides down rock—and you can, too. Put on a pair of sturdy shorts and shoes and take a fast ride down the 60-foot natural slide, landing in a seven-foot-deep pool as clear as air. People have been doing it for decades, and so have animals; Lassie supposedly took the big slide for a scene in her TV show. Kids will slide down relentlessly all day, even if the water averages 55° *in summer*. There are bathhouses and lifeguards on duty Memorial Day through Labor Day. In winter, the place is near empty. Admission.

Farther west on Route 64, near the community of Sapphire, head south on Route 281. Just before the South Carolina line, stop at **Whitewater Falls**. A most unusual cascade, it falls partly in North Carolina and partly in South Carolina. The North Carolina falls, or the upper falls, surge 411 feet down a stepped rock wall, making them the highest waterfalls east of the Rockies. Poets and writers have long attempted to capture the power and grandeur of this spot.

Just past Highlands on Route 64 are a pair of outstanding falls. You can see **Bridal Veil Falls** from the highway, a cascade of whitewater as thin and glisteny as shredded lace. The water falls in millions of little droplets upon the rocks; in winter, the droplets freeze and look like rhinestones. Angling off the highway is a little side road. Don't be shy: take it, and drive your car right under the falls.

Barely a mile west of here is the turnoff for **Dry Falls**. You can hear the thunderous torrent from the parking area, but you'll have to walk a few minutes down to where it plummets, freeform, 75 feet into the Cullasaja River. Walk around behind the mammoth falls, into the dim, damp rock grotto, and you can watch the world *through* the falls—while staying completely dry.

There are many more falls along the highway, enough, in fact, to fill up weeks of wandering. For tips on where to find them, contact **Pisgah National Forest Ranger Station**. ~ Route 276; 704-877-3265. Also try **Brevard Chamber of Commerce**. ~ 35 West Main Street, Brevard; 704-883-3700, 800-648-4523. You can also contact the **Cashiers Area Chamber of Commerce**, which publishes a Waterfall Treasure Map. ~ Route 107 North; 704-743-5191.

River is well-known for its abundance of rainbow trout. Other great spots: North Mills River, for trout and bream; and Lake Powhatan, for largemouth and smallmouth bass, bream, catfish and trout. A fishing license is required. A few areas have up to a $3 day-use fee. ~ Major access points are along Routes 64, 276, 191, and 215, and the Blue Ridge Parkway; 704-877-3265.

▲ There are nearly 300 tent and RV sites throughout the forest, plus several group camping areas. None have hookups. Most campgrounds close December through February. Fees range from $5 to $12 per night, depending on the campground.

▼▼▼▼▼▼▼▼▼▼▼
Cashiers & Highlands Area

West from Brevard to Cashiers, Route 64 is a virtual joy ride through sun-dappled mountain forest, with dips and dives and hairpin turns, and the occasional sign announcing "Boiled Peanuts" or "Trout Fishing Bait." Near Lake Toxaway, there's another sign letting you know when you cross the Eastern Continental Divide.

SIGHTS

The rural drama transforms into contemporary scenes at **Sapphire**, a community consisting mainly of a 6000-acre planned resort called **Fairfield Sapphire Valley**. Sign after sign, tucked into the woods, announce this sprawling place of townhouses and lakes, golf courses and tennis courts.

Just past here you'll find aesthetic **Cashiers**, pronounced CASH-ers, a town of a few blocks with quaint shops sitting 3486 comfortable feet up in the mountains. (Notice the little wooden building near the center of town that's a combination travel agency, video rental store, VCR repair shop and fudge factory.) Floridians love this cool summer spot and seem to have taken over the town. As soon as you arrive, you notice something is missing: the Carolinas' mountain accent. These flatlanders haven't quite learned how to say "ya'll." ~ 4000 Route 64 West; 704-743-3441.

For information on this part of the Southern Mountains, stop by the **Cashiers Area Chamber of Commerce**. Closed Sunday. ~ Route 107 North; 704-743-5191.

Keep going westward on Route 64 for a thrilling trip into the **Nantahala National Forest**. The slender road corkscrews around cliffs of exposed rocks where streams dribble down, and tunnels though great cathedrals of greenery. Random openings in the forest let you see far across horizons dotted with bluish peaks and silvery balds glinting with sun. A fortunate few people have hung homes on the mountainsides off Route 64 and given them names—Sky Watch, Sun Ledge—that hint at their extraordinary views. Very old, boldly painted pickup trucks, their mufflers in desperate need of repair, frequent this stretch of road, so don't be surprised when you meet one coming around a narrow bend.

Near the Macon County line, take the turnoff for Whiteside Mountain Road. After a mile of nothing but forest you'll arrive at **Whiteside Mountain Area Vista Point**. Take an hour or two and hike the two-mile switchback loop to the mountaintop, where you are met by sheer cliffs of white metamorphic rock climbing from 400 to 750 feet, hovering above a dark valley below and looking into the headwaters of the Chattooga River. The cliffs are formed of whiteside granite, where peregrine falcons perch.

West on Route 64, just a few minutes from where the falcons go, are places less natural and more contrived: miles of planned developments, retirement communities and golf resorts whose orderly townhomes and gardens look out of place among these wild mountains and streams. Strangely, the heart of this modern design is a town that was planned back around 1875.

Highlands was created by land developers Samuel T. Kelsey and Clinton C. Hutchinson, who bought 839 acres on this mountain plateau and published a brochure to entice investors. "No better climate in the world for health, comfort and enjoyment," it said, repeating the same words used for dozens of eastern mountain developments (folks today do admit there's a bit of pollen in the air). But the words worked, and by 1883 Highlands boasted 300 residents. Today, there are only about 2000, though you'd never know it, for up to 20,000 visitors crowd the tiny town in summer, staying in inns and manses with well-tended gardens and resorts where tee times (and tea times) are posted in the lobbies.

There is money in Highlands. You can see it in the shops of exclusive designs and hushed price tags, in the tony eateries where champagne is poured at lunch, and in the real-estate pages advertising prices you are certain must be misprints. Which is to say that Highlands is an enormously attractive town, with lush gardens and rows of perfect buildings and sidewalks overhung with colorful canopies. It is also a superior place to shop; dozens of stores, advertising highly imaginative items, crowd the downtown. And, despite the money, Highlands is far from stuffy—indeed, it is quite friendly. Even if you don't stay overnight—and you should—spend a day wandering around town.

Before you start exploring, stop by the **Highlands Chamber of Commerce** for brochures on local sights, restaurants, lodges and activities. Closed Sunday. ~ Oak and Fourth streets; 704-526-2112.

LODGING

Woodlands Inn of Sapphire is a simple roadside place, unassuming and eclectic, set on the slope of a hill. Two-story octagonal buildings feature spacious rooms and suites decorated in vivid colors and thick '80s-style carpets, and flanked by windows that look into forest. Rooms have refrigerators and coffeepots. A full breakfast is served in the gathering room. Add to that a swimming pool, a staff that's exceedingly helpful, and reasonable rates, and you have a very good value. Closed December through February. ~ 1305 Route 64 West, Sapphire; 704-966-4709, fax 704-966-4544. MODERATE.

Spread across 6000 acres of mountains and valleys and woods, offering every imaginable amenity, from golf, tennis, canoeing and horseback riding to hiking trails, cross-country ski trails, and a health club, **Fairfield Sapphire Valley Resort** is a virtual city. An excellent family retreat, it has extensive programs for children, and spacious modern condominiums and townhomes, most of them with kitchens and many with fireplaces and washers and dryers. There are several swimming pools, including an indoor Olympic pool with an huge vaulted tongue-in-groove ceiling. My favorite spot, though, is **The Library** (704-743-5512), a private restaurant and bar (open to guests and club members) built around a late-1800s farmhouse. You can read a book and have a cocktail (county laws prohibit liquor except in private clubs), a sandwich or one of the well-prepared nightly specials. ~ Route 64 West, Sapphire; 704-743-3441, 800-533-8268. MODERATE TO ULTRA-DELUXE.

Its name suggests a grand and formal lodge, but **High Hampton Inn and Country Club** is actually the opposite: warm, woody and rustic, like a huge mountain cabin. In fact, the only thing grand about the place is the trees. Two—a fraser fir and a bottlebrush buckeye near the golf course's 16th hole—are among the largest of their kind in America (both have certificates from the National Forestry Association). The lodge itself is built almost entirely out of wood, including a lot of wormy chestnut that succumbed to the blight of the 1920s (you can see the worm tunnels). A massive, four-sided stone fireplace graces the lobby. There are 130 wood-paneled rooms and 19 cottages, including a lakeside grist mill honeymoon cottage. Mountain views are everywhere. A favorite of families and company retreats, the inn features a golf course, tennis courts, a lake, summer kids' program and restaurant (coat and tie required at night). Rates include three buffet meals a day. Closed late November through March. ~ Route 107, south of Cashiers; 704-743-2411, 800-334-2551, fax 704-743-5991. ULTRA-DELUXE.

HIDDEN ► A place of great charm and solitude and style, **Millstone Inn** is situated in a 1930s former home trimmed in wood shakes and perched on a lush knoll of pine and rhododendron and mountain laurel. Birds sing from high in the treetops, and mountains and valleys are etched in the distance like a watercolor picture. In the main sitting room, an oriental rug reposes in front of a stone fireplace. In the seven bedrooms and four suites period and antique French provincial furnishings, exposed-beam ceilings and pine paneling provide an elegant ambiance. All have private baths, refrigerators and TVs. The highlight, though, is the wonderful deck off the main house with a spectacular vista of both Whiteside Mountain and Devil's Courthouse. Rates include breakfast. ~ Located off Route 64

West, Cashiers; 704-743-2737, 888-645-5786, fax 704-743-0208.
DELUXE TO ULTRA-DELUXE.

Two inns across the street from each other, both sharing the
same owners, preside over central downtown Highlands. **Highlands Inn** has seen town comings and goings since 1880, though
ongoing restorations have given the place a light and airy feel.
Plank floors, woven Persian rugs and comfortably worn sofas enhance the lobby. Three floors of rooms are decorated in country-
manor style, with antique furnishings and wallpaper stenciling by
noted local artist Donna Feltman. A gazebo room in the courtyard
is surrounded by apple trees. Just across the street, **The Old
Edwards Inn** is a prim, red-brick building with a lobby of leaded
glass and forest-green carpets. There are 19 rooms, some with canopy beds and balconies overlooking town, and some formally
adorned with antique dressers and embroidered sofas. Feltman's
fanciful stenciling is also prominent here. Both inns are closed from
November through April. ~ Main Street, Highlands; phone/fax
704-526-5036. MODERATE.

Near the quieter west end of town, the corporate-style **Highlands Suite Hotel** is for those who prefer newer accommodations
with less historical character. Rooms are spacious and modern,
with amenities such as mini-refrigerators and microwaves and gas
fireplaces. ~ 200 Main Street, Highlands; 704-526-4502, 800-221-
5078, fax 704-526-4840. MODERATE TO ULTRA-DELUXE.

DINING

Olive Oil's is really a nothing of a place, just ten tables crammed
inside and six on the front porch. But it is jammed with locals every
night who come for crispy hot disks of pizza, huge mountains of
spaghetti, and deep, bubbling casseroles of pasta. Closed Sunday.
~ Route 64, Cashiers; 704-743-9080. BUDGET TO MODERATE.

At the wildly popular **Market Basket**, you eat inside a gourmet
grocery in a smoke-free dining room with a cheery sunflower-and-

---

✔ CHECK THESE OUT—UNIQUE DINING

- *Budget:* Drink in moody views at Chimney Rock Park's **snack bar** while
  you're sipping a fruit spritzer and enjoying a tasty lunch. *page 62*
- *Moderate:* Dine inside a gourmet grocery on fresh, healthful—and
  exceedingly tasty—fare at the highly popular **Market Basket**. *page 81*
- *Deluxe:* Relish regional flights of fancy at **Expressions**, an elegant bistro
  where every dish is an elaborate, heady affair. *page 69*
- *Ultra-deluxe:* Reserve a table near the big stone hearth at **Pine Crest
  Inn** and await rich, hearty portions of beef, poultry and fish. *page 70*

Budget: under $9   Moderate: $9–$16   Deluxe: $16–$24   Ultra-deluxe: over $24

vegetable motif. The menu, printed on a paper bag, is loaded with fresh veggies (each meal comes with eight to ten) such as steamed silver queen corn and carrots cooked in apple juice. You may also find baked garlic with feta cheese spread and sun-dried tomatoes; portobello mushrooms with poblano peppers in a garlic cream sauce; and a variety of fish, seafood, chicken and meats. If you order the "Hot Rock" menu, you'll cook your own meat (if you're a vegetarian, substitute tofu) on a tabletop slab of North Carolina granite. Dinner comes with live music nightly. This spot is big fun. ~ Route 107 South, Cashiers; 704-743-2216. MODERATE.

The place for barbecue and bluegrass is **Carolina Smokehouse**, which pit cooks its chicken, ribs, pork and beef out back. The ambiance is predictably casual, with wood floors, chairs and tables, and license plates tacked to the wall. ~ Route 64, Cashiers; 704-743-3200. BUDGET TO MODERATE.

HIDDEN ► If you need a break from elaborate food, try a local soda fountain. In Highlands, **Brigitte's Soda Fountain** has an ample selection of breakfast and lunch items. Homemade soups, well-prepared sandwiches, meaty chili and extra thick malts and shakes are a few of the offerings. Closed Sunday. ~ On East Main Street, in the Blue Ridge Pharmacy Building; 704-526-9451. BUDGET.

HIDDEN ► **Highland's Back Room Deli** serves similar fare and is another good place for overhearing locals converse about golf and the stock market. Closed Sunday. ~ West Main Street, in the Highlands Pharmacy Building; 704-526-2048. BUDGET.

A venerable eatery in a beige-and-green cottage framed in tall trees and green lawn, **Wolfgang Green's** was built as a house in 1880 by town pioneer, mayor and postmaster Jay Smith. These days it's a restaurant specializing in German fare, from schnitzels and veal sweetbread to sauerbraten and *schweins haxn* (roast pork shank with Bavarian dumplings and red cabbage). Delicious pasta, fish dishes and steaks are also on the bill of fare, and sandwiches and salads are featured for lunch. Reservations are necessary for a table almost any time of day. ~ Off Main Street, Highlands; 704-526-3807. MODERATE.

HIDDEN ► **On the Veranda**, just west of Highlands, occupies a quiet spot along the Cullasaja River, barely two miles outside of Highlands. This is where premier seasonal and regional cuisine is served in a classy dining room with big windows on the woods. There are many desirable appetizers, salads and entrées—start with spicy fried calamari with an ancho-chile sauce, or apple with smoked salmon and baby arugula and cilantro-lime vinaigrette. Entrées might include sautéed lamb chops with sweet Georgia honey-roasted pecans, Thai coconut ginger shrimp, or grilled Carolina quail with wild-berry barbecue glaze. The wine bar has garnered the *Wine Spectator*'s "Award of Excellence" for the last ten years. Closed after New Year's until Easter. ~ Route 64; 704-526-2338. DELUXE.

Cashiers has a handful of shops, but Highlands has dozens. People shop here long and leisurely, easily dropping thousands (and I mean dollars) in a few hours. Browsing, of course, is nearly as much fun.

Get your smoked trout, caviar spreads and bottled gourmet sauces at **Highlands Wine & Cheese Co.** There's also a selection of fine, affordable wines. ~ Route 64, Highlands; 704-526-5210.

From June through November, **Scudder's Galleries** hosts *the* local event of the night in Highlands: an auction. Drop by during the day to peruse the offerings, everything from English and American antique furniture and art to centuries-old silver and crystal. ~ Main Street, Highlands; 704-526-4111.

The Dry Sink, open more than two decades, is stocked with every imaginable kitchen item, along with brass door knockers and Villeroy and Boch china. ~ Main Street, Highlands; 704-526-5226.

Serendipity is a showcase for handmade jewelry from around the world, including pieces crafted by Zuni, Hopi and Navajo. Pottery, sculpture and handmade dolls from international ports of call are also carried here. Like most stores in Highlands, the merchandise here is unusual, high quality and pricey. ~ Main Street, Highlands; 704-526-2564.

Two places in Cashiers have live music, but you'll have to brown bag your liquor and also order dinner.

The local favorite entertainer is guitarist and vocalist Cy Timmons, who has opened for such big names as Joan Rivers and Al Jarreau. These days he plays at **The Market Basket**. There's also bluegrass and piano music on some nights. ~ Route 107 South, Cashiers; 704-743-2216.

On weekends in the summertime, you can hear bluegrass on the front lawn of the **Carolina Smokehouse**. In spring and fall, it's a mix of acoustic and rhythm and blues. ~ Route 64, Cashiers; 704-743-3200.

For nightlife in Highlands, folks go to **Scudder's** (see "Shopping" above) for the nightly auction, sans alcohol. Or, they drive 12 miles south across the Georgia line to the **Sky Valley Resort**. ~ Off Route 106, in Georgia; 706-746-5302.

NANTAHALA NATIONAL FOREST More than half a million acres of western North Carolina, stretching north to the Great Smoky Mountains and west to the Tennessee line, Nantahala (pronounced Nan-ta-HALE-a) National Forest is a picture of drama: sheer cliffs of white granite with sharp gorges at their feet, waterfalls booming into boulder-studded rivers, slick rock outcroppings slithering with salamanders, and one area where low bogs and marshes rear up into lofty peaks and ridges. Plant and animal life is vast and varied. Among the types of trees you'll find within this national forest are Canadian and Carolina hemlock, dry pine and oak, dwarf northern red oak and beech. Among the animals are deer, bear, red-tailed and broad-winged hawks, grouse, turkey vultures, owls, wild boar and even ravens and peregrine falcons.

Near Cashiers and Highlands are several opportunities for hiking, fishing, swimming, waterfall and wildlife watching, and camping within the national forest. While no boats are allowed at **Cliffside Lake Recreation Area**, there is excellent fishing and swimming,

HIDDEN ►   in addition to a day-use-only picnic area. The 15,000-acre **Ellicott Rock Wilderness** provides miles upon miles of hiking trails. Facilities include picnic areas, restrooms and bathhouses; restaurants and groceries are nearby in Highlands and Cashiers. Swimming is excellent and fishing is good for trout and bass at Cliffside Lake Recreation Area. You'll also find good trout fishing in Whitewater River, Cullasaja River and Thompson River. ~ Route 64 serves as the access point to various forest facilities near Cashiers and Highlands, including Whiteside Mountain Area Vista Point, on Whiteside Mountain Road off Route 64, about six miles east of Highlands; and Cliffside Lake Recreation Area, off Route 64 about four and a half miles west of Highlands. To get to Ellicott Rock Wilderness, take Horse Cove Road southeast of Highlands and veer right at the fork, which is Bull Pen Road. You'll see the signs for Ellicott Rock; 704-526-3765.

▲ There are 22 sites at Van Hook Glade, off Route 64 four and half miles west of Highlands, that will accommodate tents or small pull-through and pop-up trailer; $6 per night. Various other primitive sites are also located in the area.

▼▼▼▼▼▼▼▼▼▼
Franklin Area

The drive on Route 64 from Highlands to Franklin is a zigzagging, hairpinning odyssey that skirts walls of sheer rock and presents vistas of heath-covered balds. The rock, and the intermittent waterfalls, belong to Cullasaja Gorge. If you feel a little queasy looking down and driving up and down, take a deep breath, turn up the bluegrass on the radio, and go for it!

SIGHTS   Eventually Route 64 irons out at **Franklin**, a small and simple town of five-and-dimes and beauty parlors, and seemingly hundreds of gem shops. Franklin came to gem fame back in the late 1800s when a farmer discovered a large ruby on his land in the Cowee Valley, a lovely pastoral area about five miles north of Franklin. State geologists were sent to investigate, and when they confirmed there were indeed rubies and sapphires in these hills, Tiffany & Co. came to town. The New York gem giant bought hundreds of Cowee Valley acres and dug deep mines, but after four years never struck it big, unable to find the source of the gems. They did find some pigeon-blood rubies, rarest of all rubies, known only to exist in one other place in the world, the Mogock Valley of Burma.

Commercial mining lasted only about 30 years in the Cowee Valley, but rock hounds, ever hopeful of finding "the big one," have been coming to Franklin ever since. Of course, a big find is rare these days, though travelers can find small attractive stones and gem flakes. Besides rubies and sapphires, you may come across garnet, kyanite, rhodolite, moonstone and rutile, other fairly common gemstones and minerals. Even without exciting discoveries, most people (especially kids) find it fun sifting through the gravelly mud for several hours at a time.

Basically, two kinds of mines are found here. "Native" mines are located on actual mines and give you soil only from that mine. "Enriched" or "salted" mines are rarely situated in actual mines; they're just roadside operations that say they are mines but bring in soil from other parts of North Carolina or the United States. You have a much better chance of finding something, *anything*, at the enriched mines (here's where to take the kids). However, you've a better chance of finding something more valuable and exciting at a native mine. Most mines are closed during winter.

More gem tips are available from the friendly rockophiles who run the **Franklin Gem and Mineral Museum**—stop here before you start mining. A funky, musty, glittery place inside a mid-1800s jailhouse, the museum has two floors of "theme" rooms: a North Carolina Room with garnets, sapphires, turquoise and rubies (you can't miss the 2¼-pound ruby) found around Franklin; a Fluorescent Room that showcases gems under a black light; and an Indian Room with arrowheads, peace pipes, spearpoints and obsidian. Here you can get a free guide to local gem mines and shops, most located a few miles north in the Cowee Valley. The museum staff can point out the "native" and "enriched" mines to you. Closed Sunday and Monday. ~ 2 West Main Street, Franklin; 704-369-7831.

Mine maps are also available from the **Franklin Chamber of Commerce**, which has information on area attractions. Closed on Saturday November through March; closed on Sunday year-round. ~ 425 Porter Street, Franklin; 704-524-3161, 800-336-7829.

◆◆

ROCK HOUND HINTS

Here's how to look for gems: Pick a mine, pay about five bucks (two bucks for kids) for several buckets of soil and rock, take your station at a long wooden trough lined with people and flowing with water, pour your soil and rock into the water, and sift through it. You're looking for small gem and mineral pieces, which look nothing like they do at the jewelry store, but rather are dull and crusty. The folks at the mine can provide tips on what to look for.

If you go mining and think you've found something, you can take it to **Cowee Valley Lapidary**, an independent company that will analyze, appraise and set your gem, if you desire. ~ Ruby Mine Road, east of Route 28, in the Cowee Valley; 704-524-2321.

HIDDEN ▶

Out in the rolling green Cowee Valley, one of the best gem finds is not at a mine but at **Perry's Water Gardens**. This private water-lily farm and mail-order business welcomes visitors to its ponds riotously decorated with empress lotuses, froebelises, white rushes, water lettuces, Venezuela poppies and hundreds more blooms and water plants. Check out the Hindu lotus, a colossal lily whose big pink blossom resembles a showerhead. Try to come between mid-July and mid-August, when most all the lilies are blooming. Spring is the second-best time to come, and fall is the third. Don't bother coming in the winter. ~ 1831 Leatherman Gap Road, north of Ruby Mine Road; 704-524-3264.

HIDDEN ▶

One hour west of Franklin is one of the most mysterious and compelling sights in the area: **Wayah Bald** (pronounced Why-ya-bald), a 5335-foot-high rock summit that in spring blazes with azalea, dogwood and other brilliant blooms. The Cherokee supposedly named it Wayah, meaning wolf, for the wolves that patrolled the mountaintop. ~ Route 64 west to Route 1310, then head north.

LODGING

Good lodging is limited around Franklin. The most popular way to stay here is to camp at one of the many places around the Cowee Valley. You can get a list of campgrounds from the Franklin Chamber of Commerce. ~ 180 Porter Street, Franklin; 704-524-3161.

Otherwise, in town there's **Summit Inn**, homey and rustic and scattered with multifarious antiques. As the name suggests, the 1898 house of yellow poplar wood resides on a hill and enjoys views of the surrounding mountains. Thirteen bedrooms, most with shared baths, are rather dark and peculiarly decorated with second-hand furnishings. But with low prices including a full breakfast, and a popular restaurant serving some of the best food around, it's certainly not a bad choice. ~ 210 East Rogers Street, Franklin; 704-524-2006, 800-524-3133. BUDGET.

Another Franklin bed and breakfast, **The Franklin Terrace**, is similarly rustic and cluttered with old furnishings. However, the nine rooms in this big white Carolina plantation house on a hill contain a few extras: TV, private baths and air conditioning (needed only in August and sometimes September).The low room rates include a continental breakfast. Closed from mid-November through April. ~ 159 Harrison Avenue, Franklin; 704-524-7907, 800-633-2431. BUDGET.

DINING

Other than fast food, there's not a whole lot in the way of Franklin dining. One exception is **Summit Inn**—the place for casual mountain dining. Dinner is prix fixe and full-course and there are always three entrées to choose from; they may include sautéed chicken breast with artichokes and mushrooms, trout parmesan, or German country-style ribs. Open Friday and Saturday only. ~ 210 East Rogers Street, Franklin; 704-524-2006. MODERATE.

If you're in the mood for barbecue, **Hickory Ranch** has the works. Beef and pork sandwiches and platters, barbecue chicken and spareribs are among the fixins at this casual downtown eatery. ~ 126 Palmer Street, Franklin; 704-369-9909. Closed Monday. BUDGET.

Gem shops, one after another, with their tedious, tacky facades, call to you from the highways. Most are reputable, though some have been known to falsify their merchandise. A list of gem shops is available from the **Franklin Chamber of Commerce**. ~ 425 Porter Street, Franklin; 704-524-3161.

SHOPPING

Forget it. Folks here retire to the front porch after dinner for "night-life." Bring along a few good books—or at least a companion.

NIGHTLIFE

NANTAHALA NATIONAL FOREST The westernmost—and remote—portion of this 527,000-acre forest runs from Franklin to the Tennessee and Georgia state lines. Most recreation areas and sights are west of Franklin, an hour or even three by car. But the drives are incredibly scenic and the forest deep and mysterious.

BEACHES & PARKS

Joyce Kilmer Memorial Forest Far west in Nantahala, just before the Tennessee line, lies one of the few remaining stands of virgin southern Appalachian forest. Within Nantahala National Forest is Joyce Kilmer Memorial Forest, named for the poet and World War I soldier killed in battle. Here lives big old hardwoods and Canadian hemlock, wild boar and bear, deer and salamanders. Kilmer's most famous poem was "Trees." ~ From the town of Robbinsville, head west on Route 143, then turn right onto Route 1127 until you see signs for the forest; 704-479-6431.

◄ *HIDDEN*

▲ There are tent sites nearby. Rattler Ford accepts reservations and has hot-water showers (no hookups); $15 per night. Horse Cove is first-come, first-serve (no hookups); $5 per night.

JACKRABBIT MOUNTAIN RECREATIONAL AREA The 7000-acre Jackrabbit Mountain Recreation Area, offers good swimming at its beach and a picnic area. Boating is available on Lake Chatuge in Clay County, where you might also fish for bass. Trout live in surrounding mountain streams. Closed in the winter. ~ Off Route 175 about seven miles east of the town of Hayesville; 704-837-5152.

◄ *HIDDEN*

▲ There are 103 tent and RV sites; $8 per night.

STANDING INDIAN RECREATIONAL AREA Standing Indian Recreation Area offers a picnic area and several hiking trails. Anglers try to hook some trout in Nantahala River

◄ *HIDDEN*

and Kimsey Creek, which is shallow enough for swimming. Facilities include restrooms and bathhouses at various access sites. There are a limited number of restaurants and groceries in nearby towns. Closed in the winter. ~ Take Route 64 west of Franklin for 12 miles, then go east on Old Route two miles, then south on Forest Road 67 for two miles. ~ 704-524-6441.

▲ There are 84 tent and RV sites, as well as hot-water showers, plus various primitive group sites throughout the forest; $10 per night.

▼▼▼▼▼▼▼▼▼▼▼▼▼▼
Outdoor Adventures

FISHING

Make no doubt about it—this here's trout country. More than 1500 miles of streams are swimming with trout in the Southern Mountains, where despite the abundance of hatcheries, most trout aren't farm-raised. The best time to try for a trout is March through May; the second-best time is September and October. Summer isn't bad, it's just hotter, so the fish only bite in early morning and early evening.

You can flyfish for trout, or use a rod 'n' reel baited with anything from corn kernels and crickets to nightcrawlers. You can also pond fish at one of the private trout farms in the Southern Mountains, which you should know are often way out in the country, sometimes down a series of dirt roads, so call ahead for directions. (Call ahead anyway to make sure the fish are biting.) If you fish at a private pond, you don't need a fishing license but will simply pay a per-fish fee. If you fish anywhere else, pick up a license at a local bait-and-tackle store. Other than trout, you'll find catfish, bass and bream in the Southern Mountain streams and lakes.

Most lodges will arrange a fishing trip. If you'd rather make plans on your own, these outfits sell bait and tackle and licenses, and can provide guides. **Brookings** will take you to the Nantahala National Forest to fish for small- and largemouth bass, bream, trout and walleye pike. ~ Route 64 East, Cashiers; 704-743-3768. **Main Stream Outfitters** fishes for trout in western North Carolina and North Georgia. ~ 26 East Wright Square, Highlands; 704-526-5649. **The Fish Hawk of Highlands** goes out on the Nantahala, Tuckasegee, Cullasaja and Chattooga rivers. ~ Highlands; 704-526-9256. **Blue Ridge Angler** sells fish and tackle. ~ 605 Highlands Road, Franklin; 704-369-2989. In the town of Glenville, **Glenville Country Store** has bait and tackle. ~ Route 107; 704-743-5422.

Private trout-fishing farms and ponds include **Morgan Mill Trout**. ~ Route 64 West, Brevard; 704-884-6823. In Cashiers, you can try **Lonesome Too**. ~ Route 107 North, Cashiers; 704-743-2227. In the Highlands, there's **Lisa's Trout Pond**. ~ Route 28 East, Highlands; 704-526-2333.

GOLF

The Southern Mountains are a golfer's haven, with lavishly landscaped courses and mountain views reminiscent of Scotland.

In the Hendersonville area, there's **Crooked Creek Golf Club**. ~ Kanuga Road, Hendersonville; 704-692-2011. In Fletcher, try the **French Broad Golf Center**. ~ 5 French Broad Avenue, Fletcher; 704-687-8545. Tee off at **Orchard Trace Golf Club**'s par-3, 18-hole course. ~ 942 Sugarloaf Road, Hendersonville; 704-685-1006. **Cummings Cove Golf & Country Club** is also open to the public. ~ 3000 Cummings Road, Hendersonville; 704-891-9412. There are three 9-hole courses designed by Edmund B. Ault at **Etowah Valley Country Club**. ~ Route 64 West, Etowah; 704-891-7022. In Flat Rock, there's **Lost Diamond Valley Country Club**, with a 9-hole, par-32 course. ~ 111 Highland Lake Road; 704-692-0143.

In the Brevard area, try **Sherwood Forest**. ~ Route 276, Brevard; 704-884-7825. The **Holly Forest Course** at Fairfield Sapphire Valley Resort has a waterfall hole. ~ Route 64, Sapphire; 704-743-3441. The par-71, George C. Cobb–designed course at **High Hampton Inn and Country Club** has bent-grass greens and the public is welcome in the afternoon when there's room. ~ Route 107, 2411, ext. 114. In Franklin, play at **Mill Creek Country Club**. ~ 98 Mill Creek Road, off Route 64 West; 704-524-6458. **Parker Meadows Golf Course** has a 9-hole course with seven par-3s and two par-4s. ~ Maxwell Home Road; 704-369-8008. Also try **Holly Springs Golf Course**. ~ 115 Holly Springs Golf Village; 704-369-8711.

TENNIS

Grab a racquet and head for the courts at **Silvermont**. ~ East Main Street, Brevard; 704-884-3166. Also try **Brevard Racquet Club**. ~ Country Club Road, Brevard; 704-883-3005. **Fairfield Sapphire Valley Resort** is a private club with 16 courts (fee). ~ Route 64, Sapphire; 704-743-3441. Work on your serve at **Cashiers Community Center**. ~ Route 64, Cashiers. **Highlands Recreation Park** has three courts available. ~ Cashiers Road, Highlands; 704-526-3556. There are also courts at **Franklin Parks and Recreation**. ~ Route 441 South, Franklin.

RIDING STABLES

Hundreds of trails within Pisgah National Forest and Nantahala National Forest are open to equestrians. You can rent horses and guides from **Pisgah Forest Stables**. ~ Route 276 North, Pisgah Forest; 704-883-8258. Also try **Earthshine Mountain Lodge**. ~ Golden Road, Lake Toxaway; 704-862-4207.

BIKING

Southern Mountains cycling is for those who want a workout—the terrain here is anything but flat. Many roads, however, are gently sloped and marvelously remote, offering silent pedaling through deep woods. For excellent bike trail maps, contact the North Carolina Department of Transportation's Bicycle Program. ~ P.O. Box 25201, Raleigh, NC 27611; 919-733-2804.

The first 15 miles of **Connemara Trail** offer a stomach-tingling plunge down Blue Ridge Mountains—a drop of more than 2400 feet. There are moderate hills and a few steep uphills on the 46-mile run, the first segment of the Southern Highlands Trail. Connemara commences at Wagon Road Gap on the Blue Ridge Parkway, then heads south to Route 276 east, picking up Route 176 in Brevard and winding eastward through Little River, Flat Rock, Saluda and Tryon.

Highlands Spur links the towns of Highlands and Franklin, taking scenic, little-traveled back roads for 19 miles. Start in Highlands on Route 28 west, then head north on Route 1546 to Route l545, jogging over to Route 1538, which eventually hooks up with Route 64. Here you will want to get on Route 1678, then Route 1672, and then Route 1564, following it into Franklin.

North of Franklin, the eight-mile **Cowee Valley Loop** takes you on a fairly leisurely easy tour of the area's gem mines, with pastoral views along the way. From Route 28 near West's Mill, pick up Route 1340 to Route 1341, then 1343 and 1345, winding your way back to Route 28.

It you'd care to pedal with a group, the **Highland Hiker** offers half- and full-day outings that leave from Cashiers. ~ Intersection of Routes 107 and 64, Cashiers; 704-743-1732.

Bike Rentals   Bring your bike to the Southern Mountains—bike rentals are tough to find. **Bike Ways** in Hendersonville does have a few mountain bikes for rent. Closed Sunday. ~ 607 Greenville Avenue, Hendersonville; 704-692-0613.

HIKING   All distances listed for hiking trails are one way unless otherwise noted.

From leisurely walks by waterfalls to demanding day-long treks into and out of gorges, the Southern Mountains are a hiker's paradise. Many trails are part of the Appalachian Trail stretching from Maine to Georgia. Trail maps and information are available from local chambers of commerce. **Pisgah National Forest** also has some trail information. ~ 704-877-3265. If you visit **Nantahala National Forest**, trail maps are available. ~ 704-526-3765, 704-524-6441. You can purchase trail guides and books on hiking from The **Highland Hiker**. ~ 100 East Main Street, Highlands; 704-526-5298.

CHIMNEY ROCK AREA   On the eastern end of the Southern Mountains, **Chimney Rock Park** offers three popular trails, ranging from the fairly easy **Forest Stroll** (.75 mile) to the bottom of Hickory Nut Falls to the steeper **Cliff Trail** (.75 mile) continuing onto the **Skyline Trail** (.75 mile). The latter two hikes take you on a geologic journey along ledges of gneiss rock, into a granite formation called Opera Box, and atop the fabulous Hickory Nut Falls. You'll see twisted-hair spikemoss, prickly pines, false indigo, witch hazel, false goat's beard, hairy alumroot, mountain magnolia, and many other plants, shrubs and wildflowers. Get a trail guide at the park's visitors center. ~ 607 Greenville Avenue; 704-692-0613.

HENDERSONVILLE AND FLAT ROCK AREA   In Hendersonville on Fourth Avenue East, the **Jackson Park Nature Trail** (1.5 miles) is a good way to exercise and learn about local plants and animals. The marked trail notes everything from Carolina chickadee birds and roundleaf yellow violet flowers to blackberries and wild roses.

If you take the **Talking Tree Trail** (.45 mile) at Holmes Educational State Forest, you can hear each tree "tell" you all about itself. Each one is actually outfitted with a recorder; push a button on the tree and the recording starts playing. The forest also has a more challenging hike along the **Cliffside Demonstration Trail** (3 miles). It makes a loop through hardwoods and white pine, and on the way skirts a pond and delivers you to a scenic viewpoint. The wheelchair-accessible **Soil and Water Trail** (.3 mile) takes you on a 200-foot-long boardwalk through a wetland studded with trillium and other forest flowers. To get to the forest from downtown Hendersonville, take Kanuga Road (which eventually becomes Crab Creek Road) southwest for nine miles.

◄ HIDDEN

◄ HIDDEN

BREVARD AREA   Numerous moderate to difficult trails start just north of Brevard at Pisgah National Forest's Davidson River Campground. **Farlow Gap Trail** (5.2 miles), a moderately tough hike, follows the river, studded with rocks you can slide on, and passes a former fish hatchery. The strenuous **Looking Glass Rock Trail** (6.2 miles round-trip) rewards with spectacular mountain forest views, seen from a granite dome. Much of the terrain is rocky and steep, and the trail narrows along some stomach-loosening corners. **Butter Gap Trail** (2.7 miles) runs along an old railroad grade and affords views of a waterfall and the headwaters of a creek. The hike is moderately difficult. ~ Route 276, north of Route 64.

CASHIERS AND HIGHLANDS AREA   Much of the **Whitewater Falls Trail** (2 miles round-trip) is paved, making it ideal for wheelchair travelers. The trail, which begins off Route 107, 13 miles south of Cashiers, wends past wading pools and picnic areas and culminates at the spectacular falls.

✔ **CHECK THESE OUT—UNIQUE OUTDOOR ADVENTURES**

- Wrangle for trout—use a fly or rod to reel'em in; more than 1500 miles of Southern Mountains streams await. *page 88*
- Grab a golf club and pretend you're in Scotland; the deep-green mountains and courses here are reminiscent of the Scots Highlands. *page 88*
- Let a horse bear you through the dim, moist glade of Pisgah and Nantahala national forests. *page 89*
- Take a 2400-foot plunge down beautiful Blue Ridge Mountains— by bicycle—along the Connemara Trail. *page 89*

If you only hike once in the Southern Mountains, make it **White-side Mountain** (2 miles), a switchback trail that climbs through dense forests of hemlock and dwarf northern red oak, with look-out points on the way up and possibilities for seeing broad-winged hawks, ravens and even a peregrine falcon. The climax—walls of sheer rock and mind-clearing views across the Chattooga River and endless summits. The trailhead is on Whiteside Mountain Road off Route 64 between Cashiers and Highlands.

HIDDEN ▶

One of the more challenging day hikes, **Yellow Mountain Trail** (4.8 miles) takes you up and down three peaks, including the 5127-foot Yellow Mountain, the area's highest. An old wood-and-stone fire tower presides over the summit, a popular place to camp (no facilities). To get to the trailhead from Highlands, take Route 64 three miles east to Buck Creek Road (Shortoff Baptist Church is on the corner). Turn left and go 2.3 miles on Buck Creek Road, until you see a parking area on the left and trailhead on the right.

HIDDEN ▶

Even more hidden, and offering a slice of the past, **Hurrah Ridge** (.6 mile) is on part of the historical trail used by Blue Valley ranchers to drive their cattle to "The Flats" pastures of Scaly Mountain. The trail is short but steep and the terrain is rugged, following the rocky shoulder of Hurrah Ridge. To get there from Highlands, take Route 28 south 6 miles to Clear Creek Missionary Baptist Church. Turn right at the church and go six miles until the road ends at a broken culvert in the West Fork of Overflow Creek. Cross the creek and begin looking for the trailhead on the right.

The **Chinquapin Mountain Trail** (1.6 miles) climbs to the 4160-foot summit, affording vistas across the Blue Valley along the way. The marked trailhead is located off Route 106, two miles southwest of Highlands.

FRANKLIN AREA The first half of the moderate to strenuous **Franklin to Beechertown Trail** (35.7 miles) is a National Recreation Trail. The trail lies along the 81-mile **Bartram Trail** within the Nantahala National Forest and is a wonderful walk in the woods, with vistas of cascading streams and strolls through cool, deep hardwood forest and fields of wildflowers. Directions to the trailhead are available from the national forest's Wayah District Office, on Route 1153 off Route 64 just west of Franklin. The trail begins past the office.

Much shorter and easier, the **Joyce Kilmer Memorial Trail** (1.2 miles) takes you close to the flora that Kilmer loved and wrote about. A spectacular grove of yellow poplar is here, and there are also many trillium, hemlock and crested dwarf iris. Wooden benches for resting and a footbridge for crossing a creek make this a most enjoyable hike. The trailhead starts in the parking lot of the Joyce Kilmer Memorial Forest (within Nantahala National Forest) off Route 416 west of Route 129.

The major artery of the Southern Mountains is **Route 64**, which runs east–west through the main towns. Routes 64 and **85** link the Southern Mountains with eastern North Carolina. From South Carolina, **Route 26** runs north and joins Route 64 near Hendersonville. From Tennessee on the west, **Route 64-74A** connects with Route 64 near Murphy. From Georgia to the southwest, **Route 441** travels north to Franklin.

Transportation

CAR

Asheville Regional Airport, about 12 miles north of downtown Hendersonville, is the closest commercial airport to the Southern Mountains. It is served by Atlantic Southeast, ComAir, Delta Airlines, USAir and USAir Express.

For shuttle and limousine service from the airport to various locations in the Southern Mountains, call **John Fox**. ~ 704-697-7717. Or try **Carolina Taxi**. ~ 704-693-3221.

AIR

Greyhound Lines Inc. provides bus service to Hendersonville from major points across the nation. ~ 350 East 7th Avenue, Hendersonville; 704-693-1201, 800-231-2222.

BUS

Amtrak will take you as far as Greenville, South Carolina, or Spartanburg, South Carolina, about 48 miles from Hendersonville, North Carolina. ~ 800-872-7245.

TRAIN

At the Asheville airport, there's **Avis Rent A Car** (800-331-1212), **Budget Rent A Car** (800-527-0700), **Enterprise Rent A Car** (800-325-8007) and **Hertz Rent A Car** (800-654-3131). **National Interrent** (800-327-9633) is also in Asheville though not at the airport. **U-Save Auto Rental** (704-684-8037) has an office at the airport and in Hendersonville.

CAR RENTALS

Carolina Taxi (Hendersonville; 704-693-3221), **City Taxi** (Franklin; 704-369-5042) and **Cunningham's Taxi** (Franklin; 704-524-2622) service their respective towns.

TAXIS

FOUR

The Great Smoky Mountains

The Great Smoky Mountains aren't smoky. They're damp and cool and unbelievably green. The white mantle that prompts their name is made up of fog and clouds, those swirling, shifting ghosts of high places, forever cloaking the peaks but rarely reaching down into the valleys. The ankles of the Smokies are, in fact, crisp, clear and colorful. Flowers bloom low on the mountains as late as December, when the summits are blanketed by snow.

It rains more in the Smokies than anywhere else in the southeastern United States; nearly 90 inches of rain fall in the highest forests every year. Perpetual moisture breeds life—rich, complex, inordinate plant and animal life. The virgin cove forests of the Smokies are primeval, grounded in rich soil and thronged with more variety and size of trees than any other forest in the Northern Hemisphere. Spruce fir forests rarely found south of Maine are here, too, and countless ferns and shrubs, grasses and wildflowers. Their names—witch hobble, scarlet painted cup, jack-in-the-pulpit—sound exotic to the ear.

Yet the Smokies aren't really exotic. They are soothing and sumptuous, full of warmth and mood and heights that don't soar but rise gently to five and six thousand feet. Wandering through their darkened depths feels like a mental massage, for everywhere there is subtlety: the faint trickling of streams and rain, the smooth roundness of creek stones and mountaintops, the simplicity of log cabins. White-tail deer, red squirrels, and black bear fill the forests, and trout crowd the streams. Only cars interrupt the quietude, but then that *is* the main way to see the Smokies.

More than nine million people see Great Smoky Mountains National Park every year, making it the nation's most visited national park (only half that many visit the Grand Canyon). The park's 520,000 acres are shared almost equally by North Carolina and Tennessee, though the scenery does not recognize state boundaries. The Smokies experience, unlike the Grand Canyon, does not involve seeing just one single wonder but reveling in many. Extraordinary views await visitors at every turn, and in between are old homesteads to be explored, streams to be fished, awesome summits to be scaled, trails to be taken. Visitors centers are museums focusing on mountain life, with lots of fascinating cultural and historical details on the Smokies' earliest residents, the Cherokees, who settled in the foothills some 900 years ago.

Despite all the tepees now used to promote Cherokee attractions, these early Americans were not nomadic but actually lived in homes of wood and clay. The men hunted bear, buffalo, wild turkey and other game, and fished the creeks for trout. The women grew squash, corn and beans, and gathered wild mushrooms, berries and nuts. They wrapped themselves in deerskin in summer, and buffalo and bear skins in winter. The Cherokee had seven clans and a national government, and women could vote and fight.

The Cherokee must have found it odd, then, that the Europeans considered them savage. White men began stealing Cherokee land in the 1790s and never stopped. The Smokies instantly changed—for while the Cherokee were content to live in the forest, the Europeans insisted on cutting down trees to make way for pastures, farmland and more settlers.

An acute logging push came in the early 1900s, when nearly 85 percent of current park land was owned by timber companies. Loggers, nicknamed "woodhicks" and looking precisely the part, traveled in packs and left destruction in their wake. The loggers earned a dollar for a 12-hour workday and were fed by cooks they referred to as "gut robbers." The cooks hunted during the day, though by this time elk, bison and beaver had disappeared, and deer, bear and turkey were getting more and more difficult to find.

When Congress founded Great Smoky Mountains National Park in 1926, 60 percent of the forests were gone. Patches of virgin forest remained and can be found today primarily in North Carolina.

In the past seven decades some bare lands in the Great Smoky Mountains have been renewed, though it will take a hundred years, maybe more, for some varieties of trees to return. The elk and bison will never return.

As for the Cherokee, they were nearly wiped out by smallpox and their vast lands reduced to a 56,573-acre reservation called Qualla Boundary. Today, the reservation juts into the national park like a puzzle piece and forms the park's North Carolina gateway. About 5000 Cherokees live within the boundary, some in secluded forest coves but many in the touristy town of Cherokee, which has a good museum, outdoor drama and re-created village that offer visitors an explanation of the old and new American Indian cultures.

Southwest of Cherokee, Bryson City is situated near the headwaters of the Nantahala River and hence the headquarters for whitewater rafting. In the opposite direction through the Soco Gap, the town of Maggie Valley is nearly as contrived as Cherokee, but in an old-fashioned way. Maggie's biggest attraction, Ghost Town in the Sky, is a Wild West–style theme park that hasn't changed much over the decades. Waynesville, southeast of Maggie Valley, is a genuine place with a handsome little downtown and an Old South flavor.

Except for this handful of small hamlets, and the emergence of soft mountains hovering in haze, there is nothing to suggest you are approaching the country's most popular national park.

▼▼▼▼▼▼▼▼▼▼▼▼▼▼▼▼▼

Great Smoky Mountains National Park

Plenty of roads, including paved, gravel and bumpy dirt roads, penetrate Great Smoky Mountains National Park. But only one, the paved, two-lane Newfound Gap Road, actually crosses the mountains. It's the most traveled route, cutting right through the middle of the national park, and connecting the Oconaluftee Visitor Center in North Carolina with the Sugarlands Visitor Center in Tennessee. The distance is 32 miles, but pretend it's at least 60, for the road dips and dives, backtracks and gets sidetracked along the way.

SIGHTS

Commercial vehicles are banned from **Newfound Gap Road**, but RVs and buses aren't, so traffic frequently crawls along. Which is just fine, since the point is not to stay on the road but to get off it. Dozens of overlooks, side roads and stopovers provide access to park sights—and the only way to hidden spots. Many of these stops are numbered on little wooden signposts. As you travel toward Tennessee, the numbers get lower.

Maps and information are available at the **Oconaluftee Visitors Center** near Cherokee, at the park's main North Carolina entrance. The stone building, a former town courtroom, blends nicely into the woods and offers superb displays on early mountaineer life as well as an excellent bookstore. Dozens of pamphlets, on subjects ranging from park wildflowers and wildlife to mountain people and waterfalls, are available free or sold for a minimal fee. Especially helpful are the brochures called *Auto Touring* and *Walks and Hikes*. ~ Newfound Gap Road, Signpost 21.

None of the visitors centers have phone numbers, but there is a **main park number**: 423-436-1200. Unfortunately, it's one of those touch-tone, choose-the-right-category numbers that tries desperately to keep you from talking with a live person. Plan to be on hold awhile, especially during peak seasons.

From the Oconaluftee center, a trail wide enough for wheelchair visitors wends alongside a racing river down to the **Mountain Farm Museum**. You can peek inside a number of primitive wood buildings, including an old springhouse, outhouse, blacksmith shop, meat house, sorghum mill, apple house and bee gum stand. You can look through the door of the main house and see an old sewing machine and piano, and a loom and spinning wheel. The idea is that you'll understand how rough (and uncomplicated) life was here 200 years ago. In the summer, the garden is planted with lettuce, corn and tomatoes, and surrounding fields smell of sorghum or fresh-cut hay. Always there is the rush of the river, just out of sight.

By now you may be wondering when and if you'll have to stop and pay admission to Great Smoky Mountains National Park. You

Great Smoky Mountains

won't. And you can visit almost anytime. The park is open all day and night every day of the year, except when snow shuts down the roads. Newfound Gap Road rarely closes (some folks use it to commute to work, lucky souls) but many of the side roads are blocked in winter.

The main roads are also sometimes blocked—by too much traffic—on summer weekends and during spring blooming and fall foliage seasons. Everything's more crowded—trails, picnic areas, fishing spots. Campgrounds are booked months in advance. If you don't care to share your scenic overlook with a mob, plan to visit any time *other* than these high seasons. May and September are usually wonderful months, both weatherwise and crowdwise.

After the Oconaluftee Visitors Center, the next stop north along Newfound Gap Road is **Mingus Mill**. From the parking area it's a cool walk through yellow poplar forest streaked with sunlight to the vintage 1876 cast-iron turbine mill. (The trail, unfortunately, is not paved and so there is no access for wheelchairs.) For 50 years the mill turned corn into meal and wheat into flour for the nearby hamlet of Mingus Creek. The grinding was actually done by great stones carved from the mountains and smoothed and scored by stonecutters' tools—hence the name "stoneground" meal. The mill is cranked up occasionally from April through October, but the cornmeal is stoneground at a commercial mill in Tennessee. ~ At Signpost 20.

Heading toward Tennessee, the Newfound Gap Road tunnels through enormous forest, with trees towering over five stories high and sunlight flashing from above. In summer there seems to be a thousand shades of green and a thousand angles and silhouettes passing from low to high, set against the ink-blue sky. On a more human level, a **Quiet Walkway** curls through shoulder-high wildflowers filled with the songs of crickets. Take a seat on the smooth

✦✦✦

✔ CHECK THESE OUT—UNIQUE SIGHTS

- Feel your ears pop—and the roadsides drop—as you drive seven curvy, fogbound miles toward **Clingmans Dome**. *page 99*
- Watch Cherokee artisans at work in a fragrant, deeply shaded forest community called **Oconaluftee Indian Village**. *page 105*
- Hop aboard a **Great Smoky Mountains Railway** locomotive for a smooth ride through cascading green mountains and deep river gorges. *page 105*
- Seek out **Hemphill Road** for a soothing backroad drive past whitewashed fence and tiny churches, bright-red barns and grazing cattle. *page 112*

boulder and watch the bees suck nectar from purple flowers and the orange and black butterflies duck in and out of clearings. Amid the intense aroma of fraser fir, you can look at spiderwebs so elaborate they seem to have no end, and caterpillars packaged neatly in their cocoons. ~ At the Collins Creek Picnic Area, Signpost 18.

Such subtleties are what the Smokies are all about. Along Newfound Gap Road, myriad paths invite discovery of nature—and self-discovery. Quiet walkways abound, their signs beckoning with trails that have "no particular destination, so walk as far as you like and then return."

Occasionally, the silence is interrupted by angry screams and the violent rustling of leaves. Don't worry; it's just the tiny red squirrel, the "mountain boomer," foraging for food. Much less noisy but a whole lot bigger, the black bear occasionally shows up along trails and roadsides, usually searching for food to maintain its 200- to 400-pound bulk. Don't give him any. Bears who get food become friendlier and are easy prey for poachers. How else to act? "Theories abound about how to act if you should confront a bear," says the *Great Smoky Mountains National Park Handbook*. "All such theories assume . . . that bear behavior is predictable. It is not." *Note*: Most park rangers recommend just quietly going about your business.

You don't have to leave Newfound Gap Road to see the Oconaluftee River, which presents itself again and again, sometimes as a fizzing stream and at other times as a dead-calm mirror of water. You can park at the **Oconaluftee River** stop and walk by water as clear as air and inlaid with silken smooth rocks. The river is nicknamed "The Lufty," though its real name is *Ekwanulti*, or "place-by-the-river" in Cherokee, a word white settlers butchered into Oconaluftee. ~ Signpost 17.

The displays at the **Logging Exhibit** are comical. A caption for a black-and-white photo of early loggers reads: "Definitely not soup-eating people." These bulky, craggy, rheumy-eyed henchmen for the lumber companies hacked and drank their way through the Smokies, and had a life expectancy of about 40 years. Between 1900 and 1920, they wiped out over three-quarters of the Smokies. Had the decimation not been so sudden and so deft, perhaps there would be no national park. ~ Signpost 16.

Admittedly, it is difficult to imagine the Smokies almost gone, considering their splendor today. As you drive northward, valleys are rippled and so soft looking you want to reach out to feel their greenness. Some overlooks are tightly plaited with sharp summits, others are smooth and rambling and awash in purple haze. The highest point in the park, spectacular 6643-foot **Clingmans Dome**, is up a seven-mile road that snakes across rocky precipices, which is followed by a steep half-mile hike up the mountain. The turnoff for the road comes just before the Tennessee line (you'll recognize it as the place where everyone else is turning), though it is closed in winter.

The drive to the dome is eerie. Fog and frigid air roll down the mountainsides and wash over your car, and giant trees dangle from black boulders overhead. Storms come often to this corner of the Smokies, even when the sun stays firmly over Newfound Gap. The forests change quickly, and by the time you reach the top you can see red spruce and fraser firs growing side by side—unusual outside of Central Canada.

Sadly, most of the mature fraser firs are dead, having been felled by the wee balsam woolly aphid, an insect that invaded from Maine earlier this century. More than a hundred variety of trees do surround the dome, including the mountain ash with its flaming red bunches of berries, and nearly 1500 types of flowering plants— all lovers of the constant moisture available way up here.

A half-mile trail of concrete spirals to the top of the dome (a mile round-trip) and is steep enough to make your shins ache. Still, millions of visitors have walked or taken their wheelchairs up into the clouds to be on the Clingmans Dome platform, in hopes of catching a glimpse of the thickly woven forest and creased hills and valleys that run into sheer blue sky.

Back on Newfound Gap Road, cross into Tennessee and watch the mountain balds glisten all around. Above the road, sheer, cinnamon-colored cliffs are glossy and veiled with water. Tunnels, their openings draped in luscious ferns, present themselves around turns, and you'll need your headlights to see inside their darkened lengths. As you keep driving, you'll feel the day pass in measured shades of sunlit color, like a slow technicolor dream.

The settlers of **Cades Cove** were no doubt taken by the same scenery when they arrived in the early 1800s. Making their way slowly on horses and wagons, they bought land from speculators, who had bought it from the state of Tennessee, which had taken it from the Cherokees. The settlers cleared forests, planted orchards, corn, wheat and rye, and built the most fundamental, inviting homes of hewn logs and simple wood frame. By 1850, 685 people lived in the Cove, though in ten years' time more than half had gone west in search of gold and more fertile pastures. The Cove became nearly a ghost town after that. ~ Along the Cades Cove Loop, about 23 miles from Newfound Gap Road, in Tennessee.

What you see today is not too different from Cades Cove back then. Seven simple log homes are sprinkled along the 11-mile, one-way **Cades Cove Loop**, and there are churches, barns, a blacksmith shop, mills, smokehouse and corncrib. All are accessible by wheelchair, and tell a poignant story of long, productive days spent growing and gathering food, chopping wood, milking cows, grinding corn and wheat, smoking meat, "putting up" the vegetables, helping build a house when someone needed it, helping bury someone when they needed that, too. Callused hands these people had, twentieth-century ulcers they didn't.

About half-way around the loop, the **Cades Cove Visitors Center** has information on the area, including a worthwhile auto tour booklet that's only 50 cents. The center is closed from November through mid-April, though the loop stays open except for the nastiest of winter days.

Spring through fall is the only time to explore reclusive **Rich Mountain Road** (closed in winter) and **Parson Branch Road** (closed for repairs; call ahead), which angle off from Cades Cove Loop. Rich Mountain Road heads north from the loop for seven miles and is on a path first cut by the Cherokee. It's a single-lane gravel trail, though a wide one, that fishtails up Rich Mountain, then descends into the rich woods and pastures of Tuckaleechee Cove, eventually joining Route 321 into Townsend, Tennessee.

Newfound Gap Road is so squiggly that, on a map, it looks like it was drawn by a two-year-old.

Parson Branch Road offers an entirely different drive; the road is flanked by luscious foliage, dense, wet and green, riddled with streams and waterfalls and boulders covered in furry green algae. There are some patches of pavement along the road, but most of the eight-mile stretch is gravely and skinny, heading southwest from Cades Cove through Tennessee to Route 129. Thankfully, RVs and trailers are banned from both Parson Branch and Rich Mountain roads.

Back on Newfound Gap Road, the **Sugarlands Visitors Center** is the last place before the Tennessee boundary of Great Smoky Mountains National Park. Exhibits here are more elaborate than at Oconaluftee Visitor Center; taxidermied animals are everywhere, and so are photographs of large and small Smokies critters, with lengthy details on their lives and times. The ubiquitous woodchuck, one learns, loves to graze on wildflowers along the roadways and is nicknamed "whistle pig." If you haven't already seen one, keep an eye out. They're easy to spot. ~ Signpost 1.

Right after Sugarlands, and all the solitude and silence of the Smokies, is **Gatlinburg**, Tennessee. It's a rude encounter, a town with more gimmickry and gauchery than any in western North Carolina (come to think of it, in all of North Carolina). Depending on your taste in towns, of course, you may find Gatlinburg big fun. Like a caricature of a Swiss village, it is overrun with chalets whose occupants—souvenir shops, burger joints, pinball palaces, mom-and-pop motels—cater to tourists in a not-so-subtle way. Good luck finding a parking space.

One reason to go to Gatlinburg is to get to **Roaring Fork Motor Nature Trail**. The paved, one-way loop lasts only five and

◀ HIDDEN

half miles but forges through exhilarating, eclectic scenery—first, a parade of hills, then solid green walls of woods, then light and airy poplar forest where cornfields once stood. Numbered signposts invite travelers to stop, see, feel and smell the surroundings: an old wagon trail, an 1865 dog-trot cabin, a waterfall called "The Place of a Thousand Drips." Closed in winter. ~ Off Route 441, about four miles south of Gatlinburg.

Many more back-road trips await in the national park. Most are difficult to reach, some are rough and rugged and closed in winter, but all offer a wonderful way to see the Smokies—in solitude. The isolated **Cataloochee Road**, on the park's southeastern side in North Carolina, is a six-mile trek through vast valleys decorated with pastures to **Cataloochee Historic District**, the remains of an 1800s hamlet. ~ Off Route 40.

HIDDEN ▶

Near Bryson City, North Carolina, on the park's southern end, **Lakeview Drive** goes for six scenic miles, then dead ends. The lake is Fontana Lake, framed in deep green hills and corralled by a dam 25 miles downstream, whose waters come from the Tuskaseegee River. Take a dawn drive and see fog curl off the glassy water like steam rising from a vat, a haunting morning mountain portrait. ~ Off Route 19.

HIDDEN ▶

LODGING

It makes perfect sense that the only lodge in Great Smoky Mountains National Park is thoroughly hidden. To get to **LeConte Lodge**, you have to hike five and a half miles up the third-highest Appalachian mountain, 6593 feet to be exact, and that's *after* making a reservation a year in advance. The signs at the trailheads for the lodge say: "None of the five trails should be considered a stroll. You may encounter ice and snow as late as May and as early as October." You may also encounter bears, who have figured out just what goes on at the lodge (lots of home cooking). Do not feed or approach them, but continue calmly (as possible) on the trail.

HIDDEN ▶

The lodge's seven hand-hewn cabins and three group buildings with individual bedrooms sit atop Mount LeConte and are extremely primitive—no running water or electricity (put that television right out of your mind). There are outhouses, and fresh water you carry to a metal washbasin (bring a washcloth and hand towel) for freshening up. The views are fabulous, the two meals a day fresh and filling, the mood soul-cleansing. Most people stay one night, a few stay two. Room rates include breakfast and dinner. Most important: The lodge starts taking reservations for the *following season* on October 1 of each year, and usually books up within two weeks. The season runs from late March through mid-November. ~ 423-429-5704. ULTRA-DELUXE.

Otherwise, there's camping. Ten developed campgrounds are sprinkled throughout the park and accommodate tents and some

RVs and trailers, though there are no hookups. There are picnic tables, fireplaces, restrooms and fresh water at each campground. One of the most popular campgrounds in the Smokies is **Smokemont** in North Carolina. ~ Newfound Gap Road, Signpost 19. Also try **Elkmont** campgrounds. ~ Little River Road, Signpost 3, on the way to Cades Cove. In Tennessee there is **Cades Cove**. ~ Cades Cove Loop, about 23 miles from Newfound Gap Road. These campgrounds are open year-round, but reservations are accepted only for the high season—May 15 through October 31—by contacting **Destinet**. ~ 800-365-2267. You may also want to contact **Great Smoky Mountains National Park Services**. ~ 423-436-1226. You can call up to 5 months in advance, which is a good idea for weekends in summertime and fall foliage in October. The fee is $11 per night.

For less crowded camping, try **Cataloochee** in North Carolina. ~ Cataloochee Road, off Route 40, on the park's southeastern side. Or try **Balsam Mountain** campgrounds, also in North Carolina. ~ Located on Balsam Mountain Road, off Route 19, south of Cataloochee. These and the park's other five campgrounds are open April through October, but you can't make reservations. Fees range from $6 to $8 per night.

◄ *HIDDEN*

◄ *HIDDEN*

Backcountry campsites, including 16 hike-in shelters, are also scattered throughout the park. A backcountry permit is required, though there is no fee. Pick up a permit at any of the visitors centers and ranger stations. Campers can also get a permit by contacting the park's Backcountry Office, which accepts reservations for specific backcountry sites for up to 30 days in advance. ~ 423-436-1231.

DINING

There aren't any dining establishments in these parts, so be sure to pack a picnic and find a table. Dozens of picnic tables are set among the thick green woods, beside the thunder of waterfalls and faint swish of slow-going streams, and atop mountains that look across to more mountains. Better views and atmosphere can't be had anywhere.

SHOPPING

Try the stellar bookstores at the **Oconaluftee Visitors Center**. ~ Newfound Gap Road, near the North Carolina park entrance. Also check out the **Cades Cove Visitors Center**. ~ Cades Cove Loop. There is also a good selection of materials at **Sugarlands Visitors Center**. ~ Newfound Gap Road, near the Tennessee park entrance. All of these bookstores have volumes on everything relating to the Smokies. Pioneer life, the Cherokees, photo essays, birdwatching and wildflower guides, audio tapes on Smokies' sights, children's coloring books, jigsaw puzzles—good things to fill the mind while wandering the mountains.

NIGHTLIFE   A mountaintop drenched in full moonlight, the flash of a white-tail deer vanishing into blackness, the ferocious rustling of a red squirrel, the angry grunts of wild boar—these are the night scenes of Great Smoky Mountains National Park. Spend a night in the woods and you may find it more thrilling than any nightclub.

To better understand what goes on after dusk and also during the day, rangers lead nighttime walks and host fireside chats and slide shows on the Smokies. In the fall there's a program called "Snacks and Snores" about how animals, particularly the black bear, hibernate. In the spring, you'll hear what happens when they wake up with a big appetite. Most programs are held at the **Oconaluftee Pioneer Farmstead**, **Smokemont** campground area, **Sugarlands Visitors Center** area and **Cades Cove**. For a schedule, call 423-436-1200.

▼▼▼▼▼▼▼▼▼▼
Cherokee & Bryson City

At the threshold of Great Smoky Mountains National Park and the heart of the 56,573-acre Cherokee Indian Reservation, Cherokee, North Carolina, is both tourist haven and cultural and business center. Route 441 North runs the brief length of town, strung with chain motels, putt-putt golf, sidewalk vendors, gem-mining troughs, a skylift across from the Fort Tomahawk Mall, and, as of 1995, a pair of tribal casinos whose cacophonous, neon interiors flicker with video poker, video craps and video blackjack machines (but no tables). Tour buses regularly pull up and disgorge their contents into casinos, which stay open 24 hours a day. Then there are seemingly countless roadside stands selling "Indian" souvenirs. The miniature tepees and wigwams and long feather headdresses aren't authentic; the Cherokee lived in permanent wood and clay mud homes and wore headbands with a few feathers. There's also a matter of human decency—or lack of it. The Redskin Motel and Wigwam Motel surely could be better named.

SIGHTS   There is still good reason to stop in **Cherokee**. Start with the **Museum of the Cherokee Indian**, which sets things straight about these peaceful, highly intelligent people. The video and audio displays and exhibits of artifacts tell how the Cherokee lived in the Smokies for thousands of years and let the land be. How they assembled villages along the rivers, hunted only animals they could eat or use for clothing and how, like the ancient Maya, they turned to the forest for medicine, employing more than 400 plants for healing. They were artists and craftspeople, passionate dancers and worshipers of one god called YOWA. They had seven clans (two were named Wild Potato and Long Hair) and a leader named Sequoyah who, in 1821, created the Cherokee written language. Shortly thereafter, in a holocaust called "The Trail of Tears," the

Cherokees were driven from their homes and herded like cattle to Oklahoma. More than 4000 died. Admission. ~ Route 441 North; 704-497-3481.

Oconaluftee Indian Village re-creates a 1750 Cherokee town. Take the one-hour tour (which is offered every ten minutes) and walk through cool, fragrant forest on spongy paths of peat moss, wide and firm enough for wheelchairs. You can pause at various huts and homes to watch the craftspeople and hear them tell about their works. Women make beaded necklaces using thread from hemp and needles made of deer hooves, and weave baskets of river cane and white oak, dying them with roots and bark. Men carve blowguns from river cane and demonstrate their aim, and make bear traps of logs, fish traps of hickory bark and buckskin, and teeny bird traps with teeny trap doors on top. Each exhibit is only as good as its narrators, and some are more enthusiastic than others. At the end, everyone gathers in a seven-sided council chamber (a side for each clan) to hear what they haven't heard yet about the modern Cherokees: few know the language Sequoyah created last century, most are Baptist and speak with a Southern accent, and their land is held in a federal trust. Open mid-May through late October. Admission. ~ Route 441 North, Cherokee; 704-497-2315.

> Sequoyah is thought to be the only person ever to design and perfect an entire alphabet.

For more information on the Cherokee area, stop by the **Cherokee Visitors Center**. ~ Route 441 North; 704-497-9195, 800-438-1601.

It's 15 squiggly miles on Route 19 west from Cherokee to Bryson City. Part of the way is through the thickly wooded Cherokee Indian Reservation and its speck-sized Birdtown. The road rises and falls and S-curves all over the place, and your ears pop as you careen around green caverns and mountains.

Bryson City is a country outpost, a thin wedge of town between the Nantahala River and the mountains. A handsome city hall with a four-sided clock tower presides over the downtown of red brick, and there's Clampitt Hardware, ancient-looking Na-bers Drive-In, and The Best Little Hair House in Town.

Here also is a depot for the **Great Smoky Mountains Railway**, a big attraction offering big fun around these parts. The reconditioned steam and diesel-electric locomotives, brightly painted primary colors, follow routes laid in the 1890s. Numerous trips are offered, the most popular being a four-and-a-half-hour excursion down into the deep, densely wooded Nantahala Gorge, with lunch on the train or at a restaurant in the gorge. Adventurers should opt for the seven-hour gorge trip that includes whitewater rafting on the Nantahala River. Trips are offered on varying days and times, from early April through early November. ~ Everett Street.

The railway's other popular excursion is a three-hour round-trip to the Tuckasegee River from **Dillsboro**, offered from April through December. And on summer Saturdays, there's a dinner ride in an old-fashioned dining car (on the menu: cornish game hen with peach curry sauce, filet mignon and grilled seasonal vegetables with sun-dried tomato vinaigrette). It's recommended that reservations for all excursions be made several weeks ahead. ~ Depot located on Front Street; 704-586-8811, 800-872-4681.

The other big reason people come to this part of North Carolina is the river. The Nantahala is a great whitewater river, with Class II and III rapids (Class V being the most advanced and terrifying) that are perfect for novices and families with young children. You can raft, kayak, canoe or float on an innertube down the immensely scenic river bordered with trees. Numerous whitewater outfitters line Route 19-74 about nine to 14 miles west of Bryson City, but by far the best is **Nantahala Outdoor Center**. ~ 13077 Route 19 West, about 13 miles west of Bryson City; 704-488-6737, 800-232-7238. For more on whitewater pursuits, see "Outdoor Adventures" at the end of this chapter.

LODGING

In Cherokee there are dozens of motor court-style motels, some looking more worn than others, crowded along Route 441 and just off it. Otherwise, there are about 30 private campgrounds. The Cherokee Visitors Center can provide a list of accommodations. ~ Route 441 North; 704-497-9195, 800-438-1601.

Better, though, is a stay in one of the engaging inns or bed and breakfasts around Bryson City.

HIDDEN ►

A more comfortable place than **Fryemont Inn** cannot be imagined. The fetching, 1923 bark-covered building sits on a hill, with fountain-filled ponds and a vast porch overlooking the Smoky

✔ CHECK THESE OUT—UNIQUE LODGING

- *Moderate to deluxe:* Revel in the quiet of **Balsam Mountain Inn**, a venerable Colonial Revival manse hidden in deep mountain woods. *page 114*
- *Moderate to ultra-deluxe:* Bring the family to **Fontana Village**; the kids will find days of activities—and you'll find solitude. *page 107*
- *Deluxe to ultra-deluxe:* Enter a cultured world at the **Yellow House**: European-styled rooms and well-tended gardens, evening wine and cheese, and long, luxurious baths in antique tubs. *page 113*
- *Ultra-deluxe:* Settle into a cabin at **The Swag** and take in superb mountain and meadow views from your secluded balcony. *page 113*

Budget: under $60 Moderate: $60–$100 Deluxe: $100–$130 Ultra-deluxe: over $130

Mountains. An enormous stone fireplace and long table set with
board games make the lobby extra inviting. Rich woods are rampant throughout; 37 guest rooms are paneled with chestnut and
have private baths, ceiling fans, and pocket windows that draw in
the cool mountain air. Room rates include breakfast and dinner.
Closed November through mid-April. For plusher accommodations, take one of the seven air conditioned suites in the inn's
ultra-deluxe-priced cottages, open year-round. ~ Fryemont Road,
off Spring Street, Bryson City; 704-488-2159, 800-845-4879. DE-
LUXE TO ULTRA-DELUXE.

Two miles east of Bryson City, a mile up a mountain road
through hemlock and spruce forest, is the aptly named **Hemlock**   ◄ *HIDDEN*
Inn. The low-slung, pewter-colored building resembles a mountain
motel, and there are several cabins tucked in the woods. Rooms are
plain but modern, with newish carpets, wood paneling and poster
beds. It's awfully quiet up here, except during big family-style breakfasts and dinners which are included in the rates. The inn is closed
early November through April. ~ Route 19, Bryson City; 704-488-
2885. DELUXE.

Right in whitewater country, the popular **Nantahala Village** is
surrounded by 200 acres of lush mountain forest. Choose from 14
rooms in the 1948 stone lodge along the road or drive up the hill
and stay in one of 48 cabins, many outfitted with porches that look
into trees. The decor is simple and woodsy. There's a swimming
pool and a restaurant (offering fine dining), a recreation hall and
riding stables. Closed December through February, except the week
of Christmas. ~ Route 19, about nine miles west of Bryson City;
704-488-2826, 800-438-1507, fax 704-488-9634. MODERATE TO
ULTRA-DELUXE.

Stuck way out in the western corner of the Smokies, **Fontana**   ◄ *HIDDEN*
Village is where one goes to really get away. Families in particular
have been finding this place since it opened in back in 1947, right
after the Tennessee Valley Authority built Fontana Dam and created 31-mile-long Fontana Lake. As you might expect, there are
plenty of water activities—including fishing, canoeing, boating,
scenic cruising and houseboat rentals—as well as horseback riding,
miniature golf, nightly dances and bonfires, arts-and-crafts workshops, tennis courts, shuffleboard courts, and three swimming
pools (translation: The kids will be out of your hair). Guests have
a choice of dining at one of three casual eateries, or picking up
some groceries at the general store. Accommodations vary from
older, moderately priced rooms in rustic cottages and the inn to
more contemporary, amenity-packed cottages with ultra-deluxe
price tags. ~ Located off Route 28, about 36 miles west of Bryson
City; 704-498-2211, 800-849-2258, fax 704-498-2345. MODERATE
TO ULTRA-DELUXE.

Text continued on page 110.

Best Country Cookin' in the Smokies

If mountains of mashed potatoes dripping with fresh-churned butter, peppery crusted fried chicken that crumbles to the touch, fat slabs of the sweetest ham, soup bowls bubbling with butter beans, and the fluffiest hot biscuits drizzled with honey sound like a good way to eat, then go to **The Jarrett House**.

You won't be alone. Every year tens of thousands of people eat at this venerable old house in the captivating little town of Dillsboro, along Route 441 about 13 miles south of Cherokee. Many patrons are on the way to catch a train, or are getting off a train. The popular **Great Smoky Mountains Railway** has its main depot in Dillsboro and operates three-hour sightseeing tours to the Tuckasegee River. ~ Front Street; 704-586-8811, 800-872-4681.

Most days from morning till night, you can see folks in the front-porch rockers at The Jarrett House, waiting for their turn at one of the wood tables in the dining room. The mood here is pure southern hospitality: courteous waitresses in pinafores, lacy wreaths on the doors, baskets of fresh flowers on every tables, the shine of white china, the clang of dishes, the air redolent with country-cooked food.

Things move quickly; minutes after you're seated and the sweet iced tea is poured into glasses, the waitress returns with bowls and platters burdened with so many meats and vegetables, potatoes and breads, you are certain she is heading for another table. She isn't.

The bowls and platters are left on the table, and you help yourself to all the food. If a dish starts looking empty, it's quickly refilled. *Everything* is good, right down to the legendary vinegar pie, which is made with vinegar but tastes nothing like vinegar—more like a candy custard tucked between two crumbly crusts. Alcoholic beverages are not served, but you can bring a bottle of wine. Most people don't. ~ Haywood Street, Dillsboro; phone/fax 704-586-0265, 800-972-5623. BUDGET.

Part of The Jarrett House appeal is its past as the Mount Beulah Hotel, built in 1884 by William Allen Dills after the Western North Carolina Railway starting passing through the area. In 1886, the hotel became famous after two women visited from the North Carolina coast—and smoked.

The other reason the place is so appealing are its current owners, the Hartbarger family, famous for their gracious, sincere hospitality and ability to keep things running smoothly. The Jarrett House is also their inn, with 18 guest rooms in the main, three-story building decorated with handsome antiques like clawfoot tubs, poster beds, pitchers and bowls. Three plush, modern rooms in an annex have decks that overlook the town and mountains. All of the rooms have air conditioning. Closed December through March. ~ MODERATE.

From The Jarrett House you can walk around **Dillsboro** and enjoy its charm. Peaked roofs and church steeples angle against blue mountain sky, and bakeries and coffee and tea houses open their doors to the sunshine of spring and summer. Colorful clapboard stores framed in white picket gather along two blocks of **Haywood Street** and **Front Street** and the lanes in between, and you can shop for hours.

The Imagination Station focuses on birds and wildlife, and carries imaginative handmade baskets and wood sculpture. ~ Haywood Street; 704-586-3353. Next door, **The Cheddar Box** easily satisfies a cheese fetish. The cookbooks, fudge and gourmet teas here make great gifts. ~ Haywood Street; 704-586-4442.

Bradley's General Store is just what you hope for from an old-time emporium: two rambling floors filled with bins of dime candy, homemade jams and jellies crowned with checkered cloth, rag rugs, old plows and oxen yokes and stuffed animals for the kids. Plus, there's a soda fountain. ~ Front Street; 704-586-3891.

There are two outstanding galleries. The first is **The Golden Carp**, whose watercolors, vases, baskets and other gifts lean toward the nouveau. ~ Webster Street; 704-586-5477. The other is **Dogwood Crafters**, a nonprofit cooperative where about 100 artists contribute everything from stained glass and wood sculpture to linens, baskets and pottery. ~ Webster Street; 704-586-2248.

Stop for lunch at **Maxwell's Bakery & Sandwich Shop** and have a stacked deli sandwich. Sit inside or out on the front porch. ~ Haywood Street; 704-586-5046. BUDGET.

For barbecue, go to **Dillsboro Smokehouse** and have hickory smoked beef, pork, baby back ribs or turkey attended by barbecue beans, hushpuppies, yam patties and onion rings. Low-fat, heart-healthy items are also on the menu, though the country breakfasts will blow your cholesterol for the whole day. ~ Haywood Street; 704-586-9556. BUDGET TO MODERATE.

DINING

HIDDEN ▶

In a big dining room warmed by a big fireplace, the **Fryemont Inn** serves time-honored Southern dishes with great success. There's plenty of trout on the menu, as well as roast leg of lamb with onion gravy and mint jelly, baked Virginia ham with raisin sauce and roast breast of turkey with pecan dressing, though entrées tend to change with the season. Despite the polished surroundings—gleaming wood floors, white and plum linens—dress is mountain casual. Big breakfasts are also served, but there's no lunch. Cocktails available. Closed November through late April. ~ Fryemont Road, off Spring Street, Bryson City; 704-488-2159. MODERATE.

HIDDEN ▶

Next door to Fryemont, dining is more homey at the **Randolph House**, though reservations are a must. Owners Bill and Ruth Randolph Adams serve on the terrace of their whitewashed 1895 home or inside in the little dining room. Entrées vary nightly, but might include veal Marsala, shrimp scampi, prime rib or stuffed trout. Best are the homemade desserts: apple pie, rich fruit cobblers, peanut butter supremes. There's wine, beer and limited mixed beverages. Closed November through mid-April. ~ 223 Fryemont Road, off Spring Street, Bryson City; 704-488-3472. MODERATE.

HIDDEN ▶

The folks at **Hemlock Inn** go real casual. They bring out dishes of down-home cookin'—green beans, broccoli casserole, spaghetti, country ham, carrot cake—and set them on lazy Susans in the middle of big wood tables. Then everyone helps themselves. You'll need a reservation if you're not staying at the inn. ~ Off Route 19, Bryson City; 704-488-2885. BUDGET.

Nothing seems more enjoyable after whitewater rafting on the Nantahala River than sitting on the sun porch of **Nantahala Village Restaurant**, nursing a cup of hot herbal tea, and looking out across the forest and hills. If it's lunchtime, order the Guatemalan black-bean soup and the Great Smoky Sandwich, with smoked turkey, monterey jack cheese, bacon and chive mayonnaise. There's lots of chicken and pasta on the dinner menu, plus vegetarian specials and the perennial country ham and mountain trout. The main dining room is atmospheric with its worn wood floors and granddaddy fireplace. Brown bagging. Closed December through mid-March, except for Christmas week. ~ Route 19-74, about nine miles west of Bryson City; 704-488-9616. BUDGET TO MODERATE.

SHOPPING

Bypass all those souvenir shops in Cherokee selling bogus "Indian" items and instead go to **Qualla Arts and Crafts**. The delicate and detailed pieces at this artists' cooperative include soapstone carvings, white oak baskets, soft sculpture dolls and low-fired pottery so fragile it cannot hold water. ~ Route 441 North; 704-497-3103.

NIGHTLIFE

The story of the Cherokee, from their ancestors' crossing of the Bering Straight 10,000 years ago to their being nearly decimated last century by white men, is replayed on summer nights in the outdoor pageant **Unto These Hills**. The production is both popular and well-done. During its mid-June-through-August run each year, nearly 100,000 people crowd the amphitheater, built after World War II by Cherokee stonemasons and American GIs. Call ahead for tickets or purchase them at the door. ~ Route 441 North; 704-497-2111, fax 704-497-6987.

Cherokee is a dry area (no liquor sold in establishments), so you'll have to go to Bryson City for a drink and some music.

Most relaxing is the **Fryemont Inn**, an inn/restaurant with a cozy lounge. ~ Fryemont Road, off Spring Street, Bryson City; 704-488-2159.

◄ HIDDEN

The lounge at **The Welkin** is a fine place for a drink and sometimes live acoustic and folk tunes. ~ 385 Arlington Avenue, Bryson City; 704-488-2300.

During spring and fall, visiting musicians from regional symphonies present intimate concerts at **Nantahala Village Restaurant**. Performances include a prix-fixe dinner. Brown bagging (BYOB). ~ Route 19-74, about nine miles west of Bryson City; 704-488-9616.

▼▼▼▼▼▼▼▼▼▼▼▼

Maggie Valley & Waynesville Area

Constantly linked by promotional ads and separated geographically by only 12 hilly miles, Maggie Valley and Waynesville aren't at all alike. Maggie Valley came to life around 1900 as a resort town and exists today for tourists; its main drag, Route 19, is edged with country novelty shops and motels whose neon signs give a simple "Yes" or "No." Waynesville is a real live working town with a hardware store and pharmacy and an actual downtown with a Main Street. There are places to shop and stay here, but they don't shout their presence. Rather, they are stowed under painted awnings or along side streets.

SIGHTS

In Maggie Valley you'll find **Ghost Town in the Sky**. A mile up the mountain, this is one of the oldest theme parks in the Carolinas and, unfortunately, showing its age. The imitation Wild West town is hokey all the way, from the gravely western tunes played in the train up the mountain to the painted particleboard that make up the "town." The Cherokees wear shiny lycra shorts and high-top tennis shoes for their "authentic Indian dances" and the showgirls at the Silver Dollar Saloon are rough around the edges. That said, small children do enjoy Ghost Town; there are some kiddie carnival rides and "gunfights" in the street. Be ready to fork over some serious cash—admission, as of 1996, was $16.95 for adults, $11.95 for ages 3 through 9. All shows are wheelchair accessible. Closed late October through early May. Admission. ~ Route 19; 704-926-1140, 800-446-7886.

Admission isn't nearly as painful at **Soco Gardens Zoo**, a small but pretty place with animals in small pens. Wheelchair-accessible paths wend through the gardens, with views of a bear, wallabies, a snow leopard, jaguars, emus and other creatures. Most popular with kids are the two snake shows, one venomous and one non-venomous, and the petting area. Closed November through April. ~ Route 19, Maggie Valley; 704-926-1746.

HIDDEN ►

Go the opposite direction on Route 19 to Route 276 North, then head about two miles to **Hemphill Road** for a drive through the country. You're actually climbing the mountain (switch to low gear when the car starts groaning), with panoramas of whitewashed fences and cranberry-red barns, angus cattle grazing on knolls and apple trees burdened with fruit, narrow little churches propped up on hills and homes perched across creeks, and tobacco drying in old sheds.

To get to **Waynesville**, though, you'll have to go back to Route 19 and take Route 276 South. You'll pass through a commercial area with fast-food chains before arriving in the handsome downtown of red-brick buildings, with low peaks off in the distance. Take awhile to walk around, browse the handful of shops and visit the **Museum of North Carolina Handicrafts**. Among the 2000-plus pieces of talent: river-cane baskets trimmed in honeysuckle vine, handmade flutes, fiddles and dulcimers, and fiber art colored with walnut hulls and pokeberry. Closed November through May. Admission. ~ 307 Shelton Street; 704-452-1551.

For more information on Maggie Valley or Waynesville, stop by the **Greater Haywood County Tourism Development Authority**. ~ 621 Soco Road, Maggie Valley; 704-926-5426, 800-334-9036.

LODGING

If you love golf, stay at **Maggie Valley Resort & Country Club**. The front nine holes of the picturesque, par-72 championship course lie on the valley floor, the back nine climb the mountain. All the one- and two-bedroom villas overlook the greens and fairways, and so do many of the rooms in the main lodge. The decor is contemporary country, the rates range from moderate to ultra-deluxe. In winter, you pay budget rates and play unlimited golf—but then there is the snow. A good restaurant, two all-weather tennis courts and heated pool are among the other amenities. ~ 340 Country Club Drive, off Route 19, Maggie Valley; 704-926-1616, 800-438-3861, fax 704-926-2906.

The rustic little houses at **Twinbrook Resort Cottages**, stashed in the woods, have kitchens, fireplaces and porches stacked with firewood. Owners Carl and Viola Henry have owned the place since 1946 (Carl Henry is eighty-something) and together with their extensive family provide exuberant hospitality. Cottages have pine-paneled walls and old-time decor, televisions and microwaves, all in all clean and homey. You can pitch horseshoes, play shuffleboard or swim in the indoor pool. ~ Off Route 19, Maggie Valley; 704-926-1388, 800-305-8946, fax 704-926-2943. MODERATE.

The Cataloochee Ranch is a comfy compound high on a mountain, formerly a sheep and cattle farm but now a place to ski, hike, trout fish and ride horseback. Wildflower meadows cascade down this 1000-acre property and peaks ripple across the horizon. There's a historic ranch house, a newer lodge and several cabins with decor ranging from rustic to modern. Braided rugs, patterned quilts and wood walls give a home-style ambiance. Families usually go for the cabins, which have refrigerators, fireplaces and coffeemakers. Room rates include breakfast and dinner. The Cataloochee ski area, open at night, is a mile away. Closed late November until late December. ~ Fie Top Road, three miles off Route 19, Maggie Valley; 704-926-1401, 800-868-1401, fax 704-926-9249. ULTRA-DELUXE.

◄ HIDDEN

Opened in late 1995, the Yellow House is indeed yellow, a handsome two-story home decorated with columns and chimneys and set along a knoll riotously planted with flowers, shrubs and soft green lawn. Three rooms and three suites are luxurious and beautifully adorned. The Monticeto room focuses on an oil painting by California artist Kurt Polter; the St. Paul de Vence suite has a two-sided fireplace and French doors opening onto a lily pond and private patio. You can take breakfast (included in the rate) in your room, the dining room or the veranda; wine and cheese are served in the evening and port after dinner—civilized living. ~ 610 Plott Creek Road, off of Route 23-74, one mile west of Waynesville; 704-452-0991, 800-563-1236, fax 704-452-1140. DELUXE TO ULTRA-DELUXE.

◄ HIDDEN

If one wanted to completely disappear into the woods, but in a luxurious way, there could not be a better place than The Swag. Parked on a mountaintop 5000 feet high, with gorgeous green lawn and fantastic views in every direction, this extraordinary place was put together with hand-hewn logs from numerous historic mountain buildings, including an 1800s church. Guest rooms and private cabins are stylish and woodsy, variously adorned with stone fireplaces, secluded balconies and porches, plush quilts and

ROOMS WITH A VIEW

Just west of Maggie Valley on Route 19 at Soco Gap, a number of craft shops are hinged along the mountainside, their excessive signs all announcing the "most photographed Smoky Mountains view." Some charge to look, but others just hope you'll be persuaded to step in and buy something. The view of the valley is admittedly soul-stirring: neatly plaited fields, crisp white farmhouses, soft mountains floating all around.

Appalachian art. Great Smoky Mountains National Park starts out back, and you can hike for miles and be swallowed by deep green, dark woods. On cool nights, slip into the warmth of a big hot tub beneath an inky mountain sky. Room rates include all meals—fresh, imaginative regional fare. BYOB. Closed November through mid-May. ~ Hemphill Road, six and a half miles off Route 276 North, Waynesville; 704-926-0430, 800-789-7672, fax 704-926-2036. ULTRA-DELUXE.

HIDDEN ►

Not quite as reclusive but still offering mountain privacy, the **Old Stone Inn Heath Lodge** consists of eight stone and poplar buildings tucked among several acres of woods. Rooms and suites are simply furnished, and many are paneled in wood. Two guest lounges offer opportunities for games and TV. Rates come with breakfast, and Southern cooking is available at dinnertime. Closed from January until Good Friday. ~ 900 Dolan Road, off Route 276 South, Waynesville; 704-456-3333, 800-432-8499. MODERATE TO DELUXE.

HIDDEN ►

Balsam Mountain Inn is a big place among big mountains, a Colonial Revival manse with high-ceilinged rooms, book-filled libraries and long windows looking at the tips of 6000-foot Balsams. Yet the mood here is intimate, as befitting a turn-of-the-century, weatherboard hotel that once drew travelers seeking restoration in area mineral springs. All 35 rooms have private baths and are warmly, simply decorated with wicker, oak and willow furnishings, antique iron beds and beadboard walls. The closest town, Balsam, is but a pindot in the woods, but Waynesville is only about ten miles away and the Blue Ridge Parkway is a half-mile. Hearty and healthy breakfasts (go for the French toast with sour cream and mountain blueberries) are included in the rate. ~ Off Route 74-23, a half-mile south of the Blue Ridge Parkway, Balsam; 704-456-9498. MODERATE TO DELUXE.

DINING

Maggie Valley is not known as a culinary haven, and Waynesville is only a notch better. "For a special night out," one valley chef says, "you'll have to drive to Asheville—we all do." You can, however, find filling down-home fare that satisfies on a cool mountain day.

Funky and favored by locals, **Saratoga's** serves homogenous American fare like chili-cheese fries, tuna salad plates and fried onion rings, patty melts, chopped sirloin and soup from a can. The booths are mismatched, and there are paintings planted strangely in the rafters. ~ Route 19, Maggie Valley; 704-926-1448. BUDGET TO MODERATE.

Maggie's Kountry Kitchen is the other local meeting place. It looks just like it sounds, a roadside kitchen outfitted with vinyl tablecloths and homey folk art. Breakfasts are big and Southern; lunch and dinner lean toward fried chicken, catfish and beef stew;

there are simple sandwiches as well. ~ Route 19, Maggie Valley; 704-926-2676. BUDGET.

Family-style **Snappy's** has reliable low-priced Italian food. The extensive menu lists lasagnas, calzones, chicken or eggplant parmesan, spaghetti, stromboli, and baked ziti, flounder, ham steak, loaded pizzas and hot dogs. The decor is pleasant enough, with padded vinyl booths and silk ferns dangling from the ceiling. ~ Route 19, in the Eagle Shopping Plaza, Maggie Valley; 704-926-6126. BUDGET.

With a reservation you can dine finely at **The Swag** for dinner. ◀ HIDDEN
The chef at this remote mountaintop inn selects the freshest ingredients—trout from the farm down the mountain, just-picked apples and cranberries, herbs and vegetables from the backyard garden—and turns them into luscious dishes. Tomato basil soup, grilled rainbow trout, cumin-crusted pork with red-currant wine sauce, and Kentucky Derby pie with bourbon whipped cream are examples of the everchanging menu. The dining room is an enormous wood space with a lofty ceiling. Rates include full dinner. BYOB. Closed November through mid-May. ~ Hemphill Road, 6½ miles off Route 276, Waynesville; 704-926-0430. ULTRA-DELUXE.

In a spacious house, **Bogart's** gives an open feeling with its soaring ceiling, stained-glass windows and loft dining room. The atmosphere is lively but tame enough for kids. The menu reads pub food: burgers, chili, French onion soup, broiled or fried trout, and colossal stuffed baked potatoes. Beer and wine served. ~ 222 South Main Street, Waynesville; 704-452-1313. BUDGET.

Even if you don't stay at **Balsam Mountain Inn**, consider driving out for dinner. It's about ten miles from Waynesville, stashed way in the woods with 6000-foot peaks floating all around, the air crisp and reviving. You'll need a reservation to enjoy savory, well-prepared fare such as lamb chops with lemon, leeks and garlic;

✔ **CHECK THESE OUT—UNIQUE DINING**

- *Budget:* Enjoy supreme Southern hospitality and cooking at **The Jarrett House**, an 1880s inn with a big, welcoming front porch. *page 108*
- *Budget to moderate:* Make **Nantahala Village Restaurant** your *après-river-rafting* stop; soups, sandwiches, pasta and vegetarian dishes are all quite inventive. *page 110*
- *Moderate:* Ask for a table by the big fireplace at **Fryemont Inn**, then order from a menu of robust mountain fare. *page 110*
- *Ultra-deluxe:* Dine finely at **The Swag**, a stylish mountaintop inn—try the cumin-crusted pork with red-currant wine sauce. *page 115*

Budget: under $9   Moderate: $9–$16   Deluxe: $16–$24   Ultra-deluxe: over $24

pasta with artichoke and mushroom sauce; blackened tuna; and filet mignon. Lunch served on Sunday. ~ Off Route 74-23, just south of the Blue Ridge Parkway, Balsam; 704-456-9498. MODERATE TO DELUXE.

SHOPPING Route 19 through Maggie Valley is country craft central. The stores are, for the most part, pleasant places to pour through potpourri, pottery, antiques and lovely souvenirs for the folks back home (how about a bird mobile or cake-in-a-jar?).

A stream bubbles behind **Maggie Mountaineer Crafts**, while the inside is perfumed by potpourri. Ceramics, butter churns, silk flowers and mountain apples in season are available at this agreeable place. ~ Route 19, Maggie Valley; 704-926-3129.

In the market for cowboy boots, moccasins, belts and buckles or the like? Stop in at **Jack's Leather Shop**. ~ Route 19, Maggie Valley; 704-926-1055.

How about accessories for church? **Aunt Bee's Blessing Shop** stocks Bibles, hymnals and various other religious-themed items. ~ Route 19, Market Square, Maggie Valley; 704-926-3031.

Do your Christmas shopping anytime at **Cabbage Rose**, where the ornaments, imported from around the world, number in the thousands. Victorian gifts, collectibles and floral arrangements are also available. ~ Route 19, Maggie Valley; 704-926-3079.

HIDDEN ► It's a little out of the way, but the gift shop at **The Swag** stocks some lovely local crafts, including birdhouses, jewelry, quilts and handpainted umbrellas. ~ Hemphill Road, 6½ miles off Route 276, Waynesville; 704-926-0430.

GateKeepers has antiques and collectibles, home accessories and local pottery. ~ 4 North Main Street, Waynesville; 704-456-8820.

The colored-pencil scenes at **T. Pennington Art Gallery** are of western North Carolina landmarks and scenery, and are all done by owner Teresa Pennington. ~ 15 North Main Street, Waynesville; 704-452-9284.

Main Street in Waynesville is a fine place to find high-quality artistry. **Earthworks** has a stellar selection of American Indian art and jewelry, as well as bronze sculpture, serigraphs and environmental T-shirts. ~ 110 North Main Street; 704-452-9500.

Mast General Store is a cousin of the first and famous Mast store in Valle Crucis. Spend an hour or two scanning great stuff—outdoor gear, cookware, jewelry, boots and tennis shoes, gourmet coffees, etc. ~ 148 North Main Street, Waynesville; 704-452-2101.

NIGHTLIFE Wednesday is jazz night at **Saratoga's Cafe**, while weekends bring entertainment by solo artists. The simplified soup-and-sandwich joint and local meeting spot serves beer and wine. ~ Route 19, Maggie Valley; 704-926-1448.

Put your clogging shoes on and head for **Stompin' Ground.** ~ Route 19, Maggie Valley; 704-926-1288. The big barn hosts a number of regional and national clogging teams nightly from May through October.

Maggie Valley Opry House is a wildly popular pickin' parlor. Live bluegrass and mountain music and dancing featured nightly May through October. Cover. ~ Route 19, Maggie Valley; 704-926-9336.

Sonny's Place is a pool hall, but a good one, quite clean and not too smoky. The jukebox selection leans toward country music. ~ Route 19, Maggie Valley; 704-926-2710.

Shepard's Thunder Ridge is a restaurant/nightclub that hosts weekend bands—mostly country and Southern rock, sometimes big names. There's a full bar. Cover. ~ Route 19, Maggie Valley; 704-926-9470.

Have a beer in the bar at **Bogart's,** a casual, crowded tavern serving good food and wine, as well as acoustic music on the weekends. ~ 222 South Main Street, Waynesville; 704-452-1313.

Outdoor Adventures

WHITE-WATER TRIPS

This is whitewater country. The Nantahala River, which runs southwest of Bryson City, is *the* place for rafting, kayaking, canoeing and innertubing. I like rafting the best. You can feel the smoothness of the riverbed stones under the raft's thin rubbery bottom. Anyone who has never tried whitewater rafting because of that deep-in-the-gut fear should try here: The river is kind most of the time, the rapids are easy to exciting, and the surroundings sublime. The banks of the Nantahala are smothered in Edenic forest, and the air is fragrant and brisk. Every now and then the Great Smoky Mountains Railway chugs by overhead and people wave from the colorful train cars. Otherwise, there's only the sound of water running downriver.

The premier whitewater outfitter is **Nantahala Outdoor Center.** Reputed to be one of the nation's best whitewater schools, it offers one- to seven-day courses on everything from rafting, kayaking and canoeing to "frugal floating" downriver, rock climbing and mountain cycling. Students can stay in dorm-style bunkhouses, basic motel rooms or rental homes. You can also join a half-day, all-day, or overnight trip involving any of the above. If you need to leave the little ones somewhere, the center has a day care, and there are three restaurants here, too. ~ 13077 Route 19 West, about 13 miles west of Bryson City; 704-488-6737, 800-232-7238.

Among the other whitewater companies, **Endless River Adventures** has guided kayak excursions. ~ Bryson City; 704-488-6199. Also contact **Great Smokies Rafting Company,** across from the Nantahala Village, offers guided raft trips and rental rafts and ducks, which are small canoe-shaped rafts. ~ 13077 Route 19 West, about nine miles west of Bryson City; 704-488-6302, 800-238-6302. **Tuckaseegee Outfitters** does rafting and innertube trips down the tamer Tuckaseegee River. ~ Route 74, near the junction of Route 441 South; 704-586-5050.

FISHING   The Great Smoky Mountains need no introduction to trout fishers. More than 700 miles of streams and creeks offer fishing for rainbow and brown trout, smallmouth bass and rock bass. There are also brook trout, though it is illegal to catch them. As well, there are limits on rainbow and brown trout. Only single-hook artificial lures may be used at all within the park (in other words, no live bait!), and a fishing license, available at bait-and-tackle shops outside the park, is required for anyone 13 and older. If you plan to do some serious angling, pick up a copy of *Smoky Mountains Trout Fishing Guide* by Don Kirk.

Within the Cherokee Reservation are 30 miles of streams, three ponds—and plenty of trout and bass. Call the **Fish & Game Management of the Eastern Band of Cherokee Indians** for information on fishing on the reservation. ~ 704-497-5201.

In Bryson City, **Endless River Adventures** offers guided float-fishing cruises in dories. You can fly-fish or use a spinning rod to catch smallmouth bass, walleye and trout. ~ 704-488-6199.

You don't need a license to fish at a trout farm, but you will pay a per-fish fee. Some of these places are out in the boonies, down no-name country roads, so call ahead for directions. In Cherokee, contact **Cherokee Trout Farm**. ~ Big Cove Road, Cherokee; 704-497-9227. Or try **Fontana Village Trout Farm**. ~ Route 28, Fontana Dam; 704-498-2211. Also try **Holland's Trout Pond**. ~ Holland Road, off Route 19, Maggie Valley; 704-926-7808. Fishing is open to the public at **Soco Gap Trout Farm**. ~ Route 19 West, Maggie Valley; 704-926-3635. You may also fish at **Clyde Ferguson's Trout Pond**. ~ Route 209, off Route 19, Maggie Valley;

✔ **CHECK THESE OUT—UNIQUE OUTDOOR ADVENTURES**

- Hop inside a raft, kayak, canoe or innertube and cruise down the Nantahala River—but watch out for those rapids. *page 117*
- Cast your line—trout-fishing line, that is—into over 700 miles of streams and creeks within Great Smoky Mountains National Park. *page 118*
- Sees the Smokies on horseback; five riding stables are located inside the National Park. *page 119*
- Bike along Cades Cove Loop and enjoy gentle, paved terrain and wonderful 1800s-era scenery. *page 119*

704-627-6404. In Waynesville, try your luck at **Bill's Fish Pond**. ~ Waynesville; 704-926-0501.

It's not Aspen, but there are nine runs at **Cataloochee Ski Area**, with a vertical drop of 740 feet and one chairlift. Open for night skiing, it's a good place for first-timers. ~ Off Route 19, Maggie Valley; 704-926-0285.

SKIING

What could be better than teeing up on a crisp mountain morning, while watching the fog roll off the greens? You'll find a beautiful course at **Maggie Valley Resort**. ~ 340 Country Club Drive, Maggie Valley; 704-926-1616, 800-438-3861. Check out the green at **Waynesville Country Club Inn**. ~ Country Club Drive, Waynesville; 704-452-4617. Tee off at **Springdale Country Club**. ~ Route 276, 11 miles south of Waynesville; 704-235-8451, 800-553-3027.

GOLF

The crisp, cool mountain air is ideal for tennis. There are public courts at **Maggie Valley Resort**. ~ 340 Country Club Drive, Maggie Valley; 704-926-1616, 800-438-3861. Practice your serve at the **Waynesville Country Club Inn**. ~ Country Club Drive, Waynesville; 704-425-2258, 800-627-6250. Also try **Fontana Village**. ~ Off Route 28, about 36 miles west of Bryson City; 704-498-2211, 800-849-2258.

TENNIS

◄ *HIDDEN*

Five stables within Great Smoky Mountains National Park offer guided trail rides from spring through fall. You can ride by the hour, half-day or full-day, or even take an overnight trip. Stables are located at **Smokemont Campground**. ~ North of Cherokee; 704-497-2373. Also contact **Deep Creek Campground**. ~ Near Bryson City; 704-488-8504. In Tennessee, try **Cades Cove**. ~ 423-448-6286. You may also ride at **McCarter Stables**. ~ 423-436-5354. Or try **Smoky Mountain Stables**. ~ 423-436-5634.

RIDING STABLES

Outside the park, you can saddle up at **Fontana Village**. ~ Route 28, about 36 miles west of Bryson City; 704-498-2211, 800-849-2258. Also try **Cataloochee Ranch**. ~ Fie Top Road, three miles from Route 19, Maggie Valley; 704-926-1401, 800-868-1401. If you're in Waynesville try riding at **Utah Mountain Riding Stables** and **Hayrides**. ~ Off Route 276, Waynesville; 704-926-1143. Also try **Queen's Farm Stables**. ~ 2607 Dellwood Road, off Route 19, Waynesville; 704-926-0718. All require reservations.

◄ *HIDDEN*

For excellent bike-trail maps, contact the North Carolina Department of Transportation's Bicycle Program. ~ P.O. Box 25201, Raleigh, NC 27611; 919-733-2804.

BIKING

The steep, curvy, often unpaved roads of Great Smoky Mountains National Park make bicycling tough. One place that's great to bike is the **Cades Cove Loop** (11 miles one way) in Tennessee, a trek on gentle pavement, with spectacular scenery and historic stopovers to match.

Outside the park, **Route 28** (26 miles) from Route 19-74 west to Fontana Village is a little-traveled road through fairly easy to steep mountain terrain. At **Fontana Village** are numerous short and easy bike trails.

Bike Rentals   A concession at **Cades Cove Campground** within Great Smoky Mountains National Park rents bikes. You can also rent a mountain bike from **Euchella Sport Lodge**. ~ Route 74, about 12 miles west of Bryson City; 704-488-8835. **Nantahala Outdoor Center** has mountain bikes and great trail maps, too. ~ Everett Street, Bryson City; 704-488-2446. A bike-rental concession at **Fontana Village** is open in the summer. ~ Route 28; 704-488-2211.

HIKING   All distances listed for hiking trails are one way unless otherwise noted.

GREAT SMOKY MOUNTAINS NATIONAL PARK   More than 800 miles of trails plunge into the deepest, most peaceful parts of Great Smoky Mountains National Park. Pick up a copy of the park's *Walks and Hikes* fold-out map and brochure, which lists more than 60 trails. It's only 25 cents, and is available at the park's visitors centers. The Great Smoky Mountains Natural History Association sells books that thoroughly detail all the trails, including the excellent 575-page *Hiking Trails of the Smokies*, available for $16.95. ~ 115 Park Headquarters Road, Gatlinburg, TN 37738; 423-436-7318.

HIDDEN ▶   Near the Deep Creek picnic shelter, take the moderately difficult **Juney Whank Falls Trail** (.3 mile) for a look at some beautiful cascades. Also here are two easy trails, **Indian Creek Falls Trail** (3.9 miles) and **Toms Branch Falls** (.5 mile) with more water views.

From the Smokemont Campground, two lengthy, moderate-to-rugged trails lead into the deep woods. **Chasteen Creek Trail** (4 miles) passes a 15-foot waterfall on its switchback course up Hughes Ridge. **Smokemont Loop** (3.8 miles) is a cool walk through oak and cove hardwood forest.

In early summer, the **Forney Ridge Trail** (5.7 miles) is ablaze with azaleas. A moderate trek down 600 feet to the mountain clearing, it starts at the Clingmans Dome parking area.

The sign at **Chimney Tops Trail** (2 miles) says, "The view is worth the climb." Naturally, it's a popular hike, despite the vigorous, can't-catch-your-breath trek (including some rock scrambling) up 1335 feet to the twin summits the Cherokee called *Duniskwalguni*, or "forked antlers." Early mountaineers called them chimneys, and indeed you can peer down what appears to be a flue. The big view from up here is across Sugarland Valley, looking fabulous with its peaks marbled in moss and mountain laurel and rhododendron. The trail, which starts at Signpost 6 on Newfound Gap Road in Tennessee, is along a path first worn by the Cherokee.

Hike the first mile and a half of **Alum Cave Bluffs Trail** and you've taken the easy route, a fairly carefree walk along Alum Creek through hardwood and hemlock forest to Arch Rock, a natural tunnel. Go the last, strenuous three and a half miles to the bluffs and you'll be surrounded by mysterious rocky scenery, some masked in ferns, herbs and lichens. The trailhead is at Signpost 8 on Newfound Gap Road in Tennessee.

The pace of **Upper Little River Trail** (5.1 miles) is leisurely and   ◄ *HIDDEN*
the scenery includes spectacularly clear water rushing around boulders. Pick up the trail at the locked gate just above Elkmont Campground.

You can walk behind a waterfall if you take **Grotto Falls Trail** (3 miles), an easy stroll through dense, lush hardwood forest. You'll find the trailhead near Milepost 5 on the Roaring Fork Motor Nature Trail in Tennessee.

CHEROKEE AND BRYSON CITY   South of Bryson City near Wesser, the tough **Wesser Creek Trail** (3.5 miles) gives both a good workout and good views of the Nantahala range. Parts of the trail are narrow and straight up. You'll find the beginning along Route 1107, about one and a half miles off Route 19.

▼▼▼▼▼▼▼▼▼▼
The Great Smoky Mountains begin about 40 miles west
of Asheville, North Carolina. **Route 40** heads west from   **Transportation**
Asheville, then runs north along the eastern edge of Great
Smoky Mountains National Park. **Route 23** angles off Route 40   **CAR**
toward Waynesville. **Route 19** doglegs from Route 23 to Maggie Valley and Cherokee, North Carolina's main entrance to the national park.

Newfound Gap Road, also called **Route 441**, slices through the middle of Great Smoky Mountains National Park for 32 miles, until Gatlinburg, Tennessee. The park is almost equally divided, crosswise, between North Carolina and Tennessee.

Asheville Regional Airport in Asheville, North Carolina, is about   **AIR**
40 miles from the Great Smoky Mountains. For information on airlines, airport shuttle service and car rentals, see the "Transportation" section of Chapter Two.

FIVE

The Blue Ridge Parkway

This is about a journey, not a place.

It is a long, pure journey: 252 miles of mountains rippling blue against bold bright sky, water tumbling down granite walls in luscious torrents, white clouds shifting across deep green valleys. There are no stop signs or traffic lights, no neon or billboards to sully the scenery, so high above the rest of the world.

The Blue Ridge Parkway, that soul-cleansing journey across mountain peaks, is in fact called a "highway in the sky," though highway is too harsh a name. The trip along this two-lane road is slow and soothing, full of forests and flowers and curves, and many tunnels blasted through the middle of mountains. There is also the constant rush of air, whether one is nearing a rocky summit or snaking along famous Linn Cove Viaduct, an elevated S-curve around a mountain that gives the sensation of flying.

Actually, the Blue Ridge Parkway is 469 miles long, though only 252 of those miles are in North Carolina. The rest are in Virginia, where the parkway starts. Milepost zero is a mountain pass called Rockfish Gap in Virginia's Shenandoah National Park. From here, the parkway bends southwest, crossing the North Carolina line 217 miles later at Cumberland Knob, an outpost west of Mount Airy. The road keeps heading southwest, first through gently rolling farmland, then along the humpback mountains of North Carolina's High Country and its resort areas of Blowing Rock, Boone and Linville. The parkway passes by Asheville before finishing at Great Smoky Mountains National Park. A more perfect finale cannot be imagined.

More than 20 million people take the Blue Ridge Parkway every year. Despite its popularity and closeness to resort areas, the parkway seems far from civilization, as both the road and the strips of land on either side are a national park. Unfortunately, the strips are too narrow and development has crept in on portions of the parkway, mainly in Virginia. In North Carolina, you can drive a hundred miles and see a home or two, but you will never see a fast-food chain.

Neither will you notice a gypsy moth, balsam woolly aphid or dogwood anthracnose, though you can occasionally see their destruction. The moth eats at oaks and maples and other low-elevation trees until they are ragged. The aphid strikes higher on the mountains, injecting fraser firs with a liquid that deprives them of water and nutrients. The fir holocaust is apparent on the highest ridges, where the beautiful giants lay slain, entombed in a white, woolly material.

The lovely dogwood tree is also under attack. The dogwood anthracnose has been around for decades, but only in the last few years has it gotten serious. Like so many human diseases, it has no cure, at least not yet. Neither have park officials found a way to fight the gypsy moth or woolly aphid, though they are constantly trying.

Despite human and natural predators, the parkway remains a splendorous backwoods journey, which is just how its creators intended it. In the mid-1930s, Virginia Senator Harry F. Byrd proposed a road linking the Shenandoah Valley with Great Smoky Mountains National Park. It would trace the rim of the Blue Ridge and several other mountain ranges for nearly 500 miles and it would be paved—not a simple job considering the harsh, vertical terrain. Mountain folk, accustomed to riding on bumpy dirt roads that shut down in winter, scoffed at the idea of a "hard road" through the mountains.

But President Franklin Delano Roosevelt liked the idea, having just driven on Shenandoah's Skyline Drive, where he enjoyed the scenery immensely. More importantly, it would give hundreds of post-Depression workers a job. He helped sell the idea to Congress, and Virginia and North Carolina purchased the land for the road. The parkway was placed under the control of the National Park Service and the Bureau of Public Roads.

It would be several years before short spans were built—and fifty years before the journey was complete. In 1987, long after FDR had died, the Blue Ridge Parkway was finally made whole with the Linn Cove Viaduct, the section around Grandfather Mountain.

Today, you can get on the parkway and not have the drive interrupted even once. But of course that's not what the Blue Ridge Parkway is all about, for sprinkled along its squiggly length are dozens of stopovers, places to catch a dazzling view or picnic by a stream, to explore century-old log cabins or sit at a coffee shop and hear farmers talk about putting up hay. Here, at constantly cool altitudes of 3000 to 6000 feet, are galleries where you can buy exquisite mountain art and crafts, and sprawling parks where you can fish, hike or pitch a tent and sleep close to the stars, emboldened by mountain darkness.

Along the Blue Ridge journey the scenery is forever changing, from dark to light and then dark again, from brilliantly clear to hauntingly hazy, from remote stretches of pastureland to deep woods to crowded portions peopled by sightseers in RVs.

Blossoms decorate the parkway nearly all year. Dandelions open as early as February and mask the roadsides until June. Dwarf iris, buttercups and mayapples come along in March, and then there are Indian paintbrushes and golden groundsels. The blooming of the dogwoods and mountain laurel in April and May and the rhododendrons in June is nearly celestial, as entire mountains shimmer in pink and white and yellow.

The parkway is wonderful right before and after a rain. When a storm nears, there is cool, blunt stillness, and blue darkness painting the sky. Afterward mist rises from the road, sun glints off wet leaves, animals emerge from the forest—the musky smell of renewal. During a storm, however, it is best to pull off the parkway, lest one miscalculate the sharp angle of a mountain curve.

Even on the coldest days, when the rain turns to snow and there are scant flowers, the Blue Ridge journey is both eerie and invigorating. You can drive next to waterfalls suspended by the icy breath of winter, and revel in the skeletal silhouettes of trees.

SIGHTS

Winter does shut down some parts of the road, so it's best to call ahead before setting out. Most parkway facilities are closed from November through April. For information, contact the **National Park Service**. ~ 400 BB&T Building, Asheville, NC 28801; 704-298-0398, 704-271-4779, emergencies 800-727-5928.

You can also get information at any of the visitors centers, including the one at **Cumberland Knob**, the parkway's first stopover after you cross from Virginia into North Carolina. Distances on the parkway are measured by mileposts, those little concrete markers with black numbers on the side of the road. Heading into North Carolina, the numbers get bigger. ~ Milepost 217.9.

Cumberland Knob is also the historical beginning of the Blue Ridge Parkway, the first section built back in the 1930s, 12.7 miles of lonesome road with a big view. The picnic area and hiking trails here are compliments of the Civilian Conservation Corps. The visitors center can supply all sorts of literature on the park, including excellent maps, blooming schedules and hiking trail guides. There's also a bookstore where you can pick up a copy of the *Blue Ridge Parkway Guide* by former park ranger and naturalist, William G. Lord. The thorough, two-volume guide lists every stop on the 469-mile-long parkway, delving deep into the history, flora and fauna of the mountains.

After Cumberland Knob the parkway wends southwest through North Carolina quiet country, north of the High Country and west of the Piedmont, a nowheresville where valleys run deep and long, and cows graze in pastures framed in split-log fences, crooked and weathered. It doesn't take long to get used to the parkway; who wouldn't enjoy driving through a seemingly endless Eden, pausing only to gaze at something extraordinarily beautiful, even historic?

There are motorists who, strangely, pull off at overlooks and historical markers and never roll down their car windows, preferring to take their views and history from the air conditioned, music-flooded comfort of their car. The Blue Ridge is not something to be experienced with the radio playing, nor should it be done hurriedly. The speed limit is 45 miles per hour, less on hairpin curves, though a slower pace allows better vistas. Commercial vehicles are

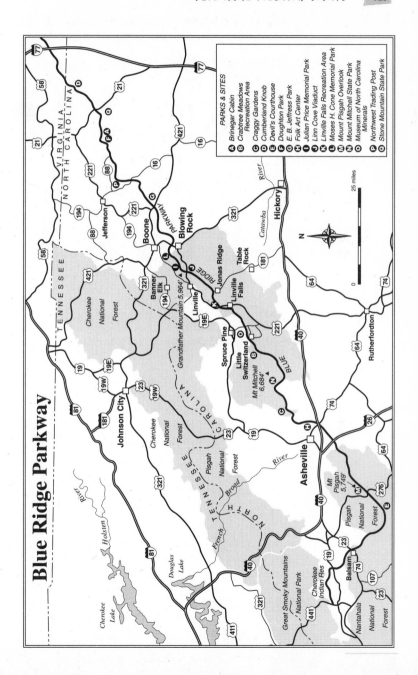

Blue Ridge Parkway

PARKS & SITES

- Ⓐ Brinegar Cabin
- Ⓑ Crabtree Meadows Recreation Area
- Ⓒ Craggy Gardens
- Ⓓ Cumberland Knob
- Ⓔ Devil's Courthouse
- Ⓕ Doughton Park
- Ⓖ E. B. Jeffress Park
- Ⓗ Folk Art Center
- Ⓘ Julian Price Memorial Park
- Ⓙ Linn Cove Viaduct
- Ⓚ Linville Falls Recreation Area
- Ⓛ Moses H. Cone Memorial Park
- Ⓜ Mount Pisgah Overlook
- Ⓝ Mount Mitchell State Park
- Ⓞ Museum of North Carolina Minerals
- Ⓟ Northwest Trading Post
- Ⓠ Stone Mountain State Park

banned from the parkway but tour buses and RVs aren't, so if you find your view blocked by one, pull over at the next scenic stop—there's one around nearly every corner. Many scenic overlooks offer a single picnic table where you can dine in peace while listening to the rush of a stream or the buzz of bumblebees. The stopovers I describe below are just a sampling of the sights you'll encounter traveling from northeast to southwest along the parkway in North Carolina.

Definitely don't miss **Stone Mountain Overlook**, where you can gaze across a valley to the granite Piedmont mountain, only 500 to 600 feet high, which in summer looks like it has a serious bald spot. In winter when the trees go naked, the baldness is rampant. A lonely picnic table, engraved with years of graffiti, invites solitary dining. ~ Milepost 232.5.

Three miles later, **Devil's Garden** is another distant view to a rocky crevice between two Piedmont hills. Best that you are not at the garden itself, as rattlesnakes and copperheads make their homes among the arid granite ledges. ~ Milepost 235.7.

Brinegar Cabin is where mountaineer Martin Brinegar and his wife, Caroline, lived in the late 1800s. Martin built the crude wood house with twin stone chimneys and the teeny springhouse down by the creek. Caroline wove on a loom, raised pole beans and gourds, and kept the place free of snakes, using rocks and sticks to subdue the rattlers and copperheads that slithered onto her turf. The cabin is normally locked, but you can peek in and see Caroline's loom. On some summer weekends there are weaving demonstrations and other pioneer happenings at the cabin. On a nearby marker is a picture of the somber-looking Brinegars, who now rest in a cemetery just off the parkway. ~ Milepost 238.5.

Pull over at Milepost 264.4 for a look at **The Lump**. Actually there are two lumps, a big one and a little one right next to it, a pair of nubby hills poking up from carpets of crisp forest. The sky seems bluer and the forest greener up here, which is why people have been finding this spot for hundreds of years—first the Cherokee, then farmers and fox hunters, and finally millions of visitors, all drinking in a big Blue Ridge view. ~ Milepost 264.4.

Keep driving southwest through sparse farm country, with sun-blistered split-rail fence trailing along the road and rhododendrons gushing from the roadside like fountains of color. There are lots of places to stop and catch your breath, then have it taken away again by some fantastic view. The mileposts keep getting higher and so does the ear-popping terrain, until you near Milepost 300 and the parkway changes. There are more cars and RVs, more exits, more homes and backyards littered with toys and swingsets within plain view of the parkway.

This is the heart of the High Country and its longtime mountain resort towns of Blowing Rock, Boone and Linville. Here, too, is famous Grandfather Mountain, a mountain with an old-man profile and a mile-high swinging bridge that dangles in the cool, treacherous mountain air. Over the next few miles, exits will direct you into these pretty, popular areas with their exclusive country clubs, old-time mountain attractions and ski resorts. You can spend a few hours or a few weeks around here, taking the parkway in measured doses while enjoying local sights.

One parkway sight that's nearly always thronged with people is **Moses H. Cone Memorial Park.** The focus is **Flat Top Manor,** a handsome whitewashed house whose rocker-lined porch faces pleated valleys and meadows and shimmering, fir-lined Bass Lake. Both the manor and compelling mountain scenes belonged to Moses H. Cone, who, in the late 1800s came from Tennessee and, with his brother, Caesar, started making blue jeans. North Carolina was a perfect place for manufacturing denim, having miles of cotton fields and railroad lines, and plenty of warehouse space as well. They built a mill in Greensboro and Moses Cone became known as "The Denim King." He soon trained his sights on the nearby Blue Ridge, bought 3600 acres of land, and began customizing his estate. He built three lakes and stocked them with trout and bass. He planted more than 75 varieties of apples. He carved 25 miles of carriage trails, and he created the 20-room Flat Top Manor. Then he died in 1908, leaving his wife, Bertha, to enjoy his Eden for the next 39 years. ~ Mileposts 292 to 295.

Today, the manor sells a stellar selection of Appalachian art and crafts, and has a small exhibit of farm tools, loom and spinning wheel, and other necessities of the Cones' era. After browsing, most folks find a chair on the porch and take in the lovely panoramic views.

The setting at **Price Lake** is equally as powerful, though different. Instead of far-reaching hills and valleys, there is the hypnotic blueness of the lake, silhouettes of elms and rhododendron reflecting along its edges, vibrantly colored mallard ducks skimming its

UNIQUE BLUE RIDGE PARKWAY EXPERIENCES

- Feel like you're flying as you drive along **Linn Cove Viaduct,** an S-curve around Grandfather Mountain. *page 128*
- Go to **Craggy Gardens** between mid-June and early July and witness an entire mountain smothered in pinkish purple. *page 130*
- Check into **Pisgah Inn** and check out the sensational, 5000-foot-high view from your cozy room. *page 131*
- Drive to the top of **Mount Mitchell** at sunset and watch surrounding mountains turn purple and orange. *page 135*

surface. From the surrounding forest comes intense birdsong, and butterflies floating against dusky sky. ~ Milepost 296.7.

Within a few miles comes the most famous curve on the parkway, the S-shaped **Linn Cove Viaduct** around Grandfather Mountain, a driving experience often compared to riding on air. Look up after the viaduct at the cliffs of exposed granite, with great evergreens sprouting like twigs, and you will feel absolutely elfish in proportion. ~ Milepost 304.4.

Pull over at Milepost 306.6 and you'll know why Grandfather Mountain was given this name. From the **Grandfather Mountain Overlook** his gnarly profile stands out; you can see the old man lying on his back, bushy eyebrows and goatee in full view. In winter, when the leaves fall away from the ridgeline trees, his features are sharper, his eyes more sunken and deeper in slumber. ~ Milepost 306.6.

The same folks you saw at Grandfather Mountain will stop at **Linville Falls**, one of the most popular and spectacular sights along the parkway. More like an angry torrent than a breezy cascade, the falls rush through Linville Gorge, its granite walls wet and worn by water and topped by vigorously growing trees. It takes some effort to get there, though. Three trails go to the falls: a 1-mile round-trip to the Upper Falls, where there's a short set of cascades down a 12-foot drop; a 1.5-mile round-trip to the Lower Falls, a forceful 60-foot gush down granite; and a 2-mile round-trip trek to Erwin's View, where you can see all the falls. In other words, the farther you hike, the better the view. ~ Milepost 316.3.

HIDDEN ► The easiest, shortest walk to the falls is, appropriately, from the town of **Linville Falls**. ~ Exit the parkway at Milepost 317.5 and follow Route 221 south about a mile. Ask around town; most anyone can direct you to the trail.

By the time you reach Milepost 325 or so, you can see apple orchards cascading down the mountainsides. If it's May, there will be pinkish-white blossoms coloring the trees and perfuming the air. Pull over at **Heffner Gap** and look down at the plaited orchards filling the landscape. ~ Milepost 326.

You can still see some orchards at the **Table Rock Overlook**, but in the far South Carolina distance there's the sharp flatness of Table Rock Mountain, its granite crown glinting above a sea of verdant forest. ~ Milepost 329.7.

The **Museum of North Carolina Minerals** is a pleasant enough place, offering a brief overview of the state's mining industry and gem finds. But if you're really into rocks, go to the extensive Colburn Gem and Mineral Museum in Asheville, a short drive from the parkway (see Chapter Two). ~ Milepost 331.

Further along the parkway, a spur road veers off the parkway and right into **Little Switzerland**, a pin-size town of the quaintest

Linn Cove Viaduct

The viaduct is 1243 feet long, 35 feet wide and shaped like an S. From underneath it looks like a giant conveyer belt that's not moving. On top, its smooth concrete surface is open to the skies, and driving the viaduct feels a little like flying. The squeamish do best to keep their eyes on the road, instead of the nothingness all around.

On one side of the road there is Grandfather Mountain, the reason for Linn Cove Viaduct. When road engineers are confronted by a mountain, they typically dynamite through it, erasing forests and ancient trees, nests of animals, even entire ecosystems. When Blue Ridge Parkway creators arrived at Grandfather Mountain, they went around him.

Linn Cove Viaduct conforms to Grandfather Mountain, obeying his every curve, dip and rise. Seven vertical piers support the roadbed, which weighs 7650 tons and is held together by wire cables and epoxy glue. The roadbed has 153 sections, no two alike, that were cast a mile away and assembled on site like a jigsaw puzzle.

There is nothing like Linn Cove Viaduct anywhere else in the world, and thus some have suggested its engineering genius is of da Vincian proportions. On a wall of the **Linn Cove Duct Visitors Center** hang many awards for the road's design, including a 1984 Presidential Award. ~ Milepost 304.4. The viaduct was completed in 1987, nearly 50 years after the Blue Ridge Parkway was begun, and was part of the final link of the 469-mile scenic road. A ceremony was held beneath the bushy brows and slumbering eyes of Grandfather Mountain.

At the visitors center you can browse among the construction exhibits and a bookstore, then take a paved trail (open to wheelchair visitors) that runs beneath the viaduct. If the road's magnitude and the surrounding blue mist of the woods inspire you, head off on one of the longer, unpaved trails up Grandfather Mountain.

order, with A-frame chalets etched into the mountain and open to hillsides and valleys in every direction. For more on visiting this lovely place, see Chapter Six. ~ Milepost 334.

By now you are deep in the Black Mountain range, presided over by Mount Mitchell, loftiest peak east of the Mississippi, its crown measuring in at 6684 feet. From 4821 feet at **Mount Mitchell Overlook**, you can look up at the forested rise. ~ Milepost 349.9.

The parkway is at its highest, 6053 feet, on Richland Balsam, though the mountain actually goes up to 6410 feet.

Farther down the parkway, if you exit at Route 128 into **Mount Mitchell State Park**, you can drive up the mountain. ~ Milepost 355.4.

"Miracle on the Mountain" is how a sign describes the blossoming of the Catawba rhododendrons at **Craggy Gardens**. Until you come face to face with an entire mountain clothed in pinkish purple, it is indeed impossible to imagine. The "miracle" happens between mid-June and early July, preceded by another show—spring wildflowers and fruit bearers opening in unison, mayapples, blackberries and violets, toothworts, mountain ash and wild crabapples, creating a technicolor display among the rocky summits. There is a visitors center here, a picnic area and trails among the gardens. ~ Milepost 363.4 to 369.6.

Keep south on the parkway and you will arrive at what George Vanderbilt called "the most beautiful land in the world." The turn-of-the-century tycoon didn't make empty exclamations; he spent millions of dollars buying and protecting the land, eventually acquiring 125,000 acres that included Mount Pisgah. At **Mount Pisgah Overlook** you'll see the massive mountain, 5749 feet high and named after the smaller peak on Jordan's Dead Sea. ~ Milepost 407.4. But it's the surrounding scenery—far-reaching forests, cloud-tipped summits, the closeness of the sky—that makes people not want to leave. If you're struck by the same feeling, consider staying at **Pisgah Inn**. ~ Milepost 408.6. Or try the **Mount Pisgah Campground**. ~ Milepost 408.8. You will not be disappointed.

After Pisgah the parkway wends west toward its terminus in western North Carolina. These last 60 miles are some of the quietest, least-crowded moments, and it is good to get out of the car and savor being alone. Look 1000 feet down at **Cherry Cove Overlook** onto black cherry groves. In early summer they fill the cove with white blossoms; by July, their dark amber fruit pops out and birds descend in droves. ~ Milepost 415.7.

At **Devil's Courthouse** you can walk up the barren granite bluff and into its cave, where the devil is said to hold court. Spruce and balsam forests climb up to the courthouse, but there is little life at the top, for the wind is too wicked to allow it. ~ Milepost 422.4.

Pull over at **Haywood-Jackson Overlook** and look across the Great Balsam Range—or what's left of it. The balsam woolly aphid, a wingless insect with a ravenous appetite for the sap of fraser firs, or she-balsams, has felled many of the great firs of Great Balsam Range. The trees lay, defeated, in abject heaps. You can see them also atop Mount Mitchell, and other high spruce-fir forests along the parkway. And so as the voracious woolly aphid, an invader from Europe, is fed, the native spruce-fir moss spider slowly starves, having fewer and fewer spruces and firs to feed on. The teensy-weensy spider, about the size of a pencil point, may soon be extinct. ~ Milepost 431.

Farther down the parkway, there's **Locust Gap**, named for black locust trees. ~ Milepost 433.3. **Licklog Gap** is named for the cows that used to gather there to lick the salt logs. ~ Milepost 435.7. There are **apple orchards** across Richland Creek. ~ Milepost 444.6. The **cross** on Mount Lynn Lowery lights up at night. This 60-foot cross serves as a memorial to Lynn Lowery, who died in 1962 of leukemia at the age of 15. ~ Milepost 445.2.

More overlooks, more tunnels, more gaps—including **Big Witch Gap** and its witchy story—await along the parkway. ~ Milepost 461.6. Then there is the end, **Oconaluftee River Bridge**. ~ Milepost 469. There is, however, no remorse at this journey's end, for if you cross the bridge you will be in the cool, sheltered depths of Great Smoky Mountains National Park.

LODGING

Only two lodges provide accommodations on the parkway in North Carolina and, not surprisingly, you often have to book months ahead to get a room.

Just off the parkway, dozens of hotels, motels and inns, many open year-round, can be found in picturesque cities and towns such as Asheville, Little Switzerland, Blowing Rock and Boone. For more on these, see Chapters Two, Four and Six.

The 24 rooms of **Bluffs Lodge** are basic and clean, but the views from 3700 feet are incredible. The location at Doughton Park means there are lots of activities: hiking, fishing and campfire parties. The coffee shop here serves good food. Closed November through April. ~ Doughton Park, Milepost 241.1; 910-372-4499, 910-982-2988. MODERATE.

Larger and higher up, **Pisgah Inn** has 50 rooms and a fireplace suite, all with sensational, 5000-foot-high panoramas. Some of the rooms were remodeled in 1994 with new carpets, bedspreads and draperies, and are wheelchair accessible. All the rooms have televisions, and VCR and video rentals are available. Closed early November through early April. ~ Located at the Mount Pisgah recreation area, Milepost 408.6; 704-235-8228, fax 704-648-9719. MODERATE TO DELUXE.

DINING

There are three places serving good, hot, home cooking along the Blue Ridge Parkway in North Carolina. Some of the waitresses have been around for ages.

At **Bluffs Lodge Coffee Shop** you get BLTs, barbecue and lots of Southern talk. ~ Doughton Park, Milepost 241.1; 910-372-4744.

A similar place is **Crabtree Meadows Restaurant**. The waitresses wear pinafores, keep the coffee cups filled and pile the bacon high for impending orders. They'll serve you soup from a can or, for a bit more change, from a homemade batch in the crockpot. Dinner's a bit more substantial, and breakfast brings eggs and grits, cornmeal cakes and country ham. Closed November through April. ~ Crabtree Meadows, Milepost 339.5; 704-675-4236. BUDGET.

The Pisgah Inn actually offers two dining choices: a coffee shop with simple breakfasts and burgers, and a dining room with full-course fare like rainbow trout, steak and fried chicken. There are daily specials, too. Closed mid-November through early April. ~ Mount Pisgah recreation area, Milepost 408.6; 704-235-8228, fax 704-648-9719. MODERATE.

SHOPPING   Few people equate great shopping with national parks, but the arts and crafts at the **Parkway Craft Center** (Moses H. Cone Memorial Park, Milepost 294; 704-295-7938) and **Folk Art Center** (Milepost 382, near Asheville; 704-298-7928) are some of the finest in the Carolinas. More than 600 artists from the southern Appalachians contribute singular, beautiful works, with price tags ranging from cheap to steep—though most people spend more than they planned. Wavy clocks, delicate stone and painted jewelry, shiny goblets and platters, zany light-switch covers, white oak baskets, luxurious rugs and throws—everything is high quality and unusual.

The Parkway Craft Center is in a gracious, whitewashed, turn-of-the-century manor built by textile magnate Moses H. Cone. Entirely different but just as engaging, the Folk Art Center is a bi-level building looking like something Frank Lloyd Wright might have designed, with a deeply overhung roof and lots of glass letting in views of the forest. On many days you can watch artisans working just outside the building.

Elsewhere on the parkway, the **Northwest Trading Post** has jams and jellies (including some excellent elderberry jelly) made by local ladies, as well as bird feeders carved from mountain woods, quilts, cookbooks, cornbread and hushpuppy mixes, and homemade breads and pastries. ~ Located at Milepost 285.6, south of Doughton Park.

Books on the parkway, wildlife, wildflowers, the history of western North Carolina and other mountain-related topics are on sale at several stopovers, including **Cumberland Knob** (Milepost 217.5), **Doughton Park** (Milepost 241.1), the **Linn Cove Viaduct** (Milepost 304.4), **Museum of North Carolina Minerals** (Milepost 331), **Craggy Gardens** (Milepost 364.6) and **Mount Pisgah** (Milepost 408.6).

There are, of course, no nightclubs along the Blue Ridge Parkway, **NIGHTLIFE**
but there is usually a nighttime show. As the sun settles down behind the mountains, the blue ridges turn ripe plum and the granite
outcroppings are softened by shadows. Blackness eases into the
woods, like a bear slipping into his winter slumber. This is a good
time to stroll beside a stream or sit upon a summit and watch for
foxes, raccoons, bobcats, skunks and other nocturnal creatures
emerging from their daytime slumber.

If you'd rather not be alone, join one of the evening walks,
campfire talks or slide shows led by parkway rangers. They're usually held on weekends from June through October. ~ 704-298-0398.

Odd as it may seem, there are several parks within Blue Ridge **PARKS**
Parkway, all run by the National Park Service. Reached by spur
roads off the parkway, they range from several hundred acres to
several thousand and offer exceptional hiking, fishing, picnicking
and camping. Mount Mitchell State Park, a state-run park the runs
alongside the parkway, is home to the highest peak in the eastern
United States.

Parkway campgrounds are open May through October on a
first-come, first-served basis. Fees for all sites are $10 for two adults
and $2 per extra adult. Children 18 and younger camp for free. If
you dislike crowds, stay away in October and on summer and holiday weekends. September and summer weekdays are wonderful.

DOUGHTON PARK 🏃 🚣 A 6000-acre chunk of Blue Ridge forest,
coves, meadows and creeks, Doughton (pronounced DOW-ton) is
the largest park on the parkway. It was once called The Bluffs, out
of respect for big Bluff Mountain that splits the park nearly down
the middle, though now it is named for the late Robert Lee "Muley
Bob" Doughton, a North Carolina congressman and advocate for
the parkway (the lodge and restaurant here are still called The
Bluffs). If you go to Wildcat Rocks and take the well-worn path
past the bronze marker honoring Congressman Doughton, you'll
come to a bluff overlooking Basin Cove. The Cove is where folks
used to (and still do?) go hog huntin'. It's also where Martin Cau-
dill built his cabin, 1500 feet below the bluff, in 1895. Look straight
down and you'll see it. For fishing try for rainbow trout in Basin
Cove and Cove Creek. Facilities include restrooms, a coffee shop,
gas pumps, a lodge, a picnic area, a camp store and a souvenir shop.
~ Located between Mileposts 238.5 and 244.7; 910-372-8568.

▲ There are 110 tent sites and 26 trailer sites (no hookups),
each with fireplace and picnic table. Restrooms and drinking water
provided; no showers. ~ 910-372-8877.

E. B. JEFFRESS PARK 🏃 These 600 acres are a monument to a
man who helped found the parkway. E. B. Jeffress was chairman

of North Carolina's state highway commission in the 1930s when he worked to secure land throughout the area. His namesake park is low on facilities but long on lush forest. Walk the half-mile Cascades Nature Trail beneath spidery limbs of magnolia, birch and rhododendron, to where Falls Creek rushes down a rocky chute, and you will know why Jeffress liked it here. Facilities include picnic tables, restrooms and a self-guided nature trail. ~ Located at Milepost 271.9; 704-295-7591.

MOSES H. CONE MEMORIAL PARK Some of the prettiest Blue Ridge country sprawls across this former turn-of-the-century estate of textile magnate Moses H. Cone. Virgin forest of hemlock and yellow poplar, great stands of fraser fir, ridge-line meadows, valleys punctuated with the liquid blue of lakes, brilliant rhododendron and mountain laurel, and two mountains fill these 3500 acres of luscious landscape. Cone and his wife, Bertha, are buried on the side of Flat Top Mountain, not far from their 20-room manor that's now the Parkway Craft Center. Their 25 miles of carriage trails still carry horseback riders in summer, but are enjoyed even more by hikers. Bass Lake and Trout Lake, which Moses Cone built and stocked, still yield plenty of catches for parkway fishers. In summer, there are ranger-led nature walks as well as pioneer programs and demonstrations at the craft center. Facilities include restrooms, nature and hiking trails and horseback rides. ~ Located from Milepost 292 to 295; 704-295-7591.

JULIAN PRICE MEMORIAL PARK Julian Price liked his employees, so he bought them several thousand acres of prime mountain country. The land was actually meant as a company vacation retreat, though after buying up numerous parcels in the 1930s and early 1940s, Price subsequently died, and the employees of Jefferson Standard Life Insurance Company never got to enjoy their mountain nirvana. Today, anyone can enjoy these beautiful wilds, 4200 acres etched with poplar and chestnut and maple forest, and secret streams snaking through darkened hollows. Some mountain headwaters have been corralled to create 47-acre Price Lake, cushioned in dense forest with many butterflies and birds. Rent a rowboat or canoe and paddle onto the lake; the trout fishing is great. Facilities include picnic grounds, restrooms, numerous nature and hiking trails, and rowboat and canoe rentals. ~ Located between Mileposts 295.1 and 298; 704-295-7591.

▲ There are 129 tent sites and 68 trailer sites (no hookups), all with fireplaces and picnic tables. ~ 704-963-5911.

LINVILLE FALLS RECREATION AREA More than 60 picnic tables edge Linville River as you enter this 440-acre park and, incredibly, most are usually filled. People like it here; the woods are moist and mind-clearing, and there is water everywhere. Linville

Falls plunge through Linville Gorge, gushing and rushing through primeval forest and walls of granite. Several trails lead to various stages of the falls. The park comes compliments of John D. Rockefeller, Jr., though it is named for William Linville and his son, who were killed in their sleep by Cherokees as they camped beside the river. It was 1766, and the pair never got to the falls or gorge that now bear their name. Brook trout, brown trout and rainbow trout are common in state hatchery-supported Linville River. You can also try for trout in Camp Creek. Facilities include a visitors center with a bookstore, a picnic area, restrooms and hiking trails. ~ Located at Milepost 316.3; 704-765-1045.

▲ Fifty tent sites and 20 trailer sites come with fireplaces and picnic tables but no hookups. Ask for tent site number 15, so secluded that park rangers call it the "honeymoon suite." ~ 704-765-7818.

CRABTREE MEADOWS RECREATION AREA 🏃 A peaceful, rambling lawn of wildflowers runs into forest, and then there are mountains in the distance. If you come in May, you will see lady's slippers, columbines and crested dwarf iris garbed in glory. A month later, mountain laurel, rhododendrons, beard tongues and goatsbeards explode with color. In summer, there are naturalist shows at the amphitheater. As parkway parks go, Crabtree is not big, only 253 acres, but it is nearly always beautiful. Facilities include a coffee shop, a souvenir shop, restrooms, gas pumps, picnic areas and hiking and nature trails. ~ Located at Milepost 339.5; 704-765-6082.

▲ There are 71 tent sites and 22 trailer sites (no hookups) with fireplaces and picnic tables. ~ 704-675-5444.

MOUNT MITCHELL STATE PARK 🏃 Six Black Mountain peaks over 6000 feet high reside within the park, though one gets all the attention. Mount Mitchell is the highest mountain in the range and also in the eastern United States, rising 6684 feet above sea level. The main parking lot of the 1677-acre park is near Mount Mitchell's summit, and an observation tower is smack on top of the summit. Down on the Blue Ridge Parkway you may be comfortable in short sleeves, but up here it's sweater weather year-round. The clouds insert themselves into the parking lots and picnic areas, and the wind blows in brisk sheets. Snow flurries have been reported in July. The park stays open year-round, but winters can be brutal and snow can close the entrance road. Average snowfall is over 100 inches. In the summer, the sunshine is brilliant. Go at dusk and watch the surrounding mountains turn purple and orange as the sun bleeds down between the peaks. A more spectacular show cannot be had in these mountains. Facilities include observation tower, picnic tables, grills and shelters, hiking trails and a restaurant that is open

May through October. ~ Exit the Blue Ridge Parkway at Milepost 355.4 and take Route 128 up Mount Mitchell. It's about a five-mile drive to the parking lot; 704-675-4611.

A Nine primitive tent sites are open May through October on a first-come, first-served basis; $9 per site.

MOUNT PISGAH 🏃 Twice as high as its Biblical namesake near the Dead Sea in Jordan, North Carolina's Mount Pisgah soars 5721 feet above a resplendent sea of velvety green valleys and foothills. The parkway runs right by the mount, with places to stay and dine among forested wilds. Facilities include a picnic area, restrooms, a gas station, a camp store, an amphitheater and hiking trails. ~ Facilities are located between Milepost 407.8 and 408.8; 704-456-9530.

A There are 140 sites divided equally between tents and trailers, all with fireplaces and picnic tables (no hookups). ~ 704-235-9109.

▼▼▼▼▼▼▼▼▼▼▼▼▼▼
Outdoor Adventures

If it's golf or tennis you seek, you'll find them in the resort towns just a few miles off the parkway. See Chapters Two and Six for places to play.

SPORT-FISHING

The streams and lakes of the Blue Ridge Parkway are prime trout waters. You must have a North Carolina or Virginia fishing license to fish on the parkway, and must abide by various state and federal rules on bait, lures and flies. Different waters have different rules, so before you cast your line in, pick up a copy of the Blue Ridge Parkway's *Fishing Regulations and Opportunities* brochure from any visitors center.

There are many places to try your luck. For brook trout, try **Chestnut Creek**. ~ Milepost 215.2 to 217. If you're looking for brook and rainbow trout there a a couple of choices. One of these is at **Big Pine Creek**. ~ Milepost 221.5 to 225.5. Head down to **Little Glade Mill Pond**, near the site of an old turbine mill, for rainbow trout and bluegill. ~ Milepost 230. The other spot is **Meadow Fork Creek**. ~ Milepost 246 to 248.5. **Bass Lake** is the place for (what else?) smallmouth bass. ~ Milepost 293. For brown trout, try **Simms Creek**. ~ Milepost 296. Three types of trout—brown, brook and rainbow—can be found at **Price Lake**. ~ Milepost 297. You'll find more of the same at **Linville River**. ~ Milepost 317.

CANOEING

You can rent a canoe or rowboat at **Julian Price Memorial Park** and paddle out onto lovely Price Lake. ~ Milepost 295 to 299; 704-963-5911.

BIKING

For excellent bike-trail maps, contact the North Carolina Department of Transportation's Bicycle Program. ~ P.O. Box 25201, Raleigh, NC 27611; 919-733-2804.

Unfortunately, the Blue Ridge Parkway was not built with bicyclists in mind, as there is no bike lane. Still, it is ever-popular with cyclists, who wear helmets and kneepads and ride single file along the edge of the two-lane road. Reflectors or white lights are required—and necessary since there are 26 pitch-black tunnels to be taken, as well as frequent fog. A headlight is the safest bet.

Cycling is most enjoyable when there aren't a lot of automobiles, usually Monday through Thursday. Avoid holidays and all of May and October, when traffic is heaviest. Stay on paved roads or in parking areas; biking is prohibited on trails and boardwalks.

Several stretches of the parkway are steeper than they seem, and you may find yourself struggling to scale 1000 feet in just three miles. The parkway's helpful *Bicycling* brochure lists the "major uphills" and can be procured at any of the visitors centers. ~ 704-259-0701.

Portions of the parkway lie within the 700-mile-long Mountains-to-Sea bike route from Murphy in the western North Carolina mountains to Manteo on the Outer Banks. The strenuous **Sliding Rock** segment begins near the Great Smoky Mountains and lasts for 55 miles. It starts with a tough 12-mile climb to Richland Balsam, then slopes down and back up to Devil's Courthouse and its circle view into four states. Shining Rock Wilderness and Mount Pisgah are among the other scenic stops. There are numerous tunnels along this stretch, so use care when riding through their darkened lengths. ~ Where Route 23-74 intersects the parkway.

The 53-mile **Craggy Pinnacle** segment of the Mountains-to-Sea route picks up the parkway just south of Asheville. For 30 miles you climb up and across the Black Mountains, then descend into Buck Creek Gap, passing through several tunnels on the way. You can rest at Craggy Gardens, Mount Mitchell State Park or Crabtree Meadows. ~ Route 25.

Farther north and a favorite of bikers, the 52-mile **Brown Mountain Lights** segment has plenty of places to stop, including the Museum of North Carolina Minerals, Linville Falls and the Linville Gorge Wilderness Area. Most of the ride, which starts near Little Switzerland, is downhill.

Bike Rentals There are no bike rentals on the Blue Ridge Parkway, but there are a few in surrounding towns. For a list of places, see Chapters Two, Four and Six.

HIKING

Hikers can choose from more than 100 trails along the Blue Ridge Parkway. Some disappear into cool, dim Edenic forest, others rear up rocky ledges into wind and sun, and still stay near the water, wending along a lake, river or creek edge. A list of parkway trails and fliers on individual trails are available from any visitors center, or by calling 704-271-4779. All distances listed for hiking trails are one way unless otherwise noted.

Park brochures describe **Cumberland Knob Trail** (.5 mile) as an ideal lazy-day walk, great for little ones who need to burn some energy. The mostly paved path starts at the Cumberland Knob Visitors Center. ~ Milepost 217.5.

Several longer trails in Doughton Park are easy enough for flatlanders. **Bluff Mountain Trail** (7.5 miles) stays near the parkway on its trek from Brinegar Cabin to Basin Cove Overlook. **Fodder Stack Trail** (1 mile) tunnels through pine and hardwood forest, with wildflowers at your feet in spring and early summer. ~ Milepost 241.

Cinnamonbush, oaks and sourwood trees crowd the popular **Jumpin' Off Rocks Trail** (1 mile). The climax, of course, is a potentially perilous bluff thrust against a vault of blue sky. ~ Starts at Milepost 260.3.

The 25 miles of turn-of-the-century carriage trails at Moses H. Cone Memorial Park are perfect for hiking. One of the most enjoyable, **Bass Lake Trail** (1.7 miles) circles the picturesque lake.

A short walk to a big view, **Beacon Heights Trail** (.44 mile) delivers hikers to a granite point with a view of the Blue Ridge foothills and streams way down below. ~ The trailhead is at Milepost 305.2.

The long and winding **Tanawha Trail** (13.5 miles) curves around Grandfather Mountain, following the parkway for several miles. Among the highlights: shady glens of birch and beech trees, tunnels of mountain laurel and rhododendron, footbridges across racing creeks, and far-reaching views across the Piedmont. Most of the trek is quite easy. ~ Begins at Milepost 305.5 below Linn Cove Viaduct.

Within Mount Mitchell State Park, **Mount Mitchell Trail** (13 miles) is the one hard-core hikers use to climb the East's highest peak. The strenuous trek connects the tops of Black Mountain and Mount Mitchell. Make it a two-day venture: one to go down Black Mountain, a strenuous 3600 feet, and another for the arduous climb up Mount Mitchell. Spend the night at the base of Black Mountain at Black Mountain Campground, operated by Pisgah National Forest. (Fee is $10 per individual site, $40 for group campsites.) ~ 704-675-9355.

More in the mood for a mountain stroll? Head down easy **Balsam Trail** (.75 mile), a self-guided nature trail on Mount Mitchell. The trailhead is at the lower summit parking lot in Mount Mitchell State Park. ~ Exit at Route 128, Milepost 355.4.

If you take the **Richland Balsam Trail** (1.5 miles), you'll walk across the highest peak on the parkway, 6053 feet high. The easy-to-moderate, self-guided loop navigates the lush forest of fraser firs and red spruce across Richland Balsam. ~ Pick up the trailhead at Milepost 431.

The Blue Ridge Parkway runs for 252 miles through western North Carolina, connecting Cumberland Knob in the north with the Great Smoky Mountains in the south. **Route 40** comes over from Raleigh in the east, running through Winston-Salem before intersecting the parkway near Asheville. **Route 26** veers up from South Carolina and joins Route 40 in Asheville.

▼▼▼▼▼▼▼▼▼▼▼
Transportation

CAR

Asheville Regional Airport is about five miles from the Blue Ridge Parkway. Exit at Milepost 388.1 and get on Route 25 south. For information on airlines, airport shuttles and car rentals, see "Transportation" in Chapter Two.

AIR

SIX

The High Country

If you want to get high, go to northwest North Carolina. The land swells more boldly here than anywhere else in the South, with big, broad mountains reaching up past 6000 feet, their peaks dressed in firs. The air is cooler, the nights blacker, the mornings coated with clouds.

Millions of people go to the High Country every year, to ski down a mountain or hike up it, to fish or canoe rock-bound rivers, to attend various folksy-themed attractions or pick apples on a hillside. Others simply come for mental and spiritual renewal, to be among "the masters," as Thomas Wolfe called these mountains, "rimmed in life. . . . absolute unity in the midst of eternal change."

Hundreds of Blue Ridge and Black mountains are packed into this tiny, extreme northwest corner of North Carolina, heart of the Southern Highlands. Their sides glint with granite and quartzite, their summits merge with sky. Ancient rivers twist along their feet, liquid highways wending across several states. The New River commences in Blowing Rock and flows northward into West Virginia. Actually, it is not new at all but extremely old, the oldest river on the continent.

The Toe River cuts through the high ragged peaks of the southern High Country—from Roan Mountain and Winter Star to Grassy Ridge and 6684-foot Mount Mitchell, the tallest mountain east of the Mississippi. At Mount Mitchell, the Toe forms the headwaters of the Nolichucky River, which tumbles down through deep Nolichucky River Gorge. Whitewater rafters take Nolichucky for a serious ride on rapids.

Some of the mountains are etched into haunting shapes. The High Country's most famous shape, the old man of Grandfather Mountain, lies sleeping on his back, his bushy brows and goatee in full view. For centuries his profile has perplexed those who look upon the 5964-foot mountain, highest in the Blue Ridge. Today it is possible to see him up close, as the entire mountain is a tourist attraction.

Long before the old man was hosting tourists, he was home to the Cherokee. Along with smaller, sometimes unfriendly tribes such as the Yeatkins, Catawbas and Sauras, the Cherokees lived low on the mountains and across the valleys. They were skilled at fishing and hunting and enduring the raw winters of this high region.

When white pioneers began pushing up into the mountains around 1670, they deftly subdued the tribes, first with disease and whiskey, eventually by murder. A hundred years later, American Indians were gone from the High Country, having retreated westward into the Great Smoky Mountains. In the 1830s they would be driven even farther west, all the way to Oklahoma, herded like cattle in a holocaust called the "Trail of Tears."

With the Cherokee out of the way, though, white men didn't rush to the mountains. Mainly rugged hunters and trappers set up camps in the 1700s, collecting pelts for trade and trading stories with flatlanders about the brutal, mysterious mountains. Daniel Boone came to the High Country in 1760 and stayed for nine years, but he spread word of "high, far-seeing places." He helped bring German, Scotch-Irish and English settlers to the area along an old buffalo trail.

By the early 1800s, settlers were growing corn and other crops, raising chickens and cows, hunting and fishing, and spinning their own clothes on wooden wheels. They dug deep into the Appalachian earth and created a folksy culture rich in music and living well off the land. They carved and strung their own dulcimers and banjos, put up their own jams, jellies and apple butter, hunted hogs, turkey and deer, and aged their moonshine in the cool confines of fern grottoes.

In a few decades the mountaineer families had grown into communities with roads firm enough for wagons and stagecoaches. By the late 1800s, mining companies invaded the area looking for minerals and ore. Then came loggers, who skinned the mountains of their fabulous firs, chestnuts, pines and other virgin forests. The federal government more or less came to the rescue, and national forests put an end to the frenzied lumbering, though some forests are still aggressively logged today.

Tourism has lately taken hold of the region (the name High Country was invented by promoters, though it is admittedly a fine name), but the mountaineers' culture survives and there are still hidden destinations to discover. Not far from the modern and moneyed country clubs and new log home developments are weathered old farmsteads with their springhouses guarding the creek, and crude cabins with apple butter for sale, stacked high on washtubs. People in the High Country still till the land, pick their banjos on the front porch, and wake well before daylight to go hunting.

The High Country tour begins and ends with the old ways. In the south, the Toe River Valley is mountain wilderness except for a few hamlets like Little Switzerland, an alpine-style village that's minuscule in size but big on mountain views. In mineral-rich Spruce Pine, massive feldspar mines feed a commercial market, while visitors can forage for gemstones. At the head of the Toe River Valley, 6285-foot Roan Mountain explodes with Catawba rhododendrons each year in late June.

North of here is the heart of the High Country, with the resort towns of Linville, Banner Elk, Blowing Rock and Boone, and four ski resorts, including the highest ski slopes in the eastern United States. Dozens of fine restaurants, grand old inns, country club communities, exclusive boutiques and golf courses appeal to year-round visitors. This is also some of the hottest real estate in the Carolinas. Flat-landers have been buying property at such a furious pace that the average price of a mountain acre has quadrupled in five years.

Northward, the High Country relaxes again. The mountains relent into foothills and folded pasture, the meticulous country clubs melt into rambling farms and scat-tered rural towns. Three remote state parks offer outstanding backwoods hiking, canoeing and scenery. Up here is also the North Carolina start of the Blue Ridge Parkway (see Chapter Five).

Whether you seek the backwoods experience or one on a golf green, you can have it in the High Country. You can stay at a plush resort or check into an 1800s farmhouse. Ride the folksy Tweetsie Railroad, or join a week-long canoe trek into wooded mountain depths. Have a croissant and cappuccino at '90s coffeehouse, or grits and gravy at a '50s coffee shop.

If it's local color you want, go for the grits.

▼▼▼▼▼▼▼▼▼▼▼▼
Toe River Valley

The Toe River does not wind lazily. It flows urgently through the southern High Country, frothing beneath lofty mountains, their sides blanketed with hardwood forest and ankles covered in wildflower meadows. Where the Toe reaches 6684-foot Mount Mitchell, it forms the Nolichucky River, tumbling down through rock-lined Nolichucky River Gorge, one of the deepest gorges east of the Grand Canyon. Whitewater rafters like the Nolichucky; the rapids are Class III and IV (Class V is high-est) and there are plenty of boulders that get in the way.

Botanists like the Toe River Valley for its inordinately rich flora. Over the centuries, Europeans have come looking for exotic Appa-lachian species to decorate the formal gardens of France and Eng-land. Artisans, too, have found inspiration in the scenery, and to-day you will find their tiny glass-blowing, weaving and pottery studios tucked down side roads.

SIGHTS

Some of their creations end up in **Little Switzerland** (Route 226A), a pin-size resort village propped atop a mountain and backing up to the Blue Ridge Parkway. The views here are mind-cleansing. The mountains cascade in waves down from the village, and the air is scented with fir and spruce. A few dozen A-frame chalets have deep wood exteriors and fanciful eaves and doors, and are charmingly arranged along sloping roads. Vast green lawns run downhill, and there are signs welcoming you to someone's "haus." Right "in town" are a handful of shops all in a row.

In the winter, Little Switzerland shuts down, and only about two dozen people live there. Spring through fall, it's a wonderful stopover, with pretty, woodsy places to stay and eat.

About 16 miles northeast from here on the Blue Ridge Park-way, take the exit for Route 221 south. Follow it about a mile to

HIDDEN ▶   the town of **Linville Falls**, named for the formidable cascade through nearby Linville Gorge (for more on getting to the falls, see Chapter Five). The town is but an eyeblink, with a gas station that is either deserted or deluged with people heading to a low-key, old-time attraction called **Linville Caverns**. Open year-round, but closed weekdays from December through February. Admission. ~ Route 221, about three miles south of Linville Falls; 704-756-4171, 800-419-0540.

The caverns were found over a hundred years ago by two fishermen who followed a trout-gorged stream inside a mountain. They purportedly described the caverns as looking like "the arch of some grand old cathedral," though today some will think themselves in the belly of the *Alien* monster. Cavern walls are brown and gooey, with stalactites and stalagmites resembling a ribcage. The floors are sopping and slick, the passageways comfortable to skinny. The guide will tell you to take care as the group files along behind him for the 20-minute tour. Trout-filled streams still run through, though they are now stocked due to past overfishing. The trout are blind because they live in the dark. The caverns are lit for human visitors, though musky blackness hovers just beyond the spotlights.

After you've seen the caverns, backtrack on Route 221 to the Blue Ridge Parkway. Head 14 miles southwest on the parkway, until you reach the **Museum of North Carolina Minerals**. This museum contains the **Mitchell County Chamber of Commerce**, which can supply maps and information on the Toe River Valley, which lies due north of here. Take Route 226 north from the museum and plunge into backcountry, where there are no tourist attractions. ~ Milepost 331; 704-765-9483, 800-227-3912.

One of the first settlements you'll come to is **Spruce Pine**, a mountain hamlet of 2500 that produces half the nation's supply of feldspar. For those not up on their feldspar, it's a chalklike rock that's blasted out of the ground and ground into a powder. The powder goes into everything from house paint and dinner plates to false teeth and toilet bowls. ~ Route 226, just north of Route 19E.

Besides feldspar, Spruce Pine is also mined commercially for quartz and mica, though dozens of gems—including aquamarine, emeralds, garnets and sapphires—have been found here. On Topaz Street in downtown Spruce Pine, the **Gunter Building** is charcoal-colored and rock-studded, fashioned in the 1930s from biotite mica. The world's only biotite mica belt is, naturally, in the area. ~ Corner of Topaz Street and Upper Oak Avenue.

Keep on Route 226 north about three miles to Penland Road and turn left. Go about a mile on Penland Road and take a right

HIDDEN ▶   at the sign for **Penland School of Crafts**. The road squiggles up a hill to several wood buildings in the woods, which house the school started in 1929 by "Miss Lucy" Morgan. Miss Lucy, new in town, thought the local ladies needed a way to earn money. She lured in Edward Worst, a nationally famous weaver, and within a few years Worst's classes had students from as far away as California and Maine. Soon other artistic skills were added, including pewter "beating" and leather tooling, and the Penland School secured a national reputation. Today, it's one of the top glass-art centers in the country. ~ 704-765-2359.

The temperature inside Linville Caverns is always a cool 52° so bring along a jacket.

You can learn all about glass making and other arts and crafts at the Visitors Center, open daily except Monday from May through October. For the best Penland experience, join one of the guided tours of the school and artists' studios, offered Tuesday mornings and Thursday afternoons May through October. Reservations are necessary.

Back on Route 226, it's another nine miles or so to the town of **Bakersville**, county seat of Mitchell County. This pleasant little place at the foot of Roan Mountain is presided over by the **Mitchell County Courthouse**, built in 1907 in Neoclassical Revival style. ~ Corner North Mitchell Avenue and Crimson Laurel Way.

From here, you can drive straight up to Roan Mountain or go the long way through teeny country towns, passing upland meadows ensconced in wildflowers and the rushing Toe River, bundled in boulders and forest. Three miles west of Bakersville on Route 226, **Loafers Glory** is best known for its name, compliments of local womenfolk who thought their husbands lazed around the general store too much—at least that's the story.

◄ HIDDEN

No doubt the area's most disgruntled wife was Frankie Silver. You can see her former house about seven miles south of Route 80 in mite-size **Kona**, where she hacked her husband, Richard, to death with an ax as he snoozed near the fireplace (maybe he, too, was a loafer?). It was 1831, and only a few days before Christmas. She cut the body into pieces and tossed them in the roaring fire, but they didn't burn too well. Her in-laws found what was left of Richard in the hearth. Frankie went to prison, escaped, was caught and finally hung from a scaffold in 1833. Her last words, according to local lore, were a 60-line poem to Richard:

◄ HIDDEN

> ". . . . *There shall I meet that mournful face, Whose blood I spilled upon this place: With flaming eyes to me he'll say: 'Why did you take my life away?'"*

You can't go inside the **Silver Homestead** to have a look at where the dirty deed occurred, but you can gaze at the outside of the two-story, poplar- and oak-log cabin, built around the turn of the eighteenth century. Therein lived seven generations of Silvers. ~ Route 80, just south of the Kona Baptist Church.

Back north on Route 80, you can wend through more hillside hamlets if you head west on Route 197. There's **Red Hill** and **Tipton**

Hill and then **Relief**, named for Hart's Relief, a medicinal potion sold here in the 1870s, and an ever-popular one it was, not in the least because it was mostly grain alcohol. A few miles past Relief is **Poplar**, a popular place for launching canoes and rafts into the Toe River for a downstream run.

At Red Hill, you can work your way north on Route 226, then northwest on Route 261 to the Toe River Valley's most compelling sight. **Roan Mountain** ripples down in waves, spreading half its deep green mass in North Carolina and half in Tennessee.

HIDDEN ▶

The mountain is most famous for its splendorous gardens of Catawba rhododendron. Around late June they explode with color, and Roan's 6285-foot summit is cloaked with purple and pink and scarlet. The gardens are vast, some 600 acres, the largest wild rhododendron patch in the world. Fraser firs cascade down from the gardens, and then there are rambling meadows. To walk among the rhododendron, park at the Rhododendron Gardens area along Route 261, just before the North Carolina–Tennessee line.

Across the state line in the town of Roan Mountain, Tennessee, is the entrance to Roan Mountain State Park. The gardens are not in the park, though many people think they are.

Back down Roan, follow Route 19E south to Route 194 south, then wind lazily through foothills and tall summits all the way to

HIDDEN ▶

Pineola. Pronounced "Pine-O-la," it's a mountain patch that has barely changed over the years, unlike touristy Linville, Boone and Blowing Rock just down the road. Pineola has nurseries that sell mountain exotics and also do a big Christmas tree business. It has a scattering of log homes that blend into the woods, a countrified

HIDDEN ▶

coffee shop, and the **Pineola Inn and Country Store**. ~ Route 221 at Route 181; 704-733-2008.

HIDDEN ▶

You can spend the night at the inn or stop in the store for a few minutes and browse the **Indian Artifacts Museum** tucked in back. Thousands of relics dating back thousands of years line the glass

---

✔ CHECK THESE OUT—UNIQUE SIGHTS

- Watch artists fashioning ethereal works of glass at **Penland School of Crafts**, one of the country's top glass art schools. *page 144*
- Walk the mile-high bridge strung between two treacherous cliffs at **Grandfather Mountain**, and feel the cold air pushing at your feet. *page 151*
- Take a stroll around the engaging town of **Blowing Rock**, sprinkled with galleries, cafes and turn-of-the-century manses. *page 156*
- Join thousands who stop by annually to see the **frescoes of St. Mary's Church**, Ben Long IV's richly painted works inside a tiny 1902 chapel. *page 165*

cases. Most of the pipes, ax heads, spearheads and beautiful arrow-heads are from the collection of Tom Dellinger, who spent several decades with his eye to the ground.

There's also a display of Confederate currency at the museum. But perhaps most intriguing is the seven-foot-long diamondback rattlesnake skin, 26 rattles and double fangs intact. You can buy it (unless someone else has by now) for several hundred dollars.

Accommodations are scarce in this secluded mountain region. The place of choice is absolutely the **Switzerland Inn**, whose chalet-style lodge nestles in the crest of a mountain, with long green lawns dotted with perfect triangles of fir and spruce trees. A warm, homey place, it has a wood-paneled lobby with a fireplace and vast windows looking across the valleys. Guest rooms in the main lodge are simple but spacious, with boxy balconies facing into the woods or offering sensational mountain panoramas. Several cottages offer more space and privacy. There's a good restaurant and a swimming pool. Rates include full breakfast. Closed early November through late April. ~ Route 226A, at Blue Ridge Parkway Milepost 334 in Little Switzerland; 704-765-2153, fax 704-765-0049. MODERATE TO DELUXE.

LODGING

Four miles north of the Blue Ridge Parkway, **Richmond Inn** is in Spruce Pine but offers the ambiance of the countryside. From the rambling flagstone terrace of this gabled house you can look down upon the North Toe River valley ringed with mountains. Seven guest rooms, all with private baths, are done in antiques and cozy accoutrements, and some have poster beds. Rates include a large country breakfast. ~ 101 Pine Avenue, Spruce Pine; phone/fax 704-765-6993. BUDGET TO MODERATE.

The basic, motel-style accommodations of **Pineola Inn** appeal mainly to cross-country skiers, fishers and anyone else looking for the low-key life. Rooms are modern, with cable TV, phones, air conditioning and heating, and several have newish kitchenettes. There's a cross-country ski shop here, and trails that start right outside the door. ~ Route 221 at Route 181, Pineola; 704-733-4979. BUDGET.

The mountaintop **Chalet Restaurant** at Switzerland Inn is a big, wood-paneled dining room with picture windows that drink in miles of mountain views. The fare is hearty, as befitting a woodsy mountain setting, with blackened prime rib, chicken pot pie and mountain trout headlining the dinner menu. Sandwiches, soups and salads are offered as well for lunch, and there's a full-course breakfast. Beer, wine and setups available. ~ Route 226A, Little Switzerland; 704-765-2153. MODERATE.

DINING

Around the corner in "downtown" Little Switzerland, the **Switzerland Cafe and General Store** has nearly a dozen tables and a dozen wonderful desserts, from fudgy, peanut-buttery tortes and cakes to dazzling fruit pies. Espresso and cappuccino, herbal teas, good soups (curried cauliflower, Italian vegetable) and sandwiches are also served at this cheery place. ~ Route 226A, Little Switzerland; 704-765-5289. BUDGET TO MODERATE.

If you hang around Pineola very long, folks will tell you to stop at the **Mountain Top Restaurant** and have yourself a Bill Burger. That would be one medium-rare beef patty with melted cheese, lettuce, tomato, onion, pickles, ham, bacon and chili. It's named for Mountain Top owner Bill Hoilman, whose past life included being a Navy chef. If the Bill Burger sounds a little like rocket fuel, go for a regular burger or the fresh mountain trout, barbecue platters, or food bar with fried chicken, mashed potatoes and mountain-grown vegetables. The breakfasts of steak and eggs, grits and gravy are gargantuan. The atmosphere is pure mountain coffee shop: linoleum on the floors, pink ruffles on the windows, pickup trucks parked outside. Closed Sunday. ~ Route 181, about a half mile from Route 221; 704-733-6375. BUDGET.

SHOPPING   Beautiful Appalachian crafts, impeccably coaxed or carved into shape by local artisans, can be found throughout the valley. One of the most famous glass-art schools, the Penland School of Crafts, is here, and there are many little-known studios where you can buy directly from artisans.

The most formal shopping is in Little Switzerland, a teeny village with a handful of shops, most closed from November through early April.

Two galleries carry exclusive items as well as homespun gifts. **The Trillium Gallery** has delicate glass works, gemstone jewelry and pottery. ~ Route 226A; 704-765-0024. **Hearthside Handmades** is for those with country leanings. ~ Route 226A; 704-765-7982.

Little Switzerland also possesses the best bookstore in the High Country. The volumes at **Grassy Mountain Book Shop** are ancient to new, and they're stacked floor-to-ceiling, musty and dusty but easy to browse. You can pick up original works by Carl Sandburg, Thomas Wolfe and other North Carolina authors, many well priced. And if you don't find what you want, the owners will search far and wide to get it. ~ Route 226A; 704-765-9070.

Next door, **Switzerland General Store** also has great browsing. Baskets, pottery, local-made jams and jellies, and gourmet coffee are among the merchandise. ~ Route 226A; 704-765-5289.

For five generations, the Woody Family has been making chairs in the woods along Grassy Creek. Author Muriel Earley Sheppard, in her 1935 book *Cabins in the Laurel*, wrote that they "turn chairs on a lathe run by a water wheel when they are not grinding meal. . . ." Today, the chairs at **Woody's Chair Shop** are still made without nails or glue and hand-rubbed to a handsome finish. ~

HIDDEN ►

The Mystery of the Brown Mountain Lights

The lights are blue and red, or purple and green. They quiver, halo-like above the mountain, or shine clear and steady like a planet's beacon. They are the ghosts of American Indians, or UFO invaders.

No two tales of the Brown Mountain Lights are the same. In fact, many people who go to Jonas Ridge and search the sky above Brown Mountain see nothing but silvery stars embedded in black night. The boulders and guardrails at Jonas Ridge, near Pineola, have been etched by disbelievers: "These lights are a fake. Go home." And: "Been here ten times. Never saw nothing."

The federal government believed enough to send weather and geological researchers to investigate. *National Geographic* magazine dispatched photographers in search of the lights. So far, nothing conclusive.

But talk to some locals and they will tell you the lights really do exist. Spring and fall nights, when the sky is crisp clear, are best, they say. Hikers, cross-country skiers and coon hunters all claim to have seen the lights. Sometimes they move across the mountaintops; other times they hover in bands of color like a rainbow.

Some old-timers say they've never witnessed the enigma after hundreds of looks at the mountain. They blame reported sightings on too much moonshine and other mind-warping substances, and human hunger for a good story. At the Mountain Top Restaurant, a few miles north of Jonas Ridge, the lights are a frequent topic at the Liar's Table, where locals come to shoot the breeze and tell questionable stories.

If you can't resist a look yourself, go to **Jonas Ridge Overlook** in Pisgah National Forest, along Route 181 about five miles south of Route 221. Arrive at sunset with a bottle of wine and watch the orange globe slink down around the mountaintops. When it's good and dark, gaze across to horseshoe-shaped Brown Mountain, 2600 feet high. Even if you don't see the lights, at least you got a great sunset.

Dale Road, just off Route 226, about two miles north of the Blue Ridge Parkway; 704-765-9277.

In downtown Spruce Pine, **Twisted Laurel Gallery** showcases the works of more than 140 area artisans. There is, of course, plenty of blown glass, stained glass and pottery, but you'll also find fiber art, clocks, paintings and sculpture. Limited hours during winter. ~ 333 Locust Avenue, Spruce Pine; 704-765-1562.

HIDDEN ▶   The **Craft Shop at Penland School** showcases exquisite blown glass, jewelry, pottery and other works by crafters at this nationally acclaimed school. Closed from November through April. ~ Off Route 226, about three miles north of Spruce Pine; 704-765-2359.

Some Penland crafters and other area artisans welcome visitors to their studios, usually by appointment. These places are often wonderfully hidden down dirt roads or sequestered in woods, and make for an enjoyable afternoon drive. A list of studios is available from the **Mitchell County Chamber of Commerce**. ~ In the Museum of North Carolina Minerals, Blue Ridge Parkway Milepost 331; 704-765-9483, 800-227-3912. You can also call the **Toe River Arts Council**. ~ 704-682-7215.

HIDDEN ▶   Of the many mountain nurseries in the valley, **Gardens of the Blue Ridge** is most renowned. Tucked down a washboard road at the 4000-foot elevation, it flourishes with Appalachian ferns, shrubs, trees and wildflowers, including many rare and exotic species. You can wander among the snow trilliums, butterfly weeds, spiderworts and other beauties that fill these six acres. Owners Robyn and Eddie Fletcher will tell you what grows best "back home," and will even ship your selections for you. ~ Pittman's Gap Road, off Route 181, near Blue Ridge Parkway Milepost 312.5, Pineola; 704-733-2417.

NIGHTLIFE   You can't buy cocktails in the valley, which puts a damper on nightlife, to say the least. Best to have dinner and curl up with a good book.

BEACHES & PARKS   **LINVILLE GORGE WILDERNESS** 🏃 ⚓ A deep, ragged crease in the mountains, Linville Gorge offers some of the most formidable terrain in the East. Stretching for 18 miles and bounded by Jonas Ridge and Linville Mountain, the gorge was carved by Linville River, which drops a fast 2000 feet into the valley. The protected wilderness spans nearly 11,000 acres, and appeals most to serious hikers, fishers and backcountry campers. Fishing for trout is excellent in the Linville River. Facilities include an information center, hiking trails, and scenic overlooks. ~ The major access roads are Routes 181 and 183 south of Pineola, and Route 221 northeast of the town of Linville Falls. The information center is along Kistler Memorial Highway, off Route 183, about three-fourths of a mile south of Linville Falls; 704-652-2144.

▲ Backcountry camping only; permit (no fee) required for weekends and holidays from May through October.

There is money in Linville. You can tell by the vast log homes set discreetly along the mountain, the country clubs with championship golf

Linville & Banner Elk

courses and private airstrips, by the expensive condominiums and villas dotting the valleys. Many are occupied only during summer months, revealing just how wealthy their owners are.

Old Linville money is the reason **Grandfather Mountain** became such a splendid attraction. Hugh Morton, whose family has lived in the area for two centuries, created a private park on this famed mount whose summit looks like an old man in repose. An accomplished outdoor photographer and avid environmentalist, Morton's mountain was declared an International Biosphere Reserve by the United Nations and is protected by the Nature Conservancy. Grandfather is the highest mountain in the Blue Ridge and one of the most treacherous. A sign near the top warns that "you are on the most rugged mountain in Eastern America. Be careful!" It seems a valid statement as you wind up the mountain road whose sides drop down into rocky chasms. Admission. ~ Route 221, just north of Linville; 704-733-4337, 800-468-7325.

SIGHTS

Since it opened in the late 1940s, millions have come to enjoy this compelling place, and families especially like it. There are hiking trails, scenic overlooks, picnic areas and a **Nature Museum** with keen displays on Appalachian flora, fauna and minerals. There's also a **Wildlife Habitat** with deer, river otters, black bears, eagles and cougars. Near the summit is the **Visitors Center** and the famed **Mile-High Swinging Bridge**. Walk out onto the suspension bridge, look way down into a ravine, and feel the cold air pushing at your feet. The feeling is a little like riding a wave.

Except for the bridge and hiking trails, Grandfather Mountain attractions are wheelchair accessible. Unfortunately, you can't see the old man's profile unless you climb up **Linville Bluffs**. Anyway, by far the best view of his shaggy brows and pointed nose is down on Route 105 south of Boone.

A little north of Grandfather Mountain, Route 184 winds up through mountains to the Carolinas' two biggest ski resorts. The first is 5300-foot **Sugar Mountain**. The road into Sugar is lined with woods and chalets rented to skiers in the winter, home to many flatlanders in the summer. Right next to Sugar Mountain, the atrocity protruding from Little Sugar Mountain's summit is a condominium tower that caused local outrage (much inaccurately vented at the ski resort, which had nothing to do with the development) and prompted the Ridge Line Law, which prevents any more mountaintop graffiti.

Four miles north on Route 184, the attractive village of **Banner Elk** is enveloped in mountains. There's a bit of a college scene here, as well as exclusivity. Pricey boutiques and restaurants blend with casual cafes and a coffeehouse. This is where skiers from Sugar Mountain and **Beech Mountain**, a couple of miles up Route 184, like to hang out. At 5505 feet, Beech has the highest downhill action in the eastern United States. (For more on skiing, see "Outdoor Adventures" at the end of this chapter.) For information on local sights, visit the **Banner Elk Chamber of Commerce**. ~ Route 184, High Country Square, Banner Elk; 704-898-5605, 800-972-2183. Another place to go for information is the **Beech Mountain Chamber of Commerce**. ~ 403-A Beech Mountain Parkway, Beech Mountain; 704-387-9283, 800-468-5506.

LODGING

The **Eseeola Lodge** is a venerable place whose longtime devotees return every summer to indulge in beautiful surroundings and sumptuous food and service. The entry of stone and bark-covered logs looks like something from the brothers Grimm; the rooms are light and airy, with pretty wallpapers and wool carpets, and colorful quilts for keeping warm on cool nights. In the evenings guests stroll across the green lawns decorated with firs and maples and arched footbridges, and there is much laughter in the expansive dining room. A swimming pool, golf course, tennis courts and croquet are among the possibilities offered. Breakfast and dinner (coat and tie required for men) are included in the price tag. Closed late October through mid-May. ~ Route 221, Linville; 704-733-4311, 800-742-6717, fax 704-733-3227. ULTRA-DELUXE.

About five minutes from the slopes of Ski Beech, **Archers Mountain Inn** is set along the mountainside overlooking the Elk River Valley. The inn has two buildings with 15 rooms and suites,

---

✔ CHECK THESE OUT—UNIQUE LODGING

- *Budget to moderate:* Tuck yourself into a four-poster bed at the gabled **Richmond Inn**. *page 147*
- *Moderate to deluxe:* Prepare for extraordinary mountain views when you check into the chalet-style **Switzerland Inn**. *page 147*
- *Deluxe to ultra-deluxe:* Sequester yourself at **Bluestone Lodge**, a handsome hideaway buried deep in the woods on a mountain. *page 158*
- *Ultra-deluxe:* Enter a cultured world of fine linens, rambling gardens and talk of tee times at **Eseeola Lodge**. *page 152*

Budget: under $60   Moderate: $60–$100   Deluxe: $100–$130   Ultra-deluxe: over $130

all with wood-burning fireplaces and most with smashing views of the valley. The presidential suite, which is warmed by a massive stone fireplace, features a king-sized canopy bed, a jacuzzi tub and a private porch where you can gaze out on the mountains. Enormous country breakfasts are included. ~ Route 184, Banner Elk; phone/fax 704-898-9004. MODERATE TO ULTRA-DELUXE.

Right next to Ski Beech, **The Inns of Beech Mountain** are the only lodges within walking distance of downhill skiing. The **Beech Alpen Inn** is the main lodge; there's a fine restaurant here and spacious, simple rooms with carpeting, window boxes and views all the way to the Tennessee mountains. Four rooms have gas fireplaces. Next door and slightly more rustic, **Top of the Beech** has a living room with vaulted ceiling and a big fireplace. Continental breakfast is set out every morning. The rates fall into the budget range on summer and fall weekdays. Special two-night budget rates are available in the winter. ~ Route 184, Beech Mountain; 704-387-2252, fax 704-387-2229. MODERATE TO DELUXE.

Villas, condominiums and homes can be rented through local lodging services. For information, call **Sugar Mountain**. ~ 704-898-4521. Or try **Ski Beech**. ~ 704-387-2011, 800-438-2093.

With reservations you can dine at **The Eseeola Lodge**, enjoying what some say is the High Country's finest cuisine. Offerings tend to change nightly, but you might find chilled Carolina peaches-and-cream soup or jumbo lump crab meat with sweet mango slaw and smoked tomato rémoulade on the four-course, prix-fixe menu. Among the possible entrées: pan-seared venison with lingonberry pear relish and black currant ginger sauce, and hickory-smoked pork tenderloin with apple, pecan and orange stuffing with balsamic vinegar and port wine sauce. Most diners are staying at the lodge—and have been here many times before. Coat and tie are required for men. Closed late October through mid-May. ~ Route 221, Linville; 704-733-4311. ULTRA-DELUXE.

DINING

The culinary experience at **Louisiana Purchase** is less formal but equally gratifying. Nawlins'-style through and through, the classy dining room is flooded with spicy smells and painted with murals of the Crescent City. Seafood leads the menu, but there's also rack of lamb, chicken and grilled duck breast. Try the pan-fried trout filet with slivered almonds, baby shrimp and Amaretto butter. The hefty, cork-bound wine list has garnered awards from the *Wine Spectator*. If you'd rather just have wine, the *cuvinét* loft upstairs features more than 15 wines by the glass. Dinner only. ~ Route 184, Banner Elk; 704-898-5656. DELUXE.

After a long day of skiing, go to **The Daily Grind** and have steamy coffee, latte or espresso. This small nook with the flavor of a soda fountain also serves sandwiches, muffins, bagels and desserts, and in winter great chilis and soups. In the summer, find a stool outside and stare up at the mountains. Closed Sunday. ~ Route 194, Banner Elk; 704-898-8686. BUDGET.

HIDDEN ▶   Banner Elk's elegant bistro is **Morels**. It's a single room colored intensely green, with linen-topped tables threatening to crowd too close, but a menu that's vastly imaginative. Spicy grilled duck sausage smothered with pan-roasted peppers, onions, potatoes, rosemary and goat cheese might start the meal. For the main course, there may be honey and tamari-seared Norwegian salmon, roast garlic–stuffed tenderloin with cabernet sauce and Gorgonzola butter, or crispy sautéed sweetbreads with mustard caper sauce. It's dinner only, and reservations are usually necessary. Closed Monday. ~ Off Route 194, down the side street beside B.J.'s Resortwear; 704-898-6866. DELUXE.

Before and after skiing, everyone goes to **Fred's General Mercantile** for coffee and muffins, sandwiches and soups—but mostly just to hang out. Fred's is most definitely an institution, a modern, airy, New American–style general store frequented by people of some affluence. On summer Sunday mornings, Floridians and other flatlanders flock to Fred's patio to sip coffee and read their hometown newspapers. ~ Beech Mountain Parkway, Beech Mountain; 704-387-4838. BUDGET.

SHOPPING   There's not much in Linville, but Banner Elk does have a few shops worth browsing.

J.W. Tweed's offers the oxford look for men (button-down shirts, leather and nubuck jackets, designer socks and belts) and a casual but elegant look for women (linen, khakis, dresses and jewelry). In the back of the store, **Eve's Leaves** is for women who need ethereal, lacy lingerie. ~ Route 184, Banner Elk; 704-898-6166.

At the ever-popular **Fred's General Mercantile**, you can buy a paintbrush or ski jacket as easily as a ham sandwich. Cookbooks, fireplace tools, kitchenry, keys made—it's all here. ~ Beech Mountain Parkway, Beech Mountain; 704-387-4838.

NIGHTLIFE   The hottest High Country nightlife is in Banner Elk—but don't expect Bourbon Street; what you're more likely to find is a cozy place to listen to music.

Louisiana Purchase is actually as close to Bourbon Street as you could want. A classy Cajun eatery, it also serves up live jazz on weekends. ~ Route 184, Banner Elk; 704-963-5087.

Folk and R&B bands play most weekends at **The Daily Grind** coffeehouse and Thursday happy hours pull in a college crowd. Cover. ~ Route 184, Banner Elk; 704-898-8686.

Rascals is the aprés ski spot. Margaritas, beer, barbecue and soup ("determined by the weather and chef's mood"), plus occasional live blues, reggae and rock-and-roll at this uproarious pub.

Cover on band nights. ~ Beech Mountain Parkway, Beech Mountain; 704-387-2266.

Olde World Grill & Still is first a steakhouse but also a bar, especially in winter, when there's live jazz and country music in the lounge. Cover. ~ 403-A Beech Mountain Parkway, Beech Mountain; 704-387-2620.

▼▼▼▼▼▼▼▼▼▼▼▼▼

Boone & Blowing Rock Area

To many people, Boone and Blowing Rock *are* the High Country, for here is the hub of vacationing: fine inns and eateries, golf greens and forays to the farmers' market, folksy attractions and outlet shopping. Only a few miles separate the two towns, though they could not be more different.

SIGHTS

Boone is the area's commercial pulse. Routes 105 and 221-321 around Boone are thronged with fast-food eateries and other suburban sprawl, so concentrate on historic **downtown**, centered around Depot and King streets. You'll see buildings of red brick housing mercantile stores and eateries, and the handsome **Appalachian State University**. Nearly 12,000 students create a vigorous campus atmosphere and fuel a pub and grub scene that's considerable for a town that allows only beer and wine to be sold. ~ Along Route 321 and Rivers Street, Boone; 704-262-2179.

Long before there was a campus here there was a log and stone cabin that belonged to Daniel Boone. For a look back at Boone (the man and the town), stop by the **Appalachian Cultural Museum**. The museum explores Boone history from its geologic development to the present. There are American Indian artifacts, exhibits of clothing, furnishings, farm tools, quilts and music from the 1700s, and more. Closed Monday. Admission. ~ University Hall, off Route 321, at Appalachian State University; 704-262-3117.

The **Daniel Boone Native Gardens** are filled with Boone details: the iron entrance gates were forged by Daniel Boone VI, the logs in the reflecting pool cabin came from a grand nephew's home, and a big cherry tree arrived in the area with Boone's brother—making it more than two centuries old. Take a leisurely walk through the woods and the rockery. Fall is the best time to be here, when the trees rage orange and yellow and purple. Some areas are not wheelchair accessible. Closed November through April. Admission. ~ Off Route 321-421, Boone; 704-264-6390.

More on Boone, and the whole High Country area, is available south of the gardens at **High Country Host**. This visitors center can also provide information and referrals for buying a Boone summer home—a popular venture these days. ~ Route 221-321; 704-264-1299, 800-438-7500.

No doubt Boone's popularity has caused interest in neighboring **Valle Crucis**, translated "Valley of the Cross." Situated a few minutes northwest of Boone along Routes 1112 and 194, the town sits where two mountain streams intersect into a cross. Only ten years ago Valle Crucis was a quiet mountain hamlet; now it's a mainly quiet mountain hamlet that's very "in." People hurrying to buy land here have driven prices way up. Secluded bed and breakfasts are booked months ahead. And the old-time general store is now a stop on the tourist track.

The frontiersman Daniel Boone lived in the High Country during the 1760s and helped bring skilled, hard-working settlers to the area.

That would be **Mast General Store** where Charles Kuralt opined that you could "find the soul of the South." Built in 1883 and going stronger than ever, Mast seems to carry everything under the sun, hornets' nests and rosebud salve included. It's the potent nostalgia, though, that draws visitors far and wide. ~ Route 194, Valle Crucis; 704-963-6511.

Southeast of Boone, the **Tweetsie Railroad** train is nearly as old as Mast General Store, though it's hard to imagine Charles Kuralt waxing nostalgic over it. In fact, I can't imagine even taking this "trip back to the Old West" lest children were involved, pesky, relentless children begging for a ride. In that case, swallow hard and cough up the admission ($13 for children, $15 for adults), then ride the train around the mountain on its three-mile run, stopping for a cancan dance and a street shoot-out. There's also a petting zoo and kiddie rides. Closed November through late May. Admission. ~ Route 321; 704-264-9061, 800-526-5740.

Not as pricey but still frightfully hokey, **Mystery Hill** is a house where gravity is supposedly askew. Objects seem to fall upward, and so does your body. Magic mirrors, glowing rocks and other funhouse oddities thrill the kids. Admission. ~ Route 221-321 southeast of Boone; 704-264-2792.

A little farther south on Route 221-321 is **Blowing Rock**, both the town and the namesake rock. The town is an engaging mountain village whose fieldstone and wood buildings rest beneath high-reaching maple and poplar trees. Turn-of-the-century manses are parked along steep crooked lanes, and mountains float in the distance. Flowers pour from window boxes along Main Street, galleries, boutiques and cafes are tucked beneath bright awnings, and park benches invite rest.

If something seems to be missing, it is. The commercial chaos of greater Boone is gone, but it did not stay away easily. Residents of this 1889 town have long fought the trappings of development—successfully. It didn't hurt that they had money.

Despite the town's apparent wealth, prices for lodging and dining are not prohibitive. Well-tended motels and lodges, neighborhood eateries and affordable shops are plentiful. And one of the most rewarding activities—walking around town—is free. Take a stroll down **Laurel Lane** to the **Annie Cannon Memorial Gardens** and **Broyhill Park**, small city parks with vigorous, immaculate plantings.

Right on Main Street, **Blowing Rock Chamber of Commerce** has information on lodging, dining and sights. Closed Sunday. ~ Beside the Town Park; 704-295-7851.

As for the biggest local sight, **The Blowing Rock**, this you will pay to see. The rock is 4000 feet high and pokes out from a mountain. It looks a bit like the head of a monster with its jaw cocked. Wind barrels up from the gorge below, and if you toss something off the rock it may get blown right back at you—hence the name. A pathway, with steps that make it impossible for wheelchairs, winds out to a platform. From here you can look over at the rock, and across mist-shrouded mountains. From January through mid-March you can only visit on weekends, weather permitting. Admission. ~ Route 321, two miles south of town; 704-295-7111.

South from the rock, Route 321 snakes down into the Piedmont, running alongside sheer cliffs with neck-craning views across the Blue Ridge. Roadside pit stops offer "hillbilly dolls," strange statuary and big jars of honey with the comb still in it.

Near Ski Hawksnest resort, **Smoketree Lodge** is a good buy. For budget prices, you get an oversized motel room with furnished kitchenette and cable TV, an indoor pool, whirlpool, dry sauna, weight room and complimentary morning coffee. Need a bottle of wine or groceries? The lodge will kindly dispatch someone for you. ~ Route 105, 11 miles south of Boone; 704-963-6505, 800-843-5581, fax 704-963-7815. MODERATE.

LODGING

Set up on an out-of-the-way hill with mountains all around, **Willow Valley Resort** is a timeshare that rents rooms by the night. Accommodations are in chalets, log cabins or condominiums, each with one, two or three bedrooms with carpeting, a kitchen and either a fireplace or a wood-burning stove. None have air conditioning. Bring your racket and clubs; there are tennis courts and a 9-hole, par-3 golf course, as well as an outdoor heated swimming pool. ~ Off Route 105, three miles south of Boone; 704-963-6551, fax 704-963-6812. MODERATE TO DELUXE.

If you prefer the exclusive confines of a country club, there are **Hound Ears Club** and the **Inn at Yonahlossee Resort & Club**. Every imaginable pursuit—golf, tennis, horseback riding, swimming, hiking—is found at Hound Ears. It offers rooms and suites in a lodge, as well as chalet, villa and home rentals. ~ Off Route 105, south of Boone; 704-963-4321, fax 704-963-8030. Yonahlossee has no golf course but it devotes 130 of its 300 acres to horseback riding, and runs one of the premier equestrian centers in North Carolina. Manicured golf greens fill the valleys, and mountain scenes fill the skies. Chalets, villas and great big homes are parked on the hillsides. Yonahlossee has cottages and villas. Winter brings moderate room rates. ~ Shulls Mill Road, off Route 105, south of Boone; 704-963-6400, 800-962-1986, fax 704-963-7902. ULTRA-DELUXE.

High Country Inn is perfect for ski digs. Cozy, rustic and kitschy (water wheel out front, ducks and trout in the concrete pond), it has 120 spacious rooms with carpeting, some with gas fireplaces. If you're traveling with several people or just want space to spread out, consider the three-bedroom, ultra-deluxe-priced cabin. It's equipped with a a full kitchen, washer and dryer, gas grill and a jacuzzi out on the porch. The inn has an indoor/outdoor pool, hot tub and sauna, laundry facility, and a restaurant serving good German food. ~ Route 105, Boone; 704-264-1000, 800-334-5605, fax 704-262-0073. MODERATE.

The name **Broyhill Inn & Conference Center** suggests a grand place (Broyhill is the furniture conglomerate), but expect something like an upscale dorm house, which makes sense, as the inn is on the campus of Appalachian State University and caters to college functions. The two-story rambling brick buildings offer some mountain views and 76 rooms and seven suites, all currently undergoing renovation. ~ 96 Bodenheimer Drive, Boone; 704-262-2204, 800-951-6048, fax 704-262-2946. MODERATE.

HIDDEN ▶   **Bluestone Lodge** is like a secret hideaway, tucked deeply in the woods, up a rutted gravel road that twists and turns around boulders and fir trees. Florida-raised owner Merry Lee Benore chose the spot because "I don't think you come to the mountains to sit on the main road." She also liked the swimming pool and the handsome wood homes on seven acres. There are two suites, two bedrooms and three cabins, all tastefully and uniquely decorated. The suites are wonderful with their whirlpool tubs, kitchens, stone fireplaces and wood stoves. Benore's breakfasts are something to look forward to: giant French toast stuffed with apricot preserves and cream cheese, Florida grapefruit halves lathered with butter, brown sugar and cinnamon then broiled. ~ Off Route 1112, about a mile from Route 105, Valle Crucis; 704-963-5177. DELUXE TO ULTRA-DELUXE.

HIDDEN ▶   If cocooning on a nineteenth-century Southern farmstead sounds appealing, stay at **Mast Farm Inn**. The front porch is lined with old rockers and a screen door that clunks. The sweeping grounds are sprinkled with a dozen rustic buildings, all on the National Register of Historic Places, including a smokehouse, springhouse, apple house and 1810 cabin where three generations of Masts lived. The main house was built in 1885 with 13 bedrooms and one bath, though today each of the nine guest rooms has a private bath. You can also spend the night in the old loom house, blacksmith shop, a granary or woodwork shop, all adorned in warm,

Beulah's
Bake Shop

There's nothing to jump-start a cold mountain morning like a cup of java and something hot from the oven at **Beulah's Bake Shop**. The teeny takeout is owned by Beulah Howell, who was born six and a half miles away on Linville Road and never left. Locals hope she never leaves, because the woman really knows how to bake. ~ Route 105, Boone; 704-265-2253.

Open the front door of the shop and you are overwhelmed by the sight and smells of buttery pound cake, pastries, muffins and breads studded with brilliant fresh fruit, cinnamon rolls drizzled with icing, lemon cakes, fudge cakes and all sorts of rolls, cookies and brownies.

Beulah's nephew, Johnny Pearson, assists with the selling. The conversation goes something like this:

> Beulah: "Now you give her the biggest, sweetest piece o' that blackberry bread you can find."

> Johnny: "Well I was gonna give her some of them cinnamon rolls and peanut-butter cookies."

> Beulah: "Well for gosh sakes, give her some of all of it!"

Folks are known to leave Beulah's full before they've bought anything. Don't leave without a piece of cheesy coffee cake oozing blackberry jam or some sourdough raisin cinnamon rolls—both easily stashed in a ski locker or hiker's backpack and retrieved for late afternoon munchies.

unassuming fashion. Innkeepers Wanda Hinshaw and Ray Hinshaw Phillip make the whole experience enjoyable, from the oatmeal cookies offered at check-in to the enormous but healthy breakfasts. Closed Thanksgiving week and during the month of March. ~ Route 1112, three miles from Route 105, Valle Crucis; 704-963-5857, 888-963-5857, fax 704-963-6404. DELUXE TO ULTRA-DELUXE.

HIDDEN ▶ The imposing white 1911 farmhouse that's **Inn at the Taylor House** has been impeccably restored. The living and dining rooms have been painted a sunny yellow, the guest rooms plushly carpeted, their beds piled with down comforters and soft pillows. All have private baths. The separate red cottage is a place to retreat to for a while; there's a sunken tub, a fireplace, satellite TV and stereo system with CD player. What more do you need? The inn even features a massage therapist. Closed mid-December to mid-April. ~ Route 194, around the corner from Mast General Store, Valle Crucis; 704-963-5581, fax 704-963-5818. DELUXE TO ULTRA-DELUXE.

A mansion in the mountains, **Westglow Spa** is the plushest place to stay in the High Country. The 1916 former home of artist Elliott Daingerfield, it's a European-style fitness and pampering spa with every imaginable extravagance, from body wraps, aromatherapies and facials to the Victorian rooms filled with antiques and objets d'art. The antebellum hilltop estate is so beautiful that the shoulder of the road has been worn away by people pulling over to stare. Inside, the white-columned manse is much as Daingerfield left it; his 2500-volume library (some books have personal notes to his daughters) and his furnishings are here, as well as his famous painting of St. Mary's of the Hills. Two-night minimum stay on Friday and Saturday nights. Rates include all meals, spa treatments and morning hikes. ~ Route 221, three miles south of Blowing Rock; 704-295-4463, 800-562-0807, fax 704-295-5115. ULTRA-DELUXE.

Right in Blowing Rock, **The Inn at Ragged Garden** is located in a one-acre setting of roses and rhododendrons, with massive trees and a walled garden. Among the eight floral-themed rooms is Monet's Garden, painted a rich burgundy and appointed with a handcrafted king-sized bed, fireplace, jacuzzi, tub, and private balcony. In the attic, the Rock Garden Garret spreads across two rooms and is highlighted by a fountain and an interesting rock garden. Other features are skylights, a jacuzzi tub, window seats and English pine antiques. ~ 203 Sunset Drive, just off Main Street; 704-295-9703. MODERATE TO ULTRA-DELUXE

Mountainaire Inn & Log Cabins will put you up for reasonable rates. The motor court with cabins is a little noisy but as neat as can be. Front doors are adorned with country wreaths, room interiors are carpeted and have cable TV and air conditioning. The cabins have fireplaces. ~ North Main Street, Blowing Rock; 704-295-7991. MODERATE.

Across from The Blowing Rock, grand old **Green Park Inn** is located at the 4300-foot elevation along the Eastern Continental Divide. Built in 1882, its long guest list includes presidents and other history makers. The sprawling, green-shuttered white manse looks down into the valleys and across mountains, and is flanked by rolling golf greens. Most of the 85 simple rooms have terrific views. There's a lounge and fine restaurant here. ~ Route 321, two miles south of downtown Blowing Rock; phone/fax 704-295-3141, 800-852-2462. DELUXE TO ULTRA-DELUXE.

DINING

Cottonwood Grill and Microbrewery, across from Appalachian State University, is where students sequester themselves for lunch, late afternoons and evenings—anytime, really. The menu's part Mexican and part New American, with grilled chicken tortillas, tofu burritos, grilled or blackened salmon, and spinach enchiladas leading the charge. The homebrewed beer is a local favorite, and there's also wine. ~ Route 321, Boone; 704-264-7111. BUDGET TO MODERATE.

As its name suggests, **Red Onion Cafe** is no run-of-the-mill place. It's a colorful, animated, smoke-free eatery with healthful offerings. The black-bean pesto lasagna and grilled chicken and fontina pizza are exceptional, and so are the Asian-baked salmon and veggie sandwich (spinach, cucumbers, cream cheese, tomatoes, carrots and sprouts on crunchy oat bread). ~ 227 Hardin Street, Boone; 704-264-5470. BUDGET TO MODERATE.

◄ HIDDEN

Any place with its own cookbook should be good, and the 1800s **Mast Farm Inn** definitely is. Dining is family style in two cozy rooms, with oil lamps and quilts on the walls, and wood tables for two or more. The menu changes nightly but there are always lots of vegetables fresh from the farm's garden, and there is a strong emphasis on healthy cooking. ("We do not have a deep-fat fryer in our kitchen!" proclaims the menu.) Sautéed mountain trout, vegetable lasagna, chicken and dumplings, moussaka, corn pudding, country ham and spinach enchiladas are dinner possibilities. Reservations required. ~ Route 1112, Valle Crucis; 704-963-5857. MODERATE.

◄ HIDDEN

The **lunch counter** in back of Mast General Store makes a great tofu sandwich, and the homemade soups are chunky and extra rich. Plenty of other deli sandwiches are offered, all generously adorned with meats and cheese and tasting extra fresh. You can eat inside or out on the porch. ~ Route 194, Valle Crucis; 704-963-6511. BUDGET.

Blowing Rock village has several prime lunch stops. **Cheeseburgers in Paradise,** owned by folks from Florida, offers both regular-size patties and gorge-yourself, one-pound burgers. The jalapeño cheese is great on top. Quesadillas, nachos, and BLTs are also on the menu—but then Jimmy Buffett never sang about those. Grab a table outside under the umbrellas. ~ North Main Street, Blowing Rock; 704-295-4858. BUDGET.

The 1918 building that's **Cosmic Coffee House** was first a hardware store and then a filling station. Now it's New Agey, a high-ceilinged space with eclectic artwork, teeny tables and hip young employees (no Southern drawl here). They make their quiches and muffins early in the mornings, and whip up an array of java choices when they're ordered. ~ South Main Street, Blowing Rock; 704-295-4762. BUDGET.

Blowing Rock Café is where folks call each by their first names, and the owners ask, "Are you OK today?" Go for lunch and order the homemade soup and sandwich—you won't be able to finish them. Pasta, seafood and chicken dishes are offered at lunch and dinner, and there's good breakfasts, too. ~ Sunset Drive, off Main Street; 704-295-9474. BUDGET.

HIDDEN ►

In an old, atmospheric log cabin hidden in the most unlikely of places—behind a Food Lion grocery—the **Best Cellar** entreats with exquisite dishes such as rack of lamb, stuffed veal chops, marinated fresh tuna and roast duckling. The homebaked breads and array of nightly vegetables, including baked acorn squash and stuffed zucchini, are superb. Stone arches and stained glass parade around the inside, and three fireplaces offer warmth. Open only on the weekend in winter. Dinner only. ~ Off Route 321, Blowing Rock; 704-295-3466. MODERATE TO DELUXE.

Woodlands Barbecue & Pickin' Parlor is the local favorite for barbecue. Upstairs and down are picnic tables, their pine tops worn to a perfect patina by years of elbows and beer mugs. Order pork or beef (sliced or chopped), chicken or turkey (smoked whole out

✔ **CHECK THESE OUT—UNIQUE DINING**

- *Budget:* Join the *après*-ski crowd for soup and sandwiches at **Fred's General Mercantile**, a hip place to hang out. *page 154*
- *Moderate:* Pass your plate for sautéed mountain trout, fresh vegetables and other tasty family-style fare at **Mast Farm Inn**. *page 161*
- *Deluxe:* Slip into an elegant bistro booth at **Morels** and enjoy vastly imaginative cuisine. *page 154*
- *Ultra-deluxe:* Take time to savor Southern flights of fancy at **Eseeola Lodge**, a coat-and-tie eatery with many longtime fans. *page 153*

Budget: under $9   Moderate: $9–$16   Deluxe: $16–$24   Ultra-deluxe: over $24

back), or opt for "The Hog," a mountain-size platter of chicken, ribs, beef and pork. Everything is served on pig-shaped wooden plates. Closed Monday in the winter. ~ Route 321 Bypass, Blowing Rock; 704-295-3651. BUDGET.

Down on Route 105 east of Route 184 are several fine shops in the **Green Mansions Village**. Among them, **Dreamfields** carries pricey, high-quality fine art, antiques and other furnishings, many European in style. ~ 704-963-8333.

SHOPPING

Next door to the village are two terrific galleries plus an artist's studio at **Creekside Galleries**. The largest space, **Carlton Gallery** (704-963-4288), is a former weaving studio that now displays works from more than 200 local and regional artists. Glass work, jewelry, paintings, sculpture and other fine art can be found here. Downstairs, potter Tim Turner turns out decorative and functional vessels at **The Potter's Gallery** (704-963-4258). ~ Route 105, ten miles south of Boone.

In downtown Boone, the **Candy Barrel** has every sweet imaginable. Make sure the kids have already eaten. ~ King Street; 704-264-0647.

Next door, you'll find the **Mast General Store and Old Boone Mercantile**. This is a satellite of the famous, century-old store in nearby Valle Crucis on Route 194 (704-963-6511). The big question at both stores is: What *won't* you find here? Hiking boots, hammered silver jewelry, duck decoys, bark bird feeders, barrels of peanuts, blue jeans, and yes, even the kitchen sink, are for sale. The folks working here are extra helpful, and prices are surprisingly decent for such a popular place. ~ Depot Street; 704-262-0000.

Blowing Rock is great for shopping. Stroll along Main Street and watch your afternoon disappear. Antiques, oriental rugs, Christmas decor, resort wear—it's all here.

Pandora's Mailbox is fairly packed with New Age and avantgarde selections. There are racks of jewelry by local artists, stacks of CDs by offbeat but terrific musicians, and loads of greeting cards. ~ Main Street, Blowing Rock; 704-295-4238.

The selection at **Starwood Gallery** is vast and varied, from pottery, stained glass and jewelry to dolls, basketry and kaleidoscopes. ~ Main Street, Blowing Rock; 704-295-9229.

The Dulcimer does have dulcimers—hammered dulcimers and mountain dulcimers, books on dulcimers and kits for making dulcimers. Closed November through April. ~ Main Street, Blowing Rock; 704-295-3616.

The jewelry at **Almost Rodeo Drive** is decidedly conservative. Jeweled sweaters, kids' fashions and silk coordinates satisfy the classy dressers in the family. Open only on the weekend from January through March. ~ Main Street, Blowing Rock; 704-295-3422.

The **Chickory Suite** has flavored coffees, fine teas, candles, baskets and decorative wine corks. ~ Main Street, Blowing Rock; 704-295-4231.

NIGHTLIFE It's beer and wine only in Boone (hard liquor sales are taboo). Everything's legal (relating to alcohol, that is) in Blowing Rock, though you won't need the leather and lycra. Most places are low-key, not wild and crazy.

One of the most enjoyable ways to spend a Boone summer night is watching **Horn in the West**. The lively outdoor pageant tells the early High Country story—from the white man's point of view, of course. Daniel Boone figures prominently and so do American Indians; a Cherokee fire dance is always a favorite. Performances are staged most nights from late June through late August. Admission. ~ Off Route 421; 704-264-2120.

Across from the Appalachian State University baseball field, **Klondike Cafe** is small, publike and college-oriented. There's music almost every night, from jazz and bluegrass to folk and grunge. Wine and beer. Cover. ~ Route 321, Boone; 704-262-5065.

Next door, **Cottonwood Grill & Microbrewery** is a lively place for sampling homemade beer. ~ 704-264-7111.

OK, it does get a little wild and crazy at **Woodlands Barbecue & Pickin' Parlor** when the banjos start cooking. Bluegrass and folk musicians play most nights—but you still won't need the lycra. Full bar. ~ Route 321 Bypass, Blowing Rock; 704-295-3651.

The weekend bluegrass and folk at **Cosmic Coffee House** is more sedate, but there's big talent here. No alcohol, only coffees and fruity "mocktails." ~ North Main Street, Blowing Rock; 704-295-4762.

Green Park Inn's **Divide Pub** has billiards and darts, and a decidedly classy atmosphere. Full bar. ~ Route 321, two miles south of downtown Blowing Rock; 704-295-3141.

BEACHES & PARKS The Blue Ridge Parkway skirts the area (it's only feet from Blowing Rock) and offers great picnicking, fishing, hiking and sightseeing. (For more information on this national parkway, see Chapter Five.)

Northern High Country

As far north and west as you can get in North Carolina, the northern High Country is what folks in Boone refer to as "out there." You won't find much lodging, dining, shopping or nightlife. What you will find is plenty of open space, hills and pasture and sky running in all directions, cows grazing beside red-roofed barns, signs for feed stores and Baptist revivals, valleys dipping and rising, and rivers running clear and clean through the countryside.

The New River flows north from Blowing Rock, splintering into a north and south fork and little creeks and streams. The oldest river in the country and one of the few that flow north, it is designated a State Scenic River. Its waters are superior for canoeing and fishing.

Several back roads wind north from Blowing Rock, including the Blue Ridge Parkway. From the parkway, Route 163 angles up through folded hills and farmlands to **West Jefferson**, home to North Carolina's only cheese factory. It's not a terribly impressive place, but **Ashe County Cheese Company** does make a whole lot of cheese, up to 24,000 pounds on some days. Walk by the factory windows and watch the curds being weighed (and squeezed of whey), then pressed, dried and sealed in wax to age. It takes three months for mild cheese, six for medium and up to two years for extra sharp. Total tour time is ten minutes. Closed Sunday. ~ 106 East Main Street; 910-246-2501.

SIGHTS

Near here, the **Ashe County Chamber of Commerce** can provide maps and information on the area. Closed weekends. ~ 6 North Jefferson Avenue, West Jefferson; 910-246-9550.

The chamber can also tell you the way to the **frescoes of St. Mary's Church**. The 1902 church is small and white, very Rockwellish, bordered by white picket fence and four gravestones. The three frescoes are inside on the walls, painted on plaster and masonry in the 1970s by Ben Long IV. A native of Statesville, North Carolina, Long trained in Italy as a fresco artist. Upon returning to his home state, he could find no church to paint, and was rejected again and again by ministers. In 1973, he approached Father Faulton Hodge at a Blowing Rock party. Hodge agreed to let Long paint his St. Mary's church, then asked: "What is a fresco?" Soon after Hodge got his frescoes, the teeny church became famous, and now thousands stop by every year to see the richly painted works of "Mary, Great With Child," "John the Baptist" and "The Mystery of Faith." ~ 400 Beaver Creek School Road, about one-half mile off Route 163, West Jefferson; 910-246-3552.

◄ *HIDDEN*

Long suddenly became sought after, and was commissioned to paint four frescoes at **Holy Trinity Church** in nearby Glendale Springs. His portrait here of "The Last Supper" is vast and sumptuous to the eye. ~ Route 16, about two and a half miles north of Route 163; 910-982-3076.

◄ *HIDDEN*

Both churches welcome visitors any time.

Chain motels and hotels are available in West Jefferson and Jefferson. For something completely out of the way, you'll have to go to Laurel Springs.

LODGING

HIDDEN ▶   There you'll find **Burgiss Farm Bed & Breakfast** on a 200-acre cattle farm ringed in deep green hills and Christmas tree farms, and crisscrossed by cold-water creeks. Few places provide such peacefulness. Nancy and Tom Burgiss have opened their 1896 farmhouse to visitors, offering a bi-level, two-bedroom suite with lots of privacy. The enormous wood-and-stone living room has a trough where water is piped in from a nearby spring. Besides the trough, you get TV, a CD player, mountain bikes, a hot tub and elaborate breakfasts (the Hawaiian pancakes are awesome). Closed January through March. ~ 294 Elk Knob Road, three miles north of Blue Ridge Parkway Milepost 246, Laurel Springs; 910-359-2995, 800-233-1505. MODERATE.

DINING   The towns of West Jefferson, Jefferson and Glendale Springs have fast-food places, pizzerias and coffee shops.

HIDDEN ▶   A few miles north of Jefferson in Crumpler, **Shatley Springs Inn** is the place of local renown. Breakfast, lunch and dinner are family-style, with sleep-inducing portions of Southern home cooking: fried chicken and country ham, mashed potatoes and creamed corn, biscuits and gravy, and tall, dewy glasses of sweet tea. Get there early, especially on weekends, or you'll wait for a seat. Closed early November through March. ~ Route 16, Crumpler; 910-982-2236. BUDGET.

SHOPPING   The locally made cheeses at **Ashe County Cheese Co.** are good quality. If it's cool out, they'll keep a few days on the road. ~ 106 East Main Street, West Jefferson; 910-246-2501.

    Shatley Springs Inn has a handful of pond-front cottages stocked with local crafts, jams, rugs and country decor. A good place for browsing while waiting for a table at the inn's ever-popular restaurant. Closed early November through March. ~ North of Glendale Springs along Route 16; 910-982-2236.

NIGHTLIFE   It's awful quiet most nights. On Saturday nights from April to December, head for the big barn at **Burgiss Farm Bed & Breakfast**. Owners Tom and Nancy Burgiss throw a huge hoedown, complete with barbecue, mountain music and "wild and crazy dancing," says Tom. Wear your blue jeans and boots. ~ 294 Elk Knob Road, three miles north of Blue Ridge Parkway Milepost 246, Laurel Springs; 910-359-2995.

PARKS   **MOUNT JEFFERSON STATE PARK** 🏃 A tiny park with all-encompassing vistas, this 555-acre wilderness caps Mount Jefferson. The

HIDDEN ▶ mountain is 4683 feet high, shooting straight up from surrounding valleys, a pinnacle amid low seas of greenery. A road winds up to the summit and parking lot, where there is a sensational Blue Ridge panorama, with views into Virginia and Tennessee. The park forests are dense oak and hickory. Sorry, no camping. Facilities include park office, picnic tables and hiking trails. ~ Off Route 221 between West Jefferson and Jefferson; 910-246-9653.

NEW RIVER STATE PARK AND SCENIC RIVER 🏃 🛶 A canoer's heaven, the 1200-acre park follows the river through remote mountain countryside. The New River is the second oldest river in the world (behind the Nile) and one of the few that flow northward. It is also intensely beautiful and barely intruded upon by humans. Two canoe outfitters (see the "Outdoor Adventures" section at the end of this chapter) provide rentals and guided trips, including overnight treks, through the park. Canoe rentals are not available in the park. The New River is excellent for smallmouth bass and redeye bass (live bait required); try for trout in the tributaries. Facilities include a park office and picnic areas. ~ The park office is eight miles southeast of Jefferson. Take Route 88 from Jefferson to Route 1590, then follow the signs; 910-982-2587.

◀ **HIDDEN**

▲ Backcountry, canoe-in camping along the New River; $5 per site per night. Permit required, available from the park office.

STONE MOUNTAIN STATE PARK 🏃 🧗 🛶 Cool woods, towering and green in summer and sparse in winter, fill this 13,450-acre park. The high point is Stone Mountain, though its glistening bald patch of granite is only about 600 feet high. Cliff climbers scramble up the stone summit, while hikers take a rugged trail up—less risky, but just as exhausting. Permit (no fee) required for rock climbing; visit the park office. More than 17 miles of streams offer good trout fishing; try for rainbow and brown trout on lower streams, brook trout on higher waters. Fishing fee is $4 per person. Facilities include park office, picnic areas, hiking and bridle trails. ~ The park's main entrance is along Route 1002, off Route 21 and the Blue Ridge Parkway, seven miles southwest of Roaring Gap. In summer, take the twisting, dirt-and-gravel John P. Frank Parkway up from Route 1002 into the park. Along this remote route are crude cabins, streams, and sometimes turtles and snakes sunning in the road. There are hardly any other cars; 910-957-8185.

◀ **HIDDEN**

▲ A family campground has 37 sites for tents or RVs (no hookups); grills, restrooms, hot showers and laundry tubs provided; $9 per family per night. A group camping area has six primitive sites with fireplaces and pit toilets; $5 per family per night.

High Country rivers, streams and lakes offer many prospects for trout, as well as small and largemouth bass, muskies and catfish. Among the top spots are: the **Toe River** and its tributaries; the **Linville River**, especially through Linville Gorge; the **Elk River** (Route 194 between Banner Elk and Elk Park); **Boone's Fork**, a tributary of the

▼▼▼▼▼▼▼▼▼▼▼▼
Outdoor Adventures

**SPORT-
FISHING**

Watauga River (above Hound Ears Club); **Howard's Creek** (off Route 194 north of Boone); the **Globe portion of the Johns River Gorge** (Globe Road, off Route 321, eight miles south of Blowing Rock); and **Anthony Creek, Johns River** and **Big Horse Creek** (located upstream from the Lower Route 1361 bridge to the Virginia state line).

There's also terrific fishing along the Blue Ridge Parkway. For information, see Chapter Five.

Among the local fishing outfits, **Foscoe Fishing Company** goes out on the Watanga and fishes for rainbow and brown trout as well as smallmouth bass. ~ Foscoe; 704-963-7431. **Wahoos** rents canoes for fishing on the New River. ~ Route 321; Boone; 704-262-5774, 800-444-7238.

Fishing licenses, available from most hardware and general stores, are required for anyone 16 and older. Various laws govern the use of lures as well as fish size. A list of regulations is available with your license.

No license is needed to fish stocked trout farms, such as **Little Switzerland Trout**. ~ Route 226 North, Marion; 704-756-4820. However, at these farms you will pay a per-fish fee. Local farms include **Grandfather Trout Farm**. ~ Route 105, near Seven Devils; 704-963-5098. Another choice is **Creekside Trout Farm**. ~ Route 19E, Elk Park; 704-733-5943.

RAFTING & CANOEING

There's superb rafting on the Nolichucky River, whose headwaters begin as the Toe River. The trip passes through the deep and deeply scenic Nolichucky River Gorge, which has Class III and IV rapids.

Carolina Wilderness offers whitewater trips on the Nolichucky River. ~ 800-872-7437. **Cherokee Adventures Whitewater Rafting** offers these trips as well. ~ 800-445-7238.

Among the repertoire of adventures offered by **High Mountain Expeditions** are whitewater rafting along the Watauga and Nolichucky rivers and "funyaking" (with one-person inflatable kayaks) through the Wilson Creek Gorge. Choose from mild to wild rapids, and half-day to overnight trips. The company also organizes hiking and caving trips. ~ North Main Street, Blowing Rock; 704-295-4200, 800-262-9036.

Wahoos offers canoeing on the Toe River and hosts a slew of outdoor expeditions. ~ Route 321, Boone; 704-262-5774, 800-444-7238.

HIDDEN ►

The New River is *the* place for canoeing. **Zaloo's Canoes** rents canoes and innertubes, and hosts overnight and week-long excursions with backcountry camping in New River State Park. ~ 3874 Route 165, about a quarter mile from Route 16S-88, Jefferson; 910-246-3066.

New River Outfitters also takes canoers on the New River. ~ Route 221, at the New River General Store between Jefferson and Sparta; 910-982-9192.

SKIING

Four major ski resorts, with High Country mountains ranging from 4000 to 5500 feet, offer downhill action, including snowboarding. A lot of the snow is machine-made, but it's groomed daily to a crumbly consistency, and sometimes it's downright powdery. The resorts are so close together—anywhere from 15 to 50 minutes apart—that it's possible to ski a different mountain each day. Most people, though, become attached to one place and never leave.

If you have children, that might be **Sugar Mountain,** where 80 percent of the 19 trails and slopes are designed for beginner or intermediate skiers. The Sugar Bear Ski School takes 5- to 10-year-olds, and the Sugar Mountain Nursery looks after the ones too little to ski. ~ Route 184, two miles east of Banner Elk; 704-898-4521, 800-784-2768.

About seven miles northeast of Sugar at the 5505-foot tip of Beech Mountain, **Ski Beech** calls itself "the highest ski area in Eastern North America." The vertical drop is only 830 feet, but it's a straight down, don't-look-now plunge. ~ Route 184; 704-387-2011, 800-438-2093.

Ski Beech has a lot going on; there's a festive little village at the base where music is played all day long, and where an assortment of restaurants and boutiques crowd around an ice-skating rink that's nearly as popular as the slopes. There's a snowboard program for kids, as well as SKIwee and PEEwee ski lessons for young skiers. You'll find a quad lift and plenty of intermediate slopes, including the long, leisurely **Oz Run** that wends down the back of ◄ HIDDEN
the mountain. You will rarely see another skier on Oz, but you may just see a deer.

Teenagers head to **Hawksnest** in the town of Seven Devils, not far from Boone. The smallest High Country ski area, it has only two short beginner runs but a testy expert run called **Top Gun** that plunges right from summit to ski lodge. There's an entire area devoted to snowboarders and two areas for "glade skiing," a kind of kamikaze skiing through thinned forest. If you like trees on your trail, this is definitely your place. ~ Route 105; 704-963-6561, 800-822-4295.

The skiing at **Appalachian Ski Mountain** is more conservative. Like Sugar Mountain, Appalachian is big with families and beginners, not in the least because of its French-Swiss Ski College. Classes are kept small (6 to 10 people) so the instructors can work one-on-one to help skiers hone their skills. The SKIwee children's school, designed by *SKI* magazine, incorporates skiing and play for kids 4 to 12 years old. ~ Route 221-321, about halfway between Boone and Blowing Rock; 704-295-7828, 800-322-2373.

The mood at Appalachian is low-key and friendly and the setting gentle, with low-lying blue ridges painting the horizon and a peak height of 4000 feet. A new-in-1994 ice-skating rink offers nonskiers a way to pass the day (other than on that slope-front barstool). The 6000-square-foot outdoor rink is parked on a knoll, with compelling views of the slopes.

All of the High Country's ski areas are open for night skiing, and sell discounted "twilight" passes good from early afternoon through the evening. This works perfectly for those who like to spend the day sightseeing and the evenings on the slopes—easiest done in March, when the mercury is well above zero at night.

Ski Rentals   You can rent equipment at all the ski resorts. Or, several private outfits rent equipment at (usually) slightly reduced rates. Check with **Ski Country Sports**. ~ Route 184, across from the entrance to Sugar Mountain; 704-898-9786, 800-528-3874. **Edge of the World Outfitters** mostly rents snowboards but also has high performance skis. ~ Route 184, about halfway between Sugar Mountain and Ski Beech; 704-898-9550. **Fred's General Mercantile** rents both skis and snowboards. ~ Route 184, Beech Mountain; 704-387-4838. Near Hawksnest is **French Swiss Ski Rentals**. ~ Route 105, near Hawksnest; 704-963-6410. **1st Tracks Ski Team** has skis and snowboards. ~ Route 105, Boone; 704-264-7368. **Farmer's Backside** only has snowboards. ~ 140 West Depot Street, Boone; 704-264-8801. **Foxfire Sports** will provide you with skis or a board. ~ 678 Route 105, Boone; 704-264-7547.

RIDING STABLES   The mountains make for wonderful trail rides. Guided horseback trips are offered through **Springmaid Mountain**. ~ Off Mckinney Gap Road and the Blue Ridge Parkway, in the Toe River Valley; 704-765-2353. You can also try **Banner Elk Riding Stables**. ~

✔ **CHECK THESE OUT—UNIQUE OUTDOOR ADVENTURES**

- Scramble up the stone summit at Stone Mountain State Park—or take the trail up: arduous, but less risky than cliff climbing. *page 173*
- Take a canoe down the New River, through a mountain countryside that's secluded and intensely scenic. *page 168*
- Saddle up a horse and set out through mountain wilderness or along turn-of-the-century carriage trails. *page 170*
- Grab your clubs and head for some of the Carolina's most compelling golf greens—and scenes. *page 171*

Shoemaker Road, off Route 194, Banner Elk; 704-898-5424. Also in Banner Elk is **Smith Quarter Horse Farm**. ~ Off Route 194, Banner Elk; 704-898-4932.

Blowing Rock Stables has rides along turn-of-the-century carriage trails at Moses H. Cone Memorial Park on the Blue Ridge Parkway. ~ Located on Laurel Lane, off Route 221, Blowing Rock; 704-295-7847.

Many stables operate from spring through fall and require reservations, so call ahead.

GOLF

High Country golf courses, like the **Grassy Creek Golf and Country Club** are famous for their mountain scenery. ~ Route 226, Grassy Creek, about two miles south of Spruce Pine; 704-765-7436. Among the courses open to the public is **Quaker Meadows Golf Club**. ~ 826 North Green Street, Morganton; 704-437-2677. For a little skiing with your golf try **Hawksnest Golf & Ski Resort**. ~ off Route 105, Seven Devils; 704-963-6561. Also in Seven Devils is **Hanging Rock Golf Course**. ~ Route 105, Seven Devils; 704-963-6565. In Banner Elk, try **Sugar Mountain Golf Club**. ~ off Route 184, Banner Elk; 704-898-6464. While in Boone, head down to the **Boone Golf Club**. ~ 433 Fairway Drive, Boone; 704-264-8760. Just south of Boone, you'll find **Willow Creek Golf Course**. ~ Route 105, three miles south of Boone; 704-963-6865. Or try the **Mountain Aire Golf Club**. ~ Off Route 221, West Jefferson; 910-877-4716.

◄ *HIDDEN*

TENNIS

Most courts are outdoors, so plan on playing spring through fall. You'll find courts at **Brad Ragan Memorial Park**. ~ School Road, Spruce Pine. In Banner Elk, you can play at **Banner Elk Community Park**. ~ Route 194, Banner Elk. **Appalachian State University** has courts. ~ River Street, Boone. In Boone, try **Watauga Recreation Complex**. ~ Complex Drive, Boone; 704-264-9511. **West Jefferson Park** is the place to go in West Jefferson. ~ Long Street, West Jefferson.

BIKING

For excellent bike-trail maps, contact the North Carolina Department of Transportation's Bicycle Program. ~ P.O. Box 25201, Raleigh, NC 27611; 919-733-2804.

Mountain bikers appreciate the High Country and its steep, muscle-building terrain that's also extremely picturesque. Try to plan your ride during the warmer months as the roads are usually too icy in winter and, anyway, who really wants to be out of doors unless it's to ski?

The **Blue Ridge Parkway** is the place of choice for many bikers. The **Brown Mountain Lights** segment of the trail starts on the Parkway just south of Little Switzerland and winds 52 miles to

Jonas Ridge at Route 191. Along the way you can stop at the Museum of North Carolina Minerals and Linville Falls.

For more on biking the Blue Ridge Parkway, see Chapter Five. **Bike Rentals**   Mountain bikes are available from **Magic Cycles**. ~ 208 Faculty Street, Suite 1, Boone; 704-265-2211. **Boone Bike & Touring** is another place to go. ~ 899 Blowing Rock Road, Boone; 704-262-5750. Also in Boone is **Rock and Roll Sports**. ~ 280 East King Street, Boone; 704-264-0765.

HIKING   A hiker's heaven, the High Country has hundreds of miles of trails through gardens and gorges, beside rivers and creeks, around lakes, and up steep rocky ledges. For an extensive list of trails, contact the **High Country Host**. ~ Route 321, Boone; 704-264-1299, 800-438-7500. All distances listed for hiking trails are one way unless otherwise noted.

TOE RIVER VALLEY   On Roan Mountain, the leisurely **Gardens Trail** (1 mile) wends through the world's largest natural rhododendron garden. The 600-acre mountaintop patch peaks in mid- to late June. The trailhead is off Route 264 just before the North Carolina–Tennessee line.

About a mile past the Gardens Trail, but still in North Carolina, **Cloudland Trail** (3 miles round-trip) is a little more challenging. It presses through fir and spruce forest to 6267-foot Roan High Bluff, where views are spectacular.

Hard-core hikers should consider the trails at Linville Gorge in Pisgah National Forest. Going down into the gorge is not too bad, but coming back out is another story: steep, ragged rocks make the hike more of a climb. Seven trails descend from the gorge's west rim, and are accessed along Route 1238 off Route 183 south of the town of Linville Falls. From the east rim, along National Forest Road 210, there are two trails. All are classified by the forest service as "more difficult" or "most difficult." Within the gorge, **Linville Gorge Trail** (11.5 miles) is a strenuous hike alongside Linville River.

Permits (there is no fee) are required for the Linville Gorge trails on weekends and holidays from May through October, and can be procured from the **Grandfather Ranger District Office**. ~ Located off Route 40, at the Nebow–Lake James exit, Nebow; 704-652-2144.

LINVILLE AND BANNER ELK   The eight trails on Grandfather Mountain are almost all rocky and strenuous, but they're unsurpassed for rugged scenery. The arduous **Grandfather Trail** (2.3 miles) has ladders and cables to help you scale various cliffs. Most of the trail is through high-elevation forest, with backcountry campsites to choose from. The **Nuwati Trail** (1.2 miles) is much easier, though rocky, with a panorama of glacier-carved Boone Fork Bowl.

A permit is required to hike and camp on Grandfather Mountain. The fee is $4.50 per day for adult hikers, $9 per day for adult campers. In addition, there is an admission to the mountain, which is a private attraction.

BOONE AND BLOWING ROCK AREA The best trails around Boone and Blowing Rock are off the Blue Ridge Parkway, which skirts both towns. For a list of hikes, see Chapter Five.

NORTHERN HIGH COUNTRY Within Mount Jefferson State Park, the **Service Road Trail** (.6 mile) goes to the top of the mountain. It's an easy gravel trail, but, unfortunately, the view from the summit is partly blocked. Keep going from here on the **Rhododendron Trail** (1.4 miles round-trip), which does reward with numerous scenic overlooks. Vegetation and outlying mountains and valleys are marked on this easy trek.

Steep and strenuous, **Stone Mountain Loop Trail** (3.3 miles) in Stone Mountain State Park curls up to the granite summit that gives the mount its name. The scenery is spartan and rocky; the forests are thin, the outcroppings windblown into futuristic shapes. The superb view from the top is across Blue Ridge Mountains and rolling Piedmont.

Also in the park, **Wolf Rock Loop Trail** (3 miles) cuts a sloping path through hardwood forest and patches of rhododendron. Parts of the trail are moderate, but most are difficult.

▼▼▼▼▼▼▼▼▼▼

Transportation

CAR

There are no major highways leading into the High Country, just scenic two- and four-lane roads that wind up through the mountains. **Route 321** is a fairly straight shot northwest from Hickory to Blowing Rock and Boone.

From Asheville, **Route 19** wends north to the southern end of the High Country. Or visitors can take **Route 40** east of Asheville for 30 miles, then veer north on **Route 221** to Linville and Boone. Route 221 also brings motorists down from Virginia into the High Country.

If time is not of the essence, use the **Blue Ridge Parkway**. The picturesque byway, part of the National Park System, curls up from Asheville and runs right through the High Country.

AIR

Tiny **Hickory Regional Airport**, in Hickory, is about 75 minutes by car from the heart of the High Country. USAir Express offers commuter services.

Larger, but about 30 minutes farther, **Asheville Regional Airport** near Asheville is serviced by Atlantic Southwest, ComAir, Delta Airlines, US Air and USAir Express.

CAR RENTALS   Budget Rent A Car (800-527-0700) and Thrifty Rent A Car (800-367-2277) are at Hickory Regional Airport.

At Asheville Regional Airport, there's Avis Rent A Car (800-331-1212), Budget Rent A Car (800-527-0700) and Hertz Rent A Car (800-654-3131).

SEVEN

The Piedmont

Between the bluish peaks of North Carolina's western mountains and the flat white expanse of its coast is the Piedmont—a ruddy, rambling region sculpted with soft hills, sprinkled with loblolly pines and mahoganies, and colored with clay. This is the geographic heart of the state and a hub of the New South, where art, education, research and industry are all growing rapidly and creating a whole new way of doing things.

Technically, the Piedmont neither starts nor ends in North Carolina but reaches down from New York's Hudson River all the way to Birmingham, Alabama, a long, lazy plateau of rolling foothills framed by mountains and sea. It is the "crescent" of Carolinas hills, however, that gives the Piedmont its name, and it is North Carolina's big cities that shape its modern image.

Winston-Salem, Charlotte, Raleigh and Durham and their environs constitute the nation's fifth-largest urban area, home to nearly six million people. Here are the factories that churn out Piedmont textiles and tobacco, and the highrises of glass that house banking, insurance and computer giants. Here, too, are the brooding Gothic college campuses of red brick, white columns and ancient gardens, and the sprawling sports arenas (and their basketball games) that are treated with the same reverence as the stately churches that decorate the landscape.

In the beginning, though, before the textile mills, skyscrapers and churches, Piedmont life was all about clay. The earliest settlers, eighteenth-century Moravians, Quakers, Shakers and Scotch-Irish, were at the mercy of the acid-rich orange soil. It wasn't much good for growing corn or any other vegetable, so the settlers had to be enterprising, concentrating on trades instead of crops. They became masons and potters, coaxing the clay into bricks and bowls—and jugs to stash moonshine. They learned blacksmithing and tinsmithing, weaving and barrel-making (called coopering). They felled trees and turned them into furniture. They built wagons, filled them with wares, and sent men out to trade them. And they grew cotton.

Cotton is a scavenger crop, prolific in even the most barren of soils. By the mid-1800s, cotton fields had taken hold of the Piedmont clay. These weren't plantations like the ones across the Carolina coastal plain, but small- and medium-size plots worked by the yeoman farmer, the backbone of Southern cotton.

Tobacco is also a scavenger, thriving in the merciless clay. American Indians had been growing and smoking tobacco for centuries, but it wasn't until the 1850s, when Piedmonters concocted the lighter, brighter "brightleaf" tobacco, that the crop became a profitable industry. An exhausted Caswell County slave helped the tobacco cause when he fell asleep in a barn, allowing a fire to smolder the bright leaves he was curing. The leaves tasted so good that the rest of the Piedmont started charcoal-curing tobacco. Soon the Civil War created an instant demand: both Rebel and Yankee troops had to have their "weed," as tobacco was called back then. Women weren't supposed to smoke but they could dip snuff, which gave them a bigger buzz, anyway.

Washington Duke was one Civil War soldier who not only enjoyed smoking tobacco but also had a mind to market it. Most every Piedmonter knows the story of how, at war's end, a broke Washington Duke walked 225 miles from New Bern, North Carolina, back to his small Durham farm. There, in a teeny, one-room barn, he started the South's first tobacco "factory," sifting the cured tobacco and packing it into cloth bags. He labeled the bags *Pro Bono Publico* ("for the good of the public"), put them in his wagon, and peddled them across the Piedmont. Cigarettes being cigarettes, Duke became wildly successful and went on to build the largest tobacco empire in the world.

The Piedmont's other tobacco magnate, R. J. Reynolds, was assembling his own cigarette empire around the same time. In 1874 he settled not far from Durham in Winston, population 400. By the early 1900s, Reynolds had built his own factory, employing more than 10,000 people. Thanks to Reynolds, Winston got so big so fast it grew right into the Moravian town of Salem. In 1913, the two officially became known as Winston-Salem.

While the tobacco fields were spreading, cotton nearly disappeared. In the 1890s, the Mexican cotton boll weevil crossed the Rio Grande River and had most of the cotton belt for lunch. Today, you'll only find small patches of cotton around the Piedmont, though there is a vast patchwork of tobacco. Much of the tobacco crop makes its way to the monstrous R. J. Reynolds Plant near Winston-Salem, where 8000 cigarettes are manufactured every minute.

Tobacco has kept the Piedmont in the national news for much of the 1990s, and not because it is *pro bono publico*. At best, tobacco is a troublesome crop; at worst, it's a deadly drug that has divided not only the South but the entire country. Cigarette sentiments run strong in these parts, and whether you're driving through brightleaf fields or eating in a restaurant (no-smoking sections have *not* caught on here), you feel tobacco's presence. Throughout the region, numerous sights and museums offer a fascinating look back at how the industry was born, right in the clay.

Clay is at least in part responsible for the region's second big industry: furniture. Ever since those early pioneers turned away from the harsh soil and to the trees for a trade, Piedmonters have been crafting furniture for folks around the country. Today, some 60 percent of all American furniture is made in the Piedmont. Furniture factories and outlets fill the landscape, and visitors converge here for deeply discounted prices.

The Piedmont

BLUE RIDGE PARKWAY

VIRGINIA
NORTH CAROLINA

John H. Kerr Reservoir

Hyco Reservoir

Tar River

Neuse River

Falls Lake

Raleigh

Durham

Chapel Hill

Burlington

Greensboro

Guilford Courthouse National Military Park

Hanging Rock State Park

Pinnacle

Mount Airy

Kernersville

High Point

Thomasville

Winston-Salem

Clemmons

Lexington

Horne Creek Living Historical Farm

Yadkin River

Wilkesboro

Love Valley

Hickory

Catawba River

Morganton

Pisgah National Forest

Statesville

Spencer

Salisbury

Mooresville

China Grove

Lake Norman

Huntersville

Gastonia

Belmont

Crowder's Mountain State Park

Lake Wylie

Kannapolis

Charlotte

Reed Gold Mine State Historic Site

Locust

Waxhaw

NORTH CAROLINA
SOUTH CAROLINA

Catawba River

Level Cross

Asheboro

Siler City

Pittsboro

Sanford

Cameron

Southern Pines

Fort Bragg Military Reservation

Pope AFB

House in the Horseshoe

Carthage

Seagrove

Uwharrie Forest

Pinehurst

Laurinburg

Fayetteville

Smithfield

Pee Dee River

Cape Fear River

N

25 miles

0

The Piedmont tour starts at the heart of furniture and tobacco land, in the Triad. A trio of big cities—Winston-Salem, Greensboro and High Point—make up the Triad, with slivers of green pasture in between.

It's easy to tell that Winston-Salem started as two cities, for it still has two distinct sides. There is the R. J. Reynolds side, with its thriving tobacco industry and its outstanding museums, parks, inns and art academies created by Reynolds money. And then there is Old Salem, one of the Piedmont's top attractions, a marvelous Moravian village of restored eighteenth- and nineteenth-century homes and workshops. The German-speaking Moravians were brilliant tradesmen who made their way to the Piedmont from Pennsylvania, after having fled religious oppression in what later became Czechoslovakia. Winston-Salem has Wake Forest University, where celebrated poet and local resident Maya Angelou is a professor.

Next door, Greensboro was the sight of several major battles, from a Revolutionary War conflict that included thousands to the nation's first lunch counter sit-ins in the fight against segregation. High Point and the neighboring towns of Thomasville and Lexington are the hub of furniture making, which extends west all the way to Hickory.

Due south of the Triad lies the Piedmont destination that has perhaps secured more national attention than any other—and not because of tobacco. In barely a decade, Charlotte has transformed itself from an obscure, unexciting textile and banking center to a lustrous New South star. Its downtown sparkles with vertical glass and metal of the most current design, and its neighborhoods of regal homes and immaculate lawns fan out for miles. Its airport connects major cities around the world, and its banking industry ranks third in the nation. The performing arts are thriving here, and so are the visual arts. Museums of every kind can be found in Charlotte, including historic neighborhoods qualifying as outdoor museums. Culinarily, it offers everything from exciting ethnic experiences to New South nouveau. The soul food here is some of the best in the South.

Why Charlotte?

Many have asked that question but few have gotten an easy answer. "There is no apparent reason, by the usual standards of urban development, why Charlotte should be doing so well," notes an editorial in the *Charlotte Observer*, the city's major daily newspaper. Perhaps part of the reason, the paper goes on to say, is that Charlotte has always invited new people and new ideas, and "is not an Old South town that moves at a crinoline and magnolia pace. . . ."

Two hundred miles east of Charlotte lie the tiny twin towns of Pinehurst and Southern Pines, where serious golf has been played for nearly a century. Three dozen courses, designed by names well known in the PGA world, are sprinkled among the sandy clay hills. Manicured country clubs, a New England–style village and a grand resort are just some of the reasons why visitors keep coming back.

North of here is the Triangle, formed by Raleigh, Durham and Chapel Hill. Despite their link in the national consciousness (mainly because of Raleigh-Durham International Airport and Research Triangle Park, a high-tech center between the two cities), Raleigh and Durham are separate cities, and not even that much alike. Raleigh is North Carolina's capital, pleasant and low-key, with a tidy downtown of classical-style state buildings and lovely historic neighborhoods. The busy North Carolina State University campus is on Raleigh's outskirts.

Durham has more bustle, taller buildings, faster-walking business people with serious looks on their faces. Like Winston-Salem, it grew up as a tobacco town; Washington Duke's homestead, now a state historic site, is minutes from downtown. Of course, his name is more often linked with Duke University, founded by his son James Buchanan "Buck" Duke. The Gothic campus is not only gorgeous to look at, it is a hub of Durham medical research.

The research continues at the 6800-acre, high-tech Research Triangle Park, whose tenants include IBM, Northern Telecom and Burroughs-Wellcome. The drug AZT was developed here, and Nobel Prizes have been awarded to park researchers. The park is a big reason *Fortune* magazine in 1993 named Raleigh/Durham the number-one U.S. city (really, cities) for business, saying "this chunk of piney-woods real estate in central North Carolina has smartened up over the past two decades and become a genuine intellectual capital."

Many of the park's employees live (or want to live) in Chapel Hill, with neighborhoods filled with princely old homes, well-tended gardens and vast oaks and sycamores. The beautiful University of North Carolina is the centerpiece of the small town and, in fact, someone just passing through might think it the town, with the constant hubbub emanating from its groomed grounds.

Despite the rich academia and industry and New South growth, the old ways can still be found across the Piedmont. You don't need to look far to find weather-worn farmhouses set amongst shaggy fields of tobacco, centuries-old curing barns emitting sweet tobacco smells, the cattle grazing in plain view of a downtown highrise. Just outside Winston-Salem, there lies a Wild West–style town, Love Valley, where no cars—only horses—are allowed on Main Street. Unmarked side roads, whose names are known only to locals, lead up to time-forgotten general stores or perhaps a pharmacy museum whose pharmacist was born in the cabin next door.

Then, too, there is still all that clay. Yankee blood, it is said, gives the soil its color, though of course it comes from something much more prosaic—an overdose of iron oxides.

Wet clay sticks to your shoes and squishes between your toes. Dry, it's as tough as cement. Clay attaches itself to a person and won't let go, staining fingers for days and shoes forever. If you drive around the Piedmont for very long, both your car and mind will be indelibly rouged.

Winston-Salem Area

The R. J. Reynolds empire put Winston-Salem on the modern map in the 1950s when it named its cigarettes after the city (both Winstons and Salems). But two centuries earlier, a hard-working, health-minded band of Protestants put it on the geographic map.

When the Moravians came to the Piedmont from Bethlehem, Pennsylvania, in 1752, there was nothing here but trees, bears and rattlesnakes. The German-speaking people, religious dissidents from Bohemia and Moravia (later Czechoslovakia), instantly loved the land. They bought nearly 100,000 acres and called it *der Wachau*, after their leader's ancestral estate. The word soon became Wachovia, pronounced Wa-KO-ve-a, and today everything from banks to dry cleaners has taken the name Wachovia.

SIGHTS   Within shouting distance of those modern Wachovias, and a few blocks from the highrises of downtown Winston-Salem, is the original Wachovia's main town, remarkably preserved as **Old Salem**. Admission. ~ 600 South Main Street; 910-721-7300. Pick up a map at the **visitors center** and start walking these tranquil streets, exploring the homes and trade shops of proper red brick and deep-toned clapboard, with their crisp white-picket borders, gushing gardens and steeply pitched roofs. ~ Old Salem Road at Academy Street.

Nearly 80 buildings have been restored from the 1700s and 1800s. Seven feature guided tours, with Moravian history and culture passionately related by docents, and with coopers, blacksmiths, weavers,and others demonstrating their trades. If you were to take all seven tours, wander leisurely through several more restored buildings and have lunch at the village's **Salem Tavern** (which you must), you would need two days. Not coincidentally, tickets are good for two days. You can stroll and drive through the village without paying admission (and of course visit the tavern and shops), but to really get the gist of things, you'll have to take the guided tours.

There is an ancient quality to Old Salem, though the streets, buildings and cobbled paths look freshly scrubbed. The workers pad about in eighteenth-century garb and speak in hushed, respectful tones as would have been done in the town's beginning. Like the Quakers and Mennonites, the Moravians lived a peaceful, structured, productive existence, though unlike those other communities, theirs focused on trades instead of farming. Men and women lived separately until marriage, leaving home when they turned 14 to live in dormitories and learn a trade.

The **Single Brothers House**, for instance, housed up to 50 men and boys teaching and attending workshops on everything from tailoring and tannery to blacksmithing and pottery making. Built in 1769 and expanded in 1786, the brick-and-timber house has much that's original, including the great hearth where the brothers cooked their five daily meals. Around the corner, the Federal-style **John Vogler House** belonged to early Salem's most famous silversmith. Vogler's signature door handle, a hand gripping a bar and representing "the hand of hospitality," became the rage back then. Today, one still greets visitors to his 1819 house.

From Vogler's place, one is overwhelmed with the doughy, sugary smells so singular to Moravian baking. Walk down a block and a half to the **Winkler Bakery** and observe the robust women feeding their hand-kneaded dough into a wood-fired brick oven. The domed oven, connected to the house by a trap door, is just like the one put here in 1800 by master builder Johann Gottlob Krause. Today's women imitate their predecessors, raking the hot coals in early morning, laying out the dough on big trays of sheet iron, using long-handled paddles to extract the shapely loaves of bread

dark as midnight, and the cakes and cookies dusted white with
sugar. The baked stuff is for sale, by the way, though you'll have
to wait in line behind all the other folks lured here by their noses.
Sunday is the only day they don't bake. ~ 525 South Main Street,
Winston-Salem; 910-721-7302.

There is more to see in Old Salem, including the **Museum of
Early Southern Decorative Arts** (separate admission), where two
dozen rooms and galleries splendidly showcase the furniture and
architecture of the Old South. There's also the **post office**, where
you can have your letters postmarked "Salem," and **God's Acre
cemetery**, where you can see how Moravians are buried, segregated
by gender.

Nothing, however, is as fitting an ending to Old Salem as the
World's Largest Coffeepot. Right on the line between Old Salem
and Winston-Salem, it stands tall and strange, like something the
Mad Hatter might have concocted, though it was, in fact, created

◀ HIDDEN

by Moravian brothers Samuel and Julius Mickey. Built in 1858 of tin, the coffeepot stands seven feet and three inches high, an advertising ploy for their tinmaking business. It is not known if it worked. ~ Main Street at Brookstown Avenue.

HIDDEN ► The idea for Old Salem was actually born six miles away at what is now **Historic Bethabara Park**. More of an archaeological site than restored village, the serene, forested, 110-acre park is speckled with the wood and stone remains of one of the Piedmont's first frontier settlements. There's a film to tell you about the place, and a guided tour of two buildings: the 1782 Potter's House, and 1788 Gemeinhaus House, where religious services were held. Here also is another God's Acre, with timeworn epithets scripted in German. ~ 2147 Bethabara Road, just north of Silas Creek Parkway, Winston-Salem; 910-924-8191.

A century after the Moravians began building their Salem, Richard Joshua "R. J." Reynolds was creating the city of Winston. There the tobacco giant opened a factory, and by the early 1900s was mass-producing cigarettes, bringing in thousands of new residents. In 1917, Reynolds and his wife, Katherine, used some of their new fortune to buy an estate that's now the **Reynolda House Museum of American Art**. The manor and its 100 rooms and galleries are positively exquisite, and yet done with such warmth and familiarity as to seem like the Reynolds just stepped out for a carriage ride.

In R. J. Reynolds' former den, wall lamps shimmer against fine Georgian oak paneling, a Gothic Revival oak desk and walnut armchairs. The art on the walls seems secondary, though it includes such intriguing pieces as a nineteenth-century oil by Edward Hicks, a sign painter and Quaker preacher. In fact, all three floors of the house are filled with architectural and artistic intrigue, with hundreds of paintings, prints and sculptures spanning 300 years, each

---

✔ CHECK THESE OUT—UNIQUE SIGHTS

- Travel back to 1700s Mennonite country at **Old Salem**, where docents, artisans and nearly 80 historic sites paint a picture of the past. *page 180*
- Check out the zebras, rhinoceros, gorillas and roadrunners—and other wild, wonderful creatures at **North Carolina Zoological Park**. *page 185*
- Go where America's first gold was found—**Reed Gold Mine State Historic Site**—and delve into dim, damp shafts veined with quartz. *page 208*
- Pore over old photos, wardrobes and movie posters at the **Ava Gardner Museum**, starring a poignant collection devoted to a native Carolinian who went Hollywood. *page 227*

piece marvelously varied and accompanied by a one-page background on the art and artist. In one stair corridor there's a 1922 abstract of Lake George, New York, by Georgia O'Keefe along with a 1957 watercolor by Andrew Wyeth depicting a farm scene near his Pennsylvania home. In a second-floor gallery there's a wonderful painting of Mount Whitney by nineteenth-century landscape artist Albert Bierstadt. And, in the attic, a costume collection that includes the wedding "suit" Katherine Smith made and then wore when she married R. J. Reynolds in 1905, in nearby Mount Airy.

The tour of Reynolda House is self-guided and accompanied by a booklet detailing every room. Docents roam the place hoping you'll ask questions, and they know *a lot*, including gossipy anecdotes about the Reynolds men and their womanizing, scandalous ways, so don't hesitate to ask! Closed Monday. Admission. ~ Reynolda Road, south of Silas Creek Parkway, Winston-Salem; 910-725-5325.

Much less attractive than the house, but interesting even if you absolutely abhor cigarettes, is a tour of the **R. J. Reynolds Tobacco Company plant**. Located in the 65-acre Whitaker Park, the plant has 26 acres under roof. You enter a lobby decorated by a 200-pound collage of tobacco leaves. Then you are escorted through giant rooms filled with huge bales of cellulose (wood fiber from loblolly pines, used for making filters), and endless conveyer belts of Dorals and Camels and Winstons. You hear how the tobacco leaves are blown through a labyrinth of ductwork in the plant's ceiling, and how 25 percent of the company's cigarettes are shipped abroad. You are told that cigarette manufacturers pay millions of dollars in taxes every single day, and that smokers are voters, too. If you ask the guide with the chainsaw-voice if she really believes smoking can't hurt you, she will not like it.

The R. J. Reynolds Tobacco Company, by the way, is a subsidiary of RJR-Nabisco, which was purchased through a leveraged buyout by a conglomerate in 1989. At the end of the tour, you are offered complimentary cigarettes in a dizzying choice of brands. Or you can opt for one of the Nabisco snacks from a vending machine. Closed weekends. ~ 1100 Reynolds Boulevard, off Route 52 South, Winston-Salem; 910-741-5718.

For more on other tours, and loads of information on places to stay and eat and play, stop by the **Winston-Salem Visitors Center.** ~ 601 North Cherry Street, Winston-Salem; 910-777-3796, 800-331-7018.

Driving north from Winston-Salem, it's less than 30 minutes before the city scenes transform into bucolic ones. From the lonely two-lane stretches of **Routes 66** and **89**, you can look into forests with feet of clay and across open fields laced with white plank fence. Church steeples spire upward, wash flaps in the wind and feed stores are attended by hound dogs and old farmers idly chewing pieces of straw. And then there will be mountains.

West of these byways, the four lanes of **Route 52** head northwest of Winston-Salem and eventually run smack into the Blue Ridge Mountains. On the way is a perfectly hidden stop, **Horne Creek Living Historical Farm**. The way to Horne Creek is down many country roads, past rippled fields of tobacco and their rugged curing sheds, and hillside cemeteries the size of postage stamps. The farm, a state historic site, is out in the woods, which is exactly where Thomas Hauser wanted to be back in the mid-1800s. His family's 1847 log barn and 1870s house are still here; the house has the original grain bin and even some indoor paint. Initially 400 acres but now 100, the farm is being fashioned as a turn-of-the-century "living" outdoor museum, meaning the animals, crops and farm tools mimic those early ones (forget those gas-guzzling tractors!). There are plots of corn, a garden with turnips, orchards of heirloom apples and peaches, a chicken coop, feed barn and hog lot. Closed Monday. ~ From Route 52, exit at the town of Pinnacle and go about eight miles west; 910-325-2298.

Back southeast of the foothills on Route 66 is a bucolic break called **Kernersville**. The town has several big old houses nestling under giant trees, but the one that gets everyone's attention is **Korner's Folly**. It's an outrageously elaborate, somewhat crumbling house built in the 1870s by local artist and eccentric Jule Korner. Unfortunately, the tour hours are equally eccentric, and unless your visit falls on a Sunday between April and October and you arrive between 1 and 5 p.m., you will only be treated to the zany exterior, missing the fanciful carved ceilings and walls, the strange mismatched doors, and the tiny thresholds that seem made for dwarfs. Admission. ~ South Main Street, Kernersville; 910-993-4521.

About 20 miles farther east, along Route 40, **Greensboro** is plain but pleasant enough and, though not a traveler's city, it does offer a few sites for those passing through. On the north side of town, **Guilford Courthouse National Military Park** covers 220 acres of forest and is the site of a key battle of the Revolutionary War. Monuments and markers nestled under sun-streaked elms guide you through the various stages of the battle that took place on March 15, 1781, between 4400 American troops and 2000 British soldiers. ~ 2332 New Garden Road, Greensboro; 910-288-1776.

In 1960, downtown Greensboro was the sight of a different kind of protest. It was here that four African-American college students sat down at the old F. W. Woolworth's lunch counter for the nation's first protest against segregation. A **marker** on Elm Street near Sycamore Street memorializes the history-altering event.

You can learn more about the sit-down nearby at the **Greensboro Historical Museum**. A striking Romanesque building sparkling with stained glass, it has had many past lives, including church and Confederate hospital. Numerous additions have been made over the years and now three floors are packed with engaging exhibits on Piedmont life. There's a terrific display of Piedmont furniture, and rooms filled with mementos of Dolley Madison and the writer O'Henry (real name William Sidney Porter), who spent his childhood in Greensboro. Closed Monday. ~ Lindsay Street and Summit Avenue, Greensboro; 910-373-2043.

On the south side of town, **Blandwood Mansion** has the distinction of being the "earliest, still standing, Italianate Tuscan villa in the United States." It's really not a terribly impressive villa, but the docents are quite friendly and effusive about the history and architectural details. Closed Monday. Admission. ~ 447 West Washington Street, Greensboro; 910-272-5003.

South of Greensboro in a farm town called **Level Cross**, the **Richard Petty Museum** is a shrine to the local boy who became history's winningest race car driver. Older kids should like this place, in part because it's located in Petty's garages and doesn't look like a museum, but mostly because they can see several of his cars, dozens of his trophies and awards, photos of his various crashes, and his "cool suit." Closed Sunday. Admission. ~ 311 Branson Mill Road, off Route 220, Level Cross; 910-495-1143.

◄ *HIDDEN*

It only makes sense that the Carolinas' premier zoo is not near people but way out in the sticks of central Piedmont, where the elephants, giraffes and rhinoceros can really roam. Plan to spend at least half a day at the superb **North Carolina Zoological Park**, and wear some comfortable shoes (for wheelchair visitors, there are wide, paved, gently sloped paths). Admission. ~ Route 159, off Route 220, near Asheboro; 910-879-7000.

◄ *HIDDEN*

Four miles of paths cut through the 1400 acres of habitats, for the most part big, open spaces designed more for animals than spectators. A tram circles the zoo; you can ride it all the way around, but in order to see the habitats you'll have to get off the tram.

On the **African-style plain** you'll find antelope and rhinoceros; in the forest edge, giraffes, zebras and ostriches; and in the forest glade, gorillas. Elsewhere you'll see baboons, chimpanzees and lions. And you'll also encounter some state-of-the-art exhibits opened in the last few years.

Most talked about are the three polar bears who live in the imitation Arctic Rocky Coast Habitat, part of the 200-acre **North American region**, new in 1994. The bears play in their pool, licking peanut butter, smeared by zoo employees, off a glass wall so visitors can get up-close looks.

The **Sonora Desert** is a domed hothouse with special heating and cooling and ventilation to keep relative humidity at 20 percent. That's how roadrunners, Chihuahuan spotted lizards, gila (pronounced HEE-la) monsters and the hundreds of other Sonora residents like it. The gilas, by the way, are warty-looking lizards, poisonous but shy.

Nearby, the gargantuan **R. J. Reynolds Aviary** is a jungle under mesh, a damp and musky space of flamboyant foliage and dazzling birds, from the turquoise tanager to the silver-eared mesia. Bromeliads burst from the elbows of great kapok trees and leggy African spoonbills—whose pinkish bills really are spoon-shaped—scoop fish from a pond. The resplendent, watermelon-colored scarlet ibis is almost too beautiful to believe.

HIDDEN ►

About 15 miles from the zoo, at the junctions of Routes 220 and 705, the hamlet of **Seagrove** has a few thousand people and more than 75 potters. Seagrove pottery had its beginnings 200 years ago when Piedmonters turned to clay to make vessels for everyday use. During Prohibition, business picked up as people needed jugs to stash their hooch, and Seagrove thrived with some 250 potters. The law died, plastic was invented, and pottery making nearly disappeared from Seagrove. In the past ten years, tourism has brought it back, though longtime local potters warn of all the amateurs in town. "You can tell right away when you walk in (to a studio) if the quality's not there," said one potter who's been around nearly 20 years. Unfortunately, to my untrained eyes, the pottery looked pretty much the same everywhere.

For a map to the potters, stop by the **Friends of the North Carolina Pottery Center**. The center can also direct you to specific types of potters, such as those making elegant crystalline glazed pottery. Closed Sunday. ~ Route 705, near Route 220; 910-873-7887.

Other than all those potters, Seagrove has a couple of filling stations, a hardware store and two restaurants—the Dairy Breeze and the Jugtown Cafe. If you don't love pottery, you probably won't love Seagrove.

LODGING

Brookstown Inn is on the outskirts of Old Salem but has much of the same Early Americana atmosphere. In a restored 1837 textile mill that's listed on the National Register of Historic Places, it's a handsome red-brick building whose rooms are all suites, full of space and light and character, with high-beamed ceilings and exposed brick walls, and furnishings reflecting early Moravian styles. Guests here do not go hungry: rates include continental breakfast, afternoon wine and cheese, and evening cookies and milk. ~ 200 Brookstown Avenue, Winston-Salem; 910-725-1120, 800-845-4262, fax 910-773-0147. DELUXE.

HIDDEN ►

A little farther from Old Salem, **Wachovia Bed & Breakfast** is a pretty pink-and-white house in a quiet neighborhood. Owner Steve Masten is friendly, and his house is obviously well cared for and comfortable. Three of the five bedrooms have shared baths,

The Real Mayberry, U.S.A.

Sheriff Andy Taylor used to say there's no place like home, and in real life that would be **Mount Airy**. The sheriff, you may remember, was played by Andy Griffith, a fresh-faced, down-home fella who was born and raised in this upper Piedmont town just south of the Virginia line off Route 52, 51 miles northwest of Winston-Salem. That's where he fished for trout in the wooded creeks and hung out at the Snappy Lunch counter on Main Street, just like he did in Mayberry on *The Andy Griffith Show*.

Mount Airy was the inspiration (though not the setting) for the fictional town of Mayberry and, amazingly, it still resembles its TV counterpart today. There are the same big gracious oaks lining the sidewalks and the same friendly folks sitting in swings on their front porches (remember how Andy used to sit with Helen Crumb?). On Main Street there's **Floyd's City Barber Shop** where Barney might have had a shave, and **Lamm's Drug**, famous for cherry smashes, now closed but well preserved, right down to the old-fashioned scale where Andy told Barn they would "take the girls down to the drugstore and weigh on the big scales."

To really get in the Mayberry swing of things, visit Mount Airy in September during "Mayberry Days," featuring a pie-eatin' contest, a pig-pickin' cookout and Opie's Backyard playground where kids can dig for worms and play hopscotch. If you attend the festival's "Siamese Twins Lecture," you will learn about Mount Airy's other famous residents, Eng and Chang Bunker.

The twin Chinese boys, joined at the chest, had been touring in a freak show when they settled here in 1839. Desperate for a "normal" life, they bought 100 acres of farmland and married Sallie Ann and Adelaide Yates, two local sisters who were daughters of a wealthy farmer. They bought slaves, rallied for the Whig party, and fathered 21 children (which raises several questions I won't delve into at the moment). In 1874 Chang got bronchitis and died. Eng panicked and died several hours later, though an autopsy showed he was perfectly healthy and had likely died from fright. The twins are buried at the **White Plains Baptist Church cemetery** (Route 601, two miles west of Mount Airy) in a large grave.

Mount Airy has lots more history as well as some fine places to stay, shop and eat. To find out more, stop in the **Mount Airy Chamber of Commerce** and pick up brochures, a walking-tour map and a copy of *The Mayberry Confidential* newspaper. ~ 200 North Main Street; 910-786-6116.

but at the low prices are a great value. Every morning, elaborate breakfasts are served in a sunny dining room. ~ 513 Wachovia Street, Winston-Salem; 910-777-0332. BUDGET.

HIDDEN ▶ In a lovely historic neighborhood near downtown, **Lady Anne's** is a stunning house elaborately decorated with gingerbread and balconies and spindle rails. Built around 1890 and still looking very much the part of a Queen Anne beauty, it has rooms and suites plush with period furnishings and big private baths (some with double-sized showers and jacuzzis) and cable TV. One room has a private balcony underneath the magnolia tree. A full breakfast is included. ~ 612 Summit Street, Winston-Salem; 910-724-1074. MODERATE TO ULTRA-DELUXE.

Once the 1100-acre estate of William Reynolds (R. J.'s brother) and his wife, Kate, Tanglewood is now a big and beautiful county park offering many activities and several places to stay. Best is the **Manor House**, Reynolds' former home that was built in 1859 and restored. There are only 10 rooms, all with ample space and all impeccably furnished in the style of a country manor, with swag drapes, louvered wood blinds, and rich hues of cranberry and hunter green. The windows look out on lawns of dogwood trees and towering pines. When you have breakfast in the Dogwood Room, take a good look at the stone hearth: there are dogwood blooms hidden in the design. Moderate rates include breakfast. In addition to the house, there is a motel-style **lodge** where accommodations are basic and budget-priced, and several rustic **cabins** can be rented by the week. ~ Off Route 158 in Clemmons, southwest of Winston-Salem; 910-766-0591, fax 910-766-1571. BUDGET TO MODERATE.

About 30 minutes north of Winston-Salem, deep in the coolness of a forested mountain with not even a sign to announce its HIDDEN ▶ presence, is **Pilot Knob Bed and Breakfast Inn**. As soon as you see the log cabins with balconies looking into the woods, the whirlpool tubs and stone fireplaces, the swimming pool and sauna staring at the rocky knob of Pilot Mountain, you know it's a place where you could hole up for a long time. Innkeeper Jim Rouse intended it that way, for though he built the cabins from an 1800s tobacco barn, he gave them luxurious touches and plenty of spaces for whiling away long afternoons. And though hidden, the place is not far from Mount Airy, several state parks and the Blue Ridge Parkway. Closed the week before Christmas. ~ From Route 52, take the exit for Pilot Mountain State Park, then turn down New Pilot Knob Lane, the dirt gravel road immediately east of the overpass, Pilot Mountain; 910-325-2502. DELUXE.

DINING Whether it's lunch or dinner, make time for a meal at **Salem Tavern**. In the midst of Old Salem, it's a handsome place, built in 1816 as the main tavern's annex. There's a dining room simply but warmly adorned with wood floors and tables where you can enjoy old-fashioned fare like chicken pot pie and paprika schnitzel, veal stew and herb-roasted pork tenderloin. When it's warm you can eat outside on the back porch, beneath a huge hood of wisteria. No dinner on Sunday. ~ 736 South Main Street, Winston-Salem; 910-748-8585. DELUXE.

Tell someone you went to **Leon's Cafe** and they'll respond incredulously, "You found it?" It's in a warehouse district, down a side street next to the Holsum Bakery (translation: good smells), but it's a wonderful space, a bistro bright and open, with wood-framed mirrors on one long wall and bright art on the other. The brief menu changes daily, but you might try the free-range chicken stuffed with spinach and mushrooms and wrapped in phyllo pastry, or the baked salmon served with an orange-ginger sauce. Dinner only. ~ 924 South Marshall Street, Winston-Salem; 910-725-9593. MODERATE TO DELUXE.

◀ HIDDEN

With its blasé stucco exterior, the temptation is to drive by **South By Southwest** and keep going. Resist, go inside, and order some of their great southwestern cuisine. Start with grilled garlic shrimp and red chile with corncake and tequila orange butter, then progress to the cornbread-crusted salmon or smoked vegetable burrito. ~ 241 South Marshall Street, Winston-Salem; 910-727-0800. MODERATE.

Rainbow News & Café is Winston-Salem's bohemian haunt. Part newsstand, part takeout counter and part restaurant, it resides in an old house with a few tables inside and a bunch outside under the sycamore trees. There's plenty to satisfy vegetarians, gourmet coffee hounds, and even wine lovers. Sandwiches, salads, pasta and the like. ~ 712 Brookstown Avenue, Winston-Salem; 910-723-5010. BUDGET TO MODERATE.

Among the city's finer dining establishments, **Zevely House** was built around 1815 by Moravian cabinetmaker Van Neman Zevely as the centerpiece of his plantation. In 1974 the house was moved to its current downtown venue and beautifully furnished in period style. In winter, fires blaze in the hearths; in summer, the garden patio is the place for Sunday brunch. The fare is Continental and stimulating: salmon in potato crust with red wine beurre rouge, roast duck breast with white peach sauce, and scallops with apricots and jarlsberg cheese. All meals are accompanied by Moravian pumpkin muffins. No dinner on Sunday. ~ 901 West 4th Street, Winston-Salem; 910-725-6666. DELUXE.

In Greensboro, **Southern Lights** is a bistro both bright and boisterous, a good-feeling place serving fresh, inventive fare for lunch and dinner. You can order sandwiches and salads from the regular menu, or check the blackboard for something like oatmeal-crusted grouper with ginger honey glaze, cheese polenta with roasted vegetables and green chile sauce, or grilled sirloin with barbecued onions. A dozen wines are offered by the glass. ~ 105 North Smyres Place, Greensboro; 910-379-9414. BUDGET TO MODERATE.

In Mount Airy, **Snappy Lunch** has an entire wall devoted to *The Andy Griffith Show*. (Andy was from Mount Airy and based the show on his hometown.) Owner Charles Dowell, a meek and exceedingly friendly man, started working at Snappy Lunch in 1943 as a floor sweeper. He was 14. By 1961 he not only owned the place, he had created a famous pork chop sandwich. Today he sells over a thousand pork chop sandwiches every week in his tiny, time-worn lunch counter with old school desks for tables. His visitors have come from all 50 states. Dowell personally makes each sandwich, dipping the boneless chop in a not-too-thin-or-thick batter, frying it until crisp and bronze, laying it between steamed buns lathered with mustard, and mounding on tomato, onion, chili and sweet coleslaw. Price: $2.25. His menu also offers cheeseburgers (breaded or all-meat), BLTs and bologna sandwiches, all under $2. Closed Sunday. ~ 125 North Main Street, Mount Airy; 910-786-4931. BUDGET.

SHOPPING   You can buy your Moravian sugar cakes and cookies at the airport, but it's much more fun to go to **Winkler Bakery** in Old Salem. The women bake everything in a big brick oven, using the same methods and secret recipes as the original Moravians did 200 years ago. ~ 525 South Main Street, Winston-Salem; 910-721-7302.

If you'd like to try making your own Moravian treats (though they won't be quite as good), walk down a block to **Moravian Book and Gift Shop**. Cookbooks, pictorials, oil paintings, toys and other Moravian items are for sale. ~ Located at 614 South Main Street, Winston-Salem; 910-723-6262.

The most enjoyable place to shop in Winston-Salem is **Reynolda Village**. Located next to Reynolda House and part of the old Reynolds' estate, the green-roofed white cottages were once barns, cattlesheds, corncribs, smokehouses and homes to various employees. Now they house upscale restaurants, shops and galleries, including the splendid **Art Gallery Originals** (910-723-9075), owned by Winston-Salem artists and featuring paintings and sculpture from around the nation. ~ 106 Reynolda Road.

Also within Reynolda Village, **Reynolda Antique Gallery** will satisfy that yearning to redecorate your home you've been having ever since you left Reynolda House. ~ 910-748-0741. At **The Niche**, you'll find basketry, pottery, jewelry, kaleidoscopes and fabric dolls. ~ 910-724-3912.

HIDDEN ►   If you hang around the Piedmont very long, you will hear talk of **Seagrove pottery**. If you are a pottery person, you'll find Seagrove's in little studios, many of them modest, kudzu-encrusted homes along Routes 220 and 705, and down dirt and gravel side roads. At last count, there were 78 "turners and burners" making Seagrove pottery, though the numbers change weekly. ~ Located in the hamlet of Seagrove, off Route 220, about 40 miles south of Greensboro.

NIGHTLIFE

The early-evening minglers at **Shobers** are a mix of straight and gay professionals. The classy, ever-popular restaurant and bar has dining alfresco and drinking. ~ Fourth and Summit streets, Winston-Salem; 910-724-3510.

Rayne Cellar, downstairs at Bistro 900, has live jazz on weekends and is great for after-dinner drinks on weekdays. ~ 900 South Marshall Street, Winston-Salem; 910-721-1336.

Winston-Salem's burgeoning coffeehouse culture offers alternative nighttime prospects. At **The Horse's Mouth,** the entertainment might be acoustic guitar or poetry readings, or even foreign film screenings. ~ 425 West Fourth Street; 910-773-1311. **Morning Dew Herb and Coffee Co.** has acoustic entertainment 'most every night. ~ 1140 Burke Street; 910-723-5282.

The latest, greatest technorama, **Beethoven's Fourth,** cranks after 10 p.m. with Top-40 spun by a deejay. Quarter drafts, ladies' nights, and other college-type specials are offered throughout the week. Cover. ~ 638 West 4th Street, downtown Winston-Salem; 910-773-1517.

Ziggy's has the best bands around, with concerts six nights a week. Better Than Ezra, Dave Matthews Band and Hootie & The Blowfish are among the big names who've played here, but the local and regional talent is hot too. Cover. ~ 433 Baity Street, Winston-Salem; 910-748-1064.

For traditional country-and-western, go to **Iron Horse Station.** The dancefloor is gigantic—5000 square feet—and usually covered with line dancers or square dancers. Live bands are featured most nights. Cover. ~ 3170 Peters Creek Parkway, Winston-Salem; 910-785-9925.

At **Cup-A-Joe,** acoustic, blues and folk bands alternate on weekends. You can choose from a long lineup of espressos, lattes, mochas and more—there's no alcohol. ~ 411 Tate Street, Greensboro; 910-275-2386.

THEATER, OPERA AND DANCE   With more than 50 cultural and entertainment groups, the performing arts thrive in Winston-Salem. The **North Carolina School for the Arts** hosts 250 performances alone, ranging from dance to music to drama. ~ 200 Waughtown Street; 910-721-1945. The **Broadway Preview Series** showcases musicals and comedies. ~ 405 West 4th Street; 910-723-3533. The **Piedmont Opera Theatre** puts on two full-scale productions annually at the Stevens Center. ~ 610 Coliseum Drive; 910-759-2277. The **North Carolina Black Repertory Company**

produces four major shows a year, as well as the National Black Theatre Festival. ~ 610 Coliseum Drive; 910-723-7907.

GAY SCENE   Unlike most other areas of North Carolina, many of the Piedmont's fast-growing, New South cities offer a thriving young gay scene.

In Winston-Salem, the scene inside **Bourbon Street** is definitely hot. Popular with gay men and women, it features entertainment by male dancers and female impersonators. Cover. ~ 916 Burke Street, Winston-Salem; 910-724-4644.

There's plenty of gay nightlife in nearby Greensboro, where everyone's talking about **Babylon**, a New York–style progressive dance club with a tri-level bar and huge dancefloor. Primarily gay and lesbian, though straights show up, too. ~ 221 South Elm Street, Greensboro; 910-275-1006.

Equally fashionable, **Warehouse 29** is also a destination for gay men and women, with mainstream music for dancing and a patio bar for outdoor relaxing. All-male revues and female impersonators are also featured. Cover. ~ 1011 West Arnold Street, Greensboro; 910-333-9333.

Expect a boisterous crowd Monday through Friday at **The Palms**, a downtown spot with live shows every Wednesday. Cover. ~ 413 North Eugene Street, Greensboro; 910-272-6307.

BEACHES & PARKS

TANGLEWOOD PARK 🏃🐎🚣⛵⛳   As county parks go, this one's a showplace, thanks to its beginnings as the luxuriant nineteenth-century estate of Will and Kate Reynolds, brother and sister-in-law to R. J. Reynolds. Rambling green lawns, ivy-clad pines and oaks, two lakes, rose gardens and "fragrance" gardens—filled with good-smelling greenery—grace these 1200 acres, and there are thick woods filled with deer. In spring when the roses bloom, the deer come out to nibble at the buds and you can watch them eat in the early morning. There are myriad places to stay, including the historic Reynolds' manor house and a cozy motel, and myriad ways to spend your time, from golfing at one of the two championship courses to taking a hayride. The Tanglewood Steeplechase, held every May, is one of Winston-Salem's most celebrated events. Swimming is best at the swimming pool. Fishing is good in the park's two lakes; $1.50. Facilities include paddleboat, canoe, rowboat and johnboat rentals; a farm offering guided horseback rides, hayrides and riding lessons; nature trails; sandwich grill. Day-use fee, $2. ~ Off Route 158 in the town of Clemmons, about eight miles southwest of Winston-Salem; 910-766-0591.

▲ There are 100 sites for tent and RV camping; $10 per night for tents and $17 for RVs.

HIDDEN ►   **HANGING ROCK STATE PARK** 🏃🚣⛵🏊   If you just want to be in the woods, screened from civilization by 6000 acres of tall trees and the sides of mountains, come to this place less than an hour's drive north of Winston-Salem. It's in the Sauratown Mountains, low as far as mountains go (1700 to 2500 feet) but intensely scenic, as evidenced by the nubby outcropping that gives the park its name. There are many more rocks, which is why rappelers and rock climbers especially love this place. Climbing and rappelling are allowed in designated areas. A permit is required, but there's no fee. Check with the park office. For picnicking and swimming, there's a 12-acre lake edged with forest and a mocha-colored beach. Swimming is good only at the protected, shallow, sandy area in the lake in summer. The fishing is excellent for bass and bream in the Dan River. Facilities include a visitors center, picnic tables with grills, hiking trails, restrooms (pit toilets only in the winter), a bathhouse and snack bar at the lake, rowboat rentals in the summer, and a boat ramp at the Dan River. Six rustic cabins can be rented by the week only in the summer, daily the rest of the year. Many facilities are closed in the winter. ~ Located about 32 miles north of Winston-Salem, 4 miles northwest of the hamlet of Danbury. You can reach the park from several paved roads (called "hard roads" by local folk) including Routes 89, 8 and 66. From Pilot Mountain State Park, take Moore's Lake Road; 910-593-8480.

▲ Seventy-three sites accommodate tents and RVs; rates range from $4.50 to $9.

PILOT MOUNTAIN STATE PARK From a long way away, the rocky knob of Pilot Mountain looks like a bump on the head. From its summit, in turn, the landscape ripples in carpets of forest, a tremendous vista stretching into Virginia. The bump is made of quartzite and was used by American Indians and early settlers as a guidepost. It's now a national landmark. The wild and clear waters of the Yadkin River cut through this 3703-acre wilderness park, and you can follow riverside trails through luscious foliage. There is no swimming. Fishing is good in the Yadkin River for largemouth bass, sunfish and catfish. Facilities include a park office, picnic areas with grills, pit toilets and canoe and hiking and bridle trails. ~ Located about 25 miles north of Winston-Salem off Route 52, near the town of Pinnacle; 910-325-2355.

▲ Family camping area with 49 primitive sites for tents or RVs (no hookups); hot showers; $9 per site per night.

Spread between the metropolises of Winston-Salem and Charlotte is this peculiar part of the Piedmont, where a traveler's main endeavor would likely involve buying furniture.

High Point to Hickory

The furniture fun starts just south of Winston-Salem at **High Point**, which calls itself the "Furniture and Hosiery Capital of the World."

SIGHTS

Ninety-one miles west, **Hickory** is simply the "Furniture Capital of the World." Both claims would seem justified, considering more than 250 furniture manufacturers and more than 100 hosiery companies make their homes in the area. In fact, some 60 percent of all American furniture is manufactured within a 200-mile radius around High Point and Hickory.

Two times when you *don't* want to be in the area are during the two, week-long International Home Furnishings Markets held every April and October in High Point. It's open to retailers only, who arrive by the tens of thousands and fill up hotels all the way to the Blue Ridge Mountains.

Before doing any furniture shopping, you may want to bone up on furniture history and lingo at the **Furniture Discovery Center**. Located downtown in a restored fabric warehouse, it's where one discovers just how a Queen Anne Highboy begins life (with a lot of carving, cutting and staining), and how adept you must be at using an air-powered nail gun to make a love seat. At the tour's climax, "the mysteries of upholstery are unveiled." Closed Monday from November through March. Admission. ~ 101 West Green Drive, High Point; 910-887-3876.

Adjacent to the Discovery Center, the **Angela Peterson Doll and Miniature Museum** invites visitors to "See the World in Dolls!" It showcases one woman's collection of more than 1600 dolls and miniatures from 54 countries. Even if you're not a doll lover, you may be intrigued by all those pensive eyes staring at you from their faces of china, wood and wax. There's even a Princess Di doll in a wedding dress, and a doll made of seaweed. Closed Monday from November through March. Admission. ~ 101 West Green Drive, High Point; 910-885-3655.

Even odder is the **World's Largest Bureau**. More than three stories high, 27 feet long and 14 feet wide, the wooden chest of drawers was built in 1926 to keep up with neighboring Thomasville, which had (and still has) the world's biggest chair. The High Point Jaycees used to keep their offices inside the bureau, and people would show up asking to look in their drawers. Now the bureau is locked tight, though you're welcome to take pictures. ~ 508 Hamilton Street, High Point.

HIDDEN ▶

Off Route 29-70, a long skinny bridge delivers you across the Yadkin River to tiny, historic **Spencer**. Like many small Southern towns, its neighborhoods are populated with pretty Victorian and antebellum homes. But Spencer's claim to the map is **The North Carolina Transportation Museum and Historic Spencer Shops**. It's housed in a brick building that rambles along the railroad tracks, and that used to be Southern Railway Company's steam locomotive headquarters (the town is named for Samuel Spencer, first president of the railway). Exhibits trace the history of local transporta-

Barbecue Capital
of the World

Furniture gave **Lexington** its name, but barbecue gave it fame. Just south of Winston-Salem, the plain town of weathered, whitewashed homes has 16,000 residents and 18 barbecue joints—which should easily make it the barbecue capital of the world. Lexington even hosts an annual Barbecue Festival with a parade of pigs.

Lexington barbecue was born in the 1920s when local fellas Sid Weaver and Varner Swicegood set up cinderblock cookers across from the Lexington County Courthouse and started cookin' on big court days. They cooked only pork shoulders and only over hickory wood fires, and it became the way to make Piedmont barbecue. (Elsewhere in the Carolinas, whole pigs are cooked and not always on wood fires but in gas and electric cookers and ovens—methods that horrify Lexington folks.) Typically, the pork is pulled by hand off the bone, hence the term "pulled pork," a food that you will see across the Carolinas.

Exactly who in Lexington serves the best barbecue is naturally a point of contention and great competition. Some folks like their pork shoulder sliced paper thin, some insist on fine-chopped till it's nearly shredded, and yet others prefer those coarse-chopped, stew-size chunks. Lexington sauce is vinegar-based, as opposed to tomato-based in the rest of the world, and it's slathered on the meat at the table, not back in the kitchen. Sauce is usually served in plastic squirt bottles—clear for mild; red for spicy. Coleslaw is doused in the same sauce, then heaped on the meat inside a sandwich. Sandwiches, by the way, are simply called "barbecues." The ultimate barbecue, in my experience, is one that's light on the slaw, heavy on the pork, nestled between soft but sturdy buns, with just enough spicy sauce to moisten the bread but not make it mushy.

Such a sandwich can be found at **Speedy's**, advertising "The Best Barbecue Anywhere." Locals start wandering in around 10:30 a.m. every morning, sliding into the tattered vinyl booths in anticipation of getting their daily barbecue fix. There are also pork plates that come with french fries and hushpuppies, and there are burgers, but don't order the latter unless you're prepared to endure the consternation of the waitress. Closed Sunday. ~ Winston Road, on the north end of town; 704-246-2092. BUDGET.

"You all right today?" is how the waitresses greet you at **Lexington Barbecue**, opened in the 1960s and famous for its owner, nicknamed "Honey Monk," and for having Tom Cruise and Ronald Reagan as former patrons. The sauce here is wonderfully tangy and rust-colored; the sandwiches are served on the teeniest of paper plates. Closed Sunday. ~ 10 Route 29-70 South; 704-249-9814. BUDGET.

tion, from Blackbeard the pirate, who used the marshy backwaters to transport his loot, to the 1970s-era Coot-A Amphibian seaplane designed by North Carolinian Bill Motes. There's a 1913 Tin Lizzie and a 1935 gangster-style North Carolina Highway Patrol car with a bulletproof windshield. From April through mid-December, you can take a 50-minute ride around the 57-acre property in a restored steam or diesel locomotive. Admission to ride the train. ~ Salisbury Avenue, Spencer; 704-636-2889.

Next door, the bigger town of **Salisbury** is a marvelous place to spend an afternoon. First stop at the **Rowan County Convention and Visitors Bureau** and pick up a walking-tour map and information guide. The map will direct you to more than 90 historic houses and points of interest. ~ 215 Depot Street, Salisbury; 704-638-3100, 800-332-2343.

Salisbury has been around since 1747, when Scotch-Irish settlers first crossed the ruddy Piedmont. German immigrants soon followed and then others, making their way along the Great Pennsylvania Wagon Road from Lancaster County or on the Trading Path from Virginia. Daniel Boone spent his childhood here fishing the Yadkin River and hunting surrounding woods. Andrew Jackson studied law in Salisbury in the 1780s, and George Washington visited in 1791 and wrote that it was "a pleasant village."

Located in Rowan County, the village gets its name from an English cathedral town, not from the steak you're thinking of, though it did produce a locally famous beverage called Cheerwine. Created in 1917 by a man named L. D. Peeler, the wine-colored, sweet and syrupy soft drink tastes a little like Dr. Pepper and is "full of good cheer," according to the label. If you'd like to try a swig, do it in Salisbury. It's tough to find Cheerwine anywhere else.

It takes a couple of hours to explore the 30 square historic blocks of Salisbury. Make sure you walk down **South Fulton Street** for a look at the fabulous homes with their luscious gardens and long, lazy driveways. The architecture is wildly varied, from Victorian storybook with rampant filigree to Neoclassical Revival with great porticoes to Italianate and Colonial Revival.

One block over, the **Rowan Museum** gives a glimpse at life in the early 1800s inside one of these moneyed abodes. Built in 1819, the Federal-style townhouse is the handiwork of master builder Jacob Stirewalt, who designed an elaborate curved staircase and fanciful moldings. Period furnishings and many other fine Rowan County artifacts are displayed. Closed Monday through Wednesday. Admission. ~ Located at 116 South Jackson Street, Salisbury; 704-633-5946.

About 14 miles west of Salisbury, off roving rural Route 150, awaits one of North Carolina's most unexpected and rewarding hidden sights: camels, antelope, water buffalo and hundreds more

exotic animals, all roaming the range at **Lazy 5 Ranch**. Owner   ◀ HIDDEN
Henry Hampton is a wildlife collector who invites people to turn
into the pastures (but stay in the car) and take a 3.5-mile auto tour
of the animals. Along the rutted paths you're apt to see rare albino
elk from the Rocky Mountains, antelope from India, deer from the
Far East, and Watusi cattle from Africa, whose horns get as wide
as 12 feet. Horse-drawn wagon rides are available by appointment,
and there's a petting zoo where children can spend hours. Among
Hampton's list of rules for visitors: "Don't honk your horn or turn
on your lights unless you need help because it gives our animals
heartburn." Admission. ~ Route 150, Mooresville; 704-663-5100.

From here, backtracking east on narrow, lonely **Route 152** is
another real drive in the country, past vast Hereford ranches stenciled in rough-hewn fence, farmhouses and gazebos parked on
wandering lawns, and intermittent tin shacks selling such diverse
items as pottery and farm tools. You will pass a town called **China**   ◀ HIDDEN
Grove, named for chinaberry groves found here in the 1700s, and
see soft, sculpted pastures ebbing and flowing along the horizon.
You will definitely know you are outside the mainstream by all the
cow manure on the road.

In Salisbury, the magnificent **Rowan Oak House Bed and Breakfast**   **LODGING**
is a Victorian fantasy, complete with a cupola, rich wall tapestries
and elaborate carved wood. Guests are invited to stay in one of
four bedrooms, each with a private bath (one has a jacuzzi tub set
in a bay window and one a two-person marble shower), and all
plushly adorned. ~ 208 South Fulton Street, Salisbury; 704-633-
2086, 800-786-0437. DELUXE.

Almost everything else is a chain motel or hotel; for a comprehensive list, contact the **High Point Convention & Visitors Bureau**.
Closed Saturday and Sunday. ~ 300 South Main Street, High Point;

✔ **CHECK THESE OUT—UNIQUE LODGING**

- *Moderate*: Find solace just outside the big city at **Still Waters Bed and Breakfast** and its lovely, wooded setting along a lake. *page 210*
- *Moderate to deluxe*: Climb into a high, downy bed at **Oakwood Inn**, a beautiful 1871 Victorian house in Raleigh's finest neighborhood. *page 227*
- *Deluxe*: Sequester yourself inside an elegant log cabin buried in mountain woods at **Pilot Knob Bed and Breakfast Inn**. *page 188*
- *Ultra-deluxe*: Spend the night at one of the Piedmont's supreme mon-eyed retreats, **Pinehurst Resort and Country Club** (and don't forget your golf clubs). *page 219*

Budget: under $60 Moderate: $60–$100 Deluxe: $100–$130 Ultra-deluxe: over $130

910-884-5255. In Hickory, go to the **Greater Hickory Convention & Visitors Bureau**. ~ 470 Route 70 Southwest, Hickory; 704-328-6111, 800-849-5093.

DINING

Like the local lodging, dining is almost strictly a chain restaurant experience. Breaking the chain mold is **1859 Café**, where dressed-up fare is served in dressed-up surroundings. Imaginative pasta dishes, salads, seafood, fowl and duckling are featured. Try the grouper rolled in hazelnuts with Frangelica butter, or the rack of lamb with garlic herb, mustard crust and cabernet sauce. ~ 443 2nd Avenue Southwest, Hickory; 704-322-1859. DELUXE.

The same owners offer lighter fare that's just as inventive at **Jessica's Porch**, a terrific place for lunch while you're furniture shopping. ~ 2220 Route 70 Southeast, in the Hickory Furniture Mart; 704-324-7204. BUDGET.

SHOPPING

Think furniture. You'll recognize the big names—Broyhill, Lexington, Thomasville, Drexel Heritage—whose factories sprawl around High Point and Hickory. Most have showrooms attached where you can browse the latest lines and styles. Furniture retail outlets and warehouses also abound in the area. Prices are often so low that even with the cost of shipping your purchases back home, you can save up to 50 percent. The amount of savings depends on how much you buy, how far you live and how committed you are to finding the best deal. Folks are known to make furniture forays from as far away as Canada, hoping to furnish their houses at deeply discounted prices.

If this, too, is your hope, then come prepared. With hundreds of stores and thousands of styles to choose from, it's best to know what you want *before* you arrive. Furniture consultants suggest shopping stores at home and making a list of the lines and styles you like. Then you can comparison shop in High Point and Hickory. Two of the best times to shop are in March and September, right before the International Home Furnishings Market. This is when manufacturers and discounters offer clearance prices to make room for the new lines they'll show at the market.

Comprehensive lists of furniture showrooms and outlets are available from the **High Point Convention & Visitors Bureau**. Closed Saturday and Sunday. ~ 300 South Main Street; 910-884-5255. You can also get lists from the **Greater Hickory Convention & Visitors Bureau** ~ 470 Route 70 Southwest; 704-328-6111, 800-849-5093. Both places can also provide the names of furniture consultants who, for a fee, will assist with your hunt.

A couple of shopping tips: Some discounters do not accept credit cards, only cash or sometimes personal checks with proper identification. Most places require a deposit of 25 to 50 percent when you place an order; the balance is due when the furniture is ready for shipping, or upon delivery. Delivery charges are typically based on weight and distance, though some discounters charge according to the price of your order.

If you order from several stores within one furniture mart, you can usually consolidate the shipping charges. Make sure you inform each store of your other purchases, and that the sales people write "Consolidation" on your orders. This, of course, is a big advantage of shopping furniture megastores and marts, where several floors of stores have snazzy showrooms and interior designers for salespeople.

Among the megastores and furniture marts: **The Atrium**, spanning some 250,000 square feet—over five football fields—of furniture. Thirty-seven galleries represent more than 700 manufacturers. ~ 430 South Main Street, High Point; 910-882-5599. **Rose Furniture Company** is less than half the size of the Atrium but carries just as many lines. ~ 916 Finch Avenue, High Point; 910-886-6050. **Furnitureland South** boasts 230,000 square feet of furniture displays and 300 different lines. There's also a third-floor library with catalogs and fabric and wood samples, and more than 50 telephones that put you instantly in touch with a salesperson. ~ 5635 Riverdale Road, Jamestown; 910-841-4328.

The megalopolis you hear about most is **Hickory Furniture Mart**, covering 13 acres and four stories of windowed showrooms. Sixty-five galleries, outlets and discounters showcase more than 500 lines, and there are places to buy reduced-price linens, lighting, wallpaper and bath fixtures. Furniture styles range from American Colonial, Art Deco and French provincial to Queen Anne, contemporary and Louis XV. ~ 2220 Route 70 Southeast, Hickory; 704-322-3510.

If you are one of those people who would rather get in the car and drive, stopping randomly at factory showrooms and warehouse outlets, then get on **Route 321** in Hickory and head north for 20 miles. Dozens of places offer bargains, and it's a pleasant drive in the country besides. **Route 70** between Statesville and Morganton also features scores of discount furniture stores.

NIGHTLIFE

It's quiet around furnitureland. Most folks have a drink at their hotel or, in High Point, at **J. Besul Noble's Uptown**. The jazzy restaurant has a polished bar with live jazz most nights. ~ 114 South Main Street, High Point; 910-889-3354.

BEACHES & PARKS

BOONE'S CAVE STATE PARK 🚶 A tiny, primitive park set along the Yadkin River, it's where Daniel Boone hunted and fished as a child, and where he supposedly spent nights in a cave along the riverbank. Boone's Cave isn't very big or comfortable, though, only two to three feet high and eighty feet long, and you have to worm your way between dark, clammy walls. Small kids don't seem to

◀ *HIDDEN*

mind, but they'll need a flashlight. The 110-acre park also has the one-room Boone's Cabin, a replica of one Boone built here, but you'll have to hike a mile round-trip through hardwood forest to see it. Facilities include a picnic shelter, a restroom and a hiking trail. ~ Located on Boone's Cave Road, about four and a half miles east of Route 150, north of Salisbury and near the hamlet of Churchland; 704-528-6514.

▼▼▼▼▼▼▼▼▼▼▼
Charlotte Area

Anyone who knew Charlotte before the 1980s and hasn't been back is in for a big surprise. In little more than a decade the city has gone from a low-key, low-slung urban hub to an upscale, uptown metropolis of the New South. Nearly half a million people now call Charlotte home, and every day many more are moving in. It's the biggest city between Atlanta and Washington, D.C., though not at all overwhelming, either physically or traffic-wise. How long it can stay that way will no doubt depend on the abilities of city politicians and planners, and how fast the city grows.

SIGHTS

Charlotte's renaissance is most obvious downtown, where soaring, variously contoured buildings of metal and glass and granite create a modern symphony in the sky. Downtown is actually referred to as **Uptown Charlotte**, and this is where you should begin exploring, your first stop being the **Charlotte Convention & Visitors Bureau**, on the northwest side of Uptown. The bureau has more brochures than you would care to count, but you should definitely pick up the *Visitors Guide to Charlotte*, which has key-coded maps of virtually every area sight. Closed weekends. ~ 122 East Stonewall Street; 704-334-2282, 800-231-4636.

Most major Uptown sights are concentrated on the north end and are easy to see on foot. From the visitors bureau, walk east to the **intersection of Trade and Tryon streets**, and you will be where it all began. Several hundred years ago, two American Indian trading paths cut through the woods and ran right into each other at this very spot. After the Europeans arrived, mostly Scotch-Irish settlers, they took over the trading post and began building homes here. To get better trade deals from the British, they named the crossroads Charlotte, after the queen of England, then named the county Mecklenburg, after her German birthplace. Today, Charlotte calls itself "The Queen City," and calls this particular crossroads—now overshadowed by twentieth-century buildings of business and trade—**The Square**.

A couple of blocks away is Charlotte's loftiest building, **Founders Hall**. Opened in 1993 and rising 60 stories, the big banking center is the highest building in the Southeast, at least until a higher one comes along (and when one does, don't be surprised if it's in Charlotte). Head through the glass doors and you're met by an enormous glass atrium with a winter garden flooded with sunlight, and walls transformed by a trio of frescoes depicting the building's creation, as well as city scenes. The frescoes are the work of Ben Long, North Carolina's famed fresco artist whose rural church frescoes in the Blue Ridge Mountains have drawn thousands of spectators. Now just as many people are coming to experience his Founders Hall work. Founders Hall also has two floors of restaurants and shops, in case you care to browse. ~ 100 North Tryon Street; 704-386-0120.

If you have children, you must take them to **Discovery Place**. Charlotte's science showpiece, it is a science museum like no other in the South, perhaps even the nation, with engaging and engrossing exhibits lodged in big and bright rooms painted in bold, bright colors that seem never-ending, leading you on a journey through a re-created rainforest, solar galaxy, mission control and space station,

Charlotte Area

science circus, undersea world and many other worlds and places. Giant panels and whole walls beep and blink in a blaze of neon, contraptions swirl, grind and pop, and children swarm in an ecstatic frenzy, giving the distinct feel of a juvenile Las Vegas. Admission. ~ 301 North Tryon Street; 704-372-6261, 800-935-0553.

The rainforest, however, is different. It is subtle and nearly quiet, a wedge of real plants and vines and trees, all very green and very damp, lodged behind a colossal wall of glass. Step inside and stroll through the forest on a catwalk, listening to the hoots and howls emanating from the tangle of luscious greenery. The noises are compliments of the rainforest residents: birds such as the Latin American aracari, deeply colored with a banded breast; the Victoria crowned pigeon, from New Guinea; and the wonderfully named "touraco-go away" from Africa. Some of the birds are involved in daily shows put on by the museum's animal trainers. Daily, five-minute thunderstorms also happen in the forest; check the front desk for times.

In an adjacent room, sea exhibits are just as absorbing. There's a simulated wave that rolls behind glass, giant tanks with everything from queen triggerfish and loggerhead turtles to camouflage fish (which become transparent when enemies come around) and nurse sharks who seem to be only inches away. Children especially love the shallow pool where they can touch snails and hermit crabs underwater.

There are, of course, plenty of other exhibits in this two-level museum, enough to keep a visitor busy at least two days. You can duck into a kaleidoscope and see hundreds of images of yourself (frightening for some folks), build a simulated sandwich on a computer and learn its nutritional details (much healthier without the cheese), and search for cavities in a mouthful of teeth.

The Discovery Place is also home to the **Omnimax Theatre** and the **Space Voyager Planetarium**, both exceptional places with frequent, everchanging shows. The Omnimax, with its overwhelming, omnipresent dome of screen and six-track sound system, feels more like a ride than a theater. Sink down into a cushiony seat, recline all the way back, and look up and around at the screen. The shows are often cosmic in nature, taking you on mental trips through time and space, and causing many to pitch and scream at various points (and some even to get seasick; just close your eyes for a few minutes if you feel woozy).

You can buy separate tickets for the museum, theatre and planetarium, or pay a combined admission for two or all three—definitely the best deal.

From Discovery Place, you can walk two blocks north and one block east to Charlotte's most famous neighborhood: **Fourth Ward**. Victorian fantasy homes, painted in sherbet colors and amusingly adorned with turrets and gables, high-peaked roofs and wood-shakes, and spectacular stained glass, parade up and down the lamp-lined brick streets. Parks the size of postage stamps offer benches for resting and fountains that bubble at your feet. Mint-colored liriope grass spills over the sidewalks, and rose gardens perfume the air. All in all, an enlightening place to stroll, and no doubt live, though quite expensively. ~ Northeast corner of Uptown, bounded roughly by Seventh, Graham, Tenth and Church streets.

Before you start exploring the restored homes of the Fourth Ward, pick up the guide *A Walk Through Historic Fourth Ward* from the Charlotte Convention & Visitors Bureau.

Fourth Ward began life as an upscale place in the mid-1800s, but did not stay that way. One of the city's four political wards, it was established by doctors and merchants and other well-to-do people. Time passed, the original owners eventually died, and the homes were not maintained. After World War II, many houses were divided into apartments or became boarding-houses or trade schools for veterans. By the early 1970s, some places were even selling liquor and sex. But the brothels and boarding-houses were soon bought up by citizens committed to saving the Fourth Ward, and during the 1980s, an extraordinary restoration took place.

On the south end of Uptown, a short drive from Fourth Ward, the **Afro-American Cultural Center** is a striking, early 1900s building of red brick with great Greek Revival columns and stained-glass windows shimmering all around, looking very much like the church it used to be. There's a small theater and larger amphitheater, and a gallery with changing exhibits of African and African-American art of stellar quality. Closed Monday. ~ 401 North Meyers Street; 704-374-1565.

There are a lot of old houses around Charlotte, but none as old as the one stuck out in the sprawling suburbia just east of Uptown at the **Charlotte Museum of History & Hezekiah Alexander Home-site.** The shuttered, unassuming, two-story rock house was built in 1774 by Hezekiah Alexander, who called himself a planter but was a whole lot more—including a justice of the peace and signer of the Mecklenburg Declaration of Independence, which created North Carolina's state government. He had a wife and ten kids, the latter sharing three bedrooms upstairs who must have loved roving the woods around the house.

◄ HIDDEN

As you stroll through the forest of black walnut and rhododendron today, notice the "placer pits," little craters dug by prospectors searching for gold. Though none of the original belongings remain, the house has been furnished with Piedmont antiques, and likely looks much as it did two centuries ago. Similar antiques can be seen in the Museum of History adjacent to the home. Wheelchair visitors can easily tour the museum and grounds, but do not have access to the inside of the home. Wheelchairs are available at the front desk. Closed Monday. Admission for the tour. ~ 3500 Shamrock Drive; 704-568-1774.

HIDDEN ► South of Uptown Charlotte, hidden in a moneyed neighborhood of elegant, vast homes whose roofs reach up into the treetops, is the inspirational **Wing Haven Gardens and Bird Sanctuary**. After decades of hard work, Elizabeth and Edwin Clarkson transformed a barren field of clay into a lush three-acre bird habitat. More than 100 varieties of birds have visited the brick-walled gardens since they opened in 1927. Hummingbirds, woodpeckers, mockingbirds, hawks, and warblers come here, and so do brown-headed nuthatches, great horned owls, and blue-gray gnatcatchers. An illustrated brochure guides you through the luxuriant flowers and trees, describing the history of the fountains and statuary and marking important places (such as where the Clarksons were sitting when they chose the name Wing Haven). Among the reflective inscriptions scattered throughout the greenery: "A garden is the mirror of a mind," by Henry Beston. Open on Tuesday and Sunday afternoons and on Wednesday mornings. ~ 248 Ridgewood Avenue; 704-331-0664.

With all the gold being discovered around the Piedmont in the 1800s, it's not surprising that the first branch of the United States Mint opened in Charlotte. Built in 1836 in what's now Uptown, it churned out $5 million in gold coins—a lot of dough in those days, but today not even enough to build the SouthPark Mall down the road. The Mint stopped being a mint around 1913, and 20 years later was nearly demolished before history lovers rescued it. They moved the low-lying building to the south end of town and made it the **Mint Museum of Art**, opening in 1936 as North Carolina's first art museum.

Today, the museum's permanent collection includes a fine sampling of American and European art, as well as outstanding pre-Columbian and Decorative art, spread across two floors. Among the diverse American selections are twentieth-century blown glass, papier-mâché, and metal collages; a Hudson River scene by Thomas Doughty, one of the founders of the Hudson River School of Art; and an 1836 portrait of a roseate spoonbill by Audubon. There are also some spectacularly ornate pieces of nineteenth- and twentieth-century furniture. Closed Monday. Admission. ~ 2730 Randolph Road; 704-337-2000.

If you want to see a prime example of New South growth, take a drive around **SouthPark**. Just 20 years ago, promotional brochures tell us, this was a cow pasture. Thanks to the daring dreams of big businessmen, including Charlotte mover-and-shaker John Belk of Belk Department Stores, the area is now a "masterpiece community," with miles of glossy retail and corporate buildings and reproduction antebellum homes and condos, and a complex grid of asphalt that constantly hums with New South traffic. Today, if you want to see the cows, you'll have to travel another ten miles south. ~ Four miles south of Uptown Charlotte; major SouthPark routes are Park, Sharon, Tyvola, Fairview and Woodlawn roads.

Which is not a bad way to go, considering there are many terrific sights on the outskirts of metropolitan Charlotte and just beyond, side trips ranging up to 30 miles that can easily be undertaken in an afternoon. Here are just some of the possibilities:

About ten miles south of downtown Charlotte, the **James K. Polk Memorial** remembers the birthplace of the eleventh president of the United States. Nicknamed "Young Hickory," Polk lived here with his family until he was 11. Polk's original homestead was destroyed, but a similar, authentic log cabin has been moved here. Notice that the cabin has no nails; it was built in the half-dovetail design popular during the late 1700s. Guides offer tours of the cabin and the cookhouse, describing the furniture, farm tools and other items of Polk's day. Closed Monday from November through March. ~ Route 521, Pineville; 704-889-7145.

Just west of here, **Paramount's Carowinds** straddles the line between North and South Carolina. The 91-acre theme park boasts six rollercoasters and a simulated NASCAR race ride, though in fact the place is more folksy than fantasy. Most of the rides work on the gravity principle as opposed to the high-tech Disney principle, and most of the entertainment is down-home country.

A family-pleaser since it opened in 1973, the park was bought in 1992 by Paramount Communications, which has added some movie-themed touches, including *Wayne's World* (after the movie of the same name) with its *Hurler* rollercoaster. While most of Carowinds re-creates Carolinas' scenes, Wayne's World re-creates the "most excellent" town of Aurora, Illinois, where Wayne and Garth hail—and hurl—from. Wayne's World is also home to the Drop Zone, which lets riders experience the sensation of freefall as they drop 100 feet at 56 mph.

Carowinds can be easily enjoyed in a day—and a day is what you should spend after forking over the hefty admission ($27.95 for ages 7 through 59). Among the rides worth repeating in a day: the *VORTEX*, a mind-scrambling rollercoaster you ride standing up; *Whitewater Falls*, a wet plunge down a 45-foot chute; and the *Carolina Cyclone*, a rollercoaster with four (count them) 360° loops and a 450° uphill helix for a finale. The *Skytower*, an air conditioned cabin that climbs 32 stories high, provides the best view around. For the little ones, *Hanna-Barbera Land* offers pint-sized rides and *Echo Park* has a giant playground.

Carowinds is closed in the fall and winter, and open weekends-only during spring. Dates and times vary, so call for hours of operation. Admission. ~ Located off Route 77; 704-588-2606, 800-888-4386.

Leave theme-park land and head for the country, traveling east on Route 51, then south on Route 16 about 13 miles, until you reach the small and engaging town of **Waxhaw**. The population is only 1300, but the town is home to upwards of 50 antique shops. Main Street proper is only about three blocks long, though it is split by railroad tracks, and there's an arched wooden bridge to take you from one side of the road to the other. You will definitely want to cross the road, lest you miss some of the antique shops that parade up and down each side, waiting behind gaily painted store-fronts in red-brick buildings.

HIDDEN ►

Just east of downtown Waxhaw off Route 75, you'll find the headquarters for JAARS Bible translators and their interesting **Museum of the Alphabet**. A series of decorative panels details the history and logic of language, from Maya and Egyptian hiero-glyphs to the Cherokee alphabet developed by Sequoyah, the only illiterate person known to have created a language. Definitely not a place to take the kids, as the displays are erudite, though fasci-nating. Despite the Biblical connection, there's no religious hype, here. In fact, the friendly volunteer docents aren't even JAARS mem-bers. Closed Sunday. ~ Davis Road, Waxhaw; 704-843-6066.

HIDDEN ►

To the west of Charlotte on Route 85, in the unexciting town of **Gastonia**, is an exciting place called the **Schiele Museum of Natural History**. Rooms and exhibits are given over to the natural world, including plants, animals, minerals and native peoples both near and far. The North American Wildlife Hall is filled with taxi-dermied beasts, from a moose and mountain goat to grizzly bear and antelope. The Hall of Earth and Man hones in on the geolog-ical and biological sides of things, and includes models of what some of the earliest, hairiest humans might have looked like. There's also a planetarium and a one-mile nature trail that's a good introduction to Piedmont plants. Closed Monday. Admission to the planetarium. ~ 1500 East Garrison Boulevard, Gastonia; 704-866-6900.

HIDDEN ►

Hidden along the banks of Catawba Creek, **Daniel Stowe Botanical Garden** is splendid for those with a fondness for flowers. In spring, the beds are bursting with azaleas, begonias, caladium and bleeding hearts. By fall, the chrysanthemums and asters have taken over. And even the depths of winter feature some decor: pan-sies and ornamental cabbages. In case you don't know a caladium from a chrysanthemum, all the flowers are labeled. ~ 6500 South New Hope Road, south of Gastonia in the town of Belmont; 704-825-4490.

For a look at how wealthy Piedmonters lived in the early 1800s, check out **Latta Place**, within Latta Plantation Park, off of Beatties

The Valley
of Love

Love first came to the valley in 1954 when Charlotte developer Andy Barker chucked city life for some benevolent green Piedmont pastures. He and his wife, Ellenora, bought a chunk of land north of Statesville but nowhere near anything in particular, save some scattered farmhouses and tobacco fields. Then they threw up some wood shacks and began building a Wild West utopia. It was Andy's lifelong dream, and he and Ellenora called it **Love Valley**.

Throughout the 1960s, love kept coming to the valley as hippies dropped out of society and pitched wigwams and tents and planted gardens. Soon "downtown" Love Valley began to take shape. Log and bark buildings and split-rail fences lined the one-block Main Street, and there was even a general store. Townsfolk lived mostly in tents or trailers and hardly ever drove cars, preferring to ride horses. Andy became the mayor and hired a town marshal, head shop owner Joe Ponder.

Little has changed today. In fact, cars aren't allowed on the sawdust Main Street, though you're welcome to tie your horse to one of the many hitchin' posts—everyone else does. The **General Store**, decorated with old wagon wheels, sells hot dogs, barbecue and Cheerwine; a toy horse out front runs on a dime. Open Friday through Sunday. ~ 704-592-5425. The ramshackle **Gracie's Kitchen** serves breakfast and barbecue. Open Friday through Sunday. ~ 704-592-4871. Andy's still the mayor, except for those intermittent years when he's voted out by Love Valley's 100 or so residents.

Joe Ponder, now the town deputy, traded his head shop for a leather store where he custom-makes saddles. If you step in the back of **Ponder Leather**, Joe will show you his "strong man" photos from the days when he lifted a 606-pound pumpkin with his teeth (he's listed in *Ripley's Believe It Or Not* and *The Guinness Book of World Records*). ~ 704-592-2010.

On weekends, there's usually a rodeo at the **Love Valley Arena** and there's always a big square dance. People come from surrounding states to dance and to join the weekend trailrides, arriving en masse on Friday nights with their horse trailers and RVs, setting up camp on the picturesque pastures around Love Valley. ~ 704-592-9413. For information on campsites, call Betty and Ron Trivette. ~ 704-592-9431. To rent a horse, call Buddy and Debbie Price. ~ 704-592-2024.

To get to Love Valley, you must drive down no-name country roads that squiggle through gentle hills speckled with whitewashed farmhouses sporting weathervanes. Fields of tobacco stretch to the horizon. *Directions:* From Route 40 just west of Statesville, take Route 115 North. Then follow the faded red heart-shaped signs to Love Valley.

Ford Road, northwest of downtown Charlotte. The restored clap-board, two-story plantation manse, furnished with Federal period pieces, was home to James Latta, a prosperous lawyer, merchant and planter, and his wife, Jane Knox. A smokehouse, log cabin and barn are being restored so that the park can become a working farm. Donkeys, sheep and chickens are among the current residents. Closed Monday. Admission. ~ 5225 Sample Road, Hunters-ville; 704-875-2312, 704-875-1391.

Birds of prey also live at Latta Plantation Park. Each year, the **Carolina Raptor Center** receives about 500 injured birds from across the Carolinas, most having been struck down by a car. About half are nursed back to health and set free. Eagles and owls, vultures and falcons all live in mesh enclosures, peering down from perches with their powerful raptor eyes. You will learn about raptor habits, including how they swallow whole mice and chicks and then regurgitate what their bodies can't digest. The regurgitated part is called a pellet. Closed Monday. Admission. ~ 704-875-6521.

HIDDEN ► Nearby, the **University of North Carolina at Charlotte Botanical Gardens** combines indoor and outdoor gardens. Begin your visit at the **McMillan Greenhouse**, a research and education center with maps to the gardens. Within the greenhouse are rooms simulating five of the world's growing environments. In the moist "tropical" room, there's sugarcane, coffee and papaya; in the dry and sunny "desert" room grow cactus and other succulents. Outside are plants native to the southeast United States, such as carnivorous pitcher plants, sundews and Venus flytraps. Next door, you'll find showy bromeliads and orchids from Guatemala, Venezuela and Mexico. Even more intriguing is the two-story "rainforest" with more than 400 plant species. Closed Sunday. ~ Mary Alexander Road, off Route 49 southeast of Huntersville; 704-547-2364.

HIDDEN ► From here, take Route 49 east to Route 601, then head south to Route 200. By this time you will know you're way out in the sticks, beyond any likeness of Charlotte, but keep pressing deeper into the country by taking the turnoff at Route 200 for **Reed Gold Mine State Historic Site**. The gold mine is in the woods, between the eye-blink hamlets of Georgeville and Locust, precisely where young Conrad Reed found a 17-pound hunk of gold—America's first nugget. The year was 1799, and Conrad showed the big "yellow rock" to his pa, a poor farmer named John Reed, who promptly used it as a doorstop.

Three years later, a Fayetteville jeweler noticed the doorstop and asked John Reed to name his price. Reed got $3.50 for the nugget but later discovered it was worth $3600, so he feverishly took to panning his creek. By 1824, he and a small crew of slaves and unsavory miners had dug up more than $100,000 in gold, including a 28-pound nugget found by Peter, a slave who didn't even enjoy a last name, but whose find set off the nation's first gold rush.

A film at the historic site, located on the old Reed farm, tells you this story and its ending (not a great one, as the farm was eventually closed due to a Reed family squabble, though John did die a wealthy man). After the film, a guide will take you five stories down into the dim, clammy shafts and wormy tunnels where Reed and his crew dug for gold as well as other minerals and gems. He'll show you the "veins" running along the quartz rock where gold and silver are born, and tell you how the Reeds used candles and oil lanterns to find their riches. During the summer, for a small fee, visitors can try their own luck at panning the Reed creek (something kids really enjoy), though you should know there have been no major finds reported lately. Closed Monday from November through March. ~ 9621 Reed Mine Road; 704-786-8337.

LODGING

Most downtown Charlotte hotels are highrises of the chain variety, which makes the **Dunhill Hotel** especially inviting. Since its opening in 1929 as the Mayfair Manor, the hostelry has been providing intimate accommodations and stellar service. Today there's a piano player in the lobby and original art by North Carolinian Philip Moose on the walls. Every room is desirable, having been restored with reproduction period pieces, poster beds and pedestal sinks. ~ 237 North Tryon Street, Charlotte; 704-332-4141, 800-354-4141, fax 704-376-4117. MODERATE TO DELUXE.

A fanciful brick manse on the edge of downtown Charlotte, **The Inn Uptown** was built in 1890 as one of the city's first speculative houses. In 1992 it became a stylish inn with seven rooms perpetually booked by business travelers. Every room has a TV and telephone with modem opportunities, and is decorated with real flair. Most desirable is the tower suite with its iron four-poster bed and staircase that spirals up to a loft with a jacuzzi under a massive chandelier. Four rooms have gas fireplaces. Rates include full breakfast in the morning and cookies at night. ~ 129 North Poplar Street, Charlotte; 704-342-2800, 800-959-1990, fax 704-342-2222. DELUXE TO ULTRA-DELUXE.

One of Charlotte's best lodging values can be found in a lovely lavender house called **The Elizabeth**. The bed and breakfast is named for the surrounding turn-of-the-century neighborhood of charming cottages and grand homes. There are but four rooms. One has an antique brass double bed and Laura Ashley bed linen, and a private entrance to a garden courtyard; the suite, with a blue, white and yellow color scheme, features a four-poster bed and separate sunroom. Breakfast is served in the dining room. ~ 2145 East 5th Street, Charlotte; 704-358-1368. MODERATE.

◀ HIDDEN

Amid posh SouthPark's highrise silhouettes and snazzy shops is the **Park Hotel**. Here things are polished and refined, from the lavish bouquets adorning the lobby to the hotel initials perfectly imprinted in the ashtray sands. Rooms are furnished with English reproductions, and turndown service includes a weather forecast card for the next day. There's a small gym, outdoor swimming pool and a restaurant. ~ 2200 Rexford Road, Charlotte; 704-364-8220, 800-334-0331, fax 704-365-4712. ULTRA-DELUXE.

HIDDEN ►

In a few minutes' drive, you can abandon the city for something silent and deeply wooded and lakeside. That would be **Still Waters Bed and Breakfast** at the upper end of Lake Wylie, where red-bellied woodpeckers play in tall maple and dogwood trees and blue herons swoop low over the water. The 1920s-era log-veneer house has two bedrooms and a suite, all decorated in homey style. One has a queen four-poster bed and plank walls, another a waterbed with mirrored canopy. A separate wooden cottage features a queen-sized bed, free-standing fireplace and jacuzzi tub in the private bath. Breakfast is served in the glass sunporch with views of the lake. ~ 6221 Amos Smith Road, near Charlotte-Douglas International Airport; 704-399-6299, fax 704-399-5406. MODERATE.

DINING

You would expect the Carolinas' largest city to have the most and best restaurants, and it does. You can have wholesome health food or wonderful deep-fried chicken with mashed potatoes and gravy, fiery Jamaican fare or something cucumbery from the Middle East or French country with a Southern twist—the list won't quit. Here are a few suggestions.

On the edge of historic Fourth Ward, in an exquisite, century-old house painted in purples, greens and pinks, is one of Charlotte's best places to dine. Jackets *and* reservations are required at the **McNinch House Restaurant**, the latter required several days in advance. Dining here is French and fabulous, and not to be undertaken with a skinny wallet. The six-course prix-fixe menu includes choices such as red bell-pepper bisque or shiitake mushroom and wild-rice soup, rack of lamb or Maine lobster tail in tomato vodka cream sauce over ravioli (some entrées have a Continental twist). Chocolate rules the desserts: go for the flourless Victorian chocolate cake. ~ 511 North Church Street, Charlotte; 704-332-6159. ULTRA-DELUXE.

Over the years, young downtown professionals have worn a path to **Alexander Michael's**, a popular, publike Fourth Ward eating and meeting place. The long, polished walnut bar is trimmed in brass, the ceiling is low and wood-paneled, and a bay window overlooks the lovely Victorian neighborhood. There are cocktails and wine and light eats—dressed-up sandwiches and burgers, pasta and salads—though the food is really secondary to the friendly atmosphere. Parking's a pain, so expect to walk several blocks. Closed Sunday. ~ 401 West 9th Street, Charlotte; 704-332-6789. MODERATE.

Located in the Dilworth area, **The Lamplighter** has long offered Charlotte premier dining experiences. Inside the 1926 Mediterranean mansion, in darkened dining nooks flickering with gaslights, black-tied waiters deliver exceptional French-Continental treatments of seafood, fowl and meats. For starters, there's buttermilk-fried quail with cheese grits. Then move on to lamb loin stroganoff with saffron linguine or mahimahi crusted with nuts and poppy seeds. Reservations required. ~ 1065 East Morehead Street, Charlotte; 704-372-5343. ULTRA-DELUXE.

For those who must have their paella, **Olé Olé** serves the real ◄ *HIDDEN* thing: a sizzling skillet of saffron rice loaded with lobster, shrimp, clams, chicken, sausages and other good things. There are lots of great Spanish and Latin eats here, including Nicaraguan pork tenderloin, Chilean seafood stew and Azturiana white-bean soup with chorizo, all served to a backdrop of salsa music and minimalist decor. No lunch served on Saturday or Sunday. ~ 709 South Kings Drive, Charlotte; 704-358-1102. MODERATE.

Anthony's Caribbean Cafe is in the most unlikely of places (the ◄ *HIDDEN* back corner of a strip shopping center) serving the most unlikely cuisine—island spice. Naturally, the place is wildly popular, especially with yuppies, who crowd in for Anthony's rotisserie chicken, basted with a secret sauce he concocted in Trinidad and served with heaps of calypso rice and callaloo greens. The Guayanese man is there at the door, wearing his tropical flowered shirt, smiling at diners before they're seated beneath bright umbrellas next to walls painted colors reminiscent of the tropics. Anthony's sauce, by the way, is for sale—either by the bottle or by the case. No lunch served on Saturday. Closed Sunday. ~ 2001 East 7th Street, Charlotte; 704-342-0749. BUDGET TO MODERATE.

The legendary **Lupie's Cafe** is cluttered and crazy, and not a lit- ◄ *HIDDEN* tle worn-out, residing in a soot-stained building with ductwork running along the ceiling and walls papered with fliers and posters and photos of known and unknown people. Lupie's is famous for

---

✔ CHECK THESE OUT—UNIQUE DINING

- *Budget*: Bring your appetite to **McDonald's Cafeteria**; the fried chicken is wonderful, as are the rib roast, mashed potatoes and more. *page 212*
- *Budget to ultra-deluxe*: Enjoy bistro fare at the **Fearrington Market Cafe** or Southern flights of fancy at **Fearrington House Restaurant**—both are outstanding. *page 243*
- *Deluxe*: Savor Southern dishes— like black-eyed-pea soup with cornmeal dumplings—at the highly esteemed **Magnolia Grill**. *page 236*
- *Ultra-deluxe*: Dine in a century-old home at **McNinch House Restaurant**; the cuisine is strictly French—and fabulous. *page 210*

Budget: under $9   Moderate: $9–$16   Deluxe: $16–$24   Ultra-deluxe: over $24

big chili—order it vegetarian, Cincinnati- or Texas-style—and other gratifying fare like chicken 'n' dumplings, macaroni 'n' cheese and banana pudding. Closed Sunday. ~ 2718 Monroe Road at 7th Street, Charlotte; 704-374-1232. BUDGET TO MODERATE.

HIDDEN ►   If you hanker for hot dogs, fried bologna, grilled cheese, Coke floats and fresh-squeezed orangeade, have a seat in one of **Dilworth Diner**'s red vinyl booths. Opened in 1952, this Charlotte institution was originally a soda shop, selling sundries and serving customers at the lunch counter. In 1996 all merchandise was removed and more tables brought in to accommodate the crowds of folks who love this place. ~ 1608 East Boulevard, Charlotte; 704-333-0137. BUDGET.

Downtown Charlotte's best soul kitchen is the **Coffee Cup**. Country-fried steak, chicken 'n' dumplings, pork chops, pigs' feet, corn bread and the like are fixed for lunch. There's no breakfast menu, but mention something Southern like fried eggs, grits and sausage patties, and you're sure to get it. Closed Sunday. ~ 914 South Clarkson Street, Charlotte; 704-375-8855. BUDGET.

When **McDonald's Cafeteria** opened in 1971, it was instantly the place for awesome cafeteria food. Over the years it has expanded and is still going strong, daily feeding more than 2000 customers such country wonders as teeny crispy-fried chicken pieces and volcanoes of mashed potatoes, slow-stewed black-eyed peas and lima beans, and the tenderest rib roast in the universe. The pies are also celestial. ~ Route 85 and Beatties Ford Road; 704-393-8823. BUDGET.

If you go antique shopping in Waxhaw, have lunch at the **Bridge and Rail**. It's Carolinas country all the way. Dating back to 1904, the downtown diner offers two daily lunch and dinner entrées (chicken pie, spaghetti and meatloaf are possibilities) accompanied by green beans, fried okra, corn, squash—whatever's in season. Breakfast buffet on Saturday morning. Closed Monday. ~ 112 East South Main Street, Waxhaw; 704-843-5005. BUDGET.

SHOPPING   If you're looking for arty, New Age stuff, try **Seventh Street** between Hawthorne and Pecan streets, southeast of downtown Charlotte. Nestled under the magnolias are great galleries and shops selling crystals, tie-dye, African tribal prints, bangle and beaded jewelry and more.

It would be easy to spend hours at the **Paper Skyscraper** pouring through the wonderfully peculiar housewares, books, cards and sundry gifts. Think Christmas shopping! ~ 330 East Boulevard, Charlotte; 704-333-7130.

Books, clothing and gifts relating to gays and lesbians are the specialty at **Rising Moon Books and Beyond**. A bulletin board in back features a calendar of local gay events. ~ 316 East Boulevard, Charlotte; 704-332-7473.

For Charlotte's best assortment of gay books, magazines and newspapers, head to **White Rabbit Books and Things**. One in a chain of stores around the Piedmont, White Rabbit also stocks clever gifts and T-shirts with gay themes. ~ 834 Central Avenue, Charlotte; 704-377-4067.

For power shopping, head to the SouthPark area. The sprawling **SouthPark Mall** has four department stores and a slew of boutiques, galleries and music stores. ~ Sharon and Fairview roads, Charlotte; 704-364-4411. Just across the street, **Specialty Shops of SouthPark** offers even more exclusive places to drop your cash, in a setting of fountains, stone piazzas and bubble canopies.

If you're interested in antiques, there's no place like the town of **Waxhaw**, about 23 miles south of Charlotte on Route 16. More than two dozen antique stores line up along downtown Main Street, and there's more on the outskirts of town. Most places are open from 10 a.m. to 5 p.m., Wednesday through Sunday, though some close for lunch, their owners wandering over to the Bridge and Rail Restaurant for chicken pot pie and fried okra.

◀ HIDDEN

Right on Main Street, **The Victorian Lady** specializes in that frilly era, with pillows, china and vintage clothing. ~ 102 South Main Street, Waxhaw; 704-843-2917.

Want something more offbeat? Step inside **The Junction** and take a look at its funky furniture and art pieces. ~ 100 South Main Street, Waxhaw; 704-843-3350. Similarly strange, the three-story **Red Barn Gallery** has racing collectibles. ~ 103 South Church Street, Waxhaw; 704-843-1309.

The Rusty Hinge purveys pottery and porcelain, silver and glass, lamps and toys. ~ 107 Southwest Main Street, Waxhaw; 704-843-4777.

Switch gears and head 30 miles northeast of Charlotte on Route 85 to the textile town of **Kannapolis**. Since the late 1800s, it's been the headquarters for Cannon Mills, the well-known maker of towels and linens, which operates **Cannon Village**. The village draws shoppers from miles around who come for discount prices

◆◆

PORK BY MAIL

You don't have to be in North Carolina to eat great North Carolina barbecue. **Exclusively Bar-B-Q**, a mail order outfit northeast of Charlotte, ships pulled-pork barbecue frozen in five-pound containers. The meat is pit-cooked slowly over hickory coals and pulled from the bone by hand. Pick your sauce—vinegar-, mustard- or tomato-based—and watch the whole five pounds vanish from your refrigerator. Cost is $39.95 per container, plus shipping. ~ 3147 Boy Scout Camp Road, Kannapolis; 704-792-2489, 800-948-1009.

not only on bed and bath items but on furniture, clothing, shoes, hosiery and toys. More than 35 factory outlet stores and boutiques are located here along pleasant streets with lushly landscaped medians and brick sidewalks. ~ 200 West Avenue, Kannapolis; 704-938-3200.

NIGHTLIFE   Charlotte has many ways to spend an evening, from the grittiest, get-down honky-tonks with great country and blues to cool-aired, after-work lounges where Southern yuppies linger over their imported beer. Some places import reggae from the sub-tropical south, others bring in big-name entertainers and acts.

Some of the city's most elaborate productions are at the **North Carolina Blumenthal Performing Arts Center**, opened in 1993. Three theaters, including a beautiful European-styled opera hall and a proscenium fashioned in a courtyard, host Broadway performances, national and international dance (including lavish cabaret) and symphony concerts. Locally, **Opera Carolina**, the **Charlotte Symphony**, **Charlotte Repertory Theater** and **Oratorio Singers**, among many others, perform at Blumenthal. ~ 130 North Tryon Street, Charlotte; 704-333-4686.

In the heart of downtown Charlotte and open weekends only, **The Moon Room** boasts both eclectic entertainment and eclectic clientele. On Friday and Saturday nights, it's usually jazz or blues, while Sundays feature poetry readings or perhaps a psychic and her tarot cards. Beer and wine only. Cover. ~ 433 South Tryon Street, Charlotte; 704-342-2003.

Downtowners head over to the classy piano bar at **Lizzie's Restaurant and Cocktail Lounge**, owned by a popular local singer of the same name. There is a small dancefloor. ~ 4809 South Tryon Street, Charlotte; 704-527-3064.

Offering top-notch blues in no-nonsense surroundings, the **Double Door Inn** books bands from all over the country. Eric Clapton and Stevie Ray Vaughn are among those who have stopped in over the past 20 years. Cover. ~ 218 East Independence Boulevard, Charlotte; 704-376-1446.

For microbrewed beer and a loud college crowd, head to the **Dilworth Brewing Company**. This place packs 'em in on the weekends with live local and regional bands playing everything from folk and acoustic to Irish. There's occasional live music during the week. Cover. ~ 1301 East Boulevard, Charlotte; 704-377-2739.

A spacious brick building that was once a skating rink is now the **Graduate Food & Pub**. For the past five years it has been voted the "Best College Bar" by a local paper. Rock bands play on Friday and Saturday nights. ~ 911 East Morehead Street, Charlotte; 704-532-2562.

In the midst of happenin' Seventh Street, **Jack Straw's** is the spot for live reggae and alternative music, delivered by bands from

New York, Texas and other netherlands. Popular with those in their 20s and 30s. Cover. ~ 1936 East 7th Street, Charlotte; 704-347-8960.

In Charlotte, the only spot offering live Dixieland jazz every single night of the week is the **Cajun Queen**. This New Orleans–style restaurant and bar crowds both stories of a renovated house with happy patrons. The atmosphere is always fun and festive and there is never a cover. ~ 1800 East 7th Street, Charlotte; 704-377-9017

The **Palomino Club** is essentially two clubs under one roof, with live music four nights a week. One club showcases national country bands, while the other hosts pop and rock bands. Cover. ~ 9607 Albermarle Road, Charlotte; 704-568-6104.

GAY SCENE   Charlotte's upscale gay crowd gathers at **Liaison's**. The old Victorian house features an upper-level veranda with a commanding view of the city skyline. Go early; the party moves elsewhere after about 11 p.m. Cover. ~ 316 Rensselaer Avenue, Charlotte; 704-376-1617.

The enormous **Scorpio** could well be North Carolina's most popular gay and lesbian nightspot, consisting of several clubs within a club, including a vast dance bar and a down-home country bar called the Queen City Saloon. On weekends, its an endless sea of bodies. Cover. ~ 2301 Freedom Drive, Charlotte; 704-373-9124.

At **Mythos** the music is a mix of rave and progressive; the crowd, a mix of gays and straights. Thursday is by far the "gayest" night, when there are drag shows and martini specials. Friday and Saturday nights bring progressive music and a mixed crowd, and on Sunday night Charlotte's Latin American crowd shows up for salsa and merengue. Cover. ~ North College and 6th streets, Charlotte; 704-375-8765.

Chasers bills itself as "Carolina's first and hottest cruise bar," and it is indeed a cruisy place, with an assortment of exotic dancers constantly performing. Men only. Cover. ~ 3217 The Plaza, Charlotte; 704-339-0500.

One of the Carolinas' only leather bars, the **Brass Rail Lounge** is a small, friendly rendezvous for those who enjoy chaps and chains. Cover. ~ 3703 Wilkinson Boulevard, Charlotte; 704-399-8413.

For top-notch drag shows, **Oleen's Lounge** is the place to be. Various female impersonators perform throughout the weekends. Cover. ~ 1831 South Boulevard, Charlotte; 704-373-9604.

MCDOWELL PARK AND NATURE PRESERVE   Meck-lenburg County's first nature preserve spans 956 acres with more than 100 species of wildflowers and ferns. The centerpiece is pretty Lake Wylie, with its verdant, steep shoreline featuring a patch of white-sand beach. Ten miles of trails, including one designed for wheelchair visitors, lead through the hardwood forest, and there's a nature center with hands-on exhibits that kids love. Swimming is

BEACHES & PARKS

not permitted. Fishing is good for bass, bream, carp, catfish and crappie. Facilities include picnic areas, restrooms, hiking trails, paddleboat and canoe rentals, and a boat launch. Day-use fee weekdays beginning of March through end of October, $5 on weekends and holidays. ~ Located about 12 miles south of downtown Charlotte on Route 49; 704-588-5224.

▲ There are 14 RV sites and 29 drive-to tent and pop-up camper sites, all at $18 per night; 30 primitive tent sites that require a short hike are $9 a night. In addition, the park has several tents already set up, for rent for $35 per night. Campsites must be reserved in advance; 704-831-2285.

HIDDEN ▶   **CROWDER'S MOUNTAIN STATE PARK** 🛶🛶⛵ This 2279-acre wilderness is ruled by the twin 800-foot peaks of Crowder's Mountain and Kings Pinnacle. The rocky monadnocks are an oddity in an otherwise flat land, having survived eons of erosion while the remaining Piedmont succumbed. Rock climbers seek out their jagged faces for a windblown experience. Clear, fast-flowing streams elbow through the park, and there's also a nine-acre lake that entices both boaters and anglers. Try fishing for bass, crappie and bream. Animal life in the park is abundant but subtle; though you may spot a gray squirrel or chipmunk, it is doubtful you will see one of the shrews, foxes or salamanders that make their homes here. More than 160 species of birds have also been sighted in the park, a big draw for birders. Swimming is not permitted. Facilities include a visitors center, restrooms, picnic areas, hiking trails and canoe rentals. ~ Located on Sparrow Springs Road 5 miles south of Route 29-74, about 25 miles west of Charlotte and six miles southwest of Gastonia. 704-853-5375.

▲ There are 16 primitive, hike-in tent sites; $1 per person per night, with a $5 minimum per site.

LATTA PLANTATION PARK 🚶🐎🛶🛶⛵ This is Mecklenburg County's biggest park and also its showpiece, with 2247 acres almost entirely devoted to nature. Waterfowl flock to the shores of manmade Mountain Island Lake, and so do canoers and those with johnboats. There's an equestrian center where you can rent horses; seven miles of horseback trails wend through the woods. There's also Latta Place, a historic plantation home, and the Carolina Raptor Center that's home to injured birds of prey. There's bass and catfish in the lake; fishing permit is $1 per day. Swimming is not permitted in Mountain Island Lake. Facilities include a nature center, a playground, volleyball courts, ten miles of hiking trails, picnic areas, and canoe, johnboat and paddleboat rentals. ~ Located at 5225 Sample Road in Huntersville, 12 miles northwest of downtown Charlotte; 704-875-1391.

HIDDEN ▶   **JETTON PARK** 🚲 Opened in 1992, this outstanding park offers one of the few public accesses to colossal Lake Norman. On a map the 32,500-acre lake looks like a miniature sea ready to burst in on Charlotte. Much of Jetton's 105 scenic acres ramble along a peninsula, and there are fancy wood picnic decks parked right along the water. There's also a gazebo for picnicking, a small, white-sand beach for sunning, bike trails for sightseeing, and many fine spots for catching a lovely liquid sunset. Swimming is not permitted. Facilities include picnic tables, restrooms, bike rentals, concessions, a playground, paved trails that are wheelchair-accessible, and lighted tennis courts. Day-use fee, $5 on weekends and holidays. ~ Located at 1900 Jetton Road in Huntersville, off Route 77 north of Charlotte; 704-896-9808.

▼▼▼▼▼▼▼▼▼▼▼▼▼▼

Pinehurst & Southern Pines Area

A hundred miles of seamless back roads and rambling rivers separate Charlotte from Pinehurst and Southern Pines. Then there is golf. More than 35 championship-caliber courses pepper these sandhills, their soothing names—Whispering Woods, Legacy Links, Hyland Hills—suggesting long, languid days on well-tended turf. They hint at the money that's been coming to Pinehurst and Southern Pines ever since James Walker Tufts got it in his mind to build something great here.

It was the late 1800s when the Boston inventor and philanthropist bought 5500 acres near a speck of a village called Southern Pines. He began building a health retreat, hiring famed landscape architect Frederick Law Olmstead to design the grounds and a neighboring New England–style village. In 1901 Tufts opened the most opulent resort for miles around. He called it The Carolina.

Originally, wealthy folks came to relax, play croquet and take shooting lessons from Pinehurst Gun Club instructor Annie Oakley. But with the popularity of golf in the early 1900s, guests were soon bringing along their clubs and little white balls. Never a man to ignore a business opportunity, Tufts hired Donald Ross—the Frederick Law Olmstead of golf course designers—to create a couple of courses.

Now there are eight courses, including the famously challenging Course Number Two. The Carolina, restored and just as spectacular, has been given the more contemporary moniker **Pinehurst Resort and Country Club**. Its grand white walls and copper cupola reign over charming Pinehurst, Olmstead's lovely little village, which attracts shoppers and strollers. ~ Carolina Vista Drive; 910-295-6811.

The entrance to **Pinehurst Village** is through a throng of tall loblolly pines, magnolias and dogwoods, with handsome homes set within their shady recesses. The village is an orderly place, very proper, with traffic circles and lots of white picket and pine mulch, and more trees than concrete. There are cafes and confectionaries,

SIGHTS

antique emporiums and a bank with a "garden walkup." Before looking around, stop by the **Pinehurst Area Convention & Visitors Bureau** for information. ~ 1480 Route 15-501, Southern Pines; 910-692-3330, 800-346-5362.

> Last century, the pretty little town of Cameron was the "Dewberry Capital of the World."

For strolling among beautifully sculpted greenery, make your way over to **Sandhills Horticultural Gardens**. The highlight is the Sir Walter Raleigh Gardens, a one-and-a-half-acre replica of a formal English garden, though if you are interested in hollies or conifers you will also find the rest of the place worthwhile. Take a look at the Ebersole Holly Collection, said to be the East Coast's largest array of hollies, and the Conifer Garden, with its assembly of firs and pines. Conifers, by the way, are cone-bearing trees. ~ 2200 Airport Road at Sandhills Community College, Pinehurst; 910-692-6185.

A few miles east you'll encounter the town of **Southern Pines** (along Route 1). Not nearly as gentrified as Pinehurst, it embraces more of the simple Southernness found in most small Carolina towns. Golf may be the point of it all in Pinehurst, but in Southern Pines, folks experience real workdays, funneling into storefronts of red brick and painted plank. There are bakeries and a jeweler, a barber shop and banks, and trains that trundle through town regularly. The train tracks run right through downtown, slicing through a median planted with magnolias and awash with the orange-red of azaleas.

To the east and south of Southern Pines, **Fort Bragg Military Reservation** is a giant yawn in the landscape, covering over 200 square miles that finally end at the city of **Fayetteville**. As you'd expect, Fayetteville's economy is fueled by the military (there is also the nearby Pope Air Force Base), and the area is more oriented to those in the service than those out for a Sunday drive. But if you'd like a peek at this side of life, stop by the **Fort Bragg/Pope Air Force Base Welcome Center** for driving-tour maps of the military reservation. ~ Randolf and Knox streets, Fayetteville; 910-396-2473. To find out if there are any scheduled parachute jumps, call 704-366-6366.

Within the base, the **82nd Airborne War Memorial Museum** follows the missions of the 82nd Airborne from World War I through the Persian Gulf War and the Haitian Civil War. A section focusing on the Battle of Normandy will excite D-Day buffs. Closed Monday. ~ Corner of Ardennes and Gela streets, Fayetteville; 910-432-5307.

HIDDEN ►

From battle history to dewberries—that's what happens if you drive north from Fort Bragg to **Cameron**, once the hub of dewberry growing, harvesting and shipping. Unfortunately, the dewberry's fate was sealed when strawberries and blackberries came along, as these were not only sweeter but easier to grow. These days, only a few backyard patches remain, but there are many antique shops in Cameron—the reason most travelers find it. Take a stroll around town and check out the terrific finds. ~ On Route 24-27, just east of Route 1.

From Cameron, wind west on Route 24-27 to Carthage and pick up Route 1006 for ten miles through lonesome sandhill country. Here you'll come to a place where the Whigs and Tories had a nasty encounter. The bullet holes in the **House in the Horseshoe** **◄ HIDDEN** testify to the 1781 shootout between Whig Philip Alston and Tory David Fanning and their respective bands of troops. It was Alston's home, and Fanning was threatening to firebomb it. After ten men were killed, Alston's wife, Temperance, negotiated a deal with Fanning: her husband would stop his rebellions against the British crown if Fanning retreated. All this history and more is part of the tour of the gabled, double-shouldered, whitewashed plantation house, built in 1772 at the horseshoe bend in the Deep River. Closed on Monday from November through March. ~ 324 Alston House Road, 12 miles north of Carthage; 910-947-2051.

Ever since its New Year's Day opening in 1901 as The Carolina, **LODGING** the **Pinehurst Resort and Country Club** has ruled as the area's supreme moneyed retreat. James Walker Tufts' palatial creation is crowned with a sparkling copper roof and cupola and cushioned in thick forest. Wide, whitewashed porches overlook gnarled limbs of magnolias alive with birdsong. The resort offers every imaginable pursuit, from swimming in one of five outdoor pools to carriage rides, croquet and lawn bowling—very Southern and very clubby. Of course, most guests come to chase the little white ball around one of the resort's seven golf courses. Within the hotel's ivory walls are 500 attractive rooms and suites; sprinkled in surrounding woods and around a lake are 140 condominiums and villas especially suited to families. ~ Carolina Vista Road, Pinehurst; 910-295-6811, 800-678-8946, fax 910-295-8503. ULTRA-DELUXE.

Tufts' first Pinehurst hostelry, the **Holly Inn**, opened in 1895 with electric lights, steam heat and its own orchestra. Tufts assured guests they'd get a good sleep on the "best hair mattress." Entirely renovated in 1985 and looking a tad timeworn, the inn still boasts bold white columns and its signature red brick porch strung with comfy old rocking chairs. The architecture is intricate, with dormers and peaks, arches and chimneys accenting the inn. Seventy-six rooms and suites are furnished in handsome Victorian style, and there's a superb restaurant. Located in the village, with shops and eateries in every direction. ~ Cherokee Road, Pinehurst; 910-295-2300, 800-682-6901, fax 910-295-0988. DELUXE TO ULTRA-DELUXE.

Magnolia Inn looks just like it sounds: a whitewashed, gabled turn-of-the-century house with a rambling porch and three magnolia trees parked on the front lawn. Right in the village of Pinehurst, it is naturally a golfers' haven ("Golf attire is always accept-able dress," says the inn brochure). Rooms and public areas are Southern-comfortable, the walls prettily papered and the floors laid with wood plank. There's fine dining, a small pub and a swim-ming pool to keep the kids happy. The inn also has condos facing golf greens. ~ Magnolia and Chinquapin roads, Pinehurst; 910-295-6900, 800-526-5562, fax 910-215-0858. ULTRA-DELUXE.

HIDDEN ▶   **Inn at the Bryant House** is hidden off the main highway between Aberdeen and Southern Pines, sequestered in a neighborhood of handsome antebellum homes. The bed and breakfast is well run—owners Abbie and Bill Gregory make you feel at home but provide plenty of privacy—and the rooms are extra-comfortable, decorated with sponge-painted nightstands and pretty linens, and thick ter-rycloth robes hang in the closet. There's courtyard parking and a good breakfast included in the rate—all in all, great value for an ex-pensive area. ~ 214 North Poplar Street, Aberdeen; 910-944-3300, 800-453-4019, fax 910-944-3300. BUDGET TO MODERATE.

Your best bet for lodging in Fayetteville is the **Radisson Prince Charles Hotel**, built in 1925 and renovated in 1992 to the tune of $7.5 million. Marble floors, Palladian windows, columns and pi-lasters adorn the eight-story hotel, and the 84 rooms and suites all have modern comforts. ~ 450 Hay Street, Fayetteville; 910-433-4444, 800-333-3333, fax 910-485-8269. MODERATE.

DINING   A little bit fancy and festive, **Theo's Taverna** is great for traditional Greek dishes like moussaka, *souvlaki* and *pastitsio*, plus nightly specials such as grilled veal chops or blackened striped bass with tomatoes. Take a linen-topped table in the main dining room, or opt for a chair at the long polished bar. ~ 140 Chinquapin Road, Pinehurst; 910-295-0780. BUDGET TO MODERATE.

For a quick and simple Pinehurst lunch, go to the **Pinehurst Playhouse Restaurant** and sit outside under the umbrellas. Choose from fresh soups, salad plates and filling sandwiches. There is indoor dining in winter. Closed Sunday. ~ 100 West Village Green, Pinehurst; 910-295-8873. BUDGET.

HIDDEN ▶   **Nature's Own Market & Cafe** isn't much on atmosphere (the tiny dining room is right beside a market selling Birkenstocks and vitamins) but the fare is fresh, imaginative and organic, different from anything else around. The menu changes daily, but for lunch you may find organic miso summer vegetable soup and pan-fried fresh salmon cake sandwich. At dinner, try the Yucatán marinated free-range chicken fajitas with black beans, or the grilled halibut with curried corn sauce and chive mashed potatoes. Closed Sun-day. ~ 1150 Old Route 1 South, Southern Pines; 910-692-3811. MODERATE TO DELUXE.

Over in Southern Pines, **Sleddon's** is a sure bet for fine dining. The menu changes quite frequently but always includes some tasty preparations of seafood, lamb, chicken, steak and veal. The roasted duck is a local favorite. The venue is a 1970s home-turned-restaurant, with various small rooms set for elegant eating. Closed Sunday and Monday. ~ 275 South Bennett Street, Southern Pines; 910-692-4480. MODERATE TO DELUXE.

In tiny, farflung Cameron, the **Dewberry Deli** is an old-fashioned soda fountain and eatery, full of nostalgia and warmth with its checkered floor, wood-beamed ceiling and assorted curios. People crowd into the cozy booths and out to sunny patio tables for salads and burgers, pita sandwiches and soups, lemonade and sweet dewberry cobbler (the dewberries come from local backyards). A favorite lunch stop for Cameron antique hounds. Closed Sunday and Monday. ~ 129 Carthage Street, Cameron; 910-245-3697. BUDGET.

◄ HIDDEN

Start in **Pinehurst Village**, a perfectly pleasant place to shop and browse among galleries, boutiques and antique shops. You instantly sense the shops' pedigree by their dressy scalloped awnings, sobering price tags, and signs that announce branches in Palm Beach and Greenwich, Connecticut.

SHOPPING

Razook's has such a sign. Step inside to cultured couture for women—extremely prim, chic styles, suits and dresses and accessories with that Jackie O. look. ~ Chinquapin Road, Pinehurst; 910-295-6141.

If you're inclined to investigate the history of Pinehurst, **The Book Place, Ltd.** has several volumes for sale, along with other local-interest books and bestsellers. ~ Chinquapin Road, Pinehurst; 910-295-1108.

River Kwai Collection has beautiful furniture, rugs and objets d'art; much of the merchandise is from Indonesia, Thailand and Malaysia. ~ Chinquapin Road, Pinehurst; 910-295-9029.

The vintages at **Village Vineyards** are well selected, the bottles well priced, and the owner knowledgeable and anxious to help. ~ Village Court Building, Pinehurst; 910-295-1004.

Grounds & Pounds has gifts for the java junkie, mugs and trivets and funky coffeepots, plus assorted gourmet roasts. ~ Market Square, Pinehurst; 910-295-0047.

Where but in Pinehurst would you find an entire store devoted to golf art? At **Burchfield's Golf Gallery** you can buy a sketch of Jack Nicklaus or a painting of Greg Norman. There's even an oil of a cowboy riding into the sunset, clubs nestled behind the saddle. ~ 1 Market Square, Pinehurst; 704-488-2175.

Just outside Pinehurst Village, **Midland Crafters** is a low-slung building nearly obscured by pines, filled with thousands of fine crafts: candles, pottery and glassware, chess sets, stone garden accessories and sculpture. ~ 2220 Midland Road, one mile east of the Pinehurst traffic circle; 910-295-6156.

Downtown Southern Pines does offer some shopping prospects, mainly shoes, cookware and antiques. Most are along **Broad Street,** on both sides of the railroad tracks (the tracks and a broad median split the road in half). A store directory can be found at the corner of North Hampshire Avenue and Northwest Broad Street.

About ten miles northeast of Southern Pines, Cameron is an attractive little town with nine or so antique stores. They're all on **HIDDEN ►** **Carthage Street,** Cameron's main drag, so you can park and prowl the showrooms for old furniture, pottery and jewelry, glassware, trains and artwork. Much has been beautifully restored—with price tags that reflect it.

Definitely make a stop at **The Old Hardware,** in a 1920 building whose past lives include housing a Ford agency and mule auction center. Today it holds unusual, good-quality antiques: perhaps a camel-back trunk, English cottage bed or a Scottish hunting horn. ~ Carthage Street, Cameron; 910-245-7001.

NIGHTLIFE The word "nightlife" is a stretch for this area. You can, however, have a drink at **The Coves,** where there's usually acoustic guitar or light jazz on weekends. ~ Market Square, Pinehurst; 910-295-3400. Or try **Theo's Taverna,** where a long, polished wood bar and a friendly bartender make for pleasant before- or after-dinner relaxation. ~ 140 Chinquapin Road, Pinehurst; 910-295-0780.

In Southern Pines, **Brooks** is one option for a drink. The locals' bar hosts bands occasionally, usually country or Southern rock. ~ 155 Northeast Broad Street, Southern Pines; 910-692-3515.

Your best bet for live music is **Firehouse Pub,** where rock-and-roll or blues bands play most weekends. Cover. ~ 241 Northeast Broad, Southern Pines; 910-695-2635.

BEACHES & PARKS

WEYMOUTH WOODS NATURE PRESERVE 🏃 These 571 acres of woods are dotted with wildflower fields and crisscrossed with streams. There's a beaver pond, though the critters are usually in hiding. Look for their woodwork along the pond's edges and trails. Four and a half miles of trails wind through the preserve. You'll find a park office, picnic tables, restrooms and hiking trails; a naturalist is available by appointment. ~ 1024 North Fort Bragg Road, across from Highlands Trails, in Southern Pines; 910-692-2167.

▼▼▼▼▼▼▼▼▼
Raleigh

It would seem logical to begin exploring North Carolina's capital city from the downtown hub of state government, but it is entirely more pleasant to start in Historic Oakwood. This engaging Victorian neighborhood on the northeast corner of town is filled with lyrical architecture and dashing color, a meld of Neoclassical style and Second Empire and Steamboat Gothic. In a span of about 22 blocks are more than 100 homes, most beautifully restored and many dating back to the 1800s.

Bounded roughly by East Edenton Street, North Person Street, Franklin Street and the Oakwood Cemetery, **Historic Oakwood** is an oasis from downtown hubbub, with birds trilling from massive magnolias and oaks, children playing along sloping sidewalks, and passersby waving at everyone they see.

Each home is different, yet many share the same Southern features: wide porches for staying cool in summer, high-pitched roofs for attic insulation in winter, and porch ceilings painted blue to match the sky—and supposedly chase the flies away.

One of the many eye-catching residences is the **Wayne Allcott House** with its bright lavender paint, fanciful gingerbread and scalloped shingles. ~ 414 North East Street. Allcott also owned the house two doors down, at **500 Polk Street**, now painted bubblegum pink and trimmed in forest green shutters and wavy shingles.

Down the way are a pair of **shotgun houses**, only one room wide, narrow enough for a bullet fired at the front to travel cleanly through the back. Built as spec homes for the working class, the tunnel-like designs saved developers money since less street frontage meant fewer taxes. ~ 407 and 409 North East Street.

Anything but narrow, the big and bold **Charles B. Hart House**, built around 1897, offers high drama with its great metal-wrapped tower, bold gables trimmed in bargeboard, delicate lancet windows and exterior of purple haze. ~ 412 Oakwood Avenue.

Along the neighborhood's eastern border is the **Oakwood Cemetery**, wherein lie the remains of many of the people responsible for creating the neighborhood. Some of the people responsible today for preserving the neighborhood—The Society for the Preservation of Historic Oakwood—publish a handy walking-tour guide to the area. The guides are available at the **Capital Area Visitors Center**, which also offers a free 15-minute slide show on Raleigh's historic buildings. ~ 301 North Blount Street; 919-733-3456.

Kitty-corner to the visitors center is Raleigh's premier historic building, the **Executive Mansion**. Fashioned in Queen Anne cottage style and home to North Carolina's governor, it is a red-brick house of tremendous design and beauty, with whimsical eaves, great steps of granite and many gables. The immaculate grounds are shaded by giant trees. Inside awaits a showcase of North Carolina wood, elaborately carved and polished to a high sheen, and opulent chandeliers and works of art. Here, too, is much history. In 1891, then-governor Daniel Fowle moved into the Queen Anne manse after prisoners and craftsmen labored on the place for nine years (some of the bricks bear the initials of the prisoners who made them). Fowle's ghost is said to inhabit the building, for subsequent governors have been awakened by a knocking noise at precisely the same time each night. Extensive investigations have produced no explanation for the knocking. ~ 200 North Blount Street; 919-733-3456.

Free half-hour tours of the mansion's interior are offered only during the spring, the fall and part of December, though dates and times are sporadic. For tour schedules and reservations, call the Capital Area Visitors Center. ~ 919-733-3456.

A few blocks away is the heart of state government, an assemblage of low-slung, somber, sand-colored buildings. The classic-style **State Legislative Building**, carved of homegrown granite and laced with square columns, offers free guided tours if you call ahead—not a bad idea, since the building's interior is a maze of look-alike rooms, corridors and courtyards famous for confounding even those with the keenest sense of direction. "Some visitors to the legislature become so hopelessly confused they become desperate," notes the book *Raleigh: A Guide to North Carolina's Capital*. "One legislative aide advises visitors to bring a bag of popcorn and leave a trail." ~ Located at Jones and Salisbury streets; 919-733-7928.

When the Greek Revival **State Capitol** was built in the 1830s, someone called it "a Grecian temple on a hog pasture." The hogs have since been crowded out by sprawl, and the capitol's great stone walls and copper rotunda now enjoy a more somber setting. ~ Capitol Square, bounded by Edenton, Salisbury, Morgan and Wilmington streets; 919-733-4994.

In 1993, the **North Carolina Museum of History** moved into its new, $30 million quarters, where sunlight streams in on spacious high-ceiling galleries, spotlighting some 250,000 artifacts that tell a story of the Tarheel State. In the lobby you can view a replica of the Wright Brothers' plane and a hang glider built by hang glider inventor Francis Rogallo; in the Sports Hall of Fame are Richard Petty's race car and Arnold Palmer's Ryder Cup golf bag; and in the folklife area, there are African-American wood carvings and Cherokee baskets. There's a currency display with more than 20,000 pieces, from Colonial to Confederate to current times, as well as 14,500 photographs, 177 handguns, 300 shoulder weapons, 399 flags and 11,000 articles of clothing. By now, you should realize you could spend all day here, and you didn't even have to pay to get in. Closed Monday. ~ 5 East Edenton Street; 919-715-0200.

The **North Carolina Museum of Natural Sciences** is also free but not nearly as absorbing, though kids love it. They can stare at taxidermied northern hogsuckle fish and finger-size short-tailed shrews in the Piedmont Plateau exhibit, and walk through an imitation mine where ultraviolet light is beamed at brilliant gems. In the Discovery Room, they can actually touch live animals and work on fossils. ~ 102 North Salisbury Street; 919-733-7450.

Even more fun for children, **Playspace** is an indoor and outdoor playground located in Raleigh's restored City Market. Parents pay

Raleigh-Durham-Chapel Hill

Falls Lake State Recreation Area

Eno River State Park

Falls Lake Reservoir

West Point on the Eno

Duke Forest

Hillsborough

Chapel Hill

Carrboro

Durham

Oak Grove

Research Triangle Park

William B. Umstead State Park

Cary

Raleigh

Pullen Park

Fearrington Village

Jordan Lake

Farrington

Pittsboro

N

0   5 miles

Raleigh

State Legislative Building

North Carolina Museum of Natural Sciences

North Carolina Museum of History

State Capitol

Capital Area Visitors Center

Executive Mansion

	North St		Oakwood Ave		East St
Lane St			Bloodworth St		St
			Jones St		St
			Person St	Edenton St	
				New Bern Ave	
		Blount St			Morgan St
		Wilmington St			St
	Salisbury St				St

POINTS OF INTEREST

CHAPEL HILL
A *Morehead Planetarium*
B *North Carolina Botanical Garden*
C *Patterson's Mill Country Store*
D *University of North Carolina at Chapel Hill*

DURHAM
E *Duke Homestead*
F *Duke University*
G *North Carolina Museum of Life and Science*

RALEIGH
H *Mordecai Historic Park*
I *North Carolina Museum of Art*
J *North Carolina State University*

by the hour and kids play by the hour, dressing in costumes and performing on stage, "working" in the imaginary hospital and grocery store, and climbing triple-tiered sand tables. *Note:* In case you're tempted to leave the little dears, you can't. All Playspace kids have to be supervised. Admission. ~ 400 Glenwood Avenue; 919-832-1212.

To see what life was like in the old days, drive to the north end of town and tour **Mordecai Historic Park**. It occupies a single city block, the remnant of a huge plantation that before the Civil War sprawled for thousands of acres in every direction, taking in much of what is now downtown Raleigh. You can tour the time-beaten 1785 **Mordecai House** (with additions in 1826), named for its second occupant, Moses Mordecai, one of Raleigh's first Jews. Behind the house is a lane lined with six historic buildings, moved here from other parts of Wade County. Smallest and most significant is the humble log kitchen apartment where Andrew Johnson, the seventeenth president of the United States, was born in 1808. Another plantation kitchen, built in 1842, is strung with dried herbs and outfitted with great antique cookware, from old butter churns and pie safes to tin candlemakers and spice grinders. Admission. ~ 1 Mimosa Street, off Wake Forest Road; 919-834-4844.

Raleigh is not exactly a place you associate with great art—which makes the **North Carolina Museum of Art** such a welcome surprise. Thanks to avid art collector and philanthropist Samuel Kress (of Kress & Co. five-and-dimes), the museum not only exists, it boasts more than 500 pieces by masters such as Botticelli, Titian, Giotto, Rubens, Cellini and Canaletto. You'll find them in the vast European art wing, where ten galleries spanning 600 years of works dazzle the eye. Most people spend all their time here, but save an hour to peruse the other galleries, featuring classical, Egyptian, African, Oceanic, New World and Judaic art as old as 450 B.C. The museum, which is free by the way, also has a great little cafe and gift shop. Closed Monday. ~ 2110 Blue Ridge Road, off Route 40; 919-839-6262.

For an entirely different look at the past, drive about 30 miles east of Raleigh to the far-flung country town of **Bailey**. Here the

HIDDEN ► **Country Doctor Museum** is in a building made of two real rural doctors' offices, where rooms are filled with strange and incredible cures and their containers. There are antidotes for toothaches, fevers and freckles, and even one marked Manhood Cure, for an ailment one can only ponder. Among the fascinating and fearsome items in the surgical office are the implements Dr. Matthew Moore Butler used to amputate Stonewall Jackson's arm after the Battle of Chancellorsville in 1863. Alas, the Confederate general did not survive the ordeal. In a 100-year-old house next to the doctor's offices, 1500 volumes of medical books span two centuries, from the 1700s to the early 1900s. Closed Monday. Admission. ~ Vance Street, just off Route 581 South; 919-235-4165.

Different, but equally engrossing, is the **Ava Gardner Museum** in **Smithfield**, about two dozen miles southeast of Raleigh. A far- ◀ HIDDEN mer's daughter and youngest of five children, Ava was born right outside Smithfield in a place called Grabtown. She owed her Hollywood career at least in part to her sister, who married a New York photographer. He displayed Ava's picture in his studio; a scout for Metro-Goldwyn-Mayer saw the photo and liked it, and Ava waved goodbye to Smithfield for a big Hollywood career. Ava Gardner died of pneumonia in 1967. She is buried in a cemetery on the edge of Smithfield.

The museum is a modest place, but deeply atmospheric, largely because of Mary Edna Grantham, Ava's niece, who acts as docent. Grantham is similarly beautiful, very graceful. She'll show you a 1941 family photo, Ava a teenager and she a little girl, and dozens of other photos of Ava's Smithfield and Rock Ridge days. She'll walk you through original movie posters from some of Ava's 61 films, and show you some of Ava's wardrobe, including the black velvet and chiffon gown she wore in 1949's *The Great Sinner*, with Gregory Peck. Admission. ~ 210 South Third Street, Smithfield; 919-934-5830.

Only a few Raleigh lodges break out of the chain mode. One place **LODGING** that's truly unusual is the **Oakwood Inn**, an 1871 Victorian house located in Historic Oakwood, Raleigh's finest neighborhood, and within walking distance from downtown. From the parlor of mahogany and leaded glass to the fancy Italian Revival eaves and big wraparound porch, it's a most appealing place inside and out. Six handsome bedrooms have private baths, thick throw rugs, clawfoot tubs, and high, downy beds to climb into at night. Owners Vara and Jim Cox see to your every need, offering cordials and "sweets" at night and hearty but healthy breakfasts (whole-wheat pancakes, stewed fruit hinting of nutmeg). ~ 411 North Bloodworth Street; 919-832-9712, 800-267-9712, fax 919-836-9263. MODERATE TO DELUXE.

Raleigh's only other bed and breakfast, the **William Thomas House**, opened in late 1993 after a year-long restoration by owners Jim and Sarah Lofton. Now the 1881 vintage, vanilla-washed house boasts an elegant parlor and high-ceiling library, and a dining room where breakfasts are served on a long clawfoot table. Four bedrooms with private baths are decorated with antique reproductions such as poster and spindle-post beds and grand armoires. Located a few blocks from downtown, though, unfortunately, on a busy street. ~ 530 North Blount Street; 919-755-9400, 800-653-3466, fax 919-755-3966. DELUXE.

The **Holiday Inn Downtown-State Capital** looks like a cylinder rising in the middle of downtown Raleigh. With a pleasant lobby, tidy rooms and a central location, it's not a bad choice. ~ 320 Hillsborough Street; 919-832-0501, 800-465-4329, fax 919-833-1631. BUDGET TO MODERATE.

Near Saint Mary's College and North Carolina State University, the **Velvet Cloak Inn** is a lodging phenomenon, being both elegant and motelish. Mozart streams through the lobby hung with gilt-frame portraits and adorned with rhinestone lamps. But the 171 rooms are small and laid out like a motor court, with 1960s-era, low-slung buildings facing a parking lot. Among the unexpected pluses: a heated pool in a huge atrium, and the first-rate Baron's restaurant. ~ 1505 Hillsborough Street; 919-828-0333, 800-334-4372, fax 919-828-2656. MODERATE TO DELUXE.

Many of the guests at **Brownestone Hotel** have children or business at the adjacent North Carolina State University. The building is a midrise brownstone with dated, comfortably clubby decor, and the 212 rooms are outfitted in standard hotel issue. (Ask for an upper floor, with views of the campus or city.) There's an outdoor swimming pool, and the YMCA is next door. ~ 1707 Hillsborough Street; 919-828-0811, 800-237-0772, fax 919-834-0904. BUDGET TO MODERATE.

DINING

Many people come to Raleigh with low culinary expectations only to be amazed by the variety of eateries. In case you're wondering who supports all these great places, remember that Raleigh is not only the state capital but home to Research Triangle Park and its 30,000-plus scientists, computer programmers, etc.

HIDDEN ►

If it weren't for the big red Coca-Cola mural on the side, you might drive right by the funky building called **Side Street**. It's better to stop and take a seat inside the little neighborhood cafe, crowded with regulars assaulting huge, elaborate sandwiches and dense desserts (the black-bottom pecan pie and fudge pie are definite winners). Located in Historic Oakwood, Side Street serves lunch and dinner. Closed Sunday. ~ 225 North Bloodworth Street; 919-828-4927. BUDGET.

HIDDEN ►

With so many historic buildings around downtown, it seems only logical to dine at an old-time eatery. **Person Street Pharmacy Soda Fountain** is just the place (its motto: "Old Fashioned Goodness The Way You Remember!"). The rock-bottom budget prices definitely remind of bygone days: a burger is $1.69; a hot dog, 99 cents. Meals, which also include tasty breakfasts, deli sandwiches, soups and ice cream, are prepared by a cheery girl behind the counter. Dining is on little tables facing the pharmacy aisles but, at these prices, who cares? Closed Sunday. ~ 702 North Person Street; 919-832-6432. BUDGET.

If you crave Italian, go to **Est Est Est Trattoria**, where the hand-rolled pastas are supple and piled with all manner of sauces, the osso buco extra hearty, and the seafood dependably fresh. Try the pumpkin fettuccine, mussels in alfredo sauce or sweet potato ravioli in nutmeg cream sauce. The ultramodern decor seems a little contrived, but the lunch and dinner crowds don't seem to mind. There's a good wine list, as well as a full bar. Closed Sunday. ~ 19 West Hargett Street; 919-832-8899. MODERATE.

Weird, whimsical and wildly popular, **The Black Dog Cafe** is overrun daily by downtown professionals, including a gay and lesbian crowd. The decor has gone to the dogs, with painted paw prints running along the edges of the tables and toy dogs and dog beds crowding around the cash register. Burgers, salads, pasta, vegetarian and seafood specials are on for lunch and dinner. No dinner served Sunday through Tuesday. Closed Monday. ~ 208 East Martin Street, in downtown's City Market; 919-828-1994. BUDGET TO MODERATE.

The homegrown beers at **Greenshields Brewery and Pub** come from the giant steel fermentation tanks occupying the center of the restaurant. There are usually five brews on tap, and a terrific pub menu ranging from pork tenderloin and bangers and mash to Jamaican jerk chicken and seafood jambalaya. Decor is equally publike, with lots of oak and brass and rich green carpets. Go for lunch or dinner. ~ 214 East Martin Street, in downtown's City Market; 919-829-0214. BUDGET TO MODERATE.

Amid the sidewalk prowl created by North Carolina State University, **The Rathskeller** is where you can get black-bean "protein" nachos; "tree frog" sandwiches of turkey, bacon and bermuda onion; and hummus or baked artichoke and cheese dip. There's wood all around, from the booths and laminated tables to the floors and ceilings. Despite the attempt at a "No Smoking" section, "The Rat" is one smoky skeller. ~ 2412 Hillsborough Street; 919-821-5342. BUDGET TO MODERATE.

Cup A Joe is the unofficial college hangout for both gay and straight students. You'll see them huddled over homework at the schoolhouse desks, tossing back their third espresso, Janis Joplin wailing on the stereo, traffic buzzing outside big open windows. The *focaccia* and pastries are homemade, the coffees available in a variety of concoctions. ~ 3100 Hillsborough Street; 919-828-9665. BUDGET.

Upon entering **Neomonde Bakery & Deli**, you are assaulted by ◄ HIDDEN a sea of smells so good you desperately want to order one of everything in the glass case. Impossible, unfortunately, as there are dozens of choices, all Middle Eastern and all just made, from the meat and cheese pies, stuffed grape leaves and tabbouleh to spinach *fatayer* (spinach, onion and tomato baked inside pita dough) and *kibbeh* (ground beef, onions, hummus and pine nuts on a sub roll). There are also regular deli sandwiches, loaves upon loaves of fresh bread, and "sweets" such as *ballouria*, layered with egg noodles and pistachios and sprinkled with rose water. Go early or late for lunch or dinner; otherwise, expect to wait for a table. ~ 3817 Beryl Road, off Hillsborough Street near North Carolina State University; 919-828-1628. BUDGET TO MODERATE.

SHOPPING   Downtown Raleigh's **City Market**, centered around a restored 1914 markethouse, is where you'll find unusual and offbeat shops and galleries. ~ Bounded by Martin, Person, Davie and Blount streets; 919-828-4555.

Foremost for gallery shopping is **Artspace**, home to nearly 70 artists and their studios. Within three floors are all sorts of paintings—silkscreen, acrylic, pastel, oil, portraiture—running the gamut from traditional to experimental. There's also jewelry, photography and even sculpted stones (whose sculptor is sometimes out stone hunting). ~ 201 East Davie Street; 919-821-2787.

The Brass Key has brass galore, as well as candles, trinkets, greeting cards, lightswitch covers and crystal. ~ 317 Blake Street; 919-828-9126.

Displaying the works of both Carolinian and national artists, the **Raleigh Contemporary Gallery** has a diverse selection of paintings, lithographs, sculpture and contemporary stained glass. ~ 323 Blake Street; 919-828-6500.

On the other side of City Market, the **American Indian Company** carries goods made by tribes all across the county. Their pottery collection is one of the largest in the state. Also available are jewelry, original artwork, wooden flutes and tapes and CDs of both traditional and contemporary American Indian music. ~ 308 Parham Street; 919-834-9655.

Nearby, Raleigh's gay literary crowd gathers at **White Rabbit Books**, a charming establishment with extensive gay readings, including periodicals from around the world, as well as specialty items and gifts. A bulletin board lists local gay happenings. ~ 309 West Martin Street; 919-856-1429.

A little west of downtown, **Cameron Village** is not a real village but six blocks of low-slung buildings lined with brick walkways and brimming with shopping possibilities. The 80-plus stores include a Talbots and several other chains, but you will also encounter the unusual. ~ 1900 Cameron Street; 919-828-2553.

Accipiter, for example, focuses on folk art and beaux-arts—things like crazy clocks, boldly painted furniture and placemats, and wavy wine glasses. ~ 2046 Clark Avenue; 919-755-9309. Down the way, **Chinese Arts** has gorgeous things to put in your home, from handpainted blue-and-white porcelain to rosewood chests inlaid with mother of pearl. ~ 2014 Clark Avenue; 919-832-0652. **Cook's Choice** carries everyday cookware plus the kind of stuff only a chef would use. ~ 2028 Cameron Street; 919-821-8450.

With three major universities and a history steeped in blues, the **NIGHTLIFE** Triangle is a nucleus of nightlife. Piedmont Blues, a softer sounding, more melodic blues, got its start in the tobacco houses of the Triangle, and there are still many places to to go to hear a harmonica really wail.

The **Berkeley Cafe** is definitely one of those places. The bands play traditional stuff as well as the newer R&B and folk rock, and there's a patio bar for hanging out when it's warm. Cover. ~ 217 West Martin Street; 919-821-0777.

Comedy or disco, take your pick at the mammoth **Charlie Goodnight's**. Jay Leno and Rich Hall are among the greats to perform here and autograph the wall in the comedy club, though lesser knowns are usually featured. ~ 861 West Morgan Street; 919-828-5233. In the adjacent **NewBar**, the disco's loud, the hair big, and the attire heavy on black lycra. Cover.

Rap, disco, reggae and bubblegum music are spun by a deejay at the Soho-style **Five-O Cafe**. Abutting North Carolina State University, it's definitely a college scene. Cover. ~ 2526 Hillsborough Street; 919-821-4419.

Melissa Etheridge, Bruce Hornsby and Living Colour are among the acts who've graced **The Brewery**. It's mainly a rock-and-roll club, though, with local and regional bands jamming on a sound system that's just short of nuclear. Cover. ~ 3009 Hillsborough Street; 919-834-7018.

GAY SCENE   Opened in 1976 and one of North Carolina's oldest gay clubs, **CC** is a friendly cruise bar with video screens, a big dancefloor and live entertainment every Wednesday and Saturday. Cover. ~ 313 West Hargrett Street; 919-755-9599.

Across the street from Capital Corral, the tastefully decorated **Legends** is the place to dance, dance, dance. Those dancing are typically gay men with astonishingly well-toned torsos; the music is typically progressive. Lesbians and straights also come to Legends. Cover. ~ 330 West Hargrett Street; 919-831-8888.

1622 is low-key and friendly, a neighborhood stomping ground popular with both gay men and women. Thursday nights, however, are the exception, as men get up on the tables and dance. And on Saturday and Sunday the place is packed for women's night. Cover. ~ 1622 Glenwood Avenue; 919-832-9082.

PULLEN PARK   Local families and college students love this **BEACHES** park, spread across 65 pretty green acres next to North Carolina **& PARKS** State University. There are many good picnic spots as well as a pool

and tennis courts, but the draws are definitely the 1912 Dentzel
Menagerie Carousel and the miniature train that chugs around the
park. Listed on the National Registry and kept sparkling by two
artists, it's one of only 170 in existence. Kids love taking the beautiful tigers, horses and other animals for a spin. One ride will set
you back 65 cents. There is swimming in the swimming pool. Facilities include picnic shelters, tennis courts, pedal-boats and a kiddie boat. Day-use fee, $3. ~ 410 Ashe Avenue, next to North
Carolina State University; 919-831-6468.

WILLIAM B. UMSTEAD STATE PARK
Physically, there is nothing particularly compelling about this park.
Its mere existence, however, is enough, for it is a breath of green
amid the gaseous traffic and concrete sprawl of Raleigh, Durham
and Research Triangle Park. During segregation, Umstead was actually two parks, Reedy Creek and Crabtree. Today Ulmstead is
one park but no roads connect the two sections, only hiking trails.
Both have woodsy areas for hiking and horseback riding and picnicking. Crabtree has Big Lake, where you can rent boats and fish.
Mostly, though, you can just relax before getting back on the interstate. You can get groceries about three miles from either park.
Swimming is not permitted, except at one of the group campsite
lakes. Fishing is best at Big Lake. Try for bluegill, crappie and bass.
At Crabtree, facilities include a visitors center, picnic tables and
covered pavilions, hiking, biking and bridle trails, and boat rentals.
At Reedy Creek there is a park office, a picnic area and hiking trails.
~ To reach the Crabtree Park section, take Route 70 six miles north-
west of Raleigh; to reach Reedy Creek, take Route 40 west of
Raleigh for 11 miles and exit at Harrison Avenue; 919-787-3033.

▲ Crabtree features 28 family tent sites; $9 per night per site.
Reedy Creek has a group site, maximum 64 people, with varying
rates depending on length and time of stay and number of people.

▼▼▼▼▼▼▼▼▼
Durham

Durham is a working city, a hustling hub of research, technology and—foremost—medicine. Dubbed "The City of
Medicine," it is home to numerous hospitals, clinics and
laboratories and boasts five times more physicians per person than
the national average. Keeping this in mind, then, unless you are inordinately interested in the medical field, you would do best to
focus your explorations away from downtown and toward the
more scenic parts of Durham.

SIGHTS

One site not to be missed would be **Duke University**. "Gothic won-
derland" is the cliché applied to this renowned campus. Indeed, it
is not an untrue moniker, as the quixotic buildings of stone, spires
and arches, cloaked deeply in forest, look pulled from the pages of
a medieval tale. Wending along the streets overhung with mammoth

oaks, hickories and gum trees, there is the sense of the ancient and surreal, and the only things out of place are the students, with their cutoff jeans and neon backpacks.

The school goes back to 1838 when some Quakers and Methodists started Union Institute in nearby Randolph County. Over the years, it was reorganized and renamed (at one point called Normal College), and then in 1897 tobacco king Washington Duke offered $100,000 if the school would admit women and move to Durham. Having let a few females slip in before, and not minding the sound of a hundred grand, the institution accepted. But it was Washington's son, Buck Duke, who in 1924 transformed it from a small-time college to a major university. All it took was $46 million—$6 million initially and $40 million in an endowment—and the Duke name was forever imprinted on the school and on Carolinians' minds. ~ Just west of downtown Durham, with main entrances off Main Street, Duke University Road, and Cameron Boulevard; 919-684-8111.

Duke is actually three separate campuses: west, central and east. The west is the main campus, the heart of Gothicism, presided over by **Duke Chapel**. When you turn onto Chapel Drive and face the chapel squarely in the distance, you have no choice but to admit that it is, quite simply, spectacular. Its jagged finials aim heavenward, its arched windows are bathed in glittering stained glass, its bell tower soars 21 stories. Modeled after *the* Canterbury Cathedral, the chapel is just as exquisite inside, with a 73-foot-high nave that overwhelms, a breathtaking sea of stained glass and an endless stream of pews. It is strangely silent and echoey in here, and when the front door opens it makes a thunderous sound. ~ 919-684-2572.

If by now you are feeling pensive, take a stroll through the **Sarah P. Duke Gardens** near the chapel. Its 55 acres are marbled with more than 1500 varieties of flora. Pond banks explode with lilies, dawn redwood trees spiral in the sky and azaleas form waves of raging color in spring. The terraced garden, designed in the 1930s by noted landscape architect Ellen Shipman, is decorated with Southern magnolias and impatiens. The Asiatic arboretum features trees and shrubs from the Far East. Paved paths and ramps allow wheelchair visitors access to most everything. ~ Anderson Street; 919-684-3698.

In keeping with the medieval mood, the **Duke University Museum of Art** possesses a vast collection of medieval stained glass and sculpture. In the South Gallery you can also gaze at the largest collection of pre-Columbian art held by any university. There are American and European paintings and sculpture and Greek and Roman artifacts in the Western Gallery. Closed Monday. ~ On the east campus, off Campus Drive; 919-684-5135.

To really get back to the beginning of Duke University and even Durham, head north several miles to **Duke Homestead**, a state historic site and keen place. Exhibits in the visitors center explore the history of tobacco and there's plenty of nostalgia here. Old TVs play old cigarette commercials. (Remember Marlboro Man and Marlboro Country? The man eventually died of lung cancer; the cigarettes still make millions.) A wall detailing the age-old tobacco debate quotes an 1884 *New York Times*, which decreed that "the decadence of Spain began when the Spaniards adopted cigarettes and if this pernicious practice obtains among adult Americans it will bring the ruin of the Republic."

Washington Duke began the first tobacco "factory" (a rickety, one-room barn) on his meager farm and parlayed his business into the world's biggest tobacco empire.

After the exhibits, you'll follow a guide out back for a walk under the trees to the old Duke house, dating to 1852; to their third factory, built in 1869; and to their early-1900s packing house, where the women had to check each tobacco leaf for quality and grade it. There's also a late-1800s curing barn, moved here from another farm. Closed Monday from November through March. ~ 2828 Duke Homestead Road, off Guess Road north of Route 85; 919-477-5498.

A short drive east of the homestead, the **North Carolina Museum of Life and Science** brings you back to the present, with more than 50,000 square feet of fun for kids. Hundreds of gizmos, gadgets and giant apparatus teach and entertain; there's a cloud you can stick your hand into, a tiger skeleton to be touched and a space shuttle you can guide to catch a satellite. Outside, kids can romp in the playground, explore nature trails, pet farmyard animals and take a train ride. Admission. ~ 433 Murray Avenue; 919-220-5429.

West Point on the Eno is a historic city park that highlights a nineteenth-century milling community. An extension of Eno River State Park, it features a reconstructed 1778 corn and wheat mill in full operation, a restored 1850 farmhouse and an original 1800s tobacco barn that is now a photography museum. Hiking trails, picnic areas and natural history programs are offered here. The state park is open year-round; the historic buildings are open only on weekend afternoons from March through December. ~ 5101 North Roxboro Road, six miles north of downtown Durham; 919-471-1623.

If you would like to explore further around Durham, stop by the **Durham Convention & Visitors Bureau**. Located downtown and run by the friendliest people, it's the best source for information and maps, including walking-tour maps of the downtown historic district. Closed Sunday. ~ 101 East Morgan Street; 919-687-0288, 800-446-8604.

In Durham's historic Holloway neighborhood not far from downtown, the **Blooming Garden Inn** was built in the late 1800s and restored in the 1990s. The Victorian venue has the feel of a dollhouse,
painted in bright pastels, trimmed in antique lace and stained glass
and festooned with clever keepsakes. There are three attractive
bedrooms as well as two suites with whirlpool tubs. Guests are
treated to an extraordinary gourmet breakfast, after which they
usually find a comfortable spot on the big wraparound porch. ~
513 Holloway Street; 919-687-0801, fax 919-688-1401. MODER-
ATE TO ULTRA-DELUXE.

"Inn" hardly seems an appropriate description for the **Washington Duke Inn**, Durham's grandest hotel. Presiding over the Duke
University campus and its 18-hole golf course, the imposing red-
brick manse is named for the man who built the world's biggest tobacco empire and along the way built much of Durham. Duke family belongings, including Washington's antique desk, decorate the
lobby. The guest rooms are contemporary, with fine linens, mahogany and cherry headboards and leather-back chairs. There are two
restaurants, as well as an outdoor pool, jogging path and tennis
courts. ~ 3001 Cameron Boulevard; 919-490-0999, 800-443-3853,
fax 919-688-0105. ULTRA-DELUXE.

An eighteenth-century, white-columned farmhouse, the **Arrow-**
head Inn offers relaxed, home-style accommodations several miles
north of downtown Durham. The Inn maintains seven guest rooms,
two with working fireplaces, embellished with both period pieces
and modern comforts such as telephones. All have private baths.
There's also the spacious Land Grant Cabin, with a sitting room,
large fireplace and bedroom loft. After a full country breakfast,
guests can mix and mingle in the big family room stocked with
puzzles, board games, and TV. ~ 106 Mason Road, off Route 501;
phone/fax 919-477-8430, 800-528-2207. MODERATE TO DELUXE.

Located across the street from Duke Medical Center and Duke
University, the **Brownstone MedCenter Inn** is a friendly place
catering primarily to patients and visitors of the hospital as well as
to the university folks. However, travelers will find comfortable,
bright rooms with cable TV, an indoor swimming pool and sauna.
A generous continental breakfast is included in the rates. ~ 2424
Erwin Road; phone 919-286-7761. MODERATE TO DELUXE.

Fishmonger's would look more at home parked at the end of a pier,
but it's in downtown Durham, filled with the salty smells of the
sea. The restaurant smokes its own bluefish, tuna, salmon and also
chicken, and sells fresh seafood from a glass case. The decor is picnic tables covered with plastic—all the better for delving into the
crabs, mussels, clams and oysters that come out of the steamer.
Grilled and fried fish are also for dinner; lunch features fish, oys-

ter and crab cake sandwiches. ~ 806 West Main Street; 919-682-0128. MODERATE.

A local favorite for Mexican and Southwestern food, **Papagayo** is where you'll find simple but good-tasting dishes like shrimp enchilada and black-bean tostadas. Right downtown and open for lunch and dinner, it looks a little like an upscale fern bar, with hanging plants and lots of wood around. When it's warm outside, you can eat on the wood deck. Sundays are "smoke-free." ~ 501 Douglas Street; 919-286-1910. MODERATE.

The same family has owned **Hartman's Steak House** for more than half a century. Which explains why the country cookin' here has been so good so long. Famous for its fried banana peppers and cheese salad dressing, Hartman's also dishes up rib-eye steaks and fried seafood platters, frogs' legs and oyster stew. Surroundings are spartan: cedar walls, ceiling fans and wood tables. Closed Sunday and Monday. 1703 East Geer Street; 919-688-7639. MODERATE.

You can't leave Durham without stopping in at the **Ninth Street Bakery**, if for no other reason than to breathe the wonderful aromas of flavored coffees, piping popovers and steamy soups. Next door to Duke University and in the Ninth Street stretch of funky shops and eateries, the bakery is big and bohemian, with high ceilings and wood tables everywhere. Order from the counter—choices include roasted pesto rounds, flatbread with bean dip, shrimp Creole and Chesapeake Bay crab cakes. ~ 776 9th Street; 919-286-0303. BUDGET.

The place with the culinary reputation is **Magnolia Grill**, a simple brick building parked along a busy road, with an interior of peach walls and white tablecloths. The star is absolutely the menu, vast and varied every day depending on whatever chef-owners Ben and Karen Barker conjure up. Expect such Southern-inspired creations as black-eyed pea soup with cornmeal dumplings, country ham and greens, or grilled yellowfin tuna with smoked tomato barbecue vinaigrette on red-pepper grits and Southern greens "sandwich." Save room for the stellar desserts. Closed Sunday. ~ 1002 9th Street at Knox Street; 919-286-3609. DELUXE.

Famed around Durham for its gourmet menu, **Nana's** combines Italian, country French and American nouveau cuisine. Chef Scott Howe's entrées include his own cured swordfish served with roasted purple potato salad and a roast Long Island duck with lentils and field greens. Choose a wine from one of the many bottles on display in the dining room—a classy place with white linen, fresh-cut flowers and everchanging local artwork. Reservations mandatory. Closed Monday. ~ 2514 University Drive; 919-493-8545. DELUXE.

Since 1952, **Bullock's Barbecue** has been churning out savory Southern edibles to anyone who wanders in, which would include celebrities Robert Duvall and Dolly Parton. Most everything on the menu is fattening, filling—and delicious. Barbecue platters come with brunswick stew; fried chicken and spareribs are served with a heap of fries, cole slaw and hushpuppies. You can also order salisbury steak or meatloaf. The vegetables, from stewed corn to black-eyed peas, have that incredible fresh flavor. Closed Sunday and Monday. ~ 3330 Quebec Street; 919-383-3211. BUDGET.

SHOPPING

At the turn-of-the-century, the buildings of **Brightleaf Square** were warehouses for the American Tobacco Company. (In case you've forgotten, the company was run by Washington Duke and produced 90 percent of the world's tobacco at the time.) Now you can stroll along the lengthy red-brick corridors in the hopes of finding a book, an artpiece or even some clothing. ~ Main and Gregson streets.

In the Square, **Wentworth & Leggett Rare Books** is packed floor-to-ceiling with wonderful old volumes, prints and world maps. ~ 919-688-5311.

Durham's hippest browsing and buying are along **Ninth Street** across from Duke University's east campus. Bookstores and bakeries, music stores and vintage boutiques appeal to both straight and gay shoppers.

The Regulator Bookshop is a place of local renown where you can find reams on every subject, from the Civil War and Old South to New Age and gay studies. The children's section is outstanding. ~ 720 9th Street; 919-286-2700.

Vaguely Reminiscent has women's jewelry, shoes and clothing updated from the '60s for the '90s. ~ 728 9th Street; 919-286-3911.

Headquarters for New Age gear is **Earth & Spirit,** carrying candles, cards, music and nose pins. ~ 754 9th Street; 919-286-4250.

If you are in need of medicinal herbs, organic vegetables and cheese, aromatherapy oils, or antibiotic- and hormone-free meat, stop by **Wellspring Grocery**. The health-oriented emporium has much more, including wonderful baked breads. ~ 621 Broad Street; 919-286-2290.

NIGHTLIFE

A gleaming, grand, beaux-arts beauty, the **Carolina Theater** began life in 1926 and enjoyed a thorough renovation in 1994. It hosts the North Carolina Symphony series every fall, plus everything from international choirs to chamber blues. ~ 309 Morgan Street; 919-560-3030.

Next door and just as palatial, the **Durham Arts Center** is headquarters to a vast performing arts network that includes the Durham Symphony, African-American Dance Ensemble, Young People's Performing Company and Durham Civic Choral Society. ~ 120 Morris Street; 919-560-2787.

Open on Friday and Saturday nights, **The Palace International** focuses on African music, from calypso to tribal to reggae, and serves African fare to match. Cover. ~ 117 West Parrish Street; 919-687-4922.

Within Brightleaf Square, **Satisfaction Restaurant & Bar** is a lively restaurant by day and a livelier bar by night, first with the after-work professional crowd and later with college students making the bar rounds. Food is served throughout the evening, of course. ~ 905 West Main Street; 919-682-7397.

Right next to the square, you can dance out on the patio at **Devine's Restaurant & Bar** when the weather's warm. In winter, all the action's inside. Rock-and-roll and Top-40 are standard band fare, but there's jazz sometimes, too. Cover. ~ 904 West Main Street; 919-682-0228.

Ninth Street Bakery, a big and friendly coffeehouse, serves folk and acoustic with its cafe lattes. ~ 776 9th Street; 919-286-0303.

GAY SCENE   For the latest on the gay night scene, pick up a copy of *The Front Page* newspaper, available from stores along Ninth Street.

With a dancefloor and light show to rival the best big-city bars, the tri-level **Power Company** brings in a diverse crowd of both gays and straights. Friday night is the hottest. Cover. ~ 315 West Main Street; 919-683-1151.

If conversation, good music and a game of pool are what you seek, you should head on over to **Boxers**. The congenial, publike atmosphere draws mostly gay men. ~ 5504 Chapel Hill Boulevard; 919-489-7678.

All About Eve is easily the most popular lesbian meetingspot in the Carolinas. Featuring a patio bar, volleyball court and huge dancefloor, it's super-crowded on weekends. Cover. ~ 711 Rigsbee Avenue; 919-688-3002.

BEACHES & PARKS

ENO RIVER STATE PARK 🏃‍♂️ Coming upon this park, you feel like you might have left the Piedmont for the mountains. Cool forest carpeted with ferns and wildflowers and studded with mountain laurel frame the rocky, rippling Eno River. Fishers and naturalists love these 2280 acres, a nature break from Durham's urban sprawl. A self-guided trail introduces visitors to the wild array of flora, and perhaps even some of the wild park residents, like barred owls, box turtles, beavers and river otters. The fishing is excellent, with lots of good fishing holes along the Eno River banks. Try for largemouth bass, bluegill, crappie and chain pickerel. There is no swimming. Facilities include a park office, a picnic area, restrooms, hiking trails and a self-guided nature trail. A convenience store is located three miles away. ~ Located at 6101 Cole Mill Road, off Route 85, about seven and a half miles northwest of downtown Durham; 919-383-1686.

▲ There are five primitive riverfront sites, reached by a one-mile hike from the parking lot; $5 per site per night. There is also a primitive group site with a maximum of 20 persons; $1 per person per night.

FALLS LAKE STATE RECREATION AREA

This enormous park reaches into three counties and is largely underwater—some 12,000 of its 38,000 acres belong to Falls Lake. There are numerous places around the lake to have fun, including three beaches with clayish sand (one with a concrete ramp for wheelchair access), and there are many possibilities for landing a fish. A marina rents boats for getting out on the water. Away from the lake, the forest is typical of the Piedmont: loblolly pine, yellow poplars, hickories and oaks. Swimming is good from all three beaches, with shallow water sloping gently over hard-packed sand. Fishing is good year-round. Try for bluegills, crappie, sunfish and largemouth bass. Facilities include the park office, several picnic areas and boat ramps, marina with boat rentals and restrooms. Day-use fee, $3. ~ The main entrance is at 13304 Creedmoor Road, off Route 50, east of Durham and north of Raleigh. Other entrances are off of Route 50 just north of Route 98, and off Route 98 west of Route 50; 919-676-1027.

▲ There are 117 sites for tents and RVs, including hookups; tent sites are $9 per night, RVs are $14 per night.

Chapel Hill Area

Chapel Hill has been called "the southern part of heaven" and it's easy to see why, for it is an instantly pleasurable place, small and personable and well-established, with lofty trees sheltering the dignified brick and stone manses and filigreed clapboard homes that make up some of the Piedmont's most desirable neighborhoods. The lovely University of North Carolina (just call it UNC) sprawls across the center of town, and in fact is *the* town, for beyond the red-brick campus and the hubbub it generates, there are mainly homes and woods and then the neighboring town of Carrboro.

A lot of people who live in Chapel Hill and Carrboro aren't from the South (you'll be hard-pressed to find a southern drawl here) but have come from the Northeast and the West to work at UNC, nearby Research Triangle Park or one of the dozen or so publishing houses. People walk around Chapel Hill carrying books—and not just the students, but everyday people. Coffeehouse conversation churns over the latest releases and bookstores brim with literary finds.

SIGHTS

Most Chapel Hill action happens on **Franklin Street**, lined on one side with columned brick houses, pizza joints, yuppie-ized head shops, coffeehouses, chain stores like The Gap, and women selling cut flowers on the sidewalk. On the other side is **University of**

North Carolina and *the wall*, made of stone and decorated for blocks with students, studying and chatting and people-watching. If you want to meet someone in Chapel Hill, don't go to a night-club. Go sit on the wall.

Parking around here is horrendous, and the least stressful thing to do is to find a spot in one of the UNC's visitor lots (the main lot is off Cameron Avenue) and pay by the hour. While you're here, take at look at the **Ackland Art Museum**, with its extensive collection of sculpture dating from the Renaissance to the present, along with European and American paintings, ancient Greek and Roman art and North Carolina pottery. Closed Monday and Tuesday. ~ South Columbia and East Franklin streets; 919-966-5736.

There's more art inside the grand rotunda of UNC's **Morehead Planetarium**, including a 1632 portrait Rembrandt painted of his sister, Liesbeth Van Rijn. The planetarium also hosts regular astronomical shows (admission) on everything from wormholes to flying objects that show up on Earth. Closed Monday evening. ~ East Franklin Street; 919-962-1236. In the building's west lobby, the UNC **Visitors Center** dispenses maps and information and arranges walking tours of the campus. Closed weekends. ~ 919-962-1630.

For more information on the area, be sure to check with the **Chapel Hill/Carrboro Chamber of Commerce**, a little north of UNC. Closed weekends. ~ 104 South Estes Drive, Chapel Hill; 919-967-7075.

On the southeast edge of UNC, the **North Carolina Botanical Garden** is set in and around 80 acres of Piedmont woods. From the many walking trails, visitors can learn about vegetation native to the Southeast. In the main garden, plants grow geographically by coastal, Piedmont and mountain habitats. Bog and aquatic plants such as waterlilies, pondweed and spatterdocks decorate ponds and streams; endangered plants, including the bunched arrowhead, are also here, as are carnivores like the Venus flytrap. Good-smelling herbs, wildflowers, ferns and brick walkways surround the visitors center. Some of the gardens are wheelchair accessible; special assistance can be arranged by calling ahead. ~ Off Old Mason Farm Road, just south of Route 15-501 and 54 bypass; 919-962-0522.

From here, jog over to Route 54 east and go three and a half miles to Farrington Road. Go north on Farrington Road (turning at the Hardees) and drive through rural countryside for one and a quarter miles until you see it, set up on a hill with its old Esso gas tank, looking like something out of an old photograph. **Patterson's Mill Country Store** is actually a 1973 replica of the original store that opened in 1870, but you could never tell it. Inside the wonderfully cluttered clapboard building is the real thing—moonshine jugs, bonnets, seed bins, cornshuckers, homemade lye soap, pioneer

HIDDEN ▶

dolls, dough bowls, old Coca Cola posters, you-name-it, stacked and strung and hung everywhere.

The woman in charge, Gail Booker, is the daughter-in-law of Elsie Booker. Elsie was born in the green farmhouse next door, and the surrounding farmland has been in her family "better than 200 years." A feisty woman with a voice that booms, Elsie was one of the first female pharmacists in North Carolina, receiving her degree from UNC in Chapel Hill in the 1940s and practicing for 40 years. Her memento to those times is her Pharmacy Museum filled with ancient-looking medicinals: well-dusted potions and vials, mortars and pestles, pillboxes, tattered prescriptions. Here one discovers that BC Tablets and Headache Powder originated in Durham, Bromo Seltzer in Chapel Hill, and Vicks Vapor Rub in Greensboro.

Elsie's husband, John, has his own place of nostalgia upstairs, a Tobacco Museum with thousands of items he collected while working more than 30 years for Liggett & Myers. There's a 1910 Piedmont cigarette sign and packs of bizarre brands like Vello, Total, Stage III and System III. If you've never seen generic cigarette packs, you'll see them here. Closed Monday. ~ 919-493-8149.

From Chapel Hill, you can instantly be in **Carrboro** in your car, and in fact not realize you had switched cities except for the small "Welcome to Carrboro" sign along West Franklin Street. Carrboro is as New Agey as its neighbor, though smaller. The little downtown is strung with arty storefronts advertising holistic foods and treatments, organic groceries and colorful galleries, and small publishing houses.

It takes longer to arrive in **Hillsborough**, about 20 minutes.   ◄ HIDDEN
From Carrboro, Old Route 86 dips and climbs and winds ten miles northwest through piney countryside, woods and hayfields. You see whitewashed homes, trailers parked along the highway, lawns planted with tulips in spring and pumpkins in fall.

The town of Hillsborough dates to 1754, and it feels like it. Handsome old clapboard homes with brick chimneys are set up along the slopes of town, just off cobbled stone sidewalks. Kudzu swarms over massive pecan and elm trees, and in the spring daylilies and hot pink azaleas ripple in the breeze. There are a handful of historic inns, fine spots for lunching and shopping.

Before exploring, stop in the **Orange County Historical Museum** and pick up a walking-tour map and brochures on antiquing and local sights. Closed Monday. ~ Located inside the Confederate Memorial Building, 201 North Churton Street, Hillsborough; 919-732-2201.

With its coat of red brick and rows of gables and tall chimneys, the   **LODGING**
Carolina Inn fits right into its UNC setting. The lobby is decorated with white columns, antiques and overstuffed chairs; the guest

Text continued on page 244.

Fearrington Village

Eight miles south of Chapel Hill off Route 15-501, Fearrington Village comes as a surprise. For it rises up from the North Carolina countryside, its meticulous shuttered buildings of white plank and flourishing arbors strangely juxtaposed against Piedmont scrubland and forgotten mill towns, and pine woods sheltering shacks and hound dogs and old pickup trucks.

Drive inside the village, park in the raked gravel, and step beneath the wash of crabapple trees. It does not take long to become accustomed to the place, where everything speaks to the art of living: the handsome inn and fountained courtyards, rambling dovecote and tiny white potting shed, the music room where Verdi reigns, the bookstore that invites all-day browsing, the sun-warmed bistro and market that carry the *New York Times*, delicate scents, and shelf after shelf of unusual wines.

Flowers engulf all the buildings—tall rugosa roses and fountains of lavender, ribbons of geraniums and pansies, tulips and iris—and in between the buildings are knot gardens, shrubs that are woven over and under each other in tight bond. Pecan trees with enormous arms serve as a cathedral for warm-weather weddings. There are hollyhocks that were seeded from Monet's garden in France. The herb garden is a daily source for the village restaurants, and if you order a summer salad, you may well find violas or passion flowers on your plate.

Much of Fearrington's style and mood are linked to Europe, where owner R. B. Fitch and his late wife, Jenny, made dozens of visits, researching architecture and horticulture, food and wine, and ways to run a place. They had purchased the 1786 Fearrington family farmstead in 1974 and started building homes on its 640 acres. But they were determined not to end up with a typical subdivision, the kind of development that infests suburbs across the country.

Now their singular village draws thousands of yearly visitors who come to shop and dine, play croquet and bocce, or bike along leafy streets hooded with elms and maples.

Some stay at **Fearrington House Inn**, in one of 24 handsome rooms, spacious and adorned with plank floors, canopied beds, antiques and original paintings. Styled like an English country manor, and somewhat lavish, it is a favorite of Europeans, who use their "Relais & Chateaux" guides (in which the inn is listed) to find their way to Fearrington. ~ 2000 Fearrington Village Center, Pittsboro; 919-542-2121, fax 919-542-4202. ULTRA-DELUXE.

Next to the inn, **Fearrington House Restaurant** is a formal place to dine, with small, intimate rooms whose walls are prettily stenciled and whose windows look out onto lush gardens. The prix-fixe dinner menu changes monthly, but selections are supremely Southern. Among the possibilities: baked Chatham County goat cheese on black-eyed-pea salad; catfish fritter with sweet-potato chips and maple hard sauce; and pecan-crusted pork tenderloin with red-onion confit and honey-thyme sauce. Closed Monday. ULTRA-DELUXE.

Across the street, in the old farm granary, the bistro-style **Fearrington Market Cafe** has sage-green walls, flowery Provençal tablecloths and sunlight streaming from windows up high. My favorite fare here is portobello mushroom sandwich, tricolored ravioli with pesto and goat cheese, and chicken pot pie. There's also a deli for takeout sandwiches and soups. Brunch is served on the weekend. ~ 2000 Fearrington Village Center, Pittsboro; 919-542-5505. BUDGET TO MODERATE.

Once a week, people come from all around to browse the bins of fresh produce and locally made cheeses and artistry that line Fearrington's country lanes. Tuesday there is a farmer's market in the village, and it is a festive few hours, with people crowding the shops and market and gardens, stirring around the 1700s barn and silo, eating creamy, herb-crusted rounds of goat cheese and sipping pinot noir on the lawns.

rooms look very Southern with their easy chairs, armoires and desks. The 77 rooms in the historic section of the inn are most desirable; each one has a unique shape and features a pedestal sink in the bathroom. Owned by the university, the hotel boasts a great location. ~ 211 Pittsboro Street at the corner of Cameron and Columbia, Chapel Hill; 919-933-2001, 800-962-8519, fax 919-962-3400. DELUXE.

The Siena is as jazzy as lodging gets around Chapel Hill, and it is in fact a fine place, though a little odd (its brochure inviting guests to "Experience Italy right in the heart of North Carolina."). The owners love Italy and return home with their finds, so the experience includes Italian gilt-frame paintings and fine sculpture, armoires and embroidered chairs decorating the large, lively lobby and 80 rooms. Guest rooms are spacious, with marble baths and cushy carpets. There's a complimentary breakfast and also shuttle service around town. ~ 1505 East Franklin Street, Chapel Hill; 919-929-4000, 800-223-7379, fax 919-968-8527. DELUXE TO ULTRA-DELUXE.

HIDDEN ►   If you stay at **Windy Oaks Inn**, you'll be sleeping in the former home of Paul Green. The Pulitzer Prize–winning playwright no doubt found inspiration in these deep wood surroundings, which now cover 25 acres. The driveway is lined with magnolias, the backyard graced with gardens and picket fence. The four guest rooms, two with shared bath, are warmly decorated. Rates include a country breakfast and afternoon wine and cheese. ~ Take Route 15-501 three miles south of Route 54 to Old Lystra Road and go one mile; 919-942-1001. MODERATE.

HIDDEN ►   Twelve miles west of Chapel Hill, **The Inn at Bingham School** is a tranquil place set among rolling Piedmont hills. The Greek Revival and Federal bed and breakfast was home to Bingham's headmaster during the mid-1800s. Now it has been restored to a polished patina, with five bedrooms furnished in period antiques. All have private baths. There's also the restored milkhouse with a large bedroom, sitting room and whirlpool tub. Full breakfast and afternoon wine and cheese are included in the rates. ~ Located at 6720 Mebane Oaks Road, off Route 54; 919-563-5583. MODERATE TO DELUXE.

HIDDEN ►   Of the trio of inns in Hillsborough, the **Hillsborough House Inn** is by far the prettiest and plushest. It sits up on a hill, white and ornate, with a soft green lawn shimmering in the sun and a swimming pool sparkling out back. All six bedrooms are different; one has a private porch and view into the woods, another has a queen bed where you can sleep beneath a cathedral of white voile. A beautiful suite is located in the adjacent, 1790s brick kitchen— the town's oldest freestanding brick building. ~ 209 East Tryon Street, Hillsborough; 919-644-1600. DELUXE TO ULTRA-DELUXE.

The best breakfast in town is at **Carolina Coffee Shop**. Small and inviting with tall, straight-back booths, the eatery has been a Franklin Street favorite since 1922. There are eggs Benedict and other extravagant day starters, and lots of gourmet coffees. There's also lunch (homemade soups, sandwiches) and dinner (London broil, stuffed rainbow trout), and even a full bar. ~ 138 East Franklin Street, Chapel Hill; 919-942-6875. BUDGET TO MODERATE.

If it's lunchtime, go to **Judges Coffee Roastery** and have a salad or sandwich. The cobb and spinach salads, tarragon chicken salad sandwich and Carolina club are the best; the cappuccino is served in cups the size of soup bowls. The brick-walled eatery has a view to the sidewalk buzz. ~ 161 East Franklin Street, Chapel Hill; 919-929-1727. BUDGET.

The Pyewacket, one of Chapel Hill's most popular eateries, specializes in seafood, poultry, pasta and vegetarian fare, but you will also hear about its desserts: chocolate cake and black-bottom pie being just two in the luscious lineup. Catering to local yuppies rather than college students, the place is light and open and a little refined. No lunch on Saturday. ~ 431 West Franklin Street; 919-929-0297. MODERATE.

The Weathervane is enormously popular for lunch and dinner. The atmosphere is quite calm—comfy booths brightened by oil lamps, jazz pouring from the speakers, diners a little dressed up—and there's a spacious patio for warm-weather dining. Menus focus on seasonal fare and feature many vegetarian dishes. Try the grilled portobello sandwich made with sun-dried tomato bread, the spring salad with Granny Smith apples or the shrimp BLT. The wine list is excellent. ~ Located within the stellar store, A Southern Season, Eastgate Shopping Center, off East Franklin Street and Route 15-501; 919-929-9466. MODERATE.

Four Eleven West has good pasta and burgers and wood-grilled pizza, but mostly it gives good atmosphere: waitresses with wisps for waists, students in tall black platforms, walls of exposed brick and ceilings high and lofty. Go even if you're not hungry and have a cocktail or espresso. ~ 411 West Franklin Street, Chapel Hill; 919-967-2782. MODERATE.

Crook's Corner is everybody's favorite for '90s-inspired Southern cooking: jalapeño cheddar hushpuppies, fiddlehead fern salad, baked catfish filet in cheese crust with herb butter, fluffy cornbread with a hood of black pepper. The atmosphere is bluesy, a little funky, with little bottles of Tabasco on silver-rimmed tables and a patio that's full as soon as the place opens. ~ 610 West Franklin Street, Chapel Hill; 919-929-7643. MODERATE.

The fill-you-up country cookin' at **Dip's** is good stuff, not too greasy or heavy. Slip into a vinyl booth and order chicken and dumplings or cured country ham, okra and tomatoes, turnips and black-eyed peas and biscuits, and the best mashed potatoes you ever had. Old ceiling fans circulate good kitchen smells, and grilled corn cobs fill ceramic pitchers. ~ 405 West Rosemary Street, Chapel Hill; 919-942-5837. BUDGET.

In Carrboro, **Aurora** is an Italian bistro, modern and somewhat elegant, with cranberry walls, exposed wood and painted metal on the ceilings. The prevailing scent of garlic and olive oil is very pleasant. The fare is different each day, but expect seasonal, imaginative creations and lots of choices. Possibilities include spinach salad with almonds, blue cheese, apricots and tomato vinaigrette; seared, soy-marinated salmon with a garlic-infused pinot grigio sauce with capers and mustard; beef tenderloin with baby artichokes and Madeira glaze over Gorgonzola polenta. ~ Carr Mill Mall, at the corner of Greensboro and Weaver streets, Carrboro; 919-942-2400. DELUXE TO ULTRA-DELUXE.

Go casual at **Elmo's Diner** with "square meals" like Italian meatloaf, turkey and gravy with mashed potatoes, or chicken and dumplings. There are also burgers and salads and breakfast anytime. The diner is clamorous, a big, open room with brick walls and a ceiling floating somewhere high overhead, steam drifting up from soup bowls. Locals like it here. ~ Carr Mill Mall, 100 North Greensboro Street, Carrboro; 919-929-2909. BUDGET.

In downtown Hillsborough, **Saratoga Grill** occupies a second-floor perch, with big arched windows overlooking the street. Ambiance is country-casual, with cane-laden chairs, Southern prints on the walls and classical music filling the air. The fare is uncomplicated Continental—barbecue shrimp, mozzarella bread for appetizers, assorted fish and seafood, chicken, lamb and steaks for entrées. Best of all, you can order smaller size portions of many dishes. ~ 108 South Churton Street, Hillsborough; 919-732-2214. MODERATE.

WU WEI TEA AND BUMBLEBEES

On a Chapel Hill afternoon, go to **Caffé Driade** and sit outside at one of the little round tables in the woods. Order a cup of wu wei tea, a hot and heady elixir plied with lavender and orange peel, and watch the bumblebees drink nectar from wildflowers. The music will be moody and so will the crowd at this former bookbindery, reincarnated as an Asian-aura coffee- and teahouse. Driade sits back off the highway, an infinitesimal sign announcing its existence, and can be maddening to find. Don't miss it. ~ 215-A Franklin Street, behind Traditions Bridal Salon; 919-942-2333.

On the third Sunday of the month you can drive to **Celebrity** ◄ *HIDDEN*
Farm and have a goat cheese dinner. The farm is out in the piney
Piedmont woods between Pittsboro and Siler City, about 30 miles
west of Chapel Hill. The afternoon dinner is a prix-fixe family-style
affair, with two dozen diners gathered at long tables inside Fleming
and Britt Phann's farmhouse. Every course the Phanns serve will
have goat cheese, perhaps a butternut squash soup with goat cheese
curd, a chicken breast stuffed with rice and herbed goat cheese, and
finally a goat cheese pound cake or cheesecake or flaming banana-
cheese surprise!

The cheese comes from the goats out in the Phanns' barn (well,
it actually comes from their milk). You can have a look at the goats
after dinner, but be prepared for some affection: "Goats like to be
held," explains Britt, "and happy goats make good milk." Reservations required. ~ Located two miles north of Route 64 on Mount
Vernon–Hickory Mountain Road; 919-742-5176. ULTRA-DELUXE.

In Chapel Hill, a stroll down **Franklin Street** delivers you to every-   **SHOPPING**
thing from The Gap to head shops to bookstores and places sell-
ing nothing but Tar Heel (UNC's revered basketball team) accessories.

Then, too, you can buy great clothes and shoes in Chapel Hill.
For haute male couture, it's **The Hub, Limited,** with blazers, sus-
penders, oxford shirts and leather briefcases with that rich, buttery
feel (and frightful price tags). ~ 103 East Franklin Street, Chapel
Hill; 919-929-0343.

Women should start at **Shoes on the Square**, whose inventory
of women's platforms, chunky-heel loafers and high-heeled tennis
shoes are as cool as can be. ~ In University Square, 133 West Franklin Street, Chapel Hill; 919-942-2044.

Owner Lisa Heyward designs much of the hip female garb at
Modern Times—soft, flowing skirts and chenille vests, satiny pants
and stunning little jackets. Great jewelry and handbags, too. ~ 402
West Franklin Street, Chapel Hill; 919-929-8119.

Internationalist Books has a small but interesting selection of   ◄ *HIDDEN*
gay and lesbian reading as well as other progressive and alternative books. The place is run by knowledgeable gay volunteers who
are happy to tell visitors about local gay events. ~ 405 West Franklin Street, Chapel Hill; 919-942-1740.

Gowns of velvet, microdresses, hiphuggers that flare at the bottom, satin shoes Audrey Hepburn would have worn—**Uniquities**
does have unique stuff. Plus the salesgirls are gorgeous waifs that
seem to drift among the merchandise. ~ 425 West Franklin Street,
Chapel Hill; 919-933-4007.

At the eastern end of Franklin Street, just outside downtown
Chapel Hill, **A Southern Season** is an enormous space filled with

beautiful and unusual items, from kitchenry, candles and coffee mugs to cookbooks and greeting cards. There's even an espresso bar and a wine "corner" with a superb selection. ~ Eastgate Shopping Center, off East Franklin Street and Route 15-501; 919-929-7133.

Next door to Chapel Hill in downtown Carrboro, **Carr Mill Mall** is an 1898 cotton mill that's been recycled into a shopping arcade. Beamed ceilings, wood floors and exposed brick walls lend atmosphere to the shopping experience. Stores inside the mall run the gamut from used books and local arts and crafts to designer duds. ~ Corner of Greensboro and Weaver streets; 919-942-8669.

Perhaps most singular at Carr Mill is **Gallery Americas**, whose furnishings and objets d'art might include a Bubinga chest, Barcelona chair, elm bowls and screens of mahogany, sycamore and ebony. ~ 919-929-1002.

Stephen White Gallery focuses on Japanese art, screens and apparel. The kimonos are luxurious, the boxes delicate and decorative. ~ 919-967-1611.

HIDDEN ►   If you've never experienced an old-time Southern store, go to **Patterson's Mill Country Store**. The crafts, kitchenwares and pieces of nostalgia fill every nook and cranny, and the owner is a character who was born in the house next door. ~ Farrington Road, one and a quarter miles north of Route 54, east of Chapel Hill; 919-493-8149.

Fearrington Village, designed like a European village in the countryside, is a most enjoyable place to shop. ~ Route 15-501, eight miles south of Chapel Hill, Pittsboro.

In the village, the warm and personal **McIntyre's Fine Books and Bookends** is designed for hours of browsing, with entire rooms devoted to travel, children's readings, and home and garden. There's a big selection by local authors, who give frequent readings here. ~ 919-542-3030.

Walking into the **Dovecote** is like stepping into the pages of a British *Home & Garden* magazine. Flowers, birdhouses, porcelain boxes, painted garden tables—everything here is artfully done. ~ 919-542-1145.

A Stone's Throw has gemstones set every imaginable way, even as the top of a wine cork. ~ 919-542-1055. **The Market** is perennially abuzz with customers gushing over all the unusual things to buy, from local beers and hard-to-find wines to green tomato relish and tangerine marmalade. ~ 919-542-5505.

NIGHTLIFE   Chapel Hill is wonderful at night (picture a small Berkeley, with a Southern twist). Clubs and cafes crowd along Franklin Street and just off it, and you can prowl for hours and not experience everything. Good bands play here, too—artists on the verge of making it (or who should be) and experimental musicians with new sounds. Expect the whole spectrum of music, from roots and reggae to Southern rock and alternative country. One music junkie in his 50s says he moved to Chapel Hill because "I can see the same groups I saw in New York and L.A. without all the crowd hassle. The people here are great."

To find out who's playing where, pick up a copy of the *Independent*, a weekly tabloid at bookstores and cafes around town.

The place to be for university students is **He's Not Here**. In warm weather, the outdoor courtyard with picnic tables and benches is packed to the hilt during happy hour. Classic rock is played real loud, and beer is dispensed in the ever-popular "Big Blue Cup." There's live music on Friday and Saturday nights during the spring and summer and they charge a cover then. ~ 112½ West Franklin Street, Chapel Hill; 919-942-7939.

On the nights He's Not Here is too jammed with people, try **Spanky's**, just a block away. Same casual college atmosphere, but quieter and a bit cleaner. Cover on nights with live music. ~ 101 East Franklin Street, Chapel Hill; 919-967-2678.

The **Dead Mule** is where UNC grad students go to escape the undergrads; professors and professionals come here, too, for afternoon scotch-on-the-rocks and jazz. Local alternative and rock bands crank up at night. Members only—though, if you fit the clientele, a member will usually sign you in. ~ 303 West Franklin Street, Chapel Hill; 919-969-7659.

Local musicians hang out at **Local 506**, listening to live everything, from surf and garage to roots and country alternative. Private club, but visitors won't have a problem getting a pass. Cover. ~ 506 West Franklin Street, Chapel Hill; 919-942-5506.

The Pyewacket caters to a slightly more upscale clientele than its neighbors on Franklin Street. The bar offers live music, mostly jazz and blues ensembles, several nights a week. Great for after-dinner drinks. ~ 431 Franklin Street, Chapel Hill; 919-929-0297.

In the glittery back bar at **Henry's Bistro**, among pale yellow walls and abstract art, there are beautiful people late at night smoking and sipping martinis. Classy. ~ 403 West Rosemary Street, Chapel Hill; 919-967-4720.

One of the best concert venues around is a minute from Chapel Hill in Carrboro. **Cat's Cradle**, a beer-only SRO club that's a black-on-the-inside warehouse, brings in local, regional and national talent. Zen Frisbee, Purple Schoolbus, Kilgore Smudge—they all play here. Cover. ~ 300 East Main Street, Carrboro; 919-967-9053.

The closest major park is Eno River State Park near Durham. For information, see the "Durham Beaches & Parks" section in this chapter.

**BEACHES
& PARKS**

There are plenty of open green spaces around Chapel Hill perfect for picnicking, the premier place being the **University of North Carolina campus** in the middle of town. Try along Franklin Street. There's also the **North Carolina Botanical Garden.** ~ Off Old Mason Farm Road, just south of Route 15-501 and 54 bypass. Or try the grounds of **Fearrington Village.** ~ Route 15-501, eight miles south of Chapel Hill.

▼▼▼▼▼▼▼▼▼▼▼▼▼▼▼

Outdoor Adventures

GOLF

Piedmonters take their clubs seriously—more than 150 courses can be found in these clay and sand hills. In Winston-Salem, you can tee off at **Reynolds Park Golf Course.** ~ 2931 Reynolds Park Road; 650-7660. **Heather Hills Golf Course** is another choice. ~ 3801 Heathrow Drive; 910-788-5785. Also in the area is **Long Creek Club.** ~ Rural Hall–Tobaccoville Road; 910-924-5226. **Or try the Hillcrest Golf Club.** ~ 2450 Stratford Road; 910-765-5269. At the beautiful **Tanglewood Park,** one of the two 18-hole courses was designed by Robert Trent Jones. ~ Route 158, Clemmons; 910-766-0591.

Other Triad courses include the **Bel Air Golf Club.** ~ Pleasant Ridge Road at Regional Road, near the Piedmont Triad International Airport; 668-2413. In Pfafftown, go to **Grandview Golf Course.** ~ 3401 Grandview Road, Pfafftown; 910-924-8229. Try the **Jamestown Park Golf Course.** ~ 7041 East Fork Road, Jamestown; 910-454-4912. While in Kernersville try the **Pine Tree Golf Club.** ~ 1680 Pine Tree Lane, Kernersville; 910-993-5598. In Brown Summit, go to **Bryan Park.** ~ 6275 Bryan Park Road, Brown Summit; 910-375-2200. The **Oak Hollow Golf Course's** 18 holes, designed by Pete Dye, have been ranked among the nation's best by *Golf Digest.* ~ 1400 Oakview Road, High Point; 910-883-3260.

Charlotte's newest, most-talked-about course is the Scottish-style **Charlotte Golf Links.** ~ 11500 Providence Road; 704-846-7990. The Queen City also has courses open to the public at **Highland Creek Golf Club.** ~ 7001 Highland Creek Parkway; 704-875-9000. The **Renaissance Park Golf Course** is also open to the public. ~ 1525 West Tyvola Road; 704-357-3373. Another option is the **Sunset Hills Golf Club.** ~ 800 Radio Road; 704-399-0980.

Pinehurst and Southern Pines have been called the "World's Most Famous Birdie Sanctuary," and there is definitely no lack of great greens. Lovely links in the area include **The Club at Longleaf.** ~ Route 2, Pinehurst; 910-692-6100, 800-889-5323. Also in Pinehurst you'll find **The Pit Golf Links.** ~ Route 5, Pinehurst; 910-944-1600, 800-574-4653. There are many courses in Southern Pines, such as at the **Mid Pines Resort.** ~ 1010 Midland Road, Southern Pines; 910-692-2114, 800-323-2114. **Talamore** is another. ~ 1595 Midland Road, Southern Pines; 910-692-5884. Along Route 2, you'll find **Pine Needles Resort.** ~ Route 2, Southern Pines;

910-692-8611. And a final course in Southern Pines can be found at the **Hyland Hills Resort**. ~ 4100 Route 1 North, Southern Pines; 910-692-3752. In Aberdeen, the place to go is **Legacy Golf Links**. ~ Route 15-501, Aberdeen; 910-944-8825, 800-344-8825.

In the Raleigh area, you'll find **Cheviot Hills Golf Course**. ~ Route 1 North, Raleigh; 919-876-9920. **Eagle Crest** is also in the area. ~ 4400 Auburn Church Road, Garner; 919-772-6104. Durham has the **Duke University Golf Course**, designed by Robert Trent Jones. ~ Cameron Boulevard and Science Drive; 919-681-2288. Also in Durham is the **Hillandale Golf Course**, whose architect was George Cobb. ~ Hillandale and Sprunt roads; 919-286-4211. In Chapel Hill, try **Finely Golf Course**. ~ Finely Golf Course Road, off Route 15-501; 919-962-2349. In neighboring Hillsborough, you'll find **Cedar Grove**. ~ 619 McDade Store Road; 919-732-8397.

There are more than 100 courts in Winston-Salem, including 20 at **Joe White Tennis Center**. ~ 625 West End Boulevard; 910-727-2137. You might also enjoy playing at **Tanglewood Park**, which has lighted clay courts as well as hard ones. ~ Route 158, Clemmons; 910-766-0591. In neighboring Greensboro, the **J. Spencer Love Tennis Center** has 12 championship courts and is home to the North Carolina Tennis Foundation's Hall of Fame. ~ Jaycee Park, on Forest Lawn Drive; 910-545-5320.

TENNIS

A number of public courts exist in Charlotte, such as **Hornets Nest Park**. ~ 6301 Beatties Ford Road; 704-336-3854. **Kilborne Park** also has public courts. ~ 2600 Kilborne Road. Or try **Mason Wallace Park**. ~ 7301 Monroe Road. A final option for the Charlotte area is **Jetton Park**. ~ 1900 Jetton Road, Huntersville; 704-896-9808. In Pinehurst, try **The Lawn and Tennis Club of North Carolina**. ~ 1 Merrywood, Pinehurst; 910-692-7270. The **Moore County Parks and Recreation Department** has courts at various locations. ~ 910-947-2504.

Raleigh has tennis courts at **Pullen Park**. ~ 410 Ashe Avenue; 919-831-6468. Also in Raleigh is **Millbrook Exchange**. ~ Off Spring Forest Road; 919-872-4128. Over in Durham, you can play at **Duke Park**. ~ Knox and Roxboro streets. In Durham you will also find **East End Park**. ~ 1204 Alston Avenue. Or try **Forest Hills Park**. ~ 1639 University Drive. In Chapel Hill, there's **Phillips Park**. ~ Estes Drive, Chapel Hill.

For excellent bike-trail maps, contact the North Carolina Department of Transportation's Bicycle Program. ~ P.O. Box 25201, Raleigh, NC 27611; 919-733-2804.

BIKING

The Piedmont's hard-packed, gently sloped terrain makes for ideal cycling. One of Winston-Salem's most scenic tours is through

Historic Bethabara Park. ~ 2147 Bethabara Road, off University Parkway; 910-924-8191. The other is Tanglewood Park. ~ Route 158, Clemmons; 910-766-0591. Greensboro has nine designated bicycle routes, including the 13.4-mile Battleground Loop through pretty neighborhoods and historic battle sites. For a map of the various routes, call the City of Greensboro Department of Transportation. ~ 910-373-2863.

Around Charlotte, McAlpine Creek Park features a two-mile trail for bicycling. ~ 8711 Monroe Road, Charlotte; 704-568-4044. Jetton Park has a one-mile trail along the shores of Lake Norman. ~ 1900 Jetton Road, Huntersville; 704-896-9808. If you care for more challenging terrain, get on the mountain bike trails at York Road/Renaissance Park, which trudges through mudholes, up steep hills and over downed trees. ~ 1536 Tyvola Road, Charlotte; 704-523-2862.

Pinehurst and Southern Pines are ideal for leisurely cycling; their village settings offer lonely lanes and quiet neighborhoods.

Duke Forest, in Durham, covers 7700 acres crisscrossed with bike trails. For information on trails, call 919-613-8013.

Bike Rentals   Despite the abundant bike trails, rentals are tough to find. In Southern Pines go to Rainbow Cycles. ~ Northeast Broad Street; 910-692-4494. In Durham, try Lifecycle Sports. ~ 3156 Hillsborough Road; 919-383-6609.

RIDING STABLES   Several equestrian centers offer opportunities for a romp in the woods. The stables at Tanglewood Park, near Winston-Salem, not only rent horses, they'll take you on a carriage ride through lovely gardens and forests. ~ Route 508, Clemmons; 910-766-0591.

The best place to saddle up in Charlotte is Latta Plantation Park. The equestrian center here offers hourly rentals and guided tours along the park's seven miles of trails. Horse shows are held on summer weekends. ~ Sample Road, off Beatties Ford Road; 704-875-0808.

In Pinehurst, the Pinehurst Livery Stable features pony rides and carriage tours with advance reservations. ~ Route 5; 910-295-8456. In nearby Cameron, the Prancing Horse specializes in therapeutic horseback riding for the physically and emotionally challenged. ~ 919-245-3220.

In Durham, Norman Stables will outfit you with horses. ~ Norman and Guess roads; 919-732-5739.

HIKING   The Piedmont may be the most urban stretch of the Carolinas, but it does not lack in nature trails. Hundreds of miles of hikes exist within the parks, offering everything from a lakeside stroll to a steep mountain climb. All distances listed for hiking trails are one way unless otherwise noted.

WINSTON-SALEM AREA North of Winston-Salem in Hanging Rock State Park, the **Hanging Rock Trail** (1.4 miles round-trip) is a moderate trek through sun-streaked forest, along drop-off ridges up to the top of the dangling rock itself. From the summit on clear days you can see the Reynolds Building in Winston-Salem, 30 miles away. The trailhead starts near the end of the first parking lot.

Near here, take the trailhead for **Window Falls and Hidden Falls Trail** (1 mile) and you will not be disappointed. Two sets of falls form myriad shapes, and you can even walk under one cascade.

In the northern part of the park, the **Lower Cascades Trail** (.6 mile) is an easy, scenic walk down to the bottom of Cascade Creek Falls, where water gushes, tier-like, for 120 feet. The trailhead is at the parking lot on Hall Road.

Tougher but even more panoramic, **Ledge Springs Trail** (1.6 miles) in Pilot Mountain State Park skirts the edge of high cliffs with stunning vistas across rippled blue horizons. Mountain laurel and rhododendron are thick, and the steep, rugged terrain requires a bit of rock scrambling. The trailhead begins at the main parking lot.

The **Lake Brandt Trail** (10 miles) in Greensboro is truly unusual, first because few people know about it, and second because it is one of the few trails to circle an undeveloped North Carolina lake. The 785-acre lake provides water to Greensboro; the trail looks across the watery expanse but also wends into deep, old forests. The trailhead is in Bur-Mil Park, off Owl's Roost Road.

CHARLOTTE AREA McDowell Park in Charlotte has nine easy to moderate walks in the woods and along Lake Wylie, ranging from .25 mile to 1 mile. The **Four-Season Trail** (.33 mile), designed for wheelchair visitors, is a combination paved path and boardwalk that even juts out over the lake.

Crowder's Mountain State Park near Gastonia has a network of trails that start at the main parking lot. Pick up a brochure for **Fern Nature Trail** (.9 mile) to learn about the birds, animals, trees

● ●

✔ CHECK THESE OUT—UNIQUE OUTDOOR ADVENTURES

- Go golfing in Pinehurst or Southern Pines, famed as the "World's Most Famous Birdie Sanctuary." *page 250*
- Saddle up at Tanglewood Park stables and ride through lovely gardens and forests, or opt for a horse-drawn carriage tour. *page 252*
- Climb a rock at Hanging Rock State Park, joining hundreds of rappelers who love this craggy, extremely scenic terrain. *page 253*
- Follow the edge of high cliffs on the Ledge Springs Trail, a fairly strenuous hike with stunning vistas. *page 253*

and plants that thrive in the woods and creek along the easy path. If you take **Crowder's Trail** to **Rocktop Trail** (5.3 miles together), you'll scale the summit of Crowder's Mountain, along the way navigating rugged, rocky terrain with stomach-turning views down the sides of cliffs. The trek is moderate to strenuous.

RALEIGH   Seventeen miles of trails follow rocky creeks and forest ridges through William B. Umstead State Park. In the Crabtree section there is a **self-guided trail** (1 mile) that is marked with signs describing the forest. Over in Reedy Creek, get on the **Loop Trail** (.5 mile) near the picnic shelter and follow it to **Beech Trail** (1.6 miles round-trip), which meanders past granite outcroppings to remnants of an old gristmill, and the surging creek where it once drew water.

DURHAM   Of the trails in Eno River State Park, **Cox's Mountain Trail** (2.3 miles) loop is the most contemplative, wending through wooded quietude to the Cox's summit, the highest place in the park. Portions of the trail are pretty steep, but the view from the top is worth it.

Nearly 40 miles of trails delve into the 7700-acre **Duke Forest**, with entrances off Routes 571, 15-501 and 70. For a map, call 919-613-8013.

▼▼▼▼▼▼▼▼▼▼
Transportation

CAR

Several interstate highways connect the Piedmont with the rest of the South. From Atlanta, **Route 85** cuts through South Carolina and into Charlotte, then makes its way up to Greensboro and over to Durham. **Route 77** comes up from Columbia, South Carolina, and into Charlotte, continuing north through Statesville and Mount Airy.

Route 40 connects North Carolina's coast with its mountains, arching through the heart of the Piedmont on the way. Winston-Salem, Greensboro, Hickory, Raleigh and Chapel Hill are all linked by Route 40.

AIR

Three major airports serve the Piedmont: the Piedmont Triad International Airport, the Charlotte-Douglas International Airport and the Raleigh-Durham International Airport.

Piedmont Triad International Airport, centrally located to Winston-Salem, Greensboro and High Point, is serviced by American Airlines, Continental Airlines, Delta Airlines, Northwest Airlines, United Airlines and USAir.

Flying into **Charlotte-Douglas International Airport** are American Airlines, British Airways, Delta Airlines, Northwest Airlines, United Airlines and USAir.

Raleigh-Durham International Airport is served by American Airlines, Continental Airlines, Delta Airlines, Northwest Airlines, TWA and United Airlines.

For shuttle service from Piedmont Triad International Airport to area cities, contact **Airport Ground Transportation**. ~ 910-668-0164.

Queens Airport Transportation (704-531-2223) and LATCO **Local Airport Transportation Company** (704-597-9440) offer shuttle service around Charlotte.

To get to the Triangle area from Raleigh-Durham Airport, call **Carolina Trailways** (919-833-3601) or **Triangle Transit Authority** (919-549-9999).

BUS

Greyhound Bus Lines (800-231-2222) has several locations around the Piedmont area. There are stops in Greensboro at 501 West Lee Street, 910-272-8950; in Winston-Salem at 250 Greyhound Court, 910-724-1429; in Charlotte at 601 West Trade Street, 704-375-9536; in Raleigh at 314 West Jones Street, 919-834-8275; in Durham at 820 Morgan Street, 919-687-4800; and in Chapel Hill at 311 West Franklin Street, 919-942-3356.

TRAIN

Intrastate and interstate service is provided by **Amtrak** (800-872-7245). Stops are in Greensboro at 2603 Oakland Avenue, 910-855-3382; in Charlotte at 1914 Tryon Street, 704-376-4416; and in Raleigh at 320 West Cabarrus Street, 919-833-7594.

CAR RENTALS

If you fly into Piedmont Triad International Airport, you can rent a car from **Alamo Rent A Car** (800-327-9633), **Budget Rent A Car** (800-527-0700), **Hertz Rent A Car** (800-654-3131), **Thrifty Rent A Car** (910-668-3488) or **Triangle Rent A Car** (910-668-3400).

Rental agencies providing service to Charlotte-Douglas International Airport include **Alamo Rent A Car** (800-327-9633), **Avis Rent A Car** (800-331-1212), **Budget Rent A Car** (800-527-0700), **Dollar Rent A Car** (800-800-4000), **Enterprise Rent A Car** (800-325-8007), **Hertz Rent A Car** (800-654-3131), **Payless Car Rental** (800-729-5377), **Thrifty Car Rental** (800-367-2277) and **Triangle Rent A Car** (704-359-0541).

Raleigh-Durham International Airport has **Alamo Rent A Car** (800-327-9633), **Avis Rent A Car** (800-331-1212), **Dollar Rent A Car** (800-800-4000), **National Interrent** (800-227-7368), **Budget Rent A Car** (800-527-0700), **Hertz Rent A Car** (800-654-3131), **Thrifty Car Rental** (800-367-2277) and **Triangle Rent A Car** (919-643-7368).

PUBLIC TRANSIT

The **Winston-Salem Transit Authority** will get visitors around Winston-Salem. ~ 910-727-2000. In Greensboro, there's SCAT. ~ 910-605-3369.

The Greater Charlotte area is served by **Charlotte Transit**. ~ 704-336-3366.

Capital Area Transit operates public buses around Raleigh. ~ 919-828-7228. The Durham Area Transit Authority handles the routes around Durham. ~ 919-688-4587. If you need a bus ride across Duke University, call Duke University Transit. ~ 919-684-2218. Around Chapel Hill, catch one of the Chapel Hill Transit buses. ~ 919-968-2769.

TAXIS

Blue Bird Cab Company (910-722-7121) and Triad Transit, Inc. (910-724-1906) have taxi service into Piedmont Triad International Airport. Around Greensboro, try Bluebird-Diamond (910-272-5112) or United Yellow Taxi (910-273-9421).

For taxi service to Charlotte-Douglas International Airport, call Crown Cab Company (704-334-6666) or Yellow Cab Company of Charlotte (704-332-6161).

At Raleigh-Durham International Airport, there's American Cab Company (919-821-0095), Cardinal Cab Company (919-828-3228), City Taxi Company (919-832-1489) and Yellow Cab Company (919-832-5811). Around Durham, you'll find Associated Cab Company (919-682-0437) and Pine Street Taxi (919-688-1394). In Chapel Hill, try Tar Heel Taxi (919-933-1255).

EIGHT

The North Carolina Coast

Where North Carolina meets the Atlantic Ocean the state opens big and wide, taking a huge hunk of coast that stretches for nearly 300 miles between Virginia and South Carolina. A vast scrollwork of swamp and scrubland, sounds and rivers, it was once the bed of a sea. Now called the Coastal Plain, it is dotted with small towns and even a few big ones, and many fishing villages attended by shrimp boats whose nets fan out like wings.

Then there are the Outer Banks, a scant strand of sand and dunes lying offshore, a half-dozen islands elbowing out to sea. The Banks are forever being shaped and reshaped by whipping winds, simmering surf and tides that get out of bounds. On a cold full moon, the water may rear up and cross the road, smothering whole islands in its wavy froth. The seafood shack that's now on the sound used to sit at the dunes—before the wind and waves erased the dunes. The row of cottages atop the dunes was claimed one day by the sea, which does not care about a developer's beachfront schemes. The Outer Banks may help protect the mainland from wicked winds and oftentimes perilous waves and currents, but there is nothing to protect the Outer Banks.

The wind is most always blowing on the Outer Banks, sweeping the sand into giant castles—the tallest dune in eastern America is here—and casting the water into strange shapes. When the water gets angry, it demands victims; more than 600 ships have been flayed by the rough seas off the Outer Banks, called the "Graveyard of the Atlantic."

On land, the winds cool your hair and whisper in your ear. After a few days on the Banks, you grow accustomed to the whispering, and returning to the mainland brings a pang of silence. Kites and hang gliders, sailboards and surfboards are the toys of the Outer Banks. If someone wants to be airborne or surfborne, then the Outer Banks are the place to go.

Orville and Wilbur Wright desperately wanted to be airborne, so they came to this windswept waterfront in 1900. They brought with them a 17-foot glider and trusted it to the wind, but it only acted like a big kite. Not discouraged, they built a shack along the dunes in a place called Kill Devil Hills and moved in with their glider, sleeping in burlap hammocks strung from the rafters. Over the next couple of years they increased the glider's wingspan and arch, and installed a small engine. In 1903, after hundreds of failed tries, Orville aimed the airplane into a serious head-wind and flew 120 feet—the first human flight.

Three centuries before the Wrights were catching air currents, two English ships made their way through wind and waves to land at what is now known as Ocracoke Inlet. It was 1584, and they had instructions from Sir Walter Raleigh to explore the New World. In a report to Raleigh, Captain Arthur Barlowe told of the "beating and surging of the sea" upon the sandy land. The shoal-studded waters, he said, "smelled so sweetly as if we had been in the midst of some delicate garden." On the mainland, the woods were rich with wildlife and "the highest and reddest cedars of the world."

Excited about the findings, Raleigh sent 107 men to establish a colony. They lasted less than a year before running out of supplies and catching a boat back to England. A second colony arrived in 1587, including 91 men, 17 women and 9 boys. Soon a child named Virginia Dare was born, the first English child born in North America. Now the Dare name appears on everything from inns and eateries to shopping cen-ters—odd, since no one knows what happened to her, or to the rest of the colonists for that matter.

For when they, too, ran low on food, they dispatched a ship to England, but it got caught up in the war with Spain. When it finally returned three years later, the colonists' cabins were gone and in their place a fort had been built. On the fort was carved the word "croatoan," the name for an Indian village. The ship sailed for Cro-atoan but got sucked into a storm and damaged, and barely made it to Trinidad for repairs before returning to England.

The conundrum of the lost colony is played out every year on Roanoke Island, in an outdoor drama written by Pulitzer Prize–winning playwright Paul Green. The fort has been reconstructed and is now a State Historic Site, though its mystery is far more intriguing than its appearance—a low-lying, grassy berm in the woods.

North Carolina's first permanent settlement happened in a place more perma-nent than the Outer Banks: the northern Coastal Plain. Planters streamed down from Virginia in the 1650s, loaded with horses, pigs, cattle and sheep, and the idea of owning huge chunks of land. They found the land they wanted around the Albe-marle Sound, where the soil was fertile and the meadows "interwoven with beauti-ful flowers, of most glorious colours, which the several seasons afford. . . ."

Over the next century more outposts were sewn into the fabric of North Caro-lina's coast. Most were fastened along the rivers and sounds, though for a long time there was no north–south route and so little sense of coastal cohesion. North Caro-lina's first town, Bath, cropped up on the Pamlico River in 1705, and by 1708 the town boasted 12 houses and a population of almost 50. Bath later lost a bid for state capital and stayed small. Today, it is a riverfront speck that looks lost in those early days—a great place for delving into coastal beginnings.

Five years after Bath was born, New Bern became North Carolina's second town. Located south of Bath where the Neuse and Trent rivers meet, it was founded by a

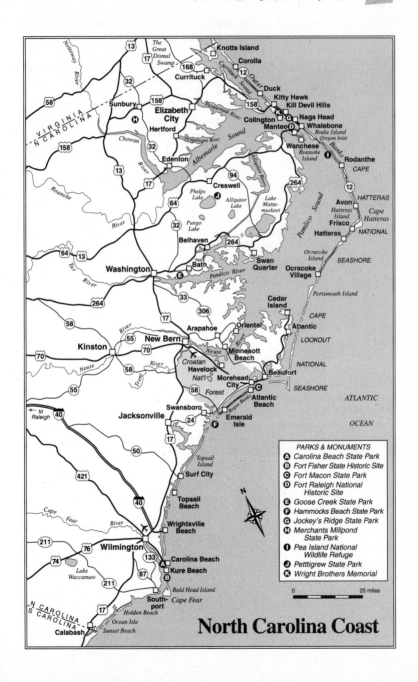

North Carolina Coast

PARKS & MONUMENTS

Ⓐ Carolina Beach State Park
Ⓑ Fort Fisher State Historic Site
Ⓒ Fort Macon State Park
Ⓓ Fort Raleigh National Historic Site
Ⓔ Goose Creek State Park
Ⓕ Hammocks Beach State Park
Ⓖ Jockey's Ridge State Park
Ⓗ Merchants Millpond State Park
Ⓘ Pea Island National Wildlife Refuge
Ⓙ Pettigrew State Park
Ⓚ Wright Brothers Memorial

0   25 miles

group of Swiss and German immigrants (the town is named after Bern, Switzerland) determined to make it great. They built beautiful homes beneath the cypress and oak trees, reveling in Georgian and Federal designs. They built docks and warehouses to service the tar and turpentine that ships would carry to England, and the rum and sugar they brought from the West Indies.

New Bern thrived so much that in the 1760s Royal Governor William Tryon declared it capital of the North Carolina colony. He immediately ordered construction of a capitol building, and when Tryon Palace opened in 1770, it was the grandest place in the Carolinas. Tryon lived there only one year before being sent to New York to be governor, but other men governed in New Bern until 1798 when the palace burned. More than 150 years passed before the palace was rebuilt, and now its imposing halls and groomed gardens see thousands of visitors every year.

While the Coastal Plain was being civilized, the Outer Banks were being ruled by pirates. After having been chased out of the West Indies by the British, Blackbeard, Stede Bonnet and dozens of other buccaneers (including several women) found the Banks' secret coves and treacherous waters a perfect place to do business. Blackbeard met his end near Ocracoke Inlet when British Navy Lieutenant Robert Maynard raided his lair and slaughtered his crew. Maynard sliced off the pirate's head and mounted it in his ship's rigging, sailed into Bath and then continued all the way to England.

The Civil War came early to the North Carolina coast. Union troops took New Bern in 1862 and then wiped out most of the plantations along the eastern plain. By the turn of the century, locals turned to lumber and textiles for a living, shipping them from their port towns all over the world.

Only a small band of gritty, gutsy folk lived on the Outer Banks, many shipwreck survivors who had nowhere else to go. They built their homes in the safety of the soundside and drew their salaries from the sea, selling fish and crabs to mainlanders.

Even now, "Bankers," as year-round residents are called, are a scarce and hardy lot, only 24,000 people scattered along 175 miles of islands. They understand and respect the winter, when the wind comes calling, and cottage walls shudder and windows clatter. If you like the idea of nature banging at your door, visit in the winter.

The majority of visitors, of course, prefer the summer, when the wind is kindest and the toast-colored sand warms the feet. Most hole up in one of the wood-shingled, long-legged cottages that huddle behind the dunes, a few seconds' stroll from the pounding surf.

The cottages are biggest, prettiest and priciest on the northernmost banks, in the towns of Corolla, Sanderling and Duck. All the action's just south of here in Kitty Hawk, Kill Devil Hills and Nags Head, and so is all the development. Wedged between here and the mainland is Roanoke Island, where Sir Walter Raleigh's first colony was lost.

Farther south, Hatteras Island has the Pea Island National Wildlife Refuge, a sliver of wide open dunes and beach and wispy seagrass, and snow geese who flock to safe shores. It also has a few small towns but scant development, thanks to the 50-mile-long Cape Hatteras National Seashore. Southwest from Hatteras, you must take a ferry to get to Ocracoke, a lovely, lost-in-time island with miles of nothing but beach and then a pretty fishing village laced around Silver Lake Harbor.

A series of sounds separate the Outer Banks from the Coastal Plain. Some, like the narrow, sheltered Currituck Sound, are calm and welcoming; others, like the vast Pamlico Sound, range from rough to treacherous. On a windy winter day, the two-and-a-half-hour ferry across the Pamlico feels like a wild ride on open seas.

Along the Coastal Plain are some of the Carolinas' most romantic names—Swan Quarter, Magnolia, Cape Fear, Emerald Isle—as well as some quirky hidden places: Frying Pan Landing, Gum Neck, Stumpy Point. The Coastal Plain tour starts north in the Albemarle Region, working southward from Virginia through the Great Dismal Swamp and then the port towns of Elizabeth City, Edenton and Bath.

The Neuse River Region takes in New Bern with its 150-plus historic homes, along with charming Beaufort, remote Cedar Island, and a string of developed beaches along Bogue Sound. At the southern foot of eastern North Carolina is the Cape Fear coast, whose centerpiece is graceful old Wilmington, where it's just as enjoyable to spend several hours or several days.

Despite its vast size, the North Carolina coast offers little glamour. There are no mind-numbing metropolises, no glitzy resorts, no possibilities for jackpot winnings. Instead, for the most part the land is given over to the intimacies of backcountry fishing, searching the shallows for crabs, settling on a harborfront porch, listening to the wind, and watching the tide roll in.

The Outer Banks

The wisps of barrier islands known as the Outer Banks begin and end in wilderness. What's in between ranges from exclusive communities nicely spaced along the sand to crowded hodgepodges of funky cottages and motels to national seashores sprinkled with eye-blink towns. Always there is subtle beauty: the curve of the dunes, the lash of the wind, the great vault of ocean and sky opening to the east.

Sitting right below Virginia are the Banks' northernmost shores, though they can be reached only by four-wheel-drive vehicles, and preferably with someone familiar with the territory, as the trek requires much beachfront driving where patches of deep sand are famed for waylaying cars. The traveler lucky enough to drive way up here is rewarded with vistas of lush green farms and lonely, wind-lashed shores that seem to have no end.

SIGHTS

The paved road goes only as far north as **Corolla** (locals say "Car-ALL-a"), a beachy village at the dead end of Route 12 that's known for two things: wild mustang ponies and an 1800s-vintage lighthouse.

No one's exactly sure how the ponies got here, though a popular story is that they came aboard Spanish ships in the sixteenth century. Others say they are offspring of early colonists' herds. Either way, they roamed wild for several hundred years, feeding on sea oats and romping in the surf. But in the mid-1980s, Route 12 was extended up to Corolla, bringing instant tourism, planned developments, and thousands of visitors who feed the beautiful animals and clamor for their photos. Naturally, the horses are no longer so wild but have become moochers (one tumbled down someone's cottage steps after being fed) and camera hams, causing traffic jams and getting themselves killed by cars. Now the fewer than two dozen remaining "wild" horses may soon find themselves corralled on 1800 government-owned acres north of Corolla, out of the tourists' camera range.

Corolla's other big attraction, **Currituck Beach Lighthouse**, is a red-brick beauty built in 1875 and restored in the 1980s. The northernmost of the Outer Banks' "famous four" lighthouses, it's a prime place to catch a sky view. Take all 212 steps spiraling up to the top and look out across swirling sea oats and surf-laced sand. The beacon still flashes every 20 seconds. Closed late November until Easter. Admission. ~ Route 12; 919-453-4939.

Route 12 is the only road out of here, indeed the only main road south for more than 20 miles. From late fall through early spring it can be a wonderfully moody drive, with few cars on the road, cottages all boarded up, the sky bundled in charcoal-colored clouds, and the sand and sea clutched by cold wind. Come summer, the road itself is clutched in traffic, cars creeping along two lanes, horns honking, tempers flaring. Weekends can be especially bad, so come prepared for crowds and allow extra travel time.

This goes for all the Outer Banks. Even remote Ocracoke, which can be reached only by ferry, is so thronged with cars on some summer days you feel certain there must be a secret bridge to the mainland. Ocracokers say there's no telling which days traffic may strike, though it usually clears up within a couple of hours—until the next ferry expels a new load of cars.

The 22 miles of Route 12 south of Corolla are designated a Wild Horse Sanctuary, so obey speed limits and be on the lookout. This stretch of northern beach is also a sanctuary for those with money, who have staked their spacious spots in well-tended dunes. Their sprawling, multilevel stilt homes are secured behind brambly foliage and at the foot of roads that stop just before the surf. Most lie within the towns of **Sanderling, Duck** and **Southern Shores**, where real estate offices with banners flapping in the wind foretell the future of this quiet, exclusive northern stretch of the Outer Banks.

South of here the future has already arrived. Starting with **Kitty Hawk** and running for 20 miles through **Kill Devil Hills** and **Nags Head**, virtually every inch of land, be it beachside or soundside, is cluttered with weathered wood-shingled cottages, cheesy motels, seafood shacks, putt-putt golf, shopping centers, surf shops, and just about every other manner of campy beach venue. This is where most Outer Banks' visitors come to play, to ride the wind on a hang glider, surfboard or windsurfer, to spread their towels cheek-to-jowl on the tawny sand, to shoot pool and eat oysters, to dangle in a hammock and be rocked to sleep by sea breezes.

On the Sea
for Free

On the North Carolina Coast, the best way to get from here to there is not always by car but by boat. State-run ferries cut across rivers and sounds, cutting travel time by hours and even days. The fleet of 22 boats range from 157-footers that can ferry 18 cars to 220-foot vessels with a capacity for 50 vehicles. They're clean and usually smooth riding, depending on weather, of course, and have air conditioned lounges to relax in. The salty fellows who run the boats are companionable and comfortingly well-informed on seafaring matters.

Best of all, some ferries are free.

If you choose the ferries between Knotts Island and Currituck, Hatteras Island and Ocracoke Island, Aurora and Bayview, or Minnesott Beach and Cherry Branch, you don't have to pay, not even if you take your bicycle or car aboard.

You should, however, be out on deck for most of the trip or you'll miss the scenes of tidal grass rippling in the breeze, the points of land capped with villages and their attendant fishing boats, the deep blues of the sound, the foggy bronze of the river. You can watch the shrimp trawlers drag their nets across the water's bottom, then unload their contents on deck. You can see the sun rise and set on the water, if you time your ferry rides right.

Trips are as short as twenty minutes and as long as two and a half hours. The three ferries that do charge fees—between Ocracoke and Cedar Island, Ocracoke and Swan Quarter, and Southport and Fort Fisher—are not expensive; pedestrians pay between 50 cents and $1. Reservations are usually required for these routes; call the **North Carolina Ferry System**. ~ 919-726-6446. You can also check weather conditions. High winds can mean a rough ride, especially on the Ocracoke routes, though ferries don't operate when it's truly high seas.

This is also where four-lane Route 158, also called "The Bypass Road" and "Croatan Highway," parallels Route 12, providing faster driving, and where distances are measured in mileposts. You'll see the little green signposts with numbers on the roadside. Heading south, the numbers get bigger. Most places give their addresses in mileposts, since it's the easiest way to find them.

When you're in Kitty Hawk, stop at the **Aycock Brown Welcome Center**, the beach headquarters for the Dare County Tourist Bureau. It's fashioned as one of the Banks' old lifesaving stations. You can load up with maps, brochures and other information on the Outer Banks. ~ Milepost 1 on Route 158; 919-261-4644. Extensive information and pamphlets can also be procured from the Dare County Tourist Bureau's main office on Roanoke Island. ~ Route 64/264; 919-473-2138, 800-446-6262.

There weren't any mileposts around when Orville and Wilbur Wright arrived in 1900 and told gravity to take a hike. You can learn how the bicycle mechanics from Dayton, Ohio, pulled off the first human flight at the **Wright Brothers Memorial**. Exhibits at the visitors center detail the ins and outs of aerodynamics, and how the Wrights first got their souped-up glider aloft in 1903. The famed event took place on Big Kill Devil Hill, which looms near the visitors center and is punctuated by a 60-foot granite pylon aimed at the sky. You can drive the loop road around the hill, but most prefer to take the slow walk up the smoothly rounded knoll where, with the wind slapping at your back, you can understand precisely why the men chose this spot. Wheelchair visitors have full access to all the sights here. Though the memorial is closed at night, the pylon is all lit up and can be seen from Route 158, looking like a great dagger in the dark. Admission. ~ Route 158, Milepost 8, Kill Devil Hills; 919-441-7430.

HIDDEN ►

A couple of miles south of the memorial, take the western turn-off for **Colington**. The way to the crusty old fishing village is along three miles of narrow road that curls around inlets and harbors

----

✔ CHECK THESE OUT—UNIQUE SIGHTS

- Hop a ferry to **Ocracoke Island** and revel in miles of wide-open sand and sea, and then a pretty village at land's end. *page 267*
- Check out the Mojave Desert–like scene at **Jockey's Ridge State Park**, home to the Eastern United States' highest sand dune. *page 278*
- Enter 1741 castle gates to arrive at **Tryon Palace**, a superb facsimile of the original royal governor's residence. *page 288*
- Take it slow on the tiny, far-flung **South Brunswick Isles**, loved by seclusionists and naturalists. *page 301*

swirling with seagrasses, roadside shacks selling softshell crabs, a hilltop cemetery, and cottages crouched beneath big oak trees.

Back on Route 158 and heading south, another side road delivers you to the little-known **Nags Head Woods Preserve**. With all   ◄ HIDDEN
the hubbub around Nags Head, it's hard to believe that these 1400 acres of forest exist, let alone harbor walnuts, hickories, maples and other big hardwoods. Visitors can take part or all of the four miles of trails through woods and swamp and along Roanoke Sound. Days and hours open vary, so call ahead. ~ Ocean Acres Drive, off Route 158, turn at Pigman's Bar-B-Q, Milepost 9½; 919-441-2525.

Farther south there's Route 64/264, where a bridge arches across Roanoke Sound to **Roanoke Island**, tucked between the Outer Banks and mainland North Carolina. The island has two contrasting sides: the south side largely smothered in marsh and punctuated by the busy little fishing village of **Wanchese**; and the north   ◄ HIDDEN
side, where the main town of **Manteo** (locals say "MAN-te-o") is haphazardly dotted with fast-food chains, car lots, and double-decker buses filled with sightseers. The most appealing part of Manteo is **The Waterfront**, where a handful of shops, eateries and inns gather along the sound. Some buildings date back to the late 1800s when Manteo was found, but most are twentieth-century replicas. ~ Route 400 East, just off Route 64/264.

Docked at The Waterfront in Shallowbag Bay, the **Elizabeth II** gives you a good idea of how North America's first colonists got to Roanoke Island in the 1500s. A visit to this State Historic Site starts with a short film about the hardships they endured on those early voyages. The regal, triple-masted ship, a replica of those early vessels, is great to explore, especially for kids, who can roam all 69 feet of polished wood deck. Admission. ~ The Waterfront in Shallowbag Bay; 919-473-1144.

The colonists actually landed down the road at a place that's now **Fort Raleigh National Historic Site**. There were 117 English settlers in all, and they were among the first Europeans to try full-time life in the New World. After several months they ran short of food and supplies and sent a ship back to England, but the vessel was forced into the war against Spain and could not return for three years. By then, the colony had vanished, and all that remained was a small earthen fort. ~ Route 64/264; 919-473-5772.

Earlier this century the fort was reconstructed and is now the centerpiece of the historic site. It's not much to see, for the fort is not big and formidable but low-lying and grassy, although the 150-acre wooded setting is certainly enjoyable. Loblolly pines form cool canopies for the trails that meander around the fort all the way to Roanoke Sound. There is wheelchair access to the fort.

Within the site is also the orderly **Elizabethan Gardens**, which explode with color year-round. Springtime is best, though depending on the season you can witness azaleas, rhododendrons, gardenias, magnolias or hydrangeas at their height. Crepe myrtles grow geometrically, and a fountain pool and whimsical stone statuary dominate the pristine Sunken Garden in the park's center. Above the garden is a handmade brick terrace dating from the late 1800s. A small gazebo reminiscent of the sixteenth century overlooks Roanoke Sound, where the colonizers first landed. Closed weekends from December to February. Admission. ~ 919-473-3234.

At the **North Carolina Aquarium on Roanoke Island**, there's an ample representation of aquatic animals native to North Carolina. Fish, alligators and turtles are on display in the freshwater aquarium. Saltwater species include lobster, stingrays and triggerfish. Kids gravitate toward the touch tank, where they can reach down and hold hermit crabs, sea stars and other small creatures. Even more popular is the shark gallery, where the sinister-looking creatures prowl along the windows of their 3000-gallon tank. Admission. ~ Airport Road, off Route 64/264, Manteo; 919-473-3493.

To keep exploring the Outer Banks, head back east on Route 64/264 to Route 12, then drive south along **Bodie Island**. Bodie (say "Body") actually was an island but isn't anymore, since the tides and winds sealed up the inlet in the 1800s. Now it's a low-key strand of pale white sand, called Coquina Beach, that's part of Cape Hatteras National Seashore. Bodie's southernmost tip is pinpointed with the **Bodie Island Lighthouse**. With black-and-white stripes racing around its 150-foot cylinder, it's a favorite of photographers. Unfortunately, you can't enter the lighthouse.

The lighthouse stands sentinel over the **Oregon Inlet**, perpetually congested with fishers hopeful of snagging a bluefish, sea bass, flounder, or dozens of other varieties that funnel through this small opening between the Atlantic Ocean and Pamlico Sound. The Herbert C. Bonner Bridge spans the inlet and delivers you to **Hatteras Island** and the solitude of **Pea Island National Wildlife Refuge**. Thousands of waterfowl such as snow geese, tundra swans, and green-winged teal have found safety on these 6000 acres running along the sides of Route 12. ~ Headquarters located on Route 12; 919-473-1131.

Seven towns are sprinkled along the skinny 58-mile length of Hatteras Island. All are little more than gathering spots for bait-and-tackle shops, campgrounds, and a handful of motels and cottages. The island owes its laid-back ambiance and abundance of silent shores to the Cape Hatteras National Seashore, which protects not only Hatteras but also Ocracoke Island to the south.

You can drive right on these shores in certain areas, provided you have a four-wheel-drive vehicle and stay well between the dunes and the surf. Access ramps are marked along Route 12 on Hatteras and Ocracoke, though before setting out you should check with the National Park Service for current weather and tide conditions. Lest you're tempted to take your two-wheel-drive car on the beach, the park's brochure says, "we think you will be sorry." ~ 919-995-5610, 919-995-4474, 919-473-5665.

Rodanthe (pronounced "Ro-DAN-thee") is Hatteras' northernmost town and also where you'll find the **Chicamacomico Lifesaving Station**. One of seven stations along the Outer Banks, it operated from 1874 until after World War II. The men who guarded the shores from this demure-looking shingled cottage were truly fearless—or crazy, depending on how you look at it. When a ship wrecked, they would launch a line out to the sinking vessel in the hopes of reeling it in. Then they would launch rowboats into the ocean's tumult and row out to collect survivors. Naturally, wrecks occurred on the nastiest of days, and even if dark thoughts of dying never crossed a lifesaver's mind, one would imagine he at least got a stomachful of saltwater. ~ Route 12; 919-987-1552.

Those heroic and hair-raising feats are remembered through exhibits at the station, open Memorial Day through Labor Day, and then sporadically through Thanksgiving weekend. Lifesaving drills are held on Thursday afternoons at 2 p.m.

Also helping steer ships to shore was the **Cape Hatteras Lighthouse** in the town of Buxton. The most famous Outer Banks lighthouse, it's the one you see in all the vacation ads looking a lot like a black-and-white striped barber's pole perched on a point of land, with whitecaps boiling at its feet. At 208 feet, it's the tallest brick lighthouse in the United States. From Easter until Columbus Day you can climb up inside the slender silhouette for the Banks' best vista (unless you go parasailing). The adjacent lighthouse keeper's quarters offer some displays on lighthouse lore. ~ Off Route 12, Buxton; 919-995-4474.

South of Buxton, the town of Frisco has perhaps the Outer Banks' quirkiest, tackiest site: a hot-dog shop called **Out of This World** that's shaped like a spaceship. (Remember the old TV series *Lost in Space*? This could be that spaceship.) ~ Route 12.

The next town south, Hatteras, is where you catch the free 40-minute ferry over to **Ocracoke Island**, the only way to Ocracoke.

Mentally, the trip seems much longer, for when you arrive on Ocracoke, it's as if you were transported to an entirely different region. Gone are the spaceships hawking hot dogs, the legions of fishing boats, the clutter of cottages. What you find here is a lonely, desolate, wind-lashed island ribboned with wide, whitish sand and bristly scrublands not burdened by a single manmade structure for nearly 14 miles. The only interlude in the scenery is the **Ocracoke Pony Pens**, where from a boardwalk you can look across pastures and watch the wild horses that once had the whole island to themselves. ~ Route 12, 7 miles south of the Ocracoke Ferry Terminal.

Ocracoke is wonderful at sunset. The great orange orb dives down across a wide-open horizon unhindered by development, leaving in its wake scarlet clouds bunched across the sky. A better day's end cannot be imagined.

Route 12 is the only road on the island until **Ocracoke Village**, near the southern end. There is nothing contrived about this tiny place of whitewashed and weathered cottages sprinkled among the gnarled boughs of live oaks. Narrow lanes curl through the neighborhoods where vegetable gardens are edged in white-plank fence. Here, too, is the **Ocracoke Lighthouse**, thickest and squattest of the Outer Banks' lighthouses. Built in 1823, its mortar walls are five feet thick, its nonrotating light still shining, making it the second-oldest operating beacon in the nation. ~ Point Road.

Ocracoke activity culminates at Silver Lake Harbor, a sort of "downtown" area of little shops, eateries and bait stores so pleasantly arranged you instantly reach for your camera. The vanilla-washed, clapboard **National Park Service Visitors Center at Ocracoke Island** provides insight on the island and tourism information. Ships' horns blow frequently as ferries head out for Swan Quarter or Cedar Island for voyages across the breadth of Pamlico Sound. The ferries bring thousands of visitors to Ocracoke in summer, though permanent residents number about 701. Says one resident: "Ten folks died last year but a bunch more were born, so it usually evens out." Closed December through March. ~ Across from the ferry landing; 919-928-4531.

LODGING

Most Outer Banks visitors rent cottages. The choices are many, from the ubiquitous two-room, cedar-shingled shacks huddling behind the dunes to the multilevel homes confronting the ocean. They are usually rented by the week or weekend, and priced according to the size of the place, the time of year and the location. Families often opt for a place on the soundside of the banks, as the water is safer for swimming.

As you might guess, the list of rental agencies is rather long. Try **Britt Real Estate** for rentals on the northern Banks. ~ 919-261-3566, 800-334-6315. **Sun Realty** also provides rentals. ~ 919-441-7033, 800-334-4745. You can also try **Carefree Cottages**. ~ 919-441-5340. Or call **Real Escapes**. ~ 919-261-3211, 800-831-3211.

If you need a place on Roanoke Island, call **20/20 Realty**. ~ 919-473-2020. On Hatteras Island, contact **Dolphin Realty**. ~ 919-986-2562, 800-338-4775. Also on Hatteras Island is **Outer Beaches Realty**. ~ 919-995-447. For rentals on Ocracoke Island, call **Ocracoke Island Realty**. ~ 919-928-6261. The alternative on Ocracoke Island is **Sharon Miller Realty**. ~ 919-928-5711.

When it comes to full-service lodging, it's tough to match the **Sanderling Inn**. Located in Duck, it bills itself as one of the most exclusive resorts in the area, and it is. Resembling the old shingled cottages dotting the island, it sits squarely on the oceanfront, with sound views from the upper floors. The lobby is a warm wooden entry with duck decoys and Audubon prints scattered across high walls. All of the 88 rooms have private porches that lend an open-air feel, as if they were secluded beach cabanas. Some rooms have kitchenettes; others offer wet bars. Tennis courts, spa facilities and indoor swimming pool are available for those not content with mere sea oats and sand. ~ Located at 1461 Duck Road, Duck; 919-261-4111, fax 919-261-1638. DELUXE TO ULTRA-DELUXE.

Generally, cottages in the northernmost Banks are most expensive, while those in Kill Devil Hills and Nags Head cost less.

The **Quality Inn Sea Ranch Hotel** is known for catering to a tourist's every whim; there's an indoor pool, beauty salon and health spa. Even as newer resorts have cropped up across the beach, the Sea Ranch is still considered one of the best. All the rooms are clean and moderately sized, many with an ocean view. ~ Beach Road, Milepost 7, Kill Devil Hills; 919-441-7126, 800-334-4737, fax 919-441-3795. MODERATE TO DELUXE.

In the lobby of **Tanya's Ocean House**, a sign reads, "We did it just for fun." Each room in this eccentric little motel is decorated in a particular theme. The walls in the "Waterloo Room" are painted with palm trees and a setting sun above the waterbed. A patch-quilt comforter, kerosene lantern and wagon wheel can be found in the "Tobacco Belt Room." If you're looking for elegance, stay away: Tanya's looks like an overnight costume party that got a little out of hand. Closed mid-October through March. ~ Beach Road, Milepost 9½, Kill Devil Hills; 919-441-2900. MODERATE.

The **Nags Head Inn** is located at the southern end of Nags Head Beach, a bit out of the congestion of mid-beach. Still, don't let the name fool you; this is no cozy B&B, but one of the largest and newest hotels on the island. Reminiscent of a big chain hotel, the inn offers such amenities as an indoor/outdoor pool and a spa and sun deck. The guest rooms are carbon-copy simple but comfortable. Ask for one with a private oceanfront balcony. ~ Beach Road, Milepost 14, Nags Head; phone/fax 919-441-0454, 800-327-8881. MODERATE.

You get a lot for your dollar at **Scarborough Inn**, where hosts Rebecca and Fields Scarborough treat guests like old family friends. Each room is decorated in antiques, collected by family members when traveling. (Microwaves, refrigerators and coffeepots are available in each room.) Though it may be quite tempting to simply lie around your room, it's far better to borrow one of the bicycles lining the wooden porch and pedal along the waterfront. There is a continental breakfast included. ~ Route 64/264, Roanoke Island; 919-473-3979. MODERATE.

Overlooking Shallowbag Bay on the Manteo waterfront, the **Tranquil House Inn** is designed like a nineteenth-century beach resort. The cypress woodworking and stained-glass windows give it a tasteful appearance, and all 25 rooms are individually decorated with accoutrements like oriental rugs and canopied beds. The most appealing rooms are on the soundside, offering a view of the docked *Elizabeth II* and shrimp boats. In the morning, there's a continental breakfast buffet; in the early evening, there are wine receptions. ~ 405 Queen Elizabeth Street, The Waterfront, Roanoke Island; 919-473-1404, 800-458-7069, fax 919-473-1526. DELUXE TO ULTRA-DELUXE.

Hatteras Island Resort is the kind of place that attracts budget-minded families. The large compound includes several cottages, a 42-unit motel, swimming pool, fishing pier and beach. All the rooms are clean, but there's no maid service in the cottages, and the motel rooms are without extras like telephones. The bonus is that there's enough here to keep the kids busy for days, without having to leave and deal with summer traffic. Closed December through March. ~ Route 12, Rodanthe; 919-987-2345, 800-331-6541. BUDGET TO MODERATE.

The **Cape Hatteras Hotel** spans from soundside to beachside. The lodging itself is nothing spectacular, just basic and comfortable. The hotel offers many different types of accommodations; standard rooms on the ocean are plainly adorned with king-sized beds and a few kitchen appliances. There are efficiencies on the oceanside and apartments on both sides of the water. There's also a sandwich shop on the property. ~ Route 12, Buxton; 919-995-5611, 800-995-0711. MODERATE.

At the southernmost tip of Hatteras Island, **The Sea Gull Motel** is a remnant of the 1950s. Other than the welcome addition of air conditioners, little has changed over the years at this bi-level brick motel. Canary-yellow bedspreads and checkered green wallpaper adorn the rooms, which include 45 oceanside units and several apartments. There's a pool here but not much else in the way of amenities. ~ Route 12, Hatteras Island; 919-986-2550. BUDGET TO MODERATE.

An Outer Banks treasure, the **Island Inn** began life in 1901 as the Oddfellows Lodge of Ocracoke and part-time schoolhouse. Since the 1950s, the gabled, whitewashed building has been welcoming overnight guests who enjoy its charm and character and slow pace (but not slow service). The inn has one of the best dining rooms on Ocracoke and the only heated swimming pool. All of the rooms are decorated differently, and though none are fancy, they are spacious, warm and welcoming—just what you'd hope from a far-flung island inn. ~ 100 Lighthouse Road, Ocracoke Island; 919-928-4351, fax 919-928-4352. BUDGET TO MODERATE.

The **Boyette House** has been a family-run hostelry since 1941. Designed in the manner of the old-time Outer Banks cottages, the cedar-shingled, two-story house has 12 rooms, all with separate entries. The decor is generic motel-style, with wall-to-wall carpets, cable TV, tubs and showers. A newer three-story cedar-shingled building has two suites equipped with steam bath, jacuzzi, refrigerator and microwave. The lobby has a selection of regional books and is a comfortable spot for reading. Closed January and February. ~ Route 12, Ocracoke Island; 919-928-4261, fax 919-928-4901. MODERATE.

Nestled behind the pine trees around Ocracoke's harbor, the **Berkley Center Country Inn** is as swanky as this little island gets— and you can still wear flip-flops. Polished hardwood floors, oriental rugs, and sink-right-in sofas dominate the lobby area. Guests gather here for conversation, or in a small den where continental breakfast is served every morning. The rooms, some with shared baths, are all graced with country antiques. Closed November through March. ~ Route 12; 919-928-5911. MODERATE.

Built in 1936, **Blackbeard's Lodge** conveys the feeling of a cozy summer camp. Barefoot children run freely through the pine-paneled lobby while older guests read the paper in wide, welcoming chairs. The rooms are rustic but comfortable and air conditioned. The harbor and beaches are but a bicycle ride away, and if you don't like the salt and sand you can splash around in Blackbeard's pool. Closed November through March. ~ Ocracoke Village; 919-928-3421, 800-892-5314. BUDGET TO MODERATE.

DINING

Small, intimate and immensely popular, **Nicoletta's** serves some of the best Italian fare on the Outer Banks. The deep antipasto salads are piled with meats and cheeses; the pasta is homemade and perfectly sauced. For something fancier, order the roasted swordfish with muscatel wine and cacciatore sauce, or the filet mignon medallions sautéed with vegetables and laced with bordelaise sauce. Dinner only. Closed January through Valentine's Day. ~ Route 12, in the Corolla Light Village Shops; 919-453-4004. MODERATE.

If you care to dine in a lovely turn-of-the-century lifesaving station, go to **Sanderling Inn Restaurant**. From the main dining room, barnyard doors open to the sand dunes. The seaside ambiance continues indoors where a brass ringing bell, wooden oars and old photos of the station adorn the walls. The fare is inventive and nearly gourmet. Pumpkin nut bread stuffed with cream cheese is on the breakfast menu. At dinner, waiters in white jackets offer specials like pan-fried crab and scallop cakes with bourbon horseradish and red bliss potatoes. ~ Route 12, Duck; 919-261-4111. DELUXE.

Blue Point Oyster Bar & Grille looks like a 1950s soda shop, with chrome tables and red-vinyl barstools lining the black-and-white checkerboard floor. The menu, which runs the gamut from simple Southern to strange, includes crab cakes, grilled Atlantic salmon, pan roast of jumbo shrimp, smoked bay scallops and fresh fish. Try the Bourbon pecan pie for dessert. Closed Monday from October to April. ~ Route 12, Duck; 919-261-8090. MODERATE TO DELUXE.

Rundown Cafe is fast becoming the best place on the beach for "fun food." Rundown is one room complete with encroaching bar and small wooden tables, ceiling fans, and bright art work on the walls. Don't expect the average fried-fish platter at this joint. The menu leans toward eastern flavors—Thai noodles with ginger and garlic and Indian garlic flatbread are staples. There are also plenty of seafood dishes. Weekends in season bring big, festive crowds, so be prepared to wait at the bar for a table. ~ Beach Road, Milepost 1, Kitty Hawk; 919-255-0026. MODERATE.

Dark and cozy, with small candles glimmering at the tables and Tiffany lamps hanging from the ceiling, **Port O' Call** is one of the Banks' fancier eateries. The dinner menu ranges from veal to prime rib to pasta. Naturally, there is seafood, though it's more elegantly prepared than the garden-variety fried type. Dinner only. Closed January to mid-March. ~ Beach Road, Milepost 8, Kill Devil Hills; 919-441-8001. MODERATE TO ULTRA-DELUXE.

HIDDEN ► Along the winding side road to Colington, look for **Colington Café** tucked up on a hill. This pretty cottage that's loved by locals delivers French-international cuisine, some of the classiest food around. The shrimp and scallops are served with a delicious cream sauce. The filet mignon, chicken filet and pork loin are equally mouth-watering. Dinner only. ~ 1029 Colington Road at Milepost 8½; 919-480-1123. MODERATE.

Seafood doesn't get any fresher than having it delivered daily from local trollers. At **Etheridge Seafood Restaurant** that's exactly what happens. Captain Will brings in the catch of the day and either "Miss Betty" Etheridge or her daughter will cook it up. Flounder, tuna and dolphin are favorites—if they're biting, that is. Closed January through March. ~ Route 158, Milepost 9, Kill Devil Hills; 919-441-2645. MODERATE.

After a morning on the waves, surfers rejuvenate at **Pigman's Bar-B-Q** over plates piled high with pork and beef, hushpuppies and sweet-potato fries. An Outer Banks institution, "The Pigman" slow-smokes its meat in the Carolinas tradition, dousing the pork in a tangy vinegar-based sauce and the beef in a spicy tomato sauce. Smoked chicken and buffalo wings are also hot items at this no-frills wood eatery. ~ Route 158, Milepost 9½, Kill Devil Hills; 919-441-6803. BUDGET.

The Dunes Restaurant is the best choice for family fare. This unimposing place packs tourists into three large dining areas. Don't be scared off if the waiting line extends out the door; turnover is usually quick. Breakfast is bountiful and served up on square, lunchroom-style platters; crab omelettes and steak and eggs are among the many choices. For lunch and dinner, there is everything from fried or broiled seafood to pasta, steak and chicken. This is no-frills dining, but the food is good and your dollar goes a long way. Closed December through February. ~ Route 158, Milepost 16, Nags Head; 919-441-1600. BUDGET TO MODERATE.

Locals frequent **Sam & Omie's** year-round, and anything goes in this joint. The sign on the screen door reads "Shirt and Shoes Required," but flip-flops and a tank top will do just fine. Looking more like a weather-beaten shack than a restaurant, Sam & Omie's serves up breakfast, lunch and dinner, and some folks stay for all three. A rarely empty bar area extends into the dining room—little more than some wooden tables and booths; a pool table reigns off to the side. Among the more popular menu items: "The Matlock" hot dog, fried-oyster sandwich and design-your-own omelettes. ~ Beach Road, Milepost 16½, Nags Head; 919-441-7366. BUDGET TO MODERATE.

A rare find in this coastal community is the **Weeping Radish Brewery and Restaurant**. Tucked behind pine trees, it's German through and through, with Bavarian meals that include veal sausage, sauerbraten, and a liverwurst and onion sandwich. The microbrewery is on display behind glass, and patrons can enjoy homemade lager with their meal. A small courtyard garden is a fine place to just have a brew. ~ On Route 64/264, Manteo, Roanoke Island; 919-473-1157. BUDGET TO MODERATE.

The **Froggy Dog** on Hatteras Island is one of the most popular places around. This three-meals-a-day joint has pine walls and low ceilings that make the dining areas somewhat dark, but the back room overlooks the reed-lined sound. The floor is tiled in slate; driftwood adorns the walls. The food is simple: eggs for breakfast, a sandwich or burger for lunch, and seafood or steak for dinner. Considering there's not much else in the way of Avon restaurants, this place is usually hopping at all hours. Closed in December. ~ Route 12, Avon; 919-995-4106. MODERATE.

At **Bubba's** the service is minimal. Just go up to the counter and order from the huge menu posted on the wall. The list leans toward barbecue; pork and chicken platters come with cornbread and two veggies. The drink of choice here is icy draft beer. Closed December through February. ~ Route 12, Frisco, Hatteras Island; 919-995-5421. BUDGET.

The **Island Inn Dining Room** has some of the best food on Ocracoke Island. The hushpuppies are sweet and light, not at all greasy, and the side dishes are many and varied, from spinach lasagna to marinated cucumbers to potatoes au gratin. Dinner entrées are long on fresh seafood, lunch features lots of sandwiches (the fried-oyster sandwich is excellent), and breakfasts are bountiful and slightly Southern. Both the main dining room and the sun-washed porch have the flavor of an intimate country inn. ~ Route 12, Ocracoke Island; 919-928-7821. BUDGET TO MODERATE.

Dining at **Captain Ben's** is like eating in a ship's galley. The main area of the restaurant is massive, decorated with potted plants and nautical kitsch. Fresh seafood, simply prepared in generous quantities, are why Ocracokers come here. Burgers, sandwiches, crab cakes and seafood platters are also popular at lunch. For dinner, prime rib, chicken and pasta are the seafood alternatives. Closed mid-November to March. ~ Route 12, Ocracoke Island; 919-928-4741. MODERATE.

Bright pink and white linens adorn the small tables at **Café Atlantic**. This tiny restaurant with vaulted ceilings and cypress walls is full of light and space. From the second floor, diners get a big view of the sound through picture windows. A great place for lunch, the cafe offers sandwiches, soups and salads at a good value. The dinner menu features the usual seafood and pasta fare. Closed November through April. ~ Route 12, Ocracoke Island; 919-928-4861. MODERATE.

A favorite among locals and visitors, the **Back Porch Restaurant** sounds just like its name. A large porch has been screened and shaded with venetian blinds and green-striped awnings, and set with little tables. Serving dinner only, the Back Porch offers seafood that departs from the mainstream, including crab beignets, sautéed crabmeat and yellowfin tuna. The homemade bread and dessert tortes and tarts are extra good. Closed mid-October to mid-April. ~ Off Route 12, Ocracoke Island; 919-928-6401. MODERATE TO DELUXE.

SHOPPING In between the gaggle of T-shirt and flip-flop shops are a few interesting boutiques and, surprisingly, several excellent art galleries.

In the Corolla Light Village Shops. In the same plaza, **Mustang Sally's** carries primitive-chic men's and women's clothing, handcrafted gifts, and accessories. Closed December to mid-March. ~ 919-453-4749.

At **Greenleaf Gallery**, paintings, prints and sculpture are just a few of the mediums on display in a bright, contemporary showroom. Closed January through March. ~ 1169 Duck Road, Duck Village; 919-261-2009.

Ghost Fleet Glenn Eure's Gallery showcases the innovative and expansive work of owner Glenn Eure, including acrylic and watercolor paintings, etchings and woodblocks. The gallery also presents special exhibits by guest artists. Closed February through March. ~ Milepost 10 on Gallery Row, Nags Head; 919-441-6584.

The most extensive and diverse collection of artwork on the Outer Banks is at **Seaside Art Gallery**. Among the everchanging offerings are works by Pablo Picasso, Winslow Homer and Mary Cassatt. Local artists are featured too, of course, and there's a large collection of animation cells from Disney and Warner Brothers. ~ Beach Road, Milepost 11, Nags Head; 919-441-5418.

Wanna go fly a kite? **Kitty Hawk Kites** can set you up with a simple, inexpensive flier or something so elaborate you'll think you've bought an airborne BMW. This beach-goods megastore has smaller locations in Corolla, Duck and Manteo, and also in Avon on Hatteras Island. ~ Route 158, Milepost 13, Nags Head; 919-441-4124.

In the colorful Caribbean Corner shopping mall, **Izit Emporium** combines the sinful with the healing; chocolate bonbons, wine biscuits and other gourmet snacks are displayed along with aromatherapy oils and lotions. Closed January through March. ~ The Causeway, Nags Head; 919-441-7754.

> Nearly two dozen stores and boutiques at Scarborough Faire handle exclusive gifts, clothing, jewelry, kitchen items and artwork. ~ Duck Road, Duck.

The Island Gallery has many small rooms loaded with floor-to-ceiling art. Paintings and prints, wood sculpture and duck decoys, woven baskets and pottery are among the finds. A special section is devoted to the paintings of P. Buckley Moss, who first displayed her works here. ~ Route 64/264, Manteo, Roanoke Island; 919-473-2838.

The best place for books, **Manteo Booksellers** has a stellar selection on seafaring subjects, as well as tough-to-find volumes on Outer Banks myths and history. ~ 105 Sir Walter Raleigh Street, Roanoke Island; 919-473-1221.

The Waterfowl Shop focuses on birds. You can buy a duck decoy or a photograph of some of the beautiful Outer Banks birds, as well as a tidal clock or wind-speed indicator. Closed Monday and the month of January. ~ Route 12, Rodanthe, Hatteras Island; 919-987-2626.

If you like those Adirondack chairs lining local porches, stop by **All Decked Out**. Hammocks, rockers and picnic tables are also for sale. All can be shipped to your home. ~ Route 12, Frisco, Hatteras Island; 919-995-4319.

Among the local artists portrayed at **Village Craftsmen** are a moon-gazer, a poet and gill-netter, and an award-winning photographer. Their whimsical creations range from fish-shaped pewter spoons and fiddle bow bread knives to teleidoscopes and bowed psalteries (triangular stringed instruments). ~ Howard Street, off Route 12, Ocracoke Island; 919-928-5541.   ◄ *HIDDEN*

Parlaying local lore into a store, **Teach's Hole** sells books, videos, flags, jewelry and other items relating to Edward Teach,   ◄ *HIDDEN* a.k.a. Blackbeard the Pirate, who lived and died on Ocracoke. Closed January and February. ~ Ocracoke Back Road, off Route 12, Ocracoke Island; 919-928-1718.

At **Over the Moon** the offerings include hammock chairs, woodworks, music boxes, pottery and beeswax impressions. Closed December through March. ~ 552 British Cemetery Road, Ocracoke Island; 919-928-3555.

HIDDEN ►   **Back Road Books** has plenty of great beach reads, from modern thrillers and humor to the old classics you've been meaning to catch up on. Closed mid-October through April. ~ Ocracoke Back Road, off Route 12, Ocracoke Island; 919-928-2665.

The locally woven hammocks at **Ocracoke Island Hammock Company** come in several styles, such as porch swing, hanging chair and deck chair. Closed December through March. ~ Across from the Historic British Cemetery; 919-928-4387.

Arts, crafts and other fare sold around Ocracoke Village celebrate island life. **The Island Ragpicker**, for instance, has pirate tales and books on nature, rag rugs and woodworks by local sculptors. Closed January and February. ~ Route 12, Ocracoke Village; 919-928-7571.

NIGHTLIFE   Alternative music and velvet Victorian decor? That's the scene at **Gaslight Salon**. Upstairs on the catwalk, you can lounge in sinking sofas overlooking the dancefloor. The crowd here is just as diverse as the atmosphere—anyone and everyone seems to find a spot. ~ In the Port O' Call Restaurant, Beach Road, Milepost 8, Kill Devil Hills; 919-441-7484.

If you'd like to relax and have a drink, the horseshoe-shaped bar at **Kelly's Restaurant** is a fine spot. The party here is low-key; the music, anything from classic rock and Motown to beach tunes. ~ Route 158, Milepost 10, Kill Devil Hills; 919-441-4116.

Rock-and-roll and alternative bands frequent **The Atlantis**, a cinderblock beach hut frequently packed elbow-to-elbow with college students. The scene resembles the basement of a frat house; the ceilings are low and the music is loud. Cover. ~ Beach Road, Milepost 11, Kill Devil Hills; 919-480-3757.

The much-acclaimed outdoor pageant, *The Lost Colony,* plays most summer nights on Roanoke Island at the **Waterside Theater**. Written by North Carolinian and Pulitzer Prize winner Paul Green, it recounts the arrival and mysterious disappearance of America's first permanent colonists. The production, complete with symphony and elaborate Elizabethan costumes, began in 1937 and has been playing to full houses every summer since. ~ Route 64/264, Fort Raleigh National Historic Site; 919-473-3414.

It's beer and wine only on Hatteras Island, and only where there's food served. However, you can show up at **Kinnakeet Tavern** for a game of pool or darts, or to watch a game on the big-screen TV. Closed in the off-season. ~ Route 12, Avon; 919-995-5959.

Nightlife on Ocracoke Island generally means finding a worn wood barstool, ordering a brew, and scanning for local color. Your best hope of finding the latter is at **Howard's Pub**, a year-round pizza joint and raw bar that even has cable TV (translation: televised sports). ~ Route 12, Ocracoke Island; 919-928-4441.

Otherwise, Ocracoke has **The Jolly Roger**, a weathered wood cottage on the harbor where bands play while the sun sinks beneath the water. Closed November through March. ~ Ocracoke Village; 919-928-3703.

As desperately as people try to define and permanently fix the shape of a beach, they cannot on the Outer Banks. What is today a wide, loosely packed swath of sand will tomorrow be narrow and hard packed—thanks to perpetual, ever-shifting winds and currents and intense tides.

Those same forces make swimming here a bit risky at times—and cold (in summer, the water temperature averages in the mid- to high-70s), though with proper precautions you can enjoy the surf of your life. Before going out, check for riptides and strong currents (for surf and weather conditions, call 919-473-2138, 800-446-6262). Dangerous seas are marked with a red flag, so if you see one don't go swimming. To be completely safe, especially if you have small children, swim only at beaches where there are lifeguards, located all along the northern Banks.

NORTHERN BANKS BEACHES The shores at Corolla are wide and windy. If you have a four-wheel-drive vehicle, you can head north toward Virginia until you find a truly deserted spot. South of Corolla, there's not much public parking until **Kitty Hawk**, where all the action starts and continues south nearly 20 miles through **Kill Devil Hills** and **Nags Head**. Cedar-shingled cottages crowd against the dunes, and so do eateries and little shops. In the height of summer, sun worshipers lay towel-to-towel, and from the air the dunes look bearded with oiled bodies. The sand is as tan as the bodies, and usually deep and finely grained, so you sink in up to your ankles. It's narrowest on the north end of Kill Devil Hills, where the water threatens the feet of the cottages.

Facilities include plenty of eateries and convenience stores in the area and lifeguards stationed throughout the beaches from Corolla down to Nags Head. Swimming is good on calmer days. King mackerel has been caught off the Outer Banks Pier in Nags Head, also a prime place for snagging flounder and red drums. From the beach you might get a bluefish or even spotted sea trout. ~ Corolla beaches are just north of the village, which has a public parking lot on Corolla Village Road. The beaches at Kitty Hawk,

Kill Devil Hills and Nags Head are off the aptly named Beach Road, which parallels Route 12. Regional beach access signs point the way to small parking lots near the dunes.

JOCKEY'S RIDGE STATE PARK 🏃 When you first see this place along Roanoke Sound, you think a chunk of the Mojave Desert landed at Nags Head. Actually it's just a sand dune, albeit the highest in the eastern United States, 30 million tons of sugar-fine grains rearing up 80 to 110 feet, depending on wind speed and direction. Your first urge is to climb it. Go ahead—everyone else does. Go barefoot or wear sturdy shoes (and plan to get lots of sand in them). Ski goggles aren't a bad idea, though sunglasses will do fine. At the top, you can watch hang gliders leaping and swooping, and sandboarders (the dune equivalent of snowboarders) cruising down the dune's rippled southwest face. Sunsets from up here are incredible. And though you can look across rippling Roanoke Sound to what is most definitely Roanoke Island, you still feel like you're in the desert.

Back near the bottom, a little museum provides sand dune trivia, like the fact that Jockey's Ridge moves three to six feet southwest every year, thanks to prevailing northeast winds. From the museum, a boardwalk wends through small dunes marbled with bayberry and southern wax myrtle and live oaks. Wheelchair travelers can take the boardwalk to the end for a big view of the big dune and the rest of the 415-acre park. Look down at the sand here and you might see tracks of park animals such as the gray fox or six-lined race runner lizard. Facilities here include a park office, a museum, restrooms, picnic tables, a hiking trail and restaurants nearby. Swimming is not allowed. This is an excellent place for hang gliding and sandboarding. These activities are allowed in designated areas and only with a permit, available from park office. ~ Off Route 158 at Milepost 12 in Nags Head; 919-441-7132.

COQUINA BEACH 🌊 A broad shell-strewn corridor of whitish brown sand at the south end of Bodie Island, Coquina is the northernmost beach within Cape Hatteras National Seashore. Families like it here; you'll see lots of tots toting buckets. They sit hopefully at the surf, hoping to pluck a coquina before the teeny mollusk digs back into the wet sand. Things get crowded in summer, so stake your towel spot early.

Facilities include restrooms, a bathhouse and picnic tables. Stores, restaurants and a marina are close by. Swimming is usually good. There is good surf fishing for whiting, pompano, small bluefish and flounder. ~ Located off Route 12, about five miles south of Whalebone Junction; 919-473-2111.

▲ There are 120 tent and RV sites just south of Coquina at Oregon Inlet, open only in summer; facilities include cold-water showers, restrooms, picnic tables and grills and are on a first-come, first-served basis; $12 per night.

HATTERAS ISLAND BEACHES To some beachgoers, Hatteras is the Outer Banks beach—58 miles of little but sand and sea oats and dunes. Only seven villages (including one named Waves) interrupt the wilderness look created here by the Pea Island National Wildlife Refuge and Cape Hatteras National Seashore, which blanket most of the island. Hatteras is so skinny that the beach tends to be narrow and the sand damp and hard-packed in most spots. You can drive on the beach in designated places, but only with four-wheel drive. **Canadian Hole**, three miles south of Avon on the soundside, has major windsurfing action. Go at sunset and watch the orange globe light up the surfers' sails. Farther south, **Cape Hatteras** is also big with windsurfers and surfers, and anyone who likes to bask beneath the famous Cape Hatteras Lighthouse. Facilities include the Pea Island National Wildlife Refuge Headquarters, located on Route 12 north of Rodanthe; Cape Hatteras National Seashore Visitors Center in Buxton; grocery stores and restaurants in nearby villages. Swimming is good on calm days. Three fishing piers offer good opportunities for bluefish, flounder, pompano, trout and croakers. ~ All facilities are accessed by Route 12, which runs the length of Hatteras Island and offers numerous beachfront parking areas; 919-473-2111.

▲ More than 320 tent and RV sites are available Memorial Day through Labor Day at campgrounds in Frisco and Cape Point. Cold-water showers, restrooms, picnic tables and grills are at each site and are on a first-come, first-served basis; $12 per night; 919-473-2111.

OCRACOKE ISLAND BEACHES Who couldn't love a beach so remote you can only get there by boat? Even in the full heat of summer when ferries discharge hundreds of cars, there is always a silent stretch of sand to be had. Cape Hatteras National Seashore covers all 14 miles of Ocracoke, offering several parking areas within steps of the sand. The beaches are some of the Outer Banks' widest, thanks to the way the island angles inland, enjoying some protection from wind and waves and therefore erosion. Shelling is good, and so is staring at miles of unencumbered coast. Facilities include Cape Hatteras National Seashore Visitors Center in Ocracoke Village at the island's south end and nature trails; groceries and restaurants are in the village. Swimming is good most everywhere, but especially near Ocracoke Village. Fishing is best close to the inlets on either end of the island; try for sea mullet, bluefish, pompano, red drum and croakers. ~ Route 12 runs the length of Ocracoke beaches; 919-473-2111.

▲ Reservations required for the 136 tent and RV sites, complete with restrooms, cold-water showers and grills; open Memorial Day through Labor Day; $12 per night; 919-473-2111.

▼▼▼▼▼▼▼▼▼▼▼▼▼
Albemarle Region

Only water—specifically the Currituck and Albemarle Sounds—separate the Outer Banks from the Albemarle Region. Yet the two places couldn't be more different, the beach with its pounding surf and raw bar scene, the Albemarle with its quiet country towns and folks resting on front porch rockers. Hound dogs rule the back roads, and sausage and grits rule the breakfast menu.

The peninsulas that edge out into the sounds are blanketed with pine woods where deer and bear roam. In some places, the distance between country stores is more than an hour, and the only radio station plays John Denver. When you stop for gas, the attendant admonishes you to watch out for the deer and bear crossing the road. The next sign you see says "Red Wolf Crossing," and you wonder why he didn't mention the wolves.

SIGHTS

The northeast corner of North Carolina's Coastal Plain, the Albemarle Region begins at Virginia and heads south to the Pamlico River, taking in more than a dozen counties but only a handful of cities. The biggest, **Elizabeth City**, is home to about 17,230 people. It curves around the Pasquotank River, which feeds into Albemarle Sound and then the ocean, a perfect locale for the country's largest Coast Guard station. ~ Junction of Routes 17 and 158.

Yachters, sailboaters and other recreational boaters also love Elizabeth City because it's at the end of the Dismal Swamp Canal, a scenic shortcut for anyone traveling the Intracoastal Waterway. None would dream of cruising past the city, lest they miss the **Rose Buddies**. Since the 1960s, a group of local seniors have been giving boats a big greeting down at **Mariners Docks**. ~ Water Street. When the boats arrive, the Buddies tool up on their golf carts, present each boater with a red rosebud, and lay out a spread of wine and cheese. The most famous Rose Buddy, Fred Fearing, got his golf cart from *Today Show* weatherman Willard Scott. The self-appointed regional historian was profiled by Scott, who then gave him the cart.

Downtown Elizabeth City is pleasant enough. Old, red-brick buildings line the streets, and shipbuilding yards pepper the waterfront. For a look back at the city's seafaring history, stop by the small but engaging **Museum of the Albemarle**. You can meander through wide corridors and see artifacts from early Colonial days, including a crude dugout canoe, farm tools and household items. There's also an 1888 ladder fire truck and blueprints and photos of the first "moth" boat, designed in Elizabeth City by Captain Joel Van Sant in 1929. Closed Monday. ~ 1116 Route 17 South, just south of downtown; 919-335-1453.

Delve even farther back in time south of Elizabeth City. North Carolina's oldest house, the **Newbold-White House,** was built in 1730 by Abraham Sanders. It's on the Perquimans River, two stories made of brick—unusual, since most homes back then were all wood. Inside, the walls are bathed in original pine, and leaded casement windows let in sunlight and crosswinds. Closed Thanksgiving through February. Admission. ~ Route 1336, off Route 17, Hertford; 919-426-7567.

South of Hertford on Route 17, **Edenton** is the quintessential small port town, with several blocks of Colonial-style clapboard crisply painted and lawns and gardens well-tended, and streets shaded by the long arms of magnolias and pecan trees. On the cusp of the Chowan River, Edenton has been around since 1722, though barely 5000 people call it home. Many of the town's residents live in and take great care of homes built before the Civil War and now on the National Register of Historic Places.

Before a walk around town, stop by the **Historic Edenton Visitors Center** for information and brochures on local sights. If you'd care to take a guided tour of the historic homes and buildings, the center can arrange it. Closed Monday from November through March. ~ 108 North Broad Street; 919-482-2637.

One of the area's most striking old homes lies southwest of Edenton near the village of Windsor. **Hope Plantation** was built in ◄ HIDDEN 1803 by David Stone, who served as North Carolina governor and also United States Senator. Fashioned with both Georgian and Federal accoutrements, the big, two-story manor is meticulously furnished to look as it did when Stone and his family lived here. In the beautiful library, Stone kept more than 1400 books, then one of the state's largest private collections. The plantation tour starts in the visitors center, housed in the King-Bazemore House, built in 1763 of red brick. Closed mid-December through February. Admission. ~ Route 308, five miles west of Route 13; 919-794-3140.

Heading back east toward the eye-blink town of **Creswell,** you'll encounter another plantation, less lavish but historically intriguing and quite hidden. **Somerset Place** was one of the biggest, ◄ HIDDEN most productive plantations of the antebellum South. Prosperous planter Josiah Collins III built the mansion in the 1830s, bought 300 slaves and put them to work harvesting rice, wheat and corn. The main house is elegant and well-maintained, but the outbuildings, including a kitchen, icehouse and smokehouse, paint the most poignant picture of life in the 1800s (you can see the foundation of the slave quarters). Except for a row of telephone poles, little has changed in 150 years. Closed Monday from November through March. ~ Off Route 64, 7 miles south of Creswell; 919-797-4560.

East and south of Creswell, coastal forest goes on for hours. Occasionally there are signs of human life, outposts with names like Stumpy Point, Frying Pan Landing and Leechville. A trio of counties—Tyrrell, Dare and Hyde—cover this vast peninsula poking into the Albemarle and Pamlico sounds. If you take the long way around the peninsula, **Route 64 to Route 264**, you'll be on lonely, two-lane roads that pass through sawgrass seas and pancake-flat farmlands studded with Colonial and antebellum farmhouses.

HIDDEN ► Eventually, you'll want to turn back west and find the place called **Bath**. It's off Route 92 and the Pamlico River, but more importantly it's the oldest town in North Carolina. When you arrive, you're not quite sure you're there, as there's nothing to denote so important a place, save for some historical markers tucked among the trees and tidy clapboard homes. One of the markers remembers **James Adams Floating Theatre**, which brought show biz to these coastal towns from 1913 to 1941. ~ Main Street.

Bath was founded in 1705 with 12 homes and nearly 50 people. Over the centuries it saw wars with Indians, pirates and Union soldiers, yellow fever outbreaks and even drought—odd, considering there's water at nearly every turn. The shore of Bath Creek squiggles along Main Street. Near Main and Carteret streets, the **Historic Bath Visitors Center** can provide maps for walking around town. To see everything, you'll need a couple of hours. Closed Monday from November through March. ~ 919-923-3971.

Make sure you look inside **St. Thomas Episcopal Church**, built in 1734 and the oldest church in the state. The prim building nestled beneath big cedar trees is made of brick shipped from England. The walls are two feet thick, the floors are battered clay. The Bible encased in glass near the entrance is a 1704 edition, donated in 1740 by King George II. ~ Craven Street.

LODGING   **Elizabeth City Bed and Breakfast** sits on a quiet, tree-lined corner one block from Main Street. Both buildings here date to 1847 and have been meticulously restored. A brick courtyard with a fish pond and gazebo is a peaceful spot for reading or sipping iced tea. There are only four guest rooms, and they get booked fast, so call

---

✔ CHECK THESE OUT—UNIQUE LODGING

- *Budget to moderate:* Enjoy old seafaring charm at the warm and welcoming **Island Inn**, a 1950s gabled home on Ocracoke Island. *page 270*
- *Moderate to deluxe:* Sleep riverside—in a luxurious room or suite, of course—at **Sheraton Grand New Bern**. *page 292*
- *Deluxe to ultra-deluxe:* Bed down where 1700s sea captains once snoozed at the stately white manse called **The Cedars**. *page 292*
- *Deluxe to ultra-deluxe:* Surround yourself with opulence—a grand staircase, music and drawing rooms—at **Graystone Inn**. *page 301*

Budget: under $60   Moderate: $60–$100   Deluxe: $100–$130   Ultra-deluxe: over $130

way ahead for reservations. ~ 108 East Fearing Street, Elizabeth City; 919-338-2177, fax 919-338-5001. MODERATE.

The Culpepper Inn is a big, brick, Colonial-style house built in 1935. Renovations have lent a modern air to the place. The spacious backyard has a swimming pool and terrace, where guests convene in the evening for wine and cheese. Eleven rooms, some outfitted with king-sized beds and fireplaces, are individually adorned, spacious and comfortable. ~ 609 West Main Street, Elizabeth City; 919-335-1993, fax 919-335-1555. MODERATE.

A lovely place to spend the night is Lords Proprietors' Inn. Three large houses, including a handsome Victorian with a charming wraparound porch, are sprinkled among these shady one and a half acres. Each building possesses an antique-filled parlor, and all of the 20 guest rooms are commodious and pleasingly furnished with an eye for detail. Telephones, TVs and VCRs are among the amenities. Breakfast is served every day; dinner is served Tuesday through Saturday. ~ Located at 300 North Broad Street, in downtown Edenton; 919-482-3641, 800-348-8933, fax 919-482-2432. ULTRA-DELUXE.

The Governor Eden Inn is conveniently situated within walking distance of the Edenton Historic District. Fashioned in Neoclassical style with large white columns parading along the wraparound porch, it offers four guest rooms, relatively small but comfortable, all with private baths and television. A hearty country breakfast and light nutritious fare are offered in the mornings. ~ 304 North Broad Street, Edenton; 919-482-2072. MODERATE.

A favorite among birders, the Trestle House Inn is adjacent to   ◄ HIDDEN
to Chris Lake Wildlife Refuge, a rest stop for migratory birds. A wooden deck serves as a lookout over the lake. The five guest rooms are named for the birds commonly seen here: heron, mallard, osprey, cormorant and egret. Each room is tastefully decorated with handcrafted quilts, oriental rugs and watercolors. ~ Soundside Road, off Route 32, south of Edenton; 919-482-2282. MODERATE.

Right at the tip of the Pasquotank River, Mulligan's Waterfront   **DINING**
Grille is a town favorite. The place is made spacious with high ceilings, airy wood floors, and large windows facing the harbor. An expansive deck out back provides a view of the boat docks. Each dish is prepared by the chef/owner, who specializes in pasta and seafood. ~ 400 South Water Street, Elizabeth City; 919-331-2431. MODERATE.

Open for breakfast, lunch and dinner, The Colonial is an Elizabeth City landmark that is always filled with locals who know each other. What they most enjoy are the breakfasts—eggs, hash browns, grits, bacon and most particularly the biscuits, which are split down the middle and then toasted on the grill. And breakfast is a bargain at less than $2.50. For lunch and dinner, you can have things like meatloaf and mashed potatoes. Closed Sunday. ~ 418 East Colonial Avenue; 919-335-0212. BUDGET.

Fresh seafood, usually fried or baked, are the mainstays of the **Marina Restaurant**, but deep South dishes like ham and liver and onions are why locals have been coming here for years. The dining-room windows offer wide views of the Pasquotank River sprinkled with sailboats. During warm weather you can eat out on the deck. Dinner only except on Sunday, when lunch is also served. Closed Monday. ~ Camden Causeway, Route 158 East, Elizabeth City; 919-335-7307. MODERATE.

With tiny tables dressed in white linen, **The Dram Tree** is as upscale as Edenton gets. Seafood, chicken, steak and pasta dominate the dinner menu, though duck and lamb are also offered. Local favorites include chicken Chesapeake and shrimp and scallops in a Cajun sauce. Lunch features salads, quiche, crab cakes and lasagna. In the summertime, the garden room offers more casual dining. No lunch on Monday or Tuesday. ~ 112 West Water Street, Edenton; 919-482-2711. MODERATE TO DELUXE.

Italian fare can be had at the **Broad Street Restaurant and Pub**. It's not much of a pub, but it does serve up a wide range of dishes, from pizza and baked cannelloni to fettuccine alfredo with scallops or shrimp. Fried seafood dinners, chicken and ribs are also on the menu. Wooden booths and stained-glass lamps help to jazz this place up a bit, but it's still family-oriented and very casual. Closed Sunday. ~ At 705 North Broad Street, Edenton; 919-482-3902. MODERATE.

SHOPPING The Albemarle Region is not a shopper's haven, though there are always ways to spend your money.

Local artisans display their works at the **Pasquotank Arts Council Gallery**. Watercolor and oil paintings reflect the region's rich seafaring past, and the gallery also has an array of pottery, jewelry and wood sculpture. ~ 609 East Main Street, Elizabeth City; 919-338-6455.

Next door to the gallery, **Bracy Books** is as much a casual hangout as it is a bookstore. This small, intimate nook has a superior selection of regional literature, as well as popular paperbacks and children's books. Reader, the resident cat, rules over all from a white wicker perch. ~ 613 East Main Street, Elizabeth City; 919-338-1056.

A block from Main Street, the **Upper Sound Supply Company** is a modern version of an old-time general store, homey and comfortably cluttered, with a good selection of outdoor wear, handmade crafts and pottery. The shop also serves as a marine hardware store and workshop where customers can watch local craftsmen

Eva Way Blount's Dried Flea Wedding

If you go to the second floor of the Town Hall building in Belhaven, you can see Eva Way Blount's dried flea wedding. You'll need to use the big magnifying glass to fully see the fleas, a happy couple decked out as bride and groom—she with parasol, he with bow tie.

Gypsies gave Eva the fleas back in the early 1900s. By then, the Belhaven woman had already begun collecting oddities, starting with a slew of buttons that grew to 30,000. A woman weighing 700 pounds gave Eva one of her dresses. Some local boys came back from World War II with a purse made of Pacific seashells. A pharmacist gave her some quinine bottles from the 1800s. Folks started visiting Eva's house in the 1940s to see what strangeness awaited within.

Eva died in 1962, and her enormous, quirky collection became the **Belhaven Memorial Museum** above Belhaven Town Hall. Belhaven, located off Route 264 between Bath and Swan Quarter in the Albemarle Region, is not a whole lot different from other small Southern coastal towns. The museum, however, is different from anything you've ever seen.

At the top of an ancient stairwell, the museum is like a giant attic filled with grandmotherly smells and papers curled and yellowed from time, every space crammed with wonderful eccentricities. There are rattles from snakes that Eva killed (34 total, including one rattle that's six inches long), a basket made from the shell of an armadillo, and her 1918 lawnmower, which looks like a stick with tiny metal wheels. Leftovers from Eva's pantry include cabbage peas, catfish, spinach and chicken fat, all nicely preserved in mason jars.

Not all the stuff here came from Eva. Dozens of folks donated furnishings, paintings, clothing, seashells, Civil War guns and other antiquities. But none had Eva's *Ripley's Believe It or Not!* style of humor.

The museum is open Monday, Tuesday, Thursday and Saturday afternoons and does not charge admission, though it's funded entirely by donations. ~ 201 East Main Street, Belhaven; 919-943-6817.

build small boats. ~ 116 North Poindexter Street, Elizabeth City; 919-331-7766.

In a recycled, turn-of-the-century mill, **Waterworks** has a cache of boutiques selling everything from designer clothing and antiques to objets d'art and gourmet coffee. ~ 400 South Water Street, Elizabeth City.

In Edenton, you can browse antique shops and boutiques along **Broad Street** and the blocks surrounding it.

NIGHTLIFE   All the action's in Elizabeth City, but don't expect much.

Aside from serving lunch and dinner, **BJ's** usually has a good party crowd at night. There's a large bar and two wide-screen TVs, and sometimes live music. When the bands aren't playing, the dance-floor is used for dart games. ~ 400 East Colonial Avenue, Elizabeth City; 919-338-5288.

Down at the docks, **Mulligan's Waterfront Grille** is a fine spot for a drink. Rock and blues bands play out back on the deck along the river on Wednesday, Friday and Saturday nights. ~ 400 South Water Street, Elizabeth City; 919-331-2431.

BEACHES & PARKS

MERCHANTS MILLPOND STATE PARK 🏃 ♨ 🚤 🛶 Perched at the northeastern head of North Carolina is this enormous vault of forest, marsh and creeks—nearly 3000 acres. For wildlife and water-fowl, it is a safe haven. For the human visitor, the thick swamp seems an eerie, endless maze. Cypress trees, laden with Spanish moss, grow out of the quagmire, and lilies waft upon the murky water. Tree frogs, snapping turtles and snakes are abundant, as are as many as 200 species of birds. Whether you intend to fish, hike, canoe or picnic, bring mosquito and tick repellent. Facilities include a park office, boat ramps, picnic tables, canoe rentals, hiking trails and restrooms. Fishing is great for largemouth bass and bluegill. ~ The park's main entrance is along Route 158 about five miles west of Sunbury; 919-357-1191.

HIDDEN ►

▲ Twenty sites are available at the family campground; $9 per night. There are also five primitive, hike-in sites; $5 per night.

THE GREAT DISMAL SWAMP ♨ 🚤 🛶 This National Wild-life Refuge spreads across more than 100,000 acres of wetlands extending from northeastern North Carolina to southeastern Virginia. A virtual animal kingdom, it harbors white-tailed deer and mink, foxes and black bears, and hundreds of bird species. Officially designated as a federal refuge in 1974, the swamp has been recognized as a valuable resource since 1763, when George Washington invested in a portion of the property to begin a logging business. In 1784, then-governor of Virginia, Patrick Henry, commissioned a 22-mile-long canal to be dug through the area, creating a trade route between Virginia and North Carolina. The canal is now popular with boaters, who enjoy its wilderness scenery. Facilities include boat docks, canoe rentals, picnic areas and restrooms. Fishing is good in Lake Drummond in Virginia, accessed by private boat from North Carolina. ~ The visitors center is on Route 17, 15 miles north of Elizabeth City; 919-771-8333, 888-872-8356.

PETTIGREW STATE PARK Most of this ◄ HIDDEN 17,500-acre park is underwater. All 25 square miles of Lake Phelps lie within Pettigrew, offering exceptional fishing, sailing and even waterskiing. The shoreline is shrouded in bald cypress and sweet gum forest, and bogs and swamps heading out to Pungo and Alligator lakes. Next door is Somerset Place, a restored antebellum plantation run by the North Carolina State Department of History that draws visitors to these swampy netherlands. Facilities include boat ramps, piers, hiking trails, a picnic area, a playing field and restrooms. Fishing is excellent for largemouth bass (particularly during spring and fall), yellow perch (also called raccoon perch) and sunfish. ~ Located off Route 64, about seven miles south of Creswell; 919-797-4475.

▲ There are 13 sites for tent and RVs, with a central bathhouse that has hot water (except in winter); fees range from $4.50 to $9 per night, depending on the season. A group campground is available for $1 per person per night.

GOOSE CREEK STATE PARK Running along ◄ HIDDEN the edges of Pamlico River and Goose Creek, the park is a subtle skein of brackish marshes, pine forest and sawgrass, and bald cypress and live oaks hung with moss. Boardwalks and boat ramps are the avenues for observing this watery cosmos. Bring mosquito repellent, even in the winter. A slice of beach along the river is good for sunning and swimming. Facilities include a park office, picnic tables, restrooms, boat ramps and hiking trails. Groceries are nearby. Swimming is good in designated areas. Fishing's good in the creek and river for largemouth bass, croaker and bluegill. ~ Off Routes 264 and 92, between Washington and Bath; 919-923-2191.

▲ Twelve primitive sites accommodate tents; $5 per night.

The south end of the Albemarle Sound meets up ▼▼▼▼▼▼▼▼▼▼▼▼ with the Pamlico Sound, which takes a great big **Neuse River Region** gulp of water between the Coastal Plain and the southern Outer Banks. The Pamlico is like a small sea, flourishing with shrimp and fish and crabs and other good things for one's dinner table, and fed by rivers that flow in from the Piedmont. The Neuse is one of the those rivers.

Several hundred years ago, American Indians built a settlement **SIGHTS** right where the Neuse and Trent rivers join before heading down to Pamlico Sound. They called it Chattawka, meaning "where the fish are." In 1710, German and Swiss colonists came poking around the area, found the settlement, and liked the idea of all those fish. They set up their own village and named it **New Bern**, after Bern, Switzerland.

New Berners were determined to have a sparkling, successful town. They built handsome homes along the shoreline, and began culling local lumber, tar and turpentine to load onto ships headed for England. In 1749, the colony's first printing press cranked up in New Bern and two years later published the colony's first newspaper.

The town-altering event came in 1770, when Royal Governor William Tryon opened a 19-room "palace" and moved in, making New Bern the colony's capital. Various governors lived in Tryon Palace until 1794, when Raleigh was made the capital. Four years later, the palace burned. For 161 years, New Bern had no palace, not until 1959, when it reopened as a public attraction.

These days, **Tryon Palace** attracts thousands of visitors to New Bern each year. Though virtually nothing is authentic, the facsimile is hauntingly identical, from the three-foot-thick walls of brick to the sienna marble fireplace pillars in the council chamber. Admission. ~ 600 block of Pollock Street; 919-514-4900, 800-767-1560.

This is how Maude Moore Latham hoped it would be. In 1944, the New Bern native gave much of her fortune to bring back Tryon Palace. Before it could be rebuilt, though, the state had to get back the land, which by then had more than 50 buildings. It took eight years before all the landowners could be persuaded (some easier than others) and the land razed, and another seven for the palace to be built and opened as a state historic site.

When you first see the palace's proper brick facade, it seems as if it's been there for centuries. Secured at the end of a tunnel of big darlington oaks, behind a pair of 1741 English castle gates, it does indeed sit upon its original foundation and retains most of its west wing. It is filled with early English art and costly antiques and ringed with formal English parterre gardens and their fountains.

But one thing Tryon Palace is not is palatial. Rather, it is orderly and symmetrical, precisely according to its Georgian architectural style. Each half of the chimneyed brick facade is identical to the other half. Every plaster molding has a match, every doorway a counterpart.

The tour of the palace, conducted by broad, buxom women in big Colonial dresses, takes about an hour. Afterward, you can wander through the luscious gardens of precisely pruned holly and bold plantings of flowers. The most famous and photographed is the Maude Moore Latham Memorial Garden, a scrollwork of dazzling flora decorated with statuary.

Tryon Palace admission includes a self-guided tour of several area gardens as well as **New Bern Academy**, four blocks away.

Here in the town's old red-brick schoolhouse, four rooms of exhibits give an incredibly detailed and vivid overview of North Carolina history, starting, of course, on the coast. You can see some fine relics of early New Bern life—early 1800s pistols, silver candlesticks—and some Civil War pieces. ~ Corner of Hancock and New streets; 919-514-4874.

For those who enjoy looking at tools of war, the **New Bern Civil War Museum** focuses on the Battle of New Bern in 1862. Numerous glass cases are lined with muskets, rifles, pistols and swords. Closed Monday; closed October through March. Admission. ~ 301 Metcalf Street; 919-633-2818.

Incredibly, the **New Bern Fireman's Museum** has even more Civil War relics. The purpose here, though, is to remember the city's early firefighting days. Among the antiques is a horse-drawn Button Steam Fire Engine that put out fires from 1884 to 1912. The bravest and most famous fire horse was Fred. Fred's head hangs in the museum. Admission. ~ 410 Hancock Street, behind the firehouse; 919-636-4087.

New Bern has several other historic sites and plenty of historic Georgian and Federal homes, some dating to the late 1700s, that are lovely to look at. The 1790 **Attmore-Oliver House** showcases exquisite eighteenth- and nineteenth-century furniture, as well as (could it be possible?) Civil War artifacts. Closed mid-December through March. ~ 510 Pollock Street; 919-638-8558.

It's easy to walk all of New Bern's sights, enjoying eateries and shops along the way. One place to pause is at **256 Craven Street**, where a historical marker recalls the beverage, known as Brad's Drink, created in the building's basement back in 1898. Today the drink is known as Pepsi-Cola.

The folks at **Craven County Convention and Visitors Bureau** have excellent walking-tour maps and are eager to provide tips and information. ~ 312 Tryon Palace Drive, New Bern; 919-637-9400, 800-437-5767.

If you head east from New Bern you can travel solitary back roads and see a slice of coastal life that hasn't changed much this century. Start east on Route 55, then head south on Route 1005 toward Arapahoe, delving through roadsides thronged with slash pines and low bush, weathered old farmhouses selling collard greens, and brambly fields of cotton. In the fall picking season, the white puffs come loose from their bushes and the roads are sprinkled with cotton balls. The road holds such emptiness that there seems no possibility of anything at its end. Yet Route 1005 eventually rejoins Route 55, which dead ends at **Oriental**.   ◄ *HIDDEN*

A mite-size village whose shores are decorated with shrimp boats and sailboats, Oriental sits where the Neuse River flows into Pamlico Sound. There's not much action around town, just loads of seafood pouring in nearly every day down at the docks.

Restaurants here serve some of the freshest-tasting sea fare on the North Carolina coast, and even the local convenience store offers fresh fish and shrimp. It's no surprise, then, that Oriental is a favorite lunch and dinner stopover for boaters cruising the Intracoastal Waterway.

From Oriental, head west to Route 306, then south to Minnesott Beach. Here, a free 20-minute ferry will take you across the Neuse River to Cherry Point. Keep going south on Route 306 until Route 101, then head southeast to the lovely port town of **Beaufort** (say BO-fort. BEW-fort is in South Carolina).

Founded in 1709, Beaufort has a rich seafaring past and a successful modern story. In recent years it has been "found" by tourists, which is no surprise, considering the town has much to offer. The orderly little harborfront is lined on one side with sailboats and on the other with pretty brick and painted clapboard storefronts and colorful awnings. Cafes, seafood houses and shops displaying clever gifts and smart attire draw strollers from early morning till evening year-round. A few roads angle off the waterfront, where neighborhoods are filled with big rambling homes and even bigger trees.

The Beaufort scene, which centers around Front Street, is awash with the salty smell of the harbor.

Before you start walking, stop by the **Beaufort Historical Association** for maps and information. The association also offers regular guided walking tours of town. Closed Sunday. ~ 138 Turner Street, Beaufort; 919-728-5225.

The association will first direct you to the **North Carolina Maritime Museum** for a look at the state's seafaring side. This roomy, modern space has well-done exhibits on whaling and oystering, and naturally all kinds of boating, taking you from the time of oars to outboards. A 1910 "deadrise sail" skiff, also called a spritsail skiff and popular around the turn of the century, is here, and there's a 1958 Silver Clipper. Don't miss the terrific maritime reference library, where copies are only ten cents. ~ 315 Front Street, Beaufort; 919-728-7317.

Many of Beaufort's earliest residents now reside at the **Old Burying Ground** within graves facing east, supposedly so they faced the morning sun when they rose for judgment. The headstones date to 1756, though there are thought to be older graves. One unmarked grave along Craven Street is said to contain a girl in a rum keg. One marked 1850 grave holds what remains of Captain Otway Burns, a naval hero in the War of 1812. Maps of the Old Burying Ground are available at the Beaufort Historic Association. ~ On Ann Street between Turner and Craven streets.

From Beaufort, it's 38 miles north along Routes 70 and 12 to **Cedar Island**. If it weren't for the ferry from Cedar Island to Ocracoke Island, few folks would find their way up here—and not too many actually do. For as Route 70 squiggles through the eye-blink villages of Otway and Williston and Stacy, the landscape courses with water and silky-looking seagrasses. There are patches of coastal woods, loblolly pines and live oaks dripping with Spanish moss, and there are tin-roofed homes tucked here and there.

West of Beaufort the scenery couldn't be any more different. Across the Beaufort Inlet is **Morehead City**, whose main drag, Route 70, rumbles with the noise of gaseous traffic. Side streets do hold some pleasant old neighborhoods, and folks in Beaufort often drive "across the bridge" to dine in Morehead City.

Morehead City is also the gateway to the **Bogue Banks**, a 30-mile-long barrier island that calls itself "The Crystal Coast" and also the "southern Outer Banks" but in no way resembles either, having been for the most part heavily developed—and not in an attractive way. Route 58 runs the length of the banks. The easternmost town, **Atlantic Beach**, is chock-a-block with cheesy motels, nondescript condos, putt-putt golf courses, and multilevel glass T-shirt shops. The beach is thin and grayish. Farther west, things improve a little in **Emerald Isle**, where folks with money have bought big attractive homes in manicured developments.

West of Emerald Isle, Route 58 veers across Bogue Sound to the mainland. Take a south turn onto Route 24 and stop in **Swansboro**. A teeny version of Beaufort, Swansboro curves along Bogue Sound, its streets angling up from the water and bordered by juniper and magnolia trees. Antique shops and art galleries look out from weathered clapboard buildings, and the adjacent neighborhood is sprinkled with shingled wood cottages. ◀ **HIDDEN**

On a tree-lined street near Tryon Palace, **The Aerie** is distinguished by a bay window and red shutters. This handsome bed and breakfast has a formal parlor feel throughout, and indeed there is a Tea Room serving public tea several days a week. Seven rooms are furnished in contemporary style with reproduction and original antiques. Country breakfasts are included. ~ 509 Pollock Street, New Bern; phone/fax 919-636-5553, 800-849-5553. MODERATE. **LODGING**

Harmony House Inn invites with a wide front porch lined with rocking chairs and a warm, prettily lit parlor. All nine guest rooms are big, offering separate sitting areas, and are tastefully appointed with antiques and reproductions made by local craftspeople. Private baths, ceiling fans, air conditioning and cable TV are standard. There's also a luxuriant suite with twin fireplaces and a queen canopy bed. Breakfast, included in the moderate to deluxe rates, might feature stuffed pancakes, orange French toast, or bacon and egg casseroles. Wine is served in the evenings. ~ 215 Pollock Street, New Bern; phone/fax 919-636-3810, 800-636-3113. MODERATE TO DELUXE.

A pair of handsome brick buildings right on the waterfront, the **Sheraton Grand New Bern** enjoys the city's premier location and accommodations. Choose from traditional hotel rooms in the main building or suites with whirlpool tubs in the newer, Georgian-style inn. All the rooms are plush, decorated in hunter green and cranberry tones, and look straight across the Neuse River. A brick promenade rambles along the river, and there's also a swimming pool and restaurant here. Tryon Palace is but a short and scenic walk. ~ One Bicentennial Park, New Bern; 919-638-3585, 800-326-3745, fax 919-638-8112. MODERATE TO DELUXE.

In the quietude of a fishing village, The **Tar Heel Inn** offers homespun bed-and-breakfast lodging. The modest 1880s white clapboard home has bright green shutters on the outside and lots of wall stenciling inside. Eight bedrooms are thickly carpeted and simply furnished. ~ 508 Church Street, Oriental; 919-249-1078, fax 919-249-0005. MODERATE.

One of the prettiest buildings along Beaufort's waterfront belongs to **The Cedars**. Built in 1768, the stately, crisp white manse once belonged to Rhode Islander William Borden, who hosted visiting sea captains. Now the home, together with a newer building next door, welcomes travelers with plush, immaculate rooms, all different and ornamented with such pleasantries as lace draperies, eyelet bedspreads and clawfoot tubs. Popular with honeymooners, The Cedars also offers gastronomic experiences in its intimate dining room. ~ 305 Front Street, Beaufort; 919-728-7036, fax 919-728-1685. DELUXE TO ULTRA-DELUXE.

For simpler accommodations, check out the **Langdon House**, located in a neighborhood across from a school and church. Friendly owner Jimm Prest has restored his two-story 1730s house to the comfortable stage and offers four guest rooms with basic furnishings. All are downstairs and have private baths, and are done in masculine maritime style. Full breakfast and taxes are included. ~ 135 Craven Street, Beaufort; 919-728-5499. DELUXE.

The **Inlet Inn**, on the east end of the waterfront, has 37 spacious rooms done in heavy woods, all-white walls, and fireplaces. French doors open onto balconies overlooking the water or onto a courtyard area. The Inlet Inn is ideal for those who prefer lodge-style hostelries over the more intimate bed-and-breakfast accommodations, though a continental breakfast is included here. ~ 601 Front Street, Beaufort; 919-728-3600, fax 919-728-5833. DELUXE.

DINING

HIDDEN ►

You'll have to look a bit for the **Bagels Plus Cottage**, tucked down a little side lane across from Tryon Palace. A perfect stop before or after the Palace, it serves hefty bagels and flavored spreads (try the cinnamon honey butter spread). If you're hungrier, the lunch menu has thick deli sandwiches and homemade soups. Closed Sunday. ~ 712 Pollock Street, New Bern; 919-636-1775. BUDGET.

The tall, white, chimneyed **Harvey Mansion** has been around since the turn of the eighteenth century—a perfect locale for classic and nouvelle European fare by a Swiss chef/owner. The specialty here is fresh seafood but the Swiss veal morsels have been a long-standing favorite. Original artwork adorns the walls of this delightful restaurant. Dinner only. ~ 221 Tryon Palace Drive, New Bern; 919-638-3205. MODERATE TO DELUXE.

Fred & Claire's is where locals gather for lunch, dinner, and—more importantly—town gossip. The tiny kitchen located downtown serves grilled-cheese sandwiches, chicken salad, chili, quiches and other homey eats. The handful of tables and booths are painted bright yellow. Closed Sunday. ~ 247 Craven Street, New Bern; 919-638-5426. BUDGET.

Publike and polished-looking, **The Chelsea** is New Bern's uptown eatery, complete with brass chairs, straight-back wood booths and a long wood bar against a brick wall. You can have a full meal (Yorkshire pie, Maryland crab cakes) or opt for fun fare like quesadillas and classic reubens. Closed Sunday. ~ 335 Middle Street, New Bern; 919-637-5469. MODERATE.

New Berners drive over to **The Trawl Door** for some of the freshest seafood on North Carolina's coast. Whatever comes off the adjacent docks—oysters, shrimp, scallops, crab, flounder, yellowfin tuna—is what's on the menu. The stuffed flounder is a favorite. The 1915 building, once a hardware store, is like a warm and inviting tavern inside, with brick walls and lots of wood. Dinner only. ~ New Street, at the foot of the bridge in Oriental; 919-249-1232. MODERATE TO DELUXE.

A longtime Beaufort favorite, **The Net House** is the perennial seafood place, nautically adorned with nets and lacquered wood tables framed in ships' lines. The fare is, of course, seafood, but it's not the heavy fried stuff. Flounder, grouper and other fresh catches come simply prepared, broiled or sautéed and ladled with light

---

✔ CHECK THESE OUT—UNIQUE DINING

- *Budget to moderate:* Wear flip-flops to **Sam & Omie's** and join Outer Banks locals for fried-oyster sandwiches and other beach fare. *page 273*
- *Budget to moderate:* Take a faux-marble table at **Caffé Phoenix** and enjoy artful eats—you'll be dining at the coast's best bistro. *page 303*
- *Moderate to deluxe:* Taste some of the coast's freshest, tastiest seafood at **The Trawl Door** in tiny, secluded Oriental. *page 293*
- *Moderate to deluxe:* Settle into the colorful, high-ceilinged **Beaufort Grocery Co.** for tasty fare that's both unusual and wonderfully prepared. *page 294*

Budget: under $9   Moderate: $9–$16   Deluxe: $16–$24   Ultra-deluxe: over $24

sauces. You can also order crab cakes and clams. Dinner only, except in spring and fall, when lunch is sometimes offered. Closed Sunday. ~ Turner Street, a half-block off Front Street, Beaufort; 919-728-2002. BUDGET TO MODERATE.

If you only dine once in Beaufort, make it **Beaufort Grocery Co.** A deli on one side and cafe on the other, this colorful, high-ceilinged venue is full of light and space and wonderful smells. Everything on the menu sounds good, from the Grecian salad with crab cakes and *gougeres* (herb pastries) for lunch to the southwestern turkey steak, free-range chicken and grilled yellowfin tuna served at dinner. Start dinner with the *sagnaki*, a wedge of *kesseri* cheese flambéed at your table. Closed Tuesday from Memorial Day to January. ~ 115–117 Queen Street, Beaufort; 919-728-3899. MODERATE TO DELUXE.

The **Sanitary Fish Market** started in 1938 as a shack that sold ice, shrimp and "shore dinners," and grew to a big rambly waterfront building selling seafood dinners daily by the hundreds. The atmosphere is crowded and noisy, the decor minimal, and the entrées listed by number. Number Eight, for instance, is a platter of broiled bluefish, jumping mullet or spots-in-the-road—whichever local fish is in season. A page explains the local fish (spots-in-the-round are sweet and flaky but require a bit of bone picking). ~ 501 Evans Street, Morehead City; 919-247-3111. MODERATE.

The island recipes at **Calypso Cafe** hail not from the Carolinas but the Caribbean. *Calaloo* (West Indian crab and spinach soup), grilled triggerfish with ginger mango relish, shrimp curry, and crab-stuffed shrimp with a calypso hollandaise are among the specialties. The scenery is casual and vibrant, with murals of island scenes on the walls and palms gushing from big pots. Dinner only. Closed Sunday. ~ 506 Arendell Street, Morehead City; 919-240-3380. MODERATE TO DELUXE.

SHOPPING   In New Bern, concentrate your shopping efforts near the waterfront along Craven, Pollock and Middle streets. **Mitchell Hardware** is a great old place, dating to 1898, whose new and not-so-new inventory ranges from quaint antique farm tools and modern cookware to Venus flytrap insecticide and seeds for growing collards, black-eyed peas and squash. ~ 215 Craven Street, New Bern; 919-638-4261.

The locally made creations at **Carolina Creations** include pottery, jewelry, fiber art, ink drawings, watercolors, stained glass and barbecue sauces, jellies and biscotti. ~ 226 Middle Street, New Bern; 919-633-4369.

Few places have such a comprehensive selection of books and material on the Carolinas, especially the coast, as **Tryon Palace Museum Shop**. ~ Pollock Street near Eden Street, New Bern; 919-514-4900.

Beaufort's boutiques and antique shops parade along the harbor and just off it. Most are on Front and Turner streets.

Included among the nautical finery at **Sea Dog Trading** are shiny brass barometers and sea-themed throws and Christmas ornaments. ~ 300 Front Street, Beaufort; 919-728-7484.

Scuttlebutt purveys "land and seaworthy gifts," things like cruising guides and charts, model ships and lighthouses, and home and galley wares. ~ 433 Front Street, Beaufort; 919-728-7765.

Among the vintage stores in Beaufort, you'll find **Waterfront Antiques and Collectibles**. ~ 121 Turner Street, Beaufort; 919-728-5452. You can also try **The Little White House With Blue Shutters**. ~ 314 Moore Street; 919-728-1647. Another choice is **Carteret Antique Mall**. ~ Beaufort Causeway; 919-728-5611.

Over in Morehead City, **Yesterdaze Closet** is a wild and crazy shrine to the '60s, jammed floor-to-ceiling with vintage attire (outrageous platforms, sequined bell bottoms) and furnishings, original posters and albums. ~ 4101 Arendell Street; 919-247-0744.

The long polished bar at **The Chelsea** restaurant is always a good place for a drink. Sometimes, there's live entertainment or karaoke nights. ~ 335 Middle Street, New Bern; 919-637-5469. **NIGHTLIFE**

Grab a cocktail at the classy **Pro Sail Pub** and stroll out along the waterfront. The stars seem extra big here on summer and fall nights. ~ Sheraton Grand New Bern, One Bicentennial Park, New Bern; 919-638-3585.

Most weekends there's live entertainment at **The Trawl Door**. Local country and blues bands, comedy acts, acoustic guitar—it's a mixed bag, but usually good quality. Cover. ~ New Street, Oriental; 919-249-1232.

In Beaufort, lots of people head to the deck at **Front Street Grill** for a drink on the harbor. ~ 419-A Front Street, Beaufort; 919-728-3118.

In a little courtyard off the waterfront, **Back Street Pub** is the town headquarters for live entertainment. Rock-and-roll, flamenco guitar, R&B, Cajun—you never know what will be playing. ~ 124 Middle Lane, just behind Clawson's Restaurant, Beaufort; 919-728-7108. ◄ *HIDDEN*

On the Atlantic Beach Causeway east of Beaufort in Morehead City, **Channel Marker** is a restaurant where waterfront decks are popular at cocktail hour. ~ 919-247-2344. **W. B. Kelli's** also has waterfront seating. ~ 919-247-1094.

CROATAN NATIONAL FOREST 🏃 🚣 ⛴ 🚢 ⛺ Few places in the world have more than one species of insect-eating plant. Croatan National Forest has five. One type, the rosette-shaped butterwort, catches bugs with its sticky leaves, then washes them in natural anesthesia. When a bug falls inside the tall, tube-shaped **BEACHES & PARKS**

pitcher plant, the plant tilts its "hairs" downward so the bug can't crawl back out. Then it splashes the bug with fluid to drown and digest him. The most common insect eater, the Venus flytrap, is also found here. Like the others, it is protected by law—so don't cut any.

Four rivers trace the edges of Croatan National Forest, and five spring-fed lakes speckle its interior. All that water seeps into swamps and bogs and marsh, utopias for wading birds, ducks, hawks and alligators. Hardwood and pine forest also marble some of these 160,000 acres. Some of the swamp cypress trees are enormous. Hiking trails and boardwalks provide access to the natural wonders.

Facilities include boat ramps, a fishing pier, picnic areas, restrooms and hiking trails in various locations throughout the park. Swimming is permitted at Neuse River campground, Route 70 south of Fishers Landing. Freshwater fishing is good in the rivers. ~ Croatan National Forest runs south of New Bern to Bogue Sound. Main access roads are Routes 70, 17 and 58. The Croatan District Forest Service Office is along Route 1101, off Route 70, south of New Bern; 919-638-5628.

▲ Free open tent camping is available year-round at Fishers Landing, off Route 70 on the Neuse River. South of Fishers Landing, 50 seasonal tent and RV sites are at the Neuse River campground off Route 70; $8 per night. At Cedar Point, on Route 24 east of Swansboro, you'll find 50 seasonal tent and RV sites; $15 per night.

MINNESOTT BEACH 🐾 Forget the roaring surf and dramatic dunes of the Outer Banks. This "beach" is a public patch of pale sand along the Neuse River near where the ferries discharge passengers coming from Cherry Point. Popular with families, it's a neighborly spot near the neighborhood of Minnesott Beach. Facilities include a picnic table; restaurant, grocery, golf course and marina are nearby. Swimming is fine in the Neuse River campground, Route 70 south of Fishers landing. ~ On Route 306 on the north side of the Neuse River, south of Oriental.

HIDDEN ► **CAPE LOOKOUT NATIONAL SEASHORE** 🛶 Arguably the most remote of all Carolinas beaches, these three thin islands last for 55 miles from Ocracoke Inlet, near the southernmost tip of Ocracoke Island, all the way to Beaufort Inlet. Accessible only by personal boat or private ferry and offering only minimal facilities, the seashore is more suited to wildlife than human life. Endangered loggerhead turtles and piping plovers (a teeny seabird) nest here, which is one reason Cape Lookout has been designated a Biosphere Reserve.

The southernmost tip of the seashore, called Cape Lookout, is punctuated by a lighthouse painted in a black-and-white diamond pattern. You can't go inside the lighthouse, but the Keepers Quarters next door has a small museum with seashell exhibits and history on the islands. Beaches go on for miles, offering secluded sunbathing and surf casting. Unfortunately, strong currents and undertow make swimming dangerous, and there are no lifeguards. On the seashore's north end, closest to Ocracoke Island, is **Portsmouth Island** and uninhabited **Portsmouth Village**, where nineteenth-century buildings have been restored and are listed on the National Register of Historic Places. Facilities include restrooms at Keepers Quarters, and picnic areas scattered throughout the seashore. Swimming is not recommended; strong currents and undertow create constant hazardous conditions. There is good surf fishing in the fall for flounder, drum, black sea bass and sea trout. ~ Private ferries provide passenger service from various locations, including Ocracoke Island, Harkers Island, Beaufort, and the towns of Davis and Atlantic. (For a complete list of ferries, see the "Transportation" section of this chapter.) Round-trip fare ranges from $10 to $30, and most operate seasonally. Only four-wheel-drive vehicles are allowed on the island; 919-728-2250.

▲ Open primitive camping, free of charge, for tents and pop-up campers; no RVs allowed. Bring your own water.

BOGUE BANKS BEACHES Not a particularly compelling example of sand and sea, the Bogue Banks have nonetheless been keenly developed and are keenly crowded in summer. A 30-mile-long barrier island along Bogue Sound, it starts east with Atlantic Beach, North Carolina's tiny version of Ocean City. Cheesy motels and T-shirt shops crowd every corner, and neon signs vie for visual space. Westward, Emerald Isle does not live up to its name, though the western point does have some exclusive homes. The beaches everywhere tend to be thin, the sand gray to pale brown, the waves big and good for surfing. Facilities include restrooms, a parking area and a boardwalk to beach in Salther Path; groceries, restaurants and bike rentals are widely available. For swimming check the surf conditions; strong currents and riptides are common. Fishing is best from one of the eight piers. Possibilities include cobia, amberjack, king mackerel and tarpon. ~ A causeway from Morehead City will guide you over to Atlantic Beach on the eastern end. Emerald Beach on the west end is accessed by Route 58 from Cape Carteret. Route 58 runs the length of Bogue Banks; 800-786-6962.

FORT MACON STATE PARK On the barren, wind-worn eastern tip of Bogue Banks sits this 1834 fort, surrounded by nearly 400 acres of marsh and desert-like dunes and beach. In summer, the landscape swells with vacationers, particularly families, who explore the five-sided, brick-and-stone fort and then hit the beach.

The fort has some history: During the Civil War, it was overtaken by Union soldiers after eleven hours of bombardment. Facilities include the Fort Macon museum, restrooms, hiking trail, picnic areas, a seasonal bathhouse and a snack bar. Swimming is good in protected area, which is patrolled by lifeguards in season. The fishing is good for drum, flounder, trout and bluefish. ~ Located off Route 58 in Atlantic Beach, on the east end of Bogue Banks; 919-726-3775.

HIDDEN ▶   **HAMMOCKS BEACH STATE PARK** Secluded and scenic, with near-empty beaches and salt marsh that last for 892 acres, the park covers all of Bear Island. Unless you have a boat, the only way there is by ferry from Swansboro, which explains its peacefulness. Even during summer, when every ferry is filled, the island does not seem crowded. Estuaries and salt marsh run along the Intracoastal Waterway and Bogue Sound–side of the island, drawing many types of birds, including willets and American oystercatchers, that nest here. The Atlantic side of the island is rimmed with beaches and high sandy ridges and dunes. Facilities include a park office, a ferry dock, a bathhouse, restrooms, picnic areas with grills, and a snack bar, open in season. Shallow sandy shores along the Atlantic side offer great swimming; lifeguards are on duty in summer. There is surf casting for puppy drum, flounder and sea trout. ~ Pontoon ferries provide transportation to the park from the dock on Route 1572 in Swansboro. The ride takes about 25 minutes. Depending on the time of year, ferries leave every half-hour or every hour. On summer weekends, the ferries fill up fast, so get there early; 910-326-4881.

▲ There are 14 primitive tent sites, as well as group camping; $5 per night for individual sites, $1 per person per night for group camping.

▼▼▼▼▼▼▼▼▼▼▼▼▼
Cape Fear Coast

The south end of the North Carolina Coast jags out into the sea as if making one last stand before succumbing to South Carolina. Where the jag is most prominent is Cape Fear, at the point of far-flung Bald Head Island, home to a private resort community. From here, you can follow the Cape Fear River north to Wilmington.

SIGHTS   The Cape Fear Coast's center of gravity, **Wilmington** is the largest city in eastern North Carolina and the one everybody's talking about. Among the publications who've paid attention lately, *Rolling Stone* magazine deemed the southern port one of the hottest spots on the eastern seaboard. Indeed, Wilmington will come as a surprise to anyone accustomed to the quietude and rural scenes of the rest of the coast.

Downtown Wilmington has a happening feeling. Cafes, fine restaurants, ornate inns and trendy boutiques, many appealing to a gay clientele, crowd along the Cape Fear River. Streets of rippling red brick run rampant through the historic area, and so do exquisite old homes of Italianate, Romanesque and antebellum design. Many buildings date to the 1800s, but have recently been painted in crimson or cranberry or hunter green, and wrapped with contrasting porches of crisp white. Mammoth sycamore, oak and pecan trees blanket the neighborhoods, giving the sense they've been here a lot longer than anyone else has.

Most sights are concentrated along the river on Water Street and in the few blocks north of the water. The **Cape Fear Coast Convention & Visitors Bureau** has excellent maps of the area with details on dozens of sights. ~ 24 North 3rd Street, Wilmington; 910-341-4030, 800-222-4757.

A block from the bureau, the **Burgwin Wright House and Garden** is among Wilmington's finest old homes, distinguished by its Palladian doorway and double porches. John Burgwin, treasurer of the Carolina Colony, built the white Georgian beauty in 1770 on the thick stone foundations of the abandoned town jail. They proved to be solid foundations, for the house has stayed true to its design, having been restored in 1937 and opened for tours in 1950. The rooms are furnished in the styles of Burgwin's day; a kitchen building and parterre garden are also on the grounds. Closed Sunday and Monday. Admission. ~ 224 Market Street, Wilmington; 910-762-0570.

Two blocks east and nearly a century later, the **Zebulon Latimer House** was built before the Civil War, when Wilmington was a bustling railway hub and port. Zebulon Latimer, a wealthy merchant, prospered in this elaborate Italianate house, and his descendants lived there until 1963. Now the home is furnished with gorgeous period pieces and artwork, and the surrounding grounds are lush in the Victorian style. Closed Monday. Admission. ~ 126 South 3rd Street, Wilmington; 910-762-0492.

Artists have also prospered in Wilmington, as evidenced by the works at **St. John's Museum of Art**. Within three historic buildings, including the 1803 Georgian-style St. John's Masonic Lodging, are paintings, prints, pottery and sculpture spanning the last two centuries. Closed Monday. Admission. ~ 114 Orange Street, Wilmington; 910-763-0281.

For the big picture of Cape Fear life, past and present, visit the **Cape Fear Museum**. Hundreds of animated exhibits trace the history of this southeastern region, many designed especially for children. A model of Wilmington's waterfront depicts the city in 1863. Admission. ~ 814 Market Street, Wilmington; 910-341-7413.

Away from Wilmington's historic downtown are, regrettably, all the trappings of suburban America. Fast-food joints, gas stations and strip shopping centers seem to swallow the perimeter of town, and then go on for miles in every direction.

And then there are beaches. East of Wilmington across the Intracoastal Waterway on Route 74, **Wrightsville Beach** spans less than one square mile but harbors some of the area's best sand and surf. Sprinkled with modern resorts, seafood houses, sun-blistered cottages and sparkling new stilt homes (on the north end), it's foremost a family destination.

The beaches that lie south of Wilmington are campy, funky and crowded. From **Carolina Beach** to **Kure Beach**, it's mostly wall-to-wall cottages along the dunes and streets crammed with cheesy mom-and-pop motels, arcades and hot-dog stands—like an amusement park that's been going on too long. The whole island, not surprisingly, has been dubbed Pleasure Island.

Kure's historic moment would be lost in all the beach regalia were it not for the **Fort Fisher State Historic Site**. Here stood the largest Confederate earthworks fort, and the last to fall in the Civil War. The moment was in January 1865, when 10,000 troops bombarded the fort and destroyed it, then headed up the Cape Fear River to take Wilmington. Little remains of the fort, but the historic site re-enacts the event through slides and museum displays. ~ Route 421, 20 miles south of Wilmington; 910-458-5538.

A mile farther south, the **North Carolina Aquarium at Fort Fisher** is a favorite of kids, who love looking at alligators, sea turtles and sharks, and handling the hermit crabs and other critters in the "touch tank." Admission. ~ Route 421; 910-458-8257.

Kids also enjoy a ferry ride, available a little farther south at the Fort Fisher Ferry Terminal. For a minimal fee, you get a 30-minute cruise across the Cape Fear River over to **Southport**, a most agreeable sight after the clutter of Atlantic and Kure beaches. In fact, from the graceful old mansions and pine trees of Southport all the way to the South Carolina line, the scenery is gentle and agreeable, the beaches isolated and sedate.

◆◆

MAN YOUR STATIONS

A big, brooding presence in Wilmington's harbor, **Battleship North Carolina** fought in Pearl Harbor. Commissioned in 1941 and called "The Showboat" of World War II, it was the fastest, most powerful battleship of the time. Today, the mammoth gray ship welcomes sightseers, including plenty of children, who explore the maze of decks and rooms, from the galley and engine rooms to sick bay and crew's quarters. Admission. ~ Route 17, Wilmington; 910-350-1817, 910-251-5797.

The southernmost necklace of North Carolina isles, the **South** ◀ *HIDDEN*
Brunswick Islands are teeny, a little tough to reach, and esteemed
by Carolinians who make summer pilgrimages to their cottages by
the sea. **Holden Beach**, north in the chain, has 600 year-round residents, most of whom fish or shrimp and live along the Intracoastal
Waterway. On the oceanside of the island, vacationers flock to
beachfront cottages.

Ocean Isle is eight miles long and the most "developed," with
a handful of shops and eateries, motels and condominiums. Most
remote and probably most loved by locals and naturalists, **Sunset
Beach** is the southernmost barrier island in North Carolina. A
one-lane swing bridge connects Sunset to civilization—which is just
fine by most folks, as it tends to scare off anyone in a hurry. At low
tide, you can wade across Mad Inlet on Sunset's west end to **Bird** ◀ *HIDDEN*
Island, a speck of ground where osprey, herons, egrets and other
beautiful birds come to nest and feed. Endangered sea turtles also
lay their eggs on the beach here, sensing the safety of such an isolated place.

The only thing between here and South Carolina is **Calabash**,
a town whose image is much bigger than its size. For out of this
nowheresville village on a river came "Calabash" seafood: seasoned,
crisp-fried niblets of fish, shrimp and clams heaped on plates and
embellished with hushpuppies, fries and slaw. Hundreds of restaurants along the Carolinas' coast hawk Calabash seafood, many of
them in Myrtle Beach, where it's served at all-you-can-eat buffets—
a strange concept for fried food.

For real Calabash seafood, you'll have to go to Calabash, of
course. At last count, more than 25 restaurants were serving here.
Most cater to tourists who unload from big air conditioned buses
and funnel inside.

The choices of lodging in Wilmington are the finest on the North **LODGING**
Carolina coast. Within the lovely historic neighborhoods more
than 15 inns, bed and breakfasts and guest houses entreat visitors
with elaborate architecture, luxuriant rooms and stellar Southern
service.

Most opulent of Wilmington's lodges, **Graystone Inn** is a magnificent Renaissance stone mansion built in 1906. Graced on the
outside with a vast three-story portico and flanked by tall chimneys, the inside is filled with exquisite touches. There's the grand
staircase of hand-carved red oak, ornate music and drawing rooms,
formal dining room, a library lined with wonderful old volumes,
and five bedrooms and two suites adorned in old-world grandeur.
~ 100 South 3rd Street, Wilmington; 910-763-2000, fax 910-763-
5555. DELUXE TO ULTRA-DELUXE.

Vickie and Greg Stringer are the congenial hosts at **The Curran
House**, a meticulously restored 1800s Victorian Italianate home.

The three bedrooms and two-room suite are wonderful spaces, each individually adorned. The Blue Harbor Room has a Polynesian/Hawaiian theme; the Gentleman's Room features a mahogany sleigh bed. All come with cable TV, air conditioning and full breakfast. ~ 312 South 3rd Street, Wilmington; 910-763-6603, 800-763-6603, fax 910-763-5116. MODERATE.

Decorated with fanciful shingles and turrets, the **Worth House** is a Queen Anne confection offering seven guest rooms. The atmosphere here is easygoing; you can relax on the porch under the pecan and magnolia trees, or walk a few blocks to the waterfront. Every room is a little different, from the Rose Suite with canopied King bed to the Azalea Suite and Hibiscus Room, located in turrets and ensconced in windows. ~ 412 South 3rd Street, Wilmington; 910-762-8562, fax 910-763-2173, 800-340-8559. MODERATE TO DELUXE.

Business travelers like **The Inn at St. Thomas Court.** Every room is a suite, bright and airy and contemporarily decorated. Some have French doors that open onto a pretty courtyard; bigger suites offer full kitchens, washers and dryers and wet bars. Downtown Wilmington is right outside the door. Moderate to deluxe rates include an extensive continental breakfast, making this place a great value. ~ 101 South 2nd Street, Wilmington; 910-343-1800, 800-525-0909, fax 910-251-1149. MODERATE TO DELUXE.

The Inn on Orange is Wilmington's only guesthouse with a swimming pool. Among the other features at this striking 1875 Italianate house are a lush courtyard and four spacious bedrooms with canopy beds, fireplaces and private baths. A Key West room is tropically furnished in wicker. The hostelry is gay-owned and attracts both gay and straight professionals. Breakfast is country-style. ~ 410 Orange Street, Wilmington; 910-815-0035, 800-381-4666. MODERATE TO DELUXE.

If you prefer less luxurious accommodations on the beach, consider staying on Wrightsville Beach.

The best place here is **Blockade Runner Resort**, where 163 airy, casual rooms and suites are geared toward families. Located in twin rectangular buildings by the sea, the rooms look out at the ocean, the Intracoastal Waterway or Wrightsville Sound. The atrium lobby is done in ethereal tropical motif; the restaurant offers good food and views of the heated outdoor pool and sand dunes. ~ 275 Waynick Boulevard, Wrightsville Beach; phone/fax 910-256-2251, 800-541-1161. ULTRA-DELUXE.

By far the best way to stay on the South Brunswick Islands is in a cottage. For a cottage rental on Holden Beach, call **Alan Holden Realty.** ~ 910-852-6061, 800-720-2200. Or try **Brunswickland Realty.** ~ 910-842-6949. On Ocean Isle, there's **Cooke Realtors.** ~ 910-579-3535. Also on Ocean Isle is **R. H. McClure Realty.** ~ 910-579-3586.

Sunset Properties handles cottages and homes on Sunset Beach. ~ 910-579-9900, 800-525-0182. **Odom Co.** deals with this area as well. ~ 910-579-3515, 800-446-3435.

DINING

Caffé Phoenix easily wins as the best bistro on the North Carolina coast. The tables are faux marble, the walls decorated with original art, and the ceilings high enough to accommodate a loft for dining. You can have lunch, dinner or cocktails and light eats. Pizzettes, salads, pasta (try the penne pasta with a chilled artichoke heart sauce), chicken and vegetarian dishes are offered. The crowd leans toward a gay, avant-garde clientele. No lunch on Sunday. ~ At 9 South Front Street, Wilmington; 910-343-1395. BUDGET TO MODERATE.

Buffets rarely offer high-quality food and ambiance, but **Taste of Country Buffet** is an exception. Lunchtime crowds pour in from downtown to eat turkey and dressing, roast pork, sweet potatoes and mashed potatoes, squash, corn, cobblers—like Thanksgiving every day. The Victorian surroundings are pleasant, but don't quite go with the food. Open for lunch Tuesday through Sunday; open for dinner on Friday and Saturday. ~ 226 South Front Street, Wilmington; 910-343-9888. BUDGET.

Anyone who savors Charleston's Lowcountry cuisine should go to **The Pilot House**. Shrimp and grits, flounder meuniere, crunchy catfish with grits, fried green tomatoes and hoppin' johns are a few of the Southern flights of fancy here. Right on the Cape Fear River in the restored historic Craig House, it has a jazzy ambiance: deep cranberry walls, linen and oil lamps on the tables. Make a reservation or you won't get in. Closed Sunday from October through March. ~ 2 Ann Street, Wilmington; 910-343-0200. DELUXE.

Solid German food served in an uproarious pub atmosphere is what you'll find at **Nuss Strasse Cafe**. Brick walls and stained glass decorate the multilevel eatery, while kielbasas, wursts and schnitzels decorate the plates. No dinner on Monday. Closed Sunday. ~ 316 Nutt Street, in the Cotton Exchange, Wilmington; 910-763-5523. MODERATE.

Trails End is so hidden, I won't even attempt to give directions. You'll have to call the restaurant, brave the maze of neighborhood roads, and hope for the best (hint: stay on the gravel road *after* the sign says "Road Ends"). A most unusual place but one that's absolutely worth finding, it's a steak house on the water. The beef is broiled over hardwood charcoal and remarkably good, the salad bar arrayed with light bites, and the service exceptional (one waiter has been here for over 20 years). The front door handles are actually shoes from the Budweiser Clydesdale horses; the cannonball pulley dates from the Civil War. Closed Sunday. ~ Located off Masonboro Loop Road near Whiskey Creek, Wilmington; 910-791-2034. DELUXE.

◄ HIDDEN

Get your grits and gravy at **The Middle of the Island,** better known as "The M.O.I." to locals who take their morning wake-up call here. The country breakfast house has fast waitresses and fast, fill-you-up fare, from butter-studded biscuits and fat pancakes to fried fish roe and eggs. ~ 216 Causeway, Wrightsville Beach; 910-256-4277. BUDGET.

With its many levels, peaked and gabled roof and pier angling out to sea, The **Oceanic Restaurant** is one of the prettiest places on the beach. This ever-popular seafood house displays its fresh catches in a glass case and dresses up its dishes. Seafood lasagna, grouper pan-seared in cashew nuts and crab-stuffed shrimp are among the specialties. Comfy booths, polished wood tables and lots of long windows create a perfect milieu for gazing at the sea. ~ 703 Lumina Avenue at the Crystal Pier, Wrightsville Beach; 910-256-5551. MODERATE TO DELUXE.

SHOPPING   The best shopping is along Wilmington's waterfront in places like **Chandler's Wharf.** ~ Corner of Ann and Water streets. The **Cotton Exchange** is another good choice. ~ 300 block of North Front Street; 910-343-9896. Also try the dozens of shops lining the streets in between these two. Both complexes offer shopping in restored buildings whose many levels are filled with eateries, pubs and interesting stores and boutiques.

In Chandler's Wharf, **A Proper Garden** will fill all your formal and informal garden needs. ~ 225 South Water Street, Wilmington; 910-763-7177. **The Quarters of Chandler's Wharf** has smart resort wear for women. ~ 3 Ann Street, Wilmington; 910-762-0970.

At the Cotton Exchange, look for **Perfect Scents,** which not only smells great but has some unusual bath oils, soaps and other toiletries. ~ 910-762-2520.

Also along the waterfront you'll find **Anasazi** with its urns, rugs, pottery and other items from Mexico and the Southwest. ~ 14 Market Street, Wilmington; 910-762-8044.

Island Passage offers men's and women's apparel that's both dressy and casual. ~ 4 Market Street, Wilmington; 910-762-1911.

The bins at **Wilmington City Market** overflow with colorful, fresh-cut flowers, just-picked produce, and arts and crafts. ~ 120 South Front Street, Wilmington; 910-763-9748.

NIGHTLIFE   The night definitely moves in Wilmington. Come ten o'clock, lines start forming along the downtown sidewalks.

An SRO club that attracts a mostly twenty-something crowd, **The Wave Hog Saloon** hosts rock-and-roll, progressive and alternative bands on weekends. Wednesdays are techno nights; Thursdays feature a variety of acoustic music. ~ 12 Dock Street, Wilmington; 910-762-2827.

The Ice House almost always has a party. The action's on a rambling outdoor patio; the music's usually live blues or jazz. ~ 115 South Water Street, Wilmington; 910-251-1158.

The music often starts early afternoon at the waterfront **Water Street**, where you can hear jazz and blues bands. ~ 5 South Water Street, Wilmington; 910-343-0042.

Stately **Thalian Hall**, built in the 1850s and designed by famed theater architect John Mantague Trimble, hosts a vast array of performing arts throughout the year. Zulu dance, big-name country and jazz artists, ballet and Far East acrobats could be on the playbill. ~ 310 Chestnut Street, Wilmington; 910-343-3660.

At **The Manor**, the local and regional bands often play to sell-out crowds, so buy your tickets early. Alternative rock-and-roll is the mainstay, but there's also some classic rock and progressive. Cover. ~ 127 College Road, in the Marketplace Mall, Wilmington; 910-251-9220.

If you're into country music and line dancing, head over to **The Palomino Club**. Live bands play frequently at this spacious, popular place. Cover. ~ 2649 Carolina Beach Road, Wilmington; 910-452-0102.

GAY SCENE   Day and night, gay men go to **Mickey Ratz** to shoot pool, drink beer, and dance. There are also regular drag shows and male strippers. The inside is smoky, but the outdoor patio is airy and open in warm weather for barbecues. ~ 115 South Front Street, Wilmington; 910-251-1289.

BEACHES & PARKS

TOPSAIL ISLAND   This 20-mile-long barrier island north of Wilmington isn't as appealing as Wrightsville Beach, but it's still a hotspot for beaching it. Fairly saturated with motels, seafood shacks and other development, it is trimmed in tan sand and dunes and sprinkled with fishing piers. Most are concentrated around Surf City near the middle and Topsail Beach on the south end. This happens to be where all the beach action is, too. Grocery stores and snack bars are located nearby. Swimming is good in most spots. From the piers you can fish for everything from king mackerel and cobia to tarpon and jack crevalles. ~ From Wilmington, take Route 17 north 26 miles to Route 50, then go east 6 miles; 800-626-2780.

WRIGHTSVILLE BEACH   The sea and sands have been very generous to Wrightsville, the prettiest, broadest beach on the Cape Fear Coast. Lasting for a mile along the Atlantic Ocean, the tawny sands are edged with dunes and sea oats, and then weathered clapboard cottages. The south end of the beach is rugged and wind-whipped, with water too rough for swimming but sands ideal for secluded sunbathing. Sailboats cruise by frequently on their way to and from Masonboro Inlet. Windsurfers like the west side of the island, where they can go fast in Banks Channel. Groceries and restaurants are located nearby. Swimming is good between Crystal Pier and Johnny Mercer Pier; lifeguards patrol in the summer. There is good fishing from both piers and good surf casting on the south end. ~ Wrightsville Beach is just east of Wilmington off Route 74. Regional beach access, with designated parking lots, are sprinkled along the island off Lumina Avenue; 800-222-4757.

CAROLINA BEACH STATE PARK 🏃 🚤 🚣 ⤵ An expansive park—1770 acres—at the northern tip of Pleasure Island, it's not really on the beach, but is flanked on one side by the Cape Fear River and on the other by the Intracoastal Waterway. Grassy ponds, swamp forest and pine savannah dominate the terrain, and you will find Venus flytraps growing here. The Venus Flytrap Trail (see "Hiking" in this chapter) promises close-up looks, but don't touch—the insect-eating plants are protected. Facilities include a park office, restrooms, a marina with boat ramps, a picnic area and hiking trails. Swimming is not permitted. ~ Located in Carolina Beach, ten miles south of Wilmington, off Route 421; 910-458-8206.

▲ A family campground features 83 tent and RV sites with two hot-water bathhouses; no hookups; $9 per night per family. ~ 910-458-8206.

HIDDEN ► **SOUTH BRUNSWICK ISLAND BEACHES** 🚣 ⤵ The Cape Fear Coast's most secluded beaches, they skirt a trio of islands: Holden Beach, Ocean Isle and Sunset Beach. Sunset is farthest south and barely developed, accessed by a single-lane bridge that swings open for passing boats. Ocean Isle has the most going on—though only 600 people call it home. Holden has a busy fishing village and a summer resort community. All have a wilderness look: fine-sand beaches washed with foamy surf, soft dunes fringed with sea oats, and water in every direction. All three islands have eateries and grocery stores. Swimming is usually excellent, just check for strong currents or undertow before going in. Fishing is good off Ocean Isle Pier and Sunset Beach Pier. ~ Located at the southern end of coastal North Carolina, the Brunswick Island Beaches are accessed from Route 17.

▼▼▼▼▼▼▼▼▼▼▼▼▼▼
Outdoor Adventures

**SPORT-
FISHING**

There are no lack of boat captains ready to take you fishing. Below are a few of the charter companies that offer everything from deep-sea to light-tackle to fly-fishing. For details on pier, jetty and surf fishing, see the section titled "Where The Fish Are" in this chapter.

Along the Outer Banks, Oregon Inlet on Bodie Island is the hub for charter fishing. The fleet at **Oregon Inlet Fishing Center** includes 37 charter boats and one headboat (holding up to 50 people) ready to take you anywhere from the sounds all the way out to the Gulf Stream. The center is a concession of the Cape Hatteras

National Seashore. ~ North side of Oregon Inlet; 919-441-6301, 800-272-5199.

On Roanoke Island, check with **Pirate's Cove Yacht Club** for charters and headboats. ~ Manteo Causeway; 919-473-3906. Down along Hatteras Island, head to **Teach's Lair Marina**. ~ Route 12, Hatteras; 919-986-2460. Teach's Lair and **Hatteras Harbor Marina** are lined with boats offering full- and half-day charters. ~ Route 12, Hatteras; 919-986-2166. In Ocracoke, get in touch with the captains of the **Drum Stick**. ~ Anchorage Marina; 919-928-5351. Also in Ocracoke is the **Miss Kathleen**. ~ 919-928-4841. Or try **The Outlaw**. ~ 919-928-4851. Finally, there is the **Rascal**. ~ 919-928-6111.

In the Neuse River Region, you'll find dozens of charter boats along at the marina on Evans Street in Morehead City. Among them is **Offshore**. ~ 919-729-3441. Next door in Beaufort there's **Abracadabra**. ~ Front Street; 919-728-5020. Also in Beaufort is **Priorities**. ~ 919-728-3907. The Causeway to Atlantic Beach is also lined with charter companies, including **Ultimate Joy**. ~ 919-726-8758. In the Causeway, you can also try **Captain Stacy VII**. ~ 919-726-4675. You can join a headboat charter on the **Carolina Princess**. ~ Morehead City; 919-726-5479. Another choice is **Continental Shelf**. ~ Morehead City; 919-726-7454, 800-775-7450.

Charter companies along the Cape Fear Coast include **Flapjack & Gung-Ho Fishing Charters**. ~ Carolina Beach Docks; 910-458-4362, 800-288-3474. **Fish Witch II Charter Fishing** is another company in Carolina Beach. ~ 1328 St. Joseph Street, Carolina Beach; 910-458-5855. In Kure Beach is **Class Action Fishing Charters**. ~ 114 Myrtle Avenue, Kure Beach; 910-458-3348.

HANG GLIDING

Persistent wind and summits of sand draw thousands of hang gliders to the Outer Banks every year. One of the largest hang-gliding schools in the world, **Kitty Hawk Kites** promises to get you off the ground within three hours. The beginner's lesson includes at least

✔ **CHECK THESE OUT—UNIQUE OUTDOOR ADVENTURES**

- Go airborne with Kitty Hawk Kites, and learn hang gliding from the world's highest sand dune at Jockey's Ridge State Park. *page 307*
- Grab a board and surf the northern Outer Banks waves, or try a sailboard; local outfits provide rentals. *page 308*
- Kayak Ocracoke by moonlight with Ride The Wind Surf Shop or, if the moon's not full, take the sunset tour. *page 308*
- Get beach-bound with your bike along Route 12, using the ferry between Hatteras and Ocracoke islands. *page 309*

five flights, though don't expect to be doing any aerial stunts. Being airborne a few feet, with an instructor right beside you, is more like it. Jockey's Ridge State Park in Nags Head, with the highest sand dunes on the East Coast, is great for launching and landing. ~ Route 158, Milepost 13, Nags Head; 919-441-4124, 800-334-4777.

On the northern Banks in Corolla, **Corolla Flight** will also take you hang gliding. ~ 1194 Ocean Trail, Corolla; 919-453-4800.

SURFING & WIND-SURFING

If you're into riding waves, the Outer Banks has some big ones. To rent the right surf stuff, call **Ocean Atlantic Rentals**, which rents boards from outlets in Corolla, Duck, Nags Head and Avon. ~ 800-635-9559. **North Beach Sailing** rents windsurfers and offers lessons on how to use them. ~ Route 12, Duck; 919-261-7100. On Ocracoke Island, you can rent a surfboard from **Ride the Wind Surf Shop**. ~ Located on the harbor in Ocracoke Village; 919-928-6311.

KAYAKING

Kitty Hawk Kites has numerous kayak tours, the most popular being a trip around Roanoke Island, that wends through narrow creeks, marsh canals and maritime forest, with a stop at the soft-shell crab docks. Other kayak destinations: Pea Island National Wildlife Refuge (including a wonderful sunset foray), Cape Hatteras National Seashore and the Audubon Society's Pine Island Sanctuary, which, naturally, is a haven for migrating birds. ~ Route 158, Milepost 13, Nags Head; 919-441-4124, 800-334-4777.

When the weather's right, the kayaking's great along the sound side of Ocracoke. **Ride the Wind Surf Shop** combines kayaking with snorkeling, wildlife watching and local history. Afternoon tours include a snorkel stop and, if the wind allows, a trip up Teach's Hole, where Blackbeard supposedly met his demise. There are sunset and sunrise tours as well, and nighttime excursions when the moon is full. ~ Located on the harbor in Ocracoke Village; 919-928-6311.

RIDING STABLES

What could be more satisfying than exploring the beach on horseback? Guided rides are offered at **Buxton Stables** on Hatteras Island. ~ Route 12, Buxton; 919-995-4659. On Ocracoke Island these rides are given by **Seaside Stables**. ~ Route 12; 919-928-3778.

GOLF

Serious sand dunes and prevailing winds make for some challenging golf along the North Carolina Coast.

On the Outer Banks you can tee up at **Duck Woods Golf Course**. ~ Dogwood Trail, off Route 158; Southern Shores; 919-261-2609. In Kitty Hawk, go to **Sea Scape Golf Course**. ~ Mile Post 2½, off Route 158, Kitty Hawk; 919-261-2158. In Nags Head, there's **Nags Head Golf Links**. ~ 5615 South Seachase Drive, Nags Head;

919-441-8074. There are also nine scenic holes on Hatteras Island at the **Ocean Edge Golf Course**. ~ Route 12, Frisco; 919-995-4100.

In the Albemarle Region, there's an 18-hole course at **Goose Creek Golf & Country Club**. ~ Route 158, Grandy; 919-453-4008. There's also an 18-hole course at **The Sound Golf Links**. ~ Albemarle Plantation, Holiday Island Road, Hertford; 919-426-5555.

Courses along the Neuse River Region include **Carolina Pines Golf & Country Club**. ~ 390 Carolina Pines Boulevard, between New Bern and Havelock; 919-444-1000. Also in the area is **Brandywine Bay**. ~ Route 70 West, Morehead City; 919-247-2541. **Bogue Banks Country Club** is also in the region. ~ Pine Knoll Shores; 919-726-1034. Another golf club is **Star Hill Golf and Country Club**. ~ 202 Clubhouse Drive, Cape Carteret; 919-393-8111. A final choice for the Neuse River Region is **Silver Creek Golf Club**. ~ Route 58, just north of Cape Carteret; 919-393-8058.

On the Cape Fear Coast, there's **Belvedere Plantation Golf and Country Club**. ~ 2368 Country Club Drive, Hampstead; 910-270-2703. **Beau Rivage Plantation Golf & Country Club** is also on this coast. ~ 6230 Carolina Beach Road, Wilmington; 910-392-9022, 800-628-7080. Another option is the **Porters Neck Plantation and Country Club**. ~ 1202 Porters Neck Road, off Route 17 north of Wilmington; 910-686-1177. Also on the Cape Fear Coast is **The Gauntlet Golf Club at St. James Plantation**. ~ Route 211 East, Southport; 910-253-3008, 800-247-4806. From Southport it's a 20-minute ferry ride to **Bald Head Island Golf Course**, a George Cobb masterpiece with ocean views and windy links. ~ Bald Head Island; 910-457-7310, 800-234-1666. A bit farther south on Ocean Isle, try **Brick Landing Plantation**. ~ Route 179; 910-754-4373.

TENNIS

If the wind's too wild on the Outer Banks, you can play indoors at **Pine Island Indoor Racquet Club**. ~ Route 12, two miles north of Sanderling; 919-453-8525. There are outdoor courts at **Dare County Recreation Center**. ~ Carolinian Circle, Kill Devil Hills. **Manteo Middle School**. also has outdoor courts ~ Route 64, Manteo.

The Albemarle Region has **Elizabeth Street Tennis Courts** in Elizabeth City. ~ Elizabeth Street.

In the Neuse River Region, grab a racquet and head for the **West New Bern Recreation Center**. ~ Pine Tree Drive, New Bern. Try **Swinson Park** if you're in Morehead City. ~ Country Club Road, Morehead City. Also in the region is **Mariner's Park**. ~ Sea Level.

There are seven courts at the city of Wilmington's **Empie Park** on the Cape Fear Coast. ~ 3450 Park Avenue.

BIKING

Flat terrain and hundreds of miles of back roads make the North Carolina coast ideal for bicycling. For excellent bike-trail maps, you should contact the North Carolina Department of Transpor-

Text continued on page 312.

Where the
Fish Are

Even on the wickedest windy days, you will see fishers along the North Carolina Coast, cocooned in down jackets, huddled against a horizon of frothy water, eyes trained on a multitude of monofilament angling out to sea. You ponder the obvious: They are either out of their minds, or they are catching a lot of fish.

It turns out to be the fish (though some would argue the former, too). Something's nearly always running off the coast of North Carolina: channel bass in spring; Spanish mackerel, whiting and flounder in summer; small bluefish in fall. Pompano, the perennial surf fish, shows up in spring and isn't chased off until wintertime, though it's often most plentiful in September. Spiny dogfish, a beach shark, prefers the winter. Sea trout can appear any time of year.

Big bluefish, one of the most exciting catches, are hunted relentlessly nearly year-round. Writes Robert J. Goldstein in his *Coastal Fishing in the Carolinas*: "Bluefish are voracious. They will hit anything that moves and most things that won't, will chop schools of baitfish to pieces, leaving gore and flesh in the water, stuff themselves like angler fish with elastic bellies, chase food up onto the beach and even strand themselves in the process, engaging in feeding frenzies like packs of sharks."

But perhaps the most exciting part of fishing off the North Carolina coast is you don't need a boat. Along the 300 miles of coast, numerous beaches, jetties and piers put you in touch with the fish. More than a quarter of all Atlantic piers are located here.

Certain piers and beaches are renowned for certain fish. On the Outer Banks, the **Nags Head Pier** draws bluefish and channel bass in spring and fall; mullet, striped bass and speckled trout in early winter; and flounder all summer. ~ Milepost 12, Nags Head; 919-441-5141. On summer nights, sharkers head for **Jennette Pier**, one of the few piers allowing shark fishing. ~ Milepost 16½, Nags Head; 919-441-6116. Years back, 600- and 700-pound sharks were pretty common here but now they're more like 50 pounds. The **Outer Banks Pier** is a haven for king and Spanish mackerel and also for flounder, spots, croakers, kingfish and cobia. ~ Milepost 18½, Nags Head; 919-441-5740.

Cast your line in the surf at **Coquina Beach** on Bodie Island and you could land a whiting, flounder or pompano. Sand fleas, those white, beetle-like bugs that burrow in the surf sand, are the bait of choice.

Oregon Inlet, between Bodie Island and Hatteras Island, is the Grand Central Station of coastal fishing. Fast currents carry a stream of fish between the ocean and Pamlico Sound. From the catwalks along the Bonner Bridge, which spans the inlet, you can hook anything from a gray sea trout, big bluefish, or puffer to a croaker, flounder or young tautog. The local way to fish the inlet is from West Point, on the southern tip of Bodie Island, but you can only get there in a beach buggy or with four-wheel drive.

On Hatteras Island, **Avon Pier** and the beaches on either side are famed for red drum. ~ Route 12, Avon. The remote beaches of **Ocracoke Island** offer good fishing for pompano, bluefish and sea mullet, with privacy to match. If you find they're not biting, try again close to the ends of Ocracoke, near the inlets.

The piers along the **Bogue Banks** in the Neuse River Region are known for big amberjack and tarpon. In the surf at **Wrightsville Beach** on the Cape Fear Coast, there's usually flounder and pompano, particularly near Carolina Beach Inlet. The southernmost beach in North Carolina, **Sunset Beach Pier** offers a secluded locale for pulling in spots, flounder, speckled trout, Spanish mackerel and even king mackerel. ~ 910-579-6630.

To find out what's biting and where, call the **Dare County Tourist Bureau**. ~ 919-473-2138, 800-446-6262. Of course, you won't need a tourist bureau to tell you when fish are biting. You'll know it by the roadways crowded with trucks whose front grills are fastened with fishing rod racks. The rods stick straight up in the racks in front of the truck and the windshield, and makes you wonder how all those fishers can see where they're going.

tation's Bicycle Program. ~ P.O. Box 25201, Raleigh, NC 27611; 919-733-2804.

If you like biking by the beach, head for the Outer Banks. Starting in Corolla, separate bike and golf cart paths parallel **Route 12** for several miles south.

The roads around Kitty Hawk and Kill Devil Hills aren't much fun in season (way too much traffic), but you can cruise the beach at low tide.

South of Kill Devil Hills, get on **Route 12** in Whalebone and head south on Hatteras Island for 58 miles. Then you can board the ferry for Ocracoke and continue another 14 miles. Remote, scenic and punctuated with a picturesque fishing village, Ocracoke is a marvelous place for a bike ride. From the village you can catch a ferry south to Cedar Island and continue biking along Route 12, or west to Swan Quarter and ride along lonesome **Route 264**.

In the Albemarle Region, you might start in Currituck on **Route 168** and head west to Elizabeth City via **Route 34**. From Elizabeth City, **Routes 37 and 137** are pleasant western rides. For a cruise through coastal forest and serene fishing towns, pick up **Route 32** near Goose Creek State Park, follow it through Bath, North Carolina's oldest town. From Bath, **Route 99** to Belhaven is also a scenic road less traveled.

Both Beaufort and Swansboro in the Neuse River Region are wonderful places to ride. Beaufort has a six-mile designated bike route that takes in historic **Front Street** along the harbor. Swansboro is only a few blocks of skinny streets along the White Oak River. Just across the river, pick up **Route 58** for a scenic stretch through Croatan National Forest.

Along the Cape Fear Coast, try the 38-mile **Venus Flytrap Route**. It starts on **Route 210** just south of Route 172 and runs along Topsail Island, then cuts inland to the woods north of Wilmington. Be on the lookout for Venus flytraps, native to the southern coast of North Carolina.

A five-and-a-half-mile route winds through scenic Southport along the Cape Fear River, taking in tranquil neighborhoods, an 1804 burial ground and a maritime museum.

The 36-mile **South Brunswick Islands Route** follows **Route 17** north from the South Carolina border, with opportunities for side trips to remote Sunset Beach, Ocean Isle and Holden Beach.

Bike Rentals   On the Outer Banks, **Ocean Atlantic Rentals** has beach cruisers at locations in Corolla, Duck, Nags Head and Avon. ~ 800-635-9559. You might also try **Bike Barn**. ~ 1312 Wrightsville Avenue, Mile Post 9½, Kill Devil Hills; 919-441-3786. In Nags Head, try **Lifesaver Rent-Alls**. ~ Route 12, Mile Post 9, Nags Head; 919-441-6048. On Hatteras Island, **Island Cycles** rents beach cruisers as well as six-speed cruisers and mountain bikes. ~ Route

12, Avon; 919-995-4336. **Lee Robinson General Store** has beach
cruisers as well. ~ Hatteras Village; 919-986-2381. **The Slushy Stand**
is the place for beach cruisers on Ocracoke Island. ~ Route 12,
Ocracoke Village; 919-928-1878.

Up in the Albemarle Region, bikes are for rent from **Cycle
Gallery.** ~ 311 South Hughes Boulevard, Elizabeth City; 919-338-
1559. You can also try **Chair and Equipment Rentals.** ~ Broad
Street, Edenton; 919-482-7368.

In the Neuse River Region, the **Surf Zone** has bikes. ~ Atlantic
Beach; 919-247-1103. So does **Ronnie's Bicycle Shop.** ~ Route 58,
Cape Carteret; 919-393-7161.

You can rent bikes on the Cape Fear Coast at **Aussie Island Surf
Shop.** ~ 1319 Military Cutoff Road, Wilmington; 910-256-5454.

All distances listed for hiking trails are one way unless otherwise
noted.

HIKING

THE OUTER BANKS   The ultimate stroll by the sea, **Cape Hatteras
Beach Trail** starts at Whalebone Junction (Route 12) south for
75.8 miles. The trail temporarily ends at land's end—the southern
tip of Hatteras Island—then picks up again on the north tip of
Ocracoke Island. Hikers need only take the scenic 2¼-hour free
ferry ride between islands.

The **Nags Head Woods Preserve Trails** (4 miles) wind through
coastal forest filled with hickories, maples and other hardwoods.
Located on Ocean Acres Drive, off Route 150 (turn at Milepost
9½, across from Pigman's Bar-B-Q). The preserve is open various
days and hours, so call 919-441-2522 before you go.

ALBEMARLE REGION   An 1800s plantation **Carriage Trail** (8.2
miles round-trip) at Pettigrew State Park is now a nature trail that
wends past Somerset Place (the plantation) and along picturesque
Phelps Lake to the west end of Cypress Point.

The **Live Oak Trail** (1.2 miles) at Goose Creek State Park tunnels through caverns of live oak trees, following the sandy shoreline of the Pamlico River.

NEUSE RIVER REGION   The **Island Creek Forest Walk** (.5 mile)
within Croatan National Forest is a leisurely loop through colossal trees, some 12 stories high. Bald cypress, American beech, black
walnut, and white and red oaks are some of the species labeled on
the trail, which begins along Route 1004, off Route 17.

Boardwalks take you part of the way on the **Cedar Point Tide-
land Trail** (1.4 miles), a walk through an estuary in Croatan
National Forest. Pine and hardwood forest and seagrasses are the
landscape here. There are platforms for getting close-up looks at
wildlife.

For a longer walk within the national forest, take the moderately difficult **Neusiok Trail** (20.4 miles) and journey through ford

palmetto swamps, sandy ridges and beaches, loblolly pine woods and the swampy bogs called pocosins. The trailhead is at the Pinecliff Recreation Area, off Cherry Branch Road near Havelock.

CAPE FEAR COAST If you've never seen a Venus flytrap, take the **Flytrap Trail** (.4 mile) at Carolina Beach State Park. For a longer jaunt the trail joins up with the **Sugarloaf Trail** (2.8 miles), **Campground Trail** (1 mile) and **Swamp Trail** (.8 mile).

▼▼▼▼▼▼▼▼▼▼▼
Transportation

CAR

The Outer Banks' main drag (and only road in some spots) is two-lane **Route 12**, which commences in Corolla and runs all the way through Ocracoke Island. The four-lane **Route 158**, known as "The Bypass," parallels Route 12 through Whalebone, Nags Head and Kill Devil Hills, providing faster but less scenic travel.

Route 17 is the common thread along the Coastal Plain. It comes in from Virginia and veers southwest through Elizabeth City, New Bern and Wilmington to the South Carolina line. **Route 40** is the interstate highway that connects the coast with the rest of North Carolina, heading northwest from Wilmington to Raleigh and Durham, then on to Winston-Salem and, finally, to Asheville in the mountains.

AIR

Two small and pleasant commercial airports are located along the North Carolina Coast: **Craven County Regional Airport** near New Bern, served by USAir Express, and **New Hanover International Airport** in Wilmington, served by Delta, Midway and USAir.

Taxis are your best bet for transportation from the airports to towns in the surrounding area.

Many people headed for the north part of the coast fly into **Norfolk International Airport** in Virginia, 90 minutes by car from the northern Outer Banks. Norfolk is served by most major domestic airlines, including American Airlines, Continental Airlines, Delta Airlines, Northwest Airlines, TWA, United Airlines and USAir.

The **Norfolk Airport Shuttle** can take you into town from the airport. ~ 804-857-1231.

BUS

Carolina Trailways, a subsidiary of **Trailways Bus Lines**, has locations in several cities. They are in Elizabeth City at 118 South Hughes Boulevard, 919-335-5183; in New Bern at 504 Guion Street, 919-633-3100; and in Morehead City at 1212 Arendell Street, 919-726-3029.

Greyhound Bus Lines (800-231-2222) has a station in Wilmington. ~ 201 Harnett Street; 910-762-6625.

FERRY

The **North Carolina Department of Transportation** operates seven year-round ferry routes along the coast: between Currituck and Knotts Island; Hatteras and Ocracoke; Ocracoke and Cedar Island;

Ocracoke and Swan Quarter; Aurora and Bayview islands; Minnesott and Cherry Branch; and Southport and Fort Fisher. ~ 919-726-6446.

Automobiles, motorcycles and bicycles are welcome on all the boats, though reservations are required on some routes. In the summer, call at least a month ahead. For departures from Ocracoke, call 919-928-3841, 800-345-1665. For departures from Cedar Island, call 919-225-3551, 800-856-0343.

Several private ferries offer service to Cape Lookout National Seashore, mainly in the summer and fall. From Ocracoke Island, **The Austins** will take you to Portsmouth Island, the seashore's southernmost island. ~ 919-928-4361. **Morris Marina Ferry Service** leaves from the little town of Atlantic, near Cedar Island. ~ 919-225-4261. **Alger Willis Fishing Camps** departs from the village of Davis. ~ 919-729-2791. From Harkers Island, you can board a ferry at **Cape Lookout Ferry Service**. ~ 919-728-3575. You can also board **Sand Dollar Ferry** here. ~ 504-3939. In Beaufort, **Outer Banks Ferry Service** has boats going over to Cape Lookout. ~ 919-728-4129.

For more on North Carolina ferries, see the section titled "On the Sea for Free" in this chapter.

CAR RENTALS

On the Outer Banks, you can rent a car from **Atlantic Auto Rental**. ~ Located on Route 158, Milepost 9, Kill Devil Hills; 919-441-7256, 800-441-2503.

In Elizabeth City, try **City Auto Rentals**. ~ 110 South Hughes Boulevard; 919-335-1224. Also in Elizabeth City is **National Interrent**. ~ 1819 North Road Street; 919-335-1860.

At the Craven County Regional Airport just outside New Bern, there's **Avis Rent A Car** (800-331-1212), **Hertz Rent A Car** (800-654-3131) and **National Interrent** (800-328-4567).

At New Hanover International Airport in Wilmington there is **Avis Rent A Car** (800-331-1212), **Budget Rent A Car** (800-527-0700) and **Hertz Rent A Car** (800-654-3131). A few minutes from the airport you'll find **Agency Rent A Car** (910-799-6622), **Enterprise Rent A Car** (800-325-8007) and **Triangle Rent A Car** (910-251-9812).

At Norfolk International Airport, you can rent a car from **Alamo Rent A Car** (800-327-9633), **Avis Rent A Car** (800-331-1212), **Budget Rent A Car** (800-527-0700) and **Hertz Rent A Car** (800-654-3131).

PUBLIC TRANSIT

As you might imagine, most coastal towns are too small to support public bus service. However, **Inter-County Public Transportation Authority** can get you around Elizabeth City and Currituck County. ~ 919-338-4480. Down south, the **Wilmington Transit Authority** operates routes in the city of Wilmington. ~ 910-343-0106.

TAXIS

In the Outer Banks, catch a ride from **Beach Cab** (919-441-2500), **Hollywood Cabs** (919-441-3777), **Island Taxi** (919-441-8803) or **Winslow Taxi Co.** (919-335-7180).

Cherry Cab Company (919-447-3101) serves Craven County Regional Airport. Around New Bern, there's also **New Taxi Service** (919-636-9000) and **Safeway Cab Co.** (919-633-2828). **Yellow Cab** (910-762-3322) is at Hanover International Airport.

At the Norfolk International Airport in Virginia you'll find **Yellow Cab** (804-622-3232), **Black and White** (804-489-7777) and **Norfolk Checker** (804-855-3333).

NINE

The South Carolina Coast

South Carolina's coast is not long, only about 200 miles, but its northern and southern stretches are nothing alike. In the north, Myrtle Beach and the Grand Strand resemble a big amusement park by the sea, all neon and newness, souvenir shops and chain eateries and golf courses appearing over and over, like a movie reel that keeps rewinding. The beaches are sugary silver, the water radiant and slurpy, the dunes silky swells of sand tracing the shore.

The south is the Lowcountry, dark, watery and mysterious, a mosaic of marshland and blackwater swamps, rivers and creeks flushed by tides. In the salty haze of a Lowcountry morning, you can see the silhouette of those wading out onto the flats to catch crabs and gather oysters. Shrimp boats, their nets spread wide much like angels' wings, slip into shore burdened with the night's bounty. Gullah women, African-Americans descended from plantation slaves, wade into the marshes to cut sweetgrass for their baskets. It is said that at night, some of them steal into the moss-sheltered depths of cypress swamps to practice voodoo.

The Lowcountry seems ancient. Gnarly cypress trees ramble low and long over rivers, and mammoth live oaks festooned with Spanish moss arch above country lanes. Bridges snake along seas of tidal grass glinting green in the sun and rippling in the wind. At low tide, the brown caps of oyster beds poke up and spread their primal scent into the air.

These are the tides of Pat Conroy's book *The Prince of Tides*, which was made into a movie. "Breathe deeply, and you would . . . remember that smell for the rest of your life," Conroy wrote, "the bold, fecund aroma of the tidal marsh, exquisite and sensual, the smell of the South in heat, a smell like new milk, semen, and spilled wine, all perfumed with seawater."

The scent of Charleston is equally as sensuous, though different. Musky sprays of Confederate jasmine perfume the sidewalks, and honeysuckle and yellow jessamine overtake the cemeteries. To walk among the tombstones is a heady experience. Magnolia trees thrust their fragrant blossoms above cobbled streets. There is the smell of loquat and wintersweet and sweet bay, of gardens growing for centuries and barely contained by walls of wrought iron and brick.

Charleston is old, the oldest city in South Carolina. The English founded the settlement in 1670 and named it Charles Town after King Charles II. He was a hedonistic king who loved women and wine, horses and the theater. Four of his many mistresses were actresses. And so his Colonial trading port grew as a place of societal pleasures, with music and art and galas lavished with food and drink. English, French and Irish immigrants poured into Charleston and got rich trading deerskins, sugar and rum. They built the grandest homes in Colonial America and planted exquisite formal gardens. Then everyone planted rice.

The Lowcountry's labyrinth of rivers and tidal creeks made it perfect for growing rice. The Europeans didn't know how to grow it but the Africans did, having cultivated it for centuries in the Congo-Angola region. Rice growing is labor-intensive, and the slave trade grew vigorously. Indigo soon joined rice as a major crop. White traders couldn't import enough slaves to work the rice and indigo plantations springing up across the Lowcountry. Crowds could be counted on at the Charleston slave market, where gaunt, shackled Africans were auctioned like livestock. The city became the Hades of Africans and slave port of America.

The Civil War brought Charleston to its knees. After a siege in February 1865, the "Cradle of Secession" was nearly in ruins, the gardens a tangle of weeds, slave markets and rice warehouses deserted, slaves finally freed. Plantations became the ghosts of the Lowcountry. Reconstruction was slow and disasters many. A hurricane struck Charleston in 1885 and a great earthquake in 1886.

Charleston's story is of a city that should not have been. It is impossibly built on a tongue of marshland with rivers on either side, threatened by tides at every turn, and by the ravages of weather and war. Fires have five times rearranged the town. But despite the tornadoes, earthquakes and hurricanes, invasions by Indians, Revolutionary forces and Sherman's Army, Charleston barely budged. By the 1920s, the city was again firmly the aristocrat of the South. Now its historic area, saturated with more than 4000 buildings, is a monument to the city's tenacity.

For centuries, writers have tried to typify Charleston, to explain its existence, but this is not an easy task. The city is complex, with attitudes and ways that can either enchant or dismay, seduce or frustrate. The place William Allen White called "the most civilized town in the world" is indeed vastly charming, slavish to manners, though proud, stubborn and eccentric.

Charlestonians have always been selective with their tolerance. In the late 1600s, Quakers and Huguenots, Jews and Baptists, and other religious rebels were warmly welcomed into town. A hundred years later, Charleston embraced slavery like no place else in the South. Today, it is the only city in South Carolina with a considerable gay scene, and the only one where, six generations removed from the Civil War, people still haven't forgiven Abraham Lincoln for interrupting their garden parties. The Civil War started in Charleston, and here it is simply called "The War" or "The Late Unpleasantness."

Today's Charleston is a walking town, its brick and cobblestone blocks filled with architectural exquisitry: glorious Gothic Revival churches, Classical Revival synagogues, Art Deco theaters, and seemingly endless manses of Georgian, Colonial,

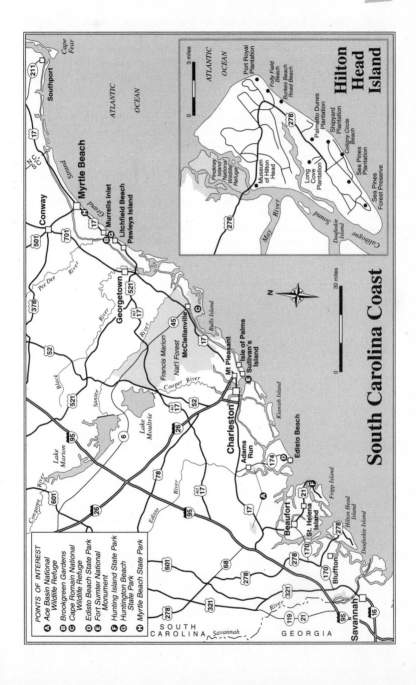

Hilton Head Island

ATLANTIC OCEAN

Port Royal Plantation
Folly Field Beach
Dunes Beach
Road Beach
Palmetto Dunes Plantation
Shipyard Plantation
Coligny Circle Beach
Sea Pines Plantation
Sea Pines Forest Preserve

Pinckney Island National Wildlife Refuge
Museum of Hilton Head
Long Cove Plantation

May River
Calibogue Sound
Daufuskie Island

0   3 miles

South Carolina Coast

Cape Fear
Southport
211
17
ATLANTIC OCEAN
N.C.
S.C.
Myrtle Beach
Conway
Murrells Inlet
Litchfield Beach
Pawleys Island
Grand Strand
501
701
17
B
Pee Dee River
378
Georgetown
521
52
Black River
Santee River
521
Francis Marion Natl Forest
45
McClellanville
C
Bulls Island
17
Lake Marion
95
Lake Moultrie
6
Cooper River
26
52
17
Isle of Palms
Sullivan's Island
E
Mt Pleasant
Charleston
Adams Run
174
D
Edisto Beach
Kiawah Island
601
Congaree River
78
Edisto River
95
17
A
Beaufort
21
St. Helena Island
F
Fripp Island
Hilton Head Island
170
278
Daufuskie Island
26
68
601
278
170
Bluffton
321
119
21
321
SOUTH CAROLINA
Savannah River
GEORGIA
Savannah
16
95

N   30 miles
0

POINTS OF INTEREST
A Ace Basin National Wildlife Refuge
B Brookgreen Gardens
C Cape Romain National Wildlife Refuge
D Edisto Beach State Park
E Fort Sumter National Monument
F Hunting Island State Park
G Huntington Beach State Park
H Myrtle Beach State Park

Federal, Italianate and Neoclassical design. The Charleston Museum, founded in 1773 and the oldest museum in the nation, looks back at the city's florid history.

The past may be worshiped in Charleston, but the present is in full force. Bohemian coffeehouses, gay cafes, extravagant inns and guesthouses, and the savviest shops in the Carolinas are here. Excellent restaurants are abundant, with many eateries focusing on distinctive Lowcountry cuisine—those sweet, sultry flavors of farm and sea.

Just outside the city and reposing across the countryside are proud old plantations, their walls reduced to cinder by the Civil War and remarkably revived this century. The enormity and elaborateness of their antebellum manors stand in harsh contrast to the cold brick cavities that were their slave quarters. Four plantations are open for touring, though it would take several days to see them all fully—and that's not counting Charleston.

As for the rest of the South Carolina coast, it can easily be canvassed in a week or two. Some people, however, prefer to park their blankets in the sand at Myrtle Beach and stay all summer. Nearly ten million visitors crowd into this beachy town every year, primarily from March through September, when the ocean is clear and clement and the boardwalk alive with amusement rides and the smell of popcorn and cotton candy.

Promoters call the Myrtle Beach area the Grand Strand, a ribbon of beach towns beginning below the North Carolina border at North Myrtle Beach and running south 60 miles to Litchfield. Besides being some of the Carolinas' best sands (some would say the best), the Strand has a lengthy parade of strip shopping centers, miniature golf courses, fast-food joints, buffet seafood houses and campgrounds—Disney World by the sea, only without the theme parks. The Strand is lately being called "Nashville by the Sea" for the country music theaters mushrooming along the coast. Families naturally love it here, and so do golfers; more than 80 courses are set along the Strand.

The Lowcountry starts nearly a hundred miles south of Myrtle Beach in Charleston, situated almost halfway down the South Carolina coast. South of Charleston, the pine and palmetto forests are immense and dense, the tourist scene slow-paced. Kiawah and Seabrook are resort islands with groomed grounds and an affluent clientele. Edisto Island, with its weathered stilt cottages, is more casual and kind of cluttered.

Then there's Beaufort (say "BEW-furt;" BO-fort is in North Carolina), antebellum all the way, a sparkling port town with beautiful old houses and a fast-growing tourist business. From Beaufort, a bridge leads to a series of secluded sea islands, including St. Helena Island, Hunting Island and Fripp Island, swirled with marshlands and trimmed in lonesome beaches.

South across the Broad River, the scenery couldn't be more different. Hilton Head Island, civilization's last fling before Savannah, Georgia, is an exclusive, expensive enclave for golfers, shoppers and beachgoers. Sprawling resorts and country club communities have been meticulously placed among the pine woods, their entrances and lawns given a Disneyesque manicure. The beaches here are long, lovely and—like the roadways—jammed in summer, though if you care to walk a bit you can always find a hidden stretch of sand.

Plenty of people who live in Myrtle Beach are older
than the city. Incorporated in 1938 with about 1200
residents, it was mostly a thick forest of pine and
myrtle trees by the Atlantic Ocean. There was a hotel as early as
1901, though guests of the Seaside Inn had to contend with razor-
back hogs rooting beneath their cottages.

▼▼▼▼▼▼▼▼▼▼▼▼▼

Myrtle Beach Area

As late as the early 1970s, Myrtle Beach was a laid-back community that slowly swelled in summer with the arrival of a few
thousand families, college students and older folks who liked to
shag. The shaggers, who started coming in the late 1940s, hung out
around North Myrtle Beach and danced their jitterbug-like dance
to beach music. The families rented quiet cottages among the dunes,
while the college students flocked to the Myrtle Beach Pavilion and
its carnival atmosphere. Winters were frightfully quiet.

Today, an estimated ten million people pack into the Myrtle
Beach area every year. They are drawn by sun, sand and surf, and
by the pop-top fun of a place swarming with pancake houses,
waterslides, all-you-can-eat seafood houses, batting cages, outlet
stores, T-shirt shops and big-name country music show houses.
The selection of golf is mind-jolting: nearly 100 regular courses and
26 miniature courses, including one of the former with a gondola
ride over water and one of the latter with an imitation erupting vol-
cano. In the bar at one course, waiters stand on your table and
throw napkins at you. A few big patches of coastal forest and
marsh remain, but they are fast being eaten by development. The
last empty oceanfront lots were for sale in 1995.

Route 17, called Kings Highway through Myrtle Beach, is the main
north–south Grand Strand thoroughfare, but it won't let you see
the beach. For the most part, it is a monument to neon and visual
chaos, with more businesses and signs crowding along than it is
possible for a motorist going a reasonable speed to glimpse. There
are also many signs for "plantations," though they hold no resem-
blance to their historic counterparts, but are sprawling modern developments and country club communities. There are numerous
restored and rebuilt plantations along South Carolina's coast, but
only a few, mainly those around Charleston, open their doors to
the masses.

SIGHTS

From Route 17, various side roads make it easy enough to cut
over to the ocean and small communities like **Cherry Grove Beach**,
near the northern end of the Strand. It's quieter, campier and less
expensive up here than in Myrtle Beach. Mom-and-pop motels
gather near the sea, and vendors sell hot dogs and pretzels.

Just south of Cherry Grove, **Ocean Drive Beach** is the heart of
shagging and beach music, pop culture of the late 1940s and 1950s.
Carolinas beach music was born of Southern black rhythm-and-

blues; shagging was born of the jitterbug, the former being a softer, sultrier dance ritual. In 1985, South Carolina made shag the official state dance. Each spring and fall, thousands of shaggers pour into Ocean Drive for the S.O.S. (Society of Stranders) weekend.

From Ocean Drive Beach, Route 65 follows the shore through the breezy, laid-back communities of **Crescent Beach**, **Atlantic Beach** and **Windy Hill Beach**, where families settle into the many cottages lining the dunes during summer. The sands are usually quieter up here than in Myrtle Beach, about ten miles south.

The central nerve of **Myrtle Beach** is the **Myrtle Beach Pavilion and Amusement Park** an old-time, horseshoe-shaped complex with carnival rides, goofy golf, a carousel, loud rock-and-roll and waterslides parked right next to the sand. Closed November through February. Admission. ~ Ocean Boulevard and 9th Avenue North; 803-448-6456.

A blur of neon and fluorescent light emanates around The Pavilion, with souvenir shops, video arcades and places selling pizza, corn dogs and fried onion rings. There is the constant prowl of traffic, which reaches deadlock during spring break and holidays and some summer weekends. Here, too, is **Ripley's Believe It or Not! museum** with such unbelievable exhibits as a four-eyed man and an eight-foot model of Cleopatra's barge made with pastry sugar. Best are the hair balls, especially the 5¾-pounder extracted from the stomach of a cow and donated by Lancaster Frozen Foods of Lancaster, South Carolina. Admission. ~ 901 North Ocean Boulevard; 803-448-2331.

A few blocks away, the **Myrtle Beach Area Chamber of Commerce** has loads of information on area sights and pursuits, including golf. ~ 1200 North Oak Street; 803-626-7444, 800-356-3016.

Only 12 miles south of Myrtle Beach, the sandy shores melt into salt marsh and the tourist trappings transform into caverns of live oaks laced with moss. Here, along Route 17 Business, **Murrells Inlet** has several thousand residents and over two dozen seafood

HIDDEN ▶

✔ CHECK THESE OUT—UNIQUE SIGHTS

- Stroll among hundreds of garden sculptures, fountains and ponds that fill the scenery at **Brookgreen Gardens**. *page 323*
- Wander down mansion-lined streets in Charleston's **Battery**, where many of the oldest and wealthiest families live. *page 338*
- Spend a few hours—or days—in the superb Southern town of **Beaufort**, filled with beautiful old homes and oaks. *page 361*
- Leave traffic and traffic lights behind as you travel the **sea islands**, Lowcountry lairs that seem lost in time. *page 363*

shacks tucked beneath the trees. The fishing village of weathered clapboard homes and sloops is much older than Myrtle Beach, having been founded in the early 1700s. Blackbeard and other pirates supposedly sailed up into the inlet.

A few miles south of the inlet lies the Strand's premier attraction and one of the finest in the state. **Brookgreen Gardens** was once home to the rice and indigo plantations of prominent Old South families, but it is now the oldest and largest public sculpture garden in the country. In 1930, New York millionaires Archer and Anna Hyatt Huntington bought the land as a winter retreat. Anna was a sculptress who needed a place to showcase her work. She designed a garden in the shape of a butterfly and set within it her bold, hauntingly detailed pieces of bronze. Soon she collected other works, and began devising a museum of American sculpture, as well as a wildlife sanctuary. Admission. ~ Route 17 South; 803-237-4218, 800-849-1931.

Today, the outdoor gallery holds more than 500 sculptures of bronze, marble, metal, limestone and granite, including 36 pieces by Anna. You'll need several hours to stroll these several hundred acres of cloistered quiet, punctuated by birdsong and tablets of poetry. There are reed-filled ponds and gushing fountains, fields of Irish ivy and flowering quinces. There are extraordinary live oaks with crazily twisted trunks trailing high into the sky, and white-barked crepe myrtles whose lithe, marble-smooth trunks are natural sculptures.

Walk down the Magnolia Allée and be overwhelmed by glossy green leaves and redolent white blossoms. Go to the Palmetto Gardens and have a look at the state tree. Walk within the Cypress Bird Sanctuary, an aviary under mesh, and watch the ibis sweep the black muck for insects. Then stroll through the other wildlife areas, where forested enclosures contain birds of prey, fox, deer, otters and alligators. You can bring a lunch and picnic at one of the tables, or eat at the Terrace Cafe, which has good, budget-priced sandwiches and breakfasts.

The cypress swamps and hammocks surrounding Brookgreen were thriving rice plantations until the Civil War. Today, Brookgreen offers a 50-minute tour aboard a pontoon boat. As you cruise the Waccamaw River you will be introduced to the flora, fauna and history of this part of the Lowcountry.

South of Brookgreen on Route 17, you know you're in **Litchfield** and **Pawleys Island** when the medians take shape, lushly planted and looking like they have their own personal gardener. On the roadsides, exclusive shopping enclaves and country club communities are sheltered in the recesses of ambling, moss-draped oaks. Two hundred years ago, the area was equally as prosperous—but because of rice. **Litchfield Plantation** was the center of

Text continued on page 326.

Taking the Country to the Sea

Myrtle Beach has gone country. In little more than a decade, six country music theaters have sprung up within stomping distance of the sand—elaborate imitations of colonial showhalls that resound with twangy tunes. The shows range from big-name country concerts and patriotic pageants to orchestral extravaganzas with a little gospel and Elvis thrown in. The entertainment is clean, feel-good fun—no booze or smoking inside. Families love the shows, and so do church and school groups. Charter buses pour in daily for matinees and nighttime shows.

Missourian Calvin Gilmore got the country show ball rolling in Myrtle Beach. A good guitar player but a much better businessman, Gilmore opened The Carolina Opry in 1986 and was instantly successful. Others were quick to open theaters, including country superstars Alabama, Dolly Parton and Ronnie Milsap. Then came developers, who fashioned elaborate entertainment complexes with showhalls that offered more than country—big-band and jazz, variety and comedy acts, Vegas-style magic shows and impersonators, and an improbable genre called rock-and-roll gospel.

Now, Gilmore's own **Carolina Opry** mixes shimmery costumes and big-band with Western swing, comedy, bluegrass and gospel. It all happens in a sparkling sandstone show house surrounded by palm trees and crowned with a cupola. Located in uptown Myrtle Beach, Carolina Opry even has a television studio. Closed January. ~ 8901-A Route 17 business, Myrtle Beach; 803-238-8888, 800-843-6779.

Country supergroup Alabama (which played its first gig in Myrtle Beach at a hole-in-the-wall called The Bowery) has **The Alabama Theatre**. They perform about ten times a year and host weekly celebrity concerts by artists such as Emmylou Harris, Merle Haggard, Charley Pride and Crystal Gayle. Most nights, there's the "American Pride Show," a vigorous song-and-dance fest by an ensemble of young, fresh-faced performers. ~ Route 17 South, in Barefoot Landing, North Myrtle Beach; 803-272-1111, 800-342-2262.

Dolly Parton's $7.8 million **Dixie Stampede** dinner theater promises "belles, beaus, bridles, buckles and big-time fun." The cast of 250 includes 32 horses and Australia's own "electric cowboy," Greg Anderson. It's a rodeo-style Civil War saga that's dreadfully hokey, but folks seem to enjoy it while they're loading up on ribs, chicken, corn on the cob and "homemade stampede bread." There's even a non-alcoholic saloon where you can have a frozen drink in a souvenir boot mug. Closed January. ~ 8901-B Route 17 business, Myrtle Beach; 803-497-9700, 800-433-4401.

In 1994, Larry Gatlin and the Gatlin Brothers settled down in Myrtle Beach and opened the **Gatlin Brothers Theatre**. They give regular shows throughout the year; otherwise, you might get to see Roy Clark, Mel Tillis, The Charlie Daniels Band or Lee Greenwood. The Gatlins' theater is located in Fantasy Harbour, an entertainment complex that also features a high-tech ice-skating arena, medieval-style dinner theater, and the Ronnie Milsap Theatre, where Milsap performs most nights, singing his ever-popular "Smoky Mountain Rain" and "Any Day Now" songs. Both the Gatlin Brothers and Milsap theaters are closed in January. ~ On Route 501, Myrtle Beach; 803-236-8500, 800-681-5209.

The biggest, priciest showplace around is **The Palace**, a $13 million theater with 2700 seats in Broadway at the Beach, yet another Myrtle Beach entertainment complex. Big-name performers like Kenny Rogers, Wayne Newton, the Righteous Brothers and Lou Rawls play at The Palace. Closed January. ~ Route 17 bypass between 21st and 29th avenues north, Myrtle Beach; 803-448-0588, 800-905-4228.

You can see unknown performers imitating superstars at **Legends in Concert**. Some of the superstars are no longer of this world—Marilyn Monroe and Elvis Presley being two that come to mind. Closed January. ~ Route 17 business, Surfside Beach; 803-238-7827, 800-960-7469.

the universe back then, and today it holds its own in country club society. The plantation's manor house, built in 1750, offers sumptuous accommodations, though you cannot enter the grounds without an appointment (or preferably, a reservation). ~ River Road, off Route 17, Pawleys Island; 803-237-9121.

Pawleys Island has long been a summer retreat. Take one of the causeways (North or South) over from Route 17 to the small spit of land and have a look at the **1800s-vintage seaside cottages.** Most are lining Myrtle Avenue. Several are made of cypress wood culled from local swamps.

Keep on Route 17 south of Pawleys and after about ten miles you'll come to **Georgetown**, parked at the confluence of six rivers. Your first impression is of a sooty port town; smokestacks spew blackness and paper mills pour an acrid scent into the air. But past the port scene lies historic Georgetown, where neighborhoods are layered with live oaks and magnolias, prim brick churches and proud old antebellum homes wrapped in big porches. Park along the harbor at Front Street, where several blocks of storefronts are washed in pink, green and blue and edged with brick walkways.

Two small museums on either end of Front Street recall the earliest days of South Carolina's third-oldest city, founded in 1729. **The Rice Museum** has modest but informative displays on the pervasive rice culture that began in the 1730s and lasted nearly 200 years. In the 1850s, Georgetown exported more rice than any other port in the world. Admission. ~ Front and Screven streets, Georgetown; 803-546-7423.

The **Kaminski House Museum** sits on a bluff overlooking the Sampit River. Built in the late 1700s and home to the town's first intendant, or mayor, the whitewashed house is warmly decorated with antiques, including a fifteenth-century Spanish wedding chest. Admission. ~ 1003 Front Street, Georgetown; 803-546-7706.

Several local people offer walking tours, the most animated being "Miss Nell" Morris Cribb, a native Georgetonian whose tales are peppered with ghost trivia. Contact **Miss Nell's Tours**. Admission. ~ 803-546-3975. If you'd rather see the city by water, **Captain Sandy's Plantation Tours** cruise the rice plantation mansions along the Sampit River and promises "history, mystery, romance and yes gators." ~ 803-527-4106.

For more information on Georgetown, visit the **Georgetown County Chamber of Commerce**. ~ 600 Front Street, Georgetown; 803-546-8437.

LODGING

Mom-and-pop motels proliferate the northern Strand, while nondescript highrises crowd along Myrtle Beach central. Sprinkled in between are a few places with character, some offering rock-bottom budget rates in winter.

At the north end of Myrtle Beach but across the street from the beach, **Mariner** is a tiny, two-story place with tin roof, wood shakes, a cupola and weather vane. The motel rooms, efficiencies and one- and two-bedroom apartments are variously decorated with crude wood beams and walls, terrazzo floors and driftwood decor— pretty funky, all in all, but completely clean. Amenities include air conditioning, television and some gas fireplaces. ~ Located at 7003 North Ocean Boulevard, Myrtle Beach; 803-449-5281. MODERATE TO DELUXE.

Also across the street from the sand, **St. John's Inn** is a pleasant compound of three-story buildings around a courtyard with a swimming pool and very green grass. The rooms are beachy and a little outdated, but extra roomy and clean as can be. Some have kitchenettes. Next to the lobby is a '50s-era coffee shop with hanging plants and chairs of yellow vinyl persuasion. ~ 6803 North Ocean Boulevard, Myrtle Beach; 803-449-5251, 800-845-0624. MODERATE.

Serendipity is entirely unexpected, a Spanish mission–style house ◄ *HIDDEN* in a sleepy neighborhood a few minutes' walk from the beach. Small and full of charm, the sand-colored stucco building with arches is enveloped by big trees (the window of one room looks into the blossoms of a magnolia). There's a heated swimming pool and a garden room where continental breakfast is served every morning. Rooms, studios and suites are tastefully decorated in different periods, some with four-poster canopy beds and carpets. Rates are somewhat more expensive here in summer. ~ 407 71st Avenue, Myrtle Beach; 803-449-5268, 800-762-3229. BUDGET TO MODERATE.

The Strand's best beach resort lies within the Radisson-owned **Kingston Plantation**, a meticulously planned community where waterways snake around condominiums and peaked-roof townhouses with fine trimmed lawns. The hotel is an all-suite affair, with kitchens and separate bedrooms and views of the ocean. The lobby is classy and subdued, the pool area sprawls along a sweet stretch of sand. There's a top-notch spa and health club and several restaurants. If you'd rather go home-style, you can reserve a condo or townhouse, too. ~ 9800 Lake Drive, off Route 17 North, Myrtle Beach; 803-449-0006, 800-333-3333, fax 803-497-1017. ULTRA-DELUXE.

The area's other big chain hotel, **Myrtle Beach Hilton** also commands ultra-deluxe summer rates but is not nearly as plush. Indeed, the whole place feels quite campy. The atrium lobby is minimally decorated, the room doors open onto breezeways. Rooms are smallish, with wall-to-wall carpets, but almost every one has a look at the ocean. Unfortunately, erosion has eaten away most of the beach here, and waves threaten the edge of the swimming pool.

~ Arcadian Shores, off Route 17 North, Myrtle Beach; 803-449-5000, 800-248-9228. ULTRA-DELUXE.

Chesterfield Inn is in the Myrtle Beach thick of things, two blocks from The Pavilion and right on the central beach. Most interesting of local motels, the red-brick building with dormer windows dates to 1946 and has attractive rooms adorned with plush green carpets, mini-blinds and ruffled shades. Many rooms don't have a view of the water. Rooms in the newer annex do, though they have generic motel decor and AstroTurf in the halls. ~ 700 North Ocean Boulevard, Myrtle Beach; 803-448-3177, 800-392-3869, fax 803-626-4736. DELUXE.

Litchfield By The Sea is a massive place, 4500 acres of low-rolling hills and ponds, villas and cottages, and beachfront tower condominiums. You can rent any of these or opt to stay in the allsuite hotel, where rooms are spacious and decorated with embroidered sofas and wallpapers of rich navy and burgundy. All have balconies overlooking a pond. Everything's geared toward families. There are swimming pools, a health club and spa, restaurants and three golf courses. Only the condos are right on the beach; everywhere else, you'll have to walk or drive to the sand. Some units rent by the week in summer. ~ Route 17, Pawleys Island; 803-237-3000, 800-845-1897, fax 803-237-4282. MODERATE TO ULTRA-DELUXE.

The drive into **Litchfield Plantation** is precisely what you'd hope for from an Old South plantation: a tunnel of live oaks lasting a quarter-mile and framing the crisp white facade of a manor house. The house, built in 1750, for a century ruled the rice fields for miles around. Today it is a country inn, regally furnished, with four lavish suites, including one in the former ballroom that has a living room, fireplace, kitchen, and veranda overlooking the lawns. It's all within a country club community, with swimming pool and cabana, tennis courts and equestrian center, and gourmet dining in the Carriage House. A reservation or an appointment is required to enter the property. Continental breakfast is included. ~ River Road, off Route 17, Pawleys Island; 803-237-9121, 800-869-1410. ULTRA-DELUXE.

Five Thirty Prince Street is sheltered within a quiet, tree-filled neighborhood only a block from the harborfront. Built in the 1920s and restored in the 1980s, the columned, two-story house has a sunroom decorated with wicker, a garden patio and a wide porch lined with rockers. Owner Nancy Bazemore has made every room attractive and comfortable, detailing them with fireplaces and ceiling fans. One has a private deck. Rates include big breakfasts. ~ 530 Prince Street, Georgetown; 803-527-1114. MODERATE.

DINING

HIDDEN ▶

Just off busy Route 17, **Hamburger Joe's** huddles beneath oaks and pines in a tin-roofed building with a wraparound gingerbread porch. You can eat on the porch or inside in full view of the guys searing burgers on a grill. Joe's patties aren't big and heavy, just juicy and tasty. If the kids don't like burgers, there's fried bologna, hot dogs and grilled cheese. There's another Hamburger Joe's at 2501 North Kings Highway in Myrtle Beach. ~ 810 Conway Street, North Myrtle Beach; 803-272-6834. BUDGET.

Behind the faux stable facade of **Thoroughbreds** you'll find warm, inviting spaces, walls of wood and brick and banquettes of leather, all prettily lit with flickering sconces and fireplaces. The leather-bound menu lists some of the Strand's finest cuisine: roast duckling and chicken Oscar, lump crab cakes with lemon dill sauce, and shrimp *boursin* (jumbo shrimp poached in white wine, cream cheese and garlic baked in puff pastry). Reserve ahead on summer weekends. ~ 9706 Route 17 North, Myrtle Beach; 803-497-2636. DELUXE.

Collectors Cafe is easy to miss, wedged in a blur of strip shopping centers bordered by chaotic traffic. But the mood inside is entirely civilized: gleaming clay tile floors, glass tables topped with radiant bouquets, original art on the walls. A good place before or after a show, the coffeehouse and gallery serves Mediterranean cuisine (grilled fish, pasta, veal, lamb and chicken dishes) as well as elaborate cafes and desserts. ~ 7726 North Kings Highway, Myrtle Beach; 803-449-9370. MODERATE.   ◀ HIDDEN

Latif's is a European-style cafe, airy, sweet-smelling and mannerly, with fresh fare and ragingly rich desserts. The lunch sandwiches and salads are prepared with flair; try the smoked ham and jalapeño grilled on oatmeal bread. Dinner is heartier, with entrées such as grilled tenderloin wrapped in bacon and served with red-onion marmalade, and the Carolina barbecued salmon in smoky vinaigrette with tomato corn relish. The only drawback: service sometimes inches along. ~ 503 61st Avenue North, off Route 17, Myrtle Beach; 803-449-1716. MODERATE.   ◀ HIDDEN

One of the few restaurants right on the beach, **Sea Captain's House** resides in a wonderful gray house built in the 1930s, with wood shakes on the sides, twin white chimneys on top and big windows looking at the ocean. The interior is homey and hospitable, the fare focused on seafood. There's shrimp baked in phyllo, Southwestern seafood pasta, broiled scallops and Lowcountry favorites like she-crab soup and fried oysters. Breakfast, lunch and dinner. ~ 3000 North Ocean Boulevard, Myrtle Beach; 803-448-8082. MODERATE TO DELUXE.

In downtown Myrtle Beach, **The Library** is about as chichi as the Strand gets. Walls are shelved with old and new volumes, the tables crowned in starched white linen. Lunch and dinner are prix fixe and not to be undertaken with a skinny wallet. The classical European treatments of cuisine range from very good to exquisite. ~ 1212 North Kings Highway, Myrtle Beach; 803-448-4527. ULTRA-DELUXE.

Among the two dozen or so Murrells Inlet seafood shacks, **Oliver's Lodge** is the oldest and, some will say, the best. The 1910 clapboard house down by the marsh serves fantail shrimp, crab cakes, softshell crab, shrimp Creole and plenty of other seafood for dinner. Lunches aren't too exciting. The dining room is comfy and rustic, with Shaker-style chairs parked on the walls, simple wood tables and a view of the pelicans out back. ~ 4204 Route 17 business, Myrtle Beach; 803-651-2963. MODERATE.

In a chimneyed white-clapboard building resting beneath loblolly pines, **Tyler's Cove** is a splendid spot for Lowcountry sampling. Shrimp creole, flounder stuffed with crabmeat and baked, fried oysters and she-crab soup are well prepared, and there's also lighter fare such as raspberry Cornish hens. Brick floors, brass lanterns and beamed ceilings provide warm, atmospheric dining for lunch and dinner. ~ Route 17, in The Hammock Shops, Pawleys Island; 803-237-4848. MODERATE.

The fare at **Frank's** is some of the best on the Strand. You never know what the chef's up to, maybe grilled yellowfin tuna on a bed of fried spinach with Moroccan barbecue sauce, or sautéed red snapper with poached oyster cream sauce on grits. The rack of lamb with garlic mashed potatoes is heady stuff. The setting—painted tin ceilings, carved mahogany bar back, and wood floors worn to a perfect patina—is funky and relaxed. If you want even more relaxed, eat out back in the courtyard. Here, the coral-washed **Out Back at Frank's** serves lighter dishes. ~ Route 17, Pawleys Island; 803-237-3030. MODERATE TO DELUXE.

There are several fine places to eat in Georgetown. The small, friendly **Kudzu Bakery** has exposed brick walls and baskets in the windows. Open for breakfast and lunch, with a lineup of pastries, muffins, sandwiches, cookies, coffees and fresh-squeezed lemonade. ~ 714 Front Street, Georgetown; 803-546-1847. BUDGET.

For fancier Georgetown dining, the **River Room** resides behind glass along the Sampit River. There's lots of brick and brass inside, and plenty of chargrilled fish on the menu. The daily specials are very good; try the grouper stuffed with crabmeat and doused with hollandaise, or Caribbean chicken with cilantro sauce. ~ 801 Front Street, Georgetown; 803-527-4110. MODERATE.

SHOPPING   Formerly marshland and now an ersatz Cape Cod by a lake, **Barefoot Landing** is where everyone who comes to Myrtle Beach simply must shop, or so it seems. It is admittedly an appealing milieu: tin-roofed buildings with cupolas and green awnings, boardwalks wending along fountain-filled ponds, paddleboats slipping silently by. There are factory outlet stores (they call them factory "direct" here), T-shirt shops, beachwear boutiques, music and children's stores, book nooks and eclectic emporiums, as well as more than a dozen eateries. ~ 4898 Route 17 South, North Myrtle Beach; 803-272-8349.

Barefoot Landing's **Sunshine Kitchen Shoppe** fills your culinary needs, as well as any that steer toward country crafts and jams. ~ 803-272-6129. **Barefoot Sandals** has strappy little shoes as well as dresses. ~ 803-272-7810.

Scents Unlimited specializes in "reformulating" popular perfumes and colognes (translation: imitation fragrances at lower prices). Within its heady, redolent recesses are French and China musks, luxuriant lotions, Italian talc and magma therapy from the Dead Sea. ~ 803-272-1796.

The merchandise at **Barefoot General Store** borders on strange: cow manure fertilizer, cow mugs, barrels of pickles beside barrels of candy. There's some normal stuff, too, like Coca-Cola collectibles. ~ 803-272-1230.

The imitation architecture at **Broadway at the Beach** includes not only New England but Caribbean styles, and you can shop among brick and cobbled avenues and painted tin roofs. Eighty-plus shops offer typical and atypical stuff, from kites, books and hammocks to sandals, trains and candles. ~ Route 17 bypass between 21st and 29th avenues north; 803-444-3200.

Within Broadway at the Beach, **Marvelous Magnets** carries only magnets—animal magnets, cartoon character magnets, celebrity magnets and magnet games. Children especially love the big section of plastic and rubber magnets that look like food. ~ 803-444-3240.

Native Spirits is a little New Agey, offering dream-catchers, mandolins, carved chests and sterling silver artistry. ~ 803-626-5511. **Thru the Garden Gate** does custom silk flower arrangements and also sells curios for the garden and home. ~ 803-626-1667.

Elsewhere around Myrtle Beach, there are souvenir and T-shirt shops. Hundreds of them line Route 17 and Ocean Boulevard, and every year they keep increasing, little neon and fluorescent cubicles mutating across the land. One T-shirt shop called Wings has 24 stores along the Grand Strand, though it is not the king of souvenirs.

That designation is reserved for the **Gay Dolphin,** opened in the 1940s in a place the size of a cubbyhole and mutated many times until reaching its current multilevel extravaganza near The Myrtle Beach Pavilion. Within this sea of silly stuff are plastic toys galore, shirts monogrammed with every imaginable slogan, sharks in a jar, baseball caps with rubber turtles protruding out . . . you get the picture. ~ 916 Ocean Boulevard, Myrtle Beach; 803-448-6550.

The shopping in Pawleys Island is considerably more cultured. There are some lovely clapboard venues at **The Hammock Shops.** ~ Route 17; 803-237-8448. These shops include **The Original**

Hammock Shop, where it is said the first Pawleys Island cotton hammock was woven in the late 1800s by a riverboat captain. Today, you can choose a cotton weave or one soft-spun in polyester, a rope swing or a cottonduck pillow. Terrific handmade jewelry and books on the Lowcountry are also for sale at The Original Hammock Shop, which does mail order, in case you can't visit. ~ 803-237-9122, 800-332-3490.

Also here is The Hammock Shop General Store, stocked with Lowcountry gifts, aprons, candles, sauces and even live hermit crabs. Other Hammock Shops stores sell everything from sporting goods and Christmas decor to ice cream and toys. ~ 803-237-9021.

Across the street, The Island Shops have a dozen more places to spend money. ~ Route 17, Pawleys Island. Among these is Van Gogh's Other Ear, with watercolor, acrylics, serigraphs, pottery and other works by more than 35 regional artists. ~ 803-237-8033.

NIGHTLIFE Dick's Last Resort promises "fun, surly help and crummy atmosphere," so don't be surprised when the waiters stand on your picnic table and throw napkins at you. There's stuff to eat, but most people come to guzzle beer and watch everyone act stupid. It's a huge hit with tourists. Live bands perform most days after 5 p.m. ~ Barefoot Landing, 4700 Route 17 South, North Myrtle Beach; 803-272-7794.

Three nightclubs reside under the roof of 2001. At Yakety Yaks comedy saloon, there are two guys on dueling pianos. Razzle's is flooded with beach music and oldies, and an older crowd. Pulsations pulsates with disco music and spinning strobe lights, and is the place to wear your painted-on lycra. Cover. ~ 920 Lake Arrowhead Road, Route 17 North, Myrtle Beach; 803-449-9434.

The latest in one-stop nightclubbing action is Celebrity Square, located within the $250 million mega-entertainment park called Broadway at the Beach. The square is imitation French Quarter, with cobblestone and brick streets, gaslamps and wrought-iron balconies overhead. Ten themed places offer drinks and possibly entertainment, after you pay a single admission, from country-style Cactus Cantina and Froggy Bottomz Jazz & Blues to Malibu Surf Bar and Beach Music Cafe. Hard Rock Cafe is here and so is Fat Tuesday, its assembly line of spinning drink machines dispensing high-octane frozen cocktails. Sloppy Joe's is yet another branch of the one in Key West, but I suspect Hemingway would have passed on this homogenized place for a dive down the road. ~ Route 17 bypass between 21st and 29th avenues north, Myrtle Beach; 803-444-3200.

The piano bar with gas fireplace at Thoroughbreds is an intimate place for drinks before or after dinner. ~ 9706 Route 17 North, Myrtle Beach; 803-497-2636.

At the Myrtle Beach Pavilion, **The Magic Attic** is a teenage nightclub with loud music and no alcohol. Cover. ~ 812 North Ocean Boulevard, Myrtle Beach; 803-448-6456.

Mother Fletchers has bikini and wet T-shirt contests, a deejay that spins pop tunes, and two-level decks right on the beach. Most summer nights, the clientele that packs this place is barely old enough to (legally) drink. Cover, with discounted tickets available in advance. ~ Ocean Boulevard and 8th Avenue, Myrtle Beach; 803-448-2545.

The other way to spend an evening in Myrtle Beach is at one of the country music theaters in town. To know where to go, see the section in this chapter titled "Taking the Country to the Sea."

NORTH MYRTLE BEACH This northern stretch of Grand Strand takes in several small seaside communities, including Cherry Grove Beach, Ocean Drive Beach, Crescent Beach and Windy Hill Beach. Most of the action's at Ocean Drive Beach, birthplace of shagging, where the spring and summer sands are jammed with sun worshipers and "The Horseshoe," a road just off the sand, is packed with cruisers. The sand is hard-packed and open to automobiles in winter. There are public beach access walkways at various spots along North Myrtle Beach and limited parking, especially around Ocean Drive Beach. The swimming is excellent. Facilities include public restrooms and showers along First Avenue South at Ocean Drive Beach, lifeguards stationed all along North Myrtle Beach, and restaurants and groceries located in various beach communities. ~ Located on Cherry Grove Beach, Ocean Drive Beach and Crescent Beach are along Route 65, off Route 17. To get to Windy Hill Beach, take 43rd Avenue east from Route 17; 803-249-3519.

MYRTLE BEACH Ten miles of hard-packed to fine brown-sugar sand make up Myrtle Beach, but it's the few yards in front of The Myrtle Beach Pavilion and Amusement Park that sticks in everyone's consciousness. From spring through fall the towels are wall-to-wall, the umbrellas vying for space beyond the blinking neon of arcades, carnival rides and cotton-candy stands. Families and beachgoers wanting mental peace head several miles north of The Pavilion, where lovely neighborhoods with luxuriant myrtle trees line the wide beaches and there are patches of public parking. Lifeguards and eateries are located at various spots along Myrtle Beach, though they're most abundant around the Myrtle Beach Pavilion and Amusement Park. There are few public restrooms, though hotels (much to their dismay) must by law allow the public to use their facilities. Wheelchair-accessible ramps cross the dunes at 15 locations, and some lifeguard stands have free beach-going wheelchairs. Swimming is good everywhere, but especially nice on the north end of Myrtle Beach, where the water is less crowded and shallow for quite a ways. ~ Along Ocean Boulevard, starting around 79th Avenue North and ending around 29th Avenue South. The Myrtle Beach Pavilion and Amusement Park is at Ocean Boulevard and 9th Avenue North; 803-626-7645, ext. 129.

MYRTLE BEACH STATE PARK 🏃 🏊 🎣 🍺 At the southern tip of Myrtle Beach, these 312 acres include generous stands of pine woods and a pretty swath of oyster-colored beach. The shore is skirted with dunes decorated with sea oats and wildflowers. It's almost always windy. The fishing pier and campground were both firsts on the Grand Strand, though the most unusual feature is the swimming pool, open only in summer. Swimming is good in both the pool and the ocean. Fishing is great from the pier for mackerel, flounder, whiting, pompano, bluefish and trout. Facilities include a park office, restrooms, picnic tables and pavilions, a snack bar, swimming pool, fishing pier, playground, nature center and trails. Day-use fee, $3. ~ Located along Route 17 at the south end of Myrtle Beach; 803-238-5325.

▲ There are 350 sites for tents and RVs, most with hookups for water and electricity; $20 to $21 per night. Families love the five cabins and two apartments, all budget-priced and requiring a three-night minimum, though you'll have to book months ahead to get one in season.

HUNTINGTON BEACH STATE PARK 🏃 🚴 🏊 🎣 🍺 The way into this 2500-acre park is through dense woods and across freshwater lagoons and saltwater marsh where oyster beds are exposed at low tide. An observation deck runs out over the marsh, and you can walk down and watch the egrets wading, waiting for fish. There are lots of sea oats and dunes, then wide, firm, lonely beach, the sand tinted orange by crushed seashells.

The coastal wilderness was once owned by sculptress Anna Hyatt Huntington and her husband, Archer, the late creators of Brookgreen Gardens, across Route 17 from the park. For their winter home they built **Atalaya** (separate fee), an enormous, Moorish-style stone-and-brick fortress by the sea that's now a National Historic Landmark. In 1930, Anna wrote in her diary that "Archer has also decided to build something and what he has in mind would probably be a hair-raiser to an architect." Indeed, there was no construction plan. The windows were randomly spaced, a watchtower perched on top, and the walls so crude that fig vines were planted to hide their harshness. Still, Anna, said to be deeply in love with Archer, sculpted one of her most significant works at Atalaya—"Don Quixote."

Swimming is good in designated areas. There's good fishing in the surf and from the jetty at the northern end of the beach; try for whiting, pompano, puppy drum and flounder. The boardwalk along the salt marsh is a prime place for snagging blue crabs. You'll need a dip net, a lead weight and string, available from the trading post, and some chicken necks and backs, available from local groceries. In case you've never crabbed before, here's how it works: You tie the chicken and weight to the string and drop it in the water. When the crabs come crawling for dinner, dip them out with the net. Facilities include a trading post, picnic areas, historic house, bike rentals, restrooms and nature trails. Day-use fee, $3 per person. ~ The beach is located along Route 17, three miles south of Murrells Inlet; 803-237-4440.

▲ Two campgrounds offer a total of 187 tent and RV sites with hookups; hot-water bathhouses are situated at both campgrounds. Two wheelchair-accessible sites are available and can be reserved in advance. Remaining sites are $20 first-come, $21 reserved from March through October; $16 first-come, $17 reserved from November through February.

▼▼▼▼▼▼▼▼▼▼▼

Charleston Area

For the 56 miles between Georgetown and Charleston, Route 17 offers leisurely, uneventful driving. Low palmetto forest and dense stands of pine, roadsides swallowed by kudzu, and scattered farmhouses whose lawns bloom with gardenias and magnolias make up much of the scenery. There is also the broad sweep of Francis Marion National Forest, stretching westward more than 40 miles from Route 17 to Lake Moultrie.

SIGHTS

◄ HIDDEN

East of Route 17 and 60 miles south of Georgetown, Pinckney Street will take you on a short detour through the scenic, strange, very small town of **McClellanville**. Small wood homes trimmed in spindle rail sit back under moss-draped oaks, their porches occupied by blank-faced people. The general store sells pantyhose along with pork ribs, and there is a very small butterfly hatchery. The Intracoastal Waterway winds through, and alongside it are shrimp boats with high-flying masts strung with nets.

Back on Route 17 South, ramshackle carts offer "Hot Boiled P-Nuts" and "Sweet P-Cans, Shelled." Just north of Mount Pleasant, the road is lined on both sides with lean-tos and stands selling sweetgrass baskets.

In Mount Pleasant, take the turnoff at Route 703 for **Patriots Point Naval and Maritime Museum**. Here, the aircraft carrier *Yorktown* looms in the Cooper River, a gray giant rimmed with guns and mounted with helicopters and planes. Kids really enjoy exploring this World War II carrier, parked here since 1975, with its hull encased in 28 feet of river silt and encrusted with weird barnacles. The depths of the ship harbor military and seafaring fascination: fire rooms and engineering flats, a torpedo workshop, combat information center, scullery (which held cookware and dishes) and Korean War Room. The Sick Bay is small and stuffy enough to make one sick. Admission. ~ 40 Patriots Point Road; 803-884-2727.

Also here is the *Savannah*, an experimental nuclear-powered ship that cost too much to operate; the destroyer *Laffey*, which fought at Normandy; the Coast Guard cutter *Ingham*; and the World War II submarine *Clamagore*. The inside of the sub is cramped and hot; the sleeping quarters a Lilliputian maze of metal and tiny bunks.

From Patriots Point you can catch a tour boat over to **Fort Sumter** on a tiny manmade island at the head of Charleston Harbor. It's an enjoyable ride across the harbor, whose waters have seen battles with the French, Spanish, British and, finally, Union soldiers. Fort Sumter is, of course, where the Civil War officially began, though it was not a terribly exciting start. Admission. ~ 803-883-3123.

Fort Sumter was occupied by a Federal garrison in 1860 when South Carolina became the first state to secede. In April 1861, renegade Confederates demanded the fort back. Union Major Robert Anderson, in charge of Fort Sumter, refused. On April 12 at 4:30 in the morning, Confederate Brigadier General Pierre Beauregard fired the first shots on the fort—and of the war. For 36 hours he shelled the fort, and then Anderson surrendered. No one was killed.

Today, the fort is a National Monument run by the National Park Service. Rangers give ten-minute talks on various details of the fort, such as how it took 11 years and 70,000 tons of rock and granite just to build the island it sits on. The fort had five-foot-thick brick walls and was originally 50 feet high, though today it is considerably less. From atop its batteries you can look across to surrounding islands and watch the harbor whipping across the horizon, and the pelicans diving for fish. Everything here is wheelchair-accessible; special elevators even deliver wheelchair visitors to the batteries.

Back in Mount Pleasant heading south, Route 17 dramatically climbs the twin steel spans of the Cooper River Bridge, whose top gird rails trace the sky like rollercoasters. You'll soon find yourself at the north end of downtown Charleston. Get on King Street going south, and you will drive through the most exquisite old city in the Carolinas.

Nothing can prepare you for **Charleston:** The processions of beautiful buildings, Italianate and Victorian, Art Deco and Gothic Revival, Federal and Colonial, most centuries old, all splendidly preserved. The Old World cathedrals with their medieval gates, stained-glass towers and spires flung against bright blue sky. The curve of magnolias wearing white, the heady walks through waist-high lilies in teeny cemeteries. The luscious gardens with marble fountains that have been flowing for more than 100 years, the outdoor markets filled with Lowcountry fruit and art and sweets. The smell of green gardens and salty ocean air, and of shrimp and sausage simmering in Lowcountry kitchens. The sun dispensing light in theatrical doses, shaping and reshaping the historical stage called Charleston.

The quietest times in Charleston are just after dawn and before dusk, when business is done and workers retreat to the suburbs. During the day there is the typical bustle of a modern city, with crowded cafes and streets, and traffic slowed by horse-drawn carriages carrying tourists (Charlestonians have their own unmentionable names for the traffic-congesting surreys). Parking is a formidable task, and it is best to park at the Meeting Street Visitors Center and either walk or take Dash downtown. The downtown historic area is extremely walkable, and even at its busiest feels scaled-down, even intimate.

Charleston Area

Charleston is also very hip. Bistros, coffee and tea houses, tony shops and pretty inns crowd along the streets, and are concealed down skinny brick alleys and in flourishing courtyards. This is a great place to go people-watching. Retro garb with a bit of '90s embellishment is in. Being young is also in. Lots of people in their 20s and 30s have lately made an exodus from Atlanta, preferring the happening scene of a small historic town to the faceless, frenzied sprawl of a Southern metropolis.

Home to just 80,000 people and host to five million annual visitors, Charleston is a low-lying city—church spires define its ceiling—that sits on a tongue of filled marsh. The Cooper River runs along its east side, the Ashley River is on the west. They meet at the southern end and proceed out into the Atlantic Ocean. Tour guides like to say that the Cooper and the Ashley form the ocean, and they also point out that plenty of people born in Charleston die there, never having ventured off the peninsula. One soon grows accustomed to such sentiments from the place Edgar Allen Poe called "the kingdom by the sea."

It is at the tip of the tongue, **The Battery**, where Charleston is most opulent. Storybook mansions washed in sherbet colors and embellished with iron fretwork and red brick march along the harbor. Many are occupied by Charleston's oldest families with some of its oldest money. The wonderful Queen Anne manse at **Two Meeting Street Inn** offers public lodging, though you can't go in without a reservation. White as a wedding cake and nearly as decorative, its gates are constantly thronged with people looking through the wrought iron and boughs of ancient oaks. ~ 2 Meeting Street; 803-723-7322.

Formerly called White Point, The Battery was created in the 1850s, when a high stone seawall and wide promenade were built. Twenty years earlier, **White Point Gardens** had been planted next to the sea, and ever since has been a wonderful place for walking. Colossal oaks shade vast green lawns sprinkled with monuments and rimmed in cannons that remember wars and other momentous times in the city's illustrious history. That would include the hanging of Stede Bonnet, British Navy major-turned-pirate who was captured with Blackbeard in 1718 at Cape Fear, North Carolina. The gentlemanly Bonnet, who claimed he became a pirate due to "domestic problems," pleaded for his life, even offering to cut off "all my limbs from my body, only reserving the use of my tongue to call continually on, and to pray to the Lord," but he was hanged anyway at White Point.

North of The Battery, lovely neighborhoods fan out, their homes residing within enormous vaults of trees. Gardens pour perfume into the air. There is the sound of fountains unseen.

Most of the homes are not of this era but of a prosperous, pre–Civil War world where European men grew absurdly wealthy trading rice, cotton and indigo through Charleston's port, and African men and women were their slaves. The merchants' money was poured into extravagant architecture that gave jobs to hundreds of builders, carpenters and designers. There were 142 cabinetmakers working in Charleston in the early 1800s, including Thomas Elfe.

Several public house museums in the area allow outsiders to walk among luxuriant gardens and see behind the fanciful facades, and to know how Old South aristocrats lived. There are guided tours that usually last about an hour or so, offered every 15 to 30 minutes.

The **Edmondston-Alston House** is located right on The Battery, its oyster-colored exterior and roomy piazzas looking across the busy harbor. Not opulent, but a handsome place with odd architecture, it was built in 1825 by Scottish merchant Charles Edmondston. His design was late Federal, though twelve years later, rice planter Charles Alston bought the house and gave it a Greek Revival makeover. He put a parapet across the front, embellished the second floor with an iron balcony, and added a third-floor piazza with Corinthian columns. Many Alston family furnishings, books, silver and paintings are on display here. Admission. ~ 21 East Battery Street; 803-722-7171.

Two blocks west, two tremendous oaks frame the entrance to **Calhoun Mansion**, and the plantings within are formal and lush. The mansion itself is magnificent, a monument to Victorian excess, with ornate woodwork and plaster moldings, an enormous ballroom with glass skylight and a staircase that soars 75 feet into a dome. The mansion is singular for Charleston: It was built in 1876, just eleven years after the Civil War crushed the city. George Walton Williams was a rich banker and merchant untouched by the war. He celebrated his own fortune, erecting the lavish mansion when the rest of Charleston was broke. Admission to Calhoun Mansion is pricier than other Charleston houses ($10, as of early 1997). Closed Monday through Wednesday. Admission. ~ 16 Meeting Street; 803-722-8205.

Walk a few blocks north on Meeting Street to Charleston's most famous, most photographed domicile, the **Nathaniel Russell House**. Russell was a prosperous merchant with a lust for architecture. He wanted a home like no other in Charleston, and when his Neoclassical "mansion house" was done in 1808, it was indeed singular in mood and design. Three floors high, three rooms deep, three bricks thick, the tour guide tells you, though there is no known architect, only a massive book on architecture memorized by Russell. His hallmark is the free-flying staircase, built on the cantilever principle and erected with wooden pegs, that swirls up three floors as though it were floating. Admission. ~ 51 Meeting Street; 803-723-1623.

Like many early Charlestonians, Russell and his wife, Sarah, were big on society and status, and they ran their house in a most formal way. English tea was served in French porcelain on Italian marble tables in the fancy front parlor. The day's main meal was promptly at 3:00, and it was a lavish affair lasting several hours and requiring many slaves to prepare, serve and clean up (the Russells had 18 slaves in all). Afterward, the men had their brandy and cigars in the drawing room or library, for it was disrespectful to smoke in front of a woman.

Before or after the house tour, have a walk around the rambling, fragrant gardens, with perfect circles of hedges, ivy climbing the walls, petite rosebuds and fat camellias, and statuary tucked here and there.

George Washington overnighted at the **Heyward-Washington House**, whose three simple stories of red brick are wedged among the row houses of Church Street. Built in 1771 by rich rice planter Daniel Heyward, it was home to his son, Thomas Heyward, Jr., one of the many signers of the Declaration of Independence. The inside is bathed in cypress and furnished with marvelous Charleston antiques, including a priceless secretary-bookcase in both Chippendale and Hepplewhite styles. The kitchens and carriage house are original, having amazingly survived centuries of fires, earthquakes, hurricanes and wars. Admission. ~ 87 Church Street; 803-722-0354.

Next door, you can look at the outside of **Cabbage Row**, where DuBose Heyward set his 1920s novel *Porgy*, though in the book the black tenement was called Catfish Row and located two blocks over on East Bay Street. A white Charleston writer hailing from New Hampshire, Heyward was one of the first American novelists to depict black life. His *Porgy* was modeled after crippled beggar "Goat Sammy" Smalls, who used to roam King Street with his goat and cart. Sammy's "woman" was Bess and his world was that of many Southern blacks: poor and segregated, cut off from the opportunities of the white elite. The novel was turned into an opera and then the musical *Porgy and Bess*, immediately a smash hit all across the country, with the now-famous first line: "Summertime and the livin' is easy." ~ 89–91 Church Street.

But living wasn't easy for Charleston blacks. From the 1930s through the 1960s there were repeated attempts to cast the musical here, but white Charlestonians insisted on segregated theaters and the blacks refused to attend. Finally, more than three decades after its initial production, *Porgy and Bess* played in Charleston.

Across the street from Cabbage Row are several privately owned **single houses** typical of 1700s Charleston. One room wide, two rooms deep and set lengthwise to the street, they were aimed into the prevailing breezes. Historian Samuel Gaillard Stoney once likened them to a sailing fleet, "trimmed to the sacred Charleston wind that every hot afternoon blows up from the southwest across the Ashley River," according to Charleston Houses and Gardens. People with a little more money and land would build "double houses," two rooms wide and often Georgian in style. ~ 90–94 Church Street.

Walk over to East Bay Street and you will see an entirely different set of row houses. **Rainbow Row** looks just like it sounds: a parade of radiant facades washed in purple, salmon and yellow, then cinnamon, aqua and olive. There are black ironwork balconies decorated with potted roses and sculpted boxwood. Built in the mid- to late-1700s as merchants' homes and stores, they were restored in the 1900s to become the private homes they are now. ~ 82–107 East Bay Street.

North from here, **East Bay Street** is a pleasant piece of road with patches of brick and cobblestone edging the Cooper River and culminating with pretty cafes, nightspots and shops. Called simply

POINTS OF INTEREST
- **Ⓐ** Aiken-Rhett House
- **Ⓑ** Calhoun Mansion
- **Ⓒ** Charleston Museum
- **Ⓓ** Edmondston-Alston House
- **Ⓔ** Four Corners of Law
- **Ⓕ** French Huguenot Church
- **Ⓖ** Gibbes Museum of Art
- **Ⓗ** Heyward-Washington House
- **Ⓘ** John Rutledge House Inn
- **Ⓙ** Joseph Manigault House
- **Ⓚ** Nathaniel Russell House
- **Ⓛ** Old City Market
- **Ⓜ** Old Exchange and Provost Dungeon
- **Ⓝ** St. Michael's Cathedral
- **Ⓞ** Two Meeting Street Inn
- **Ⓟ** Visitor Reception & Transportation Center

Charleston Historic District

The Battery

0   .2 mile

"The Bay" during the early days, the street was the pulse of eight-eenth-century Charleston, when rice, indigo and tobacco, and fine porcelain and silk passed through these docks.

Here also is the **Old Exchange and Provost Dungeon**, a strange, massive place with subterranean caverns where prisoners were kept. Completed in 1771, the stately, Palladian-style Exchange acted as town hall and hub of social, economic and political life. You can wander through the grand Colonial halls (the tour's self-guided), then slip down into the darkened dungeon honeycombed with brick arches. Admission. ~ 122 East Bay Street; 803-792-5020.

From East Bay Street you can walk west on Broad Street to **St. Michael's Episcopal Church**, whose soaring white steeple and bell tower dominate the city. It's the oldest of Charleston's churches, built between 1752 and 1761, and it is very English, designed in the same manner as Trafalgar Square's St. Martin-in-the-Fields. St. Michael's has an illustrious history involving several wars and an earthquake. It survived the 1886 quake, but its steeple sank eight inches. It was painted black and used as a lookout during the Civil War. Its eight bells have crossed the Atlantic five times (once in the American Revolution when they were stolen by the British). Robert E. Lee and George Washington have graced these pews. John Rutledge is buried beneath crepe myrtles in the cemetery here. ~ Meeting Street at Broad Street; 803-723-0603.

St. Michael's makes up one of the **Four Corners of Law** at the intersection of Broad and Meeting streets. (The church supposedly represents God's law.) The other "corners" are **City Hall**, built in 1801, **Charleston County Courthouse**, dating to 1792, and the federal **Courthouse and Post Office**, built in 1898 in the Renaissance style, after the first structure fell in the great earthquake of 1886.

More interesting than the buildings here are the **flower ladies** who gather every morning along the sidewalks to weave and sell sweetgrass baskets. They sing rich Gullah hymns, songs passed on through generations of women who've attended these sidewalks. Gullah is one of the purest forms of Creole, originating on the earliest plantations of coastal South Carolina.

Several blocks northeast of Four Corners, the **French Huguenot Church** was built back in 1844, though it was the fourth church on this plot to serve Charleston Huguenots (the first was as early as 1681). It's a stellar sample of Gothic Revival, with pointed arches and eyebrows, finials and stone tracery parading all over the sand-colored building. ~ 136 Church Street; 803-722-4385.

Just south of the church, **Chalmers Street** is one of Charleston's most charming thoroughfares, ancient curving cobblestone edged with fanciful and timeworn facades.

A couple of blocks northwest on Meeting Street, **Gibbes Museum of Art** resides in a handsome Colonial building with two rooms of permanent exhibits, mainly American art dating to the

1700s. There's a collection of miniature portraits numbering more than 400, and notable works by South Carolinians Benjamin West, Thomas Sully and Rembrandt Peale. Admission. ~ 135 Meeting Street; 803-722-2706.

The **Joseph Manigault House** is considerably north of Charleston's historic heart, so it's best to catch a public shuttle bus or drive. In 1803, wealthy French Huguenot Gabriel Manigault fashioned the house for his brother, Joseph. It was one of Gabriel's first residential creations, but it foretold his bright future as a renowned Charleston architect. The mansion is in the Adams style and designed as a parallelogram, with bows on two sides and a curving piazza on another. The interior is striking, with a flowing staircase, handsome period pieces and portraits more than 200 years old. Admission. ~ 350 Meeting Street; 803-723-2926.

The **Charleston Museum** was founded in 1773, making it the nation's first museum. Its current quarters, however, were built in 1979 and are, unfortunately, some of the city's dullest: a big block of brick. The inside is much more enlightening, with exhibits on the Lowcountry's florid history. Kids have a whole room of hands-on fun. The museum operates four of Charleston's house museums and sells discounted combination tickets. Admission. ~ 360 Meeting Street; 803-722-2996.

Across the street, the **Visitor Reception & Transportation Center** is the place for information. The friendly, well-informed people here will help plan tours, suggest dining itineraries, provide walking-tour maps (including one of King Street architecture) and even direct you to great hidden spots. This is your best bet for parking. ~ 375 Meeting Street; 803-853-8000.

Parallel to Meeting Street, **King Street** is a bustling commercial haven edged with some of Charleston's best inns and eateries and shops, especially those selling stellar antiques. The architecture is vast and varied: a German Gothic church, Art Deco theater, Georgian and Neoclassical hotel, plenty of Federal and antebellum designs, and even some Victoriana.

Before visiting Charleston, get information from the excellent **Charleston Trident Convention & Visitors Bureau** at P.O. Box 975, Charleston, SC 29402. ~ 81 Mary Street; 800-868-8118.

A few blocks northeast of the Visitor Reception & Transportation Center, the 1817 **Aiken-Rhett House** was home to South Carolina governor William Aiken, Jr., and then war room for Confederate General P.G.T. Beauregard. It began as a Greek Revival manse and was later given Rococo Revival flairs. Some of the furnishings are original; the slave quarters and stable look barely changed. Admission. ~ 48 Elizabeth Street; 803-723-1159.

There are many guided walking tours of Charleston, with seemingly endless themes. There is the **Tour De Feet**. ~ 803-556-0664. You can also try the **Rice Colony Walking Tour**. ~ 803-884-4532.

If you are interested in the Civil War go on the **Civil War Walking Tour of Charleston**. ~ 803-722-7033. Another interesting tour is the Charleston **Tea Party Walking Tour**. ~ 803-722-7033. Those interested in architecture should try the **Architectural Walking Tours of Charleston**. ~ 803-893-2327. **Chai Y'all Tours** recounts the city's Jewish heritage. ~ 803-556-0664. **Gullah Tours by Alphonso Brown** recounts the rich Gullah history. ~ 803-556-7243.

If you'd rather ride in a motor coach, consider the **Revolutionary Colonial Buildings Tour** or the **History and Ghost Tour**, both offered by Unique Tours. ~ 701 East Bay Street; 803-724-3421.

Horse-drawn carriage rides are available from numerous companies, most stationed along Market Street near Church Street. One of these companies is **Classic Carriage Tours**. ~ 803-853-3747. Another is **Charleston Carriage Company**. ~ 803-577-0042.

Outside Charleston is plantation country. Four historic plantations, including two with extraordinary gardens, are open to the public and are within a 30-minute drive of downtown Charleston. For more on these, see the section titled "Charleston Plantations" in this chapter.

Across the Ashley River from the city is the site of the original Charleston. **Charles Towne Landing** is where English settlers first set up camp and lived for several years. Today it's a pretty park and nature preserve set among wooded clearings. There's a small seventeenth-century-style village and crop garden, a 53-foot replica of a 300-year-old trading ship and a theater showing a half-hour film about Charleston's beginnings. Gravel paths wend through woods where black bears, otters, pumas and other animals live in roomy, grassy enclosures. You can have a picnic, rent a bike or stroller, or take a walk along the forested footpaths. Wheelchair visitors will want to ride the tram that regularly tours the grounds. Admission. ~ 1500 Old Town Road, Charleston; 803-852-4200.

HIDDEN ►   North of Charleston, deep in old rice plantation country, you can explore the blackwater swamp at **Cypress Gardens**. Birders and naturalists enjoy this 163-acre retreat along the Cooper River, where you can get in a little rowboat and wander along the inky, silent water studded with giant cypress trees. The gardens are a tiny remaining piece of Dean Hall, a 3000-acre antebellum plantation that flourished until the Civil War. During the spring, the shore is masked with azaleas, wisteria, dogwoods and daffodils that burst with color. This is the best time to visit, though fall is also quite pleasant. If you go in summer, take your mosquito repellent. It's muggy and very buggy. Admission. ~ 3030 Cypress Gardens Road, off Route 52 North, Moncks Corner; 803-553-0515.

South of Charleston, the Lowcountry spreads out like a watery apron, with rivers seeping through farm fields, stilt homes perched against seas of marsh, and bridges connecting a series of sea islands.

None of the islands are easy to get to. Most are cul-de-sac destinations, and you will travel the same way out as you did on the way in. The drives are atmospheric: long, silent journeys across interminable stretches of salt marsh and tidal creeks and seagrass rippling softly in the wind.

Even **Kiawah Island,** the most developed and most visited, requires a lengthy, twisting drive through the countryside, first along Route 700 south from Charleston, then southeast down Bohicket Road. Kiawah is a private, gated resort community, impeccably planned and planted with perfect shrubs and tall oaks. Four championship golf courses, several restaurants, a 150-room inn, rental cottages and villas, and tawny beaches are among the offerings. For information, call **Kiawah Island Resort.** ~ 803-768-2121, 800-654-2924.

As the crow flies, **Edisto Island** is but a few miles across the Edisto River from Kiawah. In your car, it is many miles, about 55, as you backtrack north along Bohicket Road to Route 17, then south to Route 174, which burrows eastward into Edisto. Along Route 174 is tall pine forest and modest country homes set under magnolias, and the village of **Adams Run** with a country store selling hunting and fishing supplies and a post office the size of a postage stamp.

◀ *HIDDEN*

◀ *HIDDEN*

Cathedrals of moss-draped oaks, ivy and kudzu snaking around their trunks, deliver you to the town of Edisto Island. There are no traffic lights here (the closest is 26 miles away) but there is the **Edisto Island Museum,** whose brief but well-done displays provide a portrait of sea island life. There is pottery from the island's earliest occupants, the Edistow Indians, and coil baskets made by the first Africans who were plantation slaves. The famed Sea Island Cotton, so fine it skipped local markets and was shipped straight to France to make lace, was grown here, as was rice and indigo. Several 1700s plantation homes and churches are still standing on Edisto. The museum is open afternoons on Tuesdays, Thursdays and Saturdays. ~ Route 174, at the corner of Chisolm Plantation Road; 803-869-1954.

Mostly, though, Edisto is great for beachgoers. The scene here couldn't be any more different than at Kiawah. Edisto is casual, funky, a little rundown. Rows of rental cottages line the beach and pickup trucks line their driveways. Local cafes are staffed by sweet-talking waitresses and owned by the same family for half a century.

The **Edisto Island Chamber of Commerce** can supply information on the island. ~ 547 Route 174; 803-869-3867. Marie Elliot, fifth-generation Edistonian and co-owner of **Edisto Island Tours** takes groups on tours of the island's historic churches and plantations. ~ 803-869-1937. Her husband, Coast Guard Captain Ron Elliott, leads shelling, fishing and river expeditions.

Text continued from page 348.

Charleston
Plantations

To find Charleston's four public plantations you'll have to follow the rivers out from the city, away from the commotion of downtown to cool, calming countryside ruled by mighty oaks. The rivers are the reason for the plantations. They fed the fields of rice, cotton and indigo that dominated the landscape 150 years ago. African slaves were the reason the fields thrived.

From downtown Charleston, take Route 61, also called Ashley River Road, nine miles northwest to the first of three plantations lining the Ashley River. The drive into **Drayton Hall** is typically long, lovely and oaklined, with sun pouring through massive, mossy boughs. The house is a red-brick Georgian-Palladian, built between 1738 and 1742 by young planter John Drayton and occupied by seven generations of Draytons (Draytons still live in Charleston). Though neighbors called it "Mr. Drayton's palace," it was not his primary plantation but was used as headquarters for managing his many other plantations. Extremely wealthy when he died, his possessions included some 500 slaves. He was not well-liked, and history recounts that he "lived in riches—but without public esteem."

The inside of the house is as bare as can be—which is good, as one can admire the handsome bald cypress paneling in the great hall, the intricate thistle and lotus blossom carvings around the ceilings, the mahogany garlands over the drawing room windows, and many other intricacies without being distracted by fancy furnishings. Drayton is the only Ashley River plantation the Civil War did not destroy. Admission. ~ 3380 Ashley River Road; 803-766-0188.

A mile northwest of Drayton on Route 61, **Magnolia Plantation and Gardens** is sprawling, multi-faceted, quite modern and touristy. The focus here is the gardens. The original house, built in the 1680s by the Draytons of Drayton Hall, burned and was replaced by another house, which was leveled by Union troops. The current manor dates to 1873 but it looks nothing like a Southern plantation house, more like a gingerbread confection with gables and chimneys and curving eaves.

The gardens have been growing since about 1680, though their real architect didn't come along until much later. In the 1840s. Reverend Grimke-Drayton inherited the plantation. He eschewed formal gardens, preferring the random, romantic plantings of azaleas, camellias and magnolias. His sisters were staunch abolitionists, and so Grimke-Drayton called his slaves "black roses" and taught them to read and write. They cultivated his garden, and today his wending paths are bordered by walls of flowers and greenery. Many of the blooms are higher than your head. The camellias come in 900 varieties, and there's always one in bloom. Fanciful flower-lined bridges cross the blackishgreen Ashley River, which wanders through the 50-acre gardens, and there are several lakes.

Also here is the **Audubon Swamp Garden**, a 60-acre blackwater cypress and tupelo swamp inhabited by alligators, and the small Barbados Tropical Gardens with a greenhouse burgeoning with bromeliads, pandanus and other warm-weather beauties. Paved nature and bike trails accommodate wheelchair visitors, and there's a 45-minute tram tour several times daily. Admission. ~ 803-571-1266.

Four miles farther northwest lies **Middleton Place**. The gardens are vast, French and formal, laid out in geometric patterns and embellished with long terraced lawns and twin lakes in the shape of butterfly wings. Entire embankments explode with azaleas in spring. Oaks twist toward the sky like gnarled giants. Swans repose on the glassy waters of a rice mill pond. Crabapple and myrtle trees parade around, and hidden hollows with a single bench provide cool retreats. The backdrop of all this is the dark, brooding Ashley River.

Middleton was begun in the early 1700s. Most of its buildings were burned by Sherman's troops and then finished off by the 1886 earthquake; the fault line actually runs through the gardens. Portions of a 1755 bachelor guest wing remained and were restored early in the twentieth century. Today there are guided tours of the red-brick house decorated in the manner of early Charleston.

There is much more to see at Middleton, including numerous outbuildings, a slave cemetery, sugarcane mill, and working stableyard with a smithy, horses, goats and pigs. Have lunch inside the cypress-paneled restaurant, with fresh, moderate-priced fare like fried chicken with collard greens, ham biscuits and hoppin' johns. Dinner on Fridays and Saturdays. ~ Ashley River Road; 803-556-6020, 800-782-3608.

Boone Hall Plantation lies six miles north of Charleston along the Wando River. Its high point is a half-mile alley of oaks, their spidery limbs locked high over the entrance road. The house is faux plantation, built in 1935 where once stood an eighteenth-century house. Tours of the first floor are given by women in hoop skirts; the upper floors are used by the home's current owners, no relation to the Boones. Most historic here is the 1840s slave street lined with one-room, red-brick cubicles with dirt floors. Walk along the street and look inside the dark, dank cavities. There are no tours of the slave houses. Admission. ~ Route 17; 803-884-4371.

LODGING

HIDDEN ►

Thirty miles north of Charleston, **Laurel Hill Bed and Breakfast** is hidden down a dirt road, past cornfields and country shacks. The big farmhouse sits down near the water, a great expanse of salt marsh and ocean spread before it. From the porch rockers you can breathe in the salty breeze and drink in the awesome panorama, which stretches across Cape Romain National Wildlife Sanctuary. Otherwise, there's fishing and crabbing to occupy you. Accommodations are in four comfortable guest rooms furnished with homey antiques and folk art. The house is 1990s-era; the original 1850s Laurel Hill plantation was destroyed by Hurricane Hugo in 1989. Rates include a country breakfast. ~ From Route 17, turn east at the small Laurel Hill sign just north of the Buck Hall Recreation Area, McClellanville; 803-887-3708. MODERATE.

Charleston easily has the finest lodging in South Carolina. Many inns here are old, saturated with history and judiciously restored, lavished with creature comforts and Southern pleasantries. To stay here is to enter another time, a slower mode.

If you visit in high season—spring and fall—you'll need a fat wallet. Rates at most places are deluxe and ultra-deluxe then. In summer and winter, many of those same inns offer moderate rates.

Two Meeting Street Inn is a wonderful white house right on The Battery, with views across oak-dotted White Point Gardens and Charleston Harbor. The Queen Anne manse, as fanciful as a wedding cake, was indeed a wedding gift in 1892. Carved oak paneling graces much of the interior and Tiffany stained glass fills the windows. There are lovely arched piazzas. Antiques and canopy poster beds decorate three floors of rooms, all but two with private baths. Continental breakfast, bicycles and afternoon sherry are included. There are budget rates for rooms with shared baths. ~ 2 Meeting Street, Charleston; 803-723-7322. BUDGET TO DELUXE.

The Mills House is a twentieth-century reconstruction of the 1850s antebellum hostelry once called "the finest hotel south of New York." Today's Mills House is still quite fine, its lobby bathed in floors of white marble, its 214 rooms and suites done in soothing tones of ice blue and peach and furnished with handsome reproductions. The patio rooms have French doors opening onto a private alcove above the second-floor swimming pool. ~ Meeting and Queen streets, Charleston; 803-577-2400, 800-874-9600, fax 803-722-2112. ULTRA-DELUXE.

Families like **The Meeting Street Inn**. Three stories tall and coral-washed, it's a casual place with a spacious courtyard and the faint feel of a motor court. All 56 rooms come with poster beds and simple baths with tubs, though some are showing wear. Several rooms are pet-friendly. Buffet breakfasts of ham biscuits, pecan bread and honeydew melons are served in the courtyard, and there are wine and hors d'oeuvres every afternoon. The staff is extra friendly. ~ 173 Meeting Street, Charleston; 803-723-1882, 800-842-8022. MODERATE TO DELUXE.

Many Charlestonians open their homes to visitors, offering simple to formal accommodations and prices ranging from budget to ultra-deluxe. **Historic Charleston Bed & Breakfast** can help you find a place. Most of their listings are within the historic district and so walking distance to everything. Some accommodations are in separate carriage houses with living rooms and kitchens. ~ 60 Broad Street, Charleston; 803-722-6606, 800-743-3583, fax 803-722-9773.

Charleston's most prominent lodging entrepreneur, Rick Widman, is known for his stellar yet varied taste in decorating and his affinity for impeccable service. His properties include King's Courtyard Inn, Fulton Lane Inn, Victoria House Inn, all described below, and the **John Rutledge House Inn**, which Rutledge built in 1763 for his bride, Elizabeth Grimke. Ornate ironwork and eyebrows decorate the outside of the three-story townhouse, while the inside is grandiose, endlessly detailed. All the doors and floors are original; the first-floor parquet floors are copies of European castle floors. There are eight bedrooms and three suites, the latter entirely overwhelming with its 14-foot ceilings, Italian marble fireplaces, grand canopy beds and whirlpool tubs. Eight additional rooms are spread between two carriage houses in back, though these are not as large or opulent. Pastries and coffee are delivered to your room each morning; wine and sherry are served in the grand ballroom afternoons and evenings. ~ 116 Broad Street, Charleston; 803-723-7999, 800-476-9741, fax 803-720-2615. ULTRA-DELUXE.

The Elliott House Inn is not as stylish as many other Charleston inns, but it is comfy enough and, most importantly, has rates starting in the moderate range. Twenty-six rooms gather around a brick courtyard thick with palmettos, ficus and fountains, and a big spa beneath a trellis of purple wisteria. Plush throw rugs, floral sofas, exposed plumbing, vases of fresh flowers, and small baths round out the simple rooms. Pastries and coffee are served in the morning, chocolates at night. The only drawback: occasional noise from the restaurant next door, so ask for a room across the courtyard. ~ 78 Queen Street, Charleston; 803-723-1855, 800-729-1855. MODERATE.

The 1853 Greek-Revival **King's Courtyard Inn** does indeed have a courtyard, a sunlit brick hideaway with fountains flowing and ivy climbing the walls. Rooms aren't fancy but elegant, high-ceilinged expanses with long windows and the original hardwood floors. Some rooms have lace canopy beds and fireplaces. Continental breakfast, afternoon drinks, and bedside brandy and chocolates are included in the rates. ~ 198 King Street, Charleston; 803-723-7000, 800-845-6119, fax 803-720-2608. ULTRA-DELUXE.

HIDDEN ▶

Tucked neatly down a brick alley along King Street's antique row, **Fulton Lane Inn** is a most desirable address, with three floors of sumptuous, smart-looking rooms, all totally nonsmoking. Another of Rick Widman's choice properties, Fulton Lane offers rooms and suites with poster canopy beds and big whirlpool tubs, some with fireplaces, cathedral ceilings and kitchenettes. Your Continental breakfast arrives on a silver tray every morning. ~ 202 King Street, Charleston; 803-720-2600, 800-720-2688, fax 803-720-2940. DELUXE TO ULTRA-DELUXE.

Victoria House Inn resides in a Romanesque brick building whose past lives include YMCA and boardinghouse. Impeccably restored and opened in 1992, it is an intimate, private place with a lovely parlor for a lobby and three floors of rooms painted deep plum and green and plushly carpeted. Big windows are fitted with wood blinds and lace shades, and cabinets and headboards are fashioned of rich wood. In the morning, a chambermaid brings you a champagne breakfast. ~ 208 King Street, Charleston; 803-720-2944, 800-933-5464, fax 803-720-2930. ULTRA-DELUXE.

A landmark Charleston caravanserai since 1924, the **Francis Marion Hotel** reopened in 1996 after being closed since Hurricane Hugo's unwelcome visit in 1989. Extensive refurbishing has not obscured the hotel's stunning historic features. The lobby is just as grand as ever, with its original chandeliers and marble countertops at the front desk. The 200 guest rooms, which have 24-foot ceilings, are accented with antique furnishings and burgundy floral bedspreads. Amenities here are many: weight room, sauna, art gallery, lobby bar and five-star restaurant. ~ Located at 387 King Street, Charleston; 803-722-0600, 800-433-3733, fax 803-723-4633. ULTRA-DELUXE.

Charleston Place sprawls in the midst of historic downtown, its 440 luxuriant rooms sequestered within a complex of savvy shops.

✔ CHECK THESE OUT—UNIQUE LODGING

- *Budget to moderate:* Spend a night in **Serendipity**, a Spanish mission–style house—it's a refreshing change from the blur of Myrtle Beach. *page 327*
- *Moderate:* Enjoy Lowcountry solitude at **Cassina Point Plantation**, an antebellum manse hidden on a salt marsh. *page 352*
- *Deluxe to ultra-deluxe:* Dine on English china, relax on roomy piazzas, and sleep under down comforters at the **Rhett House Inn.** *page 363*
- *Ultra-deluxe:* Settle into one of four lavish suites in the 1750 plantation house at **Litchfield Plantation**, complete with gourmet dining and equestrian center. *page 328*

Budget: under $60   Moderate: $60–$100   Deluxe: $100–$130   Ultra-deluxe: over $130

Many Charlestonians decry it for its size and newness, but in fact it has everything a visitor could want, from the grand lobby of marble and glittering chandeliers to the spacious rooms with beautiful reproduction furnishings, plush draperies and views of the city or courtyard. Service is superb. A fitness center with an indoor-outdoor pool and the excellent Louis's Charleston Grill are here, too. Not surprisingly, the rates are some of the city's highest. ~ 130 Market Street, Charleston; 803-722-4900, 800-611-5545, fax 803-722-4074. ULTRA-DELUXE.

In all of Charleston, there surely is not a more secluded, romantic place than **Jasmine House**. It's located along quiet Hasell (pronounced "Hazel") Street in Charleston's 18th-century Ansonborough neighborhood, though Jasmine was built in the 1840s. The vanilla-washed Green Revival mansion has ten luxurious rooms, with four inside a carriage house, all outfitted in grand style with antiques and finds from the Far East to England (the owner is an interior designer and collector). There's barely a hint of a hostelry here—visitors check in across the street at Indigo Inn (One Maiden Lane), which shares the same owner—and after a few hours you feel like the place belongs to you. ~ 64 Hasell Street, Charleston; 803-577-5900, 800-845-7639. ULTRA-DELUXE.   ◀ HIDDEN

Offering only one guest room, **65 Radcliffe** is a historic 1880s home set near Charleston's historic district. Furnished in antiques, the room is equipped with a private bath, cable television, a refrigerator and coffeemaker. A private porch overlooks quaint Radcliffe Street. The clientele is primarily gay men and women. Closed January and February. ~ 65 Radcliffe Street, Charleston; 803-577-6183. MODERATE.

Northwest of downtown Charleston and next door to Middleton Place plantation is the highly unusual **Middleton Inn**. Its stark granite exterior has a Gotham look, but inside, the 55 rooms are commodious spaces full of light and warmth, with lustrous wood cabinets, wood-burning fireplaces, thick glass blocks curving around sunken tubs, and floor-to-ceiling windows looking out on the woods and Ashley River. Frank Lloyd Wright fans will love it here. Continental breakfast and free admission to Middleton Place gardens (but not the house) are included in the deluxe rate (moderate on weekdays). ~ Ashley River Road, 14 miles from Charleston; 803-556-0500, 800-543-4774. MODERATE TO DELUXE.   ◀ HIDDEN

South of Charleston, the lodging choices at **Kiawah Island Resort** include a 150-room inn and myriads of cottages, villas and homes for rent. Families especially enjoy these private, landscaped environs with ten miles of beaches, several restaurants, oceanfront pool, four golf courses and 16 miles of bike trails. Reservations required to enter the property. ~ Kiawah Island; 803-768-2121, 800-654-2924. DELUXE TO ULTRA-DELUXE.

HIDDEN ▶

On Edisto Island, the venerable **Cassina Point Plantation** is tucked way off the main track along a salt marsh, its lawns dotted with pecan and live oak trees. This plantation is on the National Historic Register. The house is more than 140 years old, an antebellum manse built by newlywed planters and later occupied by Federal troops, whose etchings are apparent on the first-floor walls. Accommodations are in four cozy rooms, each with antiques, fireplaces and a half-bath. Two full baths are shared. There's not much to do here but relax in a rocker, try for crabs in the creek and watch the sun bleed down into the marsh every evening. The beach is seven miles away. You must have a reservation to enter the grounds. Breakfast is included. ~ Off Indigo Hill Road, Edisto Island; 803-869-2535. MODERATE.

Cottage and home rentals on Edisto are available by calling the **Atwood Agency.** ~ 803-869-2151, 800-476-0126. You may also want to try **Edisto Sales and Rentals Realty.** ~ 803-869-2527, 800-868-5398. Another option is **Lachicotte & Harper Realty.** ~ 803-869-1930, 800-962-1930.

With an ambiance that could be described as English country manor, the **Woodlands Resort** is situated in a lavishly restored 1906 mansion. Individually decorated, the 18 late-Victorian guest rooms are rich with antiques. Several have four-poster beds; four rooms have 17-foot ceilings. It's easy to feel pampered; there's an elegant dining room, a spa, a pool, clay tennis courts and croquet. ~ 125 Parsons Road, Summerville; 803-875-2600; 800-774-9999, fax 803-865-2603. ULTRA-DELUXE.

DINING

Lowcountry cuisine reaches its zenith in Charleston, and you'll find wonderful French and Italian food as well.

The splendid, singular **Gaulart & Maliclet,** known around the city as "Fast and French" or simply "F&F," is deep and skinny and lined with lots of little bars and counters. Grab a newspaper from a wall rack, have a seat at a bar, and choose from homemade soups, pâtés and quiches, smoked salmon and stuffed baguettes, and fruit, sandwich and cheese plates. There's petit and grand *dejeuner* every morning, and hearty dinners of escargot, fondue, chicken and fish. Go for the daily budget-priced specials with five items, including soup and a glass of wine. ~ 98 Broad Street, Charleston; 803-577-9797. BUDGET TO MODERATE.

A local critic likened **Kiva Han** to Casablanca. And with good reason: the sumptuous ambiance doesn't quit, with a warm green decor, Turkish divans with pillows and British colonial–style tables. The cuisine deserves mention as well; the lamb spring roll with feta and spinach is a delectable appetizer. For the main course, consider the Moroccan grilled snapper with shrimp falafel or the pecan-crusted lamb loin with a maple vinaigrette. ~ 235 East Bay Street, Charleston; 803-965-5282. MODERATE.

It's no coincidence that the initials of **Slightly North of Broad** spell SNOB; the restaurant is a pecan toss from Charleston's lofty old houses just off the Battery. But there's nothing stuffy about this place, so big and open and high-ceilinged and situated in a restored warehouse, with friendly waiters and arty accoutrements. The elegant Southern and regional fare includes grilled barbecued tuna topped with fried oysters and country ham, and maverick grits, a thick stew with shrimp, scallops, ham, white wine and tomatoes. Sandwiches for lunch. ~ 192 East Bay Street, Charleston; 803-723-3424. MODERATE.

Magnolia's is Charleston's premier Lowcountry haunt. The crisp linens are starched and as white as a magnolia, the light as soft and low as a Southern full-moon night. The patrons are trendy, very trendy. The chef, thirtysomething Donald Barickman, turns out such creations as sautéed black grouper filet with Cajun crawfish tails and yellow corn over creamy white grits. His signature "Down South" egg roll is stuffed with collard greens, chicken and ham and served with a trio of sauces: red pepper purée, spicy mustard sauce and peach chutney. If you can't go for dinner, go for lunch. ~ 185 East Bay Street, Charleston; 803-577-7771. DELUXE.

Adjacent to Magnolias and sharing the same owners, **Blossom Cafe** goes Mediterranean-style. The indoor-outdoor bistro is richly done in tones of hunter green and burgundy. The service is stellar, the wait staff comprised of vibrant, beautiful people. There's plenty of pasta, all hand-rolled and artfully prepared, but it's the wood-burning pizzas and their nouveau flourishes (roma tomatoes, pesto, artichoke hearts) that everyone loves. Workday crowds pack in just before noon and just after 5 p.m. ~ 171 East Bay Street, Charleston; 803-722-9200. MODERATE.

Venerable yet still chic, Charleston's **Carolinas** retains many loyal patrons. The specialty is nouveau Lowcountry fare, and there will undoubtedly be something on the menu to please you. Among the favorites are the almond-crusted grouper and the flounder in sweet potatoes. There are also plenty of poultry, pasta and beef dishes. Expect a memorable dining experience. Reservations are recommended on the weekend. ~ 10 Exchange Street, Charleston; 803-724-3800. DELUXE.

You can dine inside tony **82 Queen,** but ask for a seat out in the rambling brick courtyard with tables tucked beneath a gazebo and hoods of wisteria and rose trees. People gush about 82 Queen and its Lowcountry nouveau cooking, and this is understandable. One could eat bowls of the barbecued shrimp and grits crowned with cheddar cheese and scallions, and the pudding-thick she-crab soup laced with sherry. There are plates of oysters stuffed with Daufuskie crab and topped with melted jack cheese, roast duckling with blackberry-Cointreau glaze, and grilled Georgia lamb chops with golden pear chutney. For both lunch and dinner, the mood is momentous: waiters hurrying from the dining room, the front door mobbed with hopeful diners, the clientele Southern and smartly dressed. Don't go without a reservation. ~ 82 Queen Street, Charleston; 803-722-4428. MODERATE TO DELUXE.

Dark, small and savvy, **Fulton Five** is Italian all the way, from the platters of carpaccio, prosciutto and buffalo mozzarella that greet you at the door to the ruby wine poured in small, glittering glasses. The music is like something from a Mickey Rourke flick—fast, anxious, angst-filled. The people are polished and pretty. The pasta, chicken, veal and seafood dishes are good to great. ~ 5 Fulton Street, Charleston; 803-853-5555. MODERATE TO DELUXE.

Long, narrow and lively all day, **Baker's Cafe** has an inventive lineup of eggs and turnovers, quiches and pasta, seafood and soups (you should try the chicken soup with orzo and English sage). There's art parked on the walls and tables squeezed in tight. A back dining room offers more space—if there are any empty seats. A good place for breakfast. ~ 214 King Street, Charleston; 803-577-2694. BUDGET TO MODERATE.

HIDDEN ► In a little, blue-painted shack near the U.S. Customs House, you'll find **Your Place**. Citadel cadets and other college students have made it their place, crowding into the beat-up wood booths and ordering Charleston's juiciest, beefiest burgers. Order them plain or lavished with bacon, cheese or jalapeños. There's beer, wine and long, tall glasses of sweet tea. The waitresses wear tattoos, the walls are festooned with useless nautical items, the concrete floors flood when it rains a lot. ~ 6 Market Street, Charleston; 803-722-8360. BUDGET.

For long, leisurely, Lowcountry dining, go to **Louis's Charleston Grill**. You can listen to live jazz and eat whole baby flounder with sweet onion gravy, wild mushroom ragout with creamy grits, grilled marinated shrimp with peanut barbecue sauce, or McClellanville lump crab cakes plied with chunks of lobster and served with grained mustard. Such dishes are the inventions of chef Louis Osteen, who has a loyal following of Charlestonians. The handsome dining room is wood-paneled and prettily lit. ~ Charleston Place, 130 Market Street, Charleston; 803-577-4522. DELUXE.

A little worn-out and a lot popular, **Fannie's Diner** has a 24-hour breakfast scene: eggs and bacon on the griddle, sparkly red booths and chrome-rimmed tables hugging the walls, Elvis on the radio. Tourists, students and downtown workers are the diner's typical patrons, except for those past-midnight bloodshot hours, when bikers and drag queens and pretty young boys stop by for a cholesterol nightcap. ~ 137 Market Street, Charleston; 803-723-7121. BUDGET.

Vickeries Bar & Grill is a popular hangout serving Lowcountry cuisine with a Cuban flair. Opt for the classic Cuban sandwich or the black beans and rice and you will be transported to Havana. Or stay closer to home with the roast half-chicken or the turkey pita with mixed greens, brie and raspberry mayonnaise. The bar is lively and the outdoor patio is, regulars say, the best in town. ~ 15 Beaufain Street, Charleston; 803-577-5300. MODERATE.

In a funky, tilting pink building on a quiet street corner, **Celia's** serves hearty, gratifying Italian fare like polenta lasagna layered with spinach, marinara and béchamel sauce, and pasta with Gorgonzola, pine nuts and basil. Lasagna is the specialty, and you can also order chicken, veal, seafood and fish, including grilled tuna. Charlestonians love this cozy, conversational place with flickering candles and a piano player. ~ 49 Archdale Street, at Beaufain Street, Charleston; 803-722-9003. MODERATE.

◄ HIDDEN

If you stay on Edisto Island, have dinner at the **Old Post Office**. The cream plank board building with big blue mailboxes out front is topped with tin and surrounded by enormous live oaks. Within the high-ceiling dining rooms you can enjoy such unusual offerings as clam and jalapeño bisque with three cheeses, pecan chicken with blueberry sauce, and asparagus and blue crab pie. Shrimp Creole and ribeye steak are among the more familiar entrées, and there is fish, smoked out back over apple wood. Dinner only; reservations recommended. Closed Sunday. ~ Route 174 along Store Creek, Edisto Island; 803-869-2339. DELUXE.

Charleston has a burgeoning cafe culture, with plenty of coffeehouses to choose from when you're looking for a light meal. **Rainbow Cafe** has a young crowd, a giant chess table and plenty of newspapers to read. Choose from pastries, salads and sandwiches. ~ 282 King Street; 803-853-9777. Set in the middle of the College Street scene, **Clara's Coffee** serves veggie burgers, black-bean burgers and chicken salad. ~ 344 King Street; 803-723-9845. Near "Four Corners of Law," **Eleven Llamas** is popular with the government and business crowd. Menu favorites include a tuna salad, a turkey sandwich with Gorgonzola, and a chef's salad. ~ 58 Broad Street; 803-723-7400.

People from all over the Carolinas make shopping forays into Charleston. This isn't bargain shopping (though there are many deals to be had); we're talking antiquing and boutiquing at its very best. Whether you seek eighteenth-century English silver or Gothic garden statuary, the sassiest clothes or headiest chocolate truffles, things both bazaar and bizarre, you will find them among these brick and cobbled streets.

SHOPPING

Utopia has the ultimate in cool clothes and shoes for women. Not a big selection, but smart-looking stuff. ~ 27 Broad Street, Charleston; 803-853-9510.

Where else but Charleston would you find a store specializing in finials? **The Ground Floor** has a selection of more than 30 styles, with ornaments including puma heads, acorns and pineapples. They'll further customize yours with paint, stain or gold leaf. ~ 95½ Broad Street, Charleston; 803-722-3576.

If by now you are completely charmed by Charleston, go to the **Preservation Society of Charleston Bookstore**. Anything you could possibly want to know about the place, from floor coverings to private gardens to restoring old homes, is offered within the pages of a book. Besides that, the employees here are anxious to help you get to know the city. ~ 147 King Street, Charleston; 803-723-4381.

> Direct your energies along King Street for antiques and East Bay Street for trendy, cutting-edge gifts and apparel.

Need a tie or a blazer button? **Ben Silver** has thousands of both, with price tags reaching into the thousands. The London-based store will also sell you a sterling Chippendale photo frame, attire for your cricket or croquet match, and the "authoritative book" *The Gentlemen's Clubs of London*. ~ 149 King Street, Charleston; 803-577-4556, 800-221-4671.

George C. Birlant & Co., around since 1929, sells all manner of eighteenth- and nineteenth-century silver, china and crystal, as well as Charleston Battery benches. ~ 191 King Street, Charleston; 803-722-3842.

The Audubon Shop & Gallery is an enormous space filled with field accessories, telescopes, homewares, even candles for the yard. ~ 245 King Street, Charleston; 803-723-6171, 800-453-2473.

The great-smelling **Stella Nova** stocks luxuriant French-milled soaps and body lotions, clever cards and playful gadgets for your hair. ~ 292 King Street, Charleston; 803-722-9797.

The zany **Granny's Goodies** carries both new and used oddities, from Jerry Garcia chia heads to bizarre T-shirts and tie-dye everything. ~ 301 King Street, Charleston; 803-577-6200.

With a sister store in Atlanta, **Metropolitan Deluxe** is a purveyor of stylish furniture, fine linens, cards, truffles and fresh flowers. ~ 164 Market Street, Charleston; 803-722-0436.

The Shops at Charleston Place is downtown Charleston's chic mini-mall. In a rambling red-brick complex that includes the Charleston Place Hotel, the stores are for the most part familiar chains (Banana Republic, Godiva, Talbots, Laura Ashley), though you will find a few singular boutiques. There's a parking garage here. ~ Market Street, between Meeting and King streets.

Get your gargoyles at **The Gothic Shop**. The garden and architectural accents here also include pedestals, columns, moldings, brackets and other statuary (besides gargoyles). Originals and replicas available. ~ 223 Meeting Street, Charleston; 803-577-2938.

For flea market items and those a notch above, go to **The Old City Market**. Even if you're not buying, the market's weary old-brick walls and wood-beam ceilings are atmospheric, and you can't help but get swept along in the flush of shoppers. ~ Market Street between Meeting and East Bay streets.

Charleston cooks at night. Bar-hopping is de rigueur, and plenty of **NIGHTLIFE**
places are geared toward early or late-night crowds.

The patio at **Mesa Grill** is great for drinks and people-watching. There's also acoustic sounds on weekends. ~ 35 North Market Street, Charleston; 803-723-3770.

Wild Wing Cafe, one in a chain around the Carolinas, can get crazy most anytime, but later is better. Come for beer by the bucket, chicken wings and insanity. Bands on summer weekends. ~ 36 North Market Street, Charleston; 803-722-9464.

Save **Kaminsky's** for after dinner. The "Most Excellent Café" has brick walls and a glass case filled with tempting chocolate trappings. There's good wine and music, a gay and straight crowd, and a lineup of sassy coffee drinks. ~ 78 North Market Street, Charleston; 803-853-8270.

The classy **Chef & Clef** is the place for live jazz. Go late at night for drinks and dessert. ~ 102 North Market Street, Charleston; 803-722-0732.

Just before sunset, go to the **Library at Vendue**. The rooftop roost, peopled with pretty faces, is prime for watching the golden globe sink down along the Cooper River, with views across Waterfront Park and Charleston Harbor. ~ 23 Vendue Range, Charleston; 803-723-0485.

First a British tavern in 1778, **McCrady's Tavern** lives again, thanks to a 1993 resurrection that kept the original bricks and fireplace. A warm atmosphere, zany bartenders, savory eats and hefty, hearty brews make it a great place to hang out. ~ 2 Unity Alley, between East Bay and State streets, Charleston; 803-853-8484.

The polished, post-Modern bar at **Blossom Cafe** is tended by young men in ponytails. Young professionals settle in at the bar for happy hour, and an older crowd appears in the after-dinner hours. ~ 171 East Bay Street, Charleston; 803-722-9200.

Stop by **Kiva Han** for a nightcap and enjoy the live jazz on Saturday night. If you're concerned about your cigars spoiling while you're traveling, check them into their humidor. ~ 235 East Bay Street, Charleston; 803-965-5282.

In a big recycled warehouse and looking like a mini concert hall, the **Music Farm** hosts regional and big-name rock-and-roll, reggae, new wave and jazz bands several days a week. Advance tickets available. The scene is young and happening. ~ 32 Ann Street, Charleston; 803-722-8904.

Have a seat at the snake—the bar, I mean—at **Arizona Bar & Grill**. The 35-foot bar, shaped like a rattlesnake, slithers through this happy-hour hotspot serving Southwestern and Lowcountry eats. ~ 14 Chapel Street, Charleston; 803-577-5090.

The place to go in Edisto is **Coot's**, a funky joint situated right on the beach that hosts good blues and beach bands most summer evenings. The rest of the year, there are live acts featured on weekends. ~ The Pavilion, 102 Palmetto Drive, Edisto Island; 803-869-3063.

THEATER, BALLET AND SYMPHONY   For three weeks each spring, the **Spoleto Festival,** a Charleston-based performing-arts festival, presents internationally acclaimed opera, dance, jazz, theater and psymphonic programs at venues throughout the city. ~ 14 George Street; 803-722-2764.

Charleston's best plays come from the **Amazing Stage Theatre Company,** which produces classical and cutting-edge musicals, drama and comedy, as well as children's theater. ~ 133 Church Street, Charleston; 803-577-5967.

Dancers with the **Charleston Ballet** come from as far as Moscow, San Francisco and New York. South Carolina's only full-time professional dance company, the ballet presents traditional and contemporary dance throughout the year. ~ 280 Meeting Street, Charleston; 803-723-7334.

Classical, chamber and pop music concerts are presented September through May by the **Charleston Symphony Orchestra.** ~ 14 George Street, Charleston; 803-723-7528.

GAY SCENE   Gay and straight night owls mingle at most Charleston nightspots. For a strictly gay scene, try **Dudley's,** a "men's Cheers of Charleston." It's a "private club," so call ahead for information. ~ 346 King Street, Charleston; 803-723-2784.

With a mixed crowd, **Channel Red** is a hip spot for drinking and dancing in the upper King Street neighborhood. ~ 467 King Street, Charleston; 803-722-7009.

There's also **The Arcade,** with glitzy, Las Vegas–style drag shows. On nights when there are no shows, there is dancing—loud, pulsing and high-energy. Open Thursday through Sunday. Cover. ~ 5 Liberty Street, Charleston; 803-722-5656.

BEACHES & PARKS

Beaches are not the Lowcountry's high point, for obvious reasons: dozens of creeks and rivers delivering mud and silt out to shore and ocean. The surf gets cloudy and the sand ruddy. Near the mudflats, the beaches are littered with pesky oyster fragments. Among the few exceptions are the far-flung islands north of Charleston called Cape Romain.

HIDDEN ►

CAPE ROMAIN NATIONAL WILDLIFE REFUGE 🏃 🐊 ⬇   This 22-mile crescent of barrier islands between the Intracoastal Waterway and the Atlantic Ocean is wild, windswept—and extremely remote. You must take a ferry to the island, and it only operates three days a week. **Bulls Island,** the southern end of the refuge, is the only place you can go ashore. Here are some of the South Carolina coast's best sands, a lonesome strand of fine, deep white. Shelling is excellent. The 20-minute boat ride over is through dense salt

Sweetgrass
Baskets

Along the country roadsides of Route 17 near Mount Pleasant, you will see ebony-skinned women sitting beneath roofs of tin and plywood and selling sweetgrass baskets. They are intricate baskets, tightly woven and as resilient as the women who have spent years learning their art. Properly cared for, a sweetgrass basket will last generations. No two baskets are alike.

It is an old Lowcountry art, the making of sweetgrass baskets, originating about 300 years ago when the first Africans were shipped to the South to be slaves. The women waded into the marsh and cut the wispy, plume-like grass and took it home to dry. Its scent was good, like fresh-cut hay. They bound it with palmetto fronds, stitching the grass with slivers of frond in interlocking patterns (a maddeningly meticulous task) until it became rows of coil.

The baskets were used on the plantations; commodious ones carried produce to market, while wide, flat, winnowing trays called "fanners" separated chaff from rice. Deep baskets, which African men often made from bulrush, stored grain, cotton and fish. Ornamental baskets were filled with fruit and placed on sideboards and dining tables of plantation manors. Today, they are exhibited in museums and sold at art shows.

Mount Pleasant, across the Cooper River from Charleston, is the heart of sweetgrass country. From the humble shacks and lean-tos alongside Route 17, the Mount Pleasant Sweetgrass Basketmakers' Association sells beautiful vessels that cost up to several hundred dollars. The smallest basket (the size of a tea cup) sells for about $10. Fruit baskets with thin, graceful handles start at $50, and urn-shaped containers are over $100. Some baskets are woven with bulrush and longleaf pine needles.

Many of the women speak Gullah, a pure, rich Creole language developed by their plantation ancestors. As they sell their baskets they sing the soft, strong Gullah hymns. Besides the stalls on Route 17, you'll find Gullah basket weavers in Charleston at **The Old Charleston Market**. ~ Market Street between Meeting and East Bay streets. You can also find them at **The Four Corners of Law**. ~ Meeting and Broad streets.

In Georgetown, Mary A. Graham sells her sweetgrass baskets at **The Weavers Nook**. ~ Inside The Homecoming Store, 829-B Front Street; 803-527-6948. Down in the Sea Islands, **The Red Piano Too Art Gallery** has a small selection of baskets. ~ 751 Sea Island Parkway, St. Helena Island; 803-838-2241.

marsh populated by pelicans, egrets, herons and other shorebirds. Take along comfortable walking shoes, binoculars, insect repellent, a picnic and plenty to drink, including fresh water. This place is primitive. Swim here at your own risk; the water can be rough and the currents strong. As far as fishing goes, there is good surf casting, though it's a pain to lug the rods and tackle. Facilities include restrooms, picnic tables, and 16 miles of nature trails. ~ Ferries (there is a ferry fee of $15 per person) leave from Moores Landing, off Route 17 about twenty miles north of Charleston, just before Awendaw. From Route 17, turn east on Seewee Road; 803-928-3368. Call Cape Romain Charters (803-928-3411) for schedules and prices.

ISLE OF PALMS AND SULLIVAN'S ISLAND ⚓ These twin islands just north of Charleston are where the city folk go for sun and sand. Both were devastated in 1987 by Hurricane Hugo and so new construction is rampant. Big stilt homes line the dunes, and then there is silvery, hard-packed sand that often runs thin on high tide. Both islands are packed in summer, with traffic crawling along Route 703. Isle of Palms is favored by families and older people; there's wheelchair access across the dunes. Swimming is good along beaches at both islands. Facilities include a snack bar, restrooms, public parking lots and showers at Isle of Palms. There are restaurants and stores a few blocks from Sullivan's Island beaches. ~ The islands are located along an 12-mile stretch of Route 703, about nine miles north of Charleston.

FOLLY BEACH COUNTY PARK ⚓ 🏄 On one side of this park is Folly River and a spacious sweep of seagrass, on the other is a string of beach, silvery, silty and whipped by waves. Surfers love it here; the winds lash constantly at this land's end point of Folly Island, just south of Charleston. Wooden ramps provide wheelchair access to the beach. The gay and lesbian crowd gravitates to the southernmost end of the beach. Strong tides and currents and hidden deep areas make swimming here more challenging. Swim only in designated areas, where lifeguards patrol in summer. Facilities include picnic tables and shelter, outdoor showers and restrooms year-round; a snack bar, beach rentals and gift shop operate during the summer. Day-use fee, $4. ~ Located on the west end of Folly Island, off Route 171, about 12 miles southeast of Charleston; 803-588-2426.

HIDDEN ► **BEACHWALKER PARK** ⚓ This is the only public beach on Kiawah Island, and it is a fine one. Tremendous vistas of windblown seagrass end in forests of oak and palms, and there is the dark, snaking Kiawah River. The Atlantic Ocean borders one side of Beachwalker, complete with wide, windy beach—up to 200 feet wide at low tide. The condos and townhouses of private Kiawah

Island Resort are visible in the distance. There are strong winds and currents; swim in the designated area, staffed by lifeguards in summer. Facilities include restrooms, outdoor showers, picnic area, and a seasonal snack bar. ~ Located on the west end of Kiawah Island, off Bohicket Road, about 30 miles southeast of Charleston; 803-762-2172.

EDISTO BEACH STATE PARK 🏃 ⚓ 🚣 Spread across 1500 acres   ◄ *HIDDEN* of dunes, marsh and tidal creeks, low forest and shelly sand, the park extends from the Atlantic Ocean well into Edisto Island. It was built in the 1930s by the Civilian Conservation Corps and today is a nesting ground for endangered loggerhead turtles. The beach is a combination of brownish, dirtlike sand and crushed oyster shells, so bring a chair. Five air conditioned cabins with screened porches, picnic tables and barbecue grills overlook Scott Creek. Budget-priced, with a two-night minimum, the cabins should be booked at least six months ahead. Swimming is okay in the ocean, though the water is often cloudy. Fishing is superb. Come in late fall and fish for trout, bass, flounder, whiting, spot and even shark. Crabbing and shrimping are also excellent. Facilities include park office, restrooms and nature trails. Day-use fee, $3. ~ Located off Route 174 on Edisto Island, about 50 miles southeast of Charleston; 803-869-2156.

▲ There are 103 RV and tent campsites, including 75 with hookups; $9 to $22 per night.

On a map, the 69 inland miles between Charleston and Beaufort look empty. Route 17, which is two lanes most of the way, ambles through scrub pine and oak forest sprinkled with scant towns like Parkers Ferry, Jacksonboro and Ashepoo, then enters the hushed, hazy domain of Ace Basin National Wildlife Refuge.

▼▼▼▼▼▼▼▼▼▼
Beaufort & the Sea Islands

The **Ace Basin National Wildlife Refuge** is vast, some 350,000   **SIGHTS** acres of marsh and rivers and swamps, one of the last coastal wildernesses in the Carolinas. Alligators, wading birds and ducks (such   ◄ *HIDDEN* as blue-winged teals), nest here. There are 27 known pairs of bald eagles.

A few miles south of the basin, take the eastern turnoff for Route 21 and after 15 miles you'll arrive in **Beaufort**. It's a superb small Southern port town with rich Colonial and antebellum flourishes and only 8600 residents. Grand old mansions number more than 150. They march along a waterfront of salt marsh and frilly palmetto trees. The streets have ceilings of ancient oaks and magnolias. The air is perfumed by the sea.

Beaufort's first homes weren't grand but very simple, sturdy structures built by Barbadian planters, religious refugees, English indentured servants and others who came seeking a new life in the early 1700s. The settlers burned oyster shells with lime to make tabby, strong as cement, and used it to secure their clapboard homes. They faced the homes southward at the river, to catch prevailing breezes, and gave them Georgian, Greek Revival and tropical Spanish touches.

A hundred years later, sea island cotton came to Beaufort and neighboring islands and made a lot of people very rich. It was an unusual cotton, soft and silken and extremely prized in Europe. From 1820 to 1860, wealthy planters built furiously across Beaufort, fashioning plantation-style homes with formal gardens on big lots all over town. Today, they fill the downtown, creating a kind of outdoor, privately owned museum. Filmmakers like Beaufort. Its fanciful homes and boundaries of river and vast salt marsh and sky, so surreal and Hollywood-like, have been the backdrop for many films.

Films such as *The Big Chill*, *The Great Santini*, *The Prince of Tides* and *Forrest Gump* have been filmed in Beaufort.

Walk into the **Greater Beaufort Chamber of Commerce** and the first thing you'll hear is: "Have you seen *The Prince of Tides*? Well, right out here on this dock is where Nick Nolte was at the end of the movie," and so on about many scenes that really did or didn't take place around town. The chamber folks will explain how to best explore Beaufort and the nearby sea islands, including tips on carriage, walking and boat tours. ~ 1006 Bay Street, Beaufort; 803-524-3163.

Adjacent to the chamber is the pretty **Henry C. Chambers Waterfront Park**, dotted with oak trees and paved with brick piazzas and those made of crushed oyster shells. There are lots of benches and even swings along the seawall. Bay Street runs along the park and the water, and this is where you should start your walk around Beaufort. Shops, eateries and inns are sprinkled along Bay Street and the few blocks just off it.

The west end of Bay Street is laced with fabulous homes and manses and immense trees strung with Spanish moss. At low tide the bay reveals brown caps of oyster beds and waves of seagrass.

Near the center of Bay Street you'll find the **John Mark Verdier House Museum**. Built by a prominent merchant in 1790, it is not a prominent place but one filled with fascinating details on early Beaufort life. The Federal-style house faces south to catch river breezes and is built up high to avoid flooding (like so many early Beaufort homes, the first of its three floors is called the "garden floor"). The woodworking is outstanding, from the ocean waves carved along the staircase to cable and rope detailing along the fireplace mantles. There's a fireplace in each of the eight guest rooms. Admission. ~ 801 Bay Street, Beaufort; 803-524-6334.

You'll also find plenty of history at **The Beaufort Museum**. It's two blocks north of Bay Street in the 1798 Beaufort Arsenal, sunny yellow and Gothic in style with its pointed arches and heavy, castle-like gates. Two rooms are saturated with Lowcountry lore and arti-facts, including a tin bathtub, walnut chest and wedding dresses from the 1800s. Admission. ~ 713 Craven Street, Beaufort; 803-525-7077.

Near the east end of Bay Street, Route 21 crosses the Beaufort River and for 18 miles threads across a series of secluded **sea is-lands**. Also called the Sea Island Parkway, the road is the only way in and out of these Lowcountry lairs. It passes first along **Ladys Island** and then **St. Helena Island**, with scenes of small pastures dotted with grain silos, signs for pick-your-own tomatoes, match-book-size seafood markets, and stands of tall cabbage palm trees. No-name dirt roads trail off from the Sea Island Parkway.

On St. Helena Island, you'll find the town of **St. Helena Island**, home to a few shops, gas stations, eateries and residences. Out of town, bridges bring endless horizons of salt marsh, their grassy shallows and mudflats attended by hopeful shorebirds. Snapping turtles cross the road. Shrimp boats send out their wide nets, like birds opening their wings, and drag the bottom for the pearly pink shellfish. There is a restaurant here called the Shrimp Shack where you can eat a shrimp burger.

After St. Helena comes tiny, soon-to-be-developed **Harbor Island**, then densely wooded **Hunting Island**, where all 5000 acres are protected as a state park. The last of the sea islands, the end of the cul-de-sac, is **Fripp Island**, a private resort that you can enter only with a reservation. ~ 803-838-3535, 800-845-4100.

On the west end of Beaufort's Bay Street, **TwoSuns Inn** is a homey and inviting bed and breakfast housed in a 1917 Neoclassical Revival manse. There are five bedrooms painted deep colors and given ruffly, floral flourishes. One has an Asian theme, another is pure Victoriana. All have views of the salt marsh and bay. There is a croquet lawn in front, and a ramp that accommodates wheelchair visitors. Full breakfast is included in the rates. ~ 1705 Bay Street, Beaufort; 803-522-1122, 800-532-4244. DELUXE.

LODGING

An antebellum manse overlooking the Intracoastal Waterway, **Bay Street Inn** has eight guest rooms with water views, private baths and attractive antiques. Seven have fireplaces. The living room is embellished with gilt moldings, and a crystal chandelier presides over the dining room. Here formal breakfast is served, which is included in the rates. ~ 601 Bay Street, Beaufort; 803-522-0050. DELUXE.

One of Beaufort's most desirable guesthouse resides but a block from Bay Street and the harbor. **Rhett House Inn** is lovely, quite Southern and civilized in every way. Classical music is played at breakfast, and sugar-dusted French toast is served on English china. Guest rooms are high-ceilinged and plushly adorned with down comforters, handsome antiques and thick pile towels. There is a lush courtyard and two floors of wide piazzas wonderful for relaxing and listening to birdsong. Fine dining is offered on some nights. Owners Stephen and Marianne Harrison are former Manhattaners (her father started Anne Klein) who are completely cordial, seeing to your every need. ~ 1009 Craven Street, Beaufort; 803-524-9030, fax 803-524-1310. ULTRA-DELUXE.

As charming as a dollhouse, the award-winning **Beaufort Inn** sits in the heart of the Historic Landmark District. The common area, with mahogany trim, marble-and-slate fireplaces and pine floors, are impeccably decorated with period furniture. The inn's centerpiece is a stairway that curves around a 50-foot-high atrium and connects rooms on the second and third floors. Each of the 13 guest rooms, which vary in size and decor, is named after a Lowcountry plantation and features photographs of the room's namesake. There are modern amenities as well: wet bars, two-person jacuzzis and stocked refrigerators. Despite this modernity, the proprietors, Rusty and Debbie Fielden, retain Southern hospitality and traditions; high tea is served and rocking chairs on the front porch beckon to guests. ~ 809 Port Republic Street, Beaufort; 803-521-9000, fax 803-521-9500. DELUXE TO ULTRA-DELUXE.

HIDDEN ▶   You can rent a cottage, villa or efficiency within the private, quiet confines of **Fripp Island Resort**. The southeasternmost sea island, Fripp has more than three miles of beach, much of it secluded, and a golf course along the ocean. If you don't like golf, you can gather clams and oysters along the flats. There are tennis courts, restaurants, swimming pools, shops, a marina and a church. Nature trails and golf cart paths meander around the island, and golf carts are the vehicle of choice. Great for families, the resort even has a camp for kids. Many places rent by the week only in summer. ~ Route 21; 803-838-3535, 800-845-4100. MODERATE TO ULTRA-DELUXE.

DINING   You can sit out along the Beaufort River at **The Gadsby Tavern** and enjoy well-prepared soups, salads and sandwiches. Among the house specialties: a grouper melt, lobster and scallops *en croûte*, and Daufuskie crab cakes on a jalapeño cheese biscuit with mustard chive sauce. The environs are quite elegant: high carved ceilings, polished wood moldings, dim lighting. Steaks and seafood dishes served at dinner. ~ 822 Bay Street, Beaufort; 803-525-1800. MODERATE.

Plums, at Beaufort's Waterfront Park, is perfect for breakfast or lunch. The casual cafe with ferns strung from the ceiling and black-and-white checkerboard floors has omelettes and pancakes and very good sandwiches. Go for the shrimp roll, grilled gouda or sliced turkey with spinach, cheese and hollandaise. The lengthier dinner menu includes pasta, chicken and steak. ~ 904½ Bay Street, Beaufort; 803-525-1946. BUDGET TO MODERATE.

Emily's is Beaufort's bistro and *tapas* bar, a colorful, cozy nook with painted wood beams and small bar. Salads and soups (try the she crab or tomato Florentine) are lunch mainstays, and there's a *tapas* lineup that includes herring in wine or Cajun sausage. For dinner, there is steak *au poivre*, blackened lamb chops and duck à l'orange. *Tapas* prices are the same for dinner or lunch. ~ 906 Port Republic Street, Beaufort; 803-522-1866. BUDGET TO DELUXE.

For slow, civilized dining by candlelight, there's **Rhett House Inn**. Open Wednesday through Saturday nights, the inn serves a prix-fixe menu that's supremely Southern. You might begin with Vidalia onion and tomato pie, then an orange and red-onion salad with honey lemon vinaigrette, then move on to potato-encrusted chicken breast with bacon, figs and Madeira. There's an extensive wine list. Reservations required. ~ 1009 Craven Street, Beaufort; 803-524-9030. ULTRA-DELUXE.

For leisurely, civilized dining, try the restaurant at the **Beaufort Inn**. The atmosphere is elegant and formal, but you're not required to dress the part. Breakfast and dinner are served every day, and brunch on Sunday. The dinner menu changes twice yearly, but longstanding favorites will appear again: crispy whole flounder with a watermelon-strawberry chutney, baked salmon on a veloute sauce, sliced roast duck breast with a shallot-berry sauce. ~ 809 Port Republic Street, Beaufort; 803-521-9000. DELUXE.

Go to the sea islands and have lunch at the **Shrimp Shack**. In a humble gray house with fishnets strung out front, you can sit in a screened porch, look across the salt marsh and enjoy a shrimp burger. The shrimp are pressed into a patty, lightly battered and crisp-fried, then laid in a soft, buttery bun—very nice. Hushpuppies,

◀ HIDDEN

✔ CHECK THESE OUT—UNIQUE DINING

- *Budget:* Eat a shrimpburger on the screened porch at the **Shrimp Shack**, with views across a silent salt marsh. *page 365*
- *Moderate:* Enjoy European cafe fare and ambiance at **Latif's**, where the air is sweet-smelling and the desserts ragingly rich. *page 329*
- *Deluxe:* Savor artful, elaborate Lowcountry cuisine at **Magnolia's**; the linens are starched crisp-white, the crowd is ultra-trendy. *page 353*
- *Deluxe:* Choose from pecan chicken with blueberry sauce, asparagus-and-blue-crab pie, and other tasty New South fare at the **Old Post Office**. *page 355*

Budget: under $9   Moderate: $9–$16   Deluxe: $16–$24   Ultra-deluxe: over $24

fried sweet-potato fingers, and red rice piled with andouille sausage are possible sides. The iced tea is as sweet as honey. You could also have a hamburger, fried flounder, crab or scallops, but hardly anyone does. In summer, the shack serves a hundred pounds of shrimp a day. Dinner also served mid-April through November. ~ Route 21, east end of St. Helena Island; 803-838-2962. BUDGET.

SHOPPING   Boutiques, galleries and antique stores are plentiful in Beaufort, especially along Bay Street and the blocks immediately north. The best antiquing is on Carteret Street.

The fine **Rhett Gallery** displays paintings and prints of the Lowcountry, as well as Civil War art and memorabilia, first-edition Audubons and antique nautical charts. ~ 901 Bay Street, Beaufort; 803-524-3339.

Cherokee pottery and stones from Brazil, India and North Carolina are among the unusual finds at **Stones 'n Bones**. ~ 903 Bay Street, Beaufort; 803-521-1185.

At **Beaufort Butterfly Company & John Cody Gallery**, enthusiastic owner Steve Mix will show you his extensive collection of butterflies and moths from Beaufort and the sea islands. For sale are butterfly soaps, T-shirts, kites and many other things with winged themes. ~ 928 Bay Street, Beaufort; 803-986-0555.

Sunlight streams in the wood and glass cupola of **Firehouse Books & Espresso Bar**, which is indeed in a restored brick fire station. Browse the ample selection of hard and paperbacks and periodicals, then have a cappuccino and slice of cheesecake. ~ 706 Craven Street, Beaufort; 803-522-2665.

HIDDEN ►   If you're fond of folk art, go to the **Red Piano Gallery Too**. The old, whitewashed house in "downtown" St. Helena Island is a gallery of brightly painted birdhouses, chairs and tables, mobiles made of watermelon sculptures, jewelry, Lowcountry paintings and other fine pieces. ~ 853 Sea Island Parkway, St. Helena Island; 803-838-2241.

NIGHTLIFE   You won't get bored in Beaufort. The top spot for live jazz, reggae and blues is **Plums**. Bands can be counted on Thursday through Saturday, and the best scene is late night. Cover. ~ 904½ Bay Street, Beaufort; 803-525-1946.

The tropigalia at **Banana's** includes a big stuffed banana dangling from the ceiling. You can sit inside at the big round bar or out on the patio along the Beaufort River. Jimmy Buffett tunes (but not Jimmy Buffett) and other live music Friday through Monday nights. ~ 910 Bay Street, Beaufort; 803-522-0910.

Catch the latest game at **Ping's Sportsbar & Grill**, or stop by for happy hour and pizza. Good local crowd. ~ At 917 Bay Street, upstairs in the Old Bay Marketplace, Beaufort; 803-521-2545.

HUNTING ISLAND STATE PARK 🏃 ⛱ ⛵ At the eastern end of the sea islands, this far-flung, 5000-acre island park is filled with slash pine and palmetto forest and edged in beach that lasts more than four miles. The sand is hard-packed and silver from intruding bits of oyster shells; the beach is thin at high tide and wide at low. There is a brick-lined lighthouse, completed in 1875 and moved to its current spot in 1889 because of beach erosion. A previous lighthouse was destroyed by Confederate troops. Displays in the visitors center tell about the lighthouses, maritime and fishing history, and the island's abundant wildlife, which includes white-tailed deer. Lodging is offered in 15 furnished, budget-priced cabins near the ocean, all with air conditioning, heating and two or three bedrooms. Try to book a year in advance. Swimming is good within designated, protected areas, in season only. Paradise Fishing Pier (803-838-7437), the longest freestanding pier on the East Coast, is at the park's southern point. It is extremely popular. Try for trout, spot, drum and tarpon. Monster tarpon have been caught in previous decades. You can also fish in the lagoon near the southern end of the park. The facilities here include a visitors center, picnic areas, a snack bar, nature trails, a fishing pier and a marsh boardwalk. Day-use fee, $3. ~ Located on Route 21, 16 miles east of Beaufort; 803-838-2011.

▲ The campground has 200 sites for tents or RVs, all with electrical and water hookups. Two sites accommodate wheelchair visitors and can be booked in advance. Remaining sites are first-come; $13 to $16 per night. A trading post and hot-water showers are located in the campground.

BEACHES & PARKS

◄ *HIDDEN*

From Beaufort, Route 170 runs southwest across the Broad River for 13 miles to Route 278. Get on Route 278 heading south and then east toward Hilton Head Island, and you will see signs for Vidalia onions and Georgia peaches. Magnolia blossoms, big, fat and white, hang from 30 feet above in towering trees along the road. The city of Savannah, Georgia, is only ten miles south.

▼▼▼▼▼▼▼▼
Hilton Head Island Area

Along Route 278 take the western turnoff on Route 46 and drive two miles through pine forest to **Bluffton**. Things haven't changed much the past few decades in this Lowcountry village, which was settled around 1825 as a summer resort for rice and cotton planters and nearly leveled by Union troops in the Civil War. Folks take their noon meals at the Squat & Gobble, a roadside dive with newspaper racks parked out front.

The heart of town runs along Calhoun Street, where little clapboard homes are buried beneath the spidery branches of live oaks. Funky emporiums offer terrific art and second-hand finds. Where

SIGHTS

◄ *HIDDEN*

Calhoun ends at the river, you'll find a peaceful setting occupied by the stunning **Church of the Cross**. The Gothic wood church, built in 1854, looks like something from medieval England with its pointed arches and heavy, castle-like doors. ~ Calhoun Street; 803-757-2661.

Back on Route 278 east a few miles, the bucolic scenes evaporate when you reach **Hilton Head Island**. Twelve miles long, five miles wide and shaped like a shoe, it is foremost a resort island, heavily developed, with seemingly every chain restaurant, motel and hotel represented and many shops and real estate offices, though all in a tasteful, intensely planned and regulated setting. A band of beaches goes on for 12 miles.

Like so much of the Lowcountry, Hilton Head was once covered in plantations. Sea Island cotton was first grown here in 1790, and rice, indigo and sugarcane soon thrived. When the Civil War barreled through, there were 24 plantations on Hilton Head. More than 12,000 Union and Federal troops with 15 warships landed here in 1861 and took the island in five hours. For 90 years Hilton Head was nearly deserted. Within its dense pine woods, hot and mosquito-infested in summer, lived several hundred Gullahs, former slaves who lived simply by farming and fishing.

All that changed in 1956 when Charles Fraser, whose family owned Hilton Head land, decided to pair fairways with fancy housing. He built a bridge connecting the island with civilization, and within two decades, country club communities mushroomed across the island.

Now Hilton Head is often called "the original island green." There are 29 golf courses and room for no more. Fairways spill over the bridge to the mainland and stretch for several miles. The 11 "plantations" of Hilton Head are of recent invention, modern planned communities with homes and villas and condos, seaside resorts, restaurants and shops, tennis and golf. They all look much the same with their well-shaped pine woods, pretty plantings and homes in muted tones of gray, green and brown.

Only about 24,000 people live on Hilton Head, although more than a million and a half more visit each year. The season lasts from about mid-March through mid-November, and in summer the roads are thick with cars, the beaches thronged with sun worshipers. Families find all they need here, including kids camps, all manner of sports and an excellent network of bike paths.

Begin your exploring with a stop at **The Museum of Hilton Head Island**. Here you may meet local historian Margaret Greer, who moved to Hilton Head in 1961, when "there were 1000 black residents and 50 whites, a filling station and a liquor store." The brief exhibits here include a re-creation of a 1500s clay island house and taxidermied birds that are extinct or endangered. ~ 100

William Hilton Parkway, one mile east of the Route 278 bridge; 803-689-6767.

Sharing the same building with the museum is the **Hilton Head Island Chamber of Commerce Welcome Center**, where you can pick up information on the island, including a map, which you will need to find your way around. More extensive information is available from the chamber's main office. ~ 1 Chamber Drive, off William Hilton Parkway, just east of Long Cove Plantation; 803-785-3673, fax 803-785-7110.

Four-lane William Hilton Parkway, also Route 278, is the main drag through Hilton Head. Hundreds of roads splinter off, nary a one of them straight. From the parkway you can access the various "plantation" communities, some with security gate and officer who will take your license plate number but allow you to pass through. The parkway ends at **Sea Pines Plantation**, the toe of the Hilton Head shoe, the only community charging an entrance fee. Sea Pines is Charles Fraser's original development, the genesis of Hilton Head. Many consider it the island's most desirable setting; it is extremely wooded, dotted with beautiful homes and deer crossing signs. There are riding stables and pretty gardens. The 600-acre **Sea Pines Forest Preserve** is thick with loblolly pines (called sea pines) and live oaks and bordered by marsh. Nature trails wind through. ~ Along Greenwood Drive and Lawton Road.

Here also is an oddity called **Heritage Farm**, where gardens of   ◄ HIDDEN
sunflowers, roses and vegetables have been planted by local folks. Open the wood-slat gate and take a stroll through the farm, and you may see gardeners tending their rented plots. ~ Greenwood Drive, across from Lawton Stables.

From the northern edge of Sea Pines you can see a mile across the Intracoastal Waterway to **Daufuskie Island**. Five miles long and   ◄ HIDDEN
three miles wide, it is secluded, accessed only by boat.

Calibogue Cruises offers half-day outings to Daufuskie and provides a golf cart for getting around the island. ~ 803-681-7925.

Plantations prospered on Daufuskie in the 1800s, and timbering, oystering and a rich Gullah culture thrived during the first half of the twentieth century. In the 1950s, Savannah factories dumped pollution into the Savannah River, the oysters died and Daufuskie's oyster plants closed.

Today, the humble, picturesque village on Daufuskie's south end is occupied by a few dozen islanders, many who still cling to Gullah traditions, living in painted wood cottages. The streets are made of sand. There's only one speed-limit sign, near the two-room clapboard elementary school. Some of the homes don't have indoor plumbing. Life is slow and seabreezy most all year.

You can walk around the village, have a look at the one-room 1912 **Daufuskie Island Elementary School** (near the public dock, on the island's southwest side) and the **First Union Baptist Church** (mid-island on the south end), built in 1880 with, count 'em, *two* front doors—one for men and one for women. At the island's southern tip, buried within trees at the end of a dirt road, the teeny **Mary Dunn Cemetery** bears the 1790 gravestone of Mary Martinangele. Most of the old epitaphs are too worn to read.

LODGING
Hilton Head is famed for pricey, amenity-packed lodging. Beautiful resorts owned by big luxury chains are draped along the beaches, tucked within the lush confines of plantation communities. For these you will pay ultra-deluxe rates in season (about mid-March through mid-November) and deluxe the rest of the time. Several motels, mostly chains, offer less expensive rates, and home and villa rentals are also an option.

For a complete list of all island lodging, contact the **Hilton Head Island Chamber of Commerce.** ~ At 1 Chamber Drive, off William Hilton Parkway, just east of Long Cove Plantation; 803-785-3673.

Hilton Head Central Reservations handles bookings for hotels, motels, villas and homes on Hilton Head Island. ~ 803-785-9050, 800-845-7018, fax 803-785-8442.

Leading the list of luxury haunts, **Westin Resort Hilton Head Island** enjoys a loyal following who wouldn't think of parking their beach towels anywhere else. The tropical green tin-topped building curves against the beach among 24 acres of fantasy gardens, swimming pools and three whirlpools under waterfalls. A wooden boardwalk delivers you across the dunes to a beach that disappears in the distance. The 410 rooms are plush, handsomely decorated, and all have private balconies overlooking the ocean or island. Three golf courses, four restaurants, tennis, health club, daily family activities—it's all here. ~ 2 Grasslawn Avenue, Port Royal Plantation; 803-681-4000, 800-228-3000, fax 803-681-1087. ULTRA-DELUXE.

Hyatt Regency Hilton Head occupies a vast piece of oceanfront, with more than 500 rooms, two outdoor pools and palmy gardens spread next to a wide beach and an indoor pool tucked beneath a glass solarium. The elegant lobby has glass windows that look out to sea. Rooms are typical of the chain: thick carpets, modern furnishings, attractive drapes and fine bedspreads. Half of the rooms face the ocean, the other half look at the island. Activities are geared toward families, such as the camp for kids. Three golf courses, 25 tennis courts, several restaurants and lounges complete the offerings. ~ 1 Hyatt Circle, Palmetto Dunes Plantation; 803-785-1234, 800-233-1234, fax 803-842-4695. ULTRA-DELUXE.

The glittering lobby of **Crowne Plaza Resort** soars five floors, with glossy wood floors and balconies trimmed in theater lights.

The Holiday Inn Crowne Suites resort has a roving courtyard with swimming pools, ponds, waterfalls and streams winding through, then long green lawn running down to the dunes and beach. The 340 rooms are nicely appointed with blonde oak furniture, chintz love seats, marble vanities, and balconies overlooking the courtyard treetops or ocean. Golf, tennis, fine dining, kids' camp and anything else you care to do. ~ 130 Shipyard Drive, Shipyard Plantation, Hilton Head Island; 803-842-2400, 800-334-1881, fax 803-842-9975. ULTRA-DELUXE.

Sea Crest Oceanside Inn is old-fashioned and very motelish, with several low-slung buildings strung along the beach. The rooms, efficiencies and two-bedroom apartments are impeccably clean, adorned with wall-to-wall carpets and tropical patterned bedspreads. The grounds are landscaped with palmettos and pines. There's a good-sized pool and sundeck, and dozens of shops and restaurants within walking distance. ~ 4 North Forest Beach Drive, across from Coligny Plaza; 803-785-2121, 800-845-7014. DELUXE.

Several of Hilton Head's plantation communities offer villa lodging. For details, contact **Palmetto Dunes Resort**. ~ 803-785-1161, 800-845-6130, fax 803-842-4482. Another option for villas is **Sea Pines Villa Resorts**. ~ 803-785-3333, 800-925-4653, fax 803-842-1475.

Among the general home and villa rental agencies, you might try **Coastline Rentals, Inc.** ~ 803-842-5866, 800-752-3506, fax 803-785-9119. **ESP Home & Villa Rentals** is another choice. ~ 803-671-4700, 800-368-5975, fax 803-671-5899. Or try **Hilton Head Vacation Rentals and Sales**. ~ 803-785-4487, 800-346-0426, fax 803-785-3529.

Within the dark, clubby, regal recesses of **Carolina Cafe** you will find Hilton Head's finest beef—chateaubriand, filets, prime rib—intensely flavorful and juicy, melting in your mouth. Good seafood is served in beautiful sauces, and there is very good service. The Alaskan crab and Brie soup, a sometimes menu special, is fantastic. ~ At the Westin Resort, Two Grasslawn Avenue, Port Royal Plantation; 803-681-4000. DELUXE TO ULTRA-DELUXE.

DINING

Charlie's L'Etoile Verte is a lively cache, colorful and arty, with brick floors and stucco walls and all the verve of a Paris cafe. The lunch and dinner menus are handwritten on white paper every day. Possibilities? Omelettes, fish cakes, and lamb chili with black beans for lunch. Salmon sautéed in a parmesan crust, or perhaps filet mignon with jalapeño butter for dinner. You don't want to miss this place. ~ 1000 Plantation Center, Hilton Head Island; 803-785-9277. DELUXE.

For cultured, light lunching and a good read, you should stop by **Authors Caffé**. The little dining room is elegant and relaxing, with cushioned wrought-iron chairs and classical music pouring through. Sandwiches, soups, salads and a long list of espresso, coffees and teas. A bookstore awaits through an open door. ~ In the Village at Wexford, William Hilton Parkway, north of Sea Pines Circle, Hilton Head Island; 803-686-5020. BUDGET.

French and formal, **The Gaslight** is where you go for escargots *bourguignonne*, red snapper provençale, and sweetbreads with shallots, white wine and mushrooms. Owner and chef Serge Prat hails from New York's L'Etoile and The Rainbow Room. The decor is rich, slightly gilded, with red carpets and red banquettes and candles flickering for lunch and dinner. ~ 303 The Market Place, Sea Pines Circle, Hilton Head Island; 803-785-5814. DELUXE.

HIDDEN ► Locals wear a lunch path to **Remy's** for simple Southern and Lowcountry fare like fried chicken, fresh seafood, okra and tomatoes, mashed potatoes and sweet corn. The floors and high ceiling are unfinished wood, the TV's on in the bar, the dining room is quite small. If you can't make it for lunch, this late-night spot serves till 4 a.m. ~ 28 Arrow Road, off William Hilton Parkway, near Sea Pines Circle; 803-842-3800. BUDGET TO MODERATE.

John Braddocks is a Lowcountry seafood house, perhaps Hilton Head's best, with dining on a glass porch overlooking a marina and salt marsh, and the smell of the sea inside and out. Shrimp piccata, spicy bouillabaisse loaded with lobster and fish, and pansautéed flounder glazed with caramelized shallots, apricots and citrus are among the saucy, savory dishes. ~ Lands End Drive, at the South Beach Marina, Sea Pines Plantation; 803-671-5199. MODERATE TO DELUXE.

SHOPPING "A bit of Scotland on the road to Hilton Head"—an odder motto cannot be imagined, but when you see **Moss Creek Traders** you must agree it is steeped in all things Scottish, and it is indeed on the way to Hilton Head. Here are kilts, golf caps, Celtic jewelry, lap robes and tartans galore. ~ Route 278, Bluffton; 803-837-4696.

HIDDEN ► Don't be put off by the "Elvis Lives" sign above the door of **The Store**, for inside this quirky wood shack is some fine local art, painted sideboards, Mexican blown glass, beeswax candles and great second-hand stuff. ~ Calhoun Street, Bluffton; 803-757-3855.

HIDDEN ► An old Bluffton gas station was reincarnated as **eggs 'n tricities**, an art boutique with singular, eccentric pieces like a candle in a wine bottle. ~ Corner of Calhoun and Bridge streets, Bluffton; 803-757-3446.

You could technically shop for days on Hilton Head, though it would take a lot of driving, diving in and out of traffic between the mind-numbing array of strip shopping centers and plazas and mini-malls. The official store count is over 300, and they're scattered. Selections are typically islandy and upscale, colorful resort wear, tropical-themed art, crafts and collectibles, kitchenry and books on boating and golf.

Creative Kitchens is a well-stocked kitchen emporium with plenty for outdoor entertainers. ~ 1505 Main Street Village, off William Hilton Parkway, Hilton Head Island; 803-689-9460. A second store is in the Village at Wexford, William Hilton Parkway, north of Sea Pines Circle. ~ 803-785-8516.

If you must have a mall, there's The **Mall at Shelter Cove**. Victoria's Secret, Banana Republic, Talbots, Polo Ralph Lauren and other familiar names are located here. ~ William Hilton Parkway, one-half mile north of Palmetto Dunes Plantation entrance, Hilton Head Island; 803-686-3090.

Rare books, Art Deco glasswork, movie and sports memorabilia, and first-edition prints are among the varied finds at **Time Again, Inc.** The gallery regularly hosts collectibles shows. ~ At 14 Greenwood Drive, in the Gallery of Shops, Hilton Head Island; 803-842-6616.

The **Red Piano Gallery** has wonderful folk art and jewelry, paintings and sculptures by regional and national artists. ~ 220 Cordillo Parkway, Hilton Head Island; 803-785-2318.

Coligny Plaza, across from the island's most popular beach, has more than 20 stores assembled around courtyards and duck ponds. ~ Located at the corner of Pope Avenue and North Forest Beach Avenue, Hilton Head Island; 803-842-6050. Among them, **The Magic Puppet and Toys Too** supplies neat magic tricks and books on magic, entertaining beach games and pretty puppets. ~ 803-785-3280.

If you need a hammock, visit The **Hammock Company Home and Camp Store**, a branch of the original, locally known store at Pawleys Island. Their rope hammocks, swings and rockers are made to last. ~ Coligny Plaza; 803-686-3636.

Beneath Hilton Head's red-and-white-striped lighthouse are the colorful galleries, boutiques and plazas of **Harbour Town Shops**. ~ North end of Lighthouse Road, Sea Pines Plantation; 803-785-3333. Here, **Harbour Town Antiques** has first-edition prints by Audubon and Gould, maps and botanicals, antique oils and watercolors. ~ 803-671-5999.

NIGHTLIFE

Wild Wing Café gets crazy at night. Beer, chicken wings and a prevailing college crowd. Live bands stay mellow on weeknights, and crank it up on weekends. ~ North Forest Beach Drive in Coligny Plaza, Hilton Head Island; 803-785-9464.

The community drama, musicals and comedy at **Hilton Head Playhouse** tend to be high quality, and shows often sell out. ~ Dunnagan's Alley at Arrow Road, off William Hilton Parkway, near The Market Place; 803-785-4878.

HIDDEN ▶   The worn-wood environs of **Remy's** are a late-night local
haunt. R&B and acoustic bands play most evenings, and you can
have munchies until 4 a.m. ~ 28 Arrow Road, off William Hilton
Parkway near Sea Pines Circle; 803-842-3800.

There's always a crowd at **Salty Dog Cafe**. The shingled, peak-
roofed bar and attendant picnic tables sit outside next to a marina,
where you can hear live island music (Jimmy Buffett tunes, etc.)
nightly in summer. ~ Lands End Drive, at the South Beach Marina,
Sea Pines Plantation; 803-671-2233.

BEACHES   The best place to go to the beach is behind your hotel—it will
& PARKS   always be less crowded and chaotic than a public beach. Visitors
staying at a seaside villa or on Hilton Head will have access to even
quieter sands. The following are Hilton Head's three public beaches:

FOLLY FIELD BEACH 🏊 Here's a generous stretch of tawny sand
and a small, quiet cove where you can sometimes find shells, especially sea olives. There's a lot with metered parking. Swimming is
good. No facilities are located within a short walk, so bring food
and drinks. ~ Located at the end of Bradley Road, off William Hilton Parkway, just south of Port Royal Plantation.

HIDDEN ▶   **BURKES BEACH ROAD BEACH** 🏊 Immediately south of Folly
Field Beach and less crowded, this pretty swath of sand is reached
by a short dirt path across the dunes. The sand is hard-packed,
moist and gray, laced with dried seagrass and reeds that wash
ashore. The surf is gentle. Arrive early for parking. Stores and restrooms are only a short drive away. Swimming is excellent. ~ At the
end of Burkes Beach Road, off William Hilton Parkway.

COLIGNY CIRCLE BEACH 🏊 Next to and spilling over into the
Holiday Inn, this is Hilton Head's most popular beach, with sun-
bathers crowding in towel-to-towel spring through fall. The sands
are tan and hard-packed, the water warm in summer. There are
teenagers galore when school's out. The metered parking here is
expensive (25¢ for 5 minutes), so use the all-day lot. Get here early
in season or you won't get a parking spot. Swimming is good.
Restrooms and refreshments are nearby. ~ At Coligny Circle, at the
intersection of Pope Avenue and Forest Beach Drive.

▼▼▼▼▼▼▼▼▼▼▼▼▼▼
Outdoor Adventures

GOLF

There is great golf on South Carolina's coast.
More than 200 courses dot the Grand Strand
and Lowcountry, many created by big-name de-
signers like Jack Nicklaus, Donald Ross, George Cobb, Tom Fazio,
Robert Trent Jones and Pete Dye, who have replaced coastal
woods and wetlands and wild shores with meticulously tended
greens and holes of championship caliber.

In the Myrtle Beach area alone, there are more than 80 golf
courses and a slew of annual tournaments. (The Myrtle Beach Area

Chamber of Commerce estimates golfers spend nearly $300 million a year on their games.) Some courses run alongside pine and palmetto woods or ancient, cypress-draped rivers, others follow the windy ocean or the stillness of marshlands. Some appeal to scratch golfers, others are kind to duffers. You can play on a traditional design created in the '60s or on a cutting-edge course carved in the '90s.

Several places offer mega-golf, several courses within one club. For a detailed list of courses, pick up a copy of the *Golfer's Guide* booklet from the Myrtle Beach Area Chamber of Commerce. ~ 1301 North Kings Highway, Myrtle Beach; 803-626-7444.

You can pick from six courses at **The Legends Golf Complex**, including the Moorland Course and its 16th hole, nicknamed "Hell's Half Acre." The enormous Scottish-style clubhouse here is surrounded by 40 acres of practice and putting greens. ~ 1500 Legends Drive, off Highway 501 South, Myrtle Beach; 803-236-9318, 800-552-2660.

Pine Lakes is called the "Granddaddy" of Myrtle Beach. Built in 1927 by Robert White, the first PGA president, the Scottish-influenced course features subtle curves, contours and pitches and woodsy scenery to match. ~ Woodside Drive, off Route 17, Myrtle Beach; 803-449-6459, 800-446-6817.

Several holes at **River Hills** have a Scottish feel, as well as unexpected hills, sharp doglegs and non-parallel fairways. ~ Route 17 North, Little River; 803-399-2100, 800-264-3810.

Favorite Five Golf actually represents seven courses. ~ 803-626-1658, 800-833-6337. Among these is **Quail Creek Golf Club**, designed by Gene Hamm in 1968 with soft curving greens and fairways and riotous beds of azaleas. ~ University Drive, West Myrtle Beach; 803-347-0549. The **Burning Bridge** is another—a double course with several lakes, big bunkers and sand traps. ~ Route 501 West, Conway; 803-347-0538.

The front nine holes of **The Witch** wend through wetlands, the back nine climb along gentle hills. Designed by Dan Maples, it's not too witchy, but playable by high handicappers. ~ 1900 Route 544, Conway; 803-347-2706.

Heritage Golf Club is spread across two former rice plantations, with a tunnel of giant oaks leading to the Colonial-style clubhouse. ~ 200 Heritage Drive, Pawleys Island; 803-626-3887, 800-552-2660.

In Georgetown, **Wedgefield** course is especially scenic. The fairways snake alongside big old magnolias and oaks, and camellias punctuate the setting with color. ~ 100 Manor Drive, Georgetown; 803-448-2124.

The Charleston area has plenty of fine courses, including **Wild Dune Links** and **The Harbor Course** at Wild Dunes Resort. ~ At 5757 Palm Boulevard, Isle of Palms; 803-886-2164, 800-845-8880.

There is also **Dunes West**. ~ Route 41, Mount Pleasant; 803-856-9378. Try **Shadowmoss Plantation Golf Club** in Charleston. ~ 20 Dunvegan Drive, Charleston; 803-556-8251. At John's Island head over to **Ocean Winds**. ~ 1002 Landfall Way, Seabrook Island Resort, John's Island; 803-768-1000. Another at John's Island is **Oak Point**. ~ 4255 Bohicket Road, Hope Plantation, John's Island; 803-768-7431. On Kiawah Island try **Turtle Point** and **Osprey Point**. ~ Kiawah Island Resort, Kiawah Island; 803-768-2121. And finally there is **Fairfield Ocean Ridge Resort**. ~ 1 King Cotton Road, Edisto Island; 803-723-0325.

Around Beaufort and the Sea Islands are a couple of courses. In Beaufort is the **Country Club of Beaufort**. ~ 8 Barnwell Drive, Beaufort; 803-522-1605. On Ladys Island is **Golf Professionals Club**. ~ 93 Francis Marion Circle, Ladys Island; 803-522-9700. West of Beaufort in the town of Ridgeland, **Callawassie Island Club** has 27 holes designed by Tom Fazio. ~ Route 278; 803-522-2700.

Golf needs no introduction on Hilton Head Island. The 21 courses include some of golf's most famous and famously expensive. Green fees at **Harbour Town Golf Links** are $150, though tee times are scarce in season at this famed course. ~ 11 Lighthouse Lane, off Lighthouse Road, Sea Pines Plantation; 803-842-1892.

Designed by Pete Dye and the site of the annual PGA tournament, its trademark is the red-and-white-striped lighthouse across a canal from the 18th green. The last two holes look across Calibogue Sound.

Sea Pines Plantation also has the **Sea March** course and **Ocean Course**. The Ocean Course was Hilton Head's first fairway, built in 1962, and the country club catalyst for developers across the nation. It has only one seaside hole, despite the name. ~ Both at 100 North Sea Pines Drive; 803-842-1894.

Among the other prime public island greens on Hilton Head is **Country Club of Hilton Head**. ~ 70 Skull Creek Drive, Hilton Head Plantation; 803-681-4653. At Port Royal Plantation, you'll find **Planters Row**. ~ 10-A Grasslawn Avenue, Port Royal Plantation; 803-689-5600. In Palmetto Dunes Plantation try the **Robert Trent Jones Course**. ~ 1 Trent Jones Lane, Palmetto Dunes Plantation; 803-785-1136. In the Shipyard Plantation is **Shipyard**. ~ 45 Shipyard Drive, Shipyard Plantation; 803-689-5600.

SPORT-FISHING

Numerous outfits will take you deep-sea fishing along the coast.

In the Myrtle Beach area, **Hurricane Fleet** has six boats that go out on fishing charters. ~ Vareen's Marina, off Route 17; 803-249-3571. **Capt. Dick's Marina** has half-day and all-day trips to the Gulf Stream, as well as deep-sea overnighters. ~ Murrells Inlet; 803-651-3676, 800-344-3474.

In Charleston, several deep-sea charters leave out of the Ripley Light Marina on Ashley Point Drive, including **Capt. Ivan's Island Charters Inc.** ~ 803-588-6060. **Silver Dolphin** also leaves out of this marina. ~ 803-556-3526. As does **Blue Boy.** ~ 803-571-1830. The **Marsh Grass Charter Inc.** will take you offshore or inshore, bottom fishing or trolling. ~ 1310 Ashley Hall Road, Charleston; 803-766-1464.

Island Water Sports offers inshore and offshore trips around Edisto Island, including a three-hour shark excursion at night. ~ 803-869-0663. Coast Guard–certified Captain Ron Elliott of **Edisto Island Tours** will take you fishing on the river. ~ 803-869-1937.

SeaWolf departs from Port Royal Landing Marina near Beaufort, but will pick up customers on Hilton Head Island. ~ Beaufort; 803-525-1174. Also on Hilton Head Island, you'll find **Skipper.** ~ Shelter Cove Marina, off Route 278, across from Palmetto Dunes Plantations; 803-785-4558. On Saint Helena Island, **Captain Eddy's Fishing Charter** will take you fishing for the day. ~ 820 Salt Wind Drive; 803-838-3782.

TENNIS

You won't have trouble finding a court on South Carolina's coast. In the Myrtle Beach area, try **Sports and Health Club at Kingston Plantation.** ~ 9760 Kings Road, Myrtle Beach; 803-497-2444. Also in the area is **Myrtle Beach Tennis & Swim Club.** ~ On Route 17 Bypass North, across from Dixie Stampede; 803-449-4486.

The City of Charleston maintains a number of courts. For a list of where to play, call the **Charleston Tennis Center.** ~ 19 Farmfield Avenue, Charleston; 803-724-7402.

In Beaufort, you can play at **Beaufort Tennis Courts.** ~ Boundary and Bladen streets; 803-525-4009.

There's mega-tennis on Hilton Head Island. The courts at **Palmetto Dunes Tennis Center** include 19 clay, two hard and four artificial grass. ~ 6 Trent Jones Lane, Palmetto Dunes Plantation; 803-785-1152. **Van der Meer Tennis University** tops that with 25 hard courts (four are covered and lighted) and three of clay. ~ 19 DeAllyon Road, Shipyard Plantation; 803-785-8388, 800-845-6138. Other public courts include **Port Royal Racquet Club.** ~ 15 Wimbledon Court, Port Royal Plantation; 803-686-8803. Another is **South Beach Racquet Club.** ~ 230 South Sea Pines Drive, Sea Pines Plantation; 803-671-2215.

RIDING STABLES

Care for a waterside ride on Hilton Head Island? **Sandy Creek Stables** will take you along the Intracoastal Waterway and marshlands. ~ 102 Jonesville Road; 803-689-3423. **Lawton Stables** will take you on a guide ride through a nature preserve and wildlife habitat, with history on the island's old working plantations. ~ 190 Greenwood Drive, Sea Pines Plantation; 803-671-2586.

BIKING   With flat terrain barely above sea level, South Carolina's coast is bicycle heaven. The 227.2-mile **Coastal Route** runs from North Carolina to Georgia, curling along lonesome wooded back roads and passing through minuscule towns.

The northernmost section of the route is a 56-mile run starting on Route 17 at Little River Neck just below North Carolina. It veers off on Route 90 and then over to Route 905 south to Conway. In Conway it picks up Route 701 south to Yaukannah, then catches Route 261 to Route 513, ending near Rhems.

From Rhems, it's a 121.6-mile trek south to Givhans Ferry State Park, along the Edisto River about 31 miles west of Charleston. Routes 41, 51 and 17 are the main routes.

Charleston can be done on a bicycle, though downtown traffic can make riding tedious. The most enjoyable cycling is along **The Battery** and through the historic neighborhoods just north.

For a leisurely trek southwest of Charleston, pick up Route 17 at Route 165 and head south 35 miles to Gardens Corner.

Hilton Head Island was designed with bikers in mind. Paved bike paths wend along William Hilton Parkway from Folly Field Road to Palmetto Bay Road. On Palmetto Bay Road, the path curves south to Forest Beach Drive, then runs both north and south along the public beach.

Bike Rentals   To get rolling around Myrtle Beach, visit **Atlantic Spoke Bicycles**. ~ 4029 Route 17 South, North Myrtle Beach; 803-272-7503. Also in North Myrtle Beach is **Sun Beach Service**. ~ 525 6th Avenue South, North Myrtle Beach; 803-272-4170. The **Bike Doctor** is the place to go in Cherry Grove. ~ 8008 Sea Mountain Highway, Cherry Grove; 803-249-8152.

In Charleston, **The Bicycle Shoppe** rents bicycles. ~ 280 Meeting Street; 803-722-8168. So does the **Charles Towne Landing Nature Preserve and Historic Site**. ~ 1500 Old Town Road, off Route 171; 803-852-4200.

Beaufort has the **Lowcountry Bicycle Shop**. ~ 904 Port Republic Street; 803-524-9585.

On Hilton Head Island, bikes are available from **Fishcreek Landing**. ~ Queens Folly Road, Palmetto Dunes Plantation; 803-785-2021. Or try **Hilton Head Bicycle Company**. ~ 11-B Archer Road; 803-686-6888. **Pedals** is another choice. ~ 71 Pope Avenue; 803-842-5522. In Sea Pines Plantation, go to **Bikes Plus**. ~ Lighthouse Road, Sea Pines Plantation; 803-785-5470.

HIKING   All distances listed for hiking trails are one way unless otherwise noted.

It's easygoing along the pancake-flat coast. Every trail listed here falls in the "leisurely" category. Mosquitoes can be tenacious, however, even hellish in summer, so don't hike without repellent.

MYRTLE BEACH AREA   Beachwalking is the best way to work your legs here. The sand is wide and hard-packed in most spots.

If you'd prefer to walk through woods, the **Sculptured Oak Nature Trail** (1 mile) at Myrtle Beach State Park cuts through live oak and loblolly pine, poplar, hickory and magnolia trees. There is even a stream running through.

CHARLESTON AREA   Much of the coastal forest and marsh life is marked along the **National Recreation Trail** (2 miles) on Bulls Island, within Cape Romain National Wildlife Refuge. You're apt to see alligators and in spring, flocks of egrets, coots, warblers and painted buntings. Besides this interpretive trail, the island has 16 miles of roads that can be hiked. Bulls Island is accessed only by ferry; for information, see the "Charleston Area Beaches and Parks" section of this chapter.   ◄ *HIDDEN*

Downtown Charleston is best seen on foot and though it may not technically be hiking, you will be tired after a couple of days. Numerous companies offer guided walks around town. For a list, see the "Charleston Area Sights" section of this chapter.

A few minutes from downtown, Charles Towne Nature Preserve and Historic Site offers an enjoyable stroll. **The Garden and Animal Forest Trails** (3.2 miles) follow gravel and dirt trails through lush plantings of azaleas, camellias and myriad other bloomers, then wanders the woods where enclosures harbor black bears, otters, pumas and other animals.

The **Indian Mound Trail** (3.6 miles round-trip) at Edisto Beach State Park heads through coastal forest of palmetto and oak, red cedar and wax myrtle to a heap of shells that may (or may not) have been left by American Indians.

BEAUFORT AND THE SEA ISLANDS   At Hunting Island State Park, the **Salt Marsh Boardwalk and Nature Trail** (1.1 miles) starts out along a wooden walkway across the salt marsh, then follows

✔ **CHECK THESE OUT—UNIQUE OUTDOOR ADVENTURES**

- Book way ahead for a tee time at the famed Harbour Town Golf Links, an annual PGA tournament site with a trademark red-and-white-striped lighthouse. *page 374*
- Go shark fishing at night off Edisto Island; Edisto Oceansports offers three-hour tours. *page 376*
- Join Lawton Stables' guided horseback tours of Hilton Head Island, with history on the island's old plantations. *page 377*
- Keep a lookout for alligators, coots, warblers and other wildlife while hiking the National Recreation Trail, on extremely remote Bulls Island. *page 379*

the shore lined with dunes and sea oats. The park's **Lighthouse Trail** (.9 mile) cuts through slash pine and palmetto forest where raccoon and white-tailed deer are plentiful.

HILTON HEAD ISLAND AREA The **Pinckney Island National Wildlife Refuge main trail** (7 miles) is a dirt road, accessed on bicycle or foot, that starts at the refuge parking lot. On its trek across the island, it meanders through maritime forest with pine plantations and ponds with wading birds and rookeries. An additional ten and a half miles of trails split off from this main trail.

HIDDEN ►   The **Audubon-Newhall Nature Preserve Trail** (1.5 miles round-trip) traverses dense, sunlit woods filled with the music of birds and crickets. You'll circle a pond, passing popcorn trees (also called Chinese tallowtrees), pitcher plants and a pocosin (a boggy trough of land), all described in the brochure available at the trailhead on Palmetto Bay Road, one half-mile north of Greenwood Drive, in Sea Pines Plantation.

Seven miles of trails wend through **Sea Pines Forest Preserve**, a 605-acre woodland by the ocean on the west end of Hilton Head Island. If you'd care to hike with a group, The Museum of Hilton Head Island hosts guided treks through the preserve as well as walks along Hilton Head's beaches. ~ 803-689-6767.

▼▼▼▼▼▼▼▼▼▼▼
Transportation

CAR

Route 17, sometimes two lanes and at other times four, runs the length of South Carolina's coast and connects most major towns and metropolitan areas. Interstate highway **Route 95** comes up from Georgia, near Savannah, and runs along the eastern side of South Carolina. From Route 95, you can wind over to Hilton Head Island along **Routes 46** and **278**. Interstate highway **Route 26** connects Charleston with Columbia, South Carolina.

AIR

Several commercial airports provide service to South Carolina's coast. **Myrtle Beach Jetport,** located within Myrtle Beach Air Force Base, has regular flights via major airlines including American Airlines, American Eagle, Atlantic Southeast Airlines, United Airlines, USAir and USAir Express.

Charleston International Airport is served by several domestic and foreign airlines, including American Airlines, British Airways, Delta Air Lines, Japan Airlines, KLM Royal Dutch Airlines, Lufthansa, United Airlines, USAir and USAir Express.

The small **Hilton Head Island Airport** handles commuter flights from Charlotte, Raleigh and Atlanta via American Eagle, GP Express and USAir Express. Some visitors to Hilton Head Island fly into **Savannah International Airport,** about 45 minutes away and serviced by American Airlines, Delta Airlines, United Airlines and USAir.

Shuttle service from Myrtle Beach Jetport to points around the Grand Strand is provided by **Coastal Cab** (803-448-4444) and **Executive Coach Service** (803-448-4047).

Both **Airport Shuttle** (803-767-7111) and **North Area Taxi** (803-554-7575) provide area shuttle service from Charleston International Airport.

Lowcountry Taxi will give you a ride from Hilton Head Airport or from Savannah International Airport. ~ 803-681-8294.

BUS

Greyhound Bus Lines (800-231-2222) are located in Myrtle Beach at 511 7th Avenue North, 803-448-2471; in Georgetown at 1409 Highmarket Street, 803-546-4535; in Charleston at 3610 Dorchester Road, 803-722-7721; and in Beaufort at 1307 Boundary Street, 803-524-4646.

TRAIN

Try **Amtrak**'s "Silver Meteor" (800-872-7245). It brings visitors from surrounding regions to Charleston. ~ 4565 Gainor Avenue, Charleston; 803-744-8263.

CAR RENTALS

Myrtle Beach Jetport is serviced by several rental companies,such as **Avis Rent A Car** (800-831-2847), **Budget Rent A Car** (800-527-0700), **Enterprise Rent A Car** (800-325-8007), **Hertz** (800-654-3131), **National Interrent** (800-328-4567) and **Zippy Car Rental** (800-962-5170).

Rental agencies at or near Charleston International Airport include **Alamo Rent A Car** (800-327-9633), **Budget Rent A Car** (800-527-0700), **Dollar Rent A Car** (800-800-4000), **Hertz Rent A Car** (800-654-3131) and **Thrifty Car Rental** (800-367-2277).

On Hilton Head Island, try **Avis Rent A Car** (800-831-2847), **Budget Rent A Car** (800-527-0700) and **Enterprise Rent-A-Car** (800-325-8007).

At Savannah International Airport, you'll find **Avis Rent A Car** (800-831-2847), **Budget Rent A Car** (800-527-0700), **Hertz Rent A Car** (800-654-3131) and **National Interrent** (800-328-4567).

PUBLIC TRANSIT

Catch a **Coastal Rapid Public Transit Authority** bus along the Grand Strand. ~ 803-626-9138.

South Carolina Electric & Gas Company runs public buses in Charleston. ~ 803-747-0922. **D.A.S.H.** (Downtown Area Shuttle), makes regular city rounds, stopping often at the Visitor Reception & Transportation Center. ~ 375 Meeting Street; 803-724-7420.

For bus service around Beaufort, call **Lowcountry Regional Transit Authority**. ~ 803-846-4146.

TAXIS

The Myrtle Beach area has lots of taxis. Among them are **Carolina Cab** (803-626-2050), **City Cab** (803-448-5555), **Coastal Cab** (803-448-4444) and **Yellow Cab** (803-448-3181).

In Charleston, try **Airport Express** (803-572-2858), **Dan's Transportation Service** (803-747-1778) or **Yellow Cab** (803-577-6565).

Around Beaufort and the sea islands, call **Yellow Cab** (803-522-1121). On Hilton Head, **Lowcountry Taxi** (803-681-8294) will take you around the island or up to Savannah.

TEN

Inland South Carolina

Once you get away from the coast, South Carolina slows down. Pounding surf and golf greens transform into fuzzy fields of cotton and long-lasting forests of scrub pine. Sun-blistered farmhouses dot the horizon. Cinderblock shanties sell fresh catfish. Folks wave from their tractors and pickup trucks.

The land angles northwest 250 miles in gentle crescendo, rising to soft hills across the middle of the state and then above 3000 feet just before North Carolina. Sassafras Mountain, which peaks at 3560 feet, is South Carolina's highest place, though it is not lofty or breathtaking. Like most of inland South Carolina, it is subtle, simple, peaceful.

Inland South Carolina is also wet—very wet. A vast river system sprawls toward the ocean like a spiderweb, sending out creeks and streams and opening onto vast lakes. The most furious river, the Chattooga, runs along the Cherokee Foothills in northwestern South Carolina and is famed for whitewater rafting. The dark, disturbing movie *Deliverance* was shot on the Chattooga. Dark, secretive swamps once covered much of the state, but they were erased by loggers or drowned behind dams. Only one virgin watery wilderness, 22,000-acre Conagree Swamp, remains near the middle of the state and is protected as a National Monument.

Hundreds of small towns are sprinkled across inland South Carolina, but there are only a handful of cities. The biggest, Columbia, has 99,000 residents and is the state capital. Nestled at the confluence of three rivers, it's also a haven of history.

In February 1865, General William Tecumseh Sherman crushed Columbia on his death march through the South, nearly burning the city to the ground. He slashed telegraph wires, mangled railroad ties and ignited the bridges that linked Columbia with the rest of the world. A few homes were salvaged and restored, and today their stately Federalist, Italianate and antebellum facades are reminiscent of pre–Civil War days. The State House, half-built when Sherman arrived, now bears the shell scars of his destruction.

Just as the Civil War looms large across South Carolina, so does the American Revolution. All but one of the streets in downtown Columbia are named for Revolutionary War generals and officers. Some of those men successfully led forces in 1776 against Loyalists and Cherokees who had joined the British. Four years later, however, General Charles Cornwallis had nearly overrun the state.

Two South Carolina battles helped turn things around. In September 1780, a rugged band of "over-mountain" men trounced the Tories at Kings Mountain in northern South Carolina. Four months later, a similar defeat at nearby Cowpens helped decide the fate of the British in the war. Today, you can tour the misty green pastures and cool woods at both Kings Mountain and Cowpens National Battlefields.

You can also immerse yourself in Civil War days, and the times before and after. Immaculately tended plantation homes, some 200 years old, invite exploration across the state. Entire towns are listed on the National Register of Historic Places, their red-brick streets and marketplaces, soda fountains and steepled churches virtually unchanged for over a century. Old railroad and mill towns populate the countryside, with nothing but pastures and cornfields in between. State parks abound, but there is no blatant tourism: no enormous theme parks, no kitschy boardwalks, no towns contrived for visitors. Indeed, it seems sometimes that it's easier to find the Old South in South Carolina than the new.

Columbia is a good place to start the inland South Carolina tour. It's precisely in the center of the state, a hundred miles from either coast or mountains, and its airport is easy to get in and out of. Explore downtown and the artsy Five Points area, then head to nearby Lake Murray for golfing, boating, fishing or camping in the woods.

Southwest of Columbia, Aiken is a refined old town with big graceful homes, groomed lawns and gardens, and lots of horse racing action. Hundreds of horses train during winter in preparation for the Aiken Triple Crown competition every spring. Between Aiken and northern Abbeville, there's Sumter National Forest and four state parks, and the lonesome Savannah River Scenic Highway that wends through pine forest.

South Carolina's most dramatic landscape is in the Upcountry, the northwestern crescent of the state. Here the land swells to 2000 and 3000 feet, and water gushes down rock walls. Greenville, Spartanburg, Clemson (home to the university) and Pendleton are the main towns of the Upcountry. Greenville and Spartanburg, 30 miles apart, are a growing hub of industry in the emerging New South, with companies such as Michelin and Adidas located there. In 1994, after a worldwide search of cities, BMW selected nearby Greer as the site of its United States auto manufacturing plant.

Beyond the borders of the towns, there is little but beautiful scenery and little-traveled roads. Lodges, restaurants and shops are scarce, and six state parks stay packed during warm months.

The Upcountry also has the far-flung Chattooga River, a National Wild and Scenic River and one of the best whitewater trips in the South. Take a wild and fast rafting trip, then plan to relax. The Upcountry, like the rest of inland South Carolina, is all about downshifting into slow gear.

Inland South Carolina

PARKS & SITES

- Ⓐ Caesars Head State Park
- Ⓑ Calhoun Falls State Park
- Ⓒ Congaree Swamp National Monument
- Ⓓ Cowpens National Battlefield
- Ⓔ Devil's Fork State Park
- Ⓕ Dreher Island State Park
- Ⓖ Hamilton Branch State Park
- Ⓗ Hickory Knob State Resort Park
- ⊖ Jones Gap State Park
- Ⓙ Keowee-Toxaway State Park
- Ⓚ Kings Mountain National Military Park
- Ⓛ Kings Mountain State Park
- Ⓜ Oconee State Park
- Ⓝ Redcliffe Plantation State Park
- Ⓞ Sesquicentennial State Park
- Ⓟ Table Rock State Park

Wade across a mountain creek. Have a picnic on an abandoned bridge overhung with hickories. Witness a summer rain, when thunderclouds darken the white cotton fields and lightning licks at the tips of oak trees. Get to know the local people— they're some of the friendliest folks you'll ever meet.

On May 1, 1996, the area code for much of this region changed from 803 to 864. You can continue to call the 803 area code after this date and a recording will tell you if you need to dial the new area code.

▼▼▼▼▼▼▼▼▼▼▼
Columbia Area

Columbia is one of the few planned cities in the nation. Its meticulous design began back in 1786, when the legislature decreed that a capital would be built dead center in the state where the Broad, Congaree and Saluda rivers meet. A surveyor laid out 400 blocks, with 10 blocks equaling one square mile. He made the streets 100 feet wide, with the belief that mosquitoes could fly only 60 feet before starving to death. This being absolutely false, mosquitoes buzzed right across the new city streets. Today, however, Columbia enjoys wide, roomy streets draped in oaks and magnolias.

SIGHTS

Downtown Columbia, a gridwork of streets covering precisely two square miles, is presided over by the **State House**. The grand Classical building has a green copper dome, walls of blue granite, and elaborate columns parading along the front. Rich green lawns are ruled by vast oaks, and imposing monuments are scattered about. Some recall the three days in 1865 when General Sherman nearly leveled the city with guns and fire. Bronze stars on the building's west wall mark the wounds from Sherman's shell fire. Until 1998, the presence of construction crews will mark the ongoing renovation of this stately house. ~ Located at the corner of Main and Gervais streets; 803-734-4921.

Just west of the State House, the **Columbia Visitors Center** has maps and information on local sights. ~ 1012 Gervais Street; 803-254-0479, 800-264-4884.

The next block west on Gervais Street is the heart of **Congaree Vista**, where antiques and art galleries, artists' studios, cafes and office suites occupy restored nineteenth-century buildings. Shop and dine among the weathered red bricks and pine floors and walls worn to a warm patina. Then walk down the street and tour downtown's four public historic homes. Start at the **Richland County Historic Preservation Commission**, which sells individual or discounted combination tickets to the houses. ~ 1616 Blanding Street; 803-252-1770.

The commission is located behind **Robert Mills House and Park**, one of the historic home stops. An elegant place graced with magnolia trees, its three stories were commissioned in 1823 by prominent Columbia merchant Ainsley Hall. More prominent is the home's designer, Robert Mills, who was Federal Architect of the United States, State Architect of South Carolina and creator of the Washington Monument. Mills' trademark symmetry is everywhere; each room and door is offset by another (including some false doors added for congruity). His exquisite detailing is evident in the elaborate ceilings and curving walls, and in the columned Neoclassical porch out front. All of the doorknobs and key latches are sterling, and most of the Regency and Neoclassic furnishings are early 1800s. Unfortunately, Ainsley died before he could enjoy all this, and his widow sold the home to the Presbyterian Theological Seminary. Admission. ~ 1616 Blanding Street.

Ainsley did live across the street at the **Hampton-Preston Mansion**. Built in 1818, the antebellum address is less grandiose than its neighbor, though still stately. A curving staircase glides to two upper floors, and a grand dining room is gilded and set with finery—including china that was rolled in bedsheets and stashed in the woods during Sherman's raid on Columbia. The house itself

Downtown Columbia

POINTS OF INTEREST
- Ⓐ Columbia Museum of Art
- Ⓑ Columbia Visitors Center
- Ⓒ Hampton-Preston Mansion
- Ⓓ Mann-Simmons Cottage
- Ⓔ McKissick Museum
- Ⓕ Robert Mills House and Park
- Ⓖ South Carolina Confederate Relic Room and Museum
- Ⓗ South Carolina State Museum
- Ⓘ State House
- Ⓙ Woodrow Wilson Boyhood Home

was spared when General John Logan decided it would serve as his Union headquarters. There is much more history, most involving the Hampton family, who were sort of the Kennedys of the Old South. Wade Hampton I, a cotton plantation tycoon and general in the War of 1812, bought the manse in 1823. Wade II and Wade III, famous as their father, were raised here and enjoyed vigorous lives of wealth and politics. Wade III became governor of South Carolina in 1876. Admission. ~ 1615 Blanding Street.

A few years earlier, Woodrow Wilson was living a few blocks away in a pretty Tuscan villa. Today, the **Woodrow Wilson Boyhood Home** nestles beneath magnolias and is decorated with ivy. The inside is plush; the parlor is bathed in green, crushed-velvet draperies, the music room in red velvet. Many of the furnishings belonged to Wilson's family, who built the home in 1872. The 28th president lived there until 1875, when he was 14 years old, and the family moved out of South Carolina. Admission. ~ 1705 Hampton Street.

The last stop on the historic home tour does not speak of wealth or prominence, but the triumph of a black woman born in the plantation South. Celia Mann was a Charleston slave who also worked on the side as a midwife, saving enough money over several years to buy her freedom. She promptly left Charleston, which didn't care much for freed slaves, and walked 112 miles to Columbia. There, in the early 1850s, she purchased a small house that's now the **Mann-Simons Cottage**. She raised four daughters amid an often hostile environment, and started the Calvary Baptist Church for Blacks in her basement in 1865. Today, the white clapboard home is also the **Museum of African-American Culture**, with an art gallery and exhibits on the struggles of Southern blacks. Admission. ~ 1403 Richland Street.

The permanent exhibits at **Columbia Museum of Art** include the small but fine Kress Collection of Baroque and Renaissance art and a display of Tiffany glass and Impressionist paintings. It's the outstanding traveling exhibits, however, from photography to glass

---

✔ CHECK THESE OUT—UNIQUE SIGHTS

- Wander around **Five Points**, Columbia's hippest neighborhood, with funky shops, galleries, cool cafes and nightspots. *page 389*
- Check out the bushpigs, hartebeests, fringe-eared oryx and other bizarre wildlife (taxidermied, of course) at **Museum of York County**. *page 390*
- Immerse yourself in art at the stellar **Bob Jones University Art Gallery**, housing hundreds of outstanding religious works. *page 403*
- Spread a picnic atop the 1820 Gothic arch called **Poinsett Bridge**, and watch the river rush beneath you. *page 408*

works, that really draw lovers of art. Admission. ~ 1112 Bull Street; 803-799-2810.

Civil War aficionados will want to drop by the **South Carolina Confederate Relic Room and Museum**. Not a terribly big place, but more than a Civil War cache, it showcases clothing, money, stamps and keepsakes from Colonial to modern times. ~ 920 Sumter Street, Columbia; 803-734-9813.

Just south of here, the **University of South Carolina** is wonderful for walks. Along Greene and Sumter streets, red-brick buildings, worn to a historic patina, are enveloped in tidy gardens and lawns. Flowers spill over brick walls and planters, and sun steams through pink-blossomed myrtle trees. Streets dip way down, trailing off into neighborhoods of early 1900s cottages masked in ivy. ~ Bounded by Greene, Sumter, Pendelton and Pickens streets; 803-777-7000.

Stop inside USC's **McKissick Museum** for a look at its current art exhibit. That could be weavings, fiber art, glass works, pottery, folk art—it's always different. In permanent residence is a collection of Baruch silver. ~ Bull and Pendelton streets; 803-777-7251.

◄ HIDDEN

USC students spend a lot of time in **Five Points**, the artsy neighborhood next door to campus. It's named for the five-pronged intersection where Santee Avenue and Harden and Devine streets run together. Painted brick facades are emblazoned with bright shutters and awnings. Columbia's funkiest shopping is here, and there are some watering holes with real character.

Across town to the west, **The South Carolina State Museum** looks at the funky and serious side of state styles and history. Natural history, science, transportation, culture and art displays are spread across four floors, with plenty of hands-on fun for the kids. There are whisper dishes and strange fossils, a 1904 Oldsmobile horseless carriage and nineteenth-century decorative pottery, some made by slaves. "The Big One That Didn't Get Away" exhibit of taxidermied fish stars a 14-foot monster marlin. Admission. ~ 301 Gervais Street; 803-737-4595.

If you have kids, take them to **Riverbanks Zoological Park**. Just west of downtown and the Congaree River, it's a small but top-notch city zoo with wide paved paths (ideal for wheelchair visitors), luscious plantings (the tulips rage in spring) and roomy habitats for animals. Giraffes, ostriches and rhinos saunter around the African Plains area, sea lions dive in a pool, and polar bears snooze on refrigerated boulders. The coolest place may be the Coral Reef exhibit, where butterflyfish glide and sharks prowl around a giant pool behind glass. Admission. ~ 500 Wildlife Parkway, off Route 26, Columbia; 803-779-8717.

When Columbians want a weekend on the water, they head for **Lake Murray** about 15 miles to the west. These 78 square miles of fresh water were corralled in 1930 when a mile-and-a-half-long dam was built across the Saluda River. Electricity was made. Homes, marinas, golf courses and campgrounds cropped up on the new lakefront. Golfers, fishers and boaters were made happy, not to mention realtors.

HIDDEN ► A day trip northeast of Columbia brings you first to **Camden**, about 32 miles away. Camden enjoys the designation of "the oldest existing inland town in South Carolina," its township decreed by King George II in 1730. Fifty years later, it was a staunch Whig town captured by General Cornwallis. The British held Camden for nearly a year before retreating after nearby battle losses. Some of the British fortifications and redoubts are being unearthed today. Visitors can walk around the sites, as well as tour historic homes around town. ~ Off Routes 1 and 521. Pick up a walking-tour map at **Historic Camden**. ~ Route 521 South; 803-432-9841.

HIDDEN ► Fifty-four miles farther northeast on Route 1, **Cheraw** snoozes along the Great Pee Dee River. It started as a trading post in 1740 and became a real town in 1768. Now it's home to 6000 people and more than 50 beautiful old antebellum homes and buildings. Streets are broad and shady, the oaks dripping with moss. Before a walk around town, stop by the **Greater Cheraw Chamber of Commerce**. ~ 221 Market Street; 803-537-7681.

Straight north from Columbia, an easy 71-mile glide along Highway 77, lies the city of **Rock Hill**. Some people call it the "southern side of Charlotte," as the North Carolina metropolis has edged farther and farther southward, though Rock Hill retains its own flavor. **Winthrop University**, founded in 1886, occupies much of downtown, its imposing Georgian buildings residing behind spidery arms of oaks. ~ Oakland Avenue, Rock Hill; 803-323-2211.

HIDDEN ► The quirky **Museum of York County** is so hidden it publishes instructions on getting there. (From downtown Rock Hill, you should take Route 274 northwest to Mount Gallant Road, then go east to Museum Road. There are signs along the way.) These rural South farmlands are about the last place you'd expect to find a fringe-eared oryx, lesser kudu or Lichenstein's hartebeest—taxidermied African animals. Together with giraffes, bushpigs, teeny Kirk's dik-dik and numerous other creatures, they look out from behind museum glass, set in imitation deserts, mountains and wetlands. Even if you can't fathom why humans desire to stuff and mount animals, you'll find the display on taxidermy techniques intriguing. Admission. ~ Located at 4621 Mount Gallant Road, Rock Hill; 803-329-2121.

About 41 miles southeast of Columbia, not quite halfway to Charleston, the city of **Orangeburg** harbors the universally appeal-
HIDDEN ► ing **Edisto Memorial Gardens**. They're spread across 150 acres, with fragrant seas of azaleas, camellias and roses, arching canopies of cypress and oak, and the shadowy Edisto River cutting through.

A wheelchair-accessible boardwalk extends across the river, where the cypress "knees," or knobby exposed roots, poke out of the water. ~ Route 301, Orangeburg; 803-534-6821.

Built in 1928, **Claussen's Inn** was once a bakery but is now a handsome hostelry just off the University of South Carolina campus. Fashioned of red brick, it has a lobby full of light and space, and high-ceilinged rooms warmly decorated with reproduction Colonial furnishings. The private patios with jacuzzis are an added touch. A continental breakfast is delivered to your door, which is included in the room rate. ~ 2003 Greene Street, Columbia; 803-765-0440, 800-622-3382, fax 803-799-7924. MODERATE.

LODGING

With its stark granite exterior, worn lobby furnishings and snail-slow elevators, **The Governor's House Hotel** is dated. But the five-story downtown address is constantly booked—no doubt because of its rates. Rooms are small but clean, outfitted with stuffed leather chairs, chocolate-brown carpets, phones and televisions. Oddly, the doors open outside to the noise of downtown. ~ 1301 Main Street, Columbia; 803-779-7790, 800-800-0835, fax 803-779-7856. BUDGET.

If you're looking for mood, **Richland Street Bed & Breakfast** has it. The lovely old white house with gazebo resides in a historic neighborhood, not far from the Mann-Simons Cottage. Beautifully decorated in Victorian style, its seven bedrooms (including a bridal suite) are extra large and comfortable, offering accoutrements such as mirrored armoires and clawfoot tubs. Two rooms have jacuzzis. Big continental breakfasts are served in the expansive dining room. ~ 1425 Richland Street, Columbia; 803-779-7001. MODERATE TO DELUXE.

◄ HIDDEN

The menu at the **Capitol Restaurant** says: "Under the Same Roof Since 1905." Easy to believe, considering the hat racks at each burgundy vinyl booth, and the old-time chrome barstools lining the lunch counter. The ever-popular cafe serves breakfast, lunch and dinner, Southern style: grilled pork chops, turkey and dressing, liver and onions, BLTs and the like. Closed Sunday. ~ 1210 Main Street, Columbia; 803-765-0176. BUDGET.

DINING

The Basil Pot, behind the State Capitol, is downtown Columbia's New Age cafe. Surroundings are simple but the vegetarian fare is big on flavor. Tofu burgers, spinach tarts, falafel sandwiches and chicken salad are among the offerings. Whole-wheat pizzas can be topped with everything from shrimp and artichoke hearts to purple cabbage and tempeh sausage. ~ 928 Main Street, Columbia; 803-799-0928. BUDGET.

From auto parts to roasted Cornish hens with raspberry glaze and wild rice cakes—the merchandise has definitely changed at 920 Gervais Street. The downtown Columbia address was once an automotive store in the 1960s; now it's **Motor Supply Company Bistro**. In the hub of historic Congaree Vista, it's trendy, tastefully decorated and filled with imaginative fare that's different every day. A few lunch and dinner possibilities: potato-encrusted grouper, pink peppercorn–seared tuna with champagne and shallot beurre blanc, filet mignon with crabmeat and bearnaise, and woodland mushroom ravioli. The sculpture garden is a lovely spot for summer dining. ~ 920 Gervais Street, Columbia; 803-256-6687. MODERATE TO DELUXE.

Near the University of South Carolina, **Garibaldi's** is a friendly place with class. Jazz pours from speakers above the long glossy bar. The dining room is decorated with Art Deco statuettes and lights, booths with embroidered backs and salmon-colored walls. Pasta and gourmet pizza lead the menu. Veal, chicken and seafood dishes are also offered. Try the penne Niçoise or shrimp marinara over angel hair pasta. ~ 2013 Greene Street, Columbia; 803-771-8888. MODERATE.

In a rust-colored brick Five Points building, **Mr. Friendly's New Southern Cafe** serves some of the best and most innovative cooking around. Charleston chicken salad is a curry-spiced chicken breast topped with organic mixed greens, peach chutney, toasted almonds, shaved red onions and diced tomatoes—order it at lunchtime. For dinner there's salmon and catfish, shrimp and grits and garlic mashed potatoes, and wonderful pecan crab cakes (sans the breading) served with sherry-cayenne mayonnaise. Full bar. Closed Sunday. ~ Located at 2001 Greene Street, Columbia; 803-254-7828. MODERATE.

If you're shopping in Five Points, stop at the **Gourmet Shop Café** for wine, cheese or fresh-tasting deli sandwiches. The bright and airy eatery is kin to the gourmet cooking shop next door. ~ 724 Saluda Avenue, Columbia; 803-799-3705. BUDGET.

SHOPPING   In downtown Columbia, there's good shopping at **Congaree Vista**, a historic district bounded by Senate, Assembly and Lady streets and the Congaree River. Concentrate on Gervais Street, which runs down the vista's middle and where antique and art galleries gather beneath painted awnings.

Cucina is a smart-looking cook shop for the home chef. ~ 1001 Gervais Street; 803-779-9288. Situated across Park Street, **Mais Oui** is a chichi gallery of interior design, with reproduction and original period furnishings and objets d'art. ~ 929 Gervais Street; 803-733-1704.

The arts-and-crafts booths at **City Market Mall** purvey everything from silver, crystal and linens to glassware, original paintings and out-of-print books. ~ Located at 701–711 Gervais Street; 803-799-7722.

Southeast of downtown Columbia, the **Five Points** neighborhood has the hippest goods. Start on Saluda Avenue, the heart of funky stuff.

Joyful Alternative has far-out T-shirts, swirling candles and clever cards. ~ 747 Saluda Avenue; 803-771-9138.

The candelabra, cookbooks, jeweled T-shirts and other items at **Heritage House** are similarly singular. ~ 745 Saluda Avenue; 803-799-7946.

Gibson's stocks eclectic birdhouses, windsocks, nutcrackers and other unusual gifts. ~ 743 Saluda Avenue; 803-771-4520.

Baskets of seemingly every shape, size and color are at **Basquettes**. ~ 732 Saluda Avenue; 803-252-5656.

Volume I is a bookstore and newsstand selling normal and weird T-shirts and used goods. ~ 725 Saluda Avenue; 803-799-5390. **Circes** is loaded with balloons and other party favors. ~ 719 Saluda Avenue; 803-252-0179. **Creative Kids** has nothing but toys—stilts, stuffed animals, teeny push brooms and lots more fun. ~ 718 Saluda Avenue; 803-779-8697.

Looking for comfort? **Loose Lucy's** has loose-fitting clothes, tie-dyed jumpers and Guatemalan weaves. ~ 709 Saluda Avenue; 803-252-1390.

There is a thriving night scene in Columbia. Tammy Wynette may still croon from many a pickup truck radio, but Hootie & The Blowfish—that cool rock-and-roll foursome—are the most happening sounds around town.

NIGHTLIFE

Funky and cranking past midnight, **Art Bar** plays alternative dance music. Tuesday nights feature poetry readings, Thursdays are for live bands, and Sundays bring improv. ~ 1211 Park Street, Columbia; 803-254-4792.

Classic musicals, youth theater, cutting-edge cabaret, lesbian drama, gay falsettos—what better variety from a theater company called **Trustus**. The season culminates each year with the terrific South Carolina Playwrights' Festival in August, then starts back up in September. Every Friday there are "Late Night" shows, with possibilities ranging from solo guitarists and cello choirs to improv comedy by the "We're Not Your Mother Players." Cover on Fridays. Advance tickets available for all other events. ~ 520 Lady Street, Columbia; 803-254-9732.

In Five Points, the ever-crowded **Night Works** is "home of the $2 kamikaze and $2 fuzzy navel." A college dance bar through and through. ~ 805 Harden Street, Columbia; 803-252-8352.

Calmer and classier, **Mr. Friendly's New Southern Cafe** features live jazz every Monday night, drawing an early-evening dinner and drink crowd. Full bar. ~ 2001 Greene Street, Columbia; 803-254-7828.

The No Brainer Bar invites you to "leave your mind behind." A cramped, tattered beer joint, it's a magnet for USC students. ~ 2018 Greene Street, Columbia; 803-256-7373.

USC students like to start or end their night at a Five Points tavern called **Monterey Jack's**. No live music, but great munchies and margaritas. ~ 733 Santee Street, Columbia; 803-256-7764.

Columbia's coolest coffeehouse, **Goat Feathers** is a swanky Five Points haunt serving cocktails, foreign beers and ravishing desserts. The coffees are killer, too. ~ 2017 Devine Street; 803-256-3325.

HIDDEN ►

Rock-and-roll revelers head for **Rockefellas**, where nightly bands are some of the hottest groups around. Hootie & The Blowfish got their start at this Five Points haunt. Cover. ~ 2112 Devine Street, Columbia; 803-252-7625.

GAY SCENE The place to dance is **Metropolis**, where disco music spins until the wee hours, though there is cabaret on some nights and a patio bar for cooling off when things get overheated. Mostly gay men. Private club, so call ahead for information. Cover. ~ 1800 Blanding Street, Columbia; 803-799-8727.

Before or after the dance clubs, have a drink at **Affairs**, a neighborly, two-level place in downtown Columbia. There's a jukebox on each floor. It's a private club; call ahead for information. ~ 712 Huger Street, Columbia; 803-779-4321.

BEACHES & PARKS

FINLAY PARK 🏃 ⚓ One of the prettiest city parks anywhere, it's swirled with waterfalls, including a high one you can walk behind. People like to take off their shoes and stick their feet in one of the clear, cold streams running through these 17-plus acres. It's all manmade, of course, including the one-and-a-half-acre lake with an island stage and snack bar. Rocky terraces cascade down a hill, and crepe myrtles and weeping willows decorate lengthy lawns. A row of bench swings overlooks Columbia's skyline, and an amphitheater hosts Sunday concerts during the summer. Facilities here include a snack bar, a picnic area, a playground, restrooms and walking paths. ~ 930 Laurel Street at Gadsden Street in Columbia; 803-733-8331.

SESQUICENTENNIAL STATE PARK 🏃 🚲 ⚓ 🛶 Nicknamed "Sesqui," these 1445 acres northeast of Columbia were formerly occupied by cotton fields. Now they're oak and pine forest that sit along a strip of South Carolina sandhills running from North Augusta to Cheraw. The terrain is dry, scrubby, muggy in summer. Swimming at a 30-acre lake helps cool visitors down, while the four-mile jogging and exercise trail keeps them in shape. There's also a 1756 log house with artist's studio and gallery. Swimming is good in the lake; lifeguards are on duty in the summer. The lake has fine bream and bass fishing, though there are daily limits on each, so check with the park office. There's are picnic tables (including pavilions by the lake), a playground, nature trails and an art gallery. Day-use fee, $2 per car. ~ Thirteen miles northeast of Columbia off Route 1; 803-788-2706.

▲ A campground offers 87 tent and RV sites with water and electrical hookups. Two sites designed for wheelchair campers can be reserved in advance; remaining sites are on a first-come basis; $14 per night. A primitive camping area is available for groups; 50 cents per person.

DREHER ISLAND STATE PARK 🏃 🏖 🚤 🛥 ⚓ Columbians   ◄ *HIDDEN*
love getting away to this park on weekends. It's hidden in the woods on a peninsula poking into enormous Lake Murray, with 12 miles of shoreline and lots of ways to be on the water. You can fish, waterski or just tool around in a boat. Seven picnic areas are next to the water and there's a lakefront campground. By far the best digs are five villas, modern, roomy and right on the water, with amenities (remote-control TVs, microwaves, coffeemakers, fireplaces and porches) a hotel would offer. One villa is designed for wheelchair guests. Weekly stays only in the summer; there's a two-night minimum the rest of the year. Rates are moderate. Book several months in advance, and be flexible with your dates. Swimming is fine in the shallow areas along most of the shoreline, but there are no lifeguards. Fish from the shoreline; you might snag a bream or crappie. From a boat, the possibilities extend to largemouth bass and striped bass, called "stripers." State fishing license required. You'll find a park office, a grocery and tackle shop, a marina, boat ramps, boat rentals, a playground, picnic pavilions and a nature trail. Day-use fee, $2. ~ Located on Route 571, off Routes 231 and 48, nine miles west of the town of Chapin. From Columbia, take Route 26 northwest about 25 miles to Chapin; 803-364-4152.

▲ A lakefront campground has 112 campsites, including 97 for RVs and tents and 15 for tents only. All have hookups for water and electricity. Three sites accommodate wheelchair visitors and can be reserved ahead of time. All other sites are first-come; $16 to $17 per night.

CONGAREE SWAMP NATIONAL MONUMENT 🏃 🥾 ⚓ Stuck   ◄ *HIDDEN*
way out in the sticks south of Columbia, this 22,000-acre park is one of the last stands of virgin Southern swamp. Some of the loblolly pines are more than 300 years old; one of them is 14 stories high and 15 feet wide. The forests of sweet gum and sycamores are beautifully sunlit, the red maples and mulberries filled with bird whistles. The Congaree River squiggles along the southern side of this water-soaked wilderness, and creeks and lakes run all through it. Cypress trees drip with moss around the water's edge. There are two wooden boardwalks that let you walk across the water (only

the elevated boardwalk is wheelchair-accessible), and several trails wind along the water. Mosquitoes are vicious nearly year-round, so remember to bring repellent. Try fishing for largemouth bass, sunfish, garfish, catfish and bream; you will need a state fishing license. Certain park areas are closed to fishing, so check with visitors center. No night fishing is allowed. There's also canoeing, but you must bring your own canoe. Rentals are available in Columbia. Facilities include a visitors center, restrooms, a picnic pavilion with grills and hiking trails. ~ Located off Route 48, about 12 miles southeast of Columbia. From Route 48, park signs take you down corduroy dirt roads and gravel lanes alongside cornfields; 803-776-4396.

▲ Primitive and backcountry camping in various areas, but there are no facilities. Permit (no fee) required, available from the visitors center.

▼▼▼▼▼▼▼▼▼▼▼▼▼▼▼
Aiken to Abbeville

Sixty miles southwest of Columbia on Route 20, Aiken emerges from the cotton fields like a grand Old South dame. Antebellum mansions and palatial pine and oak trees line the labyrinthine streets. Muscled, glossy-coated thoroughbreds graze behind serpentine walls of red brick. Clay and sand trails, deeply worn by equestrians and their horses, wend through town and disappear into the woods.

Charlestonians rode the train over to Aiken and liked its cool forest environs "secure from tides and ocean mists, and free from sleet and snow," as exulted by the late Thomas H. Williamson, one of Aiken County's first treasurers. Northerners discovered Aiken after the Civil War and brought their money and horses here for the winter. Society pages told of polo matches, fox hunting forays and lively steeplechases. Men were dashing, and women were their husbands' wives (even now, you'll rarely hear a woman's first name in polite conversation). The Yankee aristocrats built magnificent manses and called them "cottages," and called themselves "The Winter Colony."

SIGHTS

Winter colonist Thomas Hitchcock was an internationally known polo player who wanted a wooded park right in the city. Together with other Aiken elite, he established **Hitchcock Woods**, today the largest urban forest in the nation. Its 1400 acres are thick with birch and pine trees and flanked by sand and clay trails designed for horseback riding and walking. ~ At Laurens Street and South Boundary Avenue, Aiken.

Running along the woods are some of the elegant Colonial "cottages" of **Aiken Winter Colony Historic District**, some with nearly a hundred rooms. Take a leisurely walk through Hitchcock Woods, then drive along South Boundary Avenue beneath its famous tunnel of live oaks. ~ Along South Boundary Avenue and Laurens and Newberry streets, Aiken.

Hopeland Gardens, set among a turn-of-the-century estate, is also a beautiful spot to walk. Fountains and shimmering ponds, weeping willows and brick walls, gigantic deodora cedars and red-berried yopon holly, and other lush flora create a pleasurable, fragrant setting. A "Touch and Scent Trail" for blind visitors has bronze markers etched in Braille. ~ At Whiskey Road and Dupree Place, Aiken.

Also at the gardens is the **Thoroughbred Racing Hall of Fame**, occupying the former carriage house of the Iselin family (Mrs. Iselin, an avid gardener who lived to be 102, used to park her Rolls-Royce here). This is the place to absorb Aiken's horse history; rooms and galleries are given over to exhibits on polo, steeple-chasing and harness, or "sulky," racing. You'll learn how hundreds of horses are trained here every winter so they can compete in the Aiken Triple Crown. The three races—Aiken Steeplechase, Aiken Trials and harness racing—are held over three weekends in late March and early April, when the town swells with thousands of equestrians and horse lovers. Open late afternoon Tuesday through Sunday from mid-October through mid-May. ~ 803-642-7758.

Of course, plenty of Aiken area folks have nothing to do with horses or big money. At the **Aiken County Historical Museum**, you discover that textiles and farming were the backbone of the region for over a hundred years. Here were lots of Southern "firsts," including the South's first cotton mill and first successful bathtub. Most intriguing, though, is the museum building, an elaborate Colonial Revival home built in 1931 by a Northern industrialist. It originally had 32 rooms, 15 bathrooms and a ballroom, though they've been altered over time. Exquisite gardens and trees fill the property, which spans an entire city block. ~ 433 Newberry Street Southwest, Aiken; 803-642-2015.

IN HONOR OF WILLIAM AIKEN

Aiken's main avenues and parkways are broad, thanks to town engineers who, in 1835, designed Aiken with extra-wide streets. Two years earlier, a railroad was completed between Charleston and Hamburg, South Carolina—at the time the world's longest tracks. William Aiken, wealthy equestrian, cotton grower and president of South Carolina Canal and Railroad Company, was thrown from his horse and killed before the tracks were finished. Railroad workers, laying line near a woodsy outpost, named it Aiken.

Aiken has many other millionaire homes, though most can be viewed only from the tree-covered sidewalks. Pick up a walking-tour map from the **Greater Aiken Chamber of Commerce**, which covers the Aiken Winter Colony Historic District. ~ 400 Laurens Street Northwest, Aiken; 803-641-1111, 800-542-4536.

For information on surrounding towns, stop by **Thoroughbred Country Visitors Center**. ~ 2748 Wagner Road, Route 302 North, Aiken; 803-649-7981.

HIDDEN ►   The nearby town of **Montmorenci**, five miles east of Aiken on Route 78, is a scattering of farmhouses enveloped by cotton, corn and peanut fields, and pecan groves. On summer afternoons, storm clouds stack up big and black over the fields, and pecans click in the pre-rain wind.

HIDDEN ►   Once 19 acres of peanut, cotton and wheat, **Montmorenci Vineyards** is now masked in brambly grape vines. Robert Scott, Sr., and son, Robert Scott, Jr., grow 60 varietals and bottle a dozen different wines. A charming, chimneyed cottage acts as tasting room, open Wednesday through Saturday. Closed the first two weeks of January. ~ Route 78; 803-649-4870.

HIDDEN ►   Northwest of Aiken, pick up Route 28 at the southern edge of Sumter National Forest. Here the road becomes the **Savannah River Scenic Highway**, trailing along the river north more than a hundred miles to South Carolina's Upcountry. The scenery is near-flat, scrub-pine forest pocketed with tiny towns, their one-room post offices and gas stations with attendant loungers. Semitrailer trucks hauling fresh-felled trees explain occasional gaps in the forest.

For the first 40 miles, the river opens wide and becomes J. Strom Thurmond Lake, though the water eludes the road and the views are mostly of trees. Four state parks provide access to the lake and forest. In the town of Calhoun Falls, you can take a 13-mile jog east on Route 72 to **Abbeville**. This timeworn town with brick streets and buildings was a frontier settlement founded in the 1730s by Patrick Calhoun. His son, John C. Calhoun, was a wealthy planter and politician who fought to keep slavery, eventually becoming vice president of the United States.

The South's Ordinance of Succession was drafted in Abbeville right before the Civil War. Near war's end, the last meeting of the Confederate War Council took place here. This is why Abbeville residents like to say the town is the "birthplace and deathbed of the Confederacy."

Despite Southern history, there's really not much to do in Abbeville. Walk around **Court Square** (bounded by Trinity, Washington, Main and Pickens streets), the heart of historic downtown, where there's the **Abbeville Opera House**. Built in 1908, the ornate brick beauty was a stop on the vaudeville circuit, hosting performers such as Jimmy Durante and Fanny Bryce. Next door, the stately

Abbeville County Courthouse was built the same year. Also here is the **Greater Abbeville Chamber of Commerce**, which can provide walking-tour maps of historic homes. ~ 104 Pickens Street, Abbeville; 864-459-4600.

The best-known historic home, **Burt-Stark Mansion**, is the official deathbed of the Confederacy. Here, in May of 1865, Jefferson Davis met with the Confederate War Council for the last time before losing to the Yanks. Tours are given on Friday and Saturday afternoons; group tours available by appointment. Admission. ~ 306 North Main Street, Abbeville; 864-459-4297.

The place to stay in Aiken is **The Willcox Inn**, right in the heart of the old-money Winter Colony neighborhood. Built in 1898 and beautifully restored, the imposing, crisp white house offers 24 spacious rooms with poster beds, ornamental fireplaces, huge baths with clawfoot tubs and separate showers, and equestrian prints on the walls. Six suites open onto porches. The Pheasant Room has fine dining, and the Polo Pub is a clubby place for a drink. ~ 100 Colleton Avenue, Aiken; 803-649-1377, 800-368-1047, fax 803-643-0971. MODERATE TO DELUXE.

LODGING

Annie's Inn is a pecan throw from cornfields and pecan groves, a big, white, antebellum house with twin columns and wraparound porch. Built in the 1830s, it was once the centerpiece of a 2000-acre cotton plantation. A Civil War cannonball took off the third floor but the house survived, and now the two-story bed and breakfast is restored just enough to be comfortable. All the bedrooms have private baths, and are variously decorated in homey style. Two cottages are rented by the week at budget prices—a great value. Rooms include a full breakfast. ~ Route 78, about five miles east of Aiken, Montmorenci; 803-649-6836. BUDGET TO MODERATE.

◄ HIDDEN

●●

✔ CHECK THESE OUT—UNIQUE LODGING

- *Budget to moderate:* Retreat to the country at **Annie's Inn,** a rambling, white antebellum house set among cornfields and pecan groves. *page 399*
- *Moderate:* Find seclusion at **Sunrise Farm** and its big, beautiful early-1900s farmhouse and cattle ranch. *page 411*
- *Moderate to deluxe:* Bring the family to **Devil's Fork State Park** and settle into a luxury villa, lakeside or in the woods. *page 415*
- *Moderate to ultra-deluxe:* Discover high style and ultimate comfort at **Pettigru Place**, a gorgeous Georgian Federal-style bed and breakfast. *page 409*

Budget: under $60 Moderate: $60–$100 Deluxe: $100–$130 Ultra-deluxe: over $130

Next door to the Abbeville Opera House, the **Belmont Inn** was heralded by the local paper as a "new and modern hotel" when it opened in 1902. Over time, it deteriorated and eventually closed, but now has been reincarnated as a no-frills, comfortable place. Twenty-four guest rooms have battered wood floors that creak with age, and doors that don't shut just right. All in all, things are basically clean. ~ Court Square, Abbeville; 864-459-9625. MODERATE TO DELUXE.

DINING

Aiken folks fuel up in the morning at **Alvano's**. The country kitchen serves eggs and grits, biscuits with sausage gravy, and intense pancakes. There's a row of booths, a counter lined with chairs, and lots of vinyl and formica. ~ 122 Laurens Street Northwest, Aiken; 803-643-9710. BUDGET.

Go to **Malia's** for lunch and have soup. Different every day but always good, you might find a cold zucchini elixir with lemon pepper and herbs, three-bean chili or—what locals crave—crabmeat bisque. The menu also lists sandwiches, salads and full-course fare. The dining room of the downtown eatery runs deep, the facade is washed with sunny yellow. Dinner on weekends. ~ 120 Laurens Street Southwest, Aiken; 803-643-3086. MODERATE.

In a restored 1840s house that's simple and elegant, **No. 10 Downing Street** serves savory Continental creations such as roasted smoked pork loin with juniper au jus, almond baked halibut with lemon beurre blanc, and rack of lamb. Save room for the whiskey road cheesecake glazed with bourbon caramel sauce, then stroll around the lovely gardens. There's a full bar. Closed Sunday and Monday. ~ 241 Laurens Street Southwest, Aiken; 803-642-9062. MODERATE.

The best eatery in Abbeville, **The Village Grill** is a comfy place with wood booths and walls painted watermelon and hunter green. Steaks, fish, shrimp and pasta selections come with side dishes like fried corn on the cob and baked beans. Among the heart-healthy items: rotisserie chicken and grilled Cajun trout. Full bar. ~ 114 Trinity Street, Abbeville; 864-459-2500. MODERATE.

SHOPPING

Look for antiques and country collectibles along Laurens and Newberry streets in downtown Aiken.

The wide range of antiquities at **Market Place Antiques** includes primitive, period and wicker furniture. ~ 343 Park Avenue South; 803-648-9696.

The merchandise at **Beam Me Up** includes gold and silver jewelry and recycled books, especially cookbooks. ~ 216 Park Avenue Southeast, Aiken; 803-642-6193.

For a comprehensive list of antique shops, stop by the **Greater Aiken Chamber of Commerce**. ~ 400 Laurens Street Northwest; 803-641-1111.

Area farmers bring their crops to **Aiken County Farmers Market**. Depending on what's in season, you'll find watermelon, silver queen corn, pecans, peanuts and cantaloupe. Call before you go; they're open only during certain times of year. ~ Richland Avenue and Williamsburg Street, Aiken; 803-648-3862.

The place to be in Aiken, especially Thursday through Sunday nights, is The Alley off Main Street. **Up Your Alley** is a neighborhood watering hole with restaurant that serves up live entertainment—from karaoke to acoustic guitar—on Friday nights. ~ 222 The Alley, Aiken; 803-649-2603.

NIGHTLIFE

Westside Bowery, a restaurant on one end and pub on the other, pulls in huge happy-hour crowds, mostly thirty- and forty-somethings. It's SRO on Thursday and Friday nights, too. Live music on occasion. ~ 151 B Lane, Aiken; 803-648-2900.

Over at the Willcox Inn, the clubby, richly paneled **Polo Pub** draws the rich and nouveau riche before and after dinner. ~ 100 Colleton Avenue, Aiken; 803-649-1377.

The Opera House Players, a stock theater company, perform year-round at **Abbeville Opera House**. The former vaudeville and "talkie" movie house is a striking turn-of-the-century showplace. ~ On Court Square, downtown Abbeville; 864-459-2157.

REDCLIFFE PLANTATION STATE PARK 🏃 Many people are surprised to discover this 1859 antebellum mansion, tucked 15 miles southwest of Aiken near the Georgia state line. South Carolina Governor James H. Hammond chose this secluded spot along the Savannah River for his two-story plantation house, calling it "Redcliffe" for the high clay bluffs running along the water. Four generations of Hammonds lived here until descendant John Shaw Billings, former managing editor for *Time* and *Life* magazines, donated it to the state. You can tour the house (admission), which has many original furnishings and art pieces, then picnic and walk along the nature trail at this 350-acre park. Facilities include the park office, the plantation home, a picnic area and a nature trail. There is a $2 fee to tour the home. ~ Located off Route 278, three miles southwest of Beech Island and 15 miles southeast of Aiken; 803-827-1473.

BEACHES & PARKS

HAMILTON BRANCH STATE PARK 🏃 🚤 🚤 ⚓ With more than 1200 miles of shoreline and a sea of fresh water teeming with bass, bream and catfish, this is a fisher's haven. The park is a 731-acre peninsula elbowing into J. Strom Thurmond Lake, pale blue water rimmed with slash pine forest rising up from the clay. Picnic tables and campsites are sprinkled along the shore of pine needles. Rarely crowded, even in the height of spring and fall seasons. There are no designated swimming areas, but plenty of shallow lakeshore with hard-packed clay bottom. Lake fishing is excellent for bass, bream and catfish; a state license is required. Facilities include the park office, picnic tables and shelters, a playground, a bath house, restrooms and boat ramps. ~ Located along Route 221 (Savannah River Highway) just north of Route 23, 12 miles south of McCormick; 864-333-2223.

▲ There are 200 tent and RV sites with electric and water hookups (most are right on the lake); $13 per site. Hot showers and restrooms available.

HICKORY KNOB STATE RESORT PARK 🏃 🚣 🛶 Just past the entrance of this vast wooded retreat, a velvety green golf course swirls against the blueness of Thurmond Lake. It's but one clue why this is called a "resort" park—and why it's wildly popular nearly year-round. Like a summer camp for adults and kids, it offers myriad activities and accommodations, including a motel-style lodge; basic but modern one-bedroom cabins with kitchenettes, TVs and telephones; and a historic, two-bedroom house with a full kitchen and fireplace. Budget rates for the lodge and cabins; moderate for the house. Book several months ahead, especially for the spring and fall. Swimming is best in the swimming pool; lake swimming is permitted, but there's no beach or lifeguards. You can catch bass, bream, yellow perch, saugers and catfish in Thurmond Lake. There are many facilities: an 18-hole golf course with putting green, a driving range, a pro shop and a clubhouse lounge; a swimming pool; two tennis courts; a skeet shooting range; an archery course; a playground; a restaurant and coffee shop; a nature center and trails; a bait-and-tackle shop and johnboat rentals. ~ Located off Route 378, seven miles west of McCormick; 864-391-2450, 800-491-1764, fax 864-391-5390.

▲ There are 75 campsites for tents or RVs, all with hookups for water and electricity, picnic tables and grills. A hot-water bathhouse is at the campground. Fee is $13 per site, available on a first-come basis.

HIDDEN ▶   **CALHOUN FALLS STATE PARK** 🏃 🚣 🚤 🛶 There aren't any waterfalls here, just miles of pine woods and pale blue Lake Russell. (The falls disappeared when the lake was created.) Everything in this enormous, 26,650-acre park is geared toward the water, with fishing and boating heading the list of park pursuits. Swimming is good off the lakefront beach, open during summer. There are excellent fishing opportunities for bass, bluegill, crappie and catfish. Facilities include the park office, a marina with 36 boat slips, boat ramps, a fishing pier, a park store and tackle shop, a modern community building, a playground, picnic areas and a bathhouse. ~ Located off Route 81, two miles north of Route 72 and the town of Calhoun Falls; 864-447-8267.

▲ Forty-one sites, all with electric and water hookups, suitable for tents or RVs; $13 to $14 per night. No reservations.

The flat pine woods and fields of central South Carolina
slowly give way to soft sculpted hills in the northwest.
Lakeshores angle against spires of trees, whitewashed
farmhouses are propped on knolls, rivers run long and lucid, and
seamless roads twist above hazy valleys. The Upcountry, as this
northwestern corner of South Carolina is called, is indeed the highest part of the state, rising more than 3000 feet, a prelude to North
Carolina's Southern Mountains just across the state line.

Upcountry

Greenville and Spartanburg are the commercial gateways to the
Upcountry. Their downtowns are separated by 30 miles but with
ever-expanding commerce and industry, their metropolitan areas
are fast merging. The nearby town of Greer was chosen over
dozens of cities worldwide as the site of BMW's new auto-manu-
facturing plant, a $5 million facility that opened in the summer of
1995. The modern and attractive Greenville-Spartanburg Airport,
almost halfway between the cities, welcomes visitors to the area.

Downtown **Greenville** is an enjoyable few blocks of tree-lined
streets, wide walkways overhung with ferns and espresso cart vendors doling out small, steamy cups. Browse the shops and have
lunch, then stop at the **Greater Greenville Convention & Visitors
Bureau** for information on the area. ~ In the City Hall lobby, 206
South Main Street; 864-233-0461. You will also find maps, brochures and assistance at the **Discover Upcountry Carolina Association**. ~ 500 East North Street, Greenville; 864-233-2690, 800-
849-4766.

SIGHTS

Two Greenville museums, both free to visitors, are worth seeking out. The permanent pieces at **Greenville County Museum of
Art** focus on Southern talent, with works by William Tylee Ranney,
Helen Turner, Washington Allston and George Healy. Traveling exhibits span ancient to modern times and are usually excellent. ~
420 College Street, Greenville; 864-271-7570.

The collection of religious art at **Bob Jones University Art Gallery and Museum** is outstanding. Twenty-seven galleries house over
400 pieces, including icons that are 4000 years old. There are vases
from ancient Egypt and Syria, an 80-foot-long Hebrew Torah scroll
written on gazelle skin, and an exquisite ecclesiastical throne. As
for the impressive sampling of Baroque and Renaissance paintings,
you'll find works by no less than Rembrandt, van Dyck, Titian,
Tintoretto and Rubens. Note that this is *not* the place to wear your
short-shorts, the university being of the Christian persuasion. Open
Tuesday through Sunday afternoons. ~ 1700 Wade Hampton Boulevard, off Route 385, Greenville; 864-242-5100 ext. 4207.

◄ HIDDEN

Northeast of Greenville toward Spartanburg, you'll come to
the town of **Greer** and, more importantly, the BMW **Manufacturing**
plant. The plant has been the biggest thing happening around
Greer ever since 1994, when BMW announced its intention to

locate here, hire several thousand workers and open a visitors center to draw tourists to town. The center (called the **Zentrum**) is where tours of the BMW factory start. The tours last about an hour, with most of the action involving actual car assembly. Open Tuesday through Thursday. Admission. ~ On Route 101, Greer; 864-989-5528.

Spartanburg lacks the contemporary edge of Greenville, but its downtown is pleasant enough. The best sightseeing is actually in the bucolic pastureland south of Spartanburg. Take Route 221 through sun-sprinkled forest and country fields until you see the signs for **Walnut Grove Plantation**. Park and follow the path beneath arches of gorgeous crepe myrtles, past the magnificent 400-year-old white oak tree, to the unassuming plantation house. It has changed little since 1765, when Charles Moore received the land by grant from King George III and built the house of local pine. He and his wife raised ten children, including daughter Kate, who was a scout for the Patriots during the American Revolution.

HIDDEN ►

Incredibly, much of the Moore's original furnishings and books are well preserved here. A closet door has its original paint—buttermilk dyed with indigo. The ruddy stains on a bedroom floor are from the blood of a Patriot captain slain by Tories. After a tour of the home and the adjacent schoolhouse (one of the first in the South), stroll the nature trail and the cemetery where Kate Moore and other family members are buried. Closed Monday and holidays. Admission. ~ Located at 1200 Otts Shoals Road, Roebuck; 864-576-6546.

HIDDEN ►

A few miles south of Walnut Grove, Thomas Price built a beautiful brick home with chimneys and a steep gambrel roof—unheard of for a 1795 plantation home. **The Price House** doesn't seem so unusual today, except that it is meticulously restored. The original plantation covered 2000 acres, with 28 slaves doing most of the farm work. Price ran the local post office and general store and entertained folks passing through by stagecoach, a good way to make extra cash and show off his place. Admission. ~ 1200 Oak View Farms Road, off Route 26, Woodruff; 864-476-2483.

Northeast of Spartanburg along rural Route 29, you will know you are in peach country when you see the **Peachoid water tower** in **Gaffney**. Painted like a peach, its ruddy, sun-faded facade is a tribute to area peach growing.

HIDDEN ►

Keep heading north on two-lane Route 29 and it will dip and climb through rolling green pastures with dirt roads that have names like Possom Trot. Turn off at Route 5 and follow the signs for **Kings Mountain National Military Park**, next door to Kings Mountain State Park. Kings is not really a mountain but a low spur of the Blue Ridge, covered in Southern hardwood forest and straddling the South and North Carolina border. The long, flat summit, rising only 60 feet, seemed an ideal place for the Tories to set up camp in October 1780. From here, they thought they could defend themselves against the Patriot "over-mountain men," a backwoods band of farmers who were marching down from Tennessee with knives and guns. But the surrounding oaks and hickories proved good cover for the mountaineers. They surrounded the Tories and "fought from tree to tree to the summit," according to one Loyalist account. In less than an hour, the over-mountain men had killed Tory commander Major Patrick Ferguson, and helped decide the end of the American Revolution.

Today, you can stroll through the forest along the ridge where the centuries-old skirmish occurred. Much of the trail is wheel-chair-accessible. Historical markers and tape recordings help bring the battle into perspective. (Basically, these guys were shooting with muskets from behind trees. Imagine their stress level every time they had to stop to reload.) There's also an 18-minute film, shown in the visitors center, that traces local battles during the war. ~ Route 21, off Route 66, Kings Mountain; 864-936-7921.

The next big skirmish was in January 1781 at nearby **National Battlefield**. Once again, the British were defeated in an hour even though they enjoyed bigger and better forces. It helped that the Colonials were led by one Daniel Morgan, a brilliant field tactician of the Revolution. The frenzied fighting went on right next to the cows and horses who grazed at Hannah's Cowpens, a frontier pasture. The battlefield originally covered only 150 acres, though the park stretches for 845 acres, providing areas for picnicking and walking. A one-and-a-quarter-mile interpretive trail (all wheelchair accessible) and three-and-a-half-mile loop road, sprinkled here and there with historical markers, take you to the heart of the battle. ~ Located on Route 11, about 11 miles west of Route 85, Chesnee; 864-461-2828.

◀ HIDDEN

If you head west from here along Route 11, you can experience the most scenic drive in inland South Carolina. For 135 miles, the road curves against the northwestern corner of the state, from Gaffney in the east to Route 85 on the west near Georgia. Called the **Cherokee Foothills Scenic Highway**, it runs alongside velvety green hills and forest-covered mountains, leafy peach orchards and bushy pea patches. Signs direct you to hidden hamlets like Pumpkintown, Pickens, Fair Play and Mountain Rest. The few rambling farmhouses, country stores and log homes are but pinpoints of civilization in this far-reaching wilderness.

Six state parks are sprinkled along the highway's hilly length, some dating back to the 1930s, when their facilities were solidly erected by the Civilian Conservation Corps. The parks provide most of the access to the vast lakes of liquid blue, the clear-as-gin streams, the rocky mountain trails.

Text continued on page 408.

The Wild Waters of Oconee

Where the Chattooga River starts in North Carolina, the water flows slow and steady, coursing south down a mountain gorge and gaining speed. Once it hits South Carolina, the Chattooga is on a rampage. The water foams and fizzes and hurls itself at boulders and trees, like a torrent in a pinball machine. It thunders down inclines in tremendous freefall, landing in silent baths.

The Cherokees called this land Oconee, or "water eyes from the hills." The Chattooga does appear to ooze from the Cherokee Foothills, the prelude to the Blue Ridge Mountains. The river races along the northwestern edge of Oconee County, separating it from Georgia. Oconee is the northwesternmost corner of South Carolina, far-flung and wild, barely inhabited by people but home to many wild animals. The forests are dim, deep and Edenic, ablaze with color in spring and fall.

It was in this watery wilderness that the 1972 movie *Deliverance* was shot. And though today you may not see any banjo-pickin' hayseeds on the porch (or you may), you will find some of the best whitewater rafting in the country. The Chattooga has Section III and IV whitewater, and is ranked as a National Wild and Scenic River. Section III, a leisurely run culminating with serious rapids, allows rafters time to enjoy the cool forest and bizarre boulder formations.

Section IV is tricky business. The water is fast and furious, the drops frequent and steep. But they deposit you into dead-calm pools where you can relax and ponder your surroundings: straight-up sides of gorges decorated with wildflowers and enormous trees. The climax of Section IV is a series of rapids called Corkscrew, Sock 'em Dog and Jawbone.

The U.S. Forest Service permits only three whitewater outfitters to offer trips on the Chattooga River. All conduct guided half- and full-day trips as well as overnight excursions. **Nantahala Outdoor Center** is located in South Carolina. ~ Chattooga Ridge Road, Mountain Rest; 800-232-7238. **Wildwater Ltd.** is a second outfitter in South Carolina. ~ Academy Road, off Route 76, Long Creek; 864-647-9587, 800-451-9972. **Southeastern Expeditions** is in Clayton, Georgia, just over the state line. ~ Route 76 East, Clayton, Georgia; 706-782-4331, 800-868-7238.

The Forest Service also limits the number of rafters, so the river rarely is crowded. It's easier to reserve a weekday; weekends are usually booked months ahead. Advance reservations are required for all trips, which are offered March through October.

If you'd prefer to enjoy Oconee's wild waters from the comfort of land, go waterfall watching. Dozens of falls can be reached by car, and then a short to long hike through the woods.

Spoonauger Falls, also called Rock Cliff Falls, are shaped like a giant spoon. You'll find them at Spoonauger Creek, a vein of the Chattooga River, near the town of Tamassee. From Route 28, take Route 107 north ten and a half miles to Burrells Fork Road. Turn left and go three miles to the Chattooga River bridge. From here it's an easy 20-minute walk to the falls.

Downriver, **Big Bend Falls** are the biggest on the Chattooga. The falls angle first in a watery sheet, then drop straight down in an angry torrent. It's a three-hour hike here, but worth it. The trailhead is at Cherry Hill Campground on Route 107 near Tamassee.

Blue Hole Falls are exquisite. Foamy white liquid freefalls 40 feet into a jewel-like pool of blue. Mist rises up and fills surrounding forest in the spring and fall. A sublime picnic spot. Getting there is a challenge, but here are the directions: From the town of Walhalla, take Route 28 north about seven miles, past the Stumphouse Ranger Station, to Route 193. Turn left and go .8 mile to Route 290 (also called Cassidy Bridge Road). Turn left and go 1.8 miles to Rich Mountain Road, a gravel road. Turn left and go .2 mile to Cedar Creek Road. Turn right and go three miles to Route 2658, a Forest Service road. From here, hike one mile to Route 2659 (also a Forest Service road) and turn right until you run into Cedar Creek. From here, you can hike down about 100 yards to the falls. If this fails, ask for directions at the Stumphouse Ranger Station!

Directions to many more hidden falls are published in *Finding the Falls*, a brochure available from **Discover Upcountry Carolina Association**. ~ 500 East North Street, Greenville; 864-233-2690, 800-849-4766.

HIDDEN ▶   Short, scenic side trips will take you to hidden places like **Campbell's Bridge**, built in 1909 and now the last covered bridge left in South Carolina. To find it, go south at Gowensville on Route 14 for four miles, then head west on Route 414 for one half mile.

A little farther west on Route 11, detour north on Route 25 for a great drive in the country. The skinny road launches through forest and farmland where a few postage stamp–size homes have corn HIDDEN ▶ patches. After a couple of miles, you'll see the turnoff for **Poinsett Bridge**, a shaded stone beauty built in 1820 and thought to be the oldest bridge in South Carolina. Its Gothic arch presides over the fast-flowing Middle Saluda River, where you can wade through the clear, brisk water embedded with black granite. Spread out a picnic atop the bridge, look into the coves crowded with kudzu, and listen to the water rush by. You will most likely have the place to yourself.

If you like twisting mountain roads with soul-gripping scenery, take Route 276 north from Route 11 and slowly squiggle up into North Carolina. It's only nine miles to the state line, and another 20 or so miles into the town of Brevard. (For more on Brevard and the Southern Mountains, see Chapter Three.)

A little farther west on Route 11, Route 178 North winds up through the woods. The trees get higher and higher, sunlight barely breaks through the tops and you'll realize you're climbing up the mountains. You can stop and wade in creeks that ramble by, or take a look at 3560-foot **Sassafras Mountain**, South Carolina's HIDDEN ▶ highest peak. The best view of the mountain is from the **Forest Service Lookout Tower** on Route 39-199, east of Route 178. If park personnel are on duty, they'll usually let you climb the tower.

Toward the western end of Cherokee Foothills Scenic Highway, Route 28 jogs north to **Walhalla**, where a sign declares "This is a Great Town." It's not really much of a town, just some whitewashed houses and patches of corn and an annual Hillbilly Festival. About eight miles north of Walhalla, through mountain gaps HIDDEN ▶ with panoramas of hazy valleys, **Stumphouse Tunnel Park** lies below the road in cool forest crisscrossed with streams.

The tunnel is part of a brief, strange attempt in 1856 to connect South Carolina with the Midwest by railroad. The Blue Ridge Railroad decided to bore through granite mountains using Irish immigrants with sledgehammers and hand drills working 12 hours a day. It took them one month to chip away 200 feet. Money ran out, the Civil War came along, and all that's left are some empty tunnels. In the 1950s, Clemson University used Stumphouse Tunnel for curing its locally renowned blue cheese, hanging the blue-veined curds in little pouches from the wet tunnel walls.

The blue cheese is gone and the tunnel is closed, due to precarious rock conditions. But you can peer through the barricades into its black, abysmal depths. Afterward, hike along nearby Issaqueena Falls and through surrounding forest, wade in the streams or picnic at the tables.

Route 11 curls south past Walhalla and crosses Route 123, which heads east to **Clemson**. The pretty, nineteenth-century town is joined in the Southern consciousness with **Clemson University** and its Tigers, and indeed the school (and mascot) is the focus of everything (there's even a Tiger Paw Car Wash). The campus is beautiful, brimming with ancient oak trees and nineteenth-century architecture and vast grassy piazzas. Drive along College Avenue and Perimeter Road, south of Route 123, and you'll get a good picture of the place. ~ 864-656-4789.

On the eastern side of campus, **The South Carolina Botanical Garden** offers a fine walk in the woods. Miles of paths cushioned with pine needles wind through forest, wooden footbridges arch over cloudy clay water, and dark, cool coves offer relief from summer heat. Over a thousand species of trees are here (unfortunately, few are labeled) and tremendous gardens of camellia, daffodils and azaleas. Wildflower, fern, bog and meditation gardens are also set among these 256 acres. ~ Perimeter Road and Route 28.

Arrive in **Pendleton** in the morning and you'll see folks out tending their gardens. This time-locked town with many lovely old homes and enormous trees is listed on the National Register of Historic Places. The big village green is embraced by colorfully painted shops and restaurants, most dating to the 1800s. ~ Route 28, three miles east of Clemson.

Farmers Hall, right on the village green, opened in the 1820s as a meeting place for Farmers Society members. It was here that Thomas Green Clemson suggested building a state agricultural college—now Clemson University. Incredibly, the Society still meets upstairs, making it the nation's oldest active farmer's hall. Downstairs is a venerable restaurant and meeting spot for Pendleton's high society. ~ East Main Street, Pendleton.

You can easily spend a day browsing, having lunch, exploring historic homes and having high tea (there's a tea room on the square). Stop by **The Pendleton District Historical and Recreational Commission,** located in an 1850 former store, for a walking-tour map to the historic area. Closed weekends. ~ At 125 East Queen Street, Pendleton; 864-646-3782.

LODGING

◀ *HIDDEN*

Most accommodations around Greenville and Spartanburg are chain hotels and motels. One exception in Greenville is **Pettigru Place,** a gorgeous bed and breakfast in a historic neighborhood near downtown. The front lawn of the Georgian Federalist house is riotously planted with flowers. Inside, the rooms are striking, just like something out of a home decorating magazine. The Brass

Giraffe has a primitive African theme, the Carolinian has a king sleigh bed and Charleston detailing, and the Greene Room has a fireplace and rich tones of cranberry and hunter green. Credit goes to Gloria Hendershot and Janice Beatty, who overhauled the 1930 house and opened it to guests in 1993. Rates include a full gourmet breakfast. ~ 302 Pettigru Street, Greenville; 864-242-4529. MODERATE TO ULTRA-DELUXE.

HIDDEN ► About 30 miles east of Spartanburg in the funky railroad town of Blacksburg, **White House Inn** is completely unexpected, a stately Greek Revival house in a simple Southern neighborhood. Pretty period pieces fill the five bedrooms, and a third-floor suite is voluminous, modern and private. Owner Jim White prepares large breakfasts and serves afternoon wine and cheese. Kings Mountain National Battlefield and Kings Mountain State Park are close by. ~ 607 West Pine Street, Blacksburg; 864-839-3000. MODERATE TO DELUXE.

Lodging is scarce along the Cherokee Foothills. Several state parks have cabins and one rents contemporary villas, but they are tough to secure (for more information, see "Beaches & Parks" later in this chapter).

HIDDEN ► It's easier to reserve a room at **The Schell Haus.** George and Sherry Schell have opened their contemporary home in the woods to visitors, offering five bedrooms with homespun decor and a swimming pool out back. One room has a sumptuous view of Table Rock Mountain. There's also a lavish suite with living room, wet bar, whirlpool tub and more panoramic scenes. Full breakfast is included in the moderate rates. ~ Off Route 11, across from Table Rock State Park; 864-878-0078. The Schells also run the adjacent **Laurel Mountain Inn,** a motel with five rooms new in 1994. All come with coffeemakers and refrigerators, and one extra-large room is wheelchair-accessible. ~ 864-878-5800. MODERATE TO ULTRA-DELUXE

✦✦

✔ CHECK THESE OUT—UNIQUE DINING

- *Budget:* Get your tofu burgers, falafels and other New Age culinaria at **The Basil Pot.** *page 391*
- *Budget:* Feeling like fresh farm fare? Head to **The Dutch Oven:** the local Mennonites really know how to cook. *page 412*
- *Moderate:* Go to **Mr. Friendly's New Southern Cafe** and order some of inland South Carolina's most innovative cooking. *page 392*
- *Moderate:* Partake of classic Continental cuisine in civilized Southern surroundings at **No. 10 Downing Street.** *page 400*

Budget: under $9   Moderate: $9–$16   Deluxe: $16–$24   Ultra-deluxe: over $24

Off the western stretch of Cherokee Foothills Scenic Highway, **Sunrise Farm** was once a cotton plantation but is now a 64-acre ◀ *HIDDEN* cattle ranch with picturesque pastures and mountains all around. The early 1900s farmhouse is big and beautiful, its lawns decorated with myrtle trees, magnolias and a split-rail fence. Owners Jean and Jim Webb are exceedingly hospitable, offering two rooms and a suite that are spacious, colorful and extra comfortable. There are also two cottages and a corncrib with Norwegian wood stove and private patio. ~ On Sunrise Drive, one mile from Route 130, Salem; 864-944-0121. MODERATE.

The four-acre grounds at **Liberty Hall Inn** are rich with apple and cedar trees, while the ten bedrooms are informal, spacious and tasteful. All have telephones, televisions and air conditioning, but these are recent additions. When a wealthy planter built the handsome, two-story home in 1850, there was little but wood floors and walls, and cotton fields all around. ~ Route 28 business, Pendleton; 864-646-7500, 800-643-7944. MODERATE.

If you like German food, go to **The Red Baron**. The downtown deli **DINING** makes great reubens, corned beef and pastramis, and the soups are scrumptious. Owner Marvin Hambleton alternates among chili, clam chowder and potato soup, though his "Chicken, By George" soup with barley and vegetables has been "made every day for 20 years," he says. Save room for the cheesecake, a 50-year-old German recipe. ~ 118 North Main Street, Greenville; 864-232-1414. BUDGET.

Seven Oaks is Greenville's top shelf. The venue is a handsome white house built in 1895 and set among big, beautiful oaks (there are only five now, thanks to storms). The cuisine is consistently superb Continental. Try the rack of lamb roasted in a dijon mustard crust or the chicken baked in puff pastry with dill and red wine sauce. ~ 104 Broadus Avenue, Greenville; 864-232-1895. DELUXE TO ULTRA-DELUXE.

You will never forget the **Beacon Drive-In**. The cafeteria line moves fast and furious, with servers hollering orders and commotion radiating from the kitchen. John White, Beacon owner for half a century, speaks like an auctioneer, running down the list of 80-plus sandwiches guaranteed to blow your cholesterol for the day. Double chili cheeseburgers with bacon, fried perch, sausage and egg—order them regular or "a-plenty" with fried potatoes and Vidalia onions. Dozens of booths and tables fill this funky, time-worn eatery. You can dine in your car, but you'll miss all the crazy goings-on. ~ 255 Reidville Road, Spartanburg; 864-585-9387. BUDGET.

Meanwhile, the ambiance at **Spice of Life** couldn't be different. ◀ *HIDDEN* Pink linens, wine racks and brick walls adorn this 1898 former foundry. Broccoli melts, vegetarian pasta and grilled chicken are among the lunch offerings. For dinner, there's roasted duckling, grilled lamb chops, swordfish steak and other well-prepared Continental fare. ~ 100 Wood Row, off St. John Street, Spartanburg; 864-585-3737. MODERATE.

There's not much cookin' along the 135-mile Cherokee Foothills Scenic Highway. For lunch, there's **Aunt Sue's Country Corner**, where organ music streams out front and waitresses are called "cousins." Deli sandwiches, BLTs, ice cream, fudge and sweet tea are the mainstays. Ladder-back chairs, rough-hewn wood walls and ruffled curtains define the decor. ~ Route 11, two miles east of Table Rock State Park; 864-878-4366. BUDGET.

The other hot dining spot is . . . a state park. **Table Rock Lodge Restaurant** is indeed jammed with patrons much of the year. The woodsy, family-style dining room and concrete patio overlooking glassy Pinnacle Lake were built in the 1930s by the Civilian Conservation Corps. The crowd-pleasing food is straightforward and Southern: fried chicken, fried flounder and trout, country ham, hushpuppies, corn-on-the-cob, french fries. Dinner is served year-round; lunch is served May through October. ~ Located at Table Rock State Park, Route 11, about 16 miles north of Pickens; 864-878-9065. BUDGET.

There's no problem finding fine food in Pendleton. To dine in cultured country style, go to **Liberty Hall Inn**. In the winter, there's a fire in the hearth; in the summer, the gardens are ablaze with flowers and crepe myrtles. The four-course, prix-fixe dinner usually features chicken, fish, seafood and tenderloin of beef. ~ Route 28 business, Pendleton; 864-646-7500. DELUXE.

At **Farmers Hall Restaurant,** you can eat beneath big trees right on the Pendleton village green. If it's wintertime, cozy indoor nooks provide the venue for the eatery's innovative lunch and dinner entrées. Sautéed trout with hazelnut butter and crab cakes piccata might be on the blackboard menu, while the regular menu features plenty of pasta and chicken. ~ East Main Street, Pendleton; 864-646-7024. MODERATE TO DELUXE.

Across from the village green, **The Dutch Oven** is a small cafeteria run by local Mennonites who definitely know how to cook. The fresh, fill-you-up farm fare features mashed potatoes, lima beans, stewed apples, stewed tomatoes, country steak, fried chicken and the best macaroni and cheese you've ever tasted. It's lunch only, so leave time for an afternoon nap. ~ 129 North Mechanic Street, Pendleton; 864-646-3301. BUDGET.

SHOPPING   Concentrate your shopping efforts in Greenville, where the area around Main Street has splendid shopping. Look for traditional and primitive furniture, funky watches, hip garb, health food items, artwork and even maps.

Pick any place in the world and **The Map Shop** will surely have a map of it. There's even a world pocket atlas for sale at this fascinating place. ~ 5-B East Coffee Street, Greenville; 864-271-6277.

The gallery of **Llyn Strong** is a prettily lit space exhibiting pricey and unusual objets d'art. Elaborate screens and jewelry, sweaters and perfume bottles are among the many items to be found here. ~ 119 North Main Street, Greenville; 864-233-0216.

Northwest of downtown Greenville, **Tempo Gallery, Art & Frame** showcases works by South Carolina artists—everything from oils, acrylics and serigraphs to pottery and works off and on paper. ~ 125 West Stone Avenue, Greenville; 864-233-1070.

Clemson University has been making blue cheese for nearly half a century, and is good at it. You can buy the blue-veined delicacy at the school's **Agricultural Sales Center**. ~ Newman Hall, Newman Road, Clemson; 864-656-3242.

Galleries and gift shops edge the Pendleton village green. The folks at **The Mercantile** will offer you coffee while you browse the pottery, porcelain, throw rugs, candles and potpourri. ~ 149 East Queen Street, Pendleton; 864-646-9431.

Greenville's after-work crowd ducks into **Henni's** pub for international beers, cocktails and light fare. ~ 103 North Main Street, Greenville; 864-370-1090.   **NIGHTLIFE**

Coffee Street, named for the FlatIron mountains of Colorado, serves up African music on Thursday nights and acoustic jazz and guitar on weekends. No alcohol. ~ 12 East Coffee Street, Greenville; 864-467-0002

From blues to bluegrass, spontaneous rock-and-roll jams to acoustic non-smoking fests, **The Handlebar** hosts some of the hottest shows in the Upcountry. Cover. Advance tickets for big shows. ~ 400 Mills Avenue, Greenville; 864-233-6173.

Greenville's $42 million **Peace Center for Performing Arts** is the venue for touring Broadway shows, national and international ballet and symphony, children's theater, and appearances by regional and big-name performers such as Mel Torme. ~ 101 West Broad Street, Greenville; 864-467-3030, 800-888-7768.

Some snacks, darts and a pint of ale perhaps? All are available at **Pendleton House Pub**, a handsome 1880 restaurant with a pub and drawing room. Full bar. ~ 203 East Main Street, Pendleton; 803-646-7795.

KINGS MOUNTAIN STATE PARK 🏃 ⛵ 🎣 🚤 Within the **BEACHES** cool, shady confines of this oak and hickory forest is a nineteenth- **& PARKS** century working farm. It's a poignant, peaceful setting, with split-rail fence running along grassy pastures and corn patches, and ◄ *HIDDEN* wildflower meadows attended by bumblebees and big grasshoppers. On weekends, a guide will take you through the 1860s log house built by a Civil War veteran and the blacksmith and carpenter shops dating to the 1820s, the cotton gin, corncrib and sorghum mill. On weekdays, you can stroll the farm by yourself. There's also a pretty lake in the park, named for a low-lying spur of the Blue Ridge—not a real mountain. Right next door, Kings Mountain National Military Park is a Revolutionary War battlefield. Swimming is good during the summer, when lifeguards are stationed at the lake. Try fishing for bass, bream and crappie in the lake. Facilities include the park office, picnic shelters, trading post, and johnboat, canoe and pedal boat rentals. Day-use fee, $2. ~ Off Route 161 north of York. From Blacksburg, take Route 29 north to Route 216 and enter through Kings Mountain National Military Park; 803-222-3209.

▲ There are 119 tent and RV sites with water and electrical hookups; $14 per night. A primitive tent camping area has no facilities.

JONES GAP STATE PARK 🏃‍♂️ The Middle Saluda River, cold and clear as air, hurries through Jones Gap mountain gorge and thus right through the park. The forest setting is immensely scenic and tranquil, filled with the rush of the river. Families love these 3346 acres; children wade in the river and play along the grassy banks sprinkled with picnic areas, including several for wheelchair visitors. A rock pond swirling with enormous trout was once the Cleveland Fish Hatchery but is now a park exhibit. The river offers excellent brown, rainbow and brook trout fishing; only artificial flies and lures permitted. Facilities include the park office, picnic areas, hiking trails and an environmental education center. ~ Located on River Falls Road, north of Route 276, about one mile west of the town of Cleveland; 864-836-3647.

▲ There are 18 primitive tent sites along Jones Gap Trail, a strenuous, five-mile hike between Jones Gap State Park and Caesars Head State Park; $2 per night.

CAESARS HEAD STATE PARK 🏃 This place is all about views. Stand on a platform of rock and a torrent of Blue Ridge mountains sweeps before you, cool winds slapping at your face. Walk down into Hell's Kitchen, a sliver of space between rocks, and look across to the granite outcropping that someone once said looks like Julius Caesar. The sad, squatty face poking from the mountain could be anyone. Facilities include the park office, gift shop, small picnic area, nature center and hiking trails. ~ Located along Route 276, just north of Route 11 near the tiny hamlet of Caesars Head; 864-836-6115.

▲ Primitive, trailside camping permitted along Jones Gap Trail, a strenuous five-mile hike between Caesars Head and Jones Gap State Park; $2 per night.

TABLE ROCK STATE PARK 🏃 ⛵ 🚤 ⛴ The flat stony summit of Table Rock Mountain looms in the distance. Lofty, fragrant forest covers the mountainsides and most of the 3068-acre park. Perennially packed from spring through fall, it's a mecca for hiking, swimming, boating and fishing. Thirty-six-acre Pinnacle Lake, framed in bluish mountains, is the focus of activity in summer. A popular restaurant serves Southern cooking. A small chapel hosts woodsy weddings. Families like the 14 budget-priced cabins with furnished kitchens, heat and air conditioning, though it's tough to get a reservation. There's a one-week minimum stay in the summer. There is swimming in the summer; Pinnacle Lake is clear but brisk. Both Pinnacle Lake and Lake Oolenoy are stocked with bass, bream and catfish. Facilities include the park office, a trading post, a restaurant, canoes, pedal boat and fishing boat rentals, picnic areas, nature and hiking trails, and carpet golf. Day-use fee, $2. ~ Located along Route 11, about 16 miles north of Pickens; 864-878-9813.

▲ One hundred sites spread across two campgrounds are open to tents and RVs; hookups for water and electricity provided, and there are hot-water bathhouses, trading post and coin laundry. Two sites for wheelchair visitors can be reserved in advance. All other sites are first-come; $14 per night.

KEEOWEE-TOXAWAY STATE PARK 🏃 ⛴ The park is a sliver of woods along 18,500-acre Lake Keeowee. The Cherokees hunted and fished around the lake for centuries, naming it "place of the mulberries." Today, the waters are an impoundment for Duke Power, which makes nuclear and electrical energy. Facilities are limited to small picnic and camping areas—unfortunately, not on the lake. It's about a one-mile hike from the campground to the lake. A three-bedroom lakeside cabin can be rented; one-week minimum in the summer. Rate is budget. Lake Keeowee has good bream, crappie, bass and trout fishing. Facilities include picnic tables and a hiking trail. ~ Located off Route 11, just west of Route 133, near the town of Salem; 864-868-2605.

▲ There are 14 tent and RV sites with hookups; $11 per night. Six additional sites accommodate tents; $6 per night.

DEVIL'S FORK STATE PARK 🏃 ⛵ 🚤 🚣 ⛴ The vast, pale blue of Lake Jocassee set against cloud-sprinkled sky and deep blue peaks—this is the scenery at Devil's Fork. Throughout these 622 acres are deep, dark woods and bright fields of wildflowers, where trout lilies, jack-in-the-pulpits and rare Oconee bells flourish. The park is one of South Carolina's most popular, not only for the stunning setting but for the 20 luxury villas set in the woods along the lake. For moderate to deluxe rates, you get two or three bedrooms, carpeting, fireplaces, screened porches, blenders microwaves, and televisions. Two villas accommodate wheelchair visitors. In the summer, minimum stay is one week. Swimming is splendid. The small clay beach along Lake Jocassee angles into clear, shallow waters. Jocassee is the only lake in South Carolina where you can fish for both smallmouth bass and trophy trout (translation: angling is exceptional). You'll also find largemouth bass, black crappie, white bass and bluegill. Facilities include the park office, a picnic area with shelters, a store and tackle shop, boat ramps and hiking trails. ~ Located on Route 25, about two and a half miles north of Route 11, near Salem; 864-944-2639.

▲ There are 59 RV sites (two wheelchair accessible) with hookups and 20 tent sites, all located lakeside. Hot showers and coin laundry are provided; $16 for RVs; $8 for tents.

HIDDEN ▶   **OCONEE STATE PARK** 🏃 🏊 ⛴ The Civilian Conservation Corps built Oconee in the early 1930s, making it one of the state's first parks. A favorite among seclusionists, it's flung deep in pine woods on a high plateau in the northwestern crook of South Carolina. There are two mountain lakes here, a family-style restaurant and an old water wheel built by the Conservation Corps. Nineteen budget-priced cabins, most of them situated along a lake, are outfitted with fireplaces, heat and air conditioning, and kitchens. A one-week minimum stay is required during the summer months; there are two- or three-day minimums the rest of the year. There's good summertime swimming in the main lake, with lifeguards provided. In the main lake, try fishing for bass, bream and catfish. Facilities include the park office and museum, picnic tables and shelters, a restaurant, carpet golf, groceries and hiking trails. Day-use fee, $2. ~ The park is located on Route 107, 12 miles northwest of Walhalla; 864-638-5353.

▲ Next to the main lake are 140 wooded sites for tents or RVs; hookups provided. Two sites are wheelchair-accessible, and can be reserved in advance. All other sites are first-come; $13 per night.

▼▼▼▼▼▼▼▼▼▼▼▼▼▼
Outdoor Adventures

BOATING

Headed for Lake Murray near Columbia? **Just Add Water** rents out pontoons, johnboats, speedboats, waverunners, houseboats and other water craft. The company has six locations on the lake, including one at Dreher Island State Park. ~ 803-345-9682, 800-951-4007.

North of Aiken, you can rent johnboats at **Hickory Knob State Resort Park** for a trip on Strom Thurmond Lake. ~ Off Route 378, nine miles west of McCormick; 864-391-2450, 800-491-1764.

Vast clear lakes and swift streams in the Upcountry make for superior boating and canoeing.

Near Devil's Fork State Park, **Hoyett's Grocery and Tackle** rents pontoon boats to take on Jocassee Lake. ~ 516 Jocassee Lake Road, Salem; 864-944-9016.

Mountain Lakes Vacation Center rents canoes to take in area waters. ~ Route 11, Fair Play; 864-972-0463, 800-610-0020.

Just Add Water, with six locations on Lake Murray, supplies guides for striped bass fishing on the lake. ~ 803-345-9682, 800-951-4007. **The Blue Heron** guide will pick you up at P&L Landing near Dreher Island State Park—or other landings on request—for an outing on Lake Murray. ~ Prosperity; 803-364-2971.

SPORT-FISHING

The Upcountry's Lake Jocassee is prime fishing turf. It's the only lake in South Carolina where you can snag a smallmouth bass as well as a trophy trout. **Fish, Inc.** will take you trolling for trout, or casting for large- and smallmouth bass, bream and crappie. Overnight trips available. ~ 348 U-Wharri Mountain Road, Pickens; 864-878-9292.

◄ *HIDDEN*

Hoyett's Grocery and Tackle, next to Devil's Fork State Park, offers guided trips on Lake Jocassee for smallmouth bass and trophy trout. ~ 516 Jocassee Lake Road, Salem; 864-944-9016.

Black Mountain Trout Farm is the only commercial trout farm in South Carolina. Visitors are invited on weekends and holidays. No license required, and there's no limit. Call for directions: It's way out in the boonies. ~ Northeast of Clemson on 198 Trout Farm Road, Westminster; 864-647-9700.

◄ *HIDDEN*

Mountain Lakes Vacation Center provides fishing guides for lakes and streams throughout the Upcountry. ~ Route 11, Fair Play; 864-972-0463, 800-610-0020.

Public courses abound across South Carolina. In Columbia, there's the P.B. Dye–designed **Northwood Golf Club**. ~ Farrow and Parkland roads, in the Carolina Research Park; 803-786-9242. There's nine-hole **Hickory Ridge Golf Club**. ~ 1300 Bitternut Drive, off Trotter Road; 803-695-2663. Also in Columbia is county-owned **LinRick Golf Course**. ~ Camp Ground Road, off Route 215 North; 803-754-6331. And finally there's 6900-yard **Oak Hills Golf Club**. ~ 7629 Fairfield Road, off Route 20; 803-735-9830.

GOLF

Not far from the city, you'll find **Indian River Golf Club**. ~ 200 Congaree Hunt Drive, West Cola; 803-955-0080. You'll also find **Coldstream Country Club**. ~ 2121 Lake Murray Boulevard, Irmo; 803-781-0114. In Chapin, go to **Timberlake Country Club**. ~ Amicks Ferry Road, off Route 26, Chapin; 803-345-9909. In Pineridge, there's **Charwood Golf Club**. ~ 4082 Bachman Road, Pineridge; 803-755-2000.

In Aiken, **Houndslake Country Club** has a 27-hole course designed around three lakes and 50,000 azaleas. ~ 1900 Houndslake Drive; 803-648-6805. Another Aiken course is at **Cedar Creek**. ~ Banks Mill Road; 803-648-4206. A third course is at **Highland Park Country Club**. ~ 555 Highland Park Avenue; 803-649-6029.

Between Aiken and Abbeville, there's superb golfing at **Hickory Knob State Resort Park,** which has an 18-hole championship course, driving range and putting green. ~ Off Route 378, nine miles west of McCormick; 864-391-2450, 800-491-1764.

Across the Upcountry, you'll find public and semi-private courses at numerous locations. In Greenville, there's one at **Bonnie Brae Golf Club.** ~ 1316 Fork Shoals Road, Greenville; 864-277-9838. Southeast of Greenville, you'll find **Carolina Springs Golf & Country Club.** ~ 1680 Scuffleton Road, Fountain Inn, southeast of Greenville; 864-862-3551. In Spartanburg, tee off at **Cotton Creek Golf Club.** ~ West Croft Circle, Spartanburg; 864-583-7084. **Falcon's Lair** is another alternative. ~ Lecroy Road, off Route 11, east of Walhalla; 864-638-0000. Try **The Gauntlet** in Tigerville. ~ 253 Chinquapin Road, Tigerville; 864-895-6758, 800-531-0098. Or in Pickens head to the **Table Rock Resort.** ~ 171 Sliding Rock Road, Pickens; 864-878-2030, 800-831-0196. **Cross Creek Plantation** is located near Clemson. ~ 130 Club Drive, Seneca, near Clemson; 864-882-0200, 800-858-8465. In Pendleton, you'll find **Boscobel Golf Club.** ~ Off Route 76; 864-646-3991.

TENNIS

Need a workout with a racquet? Head for **Columbia Tennis Center.** ~ 1630 Whaley Street, Columbia; 803-733-8440. Also in Columbia is **Greenview Park.** ~ David Street; 803-754-5223. You can also opt for **Hampton Park.** ~ 1117 Brandon Avenue; 803-776-9082. A fourth option is **Woodland Park.** ~ 6500 Olde Knight Parkway, 803-776-1096.

In Aiken, you can play at the **Weeks Tennis Center.** ~ Whiskey Road, just north of Hitchcock Parkway; 803-642-7739. North of Aiken off the Savannah River Scenic Highway, **Hickory Knob State Resort Park** has two tennis courts. ~ Off Route 378, nine miles west of McCormick; 864-391-2450, 800-491-1764.

The city of Greenville has courts at **Cleveland Park.** ~ Washington Street and Laurens Road, Greenville. There are also courts

---

✔ CHECK THESE OUT—UNIQUE OUTDOOR ADVENTURES

- Stand on the platform of rock at Caesars Head State Park—wind slapping at your face, extraordinary mountain views in all directions. *page 420*
- Raft some of the best whitewater in the country—the Chattooga River, a National Wild and Scenic River. *page 416*
- Swing a golf club at Hickory Knob State Resort Park, where a plush green championship course swirls against the azure of Thurmond Lake. *page 418*
- Drop your line into the vast pale blue of Lake Jocassee and you may get a smallmouth bass or a trophy trout. *page 417*

at **McPherson Park**. ~ Main and Park streets, Greenville. When it's cold, try the indoor courts at **The Pavilion**, a Greenville County facility. ~ Scottswood Road, off East North Street, Greenville; 803-288-6470.

Inland South Carolina rises from flat farmland to gentle hills to steep mountains. Most everywhere, you can ride for hours without the hassle of traffic, enjoying long, lonesome stretches of road and eye-blink towns.

BIKING

The 221-mile **Carolina Connector** crosses the eastern side of the state. Starting at Route 381 north of McColl, it heads southwest along country roads through Sumter, then spans several rivers before commencing at the Savannah River on Route 119.

The **Central Route** is a 165-mile run starting on the coast at McClellanville. From here, it angles northwest along Route 45, picking up Route 6 on the west side of Lake Moultrie. Near Swansea it switches to Route 178 into Saluda, then takes Route 702 to Route 246 around Greenwood. It heads into the Upcountry on Route 20, ending along Route 133 at the Cherokee Foothills Scenic Highway.

All 135 miles of the **Cherokee Foothills Scenic Highway** are ideal for bicycling. The highway arcs along northwestern South Carolina, following Route 11 from Gaffney to Lake Hartwell.

Bike Rentals In Columbia, **Outspokin' Bicycles** rents mountain bikes. ~ 1001 Harden Street; 803-254-9797. **Bob's Bicycle Shop** rents cruisers. ~ 510 Beltline Boulevard; 803-782-3932.

In the Upcountry, **Mountain Lakes Vacation Center** has mountain bikes. ~ Route 11, Fair Play; 864-972-0463, 800-610-0020.

For a comprehensive list of trails, you should try to pick up a copy of *Hiking South Carolina Trails* by Allen de Hart (Globe Pequot Press). All distances listed for hiking trails are one way unless otherwise noted.

HIKING

COLUMBIA AREA At Sesquicentennial State Park, the **Jackson Creek Nature Trail** (.25 mile) wends through pine woods with small signs describing the flora. It ends at a dam, where the **Sandhills Nature Trail** (2 miles) begins its easy-going loop around a lake. If you prefer a workout, the park's **jogging trail** (4 miles) features an obstacle course and places to stop and exercise.

Among the six scenic swamp trails in Congaree Swamp National Monument, **Weston Lake Loop Trail** (4.2 miles) is most scenic. It wends through damp, musky, centuries-old forest, passing one of the state's largest loblolly pines—14 stories high and 15 feet wide. Don't forget your mosquito repellent.

AIKEN TO ABBEVILLE Aiken's Hitchcock Woods, a premier urban forest, has 20 miles of trails coiling through lofty forests of sweet gum, oak, pine and mulberry trees and alongside wildflower meadows. Equestrians frequent these trails, so watch where you step.

Within Hickory Knob State Resort Park, the **Turkey Ridge Trail** (.3 mile round-trip) and **Beaver Run Nature Trail** (1 mile) combine for a pleasant walk through loblolly woods. Part of the trail rims a lake.

UPCOUNTRY The **Foothills Trail**, South Carolina's longest trek, runs for 120 miles, with portions reaching into North Carolina. It began as a network of trails in Sumter National Forest, along South Carolina's northwest corner, and spread across the Cherokee Foothills. Today, it passes through Oconee State Park, Caesars Head State Park and Table Rock State Park.

Many of the steps along **Table Rock Trail** (3.4 miles) were laid in the 1930s by the Civilian Conservation Corps. The strenuous trek up Table Rock Mountain crosses several creeks and granite outcroppings (some badly eroded), rewarding with numerous Blue Ridge and lake views. It connects with **Pinnacle Mountain Trail** (3.3 miles), equally as arduous. This climb up Pinnacle Mountain edges cliffs and granite overhangs and pretty waterfalls. Both trail-heads are at Table Rock State Park, and provide access to the Foothills Trail.

Jones Gap Trail (5 miles) links Jones Gap State Park with Caesars Head State Park. It's a moderate to tough trek through a rugged, rocky mountain gap, with the cold, clear Middle Saluda River coursing through. Trailside camping is available (fee charged); check with either state park.

Pick up the **Whitewater Falls Trail** (3.4 miles) at the Bad Creek Hydroelectric Station (Route 130, eight miles north of Salem). You'll hike through old-growth forest with massive fraser magnolias and tulip poplar trees, down to a platform where you can see Whitewater's Lower Falls. The Upper Falls are in North Carolina.

The **Wormy Chestnut Trail** (1.4 miles) is a stressless walk through lovely wooded lakeside at Oconee State Park.

▼▼▼▼▼▼▼▼▼▼
Transportation

CAR

All highways lead to Columbia—or so it would seem on a map. **Route 26** angles up from Charleston to Columbia, continuing northwest to Spartanburg and into North Carolina. **Route 77** comes down from Charlotte, North Carolina, and into Columbia. And **Route 20** brings motorists from Atlanta to Columbia.

Also heading up from Atlanta is **Route 85**, which passes through Greenville and Spartanburg in the Upcountry.

AIR

Columbia Metropolitan Airport in Columbia is serviced by Air South, American Eagle, Delta Airlines and USAir.

The larger, modern **Greenville-Spartanburg Airport**, halfway between Greenville and Spartanburg in the Upcountry, is served by American Airlines, American Eagle, ASA, ComAir, Delta Airlines, United Express, USAir and USAir Express.

Greyhound Bus Lines (800-231-2222) has several locations around inland South Carolina. There's a location in Columbia at 2015 Gervais Street, 803-256-6465; in Aiken at 347 Barnwell Avenue, 803-648-6894; in Greenville at 100 West MacBee Avenue, 864-235-4741; and in Spartanburg at 212 East Daniel Morgan Street, 864-583-3669.

BUS

Amtrak (800-872-7245) makes several stops around inland South Carolina. There are stations in Columbia at 850 Pulaski Street, 803-252-8246; in Denmark at 200 West Baruch Street, 40 miles southeast of Aiken; in Greenville at 1120 West Washington Street, 864-255-4221; and in Spartanburg at 290 Magnolia Street.

TRAIN

At the Columbia Metropolitan Airport, you'll find **Alamo Rent A Car** (800-327-9633), **Avis Rent A Car** (800-331-1212), **Budget Rent A Car** (800-527-0700), **Dollar Rent A Car** (800-800-4000), **Hertz Rent A Car** (800-654-3131) and **National Interrent** (800-328-4567).

If you're flying into Greenville-Spartanburg Airport, try **Alamo Rent A Car** (800-327-9633), **Avis Rent A Car** (800-331-1212), **Budget Rent A Car** (800-527-0700), **Hertz Rent A Car** (800-654-3131) or **Thrifty Car Rental** (800-367-2277).

CAR RENTALS

South Carolina Electric and Gas Co. (803-748-3019) operates bus routes in Greater Columbia.

Greenville Transit Authority (864-467-4287) provides extensive service around Greenville. In Spartanburg, hop on a SPARTA (864-583-5789) bus.

PUBLIC TRANSIT

Yellow Cab (803-799-3311) services Columbia Metropolitan Airport. **Takeout Taxi of Columbia** (803-699-1113) will take you around the city.

The **Aiken Cab Co.** (803-648-1717) and **Yellow Cab Company of Aiken** (803-642-6055) can get you around Aiken.

In Greenville, there's **Yellow Cab** (864-232-5322) and **Diamond Cab** (864-235-1713). **Checker Cab Co.** (864-583-2724) and **Spartanburg City Cab** (864-585-9395) service the Spartanburg area.

TAXIS

Recommended Reading

Blue Ridge Parkway Guide, by William G. Lord. Menasha Ridge Press, 1981. This superb two-volume guide traces all 469 miles of the parkway, starting at Rockfish Gap, Virginia, and ending at Great Smoky Mountains National Park in North Carolina. Lord, a park ranger and naturalist, delves into the folklore and history of the Blue Ridge Mountains and details most every stop, overlook and side road.

Charleston Houses and Gardens, by N. Jane Iseley and Evangeline Davis. Preservation Society of Charleston and Legacy Publications, 1975. For 20 years this glossy book has captured the exquisite architecture and luxuriant gardens of this grand Old South city. A must for any Charleston lover.

Coastal Fishing in the Carolinas, by Robert J. Goldstein. John F. Blair, 1986. Where and how to find the fish along the Carolinas' coast, with detailed information on tackle, types of fish, and surf, pier and jetty fishing.

Discovering North Carolina: A Tar Heel Reader, edited by Jack Claiborne and William Price. The University of North Carolina Press, 1991. A compendium of fascinating insights on the life and times of North Carolina, with features on history, land and people, from Daniel Boone and Andrew Jackson to Ava Gardner.

Great Smoky Mountains National Park: A Natural History Guide, by Rose Houk. Houghton Mifflin Company, 1993. Houk shares her love of the Smokies and their "green mansions" of forests, with tales of geology, flora and fauna, and streams.

Hiking South Carolina Trails, by Allen de Hart. The Globe Pequot Press, 1989. A backpacker's bible, it's a comprehensive guide to more than 200 miles of state trails.

Look Homeward, Angel, by Thomas Wolfe. Collier Books, 1957. Wolfe's first novel and possibly his most profound, the thinly veiled autobiography portrays a boy growing up in early 1900s North Carolina.

Mountain Roads and Quiet Places, by Jerry DeLaughter. Great Smoky Mountains Natural History Association, 1989. A splendid journey through the peaks and meadows, forests and farmsteads of Great Smoky Mountains National Park.

North Carolina Hiking Trails, by Allen de Hart. Appalachian Mountain Club Books, 1988. More than 750 trails, from the Smoky and Blue Ridge mountains to the Outer Banks, are floridly described in this fat but compact guide.

North Carolina Scenic Byways, North Carolina Department of Transportation, 1994. This free booklet takes drivers and cyclists along the state's roads—both hidden and better known—that guarantee good views.

North Carolina Wildlife Viewing Guide, by Charles E. Roe. Falcon Press, 1992. Well illustrated and well written, this guide tells where you're apt to see an alligator or hairy woodpecker, Venus flytrap or corn snake, or hundreds of other creatures throughout the state's parks and preserves.

The Palmetto State: Stories from the Making of South Carolina, by Louise Pettus and Ron Chepesiuk. Sandlapper Publishing, Inc., 1991. The state's history is poignantly portrayed through these vignettes on everything from early exploration and Sherman's march of terror to "The Female Factor," tales of South Carolina's most gifted women.

Plantations of the Low Country, by N. Jane Iseley and William P. Baldwin, Jr. Legacy Publications, 1987. Beautifully illustrated and written with an eye for architecture and Southern history, it's an excellent prelude to Lowcountry touring.

The Prince of Tides, by Pat Conroy. Bantam Books, 1986. Conroy's lush saga of Lowcountry life and a family's dark past is a must-read for anyone visiting the South Carolina coast.

A Short History of Charleston, by Robert Rosen. Peninsula Press, 1992. Written with wit and a keen eye for the South, Rosen's "short" history runs 175 pages, capturing both the brighter and bleaker moments of Charleston's past.

State Parks of North Carolina, by Walter C. Biggs, Jr., and James F. Parnell. John F. Blair, 1989. A complete guide to the state's parks, with extensive details on history and hiking, plant and animal life, camping, facilities and activities.

Waterfalls & Cascades of the Great Smoky Mountains, by Hal Hubbs, Charles Maynard and David Morris. Panther Press, 1992. Where to find more than 30 well-known and hidden falls of the Smokies, illustrated with maps and color photographs.

Wild Shores: Exploring the Wilderness Areas of Eastern North Carolina, by Walter K. Taylor. Down Home Press, 1993. From the Outer Banks to the Cape Fear Coast, this handy guide details the wildlife and history of coastal North Carolina.

Index

Lodging Index

Dining Index

HIDDEN GUIDES

Adventure travel or a relaxing vacation?—"Hidden" guidebooks are the only travel books in the business to provide detailed information on both. Aimed at environmentally aware travelers, our motto is "Adventure Travel Plus." These books combine details on unique hotels, restaurants and sightseeing with information on camping, sports and hiking for the outdoor enthusiast.

THE NEW KEY GUIDES

Based on the concept of ecotourism, The New Key Guides are dedicated to the preservation of Central America's rare and endangered species, architecture and archaeology. Filled with helpful tips, they give travelers everything they need to know about these exotic destinations.

ULTIMATE FAMILY GUIDES

These innovative guides present the best and most unique features of a family destination. Quality is the keynote. In addition to thoroughly covering each destination, they feature short articles and one-line "teasers" that are both fun and informative.

Order Form

Ulysses Press books are available at bookstores everywhere. If any of the following titles are unavailable at your local bookstore, ask the bookseller to order them. Or you can order them directly from Ulysses Press (P.O. Box 3440, Berkeley, CA 94703; 510-601-8301, 800-377-2542, fax: 510-601-8307).

HIDDEN GUIDEBOOKS

____ Hidden Arizona, $13.95
____ Hidden Boston and Cape Cod, $11.95
____ Hidden Carolinas, $16.95
____ Hidden Coast of California, $16.95
____ Hidden Colorado, $13.95
____ Hidden Florida, $16.95
____ Hidden Florida Keys and Everglades, $9.95
____ Hidden Hawaii, $16.95
____ Hidden Idaho, $13.95
____ Hidden Maui, $12.95
____ Hidden Montana, $12.95
____ Hidden New England, $16.95

____ Hidden New Mexico, $13.95
____ Hidden Oregon, $13.95
____ Hidden Pacific Northwest, $16.95
____ Hidden Rockies, $16.95
____ Hidden San Francisco and Northern California, $15.95
____ Hidden Southern California, $16.95
____ Hidden Southwest, $16.95
____ Hidden Tahiti, $16.95
____ Hidden Tennessee, $15.95
____ Hidden Washington, $13.95
____ Hidden Wyoming, $12.95

THE NEW KEY GUIDEBOOKS

____ The New Key to Belize, $14.95
____ The New Key to Cancún and the Yucatán, $14.95
____ The New Key to Costa Rica, $16.95

____ The New Key to Ecuador and the Galápagos, $15.95
____ The New Key to Guatemala, $14.95

ULTIMATE FAMILY GUIDEBOOKS

____ Disneyland and Beyond, $12.95

____ Disney World and Beyond, $12.95

Mark the book(s) you're ordering and enter the total cost here ⮕ [   ]

California residents add 8% sales tax here ⮕ [   ]

Shipping, check box for your preferred method and enter cost here ⮕ [   ]

❑ BOOK RATE   **FREE! FREE! FREE!**

❑ PRIORITY MAIL $3.00 First book, $1.00/each additional book

❑ UPS 2-DAY AIR $7.00 First book, $1.00/each additional book

[   ]

Billing, enter total amount due here and check method of payment ⮕ [   ]

❑ CHECK   ❑ MONEY ORDER

❑ VISA/MASTERCARD _____ EXP. DATE _____

NAME _____ PHONE _____

ADDRESS _____

_____

CITY _____ STATE _____ ZIP _____

MONEY-BACK GUARANTEE ON DIRECT ORDERS PLACED THROUGH ULYSSES PRESS.

ABOUT THE AUTHOR

STACY RITZ is the author of the award-winning *The New Key to Belize* and *Disney World and Beyond*. She writes for *Outside* and *Bride's*, and has been published in *Parents*, the *Washington Post*, *New York Post*, *Miami Herald*, *St. Petersburg Times* and *Atlanta Journal-Constitution*. She spent her childhood summers in the Carolinas and now resides in the Florida Keys.

ABOUT THE ILLUSTRATOR

HANAKO WAKIYAMA, who was born in Tokyo, moved to the United States 12 years ago with her family. She has illustrated calendars, magazines and books, including the children's book *Humphrey the Lost Whale*. She currently lives in San Francisco with her husband.